The Development of Western Thought
HUM 100-400
Mark Bailey

Custom Publication for
Seneca College

MCGRAW-HILL RYERSON LIMITED

Toronto   Montréal   Boston   Burr Ridge, IL   Dubuque, IA   Madison, WI   New York   San Francisco
St. Louis   Bangkok   Bogotá   Caracas   Kuala Lumpur   Lisbon   London   Madrid   Mexico City   Milan
New Delhi   Santiago   Seoul   Singapore   Sydney   Taipei

Western Civilization: Sources, Images, and Interpretations, Volume 1, To 1700,
Seventh Edition, by Dennis Sherman. *ISBN 0-07-328475-0.*

Western Civilization: Sources, Images, and Interpretations, Volume 2, Since 1660,
Seventh Edition, by Dennis Sherman. *ISBN 0-07-328474-2.*

Manager, Custom Learning Solutions: Jason Giles

ISBN-10: 0-07-105864-8
ISBN-13: 978-0-07-105864-3

Printed and bound in Canada

Table of Contents

Western Civilization: Sources, Images, and Interpretations, Volume 1, To 1700
Seventh Edition, by Dennis Sherman

Western Civilization: Sources, Images, and Interpretations, Volume 2, Since 1660
Seventh Edition, by Dennis Sherman

1 Civilizations of the Ancient Near East

What historians call *civilization* arose some five to six thousand years ago out of small agricultural villages in the river valleys of the ancient Near East, first in Mesopotamia near the Tigris and Euphrates rivers and shortly thereafter in Egypt around the Nile. In the delta of the Tigris-Euphrates river system, the Sumerians organized into city-states such as Ur. About 2340 B.C.E. the Sumerians were overwhelmed by the Akkadians from the north, and over the next two thousand years this area, a meeting point between Asia, Africa, and Europe, experienced great instability as in their turn the Babylonians, Hittites, Assyrians, Chaldeans, Medes, and Persians gained dominance. Egyptian civilization developed toward the end of the fourth millennium B.C.E. and is usually dated from about 3000 B.C.E., when the upper and lower Nile areas were unified under one king. Although there were some periods of change, this was a remarkably stable civilization, lasting almost three thousand years.

In many respects the Mesopotamian and Egyptian civilizations were similar. Both were dependent on rivers and the rich soil deposited by periodic floods; both had to develop and maintain organized systems of irrigation and flood control. Both eventually had powerful kings and a priestly caste. Both believed in all-powerful gods who played an active role in the world. But there were also important differences between these two civilizations. Mesopotamia was not as well protected geographically as Egypt and was thus more open to attack. Its rivers were not as navigable, nor were the floods as regular as the Nile's. Its culture and religion reflected a sense of instability and pessimism in comparison to the stability and optimism that characterized Egyptian civilization.

Between these two areas there arose a number of smaller and politically less significant states, the most important of which were the Phoenician and the Hebrew states. The Phoenicians, a mercantile people, facilitated trade, established colonies, and spread Near Eastern culture. The Hebrews developed religious and ethical ideas that would be a foundation for both Christian and Islamic civilizations.

A number of sources in this chapter deal with the origins, nature, and spread of the earliest civilizations. How should one define "civilization"? Why did civilizations arise where and when they did? What were the main characteristics of these ancient civilizations? Through what processes did civilizations spread? The rest of the documents concern each of the three main civilizations: the Mesopotamians, the Egyptians, and the Hebrews. For Mesopotamia, most of the sources center on the culture,

the legal system, and the insights they provide into the nature of civilization there. Other documents focus on the position of women in Mesopotamian societies. For Egypt, what was the relation between the Nile and religion? What were some of Egypt's main economic and social characteristics? What was the significance of the pharaoh? How did the Egyptians view death and the afterlife? For the Hebrews, how did their religion, which became so important in the development of Western civilization, compare with others?

In sum, the sources in this chapter provide an introduction to the nature of civilization and its deep roots in the ancient Near East. The more direct foundations of Western civilization in ancient Greece will be examined in the next chapter.

The sources in this and all chapters are divided into three sections: Primary Sources, Visual Sources, and Secondary Sources. In this chapter, each one of these three sections begins with a guide containing suggestions on how to use the sources, focusing on the first source within the section.

Primary Sources

Using Primary Sources: The Laws of Hammurabi

Primary sources are briefly defined and discussed in the Preface. What follows is a more specific guide to the use of primary sources. It focuses on the first primary source in this book, the *Laws of Hammurabi*, which immediately follows as an example.

1. When reading primary sources such as the following selections from the *Laws of Hammurabi*, try to think of every line as evidence. Assume that you are a historian who knows very little about the history of Mesopotamia and that this document falls into your hands. Your job is to use this document as evidence to support some conclusions about Babylonian civilization.

   Actually, you have a head start. You already know something about the peoples of Mesopotamia from the chapter introduction, the time line, and the headnote preceding the source. You can use this information to better place the source in a historical context and to gain a sense of how the evidence in the source can be used. You also can use

   information from the headnote to identify the general nature of the source, where it came from, and when it was written.

2. Think of questions as you read the source. These can keep you focused on how words and lines and sections of the source might be used as evidence. A general question to keep in mind is, "What does this tell me about this civilization, about how people behaved, how they thought, what they believed?" Try reading each line as a piece of evidence to answer part of this general question. More specific questions can be derived from the "consider" points in italics just before the beginning of the document. These points indicate that the source might be particularly useful for providing evidence about the Babylonian legal system, about Babylonian social divisions, and about Babylonian politics and economics.

3. There are several ways almost any of these selections might be used as evidence. Read Article 1, the first section of the *Laws of Hammurabi*. It might be argued that the fact that a Babylonian could bring "a charge" of murder against someone,

that this charge had to be "proved," and that consequences flowed from the outcome of the process (if the accuser does not prove it he shall be put to death) constitutes evidence that the Babylonians had a formal legal system. You may further infer that this legal system was based on some principles of fairness (having to "prove" an accusation) and justice (death to those whose accusations are "not proved"). On the other hand, we must be careful not to read too much into this article—above all, not to read our own assumptions into the past. For example, this article does not tell us what constitutes proof or whether there is a jury system, although Article 3 might provide some evidence here (testimony is used and the truth of that testimony is at least open to challenge).

Read Articles 17, 18, and 19. Clearly they reveal that there were slaves within Babylonian society. They also imply that there was a problem with slaves attempting to escape, for rewards were offered to those who caught and returned slaves to their owners (Article 17) and penalties were imposed on those who hid escaped slaves (Article 19). Article 18 can be used as evidence for the existence of an organized bureaucracy of officials who kept written records ("take him to the palace in order that his record may be investigated").

Read Articles 53 and 54. They require landowners to keep dikes against water in repair (Article 53) and impose stiff penalties against those who do not (Articles 53 and 54). Together, the articles provide evidence for the existence of extensive water control systems for agriculture that required the cooperation (voluntary or imposed) of landowners and the government (by creating and enforcing these laws). Article 54 also reveals more about slavery in Babylonia, for since a landowner could be sold into slavery ("they shall sell him") we now have evidence that the source of slaves was not only external—from other societies through war, raids, or trade—but also internal.

Read Articles 141 and 142. How can the information in these articles be used to provide evidence for marriage, family life, and the relative positions of men and women in Babylonian society?

4. After working on various parts of the source, pull back and consider the source as a whole. It can be used to provide evidence for conclusions about Babylonia's system and principles of justice (the existence of laws, what the laws were, judgment and enforcement of laws, what crimes are more serious than others), its society (the importance and sources of slavery, the existence of different social classes, relations between men and women, the institution of marriage), its government (the king, the bureaucracy or core of governmental officials), and its economy (agriculture with a flood control system, a monetary system).

The Laws of Hammurabi

Much information about the peoples of Mesopotamia comes from compilations of laws, prescriptions, and decisions that were written as early as the twenty-third century B.C.E. The best known of these are the Laws of Hammurabi (often referred to as the Code of Hammurabi), issued by an eighteenth-century B.C.E. Babylonian king who probably used older Sumerian and Akkadian laws. The laws refer to almost all aspects of life in Babylonia. The following selections are taken from this code, which originally had about 282 articles and included a long prologue and epilogue that traced Hammurabi's authority to the gods.

CONSIDER: *The principles of justice reflected by these laws; the social divisions in Babylonian society disclosed in these laws; the political and economic characteristics of Babylonia revealed in this document.*

1: If a seignior[1] accused a(nother) seignior and brought a charge of murder against him, but has not proved it, his accuser shall be put to death.

[1] The word *awelum,* used here, is literally "man," but in the legal literature it seems to be used in at least three senses: (1) sometimes to indicate a man of the higher class, a noble; (2) sometimes a free man of any class, high or low; and (3) occasionally a man of any class, from king to slave. For the last I use the inclusive word "man," but for the first two, since it is seldom clear which of the two is intended in a given context, I follow the ambiguity of the original and use the rather general term "seignior," which I employ as the term is employed in Italian and Spanish, to indicate any free man of standing, and not in the strict feudal sense, although the ancient Near East did have something approximating the feudal system, and that is another reason for using "seignior."

3: If a seignior came forward with false testimony in a case, and has not proved the word which he spoke, if that case was a case involving life, that seignior shall be put to death.

4: If he came forward with (false) testimony concerning grain or money, he shall bear the penalty of that case.

❧

6: If a seignior stole the property of church or state, that seignior shall be put to death; also the one who received the stolen goods from his hand shall be put to death.

❧

17: If a seignior caught a fugitive male or female slave in the open and has taken him to his owner, the owner of the slave shall pay him two shekels[2] of silver.

18: If that slave will not name his owner, he shall take him to the palace in order that his record may be investigated, and they shall return him to his owner.

19: If he has kept that slave in his house (and) later the slave has been found in his possession, that seignior shall be put to death.

❧

22: If a seignior committed robbery and has been caught, that seignior shall be put to death.

23: If the robber has not been caught, the robbed seignior shall set forth the particulars regarding his lost property in the presence of god, and the city and governor, in whose territory and district the robbery was committed, shall make good to him his lost property.

❧

48: If a debt is outstanding against a seignior and Adad has inundated his field or a flood has ravaged (it) or through lack of water grain has not been produced in the field, he shall not make any return of grain to his creditor in that year; he shall cancel his contract-tablet and he shall pay no interest for that year.

❧

53: If a seignior was too lazy to make [the dike of] his field strong and did not make his dike strong and a break has opened up in his dike and he has accordingly let the water ravage the farmland, the seignior in whose dike the break was opened shall make good the grain that he let get destroyed.

---

[2]A weight of about 8 g.

54: If he is not able to make good the grain, they shall sell him and his goods, and the farmers whose grain the water carried off shall divide (the proceeds).

❧

141: If a seignior's wife, who was living in the house of the seignior, has made up her mind to leave in order that she may engage in business, thus neglecting her house (and) humiliating her husband, they shall prove it against her; and if her husband has then decided on her divorce, he may divorce her, with nothing to be given her as her divorce-settlement upon her departure. If her husband has not decided on her divorce, her husband may marry another woman, with the former woman living in the house of her husband like a maidservant.

142: If a woman so hated her husband that she has declared, "You may not have me," her record shall be investigated at her city council, and if she was careful and was not at fault, even though her husband has been going out and disparaging her greatly, that woman, without incurring any blame at all, may take her dowry and go off to her father's house.

❧

195: If a son has struck his father, they shall cut off his hand.

196: If a seignior has destroyed the eye of a member of the aristocracy, they shall destroy his eye.

197: If he has broken a(nother) seignior's bone, they shall break his bone.

198: If he has destroyed the eye of a commoner or broken the bone of a commoner, he shall pay one mina of silver.

199: If he has destroyed the eye of a seignior's slave or broken the bone of a seignior's slave, he shall pay one-half his value.

200: If a seignior has knocked out a tooth of a seignior of his own rank, they shall knock out his tooth.

201: If he has knocked out a commoner's tooth, he shall pay one-third mina of silver.

202: If a seignior has struck the cheek of a seignior who is superior to him, he shall be beaten sixty (times) with an oxtail whip in the assembly.

❧

209: If a seignior struck a(nother) seignior's daughter and has caused her to have a miscarriage, he shall pay ten shekels of silver for her fetus.

210: If that woman has died, they shall put his daughter to death.

211: If by a blow he has caused a commoner's daughter to have a miscarriage, he shall pay five shekels of silver.

212: If that woman has died, he shall pay one-half mina of silver.

The Epic of Gilgamesh

Insight into a people's ideas about life and death can be gained by examining their myths and their literature. The Epic of Gilgamesh, probably written in the latter part of the third millennium (2000s) B.C.E., *was the great epic poem of Mesopotamia. Its hero, Gilgamesh, ruled the Sumerian citystate of Uruk around 2700* B.C.E. *The poem is about the mythical adventures this king, part god himself, has struggling with life, the gods, and death. In one adventure, Gilgamesh faces death by embarking on a search for immortality. As part of that search he descends into the Netherworld to find Utnapishtim, a human who has been granted immortality by the gods. In the following selection, Gilgamesh questions Utnapishtim, who tells him the story of the flood.*

CONSIDER: *The nature of the gods and their relations with humans; conclusions about life Mesopotamians might have come to reading or listening to this story; connections between this story and the Biblical story of Noah and the flood.*

"Oh, father Utnapishtim, you who have entered the assembly of the gods, I wish to question you concerning the living and the dead, how shall I find the life for which I am searching?"

Utnapishtim said, "There is no permanence. Do we build a house to stand for ever, do we seal a contract to hold for all time? Do brothers divide an inheritance to keep for ever, does the flood-time of rivers endure? It is only the nymph of the dragon-fly who sheds her larva and sees the sun in his glory. From the days of old there is no permanence. The sleeping and the dead, how alike they are, they are like a painted death. What is there between the master and the servant when both have fulfilled their doom? When the Annunaki,[3] the judges, come together, and Mammetun the mother of destinies, together they decree the fates of men. Life and death they allot but the day of death they do not disclose."

Then Gilgamesh said to Utnapishtim the Faraway, "I look at you now, Utnapishtim, and your appearance is no different from mine; there is nothing strange in your features. I thought I should find you like a hero prepared for battle, but you lie here taking your ease on your back. Tell me truly, how was it that you came to enter the company of the gods and to possess everlasting life?"

Utnapishtim said to Gilgamesh, "I will reveal to you a mystery, I will tell you a secret of the gods."

"You know the city Shurrupak, it stands on the banks of Euphrates? That city grew old and the gods that were in it were old. There was Anu, lord of the firmament, their father, and warrior Enlil their counsellor, Ninurta the helper, and Ennugi watcher over canals; and with them also was Ea.[4] In those days the world teemed, the people multiplied, the world bellowed like a wild bull, and the great god was aroused by the clamour. Enlil heard the clamour and he said to the gods in council, 'The uproar of mankind is intolerable and sleep is no longer possible by reason of the babel.' So the gods in their hearts were moved to let loose the deluge; but my lord Ea warned me in a dream. He whispered their words to my house of reeds, 'Reed-house, reed-house! Wall, O wall, hearken reed-house, wall reflect; O man of Shurrupak, son of Ubara-Tutu; tear down your house and build a boat, abandon possessions and look for life, despise worldly goods and save your soul alive. Tear down your house, I say, and build a boat.'

"When I had understood I said to my lord, 'Behold, what you have commanded I will honour and perform, but how shall I answer the people, the city, the elders?' Then Ea opened his mouth and said to me, his servant, 'Tell them this: I have learnt that Enlil is wrathful against me, I dare no longer walk in his land nor live in his city; I will go down to the Gulf to dwell with Ea my lord. But on you he will rain down abundance, rare fish and shy wild-fowl, a rich harvest-tide. In the evening the rider of the storm will bring you wheat in torrents.'" . . .

"On the seventh day the boat was complete. . . .

"I loaded into her all that I had of gold and of living things, my family, my kin, the beasts of the field both wild and tame, and all the craftsmen . . .

"For six days and six nights the winds blew, torrent and tempest and flood overwhelmed the world, tempest and flood raged together like warring hosts. When the seventh day dawned the storm from the south subsided, the sea grew calm, the flood was stilled; I looked at the face of the world and there was silence, all mankind was turned to clay. The surface of the sea stretched as flat as a rooftop; I opened a hatch and the light fell on my face. Then I bowed low, I sat down and I wept, the tears streamed down my face, for on every side was the waste of water. I looked for land in vain, but fourteen leagues distant there appeared a mountain, and there the boat grounded; on the mountain of Nisir the boat held fast, she held fast and did not budge. . . . When the seventh day dawned I loosed a dove and let her go. She flew

SOURCE: N. K. Sandars, trans., *The Epic of Gilgamesh*, 2d rev. ed. (London: Penguin Books, 1972), copyright © N. K. Sandars, 1960, 1964, 1972.

[3]Gods.

[4]God of wisdom and good fortune.

away, but finding no resting-place she returned. Then I loosed a swallow, and she flew away but finding no resting-place she returned. I loosed a raven, she saw that the waters had retreated, she ate, she flew around, she cawed, and she did not come back. Then I threw everything open to the four winds, I made a sacrifice and poured out a libation on the mountain top. Seven and again seven cauldrons I set up on their stands, I heaped up wood and cane and cedar and myrtle. When the gods smelled the sweet savour, they gathered like flies over the sacrifice. Then, at last, Ishtar also came, she lifted her necklace with the jewels of heaven that once Anu had made to please her. 'O you gods here present, by the lapis lazuli round my neck I shall remember these days as I remember the jewels of my throat; these last days I shall not forget. Let all the gods gather round the sacrifice, except Enlil. He shall not approach this offering, for without reflection he brought the flood; he consigned my people to destruction.'

"When Enlil had come, when he saw the boat, he was wrath and swelled with anger at the gods, the host of heaven, 'Has any of these mortals escaped? Not one was to have survived the destruction.' Then the god of the wells and canals Ninurta opened his mouth and said to the warrior Enlil, 'Who is there of the gods that can devise without Ea? It is Ea alone who knows all things.' Then Ea opened his mouth and spoke to warrior Enlil, 'Wisest of gods, hero Enlil, how could you so senselessly bring down the flood?' . . .

"Then Enlil went up into the boat, he took me by the hand and my wife and made us enter the boat and kneel down on either side, he standing between us. He touched our foreheads to bless us saying, 'In time past Utnapishtim was a mortal man; henceforth he and his wife shall live in the distance at the mouth of the rivers.' Thus it was that the gods took me and placed me here to live in the distance, at the mouth of the rivers."

Hymn to the Nile

Most of the earliest civilizations were located in major river valleys. The Nile River provided the Egyptians with a strip of fertile land in an area otherwise relatively arid and hostile to large long-term settlement. Moreover, its predictable annual flooding ensured the continued fertility of the land and enabled the Egyptians to irrigate the crops that supported this long-lasting civilization. Understandably, the Nile became a focus for Egyptian religious beliefs and one of the Egyptians' chief deities. In the following selection from a hymn to the Nile, *probably originating in an early period in Egyptian history, the Nile is praised for its power and deeds that have enabled the Egyptians to live in a relatively ordered, prosperous world.*

CONSIDER: *The Egyptian view of the proper relationship between themselves and this deity; the Egyptian perception of this deity and its characteristics; the information this document provides concerning Egyptian economic, social, and political life.*

When he[5] is sluggish noses clog,
Everyone is poor;
As the sacred loaves are pared,
A million perish among men.
When he plunders, the whole land rages,
Great and small roar;
People change according to his coming,
When Khnum has fashioned him.
When he floods, earth rejoices,
Every belly jubilates,
Every jawbone takes on laughter,
Every tooth is bared.

Food provider, bounty maker,
Who creates all that is good!
Lord of awe, sweetly fragrant,
Gracious when he comes.
Who makes herbage for the herds,
Gives sacrifice for every god.
Dwelling in the netherworld,
He controls both sky and earth.
Conqueror of the Two Lands,
He fills the stores,
Makes bulge the barns,
Gives bounty to the poor.

❧

When you overflow, O Hapy,[6]
Sacrifice is made for you;
Oxen are slaughtered for you,
A great oblation is made to you.
Fowl is fattened for you,
Desert game snared for you,
As one repays your bounty.

One offers to all the gods
Of that which Hapy has provided,
Choice incense, oxen, goats,
And birds in holocaust.

SOURCE: Miriam Lichtheim, *Ancient Egyptian Literature*, 3 vols., pp. 199, 206, 208–209. Copyright © 1973–1980 Regents of the University of California.

[5]The Nile.
[6]The Nile.

Hymn to the Pharaoh

The history of Egypt and the institution of kingship have been traced back to the end of the fourth millennium B.C.E., when Upper and Lower Egypt were unified apparently under one great conquering king. The Egyptian king, or pharaoh, was considered both a god and the absolute ruler of his country. These beliefs are reflected in laudatory hymns addressed to pharaohs. The following selection is from one of those hymns, dating from the reign of Sesostris III, who ruled from about 1880 to 1840 B.C.E.

CONSIDER: *The Egyptian perception of the pharaoh; what deeds or powers of the pharaoh seemed most important to the Egyptians; similarities and differences between the Egyptian perceptions of the pharaoh and of the Nile.*

How [the gods] rejoice:
    you have strengthened their offerings!
How your [people] rejoice:
    you have made their frontiers!
How your forbears rejoice:
    you have enriched their portions!
How Egypt rejoices in your strength:
    you have protected its customs!
How the people rejoice in your guidance:
    your might has won increase [for them]!
How the Two Shores rejoice in your dreadedness:
    You have enlarged their holdings!
How the youths whom you levied rejoice:
    you have made them prosper!
How your elders rejoice:
    you have made them youthful!
How the Two Lands rejoice in your power:
    you have protected their walls!

The Old Testament—Genesis and Exodus

Squeezed between the larger kingdoms of Mesopotamia and Egypt were a number of small states. For the development of Western civilization, the most important of these states was in Palestine, where the Hebrews formed Israel and Judah. Although their roots extend further into the past, the Hebrews were originally led out of northeastern Egypt toward Palestine by Moses near the end of the second millennium B.C.E. The power of the Hebrew nation reached its height during the tenth

SOURCE: Miriam Lichtheim, *Ancient Egyptian Literature*, vol. I, pp. 199, 206, 208–209. Copyright © 1973–1980 Regents of the University of California.

SOURCE: Scripture taken from the *Holy Bible, New International Version*®. NIV®. Copyright© 1973, 1978, 1984 by International Bible Society. Used by permission of Zondervan Publishing House. All rights reserved.

and ninth centuries B.C.E., but the nation's importance rests primarily in the religion developed by the Hebrews. Judaism differed in many ways from other Near Eastern religions, particularly in its monotheism, its contractual nature, and its ethical mandates. These characteristics of Judaism are illustrated in the following selections from Genesis and Exodus.

CONSIDER: *The relationship between God and people illustrated in these selections; how these Hebrew beliefs compare with Egyptian beliefs; as a set of laws, how these selections compare with Hammurabi's Code.*

12: The LORD had said to Abram, "Leave your country, your people and your father's household and go to the land I will show you.

"I will make you into a great nation and I will bless you;
I will make your name great, and you will be a blessing.
I will bless those who bless you, and whoever curses you I will curse;
and all peoples on earth will be blessed through you."

✻

19: In the third month after the Israelites left Egypt—on the very day—they came to the Desert of Sinai. After they set out from Rephidim, they entered the Desert of Sinai, and Israel camped there in the desert in front of the mountain.

Then Moses went up to God, and the LORD called to him from the mountain and said, "This is what you are to say to the house of Jacob and what you are to tell the people of Israel: 'You yourselves have seen what I did to Egypt, and how I carried you on eagles' wings and brought you to myself. Now if you obey me fully and keep my covenant, then out of all nations you will be my treasured possession. Although the whole earth is mine, you will be for me a kingdom of priests and a holy nation.' These are the words you are to speak to the Israelites."

So Moses went back and summoned the elders of the people and set before them all the words the LORD had commanded him to speak. The people all responded together, "We will do everything the LORD has said." So Moses brought their answer back to the LORD.

20: And God spoke all these words:

"I am the LORD your God, who brought you out of Egypt, out of the land of slavery.

"You shall have no other gods before me.

"You shall not make for yourself an idol in the form of anything in heaven above or on the earth beneath or in the waters below. You shall not bow down to them or worship them; for I, the LORD your God, am a jealous God, punishing the children for the sin of the fathers to the third and fourth generation of those who hate me, but showing love to a thousand generations of those who love me and keep my commandments.

"You shall not misuse the name of the LORD your God, for the LORD will not hold anyone guiltless who misuses his name.

"Remember the Sabbath day by keeping it holy. Six days you shall labor and do all your work, but the seventh day is a Sabbath to the LORD your God. On it you shall not do any work, neither you, nor your son or daughter, nor your manservant or maidservant, nor your animals, nor the alien within your gates. For in six days the LORD made the heavens and the earth, the sea, and all that is in them, but he rested on the seventh day. Therefore the LORD blessed the Sabbath day and made it holy.

"Honor your father and your mother, so that you may live long in the land the LORD your God is giving you.

"You shall not murder.

"You shall not commit adultery.

"You shall not steal.

"You shall not give false testimony against your neighbor.

"You shall not covet your neighbor's house. You shall not covet your neighbor's wife, or his manservant or maidservant, his ox or donkey, or anything that belongs to your neighbor."

When the people saw the thunder and lightning and heard the trumpet and saw the mountain in smoke, they trembled with fear. They stayed at a distance and said to Moses, "Speak to us yourself and we will listen. But do not have God speak to us or we will die."

Moses said to the people, "Do not be afraid. God has come to test you, so that the fear of God will be with you to keep you from sinning."

The Aton Hymn and Psalm 104: The Egyptians and the Hebrews

Several characteristics made the Hebrews unique in the ancient Near East. However, many civilizations have certain similarities, including their religious beliefs and practices. Moreover, Hebrews were connected to and influenced by the Egyptians in many ways. Geographically, Palestine served as a buffer zone between Egypt and the large kingdoms of Mesopotamia. Historically, the formative ordeal of Moses and the Exodus stemmed from Egypt. Less apparent but of great importance were connections between Hebrew and Egyptian religious concepts and forms of expression. The following comparison of selections from the Egyptian Aton Hymn, composed in the fourteenth century B.C.E. during the rule of Akhenaten, who attempted to change some traditional religious views, and Psalm 104 from the Old Testament, written six or seven centuries later, illustrates striking parallels between the two documents.

CONSIDER: *How the similarities between these two excerpts might be explained.*

THE ATON HYMN	PSALM 104
When thou settest in the western horizon,	Thou makest darkness and it is night,
The land is in darkness like death . . .	Wherein all the beasts of the forest creep forth.
Every lion comes forth from his den;	The young lions roar after their prey.
All creeping things, they sting.	The sun ariseth, they get them away . . .
At daybreak, when thou arisest in the horizon . . .	Man goeth forth unto his work,
Thou drivest away the darkness . . .	And to his labor until the evening.
Men awake and stand upon their feet . . .	O Jahweh, how manifold are thy works!
All the world, they do their labor.	In wisdom has thou made them all;
How manifold are thy works!	The earth is full of thy riches.
They are hidden from man's sight.	
O sole god, like whom there is no other,	
Thou hast made the earth according to thy desire.	

Visual Sources

Using Visual Sources: The "Royal Standard" of Ur

Visual sources are briefly defined and discussed in the Preface. What follows is a more specific guide to the use of visual sources, focusing on our first visual source, *The "Royal Standard" of Ur*, which immediately follows as an example (figures 1.1 and 1.2).

1. Try to look at visual sources as if they were written, primary documents. As with primary documents, assume that you are a historian who knows very

little about the history of Sumer and discovers this visual source, *The "Royal Standard" of Ur.* Your goal is to try to "read" it as evidence to support some conclusions about Sumerian civilization.

Without some guidance, "reading" a visual source as historical evidence is more difficult than using a written source. The reproduction makes the details harder to see and most people are not used to looking at a picture in this analytical way. Therefore, in the first paragraph of the headnote to *The "Royal Standard" of Ur*, there is a description that puts into words what appears in the visual source. In the second paragraph, there is an analysis of the evidence drawn from the photo. Here, as with most visual sources, it is useful to go back and forth between the photo and the written description and analysis that accompany the photo.

2. As with primary documents, think of questions as you look at the visual source and as you read the written guide to it. The general question to keep in mind is, What does this tell me about this civilization, about how people behaved, how they thought, or what they believed? Other questions are suggested in the "consider" points, such as what information the artist might have been attempting to convey to the viewer.

3. Here the first panel shows the Sumerians at war. The headnote alerts us to "read" this three-line panel from bottom to top, for that is how the Sumerian artist intended it to be viewed. With the aid of the headnote we can see the chariot charging the enemy, then the infantry, and finally the captives being led to the victorious king.

The second panel shows the Sumerians at peace. Again reading from bottom to top, we can see this society organizing in preparation for a banquet and then the banquet itself.

The second paragraph suggests some of the ways the information derived from *The "Royal Standard" of Ur* can be used as historical evidence that Ur in Sumer was a well-organized society with centralized political control, a society that at least by 2700 B.C.E. had mastered the use of various domesticated animals, tools, and instruments.

4. Now pull back and consider the source as a whole. Why might the artist have chosen to depict these scenes? What might be made of the lack of individualized differences in the figures? In what ways might a similar sort of decoration be made today and what might such a set of scenes depict?

Sumer: The "Royal Standard" of Ur

This piece of art—made of shell, lapis lazuli, and red stone inlaid on the sides of a wooden box and found in a grave dating around 2700 B.C.E.—illustrates two aspects of Sumerian life: war and peace. In the bottom line of the first panel, reading from left to right, a wooden chariot charges the enemy and knocks him over. In the second line the infantry, with protective cloaks, helmets, and short spears, captures and leads off the enemy. In the third line soldiers on the right lead captives to the king in the center. The king, who has just alighted from his attended chariot on the left, towers over the rest. In the second panel the fruits of victory or of peace are enjoyed, at least by the court. In the bottom and middle lines produce, manufactured goods, and livestock are brought to a banquet by bearers and menials. In the top line the king on the left and his soldiers drink wine while attended by servants and serenaded by a harpist and female singer on the right.

Clearly, this offers evidence for what historians consider a civilized society. Agricultural products are shown. Various animals have been domesticated for specialized purposes.

Important inventions such as the wheel are in use. Leisure activities have been cultivated, as revealed by the harp, the rather formal banquet, and the existence of this piece of art itself (which may have been a box for a lyre). The society has been organized and displays some discipline, as indicated by the use of chariots, the infantry, the porters, the musicians, the servants, and the banquet itself. Finally, the king represents centralized political authority that is directly tied to military prowess. Note that the sole female figure here is the singer.

CONSIDER: *Why there is a lack of individual differences in the people portrayed in this picture; bases for social distinction in Sumerian society revealed in this scene; things or scenes missing from this that you might have expected to find; reasons the artist chose to portray these particular scenes and to include only the things you see here.*

Egyptian Wall Paintings from the Tomb of Menna

This wall painting from the tomb of an Egyptian scribe, Menna, dating from the late fifteenth century B.C.E., illustrates the basis of Egyptian economic life (figure 1.3). This pictorial record of a harvest should be read from bottom to top. In the bottom row,

SOURCE: Reprinted in *The Burden of Egypt* by John A. Wilson, by permission of The Chicago Press. Copyright © 1951, p. 227.

FIGURE 1.1   Royal Standard of Ur, "War" Side, from the Sumerian Royal Graves of Ur, Early Dynastic Period, 2750 B.C.E. (Mosaic). (© The British Museum, London, UK/Bridgeman Art Library)

FIGURE 1.2   Royal Standard of Ur, "Peace" Side, from the Sumerian Royal Graves of Ur, Early Dynastic Period, 2750 B.C.E. (Mosaic). (© The British Museum, London, UK/Bridgeman Art Library, London)

from left to right, commoners are harvesting wheat with sickles. The wheat is then carried in rope baskets past two girls fighting over remaining bits of wheat and past two laborers (one of whom is playing a flute) who are taking a break under a date tree, to where the wheat is being threshed and raked out by laborers. In the second row, from right to left, oxen tread on the wheat, separating the kernels from the husks, and laborers remove the chaff by scooping up the wheat and allowing it to fall in the wind. The grain is then brought to the supervising scribe, Menna, standing in a kiosk. Menna is aided by subordinate recording scribes. In the top row, from left to right, the fields are being measured by

ropes as a basis for assessing taxes. In the center Menna watches as subordinates line up and whip those who have apparently failed to pay their taxes or adequately perform their duties. Finally, the grain is stacked for shipment and carried off in a boat.

The harvest seems plentiful, and Egyptian society is tightly organized around it—from the gathering, processing, and shipping of the wheat to the assessing of taxes and enforcement of laws. Menna's authority is denoted by his size, by his placement in a kiosk, and by the symbols of power placed in his hand and immediately around him. The importance of writing in early societies is also demonstrated: Menna and his immediate

FIGURE 1.3   (© Elliott Erwitt/Magnum Photos)

subordinates are in an authoritative position in part because they can write, a skill connected here to the ability of the central authority to organize the economy and exact taxes. Finally, this wall painting reveals part of the nature of Egyptian religious beliefs. The scene is painted on the inside of a tomb. Thus the paintings were not for the living public, as the tombs were not to be visited, but for the dead or the world of the dead. This implies a belief that there were strong connections between this world, what one did in it, and the afterlife.

CONSIDER: The evidence for the existence of a civilized society here; the similarities and differences between this and The "Royal Standard" of Ur.

The Environment and the Rise of Civilization in the Ancient Near East

These three maps relate weather, vegetation, agricultural sites, and civilizations in the ancient Near East. Map 1.1 shows the average annual rainfall in modern times (although weather patterns may have changed

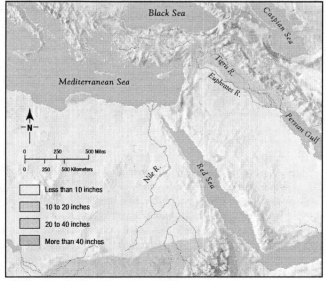

Less than 10 inches

10 to 20 inches

20 to 40 inches

More than 40 inches

MAP 1.1   Rainfall

MAP 1.2 Vegetation and Agricultural Sites

MAP 1.3 Civilization

over the last five thousand years, it is likely that they have not changed greatly). Map 1.2 shows some of the vegetation patterns and a number of the earliest agricultural sites that have been discovered in the same area. Map 1.3 shows patterns of civilization in this part of the world.

Together, these maps indicate a tendency for early agriculture sites to locate in areas of substantial rainfall and subtropical woodland, both appropriate for cereal farming. These areas often eventually supported the development of civilizations. Yet the earliest civilizations generally do not fall in these areas, but rather in areas of low rainfall that have a narrow strip of subtropical woodland along riverbanks. The rivers could compensate for the lack of rain, but low rainfall presented the challenge of developing irrigation systems along with corresponding social and political organizations. This is what happened in the earliest civilizations of Mesopotamia and Egypt.

Secondary Sources

Using Secondary Sources: The Agricultural Revolution

Secondary sources are briefly defined and discussed in the Preface. What follows is a more specific guide to the use of secondary sources, focusing on our first secondary source, *The Agricultural Revolution*, which immediately follows as an example.

1. Try to read a secondary source like *The Agricultural Revolution* by Robert J. Braidwood not as historical evidence (as you would for a primary source), but as a set of conclusions—an interpretation of the evidence from primary sources—by a scholar (usually a historian). Your job is to try to understand what the writer's interpretation is, evaluate whether any arguments or evidence the writer presents seems to support it adequately, and decide in what ways you agree or disagree with that interpretation.

2. Try to think of questions as you read a secondary source. This process can keep you alert to why the author selects and presents only certain information and what conclusions the author is trying to convey to the reader. Perhaps the two most important questions to keep in mind are, What question is this author trying to answer? and What does all of what the author has written add up to? For each secondary source, guidance for these two questions and related questions is provided in the headnote to the source and in the "consider" points.

Here the headnote to this secondary source tells us that the author, Robert J. Braidwood, is trying to interpret the agricultural revolution, particularly its spread and significance. The "consider" section alerts us to more specific aspects of what the author is trying to convince us of, such as his interpretation for the causes of the agricultural revolution and his rejection of alternative explanations (environmental determinism) for the agricultural revolution presented by other scholars.

3. Try reading and summarizing in a few words what Braidwood is trying to say or argue in each paragraph. What conclusion is he reaching?

One could summarize the first paragraph by saying that Braidwood is trying to convince us that the agricultural revolution was an extremely important achievement of our species. He also defines the agricultural revolution ("the domestication of plants and animals" and "the achievement of an effective food-producing technology") and suggests why it was so important (the "subsequent developments" that "followed swiftly"—urban societies and later industrial civilization).

In the second paragraph Braidwood concludes that the agricultural revolution was caused ("the origin") by cultural evolution ("the record of culture"). He argues that the several independent inventions ("multiple occurrence") of agriculture support ("suggests that") his conclusion.

In the third paragraph Braidwood presents a contrary interpretation for the causes of the agricultural revolution ("environmental determinism"). He then presents an argument showing why he believes this opposing interpretation is wrong (what did and did not happen in reaction to climate change).

In the following three paragraphs Braidwood presents his interpretation and the arguments to support it in greater detail. In a few words, try to summarize what he is saying in each paragraph.

In the final paragraph, he, like many other authors, again tries to convince the reader that the topic he is writing about (the agricultural revolution) is important or of great significance. How does he do this?

4. Finally, pull back and consider a secondary source as a whole. Try to formulate the author's arguments and conclusions in a nutshell.

Here you might say that Braidwood argues two things. First, the agricultural revolution was extremely important for human history because it directly led to the creation of urban civilizations. Second, the causes for the agricultural revolution were cultural differentiation and specialization (or the record of culture), not environmental determinism (circumstances).

CONSIDER: *How geographic and climatic factors help explain the rise of civilization in Mesopotamia and Egypt; how geographic and climatic factors facilitated the growth of settlements in some areas but not the blossoming of those settlements into large, organized societies.*

The Agricultural Revolution

Robert J. Braidwood

Human beings populated parts of the earth for thousands of years before the first civilizations rose five or six thousand years ago in the ancient Near East. The causes for this relatively rapid transformation in the condition of human beings have been interpreted in a variety of ways. However, most historians and anthropologists point to the agricultural revolution of the

SOURCE: From *Hunters, Farmers, and Civilizations: Old World Archaeology* by C. C. Lamberg Karlovsky. Copyright © 1979 by W. H. Freeman and Company. Reprinted with permission.

Neolithic Age, in which—through the domestication of plants and animals—human beings became food producers rather than hunters and food gatherers, as the central development in this transformation to civilization. In the following selection, Robert J. Braidwood, an archaeologist and anthropologist, analyzes the agricultural revolution, its spread, and its significance.

CONSIDER: *The origins or causes of the agricultural revolution; Braidwood's rejection of environmental determinism and his acceptance of cultural differentiation and specialization; connections between agriculture and the beginnings of cities.*

Tool-making was initiated by pre-*sapiens* man. The first comparable achievement of our species was the agricultural revolution. No doubt a small human population could have persisted on the sustenance secured by the hunting and food-gathering technology that had been handed down and slowly improved upon over the 500 to 1,000 millennia of pre-human and pre-*sapiens* experience. With the domestication of plants and animals, however, vast new dimensions for cultural evolution suddenly became possible. The achievement of an effective food-producing technology did not, perhaps, predetermine subsequent developments, but they followed swiftly: the first urban societies in a few thousand years and contemporary industrial civilization in less than 10,000 years.

The first successful experiment in food production took place in southwestern Asia, on the hilly flanks of the "fertile crescent." Later experiments in agriculture occurred (possibly independently) in China and (certainly independently) in the New World. The multiple occurrence of the agricultural revolution suggests that it was a highly probable outcome of the prior cultural evolution of mankind and a peculiar combination of environmental circumstances. It is in the record of culture, therefore, that the origin of agriculture must be sought.

Not long ago the proponents of environmental determinism argued that the agricultural revolution was a response to the great changes in climate which accompanied the retreat of the last glaciation about 10,000 years ago. However, the climate had altered in equally dramatic fashion on other occasions in the past 75,000 years, and the potentially domesticable plants and animals were surely available to the bands of food-gatherers who lived in southwestern Asia and similar habitats in various parts of the globe. Moreover, recent studies have revealed that the climate did not change radically where farming began in the hills that flank the fertile crescent. Environmental determinists have also argued from the "theory of propinquity" that the isolation of men along with appropriate plants and animals in desert oases started the process of domestication.

In my opinion there is no need to complicate the story with extraneous "causes." The food-producing revolution seems to have occurred as the culmination of the ever increasing cultural differentiation and specialization of human communities. Around 8000 B.C.E. the inhabitants of the hills around the fertile crescent had come to know their habitat so well that they were beginning to domesticate the plants and animals they had been collecting and hunting. At slightly later times human cultures reached the corresponding level in Central America and perhaps in the Andes, in southeastern Asia and in China. From these "nuclear" zones cultural diffusion spread the new way of life to the rest of the world.

As the agricultural revolution began to spread, the trend toward ever increasing specialization of the intensified food-collecting way of life began to reverse itself. The new techniques were capable of wide application, given suitable adaptation, in diverse environments. Archeological remains at Hassuna, a site near the Tigris River somewhat later than Jarmo, show that the people were exchanging ideas on the manufacture of pottery and of flint and obsidian projectile points with people in the region of the Amouq in Syro-Cilicia. The basic elements of the food-producing complex—wheat, barley, sheep, goats and probably cattle—in this period moved west beyond the bounds of their native habitat to occupy the whole eastern end of the Mediterranean. They also traveled as far east as Anau, east of the Caspian Sea. Localized cultural differences still existed, but people were adopting and adapting more and more cultural traits from other areas. Eventually the new way of life traveled to the Aegean and beyond into Europe, moving slowly up such great river valley systems as the Dnieper, the Danube and the Rhone, as well as along the coasts. The intensified food-gatherers of Europe accepted the new way of life, but, as V. Gordon Childe has pointed out, they "were not slavish imitators: they adapted the gifts from the East . . . into a new and organic whole capable of developing on its own original lines." Among other things, the Europeans appear to have domesticated rye and oats that were first imported to the European continent as weed plants contaminating the seed of wheat and barley. In the comparable diffusion of agriculture from Central America, some of the peoples to the north appear to have rejected the new ways, at least temporarily.

By about 5000 B.C.E. the village-farming way of life seems to have been fingering down the valleys toward the alluvial bottom lands of the Tigris and Euphrates. Robert M. Adams believes that there may have been people living in the lowlands who were expert in collecting food from the rivers. They would have taken up the idea of farming from people who came down from the higher areas. In the bottom lands a very different climate, seasonal flooding of the land and small-scale irrigation led agriculture through a significant new technological transformation. By about 4000 B.C.E. the people of southern Mesopotamia had achieved such increases in productivity that their farms were beginning to support an urban civilization. The ancient site at Ubaid is typical of this period.

Thus in 3,000 or 4,000 years the life of man had changed more radically than in all of the preceding 250,000 years. Before the agricultural revolution most men must have spent their waking moments seeking their next meal, except when they could gorge following a great kill. As man learned to produce food, instead of gathering, hunting or collecting it, and to store it in the grain bin and on the hoof, he was compelled as well as enabled to settle in larger communities. With human energy released for a whole spectrum of new activities, there came the development of specialized nonagricultural crafts. It is no accident that such innovations as the discovery of the basic mechanical principles, weaving, the plow, the wheel and metallurgy soon appeared.

The Process of Civilization

William H. McNeill

Historians have long been interested in how civilizations first arose and developed. Central to this question is how early civilizations influenced each other. In the following excerpt from an article, "A Short History of Humanity" (2000), noted historian William H. McNeill stresses the importance of networks of communication—especially by sea—in the process of civilization.

CONSIDER: *How McNeill defines "civilization"; why communication and transportation were so important in the process of civilization.*

Civilizations brought strangers together and separated classes of people living side by side into distinct semiautonomous groupings. Priests and rulers, warriors and artisans, merchants and travelers, masters and servants lived very differently from one another, yet all depended on exchanges of goods and services, regulated by customary rules on the one hand and, on the other, by demographic and material limits on supply and demand.

As compared to primary communities, urban-based civilizations were (and still are) tumultuous and unstable social structures, but they were also more powerful, coordinating the actions of larger numbers of persons partly by obedience to deliberate commands, and partly by negotiated, more or less voluntary, exchanges of goods and services. Larger numbers working together, whether willingly or unwillingly, deliberately or inadvertently, had the same effect that cooperation within larger bands of more or less undifferentiated individuals had had at the beginning of human history, In other words, civilized forms of society exerted power over the natural environs and over much larger human numbers than more homogeneous societies were able to do. Ever since the first civilizations arose, civilized social complexity therefore tended to spread, until in our own time almost all humankind is caught up in a single global system, exchanging messages furiously fast and upsetting traditional ways of life almost everywhere. . . .

An appropriately imaginative historian can hope to discern major landmarks in the civilizing process by focusing on breakthroughs in communication and transport that altered the range and flow of messages among human populations, and thereby accelerated the propagation of novelties far and wide that met human wishes or wants better than before. . . .

When people first learned to use paddles and sails to propel rafts and boats, possibilities for long-range encounters opened up along the coasts of easily navigable seas. Almost certainly parts of Southeast Asia (and especially the offshore islands of Indonesia) were the principal sites of this breakthrough. A vague horizon for seafaring is established by the fact that people who reached Australia some 40,000 years ago (and perhaps even earlier than that) must have used some sort of flotation device to get there. But wooden rafts and ships seldom leave archaeological traces; and since melting glaciers subsequently raised sea levels substantially, early coastal settlements in Southeast Asia and everywhere else have been inundated.

Still, it seems clear that at an early time sailing vessels began to exploit the reversible monsoon winds to sail to and fro in Southeast Asia and along the shores of the Indian Ocean. Such seafaring was well developed by the time Sumerian records offer a glimpse of the sea network that connected the land of Sumer at the head of the Persian Gulf with Indus and Egyptian societies—and with a wider world of seagoing peoples beyond.

Sumerian cities, in fact, arose where this sea network connected up with a newer network of caravan portage. Donkeys, the first important caravan animal, were domesticated about seven thousand years ago; but since caravan management was almost as complicated as seafaring it presumably took a while for overland portage to become significant. But when local peoples learned that letting caravans pass for a negotiated protection fee assured a better supply of exotic and desirable items than plundering them did, overland portage across relatively long distances began to connect diverse populations more insistently than before. And it is surely not an accident that it was in Sumer, where an already ancient seagoing network intermeshed with a newly accessible hinterland, that the first cities arose between 4000 and 3000 B.C.E. Goods and ideas moved along these communications networks and, where they converged, the Sumerians were in an optimal position to pick and choose, elaborating and improving upon skills and knowledge coming from far and near.

Sumerian achievements, such as writing, metallurgy, wheeled vehicles, and an impressive religion, spread outward along the same networks. For example, on distant northern steppes Indo-European herdsmen accepted the Sumerian pantheon of seven high gods—sky, earth, thunderstorm, sun, moon, fresh water, and salt water. And, with subsequent adjustments, their Aryan, Greek, Latin, Celtic, German, and Slavic descendants carried this pagan pantheon with them into India and across Europe.

SOURCE: William H. McNeill, "A Short History of Humanity," *The New York Review of Books,* June 29, 2000, pp. 9–11 as excerpted.

Similarly, wheeled vehicles, in the form of two-wheeled chariots, reached China by 1400 B.C.E. and helped to consolidate the power of the Shang dynasty. But of all Sumerian innovations, their resort to writing was perhaps the most significant since it added a new dimension to information storage and retrieval. Being more capacious, enduring, and reliable than human memory, written records allowed priests and rulers to collect and disburse indefinitely large quantities of material goods according to deliberate rules. As a result, government became more powerful; commands became more enforcible, even at a distance; and coordinated effort among thousands and eventually millions of persons became routine.

Freedom in the Ancient World: Civilization in Sumer

Herbert J. Muller

Historians generally see the development of cities as a sign of transformation into a civilized state and indeed an essential component of being civilized. Some of the earliest cities were formed by the Sumerians in the valley of the Tigris and Euphrates rivers, where settlers had already developed irrigation systems. In the following selection Herbert J. Muller analyzes the social, political, and religious significance of cities and irrigation systems for the Sumerians, and focuses particularly on the problems that civilization brought.

CONSIDER: *Why cities and irrigation systems require new systems of legal and political control; why Muller believes that the increased wealth and opportunity created by civilization was not an unmitigated benefit to the Sumerians; how political, economic, and social decisions made by the Sumerians were reflected in their religion.*

We must now consider the problems that came with civilization—problems due not so much to the sinful nature of man as to the nature of the city. "Friendship lasts a day" ran a Sumerian proverb; "kinship endures forever." The heterogeneous city was no longer held together by the bonds of kinship. Even the family was unstable. "For his pleasure: marriage," ran another proverb; "on his thinking it over: divorce." Hence the Sumerians could no longer depend on the informal controls of custom or common understanding that had sufficed to maintain order in the village. They had to

supplement custom by political controls, a system of laws, backed by both force and moral persuasion. In this sense the city created the problem of evil. Here, not in Eden, occurred the Fall.

More specifically, the rise of civilization forced the social question that is still with us. By their great drainage and irrigation system the Sumerians were able to produce an increasing surplus of material wealth. The question is: Who was to possess and enjoy this wealth? The answer in Sumer was to be the invariable one: Chiefly a privileged few. The god who in theory owned it all in fact required the services of priestly bailiffs, and before long these were doing more than their share in assisting him to enjoy it, at the expense of the many menials beneath them. Class divisions grew more pronounced in the divine household, as in the city at large. The skilled artisans of Sumer, whose work in metals and gems has hardly ever been surpassed, became a proletariat, unable to afford their own products. "The valet always wears dirty clothes" noted the Sumerian scribe. Other proverbs dwelt on the troubles of the poor:

The poor man is better dead than alive;
If he has bread, he has no salt,
If he has salt, he has no bread.

The poor have not always been with us. As a class, they came with civilization. There was also the new type of the slave: victors in war had discovered that it was even more profitable to domesticate human captives than other types of animals. And outside its walls the city created still another type of man—the peasant. The villager had been preliterate, on a cultural par with his fellows; the peasant was illiterate, aware of the writing he did not know, aware of his dependence on the powers of the city, and liable to exploitation by them. Altogether, the urban revolution produced the anomaly that would become more glaring with the Industrial Revolution. As the collective wealth increased, many men were worse off, and many more felt worse off, than the neolithic villager had been.

Similarly the great irrigation system posed a political problem: Who would control the organization it required, exercise the power it gave? The answer was the same—a privileged few. As the temple estate grew into a city, the priesthood needed more secular help, especially in time of war. Sumerian legend retained memories of some sort of democratic assembly in the early cities, but it emphasized that after the Flood "kingship descended from heaven." The gods had sent kings to maintain order and to assure the proper service of them upon which the city's welfare depended. This was not a pure heavenly boon, judging by the Sumerian myth of a Golden Age before the Flood: an Eden of peace and plenty in which there was no snake, scorpion, hyena, lion, wild dog, wolf—"There was no fear, no terror. Man had no rival." At any rate, the divinely appointed king ruled as an absolute monarch, and might be a terror. With him descended a plague of locusts—the tax collectors. Again civilization meant an anomaly: as the collective achieved much more effective freedom, many individuals enjoyed less freedom than prehistoric villagers had.

In Sumer these problems were aggravated by a profounder paradox. All along, we have seen, man had come to depend more and more on supernatural means of power as he extended his own power over nature. Now, with the most triumphant demonstration of his creative powers, he became convinced of his utter dependence upon the gods, his utter powerlessness without them. The monumental architecture of the Sumerians exemplifies this crowning paradox. The ziggurat, which inspired the Hebrew myth of the Tower of Babel, was by no means the symbol of human presumption that Jehovah mistook it for—it was a symbol of abject subservience. Sumerian myth taught that man had been created simply to be the slave of the gods; he did all the dirty work, that they might rest and freely enjoy. They got the credit for all the highest achievements of the Sumerians. They also got the prime benefits, since the works of the city were dedicated to the promotion of their welfare, not man's welfare.

The Intellectual Adventure of Ancient Man

Henri Frankfort and H. A. Frankfort

One of the most difficult tasks of the historian is to understand ancient peoples' assumptions and attitudes about the world and their place in it. It is much easier to gather political or social information about ancient peoples, for this is often recorded in a manner understandable to us. To come to conclusions about how individuals perceived the world when those perceptions may have been quite different from our own requires a subtler use of evidence and imaginative interpretation. In the following selection Henri Frankfort, an archaeologist and cultural historian, and H. A. Frankfort attempt to describe one of the most fundamental differences in outlook between ancient and modern peoples: the ancients' perception of the physical world not as made up of inanimate things or natural forces (each one of which modern peoples refer to as "it") but as living, dynamic, individual beings (each one of which the ancients referred to as "thou").

SOURCE: Reprinted from *The Intellectual Adventure of Ancient Man,* by Henri Frankfort and H. A. Frankfort, by permission of The University of Chicago Press. Copyright © 1946, pp. 4–6.

CONSIDER: *The religious implications of this distinction of attitudes between modern and ancient peoples; the evidence that might be used to support or attack this interpretation; the role these attitudes might play in explaining the nature of science in the ancient world.*

The ancients, like the modern savages, saw man always as part of society, and society as imbedded in nature and dependent upon cosmic forces. For them nature and man did not stand in opposition and did not, therefore, have to be apprehended by different modes of cognition. We shall see, in fact, in the course of this book, that natural phenomena were regularly conceived in terms of human experience and that human experience was conceived in terms of cosmic events. We touch here upon a distinction between the ancients and us which is of the utmost significance for our inquiry.

The fundamental difference between the attitudes of modern and ancient man as regards the surrounding world is this: for modern, scientific man the phenomenal world is primarily an "It"; for ancient—and also for primitive—man it is a "Thou." . . .

The world appears to primitive man neither inanimate nor empty but redundant with life; and life has individuality, in man and beast and plant, and in every phenomenon which confronts man—the thunderclap, the sudden shadow, the eerie and unknown clearing in the wood, the stone which suddenly hurts him when he stumbles while on a hunting trip. Any phenomenon may at any time face him, not as "It," but as "Thou." In this confrontation, "Thou" reveals its individuality, its qualities, its will. "Thou" is not contemplated with intellectual detachment; it is experienced as life confronting life, involving every faculty of man in a reciprocal relationship. Thoughts, no less than acts and feelings, are subordinated to this experience. . . .

The whole man confronts a living "Thou" in nature; and the whole man—emotional and imaginative as well as intellectual—gives expression to the experience. All experience of "Thou" is highly individual; and early man does, in fact, view happenings as individual events. An account of such events and also their explanation can be conceived only as action and necessarily take the form of a story. In other words, the ancients told myths instead of presenting an analysis or conclusions. We would explain, for instance, that certain atmospheric changes broke a drought and brought about rain. The Babylonians observed the same facts but experienced them as the intervention of the gigantic bird Imdugud which came to their rescue. It covered the sky with the black storm clouds of its wings and devoured the Bull of Heaven, whose hot breath had scorched the crops.

Daily Life in Ancient Egypt: The Afterlife

Lionel Casson

Conceptions about the afterlife can reveal much about a civilization, for these conceptions often reflect the moods, struggles, problems, and attitudes of a people. The Egyptians were greatly concerned with the afterlife, as indicated by their construction of large, elaborate pyramid-tombs. In the following selection, Lionel Casson analyzes the Egyptians' attitudes toward death and the afterlife, noting broad changes in those attitudes.

CONSIDER: *Exactly how the Egyptian view of the afterlife reflects the nature of the Egyptians; evidence for change after 1200 B.C.E.; how Sinuhe's account reflects a great concern with the afterlife.*

The Egyptians, as we have several times observed, were by nature buoyant, optimistic, and confident, and their view of the afterlife reflects this: throughout most of their history they conceived of it as something to be enjoyed, certainly not to be looked on with foreboding. Being at the same time pragmatic and material minded, they indulged in no fancies about its being a better world. As they saw it, death meant a continuation of one's life on earth, a continuation that, with the appropriate precautions of proper burial, prayer, and ritual, would include only the best parts of life on earth—nothing to fear, but on the other hand, nothing to want to hurry out of this world for. This attitude lasted from Old Kingdom times right up to the end of the Nineteenth Dynasty, about 1200 B.C.E., when change becomes noticeable. Pictures and texts in tombs from this time on no longer concern themselves with life on earth. The pictures cease portraying the deceased serenely contemplating the bustling life on his estates, and concentrate morbidly on the making of the mummy, the funeral, the judgment before Osiris, the demons the dead will see, and other aspects of death. The texts give up autobiography in favor of magical recipes for getting along in the life beyond the grave. This shift of emphasis is one of the distinctive features that mark Egypt's descent toward the religion-haunted, superstitious, ritualistic nation it was to become by the time Herodotus and other Greek and Roman authors wrote down their impressions.

But the shift did not occur until the very end of the period we are concerned with. Throughout most of the New Kingdom the Egyptians prepared for their entry into the next world with calm and confidence. It was an occupation that absorbed a man's time and resources for most of his life, since no one was able to rest easy until he was assured that the place of his final repose and its furnishings were ready. In *The Story of Sinuhe*, a Middle Kingdom tale of an official who went into exile but in his old age was recalled by the pharaoh in time to end his days happily in the fatherland, Sinuhe recounts the crowning joy of his homecoming:

There was constructed for me a pyramid-tomb of stone in the midst of the pyramid-tombs. The stonemasons who hew a pyramid-tomb took over its ground-area. The outline-draftsmen designed in it; the chief sculptors carved in it; and the overseers of works who are in the necropolis made it their concern. Its necessary materials were made from all the outfittings which are placed at a tombshaft. Mortuary priests were given to me. There was made for me a necropolis garden, with fields in it formerly (extending) as far as the town, like that which is done for a chief courtier. My statue was overlaid with gold, and its skirt was of fine gold. It was his majesty who had it made.

Women of Egypt and the Ancient Near East

Barbara S. Lesko

In the early Egyptian and Mesopotamian civilizations, women had greater access to valued political, religious, and economic positions than in civilizations that followed. What explains the changes that would make societies in the Near East more dominated by men and more oppressive to women? Barbara S. Lesko, an Egyptologist, addresses this question in the following excerpt. Here her focus is on the centuries toward the end of the third millennium and the beginning of the second millennium.

CONSIDER: *What three factors explain the decline of women's status and freedoms; how Egypt and early Sumer differed from later societies such as Assyria; other possible explanations for the decline of women's status and freedoms.*

SOURCE: Lionel Casson, "Daily Life in Ancient Egypt," *American Heritage*, pp. 107–108. Reprinted by permission of *American Heritage* magazine, a division of Forbes Inc., 1975.

SOURCE: Barbara S. Lesko, "Women of Egypt and the Ancient Near East," in Renate Bridenthal, Claudia Koonz, and Susan Stuard, *Becoming Visible: Women in European History*, 2d ed. (Boston: Houghton Mifflin Co., 1987), p. 74.

What was the real cause of the rise of patriarchy, which became increasingly oppressive to women in the Near East after Sumerian civilization waned? Several reasons suggest themselves. The first is militarism. In an early agrarian society like Egypt where internal disputes were effectively handled by the strong, centralized government, where wars usually took place beyond the borders, where no standing army existed during the first 1500 years of recorded history, and where invasion seldom affected the country, women continually shared the burdens, full rights, and obligations of citizens. However, in the newer societies, founded by the sons of ever-vigilant and suspicious desert nomads, where warfare between cities was frequent and invasion by outside hostile forces familiar, militarism developed, excluding women and rendering them dependents. Second, where commercialism held sway at the same time—as in Assyria—the worst examples of patriarchy were found. Commerce based on private initiative first appears on a well developed scale in the Old Babylonian period where the first concerted effort by men to control women for financial gain is also documented. This is seen not only in the laws of Hammurabi but in institutions like that of the cloistered *Naditu* women. Coupled with virulent militarism, as in Assyria, the rise of commercialism had a devastating effect on women's rights. In Egypt large scale commerce long remained a virtual monopoly of the state, so its impact on society remained less significant.

We might further point out that, even during the somewhat militaristic Egyptian empire of the New Kingdom, women's status and freedoms did not diminish significantly. This introduces a third factor: confidence. A supremely confident nation can afford tolerance. Egypt had confidence in its gods, in the eternity of life, and in the bounty of its land. Sumer, in its early formative years, shared these advantages too. Not so the subsequent societies. It is the threatened male and the threatened society—like Assyria, surrounded on three sides by deadly enemies, and weak impoverished Israel—which created such a restricted role for their women.

A History of the Jews

Paul Johnson

A major task of the historian is to delineate what distinguished a people, an era, or a development from others. In analyzing the Jews, most historians emphasize that the Jewish religion

SOURCE: Excerpt from *A History of the Jews* by Paul Johnson. Copyright © 1987 by Paul Johnson. Reprinted by permission of HarperCollins Publishers, Inc. and George Weidenfeld & Nicolson, Limited.

was monotheistic, recognizing only one god, and that major elements of Judaism would later be directly related to and incorporated into two other major religions founded in that area of the world: Christianity and Islam. In the following selection, Paul Johnson goes beyond the monotheism of the Jewish religion to focus on the ways the Jews were unique as ancient writers.

CONSIDER: *Whether Johnson's interpretation is supported by the primary documents on religion in the ancient Near East; why these two characteristics of ancient Jewish literature are so important; how this interpretation of ancient Jewish literature compares with Frankfort's interpretation of ancient peoples' mentality.*

The Jews had two unique characteristics as ancient writers. They were the first to create consequential, substantial and interpretative history. It has been argued that they learned the art of history from the Hittites, another historically minded people, but it is obvious that they were fascinated by their past from very early times. They knew they were a special people who had not simply evolved from an unrecorded past but had been brought into existence, for certain definite purposes, by a specific series of divine acts. They saw it as their collective business to determine, record, comment and reflect upon these acts. No other people has ever shown, particularly at that remote time, so strong a compulsion to explore their origins. The Bible gives constant examples of the probing historical spirit: why, for instance, was there a heap of stones before the city gate at Ai? What was the meaning of the twelve stones at Gilgal? This passion for aetiology, the quest for explanations, broadened into a more general habit of seeing the present and future in terms of the past. The Jews wanted to know about themselves and their destiny. They wanted to know about God and his intentions and wishes. Since God, in their theology, was the sole cause of all events—as Amos put it, 'Does evil befall a city unless Yahweh wills it?'—and thus the author of history, and since they were the chosen actors in his vast dramas, the record and study of historical events was the key to the understanding of both God and man.

Hence the Jews were above all historians, and the Bible is essentially a historical work from start to finish. . . .

Ancient Jewish history is both intensely divine and intensely humanist. History was made by God, operating independently or through man. The Jews were not interested and did not believe in impersonal forces. They were less curious about the physics of creation than any other literate race of antiquity. They turned their back on nature and discounted its manifestations except in so far as they reflected the divine-human drama. The notion of vast geographical or economic forces determining history was quite alien to them. There is much natural description in the Bible, some of astonishing beauty, but it is stage-scenery for the historical play, a mere backdrop for the characters. The Bible is vibrant because it is entirely about living creatures; and since God, though living, cannot be described or even imagined, the attention is directed relentlessly on man and woman.

Hence the second unique characteristic of ancient Jewish literature: the verbal presentation of the human personality in all its range and complexity. The Jews were the first race to find words to express the deepest human emotions, especially the feelings produced by bodily or mental suffering, anxiety, spiritual despair and desolation, and the remedies for these evils produced by human ingenuity—hope, resolution, confidence in divine assistance, the consciousness of innocence, of righteousness, penitence, sorrow and humility.

❧ CHAPTER QUESTIONS

1. What characteristics of the societies discussed in this chapter fit with what we usually consider as "civilized"?

2. How would you explain the rise of these civilizations and particularly the similarities between them?

3. Evaluate the relative importance of geographic, economic, and other factors in explaining the differing natures of these early civilizations.

4. Drawing from both primary and secondary documents, describe some of the most likely of ancient peoples' assumptions and attitudes about the world, about their societies, and about women. How might some of these assumptions and attitudes differ in the various societies of the ancient Near East?

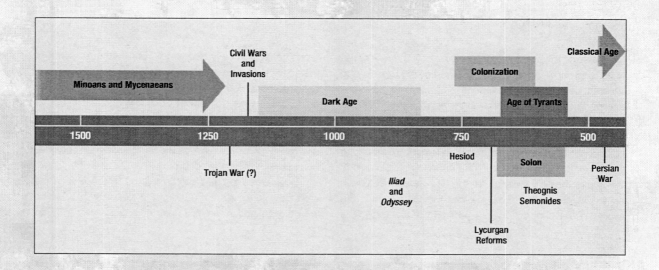

					Civil Wars and Invasions					Colonization		Classical Age

Minoans and Mycenaeans | Dark Age | Age of Tyrants

| 1500 | 1250 | 1000 | 750 | 500 |

Trojan War (?)

Iliad and Odyssey

Hesiod

Solon

Theognis Semonides

Persian War

Lycurgan Reforms

2 The Emergence of Greek Civilization

Although Western civilization was born in the ancient Near East, we can more easily recognize our own roots in Greek civilization. Before reaching its apex during the fifth and fourth centuries B.C.E., Greek civilization has a long developmental history. During the third and second millennia, the Minoans on the island of Crete developed a sophisticated maritime civilization that would have strong connections to mainland Greece. During the second millennium, the Mycenaean Greeks, a militaristic people, rose to prominence on the Greek mainland. Both of these Bronze Age peoples fell to a series of upheavals between about 1400 and 1000 B.C.E. After three centuries of cultural decline, the Greeks reemerged and entered into a period of vigorous growth. Commerce expanded and the Greeks colonized lands from the Black Sea to the western Mediterranean. At the same time the city-states entered into a period of political evolution and cultural development.

Two city-states in particular became prominent toward the end of this period: Sparta and Athens. Each represents an extreme of developments other city-states would also experience. The Spartans developed a tightly organized, militaristic, land-based state, dominating the Peloponnesian Peninsula. Athens developed a relatively open, democratic, maritime state, dominating Attica and supporting commercial and cultural expansion. During the first decades of the fifth century B.C.E., these rivals managed to ally in face of the greater Persian threat; thereafter, they were competitors in struggles that involved most of the Greek world.

23

The selections in this chapter address five major questions. First, how do we explain the end of the Bronze Age civilizations of the Mycenaeans and Minoans and the decline into the succeeding "Dark Age"? Interpretations ranging from invasions to civil wars are examined. Second, what is the historical significance of the Homeric epics? What historical information about Mycenaean times and the Dark Age do the Homeric epics provide? What was their significance for the Greeks and for Greek culture in general? Third, how did the Greek city-state evolve in the period between 800 and 500 B.C.E.? The focus here is on early Sparta and early Athens. Some of the social divisions reflected by political changes are also explored here. Fourth, what was the significance of Greek colonization between about 750 and 550 B.C.E.? How was colonization related to Greek economy and society? What role did colonization play in the spread of Greek civilization? Finally, what was the nature of Greek societies and ideals in this early period?

The sources in this chapter take us to the end of the sixth century B.C.E. At that point the Classical Age, which will be examined in the next chapter, began.

Primary Sources

The Iliad

Homer

Homer's The Iliad, a work of literature and an important cultural, religious, and social source on Greek civilization, is one of our few historical documents from the early period of Greek history. Most likely orally composed or assembled during the ninth or eighth century B.C.E., it refers to the great war between the Greeks of the Mycenaean Age and the Trojans (occupants of a city in Asia Minor near the mouth of the Hellespont), probably fought in the thirteenth century B.C.E. The social and political conditions described in The Iliad are a mixture of traditions during Mycenaean times and typical practices during the ensuing "Dark Age." The following selection refers to a shield being forged by Hephaistos, the Greek god of metalworking. The shield is decorated with scenes of two cities. In the first city, which is at peace, a trial is taking place. Around the second one, which is being besieged, are signs of a prosperous economy.

CONSIDER: *The political characteristics of these cities; the basis upon which this trial will be decided; the economic characteristics of the second city.*

On it he wrought in all their beauty two cities of mortal
    men. And there were marriages in one, and festivals.
They were leading the brides along the city from their
    maiden chambers under the flaring of torches, and
    the loud bride song was arising.
The young men followed the circles of the dance, and
    among them the flutes and lyres kept up their
    clamour as in the meantime the women standing
    each at the door of her court admired them.

The people were assembled in the market place, where
    a quarrel had arisen, and two men were disputing
    over the blood price for a man who had been killed.
    One man promised full restitution in a public
    statement, but the other refused and would accept
    nothing.
Both then made for an arbitrator, to have a decision;
    and people were speaking up on either side, to help
    both men.
But the heralds kept the people in hand, as meanwhile
    the elders were in session on benches of polished
    stone in the sacred circle and held in their hands the
    staves of the heralds who lift their voices.
The two men rushed before these, and took turns
    speaking their cases, and between them lay on the
    ground two talents of gold, to be given to that judge
    who in this case spoke the straightest opinion.
But around the other city were lying two forces of
    armed men shining in their war gear. For one side
    counsel was divided whether to storm and sack, or
    share between both sides the property and all the
    possessions the lovely citadel held hard within it.
But the city's people were not giving way, and armed for
    an ambush.
Their beloved wives and their little children stood on
    the rampart to hold it, and with them the men with
    age upon them, but meanwhile the others went out.
    And Ares led them, and Pallas Athene.
These were gold, both, and golden raiment upon them,
    and they were beautiful and huge in their armour,
    being divinities, and conspicuous from afar, but the
    people around them were smaller.
These, when they were come to the place that was set
    for their ambush, in a river, where there was a
    watering place for all animals, there they sat down in
    place shrouding themselves in the bright bronze.

SOURCE: Reprinted from Homer, *The Iliad*, trans. by Richmond Lattimore, by permission of The University of Chicago Press. Copyright © 1977, pp. 388–390.

But apart from these were sitting two men to watch for the rest of them and waiting until they could see the sheep and the shambling cattle, who appeared presently, and two herdsmen went along with them playing happily on pipes, and took no thought of the treachery.

Those others saw them, and made a rush, and quickly thereafter cut off on both sides the herds of cattle and the beautiful flocks of shining sheep, and killed the shepherds upon them. . . .

He made upon it a soft field, the pride of the tilled land, wide and triple-ploughed, with many ploughmen upon it who wheeled their teams at the turn and drove them in either direction. . . .

He made on it the precinct of a king, where the labourers were reaping, with the sharp reaping hooks in their hands. Of the cut swathes some fell along the lines of reaping, one after another, while the sheaf-binders caught up others and tied them with bind-ropes.

There were three sheaf-binders who stood by, and behind them were children picking up the cut swathes, and filled their arms with them and carried and gave them always; and by them the king in silence and holding his staff stood near the line of the reapers, happily.

And apart and under a tree the heralds made a feast ready and trimmed a great ox they had slaughtered. Meanwhile the women scattered, for the workman to eat, abundant white barley.

He made on it a great vineyard heavy with clusters, lovely in gold, but grapes upon it were darkened and the vines themselves stood out through poles of silver. About them he made a field-ditch of dark metal, and drove all around this a fence of tin; and there was only one path to the vineyard, and along it ran the grape-bearers for the vineyard's stripping.

Young girls and young men, in all their light-hearted innocence, carried the kind, sweet fruit away in their woven baskets, and in their midst a youth with a singing lyre played charmingly upon it for them, and sang the beautiful song for Linos in a light voice, and they followed him, and with singing and whistling and light dance-steps of their feet kept time to the music.

Works and Days

Hesiod

While the Homeric epics reflected many of the heroic values of the early Greeks, most Greeks faced the everyday realities of work. One of the earliest sources that describes these concerns with work and wealth was written by the Greek poet Hesiod,

who lived in the eighth century B.C.E. *In Works and Days, he includes thoughts about his own life and labor in the fields as well as fables and allegories. In the following excerpt, Hesiod discusses the importance of hard work and how wealth should be gained.*

CONSIDER: *The values Hesiod supports; the problems within Greek society that concern Hesiod; how, according to Hesiod, wealth is best obtained and guarded.*

Both gods and men are angry with a man who lives idle, for in nature he is like the stingless drones who waste the labour of the bees, eating without working; but let it be your care to order your work properly, that in the right season your barns may be full of victual. Through work men grow rich in flocks and substance, and working they are much better loved by the immortals. Work is no disgrace: it is idleness which is a disgrace. But if you work, the idle will soon envy you as you grow rich, for fame and renown attend on wealth. And whatever be your lot, work is best for you, if you turn your misguided mind away from other men's property to your work and attend to your livelihood as I bid you. An evil shame is the needy man's companion, shame which both greatly harms and prospers men: shame is with poverty, but confidence with wealth.

Wealth should not be seized: god-given wealth is much better; for if a man take great wealth violently and perforce, or if he steal it through his tongue, as often happens when gain deceives men's sense and dishonour tramples down honour, the gods soon blot him out and make that man's house low, and wealth attends him only for a little time. . . . He who adds to what he has, will keep off bright-eyed hunger; for if you add only a little to a little and do this often, soon that little will become great. What a man has by him at home does not trouble him: it is better to have your stuff at home, for whatever is abroad may mean loss. It is a good thing to draw on what you have; but it grieves your heart to need something and not to have it, and I bid you mark this. Take your fill when the cask is first opened and when it is nearly spent, but midways be sparing: it is poor saving when you come to the lees.

Let the wage promised to a friend be fixed; even with your brother smile—and get a witness; for trust and mistrust, alike ruin men.

Do not let a flaunting woman coax and cozen and deceive you: she is after your barn. The man who trusts womankind trusts deceivers.

There should be an only son, to feed his father's house, for so wealth will increase in the home; but if you leave a second son you should die old. Yet Zeus can easily give great wealth to a greater number. More hands mean more work and more increase.

If your heart within you desires wealth, do these things and work with work upon work.

SOURCE: Hugh G. Evelyn-White, trans., *Hesiod, the Homeric Hymns and Homerica.* New York: The Macmillan Co., 1914, pp. 25–31.

A Colonization Agreement

From about 750 to 550 B.C.E. Greeks from the mainland, the Aegean islands, and Asia Minor founded colonies throughout the Mediterranean region and as far east as the shores of the Black Sea. Historians speculate that this was one way for the Greeks to solve various social, political, and economic pressures, particularly resulting from population growth. In any case, the spread of colonies facilitated the growth of Greek commerce and laid the foundations for long-lasting Greek cultural influence throughout the Classical world. The following is a colonization agreement made around 630 B.C.E. by settlers sailing from Thera, an Aegean island, to Cyrene in North Africa.

CONSIDER: *The evidence for a sense of urgency or necessity in gaining support for this expedition; the kind of penalties considered legitimate and effective to enforce the will of the Assembly.*

OATH (AGREEMENT?) OF THE FOUNDERS

It was resolved by the Assembly [at Thera]. Since Apollo spontaneously ordered Battus and the Theraeans to colonize Cyrene, the Theraeans are determined to send to Libya Battus as leader and king; and the Theraeans shall sail as his companions. They shall sail on equal terms from each household, one son from each. Men in the prime of youth are to be enlisted from all the districts. Of the other Theraeans any free man may sail if he wishes. If the colonists occupy the settlement, men from the same households who later land in Libya shall share in citizenship, shall be eligible for office, and shall be allotted unoccupied land. But if they fail to occupy the settlement and if the people of Thera are unable to help them and if for five years they are beset by privation, then they may without fear leave the land [and return] to Thera, [receive back] their property and be citizens. He who refuses to sail when the city sends him shall be liable to the death penalty and his property shall be confiscated. Any father who gives refuge or asylum (?) to his son or any brother who [does the same] for his brothers shall suffer the same penalty as the person refusing to sail.

Poem on Women

Semonides of Amorgos

There are few sources in this early period of Greek history that tell us about Greek attitudes toward women. Most of the sources available were written by men, usually mentioning

SOURCE: *The Ancient World to A.D. 300*, 2d ed., edited by Paul J. Alexander. Copyright © 1963 by Macmillan Publishing Co., Inc. Reprinted by permission.

SOURCE: Hugh Lloyd-Jones, *Females of the Species: Semonides on Women* (Park Ridge, N.J.: Noyes Press, 1975), pp. 30, 32, 34, 38.

women only in passing. However there is evidence that misogyny was a common theme in early Greek literature. The following selection is an example of this theme. The selection is an excerpt from a poem about women by Semonides of Amorgos, who lived on the island of Amorgos during the seventh century. The poem emphasizes how different females are from men, describing nine negative types of women and one positive type.

CONSIDER: *What this indicates about Greek men's attitudes toward women; the ways in which the good woman differs from the bad woman according to Semonides.*

In the beginning the god made the female mind separately. One he made from a long-bristled sow. In her house everything lies in disorder, smeared with mud, and rolls about the floor; and she herself unwashed, in clothes unlaundered, sits by the dungheap and grows fat.

       ❧

Another he made from a wicked vixen; a woman who knows everything. No bad thing and no better kind of thing is lost on her; for she often calls a good thing bad and a bad thing good. Her attitude is never the same.

       ❧

Another he made from a bitch, vicious, own daughter of her mother, who wants to hear everything and know everything. She peers everywhere and strays everywhere, always yapping, even if she sees no human being. A man cannot stop her by threatening, nor by losing his temper and knocking out her teeth with a stone, nor with honeyed words, not even if she is sitting with friends, but ceaselessly she keeps up a barking you can do nothing with.

       ❧

Another is from a bee; the man who gets her is fortunate, for on her alone blame does not settle. She causes his property to grow and increase, and she grows old with a husband whom she loves and who loves her, the mother of a handsome and reputable family. She stands out among all women, and a godlike beauty plays about her. She takes no pleasure in sitting among women in places where they tell stories about love. Women like her are the best and most sensible whom Zeus bestows on men.

       ❧

Zeus has contrived that all these tribes of women are with men and remain with them. Yes, this is the worst plague Zeus has made—women; if they seem to be some use to him who has them, it is to him especially that they prove a plague. The man who lives with a woman never goes through all his day in cheerfulness; he will not be quick to push out of his house Starvation, a housemate who is an enemy, a god who is against us. Just when a man most wishes to enjoy himself at home, through the dispensation of a god or the kindness of a man, she finds a way of finding fault with him and lifts her crest for battle. Yes, where there is a woman, men cannot even give hearty entertainment to a guest who has come to the house; and the very woman who seems most respectable is the one who turns out guilty of the worst atrocity; because while her husband is not looking . . . and the neighbours get pleasure in seeing how he too is mistaken. Each man will take care to praise his own wife and find fault with the other's; we do not realise that the fate of all of us is alike. Yes, this is the greatest plague that Zeus has made, and he has bound us to them with a fetter that cannot be broken. Because of this some have gone to Hades fighting for a woman. . . .

Aristocrats and Tyrants

Theognis of Megara

Between the seventh and fifth centuries B.C.E. there was a trend in most city-states away from aristocratic political and social dominance. Often part of that trend involved the rise of tyrants who professed to be leaders of the lower classes and who succeeded, if only temporarily, against the aristocrats. The rise of tyrants was particularly common during the sixth century and the results were painful to aristocrats. This is illustrated in the following selection from the bitter poems of Theognis of Megara, a sixth-century aristocrat who lost his property and was exiled upon the rise of a tyrant in his state.

CONSIDER: *How Theognis compares commoners and aristocrats; how a commoner might respond to Theognis; how a tyrant might respond to Theognis.*

Our commonwealth preserves its former frame,
Our common people are no more the same:
They that in skins and hides were rudely dress'd
Nor dreamt of law, nor sought to be redress'd
By rules of right, but in the days of old
Flock'd to the town, like cattle to the fold,
Are now the brave and wise; and we, the rest,
(Their betters nominally, once the best)
Degenerate, debasèd, timid, mean!
Who can endure to witness such a scene?
Their easy courtesies, the ready smile,
Prompt to deride, to flatter, and beguile!
Their utter disregard of right or wrong,
Or truth or honour!—Out of such a throng
(For any difficulties, any need,
For any bold design or manly deed)

SOURCE: George Howe and Gustave A. Harrer, eds., *Greek Literature in Translation*, J. H. Frere, trans., rev. ed., Preston H. Epps, ed. (New York: Harper and Brothers, 1948), pp. 139–140. Reprinted by permission of the Estates of George Howe and Gustave A. Harrer.

Never imagine you can choose a just
Or steady friend, or faithful in his trust.
     But change your habits! Let them go their way!
Be condescending, affable, and gay! . . .
Court not a tyrant's favour, nor combine
To further his iniquitous design;
But, if your faith is pledg'd, though late and loth,
If covenants have pass'd between you both,
Never assassinate him! keep your oath!
But should he still misuse his lawless power
To trample on the people, and devour,
Depose or overturn him; anyhow!
Your oath permits it, and the gods allow. . . .
     Yet much I fear the faction and the strife,
Throughout our Grecian cities, raging rife,
And their wild councils. But do thou defend
This town of ours, our founder and our friend! . . .

Early Athens

Solon

Between the eighth and fifth centuries B.C.E. Athenian society became more complex. This affected Athens' political structure, which evolved from monarchical and aristocratic forms to more democratic institutions. A central struggle throughout this period took place between the wealthy aristocracy and the poorer classes. In the late seventh and early sixth centuries this struggle threatened to break out into civil war. In 594 Solon, a poet and wealthy aristocrat of recognized integrity, was called on to mediate and effect decisions to end this struggle. In the following document Aristotle quotes Solon and describes how Solon managed to find just solutions that recognized the issues on both sides without completely satisfying anyone.

CONSIDER: *The principal social divisions within Athenian society according to Solon; Solon's justifications for his decisions; the political and social significance of Solon's decisions.*

The truth of this view of Solon's policy is established alike by the common consent of all, and by the mention which he has himself made of it in his poems. Thus:—

I gave to the mass of the people such rank as befitted
     their need,
I took not away their honour, and I granted naught to
     their greed;
But those who were rich in power, who in wealth were
     glorious and great,
I bethought me that naught should befall them unworthy
     their splendour and state;

SOURCE: Aristotle, *The Athenian Constitution,* trans. F. G. Kenyon (London: George Bell and Sons, 1891), pp. 18–20.

And I stood with my shield outstretched, and both were
safe in its sight,
And I would not that either should triumph, when the
triumph was not with right.

Again he declares how the mass of the people ought to be
treated:—

But thus will the people best the voice of their leaders obey,
When neither too slack is the rein, nor violence holdeth
the sway:
For satiety breedeth a child, the presumption that
spurns control,
When riches too great are poured upon men of
unbalanced soul.

And again elsewhere he speaks about the persons who
wished to redistribute the land:—

So they came in search of plunder, and their cravings
knew no bound,
Every one among them deeming endless wealth would
here be found,
And that I with glozing[1] smoothness hid a cruel mind
within.
Fondly then and vainly dreamt they; now they raise an
angry din,
And they glare askance in anger, and the light within
their eyes
Burns with hostile flames upon me. Yet therein no
justice lies.
All I promised, fully wrought I with the gods at hand to
cheer,
Naught beyond of folly ventured. Never to my soul
was dear
With a tyrant's force to govern, nor to see the good
and base
Side by side in equal portion share the rich home of
our race.

Once more he speaks of the destitution of the poorer
classes and of those who before were in servitude, but
were released owing to the Seisachtheia[2]:—

Wherefore I freed the racked and tortured crowd
From all the evils that beset their lot,
Thou, when slow time brings justice in its train,
O mighty mother of the Olympian gods,
Dark Earth, thou best canst witness, from whose breast
I swept the pillars[3] broad-cast planted there,
And made thee free, who hadst been slave of yore.
And many a man whom fraud or law had sold

Far from his god-built land, and outcast slave,
I brought again to Athens; yea, and some,
Exiles from home through debt's oppressive load,
Speaking no more the dear Athenian tongue,
But wandering far and wide, I brought again;
And those that here in vilest slavery
Crouched 'neath a master's frown, I set them free.
Thus might and right were yoked in harmony,
Since by the force of law I won my ends
And kept my promise. Equal laws I gave
To evil and to good, with even hand
Drawing straight justice for the lot of each.
But had another held the goad as I,
One in whose heart was guile and greediness,
He had not kept the people back from strife.
For had I granted, now what pleased the one,
Then what their foes devised within their hearts,
Of many a man this state had been bereft.
Therefore I took me strength from every side
And turned at bay like wolf among the hounds.

And again he reviles both parties for their grumblings in
the times that followed:—

Nay, if one must lay blame where blame is due,
Wer't not for me, the people ne'er had set
Their eyes upon these blessings e'en in dreams:—
But greater men, the men of wealthier life,
Should praise me and should court me as their friend.
For had any other man, he says, received this exalted
post,—
He had not kept the people back, nor ceased
Till he had robbed the richness of the milk.
But I stood forth, a landmark in the midst,
And barred the foes from battle.

Constitution of the Lacedaemonians

Xenophon

*Sparta was one of the most powerful and well-known Greek
city-states. Located on the Peloponnesian Peninsula, it developed a reputation during the seventh and sixth centuries B.C.E.
for being conservative, disciplined, inward-looking, and devoted to military pursuits and strength. Much of this reputation
derived from events during the middle of the seventh century
when the helots, formerly the neighboring Messenians who had
been conquered by the Spartans and subjected to serfdom, revolted against the far outnumbered Spartans. With great difficulty the revolt was put down, but from that point on the Spartans committed themselves to preserving their dominance at all
costs. Various constitutional reforms were instituted to ensure
Spartan unity and military strength. Traditionally, these reforms*

---

[1]Explaining away.

[2]"Shaking off of burdens"—Solon's reform of the law of debt.

[3]These were the pillars set up on mortgaged lands, to record the fact
of the encumbrance.

SOURCE: Francis R. B. Godolphin, ed., *The Greek Historians*, vol. II, trans.
Henry G. Dakyns (New York: Random House, 1942), pp. 658–661,
666–669. Reprinted by permission.

were attributed to a perhaps legendary lawgiver, Lycurgus. Direct primary sources for these reforms are thin. The best evidence we have comes from Xenophon (c. 434–c. 355), an Athenian admirer of Sparta who wrote some two centuries after these occurrences. The following is a selection from his Constitution of the Lacedaemonians.

CONSIDER: *Xenophon's explanation for the extraordinary power and prestige of Sparta; the nature and purposes of Sparta's education system; how Sparta differed from other Greek city-states.*

I recall the astonishment with which I first noted the unique position of Sparta among the states of Hellas, the relatively sparse population, and at the same time the extraordinary power and prestige of the community. I was puzzled to account for the fact. It was only when I came to consider the peculiar institutions of the Spartans that my wonderment ceased. Or rather, it is transferred to the legislator who gave them those laws, obedience to which has been the secret of their prosperity. This legislator, Lycurgus, I admire, and hold him to have been one of the wisest of mankind. . . .

He insisted on the training of the body as incumbent no less on the female than the male; and in pursuit of the same idea instituted rival contests in running and feats of strength for women as for men. His belief was that where both parents were strong their progeny would be found to be more vigorous. . . .

Marriage, as he ordained it, must only take place in the prime of bodily vigour, this too being, as he believed, a condition conducive to the production of healthy offspring. . . .

But when we turn to Lycurgus, instead of leaving it to each member of the state privately to appoint a slave to be his son's tutor, he set over the young Spartans a public guardian, the Paidonomos, to give him his proper title, with complete authority over them. . . .

Instead of softening their feet with shoe or sandal, his rule was to make them hardy through going barefoot. This habit, if practised, would, as he believed, enable them to scale heights more easily and clamber down precipices with less danger. . . .

Instead of making them effeminate with a variety of clothes, his rule was to habituate them to a single garment the whole year through, thinking that so they would be better prepared to withstand the variations of heat and cold.

Again, as regards food, according to his regulation the prefect, or head of the flock, must see that his messmates gathered to the club meal, with such moderate food as to avoid that heaviness which is engendered by repletion, and yet not to remain altogether unacquainted with the pains of penurious living. His belief was that by such training in boyhood they would be better able when occasion demanded to continue toiling on an empty stomach. . . .

On the other hand, in order to guard against a too great pinch of starvation, though he did not actually allow the boys to help themselves without further trouble to what they needed more, he did give them permission to steal this thing or that in the effort to alleviate their hunger. . . .

It is obvious, I say, that the whole of this education was intended to make the boys craftier and more inventive in getting in supplies, while at the same time it cultivated their warlike instincts. . . .

Furthermore, and in order that the boys should not want a ruler, even in case the guardian himself were absent, he gave to any citizen who chanced to be present authority to lay upon them injunctions for their good, and to chastise them for any trespass committed. . . .

We all know that in the generality of states every one devotes his full energy to the business of making money: one man as a tiller of the soil, another as a mariner, a third as a merchant, whilst others depend on various arts to earn a living. But at Sparta Lycurgus forbade his freeborn citizens to have anything whatsoever to do with the concerns of moneymaking. As freeman, he enjoined upon them to regard as their concern exclusively those activities upon which the foundations of civic liberty are based. . . .

In Sparta, on the contrary, the stronger a man is the more readily does he bow before constituted authority. And indeed, they pride themselves on their humility, and on a prompt obedience, running, or at any rate not crawling with laggard step, at the word of command. Such an example of eager discipline, they are persuaded, set by themselves, will not fail to be followed by the rest.

Accordingly the ephors[4] are competent to punish whomsoever they choose: they have power to exact fines on the spur of the moment; they have power to depose magistrates in mid career, nay, actually to imprison and bring them to trial on the capital charge. Entrusted with these vast powers, they do not, as do the rest of states, allow the magistrates elected to exercise authority as they like, right through the year of office; but, in the style rather of despotic monarchs, or presidents of the games, at the first symptom of an offence against the law they inflict chastisement without warning and without hesitation. . . .

And yet another point may well excite our admiration for Lycurgus largely. It had not escaped his observation that communities exist where those who are willing to make virtue their study and delight fail somehow in ability to add to the glory of their fatherland. That lesson the legislator laid to heart, and in Sparta he enforced, as a matter of public duty, the practice of every virtue by every citizen. And so it is that, just as man differs from man in some excellence, according as he cultivates or neglects to cultivate it, this city of Sparta, with good reason, outshines all other states in virtue; since she, and she alone, has made the attainment of a high standard of noble living a public duty.

---

[4]Elected magistrates.

Visual Sources

Trade, Culture, and Colonization

This scene (figure 2.1) is from the inside of a Laconian cup dating from about 560 B.C.E. It shows King Arcesilas II of the Greek North African colony of Cyrene (a Dorian Greek colony originally founded by Thera around 630 B.C.E.) supervising the weighing and loading of a shipment of what is probably silphium, a medicinal plant exported from the area. On the left Arcesilas is sitting on the deck of a ship underneath a canopy, apparently arguing with his steward. On the right workers carry on the silphium and call out the weight while below workers fill the hold with it. Around are animals of the area: a lizard, a monkey, and birds.

This cup reflects the importance of trade for the Greeks and the role Greek colonies played in this trade. It also indicates a growing interconnectedness based on the Mediterranean—a familiarity with the shoreland areas in which Greeks had settled and contact with the cultures and environment they found there, as might be surmised by the use of a North African plant for medicinal purposes in the Greek homeland and by the large number of cups similar to these that were being exported from Laconia. The words on the cup provide evidence for the spread of literacy among Greeks.

CONSIDER: Connections between this cup and the colonization agreement; how this cup can be used as evidence for the importance of commerce and colonization in the Greek world.

FIGURE 2.1 (© Bibliothèque Nationale, Paris, France, Archives Charmet/The Bridgeman Art Library)

Migration and Colonization

These two maps reveal a number of relationships between history and geography in the Greek world. Map 2.1 shows some of the dialects of the Greeks; the arrows indicate some of the probable directions of Greek migrations as traced by these dialects in the aftermath of the Dorian invasions between the thirteenth and tenth centuries B.C.E. *Map 2.2 shows the extent of Greek settlement around the Mediterranean and Black seas between 750 and 550* B.C.E. *in comparison with the pre-*

viously colonized or colonizing areas originating from Phoenicia and the relatively stable Etruscans in northern Italy. This map also distinguishes the Ionian, Dorian, and Aeolian origins of some of those Greek colonies.

Comparison of these two maps shows that there is a trend for colonies to be located near, or be logical geographic extensions of, the earlier migrations of Greeks. For example, as Dorians spread south and southeast to Thera, Crete, and Rhodes, so would future colonies extend further south, such as those in North Africa (Cyrenaica), and southeast, to, for

MAP 2.1   Dialects

MAP 2.2   Colonies

example, Aspendus. Generally, the Ionians were the most mobile in face of the Dorian invasions and fled across the islands of the Aegean to the east and to the coast of Asia Minor. They were the most prolific colonizers in number and extent, stretching from Spain in the West to the extremes of the Black Sea in the North and East. Although colonies became independent city-states, some of the history of migrations and colonization affected future military alliances. For example, Greeks of the Ionic dialect tended to support each other in the Persian and Peloponnesian wars.

The extent of Greek colonization suggests the importance of colonies for diffusing culture throughout the Mediterranean.

Greeks often came into contact (at times through war) with the competing Phoenicians as well as with the established Etruscans and later the Romans in the western Mediterranean. All this helps explain how Greek and Greco-Roman civilization came to dominate most of the Mediterranean basin even when the Greeks were no longer a great military-political force and their colonies were no longer independent.

CONSIDER: How the history and geography of Greek migrations and colonization helped diffuse culture in the ancient world; how a geographic analysis of dialects can shed light on the history of a civilization.

⚓ Secondary Sources

The End of the Mycenaean World

Frank J. Frost

The highly developed Bronze Age civilizations of the Minoans and Mycenaeans seem to have collapsed suddenly between the thirteenth and twelfth centuries B.C.E. Indeed, the collapse was so complete that few records remain. This has forced historians and archaeologists to offer rather speculative interpretations for the fall. Some of these interpretations are evaluated in the following selection by Frank Frost.

CONSIDER: *The problems with the Dorian invasion interpretation; why Frost supports the civil wars interpretation.*

The return of the Greeks from Troy after such a long time caused many changes; in general, there was civil strife in the cities, and exiles from these founded other cities. . . . And eighty years after the War, the Dorians occupied the Peloponnesus with the Sons of Heracles.

Thucydides 1.12

Thus the historian Thucydides described the end of the Mycenaean world, but his brief words do little to describe the true picture: nearly every Mycenaean citadel and settlement destroyed or abandoned, an almost complete end to overseas trade, and the disappearance of a sophisticated town economy. There followed a 300-year period that may with every justification be called the "Dark Ages" of Greece.

Anyone interested in a given society must also be concerned with the reasons for the disintegration of that society. There is still disagreement about the end of the

Mycenaean world: epic tradition and archaeology combined can only hint at the great disturbances that seem to have overtaken the entire eastern Mediterranean in the twelfth century B.C. E. For many years, scholars were content to assume that the great palaces were destroyed and the surrounding lands taken over by the Dorians led by the descendants of Heracles, as tradition suggested. There can be no doubt that the Dorians occupied lands once ruled by the Mycenaeans, because in classical times, the people of these areas spoke Doric and related dialects and were proud of their tribal heritage. The difficulty comes from analyzing the archaeological evidence, which indicates only that the old society had broken down. There was no replacement of Mycenaean hardware with Dorian counterparts.

Today many scholars concentrate on the first part of Thucydides' statement, which focuses attention on internal strife. There is widespread literary tradition to support this theory because even before the war, Thebes had been destroyed by returning exiles. Furthermore, all the heroes who returned from Troy found unrest at home. Agamemnon was butchered in his bathtub; Odysseus survived only by the skin of his teeth through a bloody massacre of his rivals. In city after city new dynasties had taken over, and refugees filled the eastern Mediterranean. In 1191 B.C.E., Rameses III repelled a great invasion of "sea peoples" from the coasts of Egypt, and it is often assumed that these marauders were a product of the contemporary disturbances in Greece. We are told by tradition that only Nestor returned to safety and prosperity at Pylos. Unfortunately, the archaeological record challenges tradition at this point, showing that the palace at Pylos was one of the first to be destroyed and its destruction was awful and complete.

Civil war, therefore, may have been responsible for the destruction of many citadels, for depopulation and abandonment of other sites, and finally, for a breakdown in the Mycenaean economy. Such an elaborate social and economic structure must always depend for survival on relatively peaceful conditions: the crops must be sown and harvested at the right times, goods must exchange hands, ships must arrive at their destinations, taxes must be paid, and clerks must keep records. A generation of war can easily upset the delicate balance of such an economy. Once foreign trade ends, domestic prosperity begins to decline. Towns become isolated, driving artisans and merchants who have no more markets back to the soil as farmers—for farmers at least eat during hard times.

Greek Realities: The Homeric Epics

Finley Hooper

While the Homeric epics are significant in themselves as literature, they are doubly important for the historian. First, they supply us with much information about Greece during the late Bronze Age and the Dark Age, periods we would otherwise know little about. Second, since the epics were of tremendous educational, religious, and cultural significance to the Greeks for centuries after the Dark Age, they provide insight into Greek civilization during the Classical and Hellenistic ages. In the following selections Finley Hooper explains the importance of the Iliad *and the* Odyssey.

CONSIDER: *How Hooper compares the Homeric epics and the Bible; the ways in which it is useful to think of the epics as religious documents.*

The Homeric epics were as important to ancient Greek society as the Bible is to our own. Perhaps more so, for the *Iliad* and the *Odyssey* were the primers of Greek education. They still are. To the credit of the Greeks, their children have always learned to read and write by examples from the very best in native literature. A child may not go far with his schooling, but if he learns to read and write he knows Homer. When Socrates made his famous appeal to a large jury in Athens in 399 B.C.E. he quoted from the *Iliad*. Here at least was common ground.

Homer's writings did not comprise scripture in the sense that they were the "revealed word of God." Yet, as in the Bible, there were woven into these epics three persistent themes of human interest: the nature of the supernatural, the intervention of the supernatural in human events, and acute observations about the behavior of men toward one another.

The epics describe the province of each of the twelve Olympian gods. Nearly all of them were named in the Linear B tablets. Homer writes about the same deities as the Mycenaeans had actually worshipped. Yet the tablets mention other gods and not all of them have been clearly identified. Perhaps some of these represent the cruder aspects of religious practices, snake cults and fertility rites which Homer ignores. When the poet limited the number of gods to be given preference, he introduced order and a degree of sophistication into a highly confusing, often interchangeable, list of deities.

In the remote past, sticks and stones had been considered divine, but Homer spoke for an age when supernatural powers were personified as men and women, larger than life, living forever on special food. They acted according to the same passions and prejudices of men, even as the Hebrew Yahweh who walked and talked in the cool of the evening, and described himself as a jealous God.

The nature of God is not a matter which historians need to decide for others, but the various ways in which men have conceived of the divine is a matter of historical interest. It may be observed that although a few Greek philosophers spoke of a single creative principle, the overwhelming majority of the Greeks throughout ancient times accounted for events according to the wishes of these anthropomorphic gods which Homer describes. . . .

Homer's epics do not offer an evolutionary development toward a higher concept of God, nor any single set of answers to life's major questions. As such, these "teachings" gave the religion common to all the Greeks a totally undogmatic character. The gods of course aided men and they must be worshipped, flattered, and obeyed. The welfare of the state could depend on this. To deny the gods was dangerous, even unpatriotic. But there was no creed or set of tenets to which a man must subscribe. Although the Greeks often quarreled over the physical control of their shrines, they never fought a religious war over faith. Ironically, the adherents of the later higher religions have suffered the embarrassment of bloodshed in the name of sacred books. Homer's writings actually united the Greeks by reconciling them to the common dilemma of human existence.

Social Values and Ethics in the "Dark Age" of Greece

Sarah B. Pomeroy et al.

The Homeric epics exemplify a theme that runs throughout Greek history: the image of the good man. This image characterized Greek visions of the Mycenaeans as well as Greek ideals expressed in various cultural productions. In the following selection, Sarah B. Pomeroy, in collaboration with others, analyzes the social values and ethics that made up the essence of the "good man" during the "Dark Age" of Greece.

SOURCE: Reprinted from *Greek Realities* by Finley Hooper, by permission of the Wayne State University Press. Copyright © 1967, pp. 58–60.

SOURCE: Sarah B. Pomeroy et al., *Ancient Greece: A Political, Social, and Cultural History* (New York: Oxford University Press, 1999), pp. 60–61.

CONSIDER: *What the key components of the "good man" were; the ways these values reflect a warrior society; how this analysis compares with Hooper's interpretation.*

In all societies, the notions of good and bad, right and wrong, are largely determined by their own peculiar conditions of life. The codes of behavior for Homeric males center around war. The Greek adjective *agathos* ("good") when used of men in Homer, is almost always restricted to the qualities of bravery and skill in fighting and athletics. The opposite word, *kakos* ("bad"), means cowardly, or unskilled and useless in battle. In a society in which every ablebodied man fights to defend his community, all men are under constraint to behave bravely. The leaders are expected to be especially valiant, and in addition, to excel in public speaking and counsel.

Other traditional rules of conduct dictate that a "good man" should honor the gods, keep promises and oaths, and be loyal to friends and fellow warriors. He should exhibit self-control, be hospitable, and respect women and elders. Pity should be shown to beggars and suppliant strangers. It is proper to show pity even toward captured warriors and to refrain from defiling the corpses of the enemy. These gentler qualities are desirable, but they are not required; the sole criterion for being called agathos is good warriorship.

A warrior society is forced to breed into its future warriors a savage joy in the grim "works of Ares," a lust to annihilate the enemy. At the end of a poignant family scene in the *Iliad*, the Trojan hero Hector lifts up his baby son and prays to the gods that he may grow up to be a better warrior than his father and "bring back the bloody spoils of a dead enemy and make his mother's heart glad" (*Iliad* 6.479–481). Homeric Greeks are not only fierce in war but also savage in victory: they loot and burn captured villages, slaughter the male survivors including infants, and rape and enslave the women and girls.

A strong competitive spirit was an important part of the Greek male ethos. Homeric characters constantly compare themselves, or are compared with, one another. Men are driven to win and to be called *aristos* ("best"). One man is said to be "best of the Achaeans in bowmanship," while another "surpassed all the young men in running," or in spear throwing, or chariot racing, or speaking. This type of extracompetititve society is called agonistic, from the Greek word *agōn* ("contest," "struggle"). The instinct to compete and win permeates the society. A poor farmer is roused to work hard when he sees his neighbor getting rich, says Hesiod (c. 700);

and "potter resents potter and carpenter resents carpenter, and beggar is jealous of beggar and poet of poet" (*Works and Days* 20–26).

The sole object of competing and striving is to win *timē* ("honor" and "respect"). *Timē* is always public recognition of one's skills and achievements. It always involves some visible mark of respect: the seat of honor and an extra share of meat at a feast, or an additional share of booty, or valuable prizes and gifts, including land. To modern readers, Homeric warrior-chiefs may appear overly greedy for material things, but their purpose in acquiring and possessing many animals and precious objects was mainly to increase their fame and glory. Not to be honored when honor is due, or worse, to be dishonored, are unbearable insults. Thus, when Agamemnon in the *Iliad* grievously dishonored Achilles by taking back the captive girl Briseis, a "prize of honor" awarded to Achilles by the army, a great quarrel arose between them that led to disaster for all the Greeks.

Adherence to the competitive ethic (summed up in the motto "always be the best and be preeminent over the others") spurred men on to accomplish great things and kept the quality of leadership high. On the other hand, the relentless pursuit of personal and family honor and obsession with avenging dishonor could cause enormous political instability. For better or worse, the Homeric codes of male behavior would endure throughout antiquity, and later generations of Greek writers would continue to look to the *Iliad* and *Odyssey* for models of right and wrong conduct.

❧ CHAPTER QUESTIONS

1. How should the historical usefulness of the various primary documents, particularly those that are usually considered pieces of literature, be evaluated? What problems might arise for historians who rely on literary documents for their interpretations of early Greek civilization?

2. In what ways do the primary documents support interpretations of various ideals, such as the "good man," as particularly Greek?

3. Considering historical, geographic, and cultural factors, in what ways did the Greeks differ from the earlier civilizations of the ancient Near East? How would you explain some of these differences?

Classical Age | Hellenisitic Age

Golden Age of Athens | Decline of the Polis | Hellenisitic Kingdoms

Delian League | Athenian Empire | Macedonian Dominance

Persian War | Peloponnesian War

500 | 479 | 431 | 400 | 338 | 323 | 300

Pericles | Plato | Epicurus

Thucydides | Aristotle

Sophocles | Alexander

Hippocrates

3 Classical and Hellenistic Greece

D uring the fifth and fourth centuries B.C.E. Greek civilization reached its apex. Historians have been fascinated with this period of Greek history for several reasons. First, Classical Greece is considered the most direct foundation of Western civilization, more so than the civilizations of the ancient Near East that preceded it. Second, many Greeks took a rationalistic and naturalistic approach to almost all fundamental questions; thus they developed scientific explanations for the world around them and applied reason to questions of politics, ethics, history, and philosophy. Third, the Greeks explored and experienced the range of human emotions, above all in their literature and in the triumphant and tragic wars they fought. Fourth, they produced stunning aesthetic creations,

particularly in their sculpture, architecture, and drama. Fifth, Greeks strongly believed in the dignity and power of human beings and in balance and control as a human ideal. Sixth, the Greeks experienced and experimented with a large variety of political forms. In short, we often recognize ourselves and our own concerns when we study Classical Greece.

This chapter surveys Greek civilization as it evolved from the Classical Age (500–323 B.C.E.) to the Hellenistic Age (323–31 B.C.E.). Three overlapping topics are discussed. The first concerns the nature of the polis, of central importance to the ancient Greeks. Greeks perceived the polis as the appropriate political and geographic context for the good life, as well as the center of social, economic, religious, and cultural life. How should it be ruled? How strong was the obligation to one's own polis compared with an allegiance to the Greek world as a whole? What was the proper balance between the individual and the state? To explore these questions, it is useful to look at divisions between rival poleis of different political and social forms, as exemplified by the Peloponnesian War. It is also helpful to examine Greek ideas about the political nature of humans and in particular Greek ideas about democracy—one of the many forms of government experimented with by the Greeks. And finally, the student of Greek civilization can learn a great deal by investigating the tension between the individual and his or her obligation as a citizen of the polis.

The second topic is the nature of Greek thought. Historians have traditionally been impressed by the "modernity" of Greek thought. This is particularly the case with the scientific and rationalistic nature of Greek thought and the Greek tendency to generalize and abstract their ideas without resort to religious or supernatural assumptions. A number of questions are examined to demonstrate these traits. What was the nature of scientific thought for the Greeks? How did they apply such thought to medicine, history, and politics? What methodological differences were within this rationalistic thought? In what ways did they tend to

abstract and generalize their ideas? What was the role of irrational thought and belief in the supernatural among large portions of Greek society?

The third topic questions the validity of the traditional view of Greece during the Classical and Hellenistic ages. We usually think of the Greeks, and especially the Athenians, as being balanced, democratic, just, individualistic, rational, naturalistic, liberal, and open. Their great fault, supposedly, was in their inability to unify politically: thus the fratricidal tragedy of the Peloponnesian War, the decline of the fourth century B.C.E., the conquest of the Macedonians, the shift of a center of gravity away from the polis to the eastern Hellenistic kingdoms, and the end of the Classical Age. How true is this perception? To address this question it is necessary to examine a number of related questions: What were Greek ideals during the Classical Age, particularly in Athens, the epitome of Greek culture at its height? What was the position of women in Greek society? What was the significance of slavery for Greece? How democratic were the Greeks, and how did their greatest thinkers evaluate this democracy? How can the "decline" of the fourth century be explained, and indeed should it be considered a "decline" or simply a change?

 Primary Sources

The History of the Peloponnesian War: The Historical Method

Thucydides

The first of the great historians lived in Greece during the Classical Age. They provide us with the most useful material we have to trace events of the period. The greatest of these was Thucydides (c. 471–c. 400), a high-ranking and wealthy Athenian who was a general early in the war and who was later banished from Athens for twenty years for losing a campaign against the Spartans. In The History of the Peloponnesian War Thucydides traces the origins of the war, its course, and its consequences for the participants and for the Greek world in general. In the following selection Thucydides outlines his approach and method as a historian and analyzes the origins of the conflict, distinguishing the immediate from the underlying causes.

SOURCE: From Francis R. B. Godolphin, ed., *The Greek Historians*, vol. I (New York: Random House, 1942), pp. 576–577. Reprinted by permission.

CONSIDER: *Thucydides' assumptions and reasoning; what modern historians might point to as evidence for questionable practices of historical writing or a lack of a scientific approach; how Thucydides distinguishes the "immediate" from the "real" causes of the Peloponnesian War.*

Yet any one who upon the grounds which I have given arrives at some such conclusion as my own about those ancient times, would not be far wrong. He must not be misled by the exaggerated fancies of the poets, or by the tales of chroniclers who seek to please the ear rather than to speak the truth. Their accounts cannot be tested by him; and most of the facts in the lapse of ages have passed into the region of romance. At such a distance of time he must make up his mind to be satisfied with conclusions resting upon the clearest evidence which can be had. And, though men will always judge any war in which they are actually fighting to be the greatest at the time, but, after it is over, revert to their admiration of some other which has preceded, still the Peloponnesian, if estimated by the actual facts, will certainly prove to have been the greatest ever known.

As to the speeches which were made either before or during the war, it was hard for me, and for others who reported them to me, to recollect the exact words. I have therefore put into the mouth of each speaker the sentiments proper to the occasion, expressed as I thought he would be likely to express them, while at the same time I endeavoured, as nearly as I could, to give the general purport of what was actually said. Of the events of the war I have not ventured to speak from any chance information, nor according to any notion of my own; I have described nothing but what I either saw myself, or learned from others of whom I made the most careful and particular enquiry. The task was a laborious one, because eye-witnesses of the same occurrences gave different accounts of them, as they remembered or were interested in the actions of one side or the other. And very likely the strictly historical character of my narrative may be disappointing to the ear. But if he who desires to have before his eyes a true picture of the events which have happened, and of the like events which may be expected to happen hereafter in the order of human things, shall pronounce what I have written to be useful, then I shall be satisfied. My history is an everlasting possession, not a prize composition which is heard and forgotten.

The greatest achievement of former times was the Persian War; yet even this was speedily decided in two battles by sea and two by land. But the Peloponnesian War was a protracted struggle, and attended by calamities such as Hellas had never known within a like period of time. Never were so many cities captured and depopulated—some by barbarians, others by Hellenes themselves fighting against one another; and several of them after their capture were repeopled by strangers. Never were exile and slaughter more frequent, whether in the war or brought about by civil strife. And rumours, of which the like had often been current before, but rarely verified by fact, now appeared to be well grounded. There are earthquakes unparalleled in their extent and fury, and eclipses of the sun more numerous than are recorded to have happened in any former age; there were also in some places great droughts causing famines, and lastly the plague which did immense harm and destroyed numbers of the people. All these calamities fell upon Hellas simultaneously with the war, which began when the Athenians and Peloponnesians violated the thirty years' truce concluded by them after the recapture of Euboea. Why they broke it and what were the grounds of quarrel I will first set forth, that in time to come no man may be at a loss to know what was the origin of this great war. The real though unavowed cause I believe to have been the growth of the Athenian power, which terrified the Lacedaemonians and forced them into war; but the reasons publicly alleged on either side were as follows.

The History of the Peloponnesian War: Athens During the Golden Age

Thucydides

The most famous "speech" presented by Thucydides in his History of the Peloponnesian War *is a eulogy delivered by the Athenian leader Pericles (c. 490–429 B.C.E.) during the winter of 431–430 B.C.E. for the Athenians killed during the first campaigns. In it Pericles compares the life and institutions of Athens with those of the enemy, Sparta. He explains to his fellow Athenians what made Athens so great. This funeral oration provides a superb idealized description of the Athenian city-state at its height.*

CONSIDER: *The reliability of this report of Pericles' speech, especially considering Thucydides' description of his methods in the previous document; the description of Athens, its institutions, and its people in this document; how Pericles compares Athens and Sparta and how a Spartan leader might reply; how Pericles defines the proper balance between Athenians' freedom as individuals and their commitments as citizens.*

"I will speak first of our ancestors, for it is right and becoming that now, when we are lamenting the dead, a tribute should be paid to their memory. There has never been a time when they did not inhabit this land, which by their valour they have handed down from generation to generation, and we have received from them a free state. But if they were worthy of praise, still more were our fathers, who added to their inheritance, and after many a struggle transmitted to us their sons this great empire. And we ourselves assembled here to-day, who are still most of us in the vigour of life, have chiefly done the work of improvement, and have richly endowed our city with all things, so that she is sufficient for herself both in peace and war. Of the military exploits by which our various possessions were acquired, or of the energy with which we or our fathers drove back the tide of war, Hellenic or barbarian, I will not speak; for the tale would be long and is familiar to you. But before I praise the dead, I should like to point out by what principles of action we rose to power, and under what institutions and through what manner of life our empire became great. For I conceive that such thoughts are not unsuited to the occasion, and that this numerous assembly of citizens and strangers may profitably listen to them.

"Our form of government does not enter into rivalry with the institutions of others. We do not copy our neighbours, but are an example to them. It is true that

SOURCE: From Francis R. B. Godolphin, ed., *The Greek Historians*, vol. I (New York: Random House, 1942), pp. 648–651. Reprinted by permission.

we are called a democracy, for the administration is in the hands of the many and not of the few. But while the law secures equal justice to all alike in their private disputes, the claim of excellence is also recognised; and when a citizen is in any way distinguished, he is preferred to the public service, not as a matter of privilege, but as the reward of merit. Neither is poverty a bar, but a man may benefit his country whatever be the obscurity of his condition. There is no exclusiveness in our public life, and in our private intercourse we are not suspicious of one another, nor angry with our neighbour if he does what he likes; we do not put on sour looks at him which, though harmless, are not pleasant. While we are thus unconstrained in our private intercourse, a spirit of reverence pervades our public acts; we are prevented from doing wrong by respect for authority and for the laws, having an especial regard to those which are ordained for the protection of the injured as well as to those unwritten laws which bring upon the transgressor of them the reprobation of the general sentiment.

"And we have not forgotten to provide for our weary spirits many relaxations from toil; we have regular games and sacrifices throughout the year; at home the style of our life is refined; and the delight which we daily feel in all these things helps to banish melancholy. Because of the greatness of our city the fruits of the whole earth flow in upon us; so that we enjoy the goods of other countries as freely as of our own.

"Then, again, our military training is in many respects superior to that of our adversaries. Our city is thrown open to the world, and we never expel a foreigner or prevent him from seeing or learning anything of which the secret if revealed to an enemy might profit him. We rely not upon management or trickery, but upon our own hearts and hands. And in the matter of education, whereas they from early youth are always undergoing laborious exercises which are to make them brave, we live at ease, and yet are equally ready to face the perils which they face. And here is the proof. The Lacedaemonians come into Attica not by themselves, but with their whole confederacy following; we go alone into a neighbour's country; and although our opponents are fighting for their homes and we are on a foreign soil, we have seldom any difficulty in overcoming them. Our enemies have never yet felt our united strength; the care of a navy divides our attention, and on land we are obliged to send our own citizens everywhere. But they, if they meet and defeat a part of our army, are as proud as if they had routed us all, and when defeated they pretend to have been vanquished by us all.

"If then we prefer to meet danger with a light heart but without laborious training, and with a courage which is gained by habit and not enforced by law, are we not greatly the gainers? Since we do not anticipate the pain,

although, when the hour comes, we can be as brave as those who never allow themselves to rest; and thus too our city is equally admirable in peace and in war.

"For we are lovers of the beautiful, yet with economy, and we cultivate the mind without loss of manliness. Wealth we employ, not for talk and ostentation, but when there is a real use for it. To avow poverty with us is no disgrace; the true disgrace is in doing nothing to avoid it. An Athenian citizen does not neglect the state because he takes care of his own household; and even those of us who are engaged in business have a very fair idea of politics. We alone regard a man who takes no interest in public affairs, not as a harmless, but as a useless character; and if few of us are originators, we are all sound judges of a policy. The great impediment to action is, in our opinion, not discussion, but the want of that knowledge which is gained by discussion preparatory to action. For we have a peculiar power of thinking before we act and of acting too, whereas other men are courageous from ignorance but hesitate upon reflection. And they are surely to be esteemed the bravest spirits who, having the clearest sense both of the pains and pleasures of life, do not on that account shrink from danger. In doing good, again, we are unlike others; we make our friends by conferring, not by receiving favours. Now he who confers a favour is the firmer friend, because he would fain by kindness keep alive the memory of an obligation; but the recipient is colder in his feelings, because he knows that in requiting another's generosity he will not be winning gratitude but only paying a debt. We alone do good to our neighbours not upon a calculation of interest, but in the confidence of freedom and in a frank and fearless spirit.

"To sum up: I say that Athens is the school of Hellas, and that the individual Athenian in his own person seems to have the power of adapting himself to the most varied forms of action with the utmost versatility and grace."

Antigone

Sophocles

Much of our information about Greece comes from dramas, which played such an important educational, religious, and cultural role in Greek life. Sophocles (c. 496–406 B.C.E.), an Athenian of aristocratic birth and an important public official, was one of the greatest dramatists of the Classical Age. In Antigone, which was first staged in 441, he focused on the conflicts between social obligations and individual convictions, between political and moral conscience. The first excerpt is a speech by Creon, King of Thebes, to his counselors. He refers

Source : *Sophocles: Three Tragedies*, trans. H. D. F. Kitto (© Oxford University Press, London, 1962), pp. 8–9, 16–17, by permission of Oxford University Press.

to the recent strife in Thebes between the two sons of the tragically fallen King Oedipus. One of the sons, Polyneices, gathered Greek enemies of Thebes and attacked the city, which was defended by the other son, Eteocles. Both were killed in battle, and thus Creon, the brother of Oedipus, assumed the throne. A struggle arose between the strongwilled Antigone, Polyneices' sister, who felt compelled by dictates of blood and religion to give her brother a proper burial, and Creon, who felt that as ruler he had to uphold the authority of the state and punish rebellion. Here Creon justifies his decision to bury Eteocles honorably but to leave Polyneices unburied. In the second excerpt, Antigone justifies her burial of Polyneices and her disobeying the laws of the state.

CONSIDER: *The attitudes and ideals revealed in this selection; Creon's view of the duties of the ruler and how these duties conflict with obligations of conscience and religion; how Antigone replies to Creon; how the relation between the individual and the state presented in this document compares with the same relation presented in Pericles' funeral oration.*

CREON. My lords: for what concerns the state, the gods
Who tossed it on the angry surge of strife
Have righted it again; and therefore you
By royal edict I have summoned here,
Chosen from all our number. I know well
How you revered the throne of Laius;
And then, when Oedipus maintained our state,
And when he perished, round his sons you rallied,
Still firm and steadfast in your loyalty.
Since they have fallen by a double doom
Upon a single day, two brothers each
Killing the other with polluted sword,
I now possess the throne and royal power
By right of nearest kinship with the dead.

   There is no art that teaches us to know
The temper, mind or spirit of any man
Until he has been proved by government
And lawgiving. A man who rules a state
And will not ever steer the wisest course,
But is afraid, and says not what he thinks,
That man is worthless; and if any holds
A friend of more account than his own city,
I scorn him; for if I should see destruction
Threatening the safety of my citizens,
I would not hold my peace, nor would I count
That man my friend who was my country's foe,
Zeus be my witness. For be sure of this:
It is the city that protects us all;
She bears us through the storm; only when she
Rides safe and sound can we make loyal friends.
   This I believe, and thus will I maintain
Our city's greatness.—Now, conformably,
Of Oedipus' two sons I have proclaimed

This edict: he who in his country's cause
Fought gloriously and so laid down his life,
Shall be entombed and graced with every rite
That men can pay to those who die with honour;
But for his brother, him called Polyneices,
Who came from exile to lay waste his land,
To burn the temples of his native gods,
To drink his kindred blood, and to enslave
The rest, I have proclaimed to Thebes that none
Shall give him funeral honours or lament him,
But leave him there unburied, to be devoured
By dogs and birds, mangled most hideously.
Such is my will; never shall I allow
The villain to win more honour than the upright;
But any who show love to this our city
In life and death alike shall win my praise.

CREON. You: tell me briefly—I want no long speech:
Did you not know that this had been forbidden?
ANTIGONE. Of course I knew. There was a proclamation.
CREON. And so you dared to disobey the law?
ANTIGONE. It was not Zeus who published this decree,
Nor have the Powers who rule among the dead
Imposed such laws as this upon mankind;
Nor could I think that a decree of yours—
A man—could override the laws of Heaven
Unwritten and unchanging. Not of today
Or yesterday is their authority;
They are eternal; no man saw their birth.
Was I to stand before the gods' tribunal
For disobeying *them*, because I feared
A man? I knew that I should have to die,
Even without your edict; if I die
Before my time, why then, I count it gain;
To one who lives as I do, ringed about
With countless miseries, why, death is welcome.
For me to meet this doom is little grief;
But when my mother's son lay dead, had I
Neglected him and left him there unburied,
That would have caused me grief; this causes none.
And if you think it folly, then perhaps
I am accused of folly by the fool.

The Republic
Plato

Various city-states in Classical Greece, and particularly Athens, have been admired for their democratic institutions and practices. Yet Plato (c. 427–347 B.C.E.), the greatest

SOURCE: M. J. Knight, ed., and B. Jowett, trans., *A Selection of Passages from Plato for English Readers* (Oxford, England: The Clarendon Press, 1895), pp. 80–82.

political theorist of the time, was a harsh critic of democracy. An aristocratic Athenian who grew up during the Peloponnesian War, Plato became embittered by the trial and death of his teacher, Socrates, in 399. After an extended absence from Athens, Plato returned in 386 and founded a school, the Academy, where he hoped to train philosopher-statesmen in accordance with his ideals as expounded in The Republic. *In the following selection from that work, Plato employs the dialogue form to examine democracy and its perils. This represents more than abstract thoughts, for at the time that it was written, there was a rivalry between democratic forms of government, best represented by Athens, and more structured authoritarian forms, represented by Sparta.*

CONSIDER: *The strengths and weaknesses of Plato's argument; how Plato's view of (Athenian) democracy compares with the view of Pericles.*

And then democracy comes into being after the poor have conquered their opponents, slaughtering some and banishing some, while to the remainder they give an equal share of freedom and power; and this is the form of government in which the magistrates are commonly elected by lot.

Yes, he said, that is the nature of democracy, whether the revolution has been effected by arms, or whether fear has caused the opposite party to withdraw.

And now what is their manner of life, and what sort of a government have they? For as the government is, such will be the man.

Clearly, he said.

In the first place, are they not free; and is not the city full of freedom and frankness—a man may say and do what he likes?

'Tis said so, he replied.

And where freedom is, the individual is clearly able to order for himself his own life as he pleases?

Clearly.

Then in this kind of State there will be the greatest variety of human natures?

There will.

This, then, seems likely to be the fairest of States, being like an embroidered robe which is spangled with every sort of flower. And just as women and children think a variety of colours to be of all things most charming, so there are many men to whom this State, which is spangled with the manners and characters of mankind, will appear to be the fairest of States.

Yes.

Yes, my good Sir, and there will be no better in which to look for a government.

Why?

Because of the liberty which reigns there—they have a complete assortment of constitutions; and he who has a mind to establish a State, as we have been doing, must go to a democracy as he would to a bazaar at which they sell them, and pick out the one that suits him; then, when he has made his choice, he may found his State.

He will be sure to have patterns enough.

And there being no necessity, I said, for you to govern in this State, even if you have the capacity, or to be governed, unless you like, or to go to war when the rest go to war, or to be at peace when others are at peace, unless you are so disposed—there being no necessity also, because some law forbids you to hold office or be a dicast, that you should not hold office or be a dicast, if you have a fancy—is not this a way of life which for the moment is supremely delightful?

For the moment, yes.

And is not their humanity to the condemned in some cases quite charming? Have you not observed how, in a democracy, many persons, although they have been sentenced to death or exile, just stay where they are and walk about the world—the gentleman parades like a hero, and nobody sees or cares?

Yes, he replied, many and many a one.

See too, I said, the forgiving spirit of democracy, and the "don't care" about trifles, and the disregard which she shows of all the fine principles which we solemnly laid down at the foundation of the city—as when we said that, except in the case of some rarely gifted nature, there never will be a good man who has not from his childhood been used to play amid things of beauty and make of them a joy and a study—how grandly does she trample all these fine notions of ours under her feet, never giving a thought to the pursuits which make a statesman, and promoting to honour any one who professes to be the people's friend.

Yes, she is of a noble spirit.

These and other kindred characteristics are proper to democracy, which is a charming form of government, full of variety and disorder, and dispensing a sort of equality to equals and unequals alike.

We know her well.

Politics

Aristotle

Aristotle (384–322 B.C.E.), a student of Plato, the tutor of Alexander the Great, and the founder of the Lyceum (a school rivaling Plato's Academy), had a different approach to

SOURCE: Aristotle, *Politics,* trans. Benjamin Jowett (Oxford, England: The Clarendon Press, 1905), pp. 25–28, 239–241.

politics. Aristotle emphasized the collection and classification of facts, as in the biological and physical sciences. Although Aristotle believed that democracy was a deterioration of a more balanced, high-minded polis, his approach was more descriptive and thus seems less condemning of democracy than Plato's. This is reflected in the following selections from Politics. In the first passage Aristotle examines the political and social nature of humans, revealing the typically Greek assumption that it is part of human nature to be organized into a polis. In the second passage Aristotle analyzes democracy.

CONSIDER: *How the arguments of Aristotle and Plato compare in style and form; how Aristotle's description of democracy compares with Pericles' description of Athenian institutions; the characteristics of democracy listed by Aristotle that are generally not practiced today.*

Every state is a community of some kind, and every community is established with a view of some good; for mankind always act in order to obtain that which they think good. But, if all communities aim at some good, the state or political community, which is the highest of all, and which embraces all the rest, aims, and in a greater degree than any other, at the highest good. . . .

For governments differ in kind, as will be evident to any one who considers the matter according to the method which has hitherto guided us. As in other departments of science, so in politics, the compound should always be resolved into the simple elements or least parts of the whole. We must therefore look at the elements of which the state is composed, in order that we may see in what they differ from one another, and whether any scientific distinction can be drawn between the different kinds of rule.

He who thus considers things in their first growth and origin, whether a state or anything else, will obtain the clearest view of them. In the first place (1) there must be a union of those who cannot exist without each other; for example, of male and female, that the race may continue; and this is a union which is formed, not of deliberate purpose, but because, in common with other animals and with plants, mankind have a natural desire to leave behind them an image of themselves. And (2) there must be a union of natural ruler and subject, that both may be preserved. For he who can foresee with his mind is by nature intended to be lord and master, and he who can work with his body is a subject, and by nature a slave; hence master and slave have the same interest. Nature, however, has distinguished between the female and the slave For she is not niggardly, like the smith who fashions the Delphian knife for many uses; she makes each thing for a single use, and every instrument is best made when intended for one and not for many uses. But among

barbarians no distinction is made between women and slaves, because there is no natural ruler among them: they are a community of slaves, male and female. Wherefore the poets say,—

"It is meet that Hellenes should rule over barbarians;" as if they thought that the barbarian and the slave were by nature one.

Out of these two relationships between man and woman, master and slave, the family first arises. . . .

The family is the association by nature for the supply of men's everyday wants, and the members of it are called by Charondas "companions of the cupboard" and by Epimenides the Cretan, "companions of the manger." But when several families are united, and the association aims at something more than the supply of daily needs, then comes into existence the village. And the most natural form of the village appears to be that of a colony from the family, composed of the children and grandchildren, who are said to be "suckled with the same milk." And this is the reason why Hellenic states were originally governed by kings; because the Hellenes were under royal rule before they came together, as the barbarians still are. Every family is ruled by the eldest, and therefore in the colonies of the family the kingly form of government prevailed because they were of the same blood. . . .

When several villages are united in a single community, perfect and large enough to be nearly or quite self-sufficing, the state comes into existence, originating in the bare needs of life, and continuing in existence for the sake of a good life. And therefore, if the earlier forms of society are natural, so is the state, for it is the end of them, and the [completed] nature is the end. For what each thing is when fully developed, we call its nature, whether we are speaking of a man, a horse, or a family. Besides, the final cause and end of a thing is the best, and to be self-sufficing is the end and the best.

Hence it is evident that the state is a creation of nature, and that man is by nature a political animal. And he who by nature and not by mere accident is without a state, is either above humanity, or below it. . . .

❧

The basis of a democratic state is liberty; which, according to the common opinion of men, can only be enjoyed in such a state—this they affirm to be the great end of every democracy. One principle of liberty is for all to rule and be ruled in turn, and indeed democratic justice is the application of numerical not proportionate equality; whence it follows that the majority must be supreme, and that whatever the majority approve must be the end and the just. Every citizen, it is said, must have equality, and therefore in a democracy the poor have more power than the rich, because there are more of them, and the will of the majority is supreme. This, then, is one note of liberty which all democrats affirm to be the principle of their state. Another is that a man should live as he likes. This, they say, is the privilege of a freeman; and, on the other hand, not to live as a man likes is the mark of a slave. This is the second characteristic of democracy, whence has arisen the claim of men to be ruled by none, if possible, or, if this is impossible, to rule and be ruled in turns; and so it coincides with the freedom based upon equality.

Such being our foundation and such the nature of democracy, its characteristics are as follows:—the election of officers by all out of all; and that all should rule over each, and each in his turn over all; that the appointment to all offices, or to all but those which require experience and skill, should be made by lot; that no property qualification should be required for offices, or only a very low one; that no one should hold the same office twice, or not often, except in the case of military offices; that the tenure of all offices, or of as many as possible, should be brief; that all men should sit in judgment, or that judges selected out of all should judge in all matters, or in most, or in the greatest and most important—such as the scrutiny of accounts, the constitution, and private contracts; that the assembly should be supreme over all causes, or at any rate over the most important, and the magistrates over none or only over a very few. Of all institutions, a council is the most democratic when there is not the means of paying all the citizens, but when they are paid even this is robbed of its power; for the people then draw all cases to themselves, as I said in the previous discussion. The next characteristic of democracy is payment for services; assembly, law-courts, magistrates, everybody receives pay, when it is to be had; or when it is not to be had for all, then it is given to the law-courts and to the stated assemblies, to the council and to the magistrates, or at least to any of them who are compelled to have their meals together. And whereas oligarchy is characterized by birth, wealth, and education, the notes of democracy appear to be the opposite of these—low birth, poverty, mean employment. Another note is that no magistracy is perpetual, but if any such have survived some ancient change in the constitution it should be stripped of its power, and the holders should be elected by lot and no longer by vote. These are points common to all democracies; but democracy and demos in their truest form are based upon the recognized principle of democratic justice, that all should count equally; for equality implies that the rich should have no more share in the government than the poor, and should not be the only rulers, but that all should rule equally according to their numbers. And in this way men think that they will secure equality and freedom in their state.

Household Management

Xenophon

Public life in Greece was dominated by men. Everyday life for women, even upper-class women in Athens, rarely extended beyond the bounds of the household. An image of this life for women, from a man's point of view, is provided by the Athenian historian and essayist Xenophon (c. 434–355 B.C.E.). In this excerpt from Oeconomicus *(Household Management),* Ischomachus *and* Socrates *discuss marriage, women, and domestic life.*

CONSIDER: *How women are perceived; the relationship of husband and wife; the differing roles of men and women.*

"Here's another thing I'd like to ask you," said I. "Did you train your wife yourself or did she already know how to run a house when you got her from her father and mother?"

"What could she have known, Socrates," said he, "when I took her from her family? She wasn't yet fifteen. Until then she had been under careful supervision and meant to see, hear, and ask as little as possible. Don't you think it was already a lot that she should have known how to make a cloak of the wool she was given and how to dole out spinning to the servants? She had been taught to moderate her appetites, which, to my mind, is basic for both men's and women's education."

"So, apart from that," I asked, "it was you, Ischomachus, who had to train and teach her her household duties?"

"Yes," said Ischomachus, "but not before sacrificing to the gods. . . . And she solemnly swore before heaven that she would behave as I wanted, and it was clear that she would neglect none of my lessons."

"Tell me what you taught her first. . . ."

"Well, Socrates, as soon as I had tamed her and she was relaxed enough to talk, I asked her the following question: 'Tell me, my dear,' said I, 'do you understand why I married you and why your parents gave you to me? You know as well as I do that neither of us would have had trouble finding someone else to share our beds. But, after thinking about it carefully, it was you I chose and me your parents chose as the best partners we could find for our home and children. Now, if God sends us children, we shall think about how best to raise them, for we share an interest in securing the best allies and support for our old age. For the moment we only share our home. . . .'"

"My wife answered, 'But how can I help? What am I capable of doing? It is on you that everything depends. My duty, my mother said, is to be well behaved.'"

"'Oh, by Zeus,' said I, 'my father said the same to me. But the best behavior in a man and woman is that which will keep up their property and increase it as far as may be done by honest and legal means.'"

"'. . . And do you see some way,' asked my wife, 'in which I can help in this?'"

❧

"'. . . it seems to me that God adapted women's nature to indoor and man's to outdoor work. . . . As Nature has entrusted woman with guarding the household supplies, and a timid nature is no disadvantage in such a job, it has endowed woman with more fear than man. . . . It is more proper for a woman to stay in the house than out of doors and less so for a man to be indoors instead of out. If anyone goes against the nature given him by God and leaves his appointed post . . . he will be punished. . . . You must stay indoors and send out the servants whose work is outside and supervise those who work indoors, receive what is brought in, give out what is to be spent, plan ahead what should be stored and ensure that provisions for a year are not used up in a month. When the wool is brought in, you must see to it that clothes are made from it for whoever needs them and see to it that the corn is still edible. . . . Many of your duties will give you pleasure: for instance, if you teach spinning and weaving to a slave who did not know how to do this when you got her, you double her usefulness to yourself, or if you make a good housekeeper of one who didn't know how to do anything. . . .' Then I took her around the family living rooms, which are pleasantly decorated, cool in summer and warm in winter. I pointed out how the whole house faces south so as to enjoy the winter sun. . . . I showed her the women's quarters which are separated from the men's by a bolted door to prevent anything being improperly removed and also to ensure that the slaves should not have children without our permission. For good slaves are usually even more devoted once they have a family; but good-fornothings, once they begin to cohabit, have extra chances to get up to mischief."

Medicine and Magic

Hippocrates

By the fifth century B.C.E. the Greeks had developed a scientific approach to knowledge. One of the many subjects reflecting this development was medicine. Hippocrates of Cos (c. 460–377 B.C.E.) founded a medical school that stressed careful observation and natural causes for disease. This method involved abandoning many religious or supernatural

Source: From Hippocrates, *The Medical Works of Hippocrates*, trans. John Chadwick and W. N. Mann, 1950. Courtesy of Charles C. Thomas, Publisher, Springfield, Illinois, and Basil Blackwell, Publisher, Oxford, England.

assumptions about diseases and rejecting various forms of divine healing. In the following selection attributed to Hippocrates, or at least his school, this approach is applied to the "sacred disease," the common term for epilepsy.

CONSIDER: *How scientific the assumptions in this document are; the points that might be rejected or applauded by modern doctors.*

I do not believe that the "Sacred Disease" is any more divine or sacred than any other disease but, on the contrary, has specific characteristics and a definite cause. Nevertheless, because it is completely different from other diseases, it has been regarded as a divine visitation by those who, being only human, view it with ignorance and astonishment. This theory of divine origin, though supported by the difficulty of understanding the malady, is weakened by the simplicity of the cure consisting merely of ritual purification and incantation. If remarkable features in a malady were evidence of divine visitation, then there would be many "sacred diseases." Quotidian, tertian and quartan fevers are among other diseases no less remarkable and portentous and yet no one regards them as having a divine origin. I do not believe that these diseases have any less claim to be caused by a god than the so-called "sacred" disease but they are not the objects of popular wonder. Again, no less remarkably, I have seen men go mad and become delirious for no obvious reason and do many strange things. I have seen many cases of people groaning and shouting in their sleep, some who choke; others jump from their bed and run outside and remain out of their mind till they wake, when they are as healthy and sane as they were before, although perhaps rather pale and weak. These things are not isolated events but frequent occurrences. There are many other remarkable afflictions of various sorts, but it would take too long to describe them in detail.

It is my opinion that those who first called this disease "sacred" were the sort of people we now call witch-doctors, faith-healers, quacks and charlatans. These are exactly the people who pretend to be very pious and to be particularly wise. By invoking a divine element they were able to screen their own failure to give suitable treatment and so called this a "sacred" malady to conceal their ignorance of its nature. . . .

They also employ other pretexts so that, if the patient be cured, their reputation for cleverness is enhanced while, if he dies, they can excuse themselves by explaining that the gods are to blame while they themselves did nothing wrong; that they did not prescribe the taking of any medicine whether liquid or solid, nor any baths which might have been responsible. . . .

It seems, then, that those who attempt to cure disease by this sort of treatment do not really consider the maladies thus treated of sacred or of divine origin. If the disease can be cured by purification and similar treatment then what is to prevent its being brought on by like devices? The man who can get rid of a disease by his magic could equally well bring it on; again there is nothing divine about this but a human element is involved. By such claims and trickery, these practitioners pretend a deeper knowledge than is given to others; with their prescriptions of "sanctifications" and "purifications," their patter about divine visitation and possession by devils, they seek to deceive. And yet I believe that all these professions of piety are really more like impiety and a denial of the existence of the gods, and all their religion and talk of divine visitation is an impious fraud which I shall proceed to expose. . . .

I believe that this disease is not in the least more divine than any other but has the same nature as other diseases and a similar cause. Moreover, it can be cured no less than other diseases so long as it has not become inveterate and too powerful for the drugs which are given.

Like other diseases it is hereditary. If a phlegmatic child is born of a phlegmatic parent, a bilious child of a bilious parent, a consumptive child of a consumptive parent and a splenetic child of a splenetic parent, why should the children of a father or mother who is afflicted with this disease not suffer similarly? The seed comes from all parts of the body; it is healthy when it comes from healthy parts, diseased when it comes from diseased parts. Another important proof that this disease is no more divine than any other lies in the fact that the phlegmatic are constitutionally liable to it while the bilious escape. If its origin were divine, all types would be affected alike without this particular distinction.

Individual Happiness

Epicurus

The Hellenistic Age's greater concern for individual happiness distinguished it from the preceding Classical Age. This concern is reflected in the teachings of Epicurus (342–268 B.C.E.), who founded a school in Athens and was a very influential Hellenistic philosopher. The following selection presents an excerpt from a letter to a student, in which Epicurus describes what he means by pleasure, and a section from his Fragments, *in which he also focuses on individual happiness but broadens his comments to justice and injustice.*

CONSIDER: *Whether this document supports the common association of Epicureanism with indulgence in luxury or sensual pleasures; how this document reflects differences between the Classical and Hellenistic ages.*

SOURCE: From *Epicurus: The Extant Remains,* trans. Cyril Bailey (1926), pp. 89–91, 95–97, 103, by permission of Oxford University Press.

When, therefore, we maintain that pleasure is the end, we do not mean the pleasures of profligates and those that consist in sensuality, as is supposed by some who are either ignorant or disagree with us or do not understand, but freedom from pain in the body and from trouble in the mind. For it is not continuous drinkings and revellings, not the satisfaction of lusts, nor the enjoyment of fish and other luxuries of the wealthy table, which produce a pleasant life, but sober reasoning, searching out the motives for all choice and avoidance, and banishing mere opinions, to which are due the greatest disturbance of the spirit.

Of all this the beginning and the greatest good is prudence. Wherefore prudence is a more precious thing even than philosophy: for from prudence are sprung all the other virtues, and it teaches us that it is not possible to live pleasantly without living prudently and honourably and justly (nor, again, to live a life of prudence, honour, and justice without living pleasantly). For the virtues are by nature bound up with the pleasant life, and the pleasant life is inseparable from them.

❧

II. Death is nothing to us: for that which is dissolved is without sensation; and that which lacks sensation is nothing to us.

❧

VIII. No pleasure is a bad thing in itself: but the means which produce some pleasures bring with them disturbances many times greater than the pleasures.
IX. If every pleasure could be intensified so that it lasted and influenced the whole organism or the most essential parts of our nature, pleasures would never differ from one another.
X. If the things that produce the pleasures of profligates could dispel the fears of the mind about the phenomena of the sky and death and its pains, and also teach the limits of desires (and of pains), we should never have cause to blame them: for they would be filling themselves full with pleasures from every source and never have pain of body or mind, which is the evil of life.

❧

XII. A man cannot dispel his fear about the most important matters if he does not know what is the nature of the universe but suspects the truth of some mythical story. So that without natural science it is not possible to attain our pleasures unalloyed.

❧

XXXIII. Justice never is anything in itself, but in the dealings of men with one another in any place whatever and at any time it is a kind of compact not to harm or be harmed.
XXXIV. Injustice is not an evil in itself, but only in consequence of the fear which attaches to the apprehension of being unable to escape those appointed to punish such actions.

Visual Sources

Education

Most of the few pictorial representations of Greek life that have survived are on pottery. What is portrayed on this early fifth-century B.C.E. cup (figure 3.1) is stylized. The intention is to show an aspect of everyday life that would be recognized by the viewers—the education of Greek boys. On the left a boy is being taught to play the lyre; on the right a boy is being taught to read. The figure on the far right is probably a slave chaperon, who served as a guard and an aid in moral upbringing. On the other side of the cup (not shown) students are learning another musical instrument and writing. Since there were no state schools, instruction was limited to those who could afford a private teacher.

CONSIDER: *The connections between the scenes depicted on this cup and Pericles' description of Athenian society.*

The Women's Quarters

According to Greek social ideals, women spent most of their lives indoors at home. While the majority of Greek women were not wealthy enough to live without working, elite women might approach the ideal. The scene on this fifth-century jar used by women to fetch water from a well or communal fountain (figure 3.2) depicts the activities that form part of this ideal. Here women have gathered to share cultural activities. In the center a woman sits reading aloud from a scroll. In front of her stands another woman holding a chest of scrolls. On each side, women listen to the recitation. The perfume flask on the upper left emphasizes that this is a scene from a wealthy woman's quarters.

CONSIDER: *What this reveals about social life for upper-class Greek women.*

The Dying Niobide: The Classical Balance

The Dying Niobide (c. 440), an example of the Classical style, mixes realism and idealism (figure 3.3). The human body is depicted more or less as it appears to the human eye. Suffering shows in the mouth, perhaps fear in the eyes. Yet it is difficult to say that this is a real individual. The body is not that of a real woman but of an ideal—the artist's vision of the perfect female body. This vision fits a broader

Greek cultural ideal of the human form: It reflects a balance between the private statement and the public expression, between the individual and the community, which characterized Greeks during the Classical Age. The subject is also a lesson for the viewer. It shows the mythical story of an innocent woman being killed by the gods because of her

FIGURE 3.1 (© Bildarchiv Preussischer Kulturbesitz/Art Resource, NY)

FIGURE 3.2 (The British Museum)

FIGURE 3.3   (© Erich Lessing/Art Resource, NY)

FIGURE 3.4   (© The Metropolitan Museum of Art, Rogers Fund, 1909. 09.39 view #1)

mother's excess pride. Still, the Classical balance dominates, for while there is some action, it is not overly dramatic, not shocking. On the whole it invites the viewer to observe and contemplate as well as to enjoy.

CONSIDER: *How* The Dying Niobide *relates to the emotional and philosophical conflicts illustrated by the selection from* Antigone.

The Old Market Woman: Hellenistic Individualism

The Old Market Woman (*second century* B.C.E.) *exemplifies the Hellenistic style (figure 3.4). Gone is the mixture of realism and idealism that characterized the Classical style. Instead, individualism and emotionalism are emphasized. A realistic individual is shown. She is far from ideal in almost every detail, from her facial lines to the basket she carries. One can empathize with the pains of old age and the situation of this individual, straining under an everyday task. No reference is made to a well-known myth or a heroic trait. This statue reflects the greater concern for the individual, the focus on the material aspects of life, and the technical brilliance of the Hellenistic Age.*

CONSIDER: *The emotions, ideals, and experiences of the viewer being appealed to by the sculptors of this and the preceding statue.*

Geography and Political Configurations in Greece

Map 3.1 shows Athens and the surrounding areas during the fifth century B.C.E. *Like many other Greek city-states, Athens was located near the sea on a cultivated plain surrounded by mountains. The city was walled and surrounded an easily defensible high point (the acropolis). The Athenians extended the walls to protect their access to their port at Piraeus. The surrounding mountains facilitated the Athenian defense of their lands while discouraging regular communication by land with other Greek city-states. The smallness of the Athenian plain and its easy access to the sea encouraged maritime commerce, especially to obtain foods the Athenians could not grow themselves. A large number of the other Greek city-states were actually inhabited islands and port*

MAP 3.1   Athens in the Fifth Century B.C.E

cities lacking natural geographic protection and thus were vulnerable to attack from the sea. Athens took advantage of its own protected location and its neighbors' vulnerability to become a significant naval power.

CONSIDER: *How geography can help explain some aspects of the city-states, of the wars against Persia and between Athens and Sparta, and of the dominance over Greece achieved by Philip and Alexander.*

Secondary Sources

Goddesses, Whores, Wives, and Slaves: Women and Work in Athens

Sarah B. Pomeroy

The traditional image of Greek society is based primarily on what men did and thought. In recent decades historians have focused on the roles women played in Greek society and how those roles differed from men's roles. In the following excerpt from her well-known study of women in Greece and Rome,

SOURCE: From *Goddesses, Whores, Wives, and Slaves* by Sarah B. Pomeroy. Copyright © 1975 by Sarah B. Pomeroy. Reprinted by permission of Schocken Books, Pantheon Books, a division of Random House, Inc.

Sarah B. Pomeroy analyzes the economic roles played by women in Athens during the Classical Age. Here she emphasizes the effect of urban living on their lives.

CONSIDER: *How the position of women differed from that of men in Athens; the possible effects of urbanization on women; the kind of work women engaged in and how it was valued.*

By the late fifth century B.C.E., owing to the need for the safety afforded by city walls, urban living replaced farming for many Athenians. Thus, when one compares Sparta to Athens, it is necessary to remember that the former never comprised more than a settlement of villages, while Athens was one of the largest Greek cities. The effect of urbanization upon women was to have their activities moved indoors, and to make their labor less visible and hence less valued.

Urban living created a strong demarcation between the activities of men of the upper and lower classes, as well as between those of men and women. Men were free to engage in politics, intellectual and military training, athletics, and the sort of business approved for gentlemen. Some tasks were regarded as banausic and demeaning, befitting slaves rather than citizens. Naturally, a male citizen who needed income was unable to maintain the ideal and was forced to labor in banausic employment. Women of the upper class, excluded from the activities of the males, supervised and—when they wished—pursued many of the same tasks deemed appropriate to slaves. Since the work was despised, so was the worker. Women's work was productive, but because it was the same as slaves' work, it was not highly valued in the ideology of Classical Athens. The intimacy of the discussions between heroines and choruses of female slaves in tragedy and the depictions of mistress and slave on tombstones imply a bond between slave and free, for they spent much time together and their lives were not dissimilar.

✺

Women of all social classes worked mainly indoors or near the house in order to guard it. They concerned themselves with the care of young children, the nursing of sick slaves, the fabrication of clothing, and the preparation of food. The preparation of ordinary food was considered exclusively women's work.

✺

Transporting water in a pitcher balanced on the head was a female occupation. Because fetching water involved social mingling, gossip at the fountain, and possible flirtations, slave girls were usually sent on this errand.

Women did not go to market for food, and even now they do not do so in rural villages in Greece. The feeling that purchase or exchange was a financial transaction too complex for women, as well as the wish to protect women from the eyes of strangers and from intimate dealings with shopkeepers, contributed to classifying marketing as a man's occupation.

Wealthier women were distinguished by exercising a managerial role, rather than performing all the domestic work themselves.

✺

Poorer women, even citizens, went out to work, most of them pursuing occupations that were an extension of women's work in the home. Women were employed as washerwomen, as woolworkers, and in other clothing industries. They also worked as vendors, selling food or what they had spun or woven at home. Some women sold garlands they had braided. Women were also employed as nurses of children and midwives.

The Greeks: Slavery

Anthony Andrews

It has long been known that the Greeks, like other ancient peoples, practiced slavery. But focusing only on the glories of Greece sometimes leads one to forget how much slavery existed at that time and the role slavery played in supporting the Greek style of life. A historian who takes this into account is Anthony Andrews, a professor at Oxford University who has written a major text on the Greeks. In the following selection he examines Greek assumptions about slavery and the relations between slaves and masters in the Greek world.

CONSIDER: *How this analysis undermines an image of Athens as an open, democratic, and just society; what distinctions might be made between slavery in different times and societies—such as between slavery in Athens and in eighteenth-century America.*

In the broadest terms, slavery was basic to Greek civilisation in the sense that, to abolish it and substitute free labour, if it had occurred to anyone to try this on, would have dislocated the whole society and done away with the leisure of the upper classes of Athens and Sparta. The ordinary Athenian had a very deeply ingrained feeling that it was impossible for a free man to work directly for another as his master. While it is true that free men, as well as slaves, engaged in most forms of trade and industry, the withdrawal of slaves from these tasks would have entailed a most uncomfortable reorganisation of labour and property. . . .

No easy generalisation is possible about the relations between slave and master in the Greek world, since the slave's view, as usual, is not known. In the close quarters of Greek domestic life, no distance could be preserved like that which English middle-class families used to keep between themselves and their servants—and the Greek was unlikely to refrain from talking under any circumstances. The closer relation of nurse and child, tutor and pupil, easily ripened into affection, nor need we doubt stories of the loyal slave saving his master's life on the battlefield, and the like. But at its best the relationship was bound to have unhappy elements, as that when a slave was punished it was with physical blows of the kind that a free man had the right to resent. . . .

The domestic slave who was on good terms with his master stood some chance of liberation, and the slave "living apart" and practising his trade might hope to earn enough to buy his release. Manumission was by no means uncommon, though the practice and the formalities differed a good deal from place to place. The master often retained the right to certain services for a fixed period, or for his own lifetime. Some of those "living apart"

SOURCE: Anthony Andrews, *The Greeks* (New York: Random House, 1967), pp. 133, 138–139, 142.

prospered conspicuously, giving rise to disgruntled oligarchic comment that slaves in the streets of Athens might be better dressed than free men. . . .

But the domestic slave with a bad master was in poor case, with little hope of redress, and the prospects were altogether bleaker for those who were hired out to the mines and other work—and we are not given even a distorted reflection of their feelings. But, after the Spartans had fortified their post outside Athens in 413, Thucydides tells us that over 20,000 slaves deserted to the enemy, the bulk of them "craftsmen" (the word would cover any sort of skilled labour and need not be confined to the miners of Laurium, though no doubt many of the deserters were from there). We do not know what promises the invaders had held out to them, still less what eventually became of them, but the suggestion is clear that the life of even a skilled slave was one which he was ready to fly from on a very uncertain prospect. . . .

In the generation of Socrates, when everything was questioned, the justice of slavery was questioned also. Isolated voices were heard to say that all men were equally men, and that slavery was against nature. The defence of Aristotle, that some were naturally slaves, incapable of full human reason and needing the will of a master to complete their own, rings hollow to us, quite apart from the accident that "naturally free" Greeks might be enslaved by the chances of war. But this was a world in which slavery, in some form or other, was universal, and no nation could remember a time when it had not been so. It is not surprising that there was no clamour for emancipation. It has been convincingly argued that the margin over bare subsistence in Greece was so small that the surplus which was needed to give leisure to the minority could only be achieved with artificially cheap labour. If that is right, there was not much alternative for Greece. For Athens, it had come, by the opening of the sixth century, to a choice between reducing citizens to slavery or extensive import of chattel slaves from abroad. Only a greatly improved technology, something like an industrial revolution, could effectively have altered these conditions.

The Ancient Greeks: Decline of the Polis

M. I. Finley

Typically, the fourth century B.C.E. *is seen as a period of decline, at least for the Greek polis. This decline and the reasons for it have long fascinated historians. Some point to*

SOURCE: From *The Ancient Greeks* by M. I. Finley. Copyright © 1963 by M. I. Finley. Copyright renewed © 1991 by Paul O'Higgens and Charles Richard Watten. Used by permission of Viking Penguin, a division of Penguin Books USA, Inc.

the disillusionment following the Peloponnesian War, others to the inability of Greek city-states to control wars among themselves and ally in the face of the threat from Macedonia. In the following selection M. I. Finley, a leading historian of ancient times from Cambridge University, deals with this issue from a different point of view: The Greek polis could flourish only under unusual circumstances and only for a short period of time.

CONSIDER: *Additional factors that could explain the "decline" of the polis; what policies or developments might have delayed the decline of the polis; whether the fate of Greek civilization was tied to that of the polis.*

All this movement, like the constant *stasis*, marked a failing of the community, and therefore of the *polis*. The more the *polis* had to hire its armed forces, the more citizens it could no longer satisfy economically, and that meant above all with land, so that they went elsewhere in order to live; the more it failed to maintain some sort of equilibrium between the few and the many, the more the cities were populated by outsiders, whether free migrants from abroad or emancipated slaves (who can be called metaphorically free migrants from within)—the less meaningful, the less real was the community. "Decline" is a tricky and dangerous word to use in this context: it has biological overtones which are inappropriate, and it evokes a continuous downhill movement in all aspects of civilization which is demonstrably false. Yet there is no escaping the evidence: the fourth century was the time when the Greek *polis* declined, unevenly, with bursts of recovery and heroic moments of struggle to save itself, to become, after Alexander, a sham *polis* in which the preservation of many external forms of *polis* life could not conceal that henceforth the Greeks lived, in Clemenceau's words, "in the sweet peace of decadence, accepting all sorts of servitudes as they came." . . .

Even fourth-century Athens was not free from signs of the general decline. Contemporary political commentators themselves made much of the fact that whereas right through the fifth century political leaders were, and were expected to be, military leaders at the same time, so that among the ten generals were regularly found the outstanding political figures (elected to the office because of their political importance, not the other way round), in the fourth century the two sides of public activity, the civil and the military, were separated. The generals were now professional soldiers, most of them quite outside politics or political influence, who often served foreign powers as mercenary commanders as well as serving their own *polis*. There are a number of reasons for the shift, among which the inadequate finances of the state rank high, but, whatever the explanation, the break was a bad thing for the *polis*, a cleavage in the responsibility of the members to their community which weakened the sense of community without producing visibly better generalship. In the navy the signs took a different form. A heavy share of the costs still fell on the richest 1200 men and the navy continued to perform well, but there was more evasion of responsibility, more need than before to compel the contributions and to pursue the defaulters at law. The crews themselves were often conscripted; voluntary enlistment could no longer provide the necessary complements. No doubt that was primarily because the treasury was too depleted to provide regular pay for long periods, just as the unwillingness of some to contribute their allotted share of the expenses resulted from an unsatisfactory system of distributing the burden, rather than from lack of patriotism. Wherever the responsibility lay, however, the result was again a partial breakdown in the *polis*.

There is no need to exaggerate: Athens nearly carried it off, and the end came because Macedon, or at least Alexander, was simply too powerful. But Macedon did exist, and so did Persia and Carthage, and later Rome. The *polis* was developed in such a world, not in a vacuum or in Cloud-Cuckoo-Land, and it grew on poor Greek soil. Was it really a viable form of political organization? Were its decline and disappearance the result of factors which could have been remedied, or of an accident—the power of Macedon—or of inherent structural weaknesses? These questions have exercised philosophers and historians ever since the late fifth century (and it is noteworthy how the problem was being posed long before the *polis* could be thought of as on its way out in any literal sense). Plato wished to rescue it by placing all authority in the hands of morally perfect philosophers. Others blame the *demos* and their misleaders, the demagogues, for every ill. Still others, especially in the past century or so, insist on the stupid failure to unite in a national state. For all their disparity, these solutions all have one thing in common: they all propose to rescue the *polis* by destroying it, by replacing it, in its root sense of a community which is at the same time a self-governing state, by something else. The *polis*, one concludes, was a brilliant conception, but one which required so rare a combination of material and institutional circumstances that it could never be realized; that it could be approximated only for a very brief period of time; that it had a past, a fleeting present, and no future. In that fleeting moment its members succeeded in capturing and recording, as man has not often done in his history, the greatness of which the human mind and spirit are capable.

Alexander the Great

Richard Stoneman

If one argues that there were great individuals who changed the course of history, Alexander (356–323 B.C.E.) seems to have had the right characteristics. In his short career he led the Greeks in a stunning conquest of the Persian Empire. For most historians his death in 323 marks a convenient dividing line between the Classical and Hellenistic ages. It used to be common for historians, like W. W. Tarn, to laud Alexander's greatness in deeds as well as in dreams. But as exemplified by the following selection, most historians now reject this older view. Here Richard Stoneman evaluates Alexander's personality, plans, and accomplishments.

CONSIDER: *The connections between Alexander's accomplishments and his purposes; how Alexander, often thought of as a hero, might be criticized; why Alexander's empire did not last long.*

Alexander's career was the motive force for the spread of Hellenism throughout the western Mediterranean and the Near East, and his achievement thus provided the matrix in which the Roman Empire, Christianity and other important aspects of western civilisation could take root. . . . [However] such grandiose prospects were far from Alexander's imagining and . . . his own aims and ambitions were very different. It is time to draw some of the threads together and to bring those aims and ambitions face-to-face with his actual legacy.

On the assumption, current today among most scholars, that [Alexander's "Last Plans"] . . . represent genuine plans of Alexander, we can deduce that Alexander's megalomania was increasing. He had come to believe, in some degree, his own propaganda, that made him a son of the god Ammon and possibly divine himself. Buttressed by this sublime form of self-confidence (and he had never, at any stage of his career, been short of confidence), he had become increasingly ruthless in executing his purposes. Disloyalty was instantly punished, but corruption and peculation were treated with casualness as long as the perpetrator's loyalty was not in doubt. Opportunistic and flexible, Alexander had been as quick to lose his conquests in India as he had been to gain them, abandoning them when they no longer threatened his immediate position. Babylon and Iran had become the heartland of his empire, but what kind of empire was that to be?

Administration was never to his taste, and Augustus' observation that Alexander had done surprisingly little to set in order the vast empire he had gained is a telling

---

SOURCE: Richard Stoneman, *Alexander the Great* (New York: Routledge, 1997), pp. 92–94.

one. The king's state of mind seems to have been a strange one in his last months; besides his megalomania, he was perhaps already ill with the disease that killed him and suffering from a consequent *accidie*. The only activity he could conceive of that was worthy of his self-image was further conquest. Preparations were already far advanced for the invasion of Arabia, and it is not unreasonable to believe that he had plans to conquer the west—Italy and Carthage, and perhaps beyond. Italians and Carthaginians plainly believed it.

In hindsight it may seem inevitable that an empire based purely on rapid military conquest could not be held together. It was Alexander's pleasure to have his satraps loyal to him; he was not interested in imposing a uniform style of government on his empire, and the Greek lands were virtually forgotten. It was inevitable that such an empire would collapse once his own strong personality was removed. In addition, the fact that he did nothing to appoint a successor strengthened this inevitability. . . .

But it was a world that spoke Greek. In addition, all the successor kings revered the memory of Alexander as their founder. All minted coins with his image. . . .

If we turn now from Macedon to the wider world, we can see that, although it was far from Alexander's intention to mingle cultures for any kind of altruistic or philosophical motive, it was an end result of his actions that the cultures did mix. This happened at different rates, and in different degrees, in different parts of the empire. Greece, with its strong cultural traditions, was essentially unaffected by the empire. The city-states continued their own way under Macedonian overlordship, though they had to get used to honouring "Royal Friends." The same is largely true of the Greek cities of Asia Minor, which were able to continue as "independent cities" under the relatively weak rule of Antigonus and then Lysimachus. Some of the cities prospered remarkably, notably Pergamon which developed a literary and artistic culture to rival that of Alexandria itself. When the last Attalid king of Pergamon bequeathed his kingdom to Rome, the fate of the rest of Asia Minor was also sealed.

Greek Realities

Finley Hooper

Most historians stress the intellectual and scientific accomplishments of the Greeks, above all their extraordinary use of reason. In recent years historians have been pointing to the less rational and individualistic aspects of the Greeks. Finley

Hooper exemplifies this trend in the following selection by focusing on the context of the supernatural and the demand to conform that typified everyday life for most Greeks.

Consider: *Ways the primary documents support or refute Hooper's argument; considering this interpretation along with that of Andrews, whether it is a mistake to view the Greeks as democratic; the context Hooper is using for making his evaluation.*

For the most part, this history of the Greek people from the earliest times to the late fourth century B.C.E. is about a few men whose talents made all the others remembered. That would be true, in part, of any people. In ancient times, the sources of information about the average man and his life were very limited, yet one of the realities of Greek history is the wide disparity in outlook between the creative minority which held the spotlight and the far more numerous goatherders, beekeepers, olive growers, fishermen, seers, and sometimes charlatans, who along with other nameless folk made up the greater part of the population.

Romantic glorifications of Greece create the impression that the Greeks sought rational solutions and were imaginative and intellectually curious as a people. Actually, far from being devoted to the risks of rationality, the vast majority of the Greeks sought always the safe haven of superstition and the comfort of magic charms. Only a relatively few thinkers offered a wondrous variety of ideas in their tireless quest for truth. To study various opinions, each of which appears to have some element of truth, is not a risk everyone should take and by no means did all the ancient Greeks take it. Yet enough did, so as to enable a whole people to be associated with the beginnings of philosophy, including the objectivity of scientific inquiry.

The Greeks who belonged to the creative minority were no more like everybody else than such folk ever have been. . . .

They were restless, talkative, critical and sometimes tiresome. Yet their lives as much as their works reveal Greece, for better or for worse, in the way it really was. After Homer, lyric poets went wandering from place to place, in exile from their native cities; before the time of Aristotle, Socrates was executed. If the Greeks invented intellectualism, they were also the first to suppress it. They were, in brief, a people who showed others both how to succeed and how to fail at the things which men might try.

As has often been said, the first democratic society known to man originated in Greece. For this expression of human freedom the Greeks have deservedly received everlasting credit. Yet it is also true that democratic governments were never adopted by a majority of Greek states, and those established were bitterly contested from within and without. In Athens where democracy had its best chance, the government was always threatened by the schemes of oligarchical clubs which sought by any means possible to subvert it. Ironically, Athenian democracy actually failed because of the mistakes of those whom it benefited most, rather than through the machinations of men waiting in the wings to take over. Then, as now, beneath the surface of events there persisted the tension between the material benefits to be obtained through state intervention and the more dynamic vitality which prevails where individuals are left more free to serve and, as it happens, to exploit one another.

A historian must be careful in drawing parallels. The number of individuals in a Greek democracy whose freedom was at stake would be considerably fewer than nowadays. The history of ancient Greece came before the time when all men were created equal. Even the brilliant Aristotle accepted at face value the evidence that certain individuals were endowed with superior qualities. He saw no reason why all men should be treated alike before the law. In fact, he allowed that certain extraordinary persons might be above the law altogether. Some men seemed born to rule and others to serve. There was no common ground between them.

The egalitarian concept that every human being has been endowed by his creator with certain inalienable rights was not a part of the Greek democratic tradition. Pericles, the great Athenian statesman, said that the Athenians considered debate a necessary prelude to any wise action. At the same time, he had a narrow view as to who should do the debating. At Athens, women, foreigners and slaves were all excluded from political life. The actual citizenry was therefore a distinct minority of those living in the city.

In other Greek cities, political power continued to be vested in a small clique (an oligarchy) or in the hands of one man, and often with beneficial results. Various answers to the same political and social problems were proposed and because there were differences there were conflicts. Those who sought to reduce the conflicts also sought to curb the differences, the very same which gave Greek society its exciting vitality. Here we have one of the ironies of human history. Amid bitter often arrogant quarrelsomeness, the Greeks created a civilization which has been much admired. Yet, the price of it has been largely ignored. Hard choices are rarely popular. The Greeks provide the agonizing lesson that men do struggle with one another and in doing so are actually better off than when they live in collective submission to a single idea.

✁⤾　CHAPTER QUESTIONS

1. Evaluate the role of democracy in explaining the rise to greatness of Athens as well as the nature of Athenian society during the Classical Age.

2. Many of the documents have dealt with the nature of the city-state, emphasizing some of the tensions and changes the Greeks experienced. Basing your answers on the information and arguments presented in these sources, what do you think were the advantages and disadvantages for the Greeks of being organized into such relatively small, independent units?

3. On the one hand, the sources have focused on various admired characteristics of Greek civilization, such as their art, drama, democracy, political thought, science, and philosophy. On the other hand, the documents reveal certain criticized qualities of Greek civilization, such as the instability of the polis, the relatively common occurrence of war, the nonegalitarian attitudes of the Greeks, the negative attitude toward women, and the support of slavery. Considering this, do you think that the Greeks have been overly romanticized or appropriately admired? Why?

4 The Rise of Rome

Roman civilization arose during the middle of the first millennium B.C.E. After the Romans gained independence from the ruling Etruscans in 509 B.C.E., they slowly established control over the Italian peninsula, the western Mediterranean, the whole Mediterranean basin, and large parts of Europe. Although Rome retained its republican form of government until the first century B.C.E., there was considerable political turmoil and struggle, often reflecting tensions between the lower and middle classes and the ruling elites. Eventually, the Republic was unable to support these and other tensions. After a century of "slow revolution," Augustus took command in 27 B.C.E., making Rome an empire in all but name. By the time the Republic was transformed into the Empire, the combination of Roman political control and Greek culture had provided considerable unity to the Mediterranean basin. This Greco-Roman civilization enjoyed full maturity following the triumph of Augustus.

The Republic's most stunning accomplishments were military, political, and administrative. Rome was in the long run consistently successful in its wars, each time extending its rule. One reason for this success was her ability to develop political, administrative, and legal policies to manage newly won territories—something at which the Greeks were much less successful. During the late Republic and particularly during the Empire, these accomplishments were facilitated and symbolized by great architectural achievements—the roads, aqueducts, public facilities, and monuments that helped hold Roman lands together. Culturally, the Romans borrowed freely from the Greeks, acknowledging Greek superiority but nevertheless adding their own style to what they borrowed.

This chapter deals with two main issues. First, what was the structure of the Roman state? This involves an examination of the Roman constitution. Second, what was the nature of Roman society during the Republic? To get at this issue, a number of documents focus on the life and education of the aristocracy, the importance of Roman religious practices, the position of women, the use of slaves, and the place of Greek culture in Roman life. The sources in this chapter should provide a background for developments during the Empire, which will be covered in the next chapter.

Primary Sources

Histories: The Roman Constitution

Polybius

One of the Romans' greatest achievements was the development of political institutions that, despite problems, accommodated Rome's needs. Probably the best general description of these institutions during the Republic is provided by Polybius (c. 205–123 B.C.E.), a Greek politician and one of the greatest historians of the ancient world. He spent sixteen years in Rome, where he was in a position to observe the functioning of the Roman state and examine relevant documents. Part of his stated purpose in examining Rome's institutions was to explain why Rome had been so successful, particularly in comparison with his own Greek world. Some of his conclusions are presented in the following selection in which he describes the balanced nature of the Roman constitution.

CONSIDER: *The relative powers of the consuls, the Senate, and the people; the most important functions of the Roman government according to Polybius; the potential dangers or sources of instability in such a constitution.*

As for the Roman constitution, it had three elements, each of them possessing sovereign powers: and their respective share of power in the whole state had been regulated with such a scrupulous regard to equality and equilibrium, that no one could say for certain, not even a native, whether the constitution as a whole were an aristocracy or democracy or despotism. And no wonder: for if we confine our observation to the power of the Consuls we should be inclined to regard it as despotic; if on that of the Senate, as aristocratic; and if finally one looks at the power possessed by the people it would seem a clear case of democracy. What the exact powers of these several parts were, and still, with slight modifications, are, I will now state.

The Consuls, before leading out the legions, remain in Rome and are supreme masters of the administration. All other magistrates, except the Tribunes, are under them and take their orders. They introduce foreign ambassadors to the Senate; bring matters requiring deliberation before it; and see to the execution of its decrees. If, again, there are any matters of state which require the authorisation of the people, it is their business to see to them, to summon the popular meetings, to bring the proposals before them, and to carry out the decrees of the majority. In the preparations for war also, and in a word in the entire administration of a campaign, they have all but absolute power. It is competent to them to impose on the allies such levies as they think good, to appoint the Military Tribunes, to make up the roll for soldiers and select those that are suitable. Besides they have absolute power of inflicting punishment on all who are under their command while on active service: and they have authority to expend as much of the public money as they choose, being accompanied by a quaestor[1] who is entirely at their orders. A survey of these powers would in fact justify our describing the constitution as despotic,—a clear case of royal government. Nor will it affect the truth of my description, if any of the institutions I have described are changed in our time, or in that of our posterity: and the same remarks apply to what follows.

The Senate has first of all the control of the treasury, and regulates the receipts and disbursements alike. For the Quaestors cannot issue any public money for the various departments of the state without a decree of the Senate, except for the service of the Consuls. The Senate controls also what is by far the largest and most important expenditure, that, namely, which is made by

SOURCE: Polybius, *Histories*, vol. I, trans. Evelyn S. Shuckburgh (New York: Macmillan and Co., 1889), pp. 468–471.

[1] Official responsible for finance and administration.

the censors[2] every *lustrum*[3] for the repair or construction of public buildings; this money cannot be obtained by the censors except by the grant of the Senate. Similarly all crimes committed in Italy requiring a public investigation, such as treason, conspiracy, poisoning, or wilful murder, are in the hands of the Senate. Besides, if any individual or state among the Italian allies requires a controversy to be settled, a penalty to be assessed, help or protection to be afforded,—all this is the province of the Senate. Or again, outside Italy, if it is necessary to send an embassy to reconcile warring communities, or to remind them of their duty, or sometimes to impose requisitions upon them, or to receive their submission, or finally to proclaim war against them,—this too is the business of the Senate. In like manner the reception to be given to foreign ambassadors in Rome, and the answers to be returned to them, are decided by the senate. With such business the people have nothing to do. Consequently, if one were staying at Rome when the Consuls were not in town, one would imagine the constitution to be a complete aristocracy: and this has been the idea entertained by many Greeks, and by many kings as well, from the fact that nearly all the business they had with Rome was settled by the Senate.

After this one would naturally be inclined to ask what part is left for the people in the constitution, when the Senate has these various functions, especially the control of the receipts and expenditure of the exchequer; and when the Consuls, again, have absolute power over the details of military preparation, and an absolute authority in the field? There is, however, a part left the people, and it is a most important one. For the people is the sole fountain of honour and of punishment; and it is by these two things and these alone that dynasties and constitutions and, in a word, human society are held together: for where the distinction between them is not sharply drawn both in theory and practice, there no undertaking can be properly administered,—as indeed we might expect when good and bad are held in exactly the same honour. The people then are the only court to decide matters of life and death; and even in cases where the penalty is money, if the sum to be assessed is sufficiently serious, and especially when the accused have held the higher magistracies. And in regard to this arrangement there is one point deserving especial commendation and record. Men who are on trial for their lives at Rome, while sentence is in process of being voted,—if even only one of the tribes whose votes are needed to ratify the sentence has not voted,—have the privilege at Rome of openly departing and condemning themselves to a voluntary exile. Such men are safe at Naples or Praeneste or at Tibur, and at other towns with which this arrangement has been duly ratified on oath.

Again, it is the people who bestow offices on the deserving, which are the most honourable rewards of virtue. It has also the absolute power of passing or repealing laws; and, most important of all, it is the people who deliberate on the question of peace or war. And when provisional terms are made for alliance, suspension of hostilities, or treaties, it is the people who ratify them or the reverse.

These considerations again would lead one to say that the chief power in the state was the people's, and that the constitution was a democracy.

Such, then, is the distribution of power between the several parts of the state.

The Education of a Roman Gentleman

Cicero

Roman society during the last century of the Republic was turbulent and mobile. One way to rise in this society was through education and talent. Marcus Tullius Cicero (106–43 B.C.E.) rose in this way. Born into a moderately wealthy but nonaristocratic family, he became an extremely successful orator in the law courts, rose to the position of consul in 63 B.C.E., and became one of the most prolific, influential, and admired authors of Roman times. Cicero attributed part of his success to the excellent education he received. This is described in the following excerpt from one of his numerous letters.

CONSIDER: *The nature of this process of education; the importance of Greek culture for Cicero's education; Cicero's social and political environment.*

I daily spent the remainder of my time in reading, writing, and private declamation, I cannot say that I much relished my confinement to these preparatory exercises. The next year Quintus Varius was condemned, and banished by his own law; and I, that I might acquire a competent knowledge of the principles of jurisprudence, then attached myself to Quintus Scævola, the son of Publius, who, though he did not choose to undertake the charge of a pupil, yet, by freely giving his advice to those who consulted him, answered every purpose of instruction to

---

[2]Officials responsible for supervising the public census and public behavior and morals.

[3]A ceremonial purification of the Roman population after the census every five years.

SOURCE: From J. S. Watson, trans., *Cicero on Oratory and Orators* (London: Henry G. Bohn, 1855), pp. 495–499.

such as took the trouble to apply to him. In the succeeding year, in which Sylla and Pompey were consuls, as Sulpicius, who was elected a tribune of the people, had occasion to speak in public almost every day, I had opportunity to acquaint myself thoroughly with his manner of speaking. At this time Philo, a philosopher of the first name in the Academy, with many of the principal Athenians, having deserted their native home, and fled to Rome, from the fury of Mithridates, I immediately became his scholar, and was exceedingly taken with his philosophy; and, besides the pleasure I received from the great variety and sublimity of his matter, I was still more inclined to confine my attention to that study; because there was reason to apprehend that our laws and judicial proceedings would be wholly overturned by the continuance of the public disorders. In the same year Sulpicius lost his life; and Quintus Catulus, Marcus Antonius, and Caius Julius, three orators who were partly contemporary with each other, were most inhumanly put to death. Then also I attended the lectures of Molo the Rhodian, who was newly come to Rome, and was both an excellent pleader, and an able teacher of the art. . . .

The three following years the city was free from the tumult of arms. . . . I pursued my studies of every kind, day and night, with unremitting application. I lodged and boarded at my own house (where he lately died) Diodotus the Stoic; whom I employed as my preceptor in various other parts of learning, but particularly in logic, which may be considered as a close and contracted species of eloquence; and without which, you yourself have declared it impossible to acquire that full and perfect eloquence, which they suppose to be an open and dilated kind of logic. Yet with all my attention to Diodotus, and the various arts he was master of, I never suffered even a single day to escape me, without some exercise of the oratorical kind. I constantly declaimed in private with Marcus Piso, Quintus Pompeius, or some other of my acquaintance; pretty often in Latin, but much oftener in Greek; because the Greek furnishes a greater variety of ornaments, and an opportunity of imitating and introducing them into the Latin; and because the Greek masters, who were far the best, could not correct and improve us, unless we declaimed in that language. This time was distinguished by a violent struggle to restore the liberty of the republic; the barbarous slaughter of the three orators, Scævola, Carbo, and Antistius; the return of Cotta, Curio, Crassus, Pompey, and the Lentuli; the re-establishment of the laws and courts of judicature, and the entire restoration of the commonwealth; but we lost Pomponius, Censorinus, and Murena, from the roll of orators. I now began, for the first time, to undertake the management of causes, both private and public; not, as most did, with a view to learn my profession, but to make a trial of the abilities which I had taken so much pains to acquire. I had

then a second opportunity of attending the instructions of Molo, who came to Rome while Sylla was dictator, to solicit the payment of what was due to his countrymen for their services in the Mithridatic war. My defence of Sextus Roscius, which was the first cause I pleaded, met with such a favourable reception, that, from that moment, I was looked upon as an advocate of the first class, and equal to the greatest and most important causes; and after this I pleaded many others, which I precomposed with all the care and accuracy I was master of. . . .

[A]fter I had been two years at the bar, and acquired some reputation in the forum, I left Rome. When I came to Athens, I spent six months with Antiochus, the principal and most judicious philosopher of the old Academy; and under this able master, I renewed those philosophical studies which I had laboriously cultivated and improved from my earliest youth. At the same time, however, I continued my *rhetorical exercises* under Demetrius the Syrian, an experienced and reputable master of the art of speaking. After leaving Athens, I traversed every part of Asia, where I was voluntarily attended by the principal orators of the country, with whom I renewed my rhetorical exercises. The chief of them was Menippus of Stratonica, the most eloquent of all the Asiatics; and if to be neither tedious nor impertinent is the characteristic of an Attic orator, he may be justly ranked in that class. Dionysius also of Magnesia, Æschylus of Cnidos, and Xenocles of Adramyttium, who were esteemed the first rhetoricians of Asia, were continually with me. Not contented with these, I went to Rhodes, and applied myself again to Molo, whom I had heard before at Rome; and who was both an experienced pleader and a fine writer, and particularly judicious in remarking the faults of his scholars, as well as in his method of teaching and improving them. His principal trouble with me was to restrain the luxuriancy of a juvenile imagination, always ready to overflow its banks, within its due and proper channel. Thus, after an excursion of two years, I returned to Italy, not only much improved, but almost changed into a new man. The vehemence of my voice and action was considerably abated; the excessive ardour of my language was corrected; my lungs were strengthened; and my whole constitution confirmed and settled.

Eulogy for a Roman Wife
Quintus Lucretius Vespillo

Romans of high social rank usually married for political and economic reasons, but that did not mean affection and love were absent from such alliances. The following is an excerpt

⎯⎯⎯⎯⎯⎯
SOURCE: Dana C. Munro, ed., *A Source Book of Roman History* (Boston: D.C. Heath, 1904), pp. 201–204.

from a funeral eulogy composed in about 8 B.C.E. by ex-Consul Quintus Lucretius Vespillo for his wife Turia. In it, Vespillo discusses their life together and the qualities that made Turia such a good woman.

CONSIDER: *What this reveals about the proper role of Roman wives; the qualities that made Turia an admired and powerful figure.*

Before the day fixed for our marriage, you were suddenly left an orphan, by the murder of your parents in the solitude of the country. . . .

Through your efforts chiefly, their death did not remain unavenged. . . .

In our day, marriages of such long duration, not dissolved by divorce, but terminated by death alone, are indeed rare. For our union was prolonged in unclouded happiness for forty-one years. Would that it had been my lot to put an end to this our good fortune and that I as the older—which was more just—had yielded to fate.

Why recall your inestimable qualities, your modesty, deference, affability, your amiable disposition, your faithful attendance to the household duties, your enlightened religion, your unassuming elegance, the modest simplicity and refinement of your manners? Need I speak of your attachment to your kindred, your affection for your family—when you respected my mother as you did your own parents and cared for her tomb as you did for that of your own mother and father,—you who share countless other virtues with Roman ladies most jealous of their fair name? These qualities which I claim for you are your own, equalled or excelled by but few; for the experience of men teaches us how rare they are.

With common prudence we have preserved all the patrimony which you received from your parents. Intrusting it all to me, you were not troubled with the care of increasing it; thus did we share the task of administering it, that I undertook to protect your fortune, and you to guard mine. . . .

You gave proof of your generosity not only towards several of your kin, but especially in your filial devotion. . . . You brought up in your own home, in the enjoyment of mutual benefits, some young girls of your kinship. And that these might attain to a station in life worthy of our family, you provided them with dowries. . . .

I owe you no less a debt than Caesar Augustus [27 B.C.E.–C.E. 14, emperor of Rome] himself, for this my return from exile to my native land. For unless you had prepared the way for my safety, even Caesar's promises of assistance had been of no avail. So I owe no less a debt to your loyal devotion than to the clemency of Caesar. . . .

When all the world was again at peace and the Republic reestablished, peaceful and happy days followed. We longed for children, which an envious fate denied us.

Had Fortune smiled on us in this, what had been lacking to complete our happiness? But an adverse destiny put an end to our hopes. . . . Disconsolate to see me without children . . . you wished to put an end to my chagrin by proposing to me a divorce, offering to yield the place to another spouse more fertile, with the only intention of searching for and providing for me a spouse worthy of our mutual affection, whose children you assured me you would have treated as your own. . . .

I will admit that I was so irritated and shocked by such a proposition that I had difficulty in restraining my anger and remaining master of myself. You spoke of divorce before the decree of fate [death] had forced us to separate, and I could not comprehend how you could conceive of any reason why you, still living, should not be my wife, you who during my exile had always remained most faithful and loyal . . .

Menaechmi: Roman Slavery

Plautus

It should not be overlooked that the Romans, like other peoples in the ancient world, were supported by slaves. Indeed, slaves were a familiar component of everyday life for the Romans during the Republic. Some notion of the Roman treatment and perception of slaves can be gained from the following extract from Menaechmi *by Plautus (c. 254–184 B.C.E.), a Roman who wrote numerous comedies, often adapted from Greek originals. Here, Messenio, a slave, soliloquizes.*

CONSIDER: *What distinguished the "good" from the "bad" slave; the "right" way to treat a servant; the presence or absence of a sense of guilt or injustice about the institution of slavery.*

Mess. (*to himself*). This is the proof of a good servant, who takes care of his master's business, looks after it, arranges it, thinks about it, in the absence of his master diligently to attend to the affairs of his master, as much so as if he himself were present, or *even* better. It is proper that his back[4] should be of more consequence than his appetite, his legs than his stomach, whose heart is rightly placed. Let him bear in mind, those who are good for nothing, what reward is given them by their masters—lazy, worthless fellows. Stripes, fetters, the mill, weariness, hunger, sharp cold; these are the rewards of idleness. This evil do I terribly stand in awe of.

SOURCE: H. T. Riley, *The Comedies of Plautus*, vol. I (London: G. Bell and Sons, Ltd., 1852), pp. 364–365.

[4] *That his back—*Ver. 970. For the purpose of keeping his back intact from the whip, and his feet from the fetters.

Wherefore 'tis sure that to be good is better than to be bad. Much more readily do I submit to words, stripes I do detest; and I eat what is ground much more readily than supply it *ground* by myself.[5] Therefore do I obey the command of my master, carefully and diligently do I observe it; and in such manner do I pay obedience, as I think is for the interest of my back. And that *course* does profit me. Let others be just as they take it to be their interest; I shall be just as I ought to be. If I adhere to that, I shall avoid faultiness; so that I am in readiness for my master on all occasions, I shall not be much afraid. *The time* is near, when, for these deeds of mine, my master will give his reward.

The Conspiracy of Catiline: Decline of the Republic

Sallust

The Roman Republic came to an end during the second half of the first century B.C.E. *after a long period of conflict and civil war. Many saw this period as one of moral, social, and political decline from the more glorious and virtuous days of the Republic. Sallust (86–36* B.C.E.*) was both a participant and an observer in this period. He became a tribune of the people in 52* B.C.E. *and a close supporter of Julius Caesar in the following years. Later in his life he devoted himself more to historical writing. In the following selection he describes his own sense of disgust and disillusionment with the recent course of events.*

CONSIDER: *The main developments that disturbed Sallust; how Sallust compared characteristics of his own times with characteristics of the early Republic; the reliability of this account.*

My earliest inclinations led me, like many other young men, to throw myself wholeheartedly into politics. There I found many things against me. Self-restraint, integrity, and virtue were disregarded; unscrupulous conduct, bribery, and profit-seeking were rife. And although, being a stranger to the vices I saw practised on every hand, I looked on them with scorn, I was led astray by ambition and, with a young man's weakness, could not tear myself away. However much I tried to dissociate myself from the prevailing corruption, my craving for advancement exposed me to the same odium and slander as all my rivals.

After suffering manifold perils and hardships, peace of mind at last returned to me, and I decided that I must bid farewell to politics for good. But I had no intention of wasting my precious leisure in idleness and sloth, or of devoting my time to agriculture or hunting—tasks fit only for slaves. I had formerly been interested in history, and some work which I began in that field had been interrupted by my misguided political ambitions. I therefore took this up again, and decided to write accounts of some episodes in Roman history that seemed particularly worthy of record—a task for which I felt myself the better qualified inasmuch as I was unprejudiced by the hopes and fears of the party man. . . .

Thus by hard work and just dealing the power of the state increased. Mighty kings were vanquished, savage tribes and huge nations were brought to their knees; and when Carthage, Rome's rival in her quest for empire, had been annihilated,[6] every land and sea lay open to her. It was then that fortune turned unkind and confounded all her enterprises. To the men who had so easily endured toil and peril, anxiety and adversity, the leisure and riches which are generally regarded as so desirable proved a burden and a curse. Growing love of money, and the lust for power which followed it, engendered every kind of evil. Avarice destroyed honour, integrity, and every other virtue, and instead taught men to be proud and cruel, to neglect religion, and to hold nothing too sacred to sell. Ambition tempted many to be false, to have one thought hidden in their hearts, another ready on their tongues, to become a man's friend or enemy not because they judged him worthy or unworthy but because they thought it would pay them, and to put on the semblance of virtues that they had not. At first these vices grew slowly and sometimes met with punishment; later on, when the disease had spread like a plague, Rome changed: her government, once so just and admirable, became harsh and unendurable. . . .

As soon as wealth came to be a mark of distinction and an easy way to renown, military commands and political power, virtue began to decline. Poverty was now looked on as a disgrace and a blameless life as a sign of ill nature. Riches made the younger generation a prey to luxury, avarice, and pride. Squandering with one hand what they grabbed with the other, they set small value on their own property while they coveted that of others. Honour and modesty, all laws divine and human, were alike disregarded in a spirit of recklessness and intemperance.

---

[5] *Ground by myself*—Ver. 979. He alludes to the custom of sending refractory slaves to the "pistrinum," where the corn was ground by a handmill, which entailed extreme labour on those grinding. He says that he would rather that others should grind the corn for him, than that he should grind it for others.

SOURCE: Sallust, *The Conspiracy of Catiline*, trans. S. A. Hanford (London: Penguin Books Ltd., 1963), pp. 174–178. Copyright © 1963. Reprinted by permission of Penguin Books Ltd.

---

[6] In 146 B.C.E.

To one familiar with mansions and villas reared aloft on such a scale that they look like so many towns, it is instructive to visit the temples built by our godfearing ancestors. In those days piety was the ornament of shrines; glory, of men's dwellings. When they conquered a foe, they took nothing from him save his power to harm. But their base successors stuck at no crime to rob subject peoples of all that those brave conquerors had left them, as though oppression were the only possible method of ruling an empire. I need not remind you of some enterprises that no one but an eyewitness will believe—how private citizens have often levelled mountains and paved seas for their building operations. Such men, it seems to me, have treated their wealth as a mere plaything: instead of making honourable use of it, they have shamefully misused it on the first wasteful project that occurred to them. Equally strong was their passion for fornication, guzzling, and other forms of sensuality. Men prostituted themselves like women, and women sold their chastity to every comer. To please their palates they ransacked land and sea. They went to bed before they needed sleep, and instead of waiting until they felt hungry, thirsty, cold, or tired, they forestalled their bodies' needs by self-indulgence. Such practices incited young men who had run through their property to have recourse to crime. Because their vicious natures found it hard to forgo sensual pleasures, they resorted more and more recklessly to every means of getting and spending.

Visual Sources

Evidence from Coins

Historians can generally use coins for dating and for determining changes in dynasties and regimes. For ancient times, deposits of coins are often the best evidence for the presence of a people in a particular area. They can indicate the geographic area and quantity of trade relations. By analyzing changing patterns of deposits of coins, growing trade rivalries and changes of commercial, political, or military dominance can be discovered.

The designs and representations on coins often reveal much about a society. On this Roman coin from about 137 B.C.E. (figure 4.1), a citizen is pictured dropping a ballot into a voting urn. This reveals something about the type of political system present in Rome at the time and indicates that Romans were particularly proud of that system. In fact, Roman citizenship and voting rights were highly valued and part of what facilitated Rome's expansion. Yet too much should not be assumed: This scene could denote a limited oligarchy as much as a democracy or anything between. The writing on the coin is evidence of some level of literacy.

CONSIDER: *How modern American coins might reveal characteristics of American society to future historians.*

The Geographic and Cultural Environment

Map 4.1 shows some of the peoples and civilizations that occupied Italy and its immediately surrounding territory during the fifth century B.C.E. In the process of Rome's formation and expansion, the Romans came into direct and extended contact with these peoples. Before Rome became a dominant power, the Etruscans, Carthaginians (descendants of the Phoenicians), and Greeks had already established strong, literate, sophisticated civilizations. Understandably, then, as Rome expanded the Romans drew from and even copied many of the institutions and practices of these civilizations, particularly the closer Etruscans and Greeks. Other peoples, such as the Samnites, constituted a barrier to Roman expansion that the Romans overcame during the fifth, fourth, and third centuries B.C.E., usually by force of arms. Rome's geographic and cultural environment, therefore, played an important role in the development of the Roman Republic.

CONSIDER: *How the experience gained during the early years of the Roman Republic laid the foundations for later Roman imperialism.*

FIGURE 4.1 (© Snark/Art Resource, NY)

MAP 4.1 **Italy, Fifth Century** B.C.E.

Secondary Sources

The Ancient City: Religious Practices

Fustel de Coulanges

Ancient Rome is usually described in political, military, and cultural terms. The Romans themselves are typically described as practical, rational, disciplined, and secular. Yet like the Greeks, they were also very religious. This is emphasized in the following selection from The Ancient City, *which has become a minor classic. Here Fustel de Coulanges, a nineteenth-century French historian, shows how central religious beliefs were to the Roman's everyday life.*

CONSIDER: *How the Romans related to the gods; what the author means in arguing that the Roman patrician was a priest.*

We must inquire what place religion occupied in the life of a Roman. His house was for him what a temple is for us. He finds there his worship and his gods. His fire is a god; the walls, the doors, the threshold are gods; the boundary marks which surround his field are also gods. The tomb is an altar, and his ancestors are divine beings.

Each one of his daily actions is a rite; his whole day belongs to his religion. Morning and evening he invokes his fire, his Penates,[7] and his ancestors; in leaving and entering his house he addresses a prayer to them. Every meal is a religious act, which he shares with his domestic divinities. Birth, initiation, the taking of the toga, marriage, and the anniversaries of all these events, are the solemn acts of his worship.

He leaves his house, and can hardly take a step without meeting some sacred object—either a chapel, or a place formerly struck by lightning, or a tomb; sometimes he must step back and pronounce a prayer; sometimes he must turn his eyes and cover his face, to avoid the sight of some ill-boding object.

Every day he sacrifices in his house, every month in his cury, several months a year with his gens or his tribe. Above all these gods, he must offer worship to those of the city. There are in Rome more gods than citizens.

He offers sacrifices to thank the gods; he offers them, and by far the greater number, to appease their wrath. One day he figures in a procession, dancing after a certain ancient rhythm, to the sound of the sacred flute. Another day he conducts chariots, in which lie statues of the divinities. Another time it is a *lectisternium*: a table is set in a street, and loaded with provisions; upon beds lie statues of the gods, and every Roman passes bowing, with a crown upon his head, and a branch of laurel in his hand.

There is a festival for seed-time, one for the harvest, and one for the pruning of the vines. Before corn has reached the ear, the Roman has offered more than ten sacrifices, and invoked some ten divinities for the success of his harvest. He has, above all, a multitude of festivals for the dead, because he is afraid of them.

He never leaves his own house without looking to see if any bird of bad augury appears. There are words which he dares not pronounce for his life. If he experiences some desire, he inscribes his wish upon a tablet which he places at the feet of the statue of a divinity.

At every moment he consults the gods, and wishes to know their will. He finds all his resolutions in the entrails of victims, in the flight of birds, in the warning of the lightning. The announcement of a shower of blood, or of an ox that has spoken, troubles him and makes him tremble. He will be tranquil only after an expiatory ceremony shall restore him to peace with the gods.

He steps out of his house always with the right foot first. He has his hair cut only during the full moon. He carries amulets upon his person. He covers the walls of his house with magic inscriptions against fire. He knows of formulas for avoiding sickness, and of others for curing it; but he must repeat them twenty-seven times, and spit in a certain fashion at each repetition.

He does not deliberate in the senate if the victims have not given favorable signs. He leaves the assembly of the people if he hears the cry of a mouse. He renounces the best laid plans if he perceives a bad presage, or if an ill-omened word has struck his ear. He is brave in battle, but on condition that the auspices assure him the victory.

This Roman whom we present here is not the man of the people, the feeble-minded man whom misery and ignorance have made superstitious. We are speaking of the patrician, the noble, powerful, and rich man. This patrician is, by turns, warrior, magistrate, consul, farmer, merchant; but everywhere and always he is a priest, and his thoughts are fixed upon the gods. Patriotism, love of glory, and love of gold, whatever power these may have over his soul, the fear of the gods still governs everything.

SOURCE: Numa Denis Fustel de Coulanges, *The Ancient City,* trans. Williard Small (Boston: Lee and Shepard, Publishers, 1874), pp. 281–283.

[7]Gods of the household.

Life and Leisure: The Roman Aristocrat

J. P. V. D. Balsdon

Although it is appropriate to concentrate on the major events and the important accomplishments of the Romans, at times this leads one to forget that the Romans were real people with everyday lives. The religious aspects of their lives are brought out in the selection by Fustel de Coulanges. In the following selection J. P. V. D. Balsdon of Oxford focuses on the occupations, alternatives, and patterns of life open to a typical Roman aristocrat.

CONSIDER: *The occupations most appropriate for a Roman aristocrat and the limitations he had to face; connections between this description and Cicero's life and education as revealed in the document by Cicero; any connections between this picture of Roman life and the image presented by Fustel de Coulanges.*

By upper-class standards public service was the noblest activity of man—the life of the barrister, the soldier, the administrator and the politician; for normally the senator's life embraced all those four activities. Rhetoric was a main constituent of his education and at an early age he put his learning into practice by pleading at the Bar. He climbed the ladder of a senatorial career, absent from Rome sometimes for considerable periods in which he served as an army officer or governed a province. If he committed no indiscretion, he was a life-member of the Senate—if he held the consulship, an important elder statesman from then onwards. In the Empire he might be one of the Emperor's privy counsellors.

This was not a career in which, except in the last centuries of the Republic, great fortunes were to be made. The senator therefore needed to be a wealthy man, in particular to own considerable landed property. To this he escaped when he could, particularly if he came of a good family, for the Roman aristocrat was a countryman at heart, interested in farming well, happy in the saddle, fond of hunting. He would have been shocked by the parvenu Sallust's description of farming and hunting as "occupations fit for a slave"; and other Romans no doubt were shocked too, for in the case of the farmer (and perhaps only of the farmer) the notion of work had a wide romantic fascination. Everyone liked to be reminded of Cincinnatus in the fifth century B.C.E., of how, when they sent for him to be dictator, they found him ploughing and how, once the business of saving Rome as dictator was

accomplished, he returned happily to his farm. When Scipio Africanus found himself driven from public life, he worked on the land with his own hands.

If an aristocrat's means were not sufficient to support him in a life of public service, he might turn to business, banking, trading, tax-farming, the activities of the "Equestrian order." In this way distinguished families sometimes disappeared from politics for a generation or more and then, their wealth restored, they returned. There was nothing disgraceful about being a business man, as long as you were rich and successful enough, in which case you were likely to invest largely in land and to become one of the land-owning gentry. Equestrians, whether business men or rich country residents, were fathers of senators often and sometimes sons, frequently close personal friends, Atticus of Cicero for instance.

A man who avoided or deserted "the sweat and toil" of a public career in favour of industrious seclusion—"a shady life" (*vita umbratilis*)—could excuse himself and indeed (like Cicero and Sallust when, elbowed out of an influential position in public life, they became writers) found it desirable to excuse himself. If he became a writer, then he made it clear that he wrote as an educationalist, employing his seclusion to teach valuable lessons to his readers, particularly his young readers, a purpose which nobody disparaged. But if his retirement was the retirement of self-indulgence (*desidia*), like the later life of L. Lucullus, an obsession with fantastically expensive landscape gardening and extravagant fish ponds, he was a traitor to serious and responsible standards of living (*gravitas*) and won the contempt—however envious—of all but his like-minded friends. There was no secure happiness in such a life, as serious men like Lucretius, Horace and Seneca knew.

Roman Women

Gillian Clark

Until recently most historians presented an image of Roman life that mentioned women only in passing. This void about the experience of Roman women is being filled by new scholarship, much of it written by feminist historians. In the following selection Gillian Clark analyzes the position and experience of women during the late Republic and age of Augustus, emphasizing the political, legal, and social restraints on women.

CONSIDER: *Ways in which women might influence public life despite restraints placed on them; what the characteristics of the good woman were; how one might evaluate whether*

SOURCE: From "Life and Leisure," by J. P. V. D. Balsdon in *The Romans*, ed. by J. P. V. D. Balsdon, pp. 270–272, © 1965 by Basic Books, Inc., Publisher, New York. Reprinted with permission.

SOURCE: Gillian Clark, "Roman Women," *Greece and Rome*, 28 (1981), 206–207, 209–210.

Roman women were happy; how this description of Roman women compares with Balsdon's description of aristocratic Roman men.

Women did not vote, did not serve as *iudices*,[8] were not senators or magistrates or holders of major priesthoods. They did not, as a rule, speak in the courts. . . . As a rule, women took no part in public life, except on the rare occasions when they were angry enough to demonstrate, which was startling and shocking. . . .

Women might, then, have considerable influence and interests outside their homes and families, but they were acting from within their families to affect a social system managed by men: their influence was not to be publicly acknowledged. Why were women excluded from public life? The division between arms-bearers and child-bearers was doubtless one historical cause, but the reasons publicly given were different. Women were alleged to be fragile and fickle, and therefore in need of protection; if they were not kept in their proper place they would (fragility and fickleness notwithstanding) take over. As the elder Cato . . . said . . .

"Our ancestors decided that women should not handle anything, even a private matter, without the advice of a guardian; that they should always be in the power of fathers, brothers, husbands. . . . Call to mind all those laws on women by which your ancestors restrained their licence and made them subject to men: you can only just keep them under by using the whole range of laws. If you let them niggle away at one law after another until they have worked it out of your grasp, until at last you let them make themselves equal to men, do you suppose that you'll be able to stand them? If once they get equality, they'll be on top." . . .

A social system which restricted women to domestic life, and prevailing attitudes which assumed their inferiority, must seem to us oppressive. I know of no evidence that it seemed so at the time. The legal and social constraints detailed above may have frustrated the abilities of many women and caused much ordinary human unhappiness. But there evidently were, also, many ordinarily happy families where knowledge of real live women took precedence over the theories, and women themselves enjoyed home, children, and friends. There were some women who enjoyed the political game, and who found an emotional life outside their necessary marriages. And there were certainly women who found satisfaction in living up to the standards of the time. They were, as they should be, chaste, dutiful, submissive, and domestic; they took pride in the family of their birth and the family they had produced; and probably their resolution to maintain these standards gave them the support which women in all ages have found in religious faith. But the religious feelings of Roman women, as opposed to the acts of worship in which they might take part, are something of which we know very little. . . .

The son of Murdia, in the age of Augustus, made her a public eulogy . . . [which] may make the best epitaph for the women who did not make the history books.

"What is said in praise of all good women is the same, and straightforward. There is no need of elaborate phrases to tell of natural good qualities and of trust maintained. It is enough that all alike have the same reward: a good reputation. It is hard to find new things to praise in a woman, for their lives lack incident. We must look for what they have in common, lest something be left out to spoil the example they offer us. My beloved mother, then, deserves all the more praise, for in modesty, integrity, chastity, submission, woolwork, industry, and trustworthiness she was just like other women."

〜 CHAPTER QUESTIONS

1. Describe the circumstances, options, and everyday life of a Roman aristocrat during the first century B.C.E. as revealed in the documents in this chapter.

2. In what ways did Greeks, Greek culture, and Greek history affect Roman civilization?

3. Describe the similarities and differences between Greek and Roman civilizations. What were some of the main strengths and weaknesses of each?

---

[8]Judges.

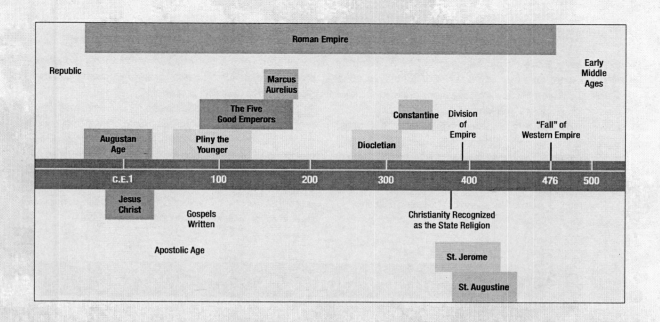

5 The Roman Empire and the Rise of Christianity

With control in the hands of Augustus by 27 B.C.E., the Augustan Age began. A variety of reforms transformed the Republic into the Empire. Rome entered a period of expansion, prosperity, cultural vigor, and relative political stability that would last until the end of the second century. This was particularly so under the long rule of Augustus (27 B.C.E.–C.E. 14) and the five "good emperors" (C.E. 96–180).

During this same period Christianity arose. Initially, it seemed only one of many religious sects and was perceived as a version of Judaism. But through the missionary work of Paul and the internal organization of the Church, Christianity spread and became institutionalized. During the fourth century it was recognized as the state religion within the Roman Empire.

By then enormous difficulties had been experienced within the Empire. Economic, political, and military problems were so great in the third century that the Empire shrank and nearly collapsed. A revival under the strong leadership of Diocletian and Constantine during the late third and early fourth centuries proved only temporary. By the end of the fourth century, the Empire was split into a Western and an Eastern half. The West was increasingly rural, subject to invasion, and generally in decline; the East evolved into the long-lasting Byzantine Empire. By the end of the fifth century, a unified, effective Western Empire was little more than a memory.

The selections in this chapter deal with three topics. The first concerns the general nature of the Empire at its height. During this time, those who predominated were the politically active Roman "gentlemen." What was their lifestyle? What were their interests? How did they relate to Classical culture? These same questions apply to some of the Roman emperors, like Marcus Aurelius, a Stoic philosopher. The documents also deal with broader questions. How was the transition from the Republic to the Empire made and what role did Augustus play in this transition? What were the connections between Roman society, culture, and religion?

The second topic is Christianity. Why was Christianity so appealing, particularly to Roman women? What explains the success of this religious movement? How did Christianity relate to Roman civilization? How did Christian theology relate to Classical philosophy?

The third topic is the decline and fall of Rome, a problem of continuing interest to historians. Some of the primary documents explore reactions to the fall. The secondary documents offer interpretations of the fall. Here the need to distinguish the Western from the Eastern Roman Empire during the decline and fall is stressed. This topic will take us up to the rise of new civilizations in lands once controlled by Rome; this will be covered in the next chapter.

Primary Sources

Letters: The Daily Life of a Roman Governor

Pliny the Younger

For a cultured, well-to-do Roman gentleman, the period between C.E. 96 and 180, when the Empire was at its height, was a good time to live. This is reflected in the letters of Pliny the Younger (c. 62–c. 113), a lawyer who rose to the position of governor of Bithynia in Asia Minor. In the following letter he describes a typical day while vacationing at one of his Italian villas.

CONSIDER: *The kinds of activities most important to Pliny, at least during his stay at the villa; Pliny's view of his life and of people around him.*

TO FUSCUS

You desire to know in what manner I dispose of my day in summer-time at my Tuscan villa.

I rise just when I find myself in the humour, though generally with the sun; often indeed sooner, but seldom later. When I am up, I continue to keep the shutters of my chamber-windows closed. For under the influence of darkness and silence, I find myself wonderfully free and abstracted from those outward objects which dissipate attention, and left to my own thoughts; nor do I suffer my mind to wander with my eyes, but keep my eyes in subjection to my mind, which in the absence of external objects, see those which are present to the mental vision. If I have any composition upon my hands, this is the time I choose to consider it, not only with respect to the general plan, but even the style and expression, which I settle and correct as if I were actually writing. In this manner I compose more or less as the subject is more or less difficult, and I find myself able to retain it. Then I call my secretary, and, opening the shutters, I dictate to him what I have composed, after which I dismiss him for a little while, and then call him in again and again dismiss him.

About ten or eleven of the clock (for I do not observe one fixed hour), according as the weather recommends, I betake myself either to the terrace, or the covered portico, and there I meditate and dictate what remains upon the subject in which I am engaged. From thence I get into my chariot, where I employ myself as before, when I was walking or in my study; and find this changing of the scene preserves and enlivens my attention. At my return home I repose myself a while; then I take a walk; and after that, read aloud and with emphasis some Greek or Latin oration, not so much for the sake of strengthening my elocution as my digestion; though indeed the voice at the same time finds its account in this practice. Then I walk again, am anointed, take my exercises, and go into the bath. At supper, if I have only my wife, or a few friends with me, some author is read to us; and after supper we are entertained either with music, or an interlude. When that is finished, I take my walk with my domestics, in the number of which I am not without some persons of literature. Thus we pass our evenings in various conversation; and the day, even when it is at the longest, is quickly spent.

Upon some occasions, I change the order in certain of the articles above mentioned. For instance, if I have lain longer or walked more than usual, after my second sleep and reading aloud, instead of using my chariot I get on horseback; by which means I take as much exercise and lose less time. The visits of my friends from the neighbouring towns claim some part of the day; and sometimes

SOURCE: Pliny, *Letters*, trans. by William Melmoth, rev. by W. M. L. Hutchinson, in vol. II of the Loeb Classical Library (Cambridge, MA.: Harvard University Press, 1924), pp. 259–263.

by a seasonable interruption, they relieve me, when I am fatigued. I now and then amuse myself with sporting, but always take my tablets into the field, that though I should catch nothing, I may at least bring home something. Part of my time, too (though not so much as they desire), is allotted to my tenants: and I find their rustic complaints give a zest to my studies and engagements of the politer kind. Farewell.

Meditations: Ideals of an Emperor and Stoic Philosopher

Marcus Aurelius

Emperor Marcus Aurelius (161–180), of great significance for what he did as well as for what he symbolized, was the last of the five "good emperors" who ruled during the relatively stable and prosperous period from the end of the first century through most of the second century. He was also an important Stoic philosopher and in his meditations captured much of the essence of the popular Hellenistic philosophy. Marcus Aurelius approached the Platonic ideal of a philosopher-king and symbolized much of what was best about Roman civilization. The following are selections from his Meditations, *written in the form of a diary toward the end of his life.*

CONSIDER: *Aurelius' standards of conduct; his attitude toward death; how he compares himself to most of those around him; the similarities between Marcus Aurelius and Pliny the Younger.*

Do not despise death, but be well content with it, since this too is one of those things which nature wills. For such as it is to be young and to grow old, and to increase and to reach maturity, and to have teeth and beard and grey hairs, and to beget, and to be pregnant and to bring forth, and all the other natural operations which the seasons of thy life bring, such also is dissolution. This, then, is consistent with the character of a reflecting man, to be neither careless nor impatient nor contemptuous with respect to death, but to wait for it as one of the operations of nature. As thou now waitest for the time when the child shall come out of thy wife's womb, so be ready for the time when thy soul shall fall out of this envelope. But if thou requirest also a vulgar kind of comfort which shall reach thy heart, thou wilt be made best reconciled to death by observing the objects from which thou art going to be removed, and the morals of those with whom thy soul will no longer be mingled. For

it is no way right to be offended with men, but it is thy duty to care for them and to bear with them gently; and yet to remember that thy departure will be not from men who have the same principles as thyself. For this is the only thing, if there be any, which could draw us the contrary way and attach us to life, to be permitted to live with those who have the same principles as ourselves. But now thou seest how great is the trouble arising from the discordance of those who live together, so that thou mayest say, Come quick, O death, lest perchance I, too, should forget myself.

He who does wrong does wrong against himself. He who acts unjustly acts unjustly to himself, because he makes himself bad.

He often acts unjustly who does not do a certain thing; not only he who does a certain thing.

Thy present opinion founded on understanding, and thy present conduct directed to social good, and thy present disposition of contentment with everything which happens—that is enough.

Wipe out imagination: check desire: extinguish appetite: keep the ruling faculty in its own power. . . .

How does the ruling faculty make use of itself? For all lies in this. But everything else, whether it is in the power of thy will or not, is only lifeless ashes and smoke. . . .

Man, thou hast been a citizen in this great state (the world): what difference does it make to thee whether for five years (or three)? For that which is conformable to the laws is just for all. Where is the hardship then, if no tyrant nor yet an unjust judge sends thee away from the state, but nature who brought thee into it? The same as if a praetor who has employed an actor dismisses him from the stage.—"But I have not finished the five acts, but only three of them."—Thou sayest well, but in life the three acts are the whole drama; for what shall be a complete drama is determined by him who was once the cause of its composition, and now of its dissolution: but thou art the cause of neither. Depart then satisfied, for he also who releases thee is satisfied.

Rome and the Early Christians

Pliny the Younger and Trajan

After the death of Christ, Christianity began to spread. Centuries would pass before it would become the major religion in the Roman world, but, by the beginning of the second century, it was a well-recognized sect to be contended with,

SOURCE: Marcus Aurelius, "Meditations," trans. G. Long in Whitney J. Oates, ed., *The Stoic and Epicurean Philosophers* (New York: Random House, 1940), pp. 554, 584–585. Copyright © 1940. Reprinted by permission.

SOURCE: From Dana Munro and Edith Bramhall, eds., "The Early Christian Persecutions," in Department of History of the University of Pennsylvania, ed., *Translations and Reprints from the Original Sources of European History*, vol. IV, no. 1 (Philadelphia: University of Pennsylvania Press, 1898), pp. 8–10.

particularly in the Eastern provinces. The more Christianity spread, the more government officials were faced with the issue of how to deal with it. Generally, various religious sects and beliefs were tolerated as long as their adherents were willing to participate in official pagan rituals, which were of a combined religious and political significance. But Christian beliefs demanded exclusivity and thus prevented acceptance of official rituals; to many this constituted both religious and political subversion. This problem and a common official response to it are revealed in the following correspondence in the year 112 between Pliny the Younger, then governor of Bithynia, and the enlightened emperor Trajan.

CONSIDER: *The circumstances under which Pliny became involved in prosecutions of Christians; what evidence this document provides about the general Roman policy toward the Christians; Roman legal practices and institutions revealed in this document; how Christians might have avoided prosecution or persecution.*

It is my custom, my Lord, to refer to you all things concerning which I am in doubt. For who can better guide my indecision or enlighten my ignorance?

I have never taken part in the trials of Christians: hence I do not know for what crime nor to what extent it is customary to punish or investigate. I have been in no little doubt as to whether any discrimination is made for age, or whether the treatment of the weakest does not differ from that of the stronger; whether pardon is granted in case of repentance, or whether he who has ever been a Christian gains nothing by having ceased to be one; whether the *name* itself without the proof of crimes, or the crimes, inseparably connected with the *name*, are punished. Meanwhile, I have followed this procedure in the case of those who have been brought before me as Christians. I asked them whether they were Christians a second and a third time and with threats of punishment; I questioned those who confessed; I ordered those who were obstinate to be executed. For I did not doubt that, whatever it was that they confessed, their stubbornness and inflexible obstinacy ought certainly to be punished. There were others of similar madness, who because they were Roman citizens, I have noted for sending to the City. Soon, the crime spreading, as is usual when attention is called to it, more cases arose. An anonymous accusation containing many names was presented. Those who denied that they were or had been Christians, ought, I thought, to be dismissed since they repeated after me a prayer to the gods and made supplication with incense and wine to your image, which I had ordered to be brought for the purpose together with the statues of the gods, and since besides they cursed Christ, not one of which things they say, those who are really Christians can be compelled to do. Others, accused by the informer, said that they were Christians and afterwards denied it; in fact they had been but had ceased to be, some many years ago, some even twenty years before. All both worshipped your image and the statues of the gods, and cursed Christ. They continued to maintain that this was the amount of their fault or error, that on a fixed day they were accustomed to come together before daylight and to sing by turns a hymn to Christ as a god, and that they bound themselves by oath, not for some crime but that they would not commit robbery, theft, or adultery, that they would not betray a trust nor deny a deposit when called upon. After this it was their custom to disperse and to come together again to partake of food, of an ordinary and harmless kind, however; even this they had ceased to do after the publication of my edict in which according to your command I had forbidden associations. Hence I believed it the more necessary to examine two female slaves, who were called deaconesses, in order to find out what was true, and to do it by torture. I found nothing but a vicious, extravagant superstition. Consequently I have postponed the examination and make haste to consult you. For it seemed to me that the subject would justify consultation, especially on account of the number of those in peril. For many of all ages, of every rank, and even of both sexes are and will be called into danger. The infection of this superstition has not only spread to the cities but even to the villages and country districts. It seems possible to stay it and bring about a reform. It is plain enough that the temples, which had been almost deserted, have begun to be frequented again, that the sacred rites, which had been neglected for a long time, have begun to be restored, and that fodder for victims, for which till now there was scarcely a purchaser, is sold. From which one may readily judge what a number of men can be reclaimed if repentance is permitted.

TRAJAN'S REPLY

You have followed the correct procedure, my Secundus, in conducting the cases of those who were accused before you as Christians, for no general rule can be laid down as a set form. They ought not to be sought out; if they are brought before you and convicted they ought to be punished; provided that he who denies that he is a Christian, and proves this by making supplication to our gods, however much he may have been under suspicion in the past, shall secure pardon on repentance. In the case of no crime should attention be paid to anonymous charges, for they afford a bad precedent and are not worthy of our age.

The Gospel According to St. Matthew

During the first and second centuries Christianity was one of many competing sects in the Empire. But by the fourth century it had become the most influential one and was finally adopted as the official faith of the Roman Empire. From a historical point of view, a crucial problem is to explain the success of Christianity. Part of the explanation comes from an analysis of the basic teachings of Christianity. One of the most useful texts for this purpose is found in the Gospel according to St. Matthew, written toward the end of the first century, about sixty years after the recorded occurrences. The rules for conduct and the general ethical message of Christianity are revealed in the following sermon of Jesus.

CONSIDER: *To whom this message was directed; the appeal of this message to people of those times; the differences in tone and content between these selections and the selections from the Old Testament in Chapter 1.*

5: Now when he saw the crowds, he went up on a mountainside and sat down. His disciples came to him and he began to teach them, saying:

"Blessed are the poor in spirit, for theirs is the kingdom of heaven.
Blessed are those who mourn, for they will be comforted.
Blessed are the meek, for they will inherit the earth.
Blessed are those who hunger and thirst for righteousness, for they will be filled.
Blessed are the merciful, for they will be shown mercy.
Blessed are the pure in heart, for they will see God.
Blessed are the peacemakers, for they will be called sons of God.
Blessed are those who are persecuted because of righteousness, for theirs is the kingdom of heaven.
Blessed are you when people insult you, persecute you and falsely say all kinds of evil against you because of me. Rejoice and be glad, because great is your reward in heaven, for in the same way they persecuted the prophets who were before you.

✌

"You have heard that it was said, 'Do not commit adultery.' But I tell you that anyone who looks at a woman lustfully has already committed adultery with her in his heart. If your right eye causes you to sin, gouge it out and throw it away. It is better for you to lose

SOURCE: *The Holy Bible, New International Version* (Colorado: International Bible Society, 1983), pp. 886–889 as excerpted.

one part of your body than for your whole body to be thrown into hell. And if your right hand causes you to sin, cut it off and throw it away. It is better for you to lose one part of your body than for your whole body to go into hell.

"It has been said, 'Anyone who divorces his wife must give her a certificate of divorce.' But I tell you that anyone who divorces his wife, except for marital unfaithfulness, causes her to become an adulteress, and anyone who marries the divorced woman commits adultery. . . .

"You have heard that it was said, 'Eye for eye, and tooth for tooth.' But I tell you, Do not resist an evil person. If someone strikes you on the right cheek, turn to him the other also. And if someone wants to sue you and take your tunic, let him have your cloak as well. If someone forces you to go one mile, go with him two miles. Give to the one who asks you, and do not turn away from the one who wants to borrow from you.

"You have heard that it was said, 'Love your neighbor and hate your enemy.' But I tell you: Love your enemies and pray for those who persecute you, that you may be sons of your Father in heaven. He causes his sun to rise on the evil and the good, and sends rain on the righteous and the unrighteous. If you love those who love you, what reward will you get? Are not even the tax collectors doing that? And if you greet only your brothers, what are you doing more than others? Do not even pagans do that? Be perfect, therefore, as your heavenly Father is perfect.

✌

"Watch out for false prophets. They come to you in sheep's clothing, but inwardly they are ferocious wolves. By their fruit you will recognize them. Do people pick grapes from thornbushes, or figs from thistles? Likewise every good tree bears good fruit, but a bad tree bears bad fruit. A good tree cannot bear bad fruit, and a bad tree cannot bear good fruit. Every tree that does not bear good fruit is cut down and thrown into the fire. Thus, by their fruit you will recognize them.

"Not everyone who says to me, 'Lord, Lord,' will enter the kingdom of heaven, but only he who does the will of my Father who is in heaven. Many will say to me on that day, 'Lord, Lord, did we not prophesy in your name, and in your name drive out demons and perform many miracles?' Then I will tell them plainly, 'I never knew you. Away from me, you evil-doers!'

"Therefore everyone who hears these words of mine and puts them into practice is like a wise man who built his house on the rock. The rain came down, the streams rose, and the winds blew and beat against that house; yet it did not fall, because it had its foundation on the rock. But everyone who hears these words of mine and does not put them into practice is like a foolish man who built his house on sand. The rain came down, the streams rose, and the winds blew and beat against that house, and it fell with a great crash."

When Jesus had finished saying these things, the crowds were amazed at his teaching, because he taught as one who had authority, and not as their teachers of the law.

Epistle to the Romans

St. Paul

Christianity owes its historical success not only to the content of its message but also to the organizing work of its early missionaries. St. Paul was the most important of these missionaries, traveling from the Near East to Greece and Rome with his message and organizing Christian groups during the decades after the death of Jesus. Paul's Epistle to the Romans was written during the middle of the first century. It had a strong influence on Christian theology. The following selection focuses on the relation of Christianity to law and authority.

CONSIDER: *The ways Paul has presented Christianity to meet the concerns of the Romans; how Christianity can be seen as compatible with Roman rule; connections between this message and the message in the Gospel according to St. Matthew.*

[21]But now, quite independently of law, God's justice has been brought to light. [22]The Law and the prophets both bear witness to it: it is God's way of righting wrong, effective through faith in Christ for all who have such faith—all, without distinction. [23]For all alike have sinned, and are deprived of the divine splendour, [24]and all are justified by God's free grace alone, through his act of liberation in the person of Christ Jesus. [25]For God designed him to be the means of expiating sin by his sacrificial death, effective through faith. God meant by this to demonstrate his justice, [26]because in his forbearance he had overlooked the sins of the past—to demonstrate his justice now in the present, showing that he is himself just and also justifies any man who puts his faith in Jesus.

[27]What room then is left for human pride? It is excluded. And on what principle? The keeping of the law would not exclude it, but faith does. [28]For our argument is that a man is justified by faith quite apart from success in keeping the law.

[29]Do you suppose God is the God of the Jews alone? Is he not the God of Gentiles also? [30]Certainly, of Gentiles also, if it be true that God is one. And he will therefore justify both the circumcised in virtue of their faith, and the uncircumcised through their faith. [31]Does this mean that we are using faith to undermine law? By no means: we are placing law itself on a firmer footing.

✑

[6]The gifts we possess differ as they are allotted to us by God's grace, and must be exercised accordingly: the gift of inspired utterance, for example, [7]in proportion to a man's faith; or the gift of administration, in administration. [8]A teacher should employ his gift in teaching, and one who has the gift of stirring speech should use it to stir his hearers. If you give to charity, give with all your heart; if you are a leader, exert yourself to lead; if you are helping others in distress, do it cheerfully.

✑

[1]Every person must submit to the supreme authorities. There is no authority but by act of God, and the existing authorities are instituted by him; [2]consequently anyone who rebels against authority is resisting a divine institution, and those who so resist have themselves to thank for the punishment they will receive. [3]For government, a terror to crime, has no terrors for good behaviour. You wish to have no fear of the authorities? [4]Then continue to do right and you will have their approval, for they are God's agents working for your good. But if you are doing wrong, then you will have cause to fear them; it is not for nothing that they hold the power of the sword, for they are God's agents of punishment, for retribution on the offender. [5]That is why you are obliged to submit. It is an obligation imposed not merely by fear of retribution but by conscience. [6]That is also why you pay taxes. The authorities are in God's service and to these duties they devote their energies.

[7]Discharge your obligations to all men; pay tax and toll, reverence and respect, to those to whom they are due. [8]Leave no claim outstanding against you, except that of mutual love. He who loves his neighbour has satisfied every claim of the law. [9]For the commandments, "Thou shalt not commit adultery, thou shalt not kill, thou shalt not steal, thou shalt not covet," and any other commandment there may be, are all summed up in the one rule, "Love your neighbour as yourself." [10]Love cannot wrong a neighbour; therefore the whole law is summed up in love.

[11]In all this, remember how critical the moment is. It is time for you to wake out of sleep, for deliverance is nearer to us now than it was when first we believed. It is far on in the night; day is near. [12]Let us therefore throw off the deeds of darkness and put on our armour as soldiers of the light. [13]Let us behave with decency as befits the day: no revelling or drunkenness, no debauchery or vice, no quarrels or jealousies! [14]Let Christ Jesus himself be the armour that you wear; give no more thought to satisfying the bodily appetites.

SOURCE: The Epistle of Paul to the Romans (III: 21–31; XII: 6–8; XIII: 1–14), *The New English Bible*. Copyright, The Delegates of the Oxford University Press and the Syndics of the Cambridge University Press, 1961, 1970, pp. 194, 204–205. Reprinted by permission.

The City of God

St. Augustine

Christianity grew in the pagan Greco-Roman world and flourished during the ensuing Middle Ages. Christianity's ability to survive and grow amid paganism is reflected in The City of God. Written by St. Augustine (354–430) in response to accusations that the sack of Rome by the Visigoths in 410 was caused by the pagan gods' anger at being displaced by the ascendant Christianity, this is one of the great works of Christian philosophy. St. Augustine, after studying Classical literature, becoming a professor of rhetoric, and being attracted to various philosophies and religious sects, was baptized in 387 and quickly rose to the post of Bishop of Hippo in his native Africa. He gained a reputation through his writings and became a very influential father of the Christian Church. Augustine argued that there were two cities, an eternal City of God awaiting the faithful and a worldly, sinful City of Men. The Christian Church more closely embodied the City of God and was preordained to replace Rome. The sack of Rome was thus part of God's divine plan and in no way tarnished the promise of the eternal city.

CONSIDER: *The differences between the "heavenly" and "earthly" cities; the "proper" relationship between the two cities; ways this philosophy was conducive to the spread of Christianity within a well-ordered empire and ways this same philosophy enabled Christianity to thrive despite the decline of that empire.*

But the families which do not live by faith seek their peace in the earthly advantages of this life; while the families which live by faith look for those eternal blessings which are promised, and use as pilgrims such advantages of time and of earth as do not fascinate and divert them from God, but rather aid them to endure with greater ease, and to keep down the number of those burdens of the corruptible body which weigh upon the soul. Thus the things necessary for this mortal life are used by both kinds of men and families alike, but each has its own peculiar and widely different aim in using them. The earthly city, which does not live by faith, seeks an earthly peace, and the end it proposes, in the well-ordered concord of civic obedience and rule, is the combination of men's wills to attain the things which are helpful to this life. The heavenly city, or rather the part of it which sojourns on earth and lives by faith, makes use of this peace only because it

SOURCE: Marcus Dods, ed., *The Works of Aurelius Augustine, Bishop of Hippo*, vol. II (Edinburgh, Scotland: T. and T. Clark, 1881), pp. 326–328.

must, until this mortal condition which necessitates it shall pass away. Consequently, so long as it lives like a captive and a stranger in the earthly city, though it has already received the promise of redemption, and the gift of the Spirit as the earnest of it, it makes no scruple to obey the laws of the earthly city, whereby the things necessary for the maintenance of this mortal life are administered; and thus, as this life is common to both cities, so there is a harmony between them in regard to what belongs to it. But, as the earthly city has had some philosophers whose doctrine is condemned by the divine teaching, and who, being deceived either by their own conjectures or by demons, supposed that many gods must be invited to take an interest in human affairs, and assigned to each a separate function and a separate department,—to one the body, to another the soul; and in the body itself, to one the head, to another the neck, and each of the other members to one of the gods; and in like manner, in the soul, to one god the natural capacity was assigned, to another education, to another anger, to another lust; and so the various affairs of life were assigned,—cattle to one, corn to another, wine to another, oil to another, the woods to another, money to another, navigation to another, wars and victories to another, marriages to another, births and fecundity to another, and other things to other gods: and as the celestial city, on the other hand, knew that one God only was to be worshipped, and that to Him alone was due that service which the Greeks call λατρεία, and which can be given only to a god, it has come to pass that the two cities could not have common laws of religion, and that the heavenly city has been compelled in this matter to dissent, and to become obnoxious to those who think differently, and to stand the brunt of their anger and hatred and persecutions, except in so far as the minds of their enemies have been alarmed by the multitude of the Christians and quelled by the manifest protection of God accorded to them. This heavenly city, then, while it sojourns on earth, calls citizens out of all nations, and gathers together a society of pilgrims of all languages, not scrupling about diversities in the manners, laws, and institutions whereby earthly peace is secured and maintained, but recognising that, however various these are, they all tend to one and the same end of earthly peace. It therefore is so far from rescinding and abolishing these diversities, that it even preserves and adopts them, so long only as no hindrance to the worship of the one supreme and true God is thus introduced. Even the heavenly city, therefore, while in its state of pilgrimage, avails itself of the peace of earth, and, so far as it can without injuring faith and godliness, desires and maintains a common agreement among men regarding the acquisition of the necessaries of life, and makes this earthly peace bear upon the peace of heaven; for this alone can be truly called and esteemed the peace of the reasonable creatures, consisting as it does in the perfectly ordered and harmonious enjoyment of God and of one another in God. When we shall have reached that peace, this mortal life shall give place to one that is eternal, and our body shall be no more this animal body which by its corruption weighs down the soul, but a spiritual body feeling no want, and in all its members subjected to the will. In its pilgrim state the heavenly city possesses this peace by faith; and by this faith it lives righteously when it refers to the attainment of that peace every good action towards God and man; for the life of the city is a social life.

The Germanic Tribes

Ammianus Marcellinus

For much of Roman history, "barbarians"—most of whom were tribes from the north and east—threatened the empire's borders. These pressures increased in the third and fourth centuries as Rome weakened and various tribes, led by warrior kings, pressed against Rome's frontiers. In the following selection, the Roman soldier and historian Ammianus Marcellinus (c. 330–395) describes one of these tribes, the Alans.

CONSIDER: *The characteristics of the Alans' nomadic life; why, according to Marcellinus, the Alans were such fierce fighters; how the Alans' daily life and culture differed from that of the Romans.*

Thus the Alans, whose various tribes there is no point in enumerating, extend over both parts of the earth [*Europe and Asia*]. But, although they are widely separated and wander in their nomadic way over immense areas, they have in course of time come to be known by one name and are all compendiously called Alans, because their character, their wild way of life, and their weapons are the same everywhere. They have no huts and make no use of the plough, but live upon meat and plenty of milk. They use wagons covered with a curved canopy of bark, and move in these over the endless desert. When they come to a grassy place they arrange their carts in a circle and feed like wild animals; then, having exhausted the forage available, they again settle what one might call their mobile towns upon their vehicles, and move on. In these wagons the males couple with the women and their children are born and

reared; in fact, these wagons are their permanent dwellings and, wherever they go, they look upon them as their ancestral home.

They drive their cattle before them and pasture them with their flocks, and they pay particular attention to the breeding of horses. The plains there are always green and there are occasional patches of fruit-trees, so that, wherever they go, they never lack food and fodder. This is because the soil is damp and there are numerous rivers. Those whose age or sex makes them unfit to fight stay by the wagons and occupy themselves in light work, but the younger men, who are inured to riding from earliest boyhood, think it beneath their dignity to walk and are all trained in a variety of ways to be skilful warriors. This is why the Persians too, who are of Scythian origin, are such expert fighters.

Almost all Alans are tall and handsome, with yellowish hair and frighteningly fierce eyes. They are active and nimble in the use of arms and in every way a match for the Huns, but less savage in their habits and way of life. Their raiding and hunting expeditions take them as far as the Sea of Azov and the Crimea, and also to Armenia and Media. They take as much delight in the dangers of war as quiet and peaceful folk in ease and leisure. They regard it as the height of good fortune to lose one's life in battle; those who grow old and die a natural death are bitterly reviled as degenerate cowards. Their proudest boast is to have killed a man, no matter whom, and their most coveted trophy is to use the flayed skins of their decapitated foes as trappings for their horses.

No temple or shrine is to be found among them, not so much as a hut thatched with straw, but their savage custom is to stick a naked sword in the earth and worship it as the god of war, the presiding deity of the regions over which they range. They have a wonderful way of foretelling the future. They collect straight twigs of osier, and at an appointed time sort them out uttering a magic formula, and in this way they obtain clear knowledge of what is to come. They are all free from birth, and slavery is unknown among them. To this day they choose as their leaders men who have proved their worth by long experience in war. Now I must return to what remains of my main theme.

The Fall of Rome

St. Jerome

The fall of the Roman Empire, though occurring over a long period of time, was experienced as a profound shock. Even those who were not part of the Roman power structure saw the invasions and decomposition of Rome as a catastrophe. This

---

SOURCE: Ammianus Marcellinus, *The Later Roman Empire,* ed. and trans. by Walter Hamilton (New York: Penguin Books, 1986), pp. 412–414.

SOURCE: From James Harvey Robinson, ed., *Readings in European History,* vol. I (New York: Ginn and Co., 1904), pp. 44–45.

reaction can be found in the letters of St. Jerome (c. 340–420), who lived through much of the decline. St. Jerome, an ascetic for part of his life and a great doctor of the Church, spent most of his life in Jerusalem and is known for his translation of the Bible into Latin.

CONSIDER: *Why Jerome was so shocked and overwhelmed by what was happening; any evidence in these letters of an incompatibility between Christianity and the Roman Empire; the methods apparently used in an effort to avoid destruction by invaders.*

Nations innumerable and most savage have invaded all Gaul. The whole region between the Alps and the Pyrenees, the ocean and the Rhine, has been devastated by the Quadi, the Vandals, the Sarmati, the Alani, the Gepidae, the hostile Heruli, the Saxons, the Burgundians, the Alemanni and the Pannonians. O wretched Empire! Mayence, formerly so noble a city, has been taken and ruined, and in the church many thousands of men have been massacred. Worms has been destroyed after a long siege. Rheims, that powerful city, Amiens, Arras, Speyer, Strasberg,—all have seen their citizens led away captive into Germany. Aquitaine and the provinces of Lyons and Narbonne, all save a few towns, have been depopulated; and these the sword threatens without, while hunger ravages within. I cannot speak without tears of Toulouse, which the merits of the holy Bishop Exuperius have prevailed so far to save from destruction. Spain, even, is in daily terror lest it perish, remembering the invasion of the Cimbri; and whatsoever the other provinces have suffered once, they continue to suffer in their fear.

I will keep silence concerning the rest, lest I seem to despair of the mercy of God. For a long time, from the Black Sea to the Julian Alps, those things which are ours have not been ours; and for thirty years, since the Danube boundary was broken, war has been waged in the very midst of the Roman Empire. Our tears are dried by old age. Except a few old men, all were born in captivity and siege, and do not desire the liberty they never knew. Who could believe this? How could the whole tale be worthily told? How Rome has fought within her own bosom not for glory, but for preservation—nay, how she has not even fought, but with gold and all her precious things has ransomed her life. . . .

Who could believe [Jerome exclaims in another passage] that Rome, built upon the conquest of the whole world, would fall to the ground? that the mother herself would become the tomb of her peoples? that all the regions of the East, of Africa and Egypt, once ruled by the queenly city, would be filled with troops of slaves and handmaidens? that to-day holy Bethlehem should shelter men and women of noble birth, who once abounded in wealth and are now beggars?

Visual Sources

Carved Gemstone: Augustus and the Empire Transformed

This onyx gemstone with a carved relief scene, known as the Gemma Augustrea (figure 5.1), portrays both a specific event and a general set of views during the early Roman Empire. Made between C.E. 10 and 20, it appears to commemorate a victory by the Romans over the Pannonians and Germans in C.E. 12. In the lower half, moving from right to left, a man and a woman are being dragged by auxiliary soldiers (probably Macedonian allies of the Romans). On the left four Roman soldiers raise a trophy; another barbarian couple will be tied to it. In the upper half, moving from left to right, Tiberius, who led the victorious Roman troops, descends from a chariot held by Victory. The youth in armor is probably his nephew Germanicus. In the center sit the goddess Roma and Augustus, between them the sign of Capricorn

FIGURE 5.1   (© Erich Lessing/Art Resource, NY)

(the month of his conception) and below them an eagle (the bird of the god Jupiter) and armor of the defeated. Augustus is being crowned as ruler of the civilized world by Oikoumene, while on the far right the bearded Ocean and the Earth with one of her children look on.

This scene is particularly revealing of political and religious information. It shows the transformation from the Republic to the Empire under a deified emperor in the making, for Augustus is being transformed into an equivalent of Jupiter and is clearly accepted by the rest of the gods. Moreover, his successor, Tiberius, appears to be in line for a similar fate. It also indicates the growing reach of the Roman Empire and the Romans' use of subordinate allies—the Macedonians—to exert their control. The religious figures and symbols, while Roman, also reveal affinities with Greek religious figures and symbols; artistically, the scene has a Hellenistic flavor. This is evidence for a merging of Roman and Greek cultures. Note also the balance between idealized form and realistic representation: The bodies are somewhat stylized, particularly Augustus' heroic body, but at the same time the individuals are clearly distinguished; these individuals were meant to be recognizable to the viewer.

FIGURE 5.2　(© Scala/Art Resource)

CONSIDER: *The political implications of this scene and of the coin of some 150 years earlier shown in Chapter 4; how contemporaries might have understood the message of this scene.*

Tomb Decoration: Death and Roman Culture

The tomb decoration in figure 5.2, known as the Sarcophagus from Acilia, dates from the mid–third century. Here, a boy, perhaps the young Emperor Gordian III, is standing next to a number of other figures. To his right are perhaps his parents, and to his left important government officials (perhaps senators) as suggested by their costumes. The bundle of scrolls at the feet of the boy and the stance of the figures indicate a dedication to Classical philosophy or scholarship. Indeed, in this period, there were many tombs with scenes representing a commitment to or glorification of pagan culture—a wish by individuals to be remembered as devotees of philosophy or literature.

This commitment to pagan culture is revealed both in what this tomb decoration shows and in what it does not show. Rather than showing mythical scenes, pagan gods, or Christian beliefs, it shows secular figures glorifying literature and philosophy. It is thus evidence for the continued strength of Classical pagan culture, at least among the elite, even during a period of decline for Rome. The style also indicates a continuing Classical balance between idealized forms and realistic representation: While the robes, the bearing, and the figures are stylized, there are clear individual differences, particularly in the head of the boy and in the balding individual to his left.

CONSIDER: *How this tomb decoration compares with the Tomb of Menna (Chapter 1), the thoughts of Marcus Aurelius, and Christian beliefs.*

Secondary Sources

The Roman Empire: The Place of Augustus

Chester G. Starr

With the rise of power of Augustus, the Republic came to an end and the Empire began. Under the long rule of Augustus, patterns were established that would endure well beyond his death in C.E. 14. During his own time Augustus was a controversial person, and ever since scholars have tried to evaluate the man and his rule. In the following selection, Chester Starr, a historian at the University of Michigan, analyzes some of the controversies over the place of Augustus in Roman history, here emphasizing his successes in the political and military fields.

CONSIDER: *The ways in which Augustus might be considered a success; how other writers and scholars might disagree with this evaluation.*

The failure of Augustus' social reforms throws into more vivid light his remarkable success in the political and military fields. Working patiently decade after decade Augustus gave the Roman world a sense of internal security based on a consciously elaborated pattern of government which embodied two principles. First came his own preeminence, and as we have seen in regard to coinage and architecture he was not bashful in stressing his own merits and achievements; no less than 150 statues and busts of the first emperor also survive. The second was his emphasis on outward cooperation with the Roman aristocracy, clothed in old constitutional forms; one may also add that on the local level Augustus, to ensure urban peace, favored the dominance of the rich and wellborn as against democracy. In sum, Augustus' reforms were essentially conservative in character. . . .

Modern historians have evaluated Augustus in many divers ways, but until recently have tended to treat him with respect, partly because of the great triumphs of literature in the "Augustan Age." Of late, however, scholars affected by the overtly arbitrary character of government in some contemporary states have approached Augustus, as the founder of a covertly arbitrary system, with little admiration. . . .

Certainly he was revered with great and genuine enthusiasm by his contemporaries both in Rome and in the provinces. In rising to the foreground as a single, unique figure Augustus had concentrated upon himself the yearnings of men for order. To this leader, more as symbol than as living creature, the subjects turned for assurance and prosperity in the material world, for a sense of security and purpose on the spiritual level. . . .

In sum Augustus steered the Empire along lines which it was to follow for centuries to come, both in its strengths and in its weaknesses; the latter often the consequence of artful compromise with the Republican past. When men of later generations looked back on Augustus, they tended to have mixed emotions. His memory among common folk stood high, and the great events of his reign were long commemorated by coins, calendars, and both public and court rites and festivals. Writers of aristocratic stamp from Seneca the Elder on accepted him as inevitable and necessary to stop the Roman revolution; yet these writers rejected almost unanimously his claim that he had restored the Republic. To them the Empire was an autocratic system, and Augustus was the first autocrat. If Augustus could have heard the voices of future generations as he lay on his deathbed and begged for the applause of the bystanders, his self-satisfaction might have been diminished.

Pagan and Christian: The Appeal of Christianity

E. R. Dodds

The beginnings of Christianity coincided with the establishment of the Empire under Augustus and the early emperors who succeeded him. Numerous attempts have been made to analyze Jesus and the rise of Christianity. In the following selection E. R. Dodds views early Christianity from a historical perspective. He focuses on the appeal of Christianity and how it compares with other religions of that period.

CONSIDER: *Typical traits of mystery religions and how Christianity differed from other mystery religions; other factors that might help explain the rise of Christianity in this early period.*

In the first place, its very exclusiveness, its refusal to concede any value to alternative forms of worship, which nowadays is often felt to be a weakness, was in the circumstances of the time a source of strength. The religious tolerance which was the normal Greek and Roman practice had resulted by accumulation in a bewildering mass of alternatives. There were too many cults, too many mysteries, too many philosophies of life to choose from: you could pile one religious insurance on another, yet not feel safe. Christianity made a clean sweep. It lifted the burden of freedom from the shoulders of the individual: one choice, one irrevocable choice, and the road to salvation was clear. . . .

Secondly, Christianity was open to all. In principle, it made no social distinctions; it accepted the manual worker, the slave, the outcast, the ex-criminal; and though in the course of our period it developed a strong hierarchic structure, its hierarchy offered an open career to talent. Above all, it did not, like Neoplatonism, demand education. . . .

Thirdly, in a period when earthly life was increasingly devalued and guilt-feelings were widely prevalent, Christianity held out to the disinherited the conditional promise of a better inheritance in another world. So did several of its pagan rivals. But Christianity wielded both a bigger stick and a juicier carrot. It was accused of being a religion of fear, and such it no doubt was in the hands of the rigorists. But it was also a religion of lively hope. . . .

But lastly, the benefits of becoming a Christian were not confined to the next world. A Christian congregation was from the first a community in a much fuller sense than any corresponding group of Isiac or Mithraist devotees. Its members were bound together not only by common rites but by a common way of life and, as Celsus shrewdly perceived, by their common danger. Their promptitude in bringing material help to brethren in captivity or other distress is attested not only by Christian writers but by Lucian, a far from sympathetic witness. Love of one's neighbour is not an exclusively Christian virtue, but in our period the Christians appear to have practised it much more effectively than any other group. The Church provided the essentials of social security: it cared for widows and orphans, the old, the unemployed, and the disabled; it provided a burial fund for the poor and a nursing service in time of plague. But even more important, I suspect, than these material benefits was the sense of belonging which the Christian community could give. Modern social studies have brought home to us the universality of the "need to belong" and the unexpected ways in which it can influence human behaviour, particularly among the rootless inhabitants of great cities. I see no reason to think that it was otherwise in antiquity: Epictetus has described for us the dreadful loneliness that can beset a man in the midst of his fellows. Such loneliness must have been felt by millions—the urbanised tribesman, the peasant come to town in search of work, the demobilised soldier, the rentier ruined by inflation, and the manumitted slave. For people in that situation membership of a Christian community might be the only way of maintaining their self-respect and giving their life some semblance of meaning. Within the community there was human warmth: some one was interested in them, both here and hereafter. It is therefore not surprising that the earliest and the most striking advances of Christianity were made in the great cities—in Antioch, in Rome, in Alexandria. Christians were in a more than formal sense "members one of another": I think that was a major cause, perhaps the strongest single cause, of the spread of Christianity.

Women of the Roman Empire

Jo Ann McNamara

Roman women, like Greek women, were usually in a subordinate position to men. Rome was and would remain a patriarchy. However, during the Empire and particularly as Christianity grew in importance, women's roles evolved. In the following selection, Jo Ann McNamara stresses how women were able to use their family roles and religion to gain new power and choices.

CONSIDER: *Why Christianity may have been so attractive to women; how Christianity played a role in improving women's power and status.*

The Roman Republic was a patriarchy in the strictest sense of the word. Private life rested upon *patria potestas*, paternal power over the subordinate women, children, slaves, and clients who formed the Roman *familia*. The Roman matron was highly respected within limits established by a strong gender system that defined her role as the supporter of the patriarch's power. Public life was conducted in the name of the Senate and People of Rome, institutionally defined as exclusively male. In the last days of the Republic, the power of these institutions was destroyed by civil war at the same time that the army, led by its emperors (originally only a military title), carried the standards of Rome to victory over the many civilizations of the Mediterranean world and ultimately took power over the city of Rome itself.

Under the Empire, the boundaries between public and private lives became porous and women began to use their familial roles as instruments of public power. Religion, in particular, offered women a bridge across class and gender differences, from private to public life.

SOURCE: Jo Ann McNamara, "Matres Patriae/Matres Ecclesiae: Women of the Roman Empire," in Renate Bridenthal, Claudia Koonz, and Susan Stuard, eds., *Becoming Visible: Women in European History*, 2d ed. (Boston: Houghton Mifflin, 1987), p. 108.

Roman women experimented widely with a variety of pagan cults, but increasingly Christianity attracted women with a vision of a community where in Christ "There is neither Jew nor Greek, . . . neither bond nor free, . . . neither male nor female." (Galatians 3:28)

Christianity was founded at about the same time as the Roman Empire was established, and for the next three centuries the imperial government and the Christian religion developed on separate but converging tracks. As an outlawed sect, the new religion was peculiarly susceptible to the influence of wealthy and noble women. Their participation was so energetic and prominent that critics often labeled Christianity a religion of women and slaves. In the fourth and fifth centuries, when the Empire had become Christian, it consolidated new political and religious hierarchies which reinforced one another. The synthesis was basically a restructured patriarchy with Christian men firmly in control of both government and church. But Roman Law and Roman Christianity contained a wider range of choices for women regarding marriage and property which passed into the hands of Rome's European successors.

The Later Roman Empire

A. H. M. Jones

Most historians who interpret the decline and fall of the Roman Empire focus on the Western half of the Empire. In fact, the Eastern half did not fall and would not, despite some ups and downs, for another thousand years. A. H. M. Jones, a distinguished British scholar of Greece and Rome, has emphasized the significance of the Eastern Empire's different fate for analyzing the decline and fall of the Western Empire. In the following selection Jones compares conditions in the two halves of the Empire, criticizing those who have theorized that the fall in the West stemmed from long-term internal weaknesses.

CONSIDER: *The primary cause for the collapse in the West according to Jones; other possible causes for the collapse in the West.*

All the historians who have discussed the decline and fall of the Roman empire have been Westerners. Their eyes have been fixed on the collapse of Roman authority in the Western parts and the evolution of the medieval Western European world. They have tended to forget, or to brush aside, one very important fact, that

SOURCE: A. H. M. Jones, *The Later Roman Empire*, vol. II (Oxford, England: Basil Blackwell, 1964), pp. 1026–1027, 1062–1064, 1066–1067. By permission of Basil Blackwell, Oxford.

the Roman empire, though it may have declined, did not fall in the fifth century nor indeed for another thousand years. During the fifth century, while the Western parts were being parcelled out into a group of barbarian kingdoms, the empire of the East stood its ground. In the sixth it counter-attacked and reconquered Africa from the Vandals and Italy from the Ostrogoths, and part of Spain from the Visigoths. Before the end of the century, it is true, much of Italy and Spain had succumbed to renewed barbarian attacks, and in the seventh the onslaught of the Arabs robbed the empire of Syria, Egypt, and Africa, and the Slavs overran the Balkans. But in Asia Minor the empire lived on, and later, recovering its strength, reconquered much territory that it had lost in the dark days of the seventh century.

These facts are important, for they demonstrate that the empire did not, as some modern historians have suggested, totter into its grave from senile decay, impelled by a gentle push from the barbarians. Most of the internal weaknesses which these historians stress were common to both halves of the empire. The East was even more Christian than the West, its theological disputes far more embittered. The East, like the West, was administered by a corrupt and extortionate bureaucracy. The Eastern government strove as hard to enforce a rigid caste system, tying the *curiales* to their cities and the *coloni* to the soil. Land fell out of cultivation and was deserted in the East as well as in the West. It may be that some of these weaknesses were more accentuated in the West than in the East, but this is a question which needs investigation. It may be also that the initial strength of the Eastern empire in wealth and population was greater, and that it could afford more wastage; but this again must be demonstrated. . . .

The East then probably possessed greater economic resources, and could thus support with less strain a larger number of idle mouths. A smaller part of its resources went, it would seem, to maintain its aristocracy, and more was thus available for the army and other essential services. It also was probably more populous, and since the economic pressure on the peasantry was perhaps less severe, may have suffered less from population decline. If there is any substance in these arguments, the Eastern government should have been able to raise a larger revenue without overstraining its resources, and to levy more troops without depleting its labour force. . . .

The Western empire was poorer and less populous, and its social and economic structure more unhealthy. It was thus less able to withstand the tremendous strains imposed by its defense effort, and the internal weaknesses which it developed undoubtedly contributed to its final collapse in the fifth century. But the major cause of its fall was that it was more exposed to barbarian onslaughts which in persistence and sheer weight of numbers far exceeded anything which the empire had previously had to face. The Eastern empire, owing to its greater wealth and population and sounder economy, was better able to carry the burden of defence, but its resources were overstrained and it developed the same weaknesses as the West, if perhaps in a less acute form. Despite these weaknesses it managed in the sixth century not only to hold its own against the Persians in the East but to reconquer parts of the West, and even when, in the seventh century, it was overrun by the onslaughts of the Persians and the Arabs and the Slavs, it succeeded despite heavy territorial losses in rallying and holding its own. The internal weaknesses of the empire cannot have been a major factor in its decline.

✣ CHAPTER QUESTIONS

1. What are the similarities and differences between Roman and Christian rules of conduct and ethics?

2. What traits of Classical culture and civilization do you find most admirable? Are these also traits of Christianity?

3. In what ways were conditions of Roman civilization conducive to the growth of Christianity? In what ways was Christianity nevertheless contradictory to Roman civilization?

4. How might the very success of the Roman Empire be related to its decline?

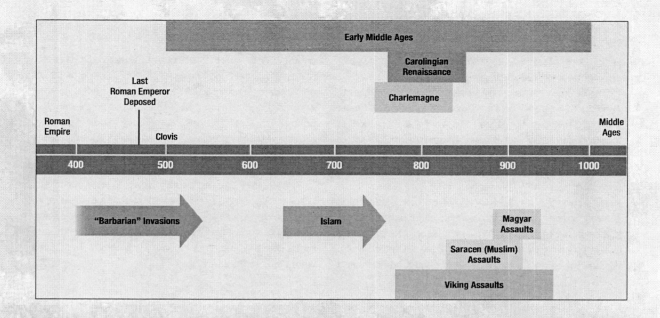

6 The Early Middle Ages

By the end of the fifth century, the Roman Empire had disintegrated in the West. In a series of invasions, various "Barbarian" peoples (mainly Germanic tribes) swept into Western Europe. Established patterns of life were disrupted and lines of communication were broken. There were great movements of population as invaders settled and were in turn threatened by new invaders. The civilization of the Early Middle Ages that formed in the West between the sixth and eleventh centuries reflected the threefold legacy of the fifth and sixth centuries: Germanic customs and institutions, Roman culture and institutions, and Christian belief and institutions.

Early medieval institutions drew from this legacy and slowly took form. The Christian Church, supported by a growing bureaucracy, numerous monasteries, and vast land holdings, became increasingly powerful. Medieval monarchies formed during this period but were generally weak. Local officials usually exercised political authority more effectively than monarchs. Europeans gradually established feudal relations among themselves based on personal contractual obligations for military service or exchange of land. An almost self-sufficient manorial economic and social system spread throughout many areas. In comparison to the preceding era, there was a broad cultural decline.

During the eighth and ninth centuries, there was a temporary revival, especially under the rule of the Carolingian King Charlemagne, who conquered vast territories, centralized his own authority, and encouraged cultural activities.

But not long after his death, fragmentation set in and Western Europe was again beset by invasions.

The sources in this chapter center on five broad topics. The first is the transition from Classical to medieval times: When did this transition occur, and what was its nature? Is this transition best viewed as occurring with the fall of Rome in the late fifth century or two centuries later with the rise of Islam? How was the transition experienced by observers of the time? The second topic is feudalism: How exactly should it be defined? What sort of relationships between people were characteristic of feudalism? What purposes did feudalism serve? How should feudalism be evaluated? The third topic is the reign of Charlemagne. What is the evidence for a revival of central authority and culture? What were the relations between Church and state during this period? The fourth topic concerns issues of gender characteristic of the Early Middle Ages: In what ways did the position of women change during this period? The fifth topic looks at the Early Middle Ages from a geographic perspective: How was the instability of the ninth and tenth centuries related to Western Europe's vulnerability to outside forces?

The aim in presenting these topics is to show the nature of the civilization that was developing during this time. Despite the disruptions, the apparent decline, and the relative disorganization of life between the fifth and eleventh centuries, long-lasting and distinctly European institutions were being formed.

 Primary Sources

History of the Franks

Gregory of Tours

In the early years of the Middle Ages, the cultures of Rome and the invading Germanic peoples merged. One way this merger took place was through Christianity, and one of the most crucial conversions was that of Clovis (c. 466–511), king of the Franks. Under Clovis, the Franks emerged as a powerful kingdom in Gaul, and Clovis's conversion to Christianity made him more acceptable to the Romans. In the following selection from his History of the Franks, *Gregory of Tours (538–594), a Christian bishop in Gaul, describes the conversion of Clovis as well as the baptism of his army.*

CONSIDER: *The role played by queen Clotilda; what convinced Clovis to convert; why so many of his followers suddenly converted.*

The queen did not cease to urge him [Clovis] to recognize the true God and cease worshiping idols. But he could not be influenced in any way to this belief, until at last a war arose with the Alamanni, in which he was driven by necessity to confess what before he had of his free will denied. It came about that as the two armies were fighting fiercely, there was much slaughter, and Clovis's army began to be in danger of destruction. He saw it and raised his eyes to heaven, and with remorse in his heart he burst into tears and cried: "Jesus Christ,

SOURCE: Gregory, Bishop of Tours, *History of the Franks*, trans. Ernest Brehaut (New York: Columbia University Press, 1916), pp. 39–41.

whom Clotilda asserts to be the son of the living God, who art said to give aid to those in distress, and to bestow victory on those who hope in thee, I beseech the glory of thy aid, with the vow that if thou wilt grant me victory over these enemies, and I shall know that power which she says that people dedicated in thy name have had from thee, I will believe in thee and be baptized in thy name. For I have invoked my own gods, but, as I find, they have withdrawn from aiding me; and therefore I believe that they possess no power, since they do not help those who obey them. I now call upon thee, I desire to believe thee, only let me be rescued from my adversaries." And when he said this, the Alamanni turned their backs, and began to disperse in flight. And when they saw that their king was killed, they submitted to the dominion of Clovis, saying: "Let not the people perish further, we pray; we are yours now." And he stopped the fighting, and after encouraging his men, retired in peace and told the queen how he had had merit to win the victory by calling on the name of Christ. This happened in the fifteenth year of his reign.

Then the queen asked saint Remi, bishop of Rheims, to summon Clovis secretly, urging him to introduce the king to the word of salvation. And the bishop sent for him secretly and began to urge him to believe in the true God, maker of heaven and earth, and to cease worshiping idols, which could help neither themselves nor any one else. But the king said: "I gladly hear you, most holy father; but there remains one thing: the people who follow me cannot endure to abandon their gods; but I shall go and speak to them according to your words." He met with his followers, but before he could speak the power of God anticipated him, and all the people cried out together: "O pious king, we reject our mortal gods, and we are ready to follow the immortal God whom Remi preaches." This was reported to the bishop, who was greatly rejoiced, and bade them get ready the baptismal font. . . . And so the king confessed all-powerful God in the Trinity, and was baptized in the name of the Father, Son and holy Spirit, and was anointed with the holy ointment with the sign of the cross of Christ. And of his army more than 3000 were baptized.

The Origins of Feudalism

During the Middle Ages a system of feudalism developed, in part to fill the void created by the collapse of Roman authority and the weakness of centralized monarchies, and in part as a pragmatic outgrowth of various Roman institutions and German concepts of personal service and loyalty. Feudalism was essentially a series of contractual relationships between individuals, backed up by various ethical and legal doctrines. This is illustrated in the following documents dating from the seventh to the eleventh centuries.

CONSIDER: *The benefits that each party to a feudal contract expected to gain; the ideals behind the feudal relationship; the conditions for termination of the contract or relationship; the social and political conditions during these centuries suggested by these documents; the ways individuals might have attempted to secure or improve their social position in this system.*

A FRANKISH FORMULA OF COMMENDATION, SEVENTH CENTURY

Who commends himself in the power of another:

To that magnificent lord *so and so*, I, *so and so*. Since it is known familiarly to all how little I have whence to feed and clothe myself, I have therefore petitioned your piety, and your good-will has decreed to me that I should hand myself over or commend myself to your guardianship, which I have thereupon done; that is to say in this way, that you should aid and succor me as well with food as with clothing, according as I shall be able to serve you and deserve it.

And so long as I shall live I ought to provide service and honor to you, suitably to my free condition; and I shall not during the time of my life have the ability to

SOURCE: Edward P. Cheyney, ed., "Documents Illustrative of Feudalism," in *Translations and Reprints from the Original Sources of European History*, vol. IV, no. 3, ed. Department of History of the University of Pennsylvania (Philadelphia: University of Pennsylvania Press, 1898), pp. 3, 5, 23–24.

withdraw from your power or guardianship; but must remain during the days of my life under your power or defence. Wherefore it is proper that if either of us shall wish to withdraw himself from these agreements, he shall pay *so many* shillings to the other party (*pari suo*), and this agreement shall remain unbroken. . . .

CAPITULARY CONCERNING FREEMEN AND VASSALS, 816

If any one shall wish to leave his lord (*seniorem*), and is able to prove against him one of these crimes, that is, in the first place, if the lord has wished to reduce him unjustly into servitude; in the second place, if he has taken counsel against his life; in the third place, if the lord has committed adultery with the wife of his vassal; in the fourth place, if he has wilfully attacked him with a drawn sword; in the fifth place, if the lord has been able to bring defence to his vassal after he has commended his hands to him, and has not done so; it is allowed to the vassal to leave him. If the lord has perpetrated anything against the vassal in these five points it is allowed the vassal to leave him. . . .

LETTER FROM BISHOP FULBERT OF CHARTRES, 1020

Asked to write something concerning the form of fealty,[1] I have noted briefly for you on the authority of the books the things which follow. He who swears fealty to his lord ought always to have these six things in memory; what is harmless, safe, honorable, useful, easy, practicable. Harmless, that is to say that he should not be injurious to his lord in his body; safe, that he should not be injurious to him in his secrets or in the defences through which he is able to be secure; honorable, that he should not be injurious to him in his justice or in other matters that pertain to his honor; useful, that he should not be injurious to him in his possessions; easy or practicable, that that good which his lord is able to do easily, he make not difficult, nor that which is practicable he make impossible to him.

However, that the faithful vassal should avoid these injuries is proper, but not for this does he deserve his holding; for it is not sufficient to abstain from evil, unless what is good is done also. It remains, therefore, that in the same six things mentioned above he should faithfully counsel and aid his lord, if he wishes to be looked upon as worthy of his benefice and to be safe concerning the fealty which he has sworn.

The lord also ought to act toward his faithful vassal reciprocally in all these things. And if he does not do this he will be justly considered guilty of bad faith, just

[1] The obligation of loyalty owed by a vassal to his feudal lord.

as the former, if he should be detected in the avoidance of or the doing of or the consenting to them, would be perfidious and perjured.

Instructions to the Subjects of Charlemagne's Empire

Charlemagne

The most successful effort to reestablish central authority and revive culture during the Early Middle Ages came under the reign of Charlemagne (768–814), who was able to gain authority over a vast area, including most of Western and Central Europe. Charlemagne pursued policies to encourage literacy and improve the quality of religious institutions. Yet his efforts resulted in only temporary success, his empire falling apart soon after his death, with authority evolving to more local levels. The two documents that follow are instructions carried throughout Charlemagne's lands by royal agents. These documents illustrate his efforts to gain strength by mobilizing military forces and to improve culture and religion through education.

CONSIDER: *How these documents reveal the strengths and weaknesses of the central monarchy; Charlemagne's justification for his demand for better education; how these documents indicate a lack of division between religious and secular affairs.*

Concerning going to the army; the count in his county under penalty of the ban, and each man under penalty of sixty *solidi* shall go to the army, so that they come to the appointed muster at that place where it is ordered. And the count himself shall see in what manner they are prepared, that is, each one shall have a lance, shield, bow with two strings, twelve arrows. And the bishops, counts, abbots shall oversee their own men and shall come on the day of the appointed muster and there show how they are prepared. Let them have breastplates or helmets, and let them proceed to the army, that is, in the summer.

❧

Be it known, therefore, to your devotion pleasing to God, that we, together with our faithful, have considered it to be useful that the bishoprics and monasteries entrusted by the favor of Christ to our control, in addition

SOURCE: Dana Munro, ed., "Laws of Charles the Great," in *Translations and Reprints from the Original Sources of European History*, vol. VI, no. 5, ed. Department of History of the University of Pennsylvania (Philadelphia: University of Pennsylvania Press, 1898), p. 11.

to the order of monastic life and the intercourse of holy religion, in the culture of letters also ought to be zealous in teaching those who by the gift of God are able to learn, according to the capacity of each individual, so that just as the observance of the rule imparts order and grace to honesty of morals, so also zeal in teaching and learning may do the same for sentences, so that those who desire to please God by living rightly should not neglect to please him also by speaking correctly. For it is written: "Either from thy words thou shalt be justified or from thy words thou shalt be condemned." For although correct conduct may be better than knowledge, nevertheless knowledge precedes conduct. Therefore, each one ought to study what he desires to accomplish, so that so much the more fully the mind may know what ought to be done, as the tongue hastens in the praises of omnipotent God without the hindrances of errors. For since errors should be shunned by all men, so much the more ought they to be avoided as far as possible by those who are chosen for this very purpose alone, so that they ought to be the especial servants of truth. For when in the years just passed letters were often written to us from several monasteries in which it was stated that the brethren who dwelt there offered up in our behalf sacred and pious prayers, we have recognized in most of these letters both correct thoughts and uncouth expressions; because what pious devotion dictated faithfully to the mind, the tongue, uneducated on account of the neglect of study, was not able to express in the letter without error. Whence it happened that we began to fear lest perchance, as the skill in writing was less, so also the wisdom for understanding the Holy Scriptures might be much less than it rightly ought to be. And we all know well that, although errors of speech are dangerous, far more dangerous are errors of the understanding. Therefore, we exhort you not only not to neglect the study of letters, but also with most humble mind, pleasing to God, to study earnestly in order that you may be able more easily and more correctly to penetrate the mysteries of the divine Scriptures.

War and Conversion Under Charlemagne

Einhard

The spread of Christianity during the Early Middle Ages sometimes involved wars and forcible conversion. Charlemagne became involved in long wars against the

SOURCE: Oliver J. Thatcher and Edgar H. McNeal, eds., *A Source Book for Mediaeval History* (New York: Charles Scribner's Sons, 1905), pp. 39–40.

Saxons, one of the Germanic pagan tribes on the borders of his Frankish kingdom. His efforts to subdue them permanently and bring them within his power included forcing them to convert to Christianity and dispersing them within Frankish lands. These events are described by Einhard (770–840), a scholar and member of Charlemagne's court who wrote a sympathetic biography of Charlemagne (Karl the Great).

CONSIDER: Possible reasons for Charlemagne forcing the Saxons to convert; whether forcible conversions would have different consequences from voluntary conversions.

Then Karl returned to the attack which he had been making upon the Saxons and which had been interrupted by the Lombard invasion. This was the longest and most severe of all his wars, for the Saxons, being barbarians and pagans like most of the tribes in Germany, were bound by the laws neither of humanity nor of religion. For a long time there had been continual disturbances along the border, since there was no natural barrier marking the boundary between the two races, except in a few places where there were heavier forests or mountains. So the Franks and the Saxons were accustomed to make almost daily raids on the territory of each other, burning, devastating, and slaying. Finally the Franks determined to put an end to this condition of affairs by conquering the Saxons. In this way that war was begun which was waged continually for thirty-three years, and which was characterized by the most violent animosity on both sides, although the Saxons suffered the greater damage. The final conquest of the Saxons would have been accomplished sooner but for their treachery. It is hard to tell how often they broke faith; surrendering to the king and accepting his terms, giving hostages and promising to accept the Christian faith and abandon their idols, and then breaking out into revolt again. This happened in almost every year of that war, but the determination of the king could not be overcome by the difficulties of the undertaking nor by the treachery of the Saxons. He never allowed a revolt to go unpunished, but immediately led or sent an army into their territory to avenge it. Finally after all the warriors had been overthrown or forced to surrender to the king, he transplanted some ten thousand men with their wives and children, from their home on the Elbe, to Gaul and Germany, distributing them through these provinces. Thus they were brought to accept the terms of the king, agreeing to abandon their pagan faith and accept Christianity, and to be united to the Franks; and this war which had dragged on through so many years was brought to an end.

Disorder and Destruction
The Annals of Xanten

Charlemagne brought some order to a large part of Europe, but that order was only relative and temporary. The period after his death in 814 was characterized by political disintegration, internal violence, and raids from outside forces such as the Vikings (Northmen) and Saracens (Moors). This disorder and destruction is reflected in the following selection from The Annals of Xanten, written by ninth-century monks. These excerpts cover the years from 846 to 852.

CONSIDER: The impact of the Northmen and Saracens on life in Christian Europe; why Western Europeans had such difficulty defending themselves against outside forces during this period.

(846) According to their custom the Northmen plundered Eastern and Western Frisia and burned the town of Dordrecht, with two other villages, before the eyes of Lothaire, who was then in the castle of Nimwegen, but could not punish the crime. The Northmen, with their boats filled with immense booty, including both men and goods, returned to their own country. . . .

At this same time, as no one can mention or hear without great sadness, the mother of all churches, the basilica of the apostle Peter, was taken and plundered by the Moors, or Saracens, who had already occupied the region of Beneventum. The Saracens, moreover, slaughtered all the Christians whom they found outside the walls of Rome, either within or without this church. They also carried men and women away prisoners. They tore down, among many others, the altar of the blessed Peter, and their crimes from day to day bring sorrow to Christians. Pope Sergius departed life this year.

(847) After the death of Sergius no mention of the apostolic see has come in any way to our ears. Rabanus [Maurus], master and abbot of Fulda, was solemnly chosen archbishop as the successor of Bishop Otger, who had died. Moreover the Northmen here and there plundered the Christians and engaged in a battle with the counts Sigir and Liuthar. They continued up the Rhine as far as Dordrecht, and nine miles farther to Meginhard, when they turned back, having taken their booty. . . .

(849) While King Louis was ill his army of Bavaria took its way against the Bohemians. Many of these were killed and the remainder withdrew, much humiliated,

SOURCE: James Harvey Robinson, *Readings in European History*, vol. I (Boston: Ginn and Co., 1904), pp. 159–161.

into their own country. The heathen from the North wrought havoc in Christendom as usual and grew greater in strength; but it is revolting to say more of this matter.

(850) On January 1st of that season, in the octave of the Lord, towards evening, a great deal of thunder was heard and a mighty flash of lightning seen; and an overflow of water afflicted the human race during this winter. In the following summer an all too great heat of the sun burned the earth. Leo, pope of the apostolic see, an extraordinary man, built a fortification round the church of St. Peter the apostle. The Moors, however, devastated here and there the coast towns in Italy.... The Normans inflicted much harm in Frisia and about the Rhine. A mighty army of them collected by the river Elbe against the Saxons, and some of the Saxon towns were besieged, others burned, and most terribly did they oppress the Christians. A meeting of our kings took place on the Maas....

(852) The steel of the heathen glistened; excessive heat; a famine followed. There was not fodder enough for the animals. The pasturage for the swine was more than sufficient.

The Wanderer: Life of a Medieval Warrior

Warfare and disorder marked much of the Early Middle Ages, particularly during the ninth and tenth centuries. In this society, local lords and their warrior followers often relied on each other for companionship as well as military and economic support. Opportunities and obligations might periodically take them far from home, and death always threatened them. Some of the values, joys, and difficulties of this life are reflected in the following excerpt from The Wanderer, *an epic poem probably written in the ninth or tenth century. Here the speaker, a warrior adrift because he has lost his lord and companions, looks back on his life.*

CONSIDER: *The values of this speaker's society; the ideal relationship of the lord and his warrior follower; the advantages and disadvantages of the warrior's life.*

"Often before the day dawned I have had to speak of my cares, alone: there is now none among the living to whom I dare clearly express the thought of my heart. I know indeed that it is a fine custom for a man to lock tight his heart's coffer, keep closed the hoard-case of his mind, whatever his thoughts may be. Words of a weary heart may not withstand fate, nor those of an angry spirit bring help. Therefore men eager for fame shut sorrowful thought up fast in their breast's coffer.

"Thus I, wretched with care, removed from my homeland, far from dear kinsmen, have had to fasten with fetters the thoughts of my heart—ever since the time, many years ago, that I covered my gold-friend in the darkness of the earth; and from there I crossed the woven waves, winter-sad, downcast for want of a hall, sought a giver of treasure—a place, far or near, where I might find one in a mead-hall who should know of my people, or would comfort me friendless, receive me with gladness. He who has experienced it knows how cruel a companion sorrow is to the man who has no beloved protectors. Exile's path awaits him, not twisted gold—frozen thoughts in his heart-case, no joy of earth. He recalls the hall-warriors and the taking of treasure, how in youth his gold-friend made him accustomed to feasting. All delight has gone.

"He who has had long to forgo the counsel of a beloved lord knows indeed how, when sorrow and sleep together bind the poor dweller-alone, it will seem to him in his mind that he is embracing and kissing his liege lord and laying his hands and his head on his knee, as it some times was in the old days when he took part in the gift-giving. Then he wakens again, the man with no lord, sees the yellow waves before him, the sea-birds bathe, spread their feathers, frost and snow fall, mingled with hail.

"Then the wounds are deeper in his heart, sore for want of his dear one. His sorrow renews as the memory of his kinsmen moves through his mind: he greets them with glad words, eagerly looks at them, a company of warriors. Again they fade, moving off over the water; the spirit of these fleeting ones brings to him no familiar voices. Care renews in him who must again and again send his weary heart out over the woven waves.

"Therefore I cannot think why the thoughts of my heart should not grow dark when I consider all the life of men through this world—with what terrible swiftness they forgo the hall-floor, bold young retainers. So this middle-earth each day fails and falls....

"Therefore the man wise in his heart considers carefully this wall-place and this dark life, remembers the multitude of deadly combats long ago, and speaks these words: 'Where has the horse gone? Where the young warrior? Where is the giver of treasure? What has become of the feasting seats? Where are the joys of the hall? Alas, the bright cup! Alas, the mailed warrior! Alas, the prince's glory! How that time has gone, vanished beneath night's cover, just as if it never had been!'"

SOURCE: Anonymous, "The Wanderer," trans. E. Talbot Donaldson, in *The Norton Anthology of English Literature*, 4th ed., ed. by M. H. Abrams et al. (New York: W. W. Norton and Co., 1979), pp. 84–85.

Illustration from a Gospel Book: Christianity and Early Medieval Culture

During the Early Middle Ages art became quite religious. Indeed, many of the paintings that survive from that period are miniatures from religious manuscripts, as in the case of this picture of the four evangelists from an early ninth-century Carolingian Gospel book. Each evangelist is shown writing his Gospel, and each is accompanied by his symbol: Matthew by a man, John by an eagle, Luke by a bull, and Mark by a lion.

This painting (figure 6.1) reveals a number of things about the Early Middle Ages. First, it suggests something about the position of Christianity. To this recently Christianized

FIGURE 6.1 (© AKG Images)

civilization, this scene could constitute a visual confirmation of biblical truth; the four evangelists are shown to have written, independently, similar accounts, thus testifying to the essential truth of the New Testament. Second, it exemplifies some of the uses of art in a strongly religious but relatively illiterate civilization: Here, the picture tells a story and important individuals are associated with identifying symbols. Third, the style and composition indicate that the artist was probably Byzantine or heavily influenced by Byzantine art. A Byzantine influence is also evident in a number of similar works that were part of the Carolingian revival initiated by Charlemagne. This could indicate a recognition of the superiority of Classical and Byzantine cultural productions and perhaps a sense of cultural inferiority in Western Europe.

CONSIDER: *What this reveals about the purposes of art during this period, and the nature of popular religion.*

Painting from an Illuminated Bible: Secular and Religious Authority

This painting (figure 6.2) shows Charles the Bald (823–877) being presented with an illuminated Bible by Count Vivian and the monks who produced it at the Monastery of St. Martin in Tours, France. It was produced around 846 and formally given to Charles in 851. The picture appears on the last page of the Bible being presented.

FIGURE 6.2 (© Bibliothèque Nationale, Paris, France/Bridgeman Art Library)

In the upper center is Charles the Bald, a grandson of Charlemagne, seated on his throne and flanked by dignitaries. His position and authority are denoted by his central position, crown, throne, and robes (which link him to past Roman authority), as well as the hand of God above him. Below Charles stands Count Vivian, surrounded on his right by the palace clergy and on his left by monks of St. Martin of Tours, three of whom are holding this Bible being presented.

The scene shows the attempted or assumed linkage between actual secular authority, which at this time was relatively fluid, Roman authority, by then a thing of the distant past, and spiritual authority, which remained unclear.

CONSIDER: Reasons for the perspective, or lack of it, in this picture; similarities and differences between this and the preceding painting; how this scene differs from the Gemma Augustrea (Chapter 5) and how this difference relates to differences between Roman and medieval civilizations.

MAP 6.1   Urban Decline, the Early Middle Ages

Contraction in the Early Middle Ages

The first map (map 6.1) offers evidence for the urban decline that occurred throughout Europe during the Early Middle Ages. It shows Trier, Germany, founded by the Romans, as it was during the Early Middle Ages. It became smaller, and the ordered street plan of the Romans was abandoned. Some of the Roman buildings were retained and used; some new churches were constructed both inside and outside the city.

Map 6.2 illustrates the relative weakness and contraction of Europe on a broader scale. Pressure was being exerted by three non-Christian groups during the ninth and tenth centuries: the Saracens (Muslims) from the south, the Magyars from the east, and the Vikings (a general term for groups of Scandinavians known by various names) from the north. The Saracens, adding to the already conquered Spanish lands, took control of the western Mediterranean from Christian hands and disrupted life with numerous raids into large areas of Southern Europe, particularly France and Italy. The Magyars made a number of destructive raids into parts of Central, Western, and Southern Europe from their eastern homelands.

The Vikings were the most mobile of all, moving into Slavic lands to the east, England to the west, and coastal areas in Northern and Western Europe, as well as competing with the Saracens in the Mediterranean region.

These two maps indicate some of the geopolitical problems affecting Western Christendom in the Early Middle Ages. The difficulty Christian monarchs had in resisting these invasions contributed to the political decentralization and corresponding feudalization of the period. Being unchristianized, these invaders did not respect Christian holy places or officials, which added to the disruption of organized life. Similarly, commerce suffered, as it could no longer be safely carried out. All this contributed to the increased turning inward and contraction in Europe that were indeed geographic and political realities on both a local and an international scale. Finally, with many of these invaders, particularly the Vikings, there was a merging of cultures and an influx of new strength as they eventually became Christianized and adapted to their new environments.

CONSIDER: The ways in which the geopolitical realities of Europe in the Early Middle Ages were conducive to the growth of feudalism; the ways in which maps can support the argument that the Early Middle Ages was a period of decline in the West.

MAP 6.2   Non-Christian Pressures, Ninth and Tenth Centuries

Secondary Sources

Mohammed and Charlemagne: The Beginnings of Medieval Civilization

Henri Pirenne

Traditionally, the break between Roman civilization and the Middle Ages in the West has been dated to the Germanic invasions during the fifth century. According to this view, by the

SOURCE: Henri Pirenne, *Mohammed and Charlemagne*, trans. Bernard Miall (London: George Allen & Unwin Ltd., 1958), pp. 284–285. Reprinted by permission.

sixth century the West had experienced such change and decline in its political institutions, commerce, social life, and cities that Rome was at best a distant memory; the Early Middle Ages had begun. During the 1920s and 1930s this assumption was challenged by the Belgian historian Henri Pirenne (1862–1935). He argued that there was relative continuity during the fifth, sixth, and first half of the seventh centuries. The transition to the Middle Ages occurred between 650 to 750 as a result of the rise of Islam. Pirenne's thesis had wide acceptance for many years. Although historians have since cast doubt on important parts of this thesis, all medievalists must still deal with this interpretation. In the following excerpt Pirenne summarizes his argument.

CONSIDER: *Pirenne's explanation of why the Germanic invasions did not create the break with antiquity; Pirenne's rationale for arguing that the transition was completed by 800; Pirenne's view of the most important ways in which the civilization of the Middle Ages differed from that of the fifth and sixth centuries.*

From the foregoing data, it seems, we may draw two essential conclusions:

1. The Germanic invasions destroyed neither the Mediterranean unity of the ancient world, nor what may be regarded as the truly essential features of the Roman culture as it still existed in the 5th century, at a time when there was no longer an Emperor in the West.

Despite the resulting turmoil and destruction, no new principles made their appearance; neither in the economic or social order, nor in the linguistic situation, nor in the existing institutions. What civilization survived was Mediterranean. It was in the regions by the sea that culture was preserved, and it was from them that the innovations of the age proceeded: monasticism, the conversion of the Anglo-Saxons, the *ars Barbarica*, etc.

The Orient was the fertilizing factor: Constantinople, the centre of the world. In 600 the physiognomy of the world was not different in quality from that which it had revealed in 400.

2. The cause of the break with the tradition of antiquity was the rapid and unexpected advance of Islam. The result of this advance was the final separation of East from West, and the end of the Mediterranean unity. Countries like Africa and Spain, which had always been parts of the Western community, gravitated henceforth in the orbit of Baghdad. In these countries another religion made its appearance, and an entirely different culture. The Western Mediterranean, having become a Musulman lake, was no longer the thoroughfare of commerce and of thought which it had always been.

The West was blockaded and forced to live upon its own resources. For the first time in history the axis of life was shifted northwards from the Mediterranean. The decadence into which the Merovingian monarchy lapsed as a result of this change gave birth to a new dynasty, the Carolingian, whose original home was in the Germanic North.

With this new dynasty the Pope allied himself, breaking with the Emperor, who, engrossed in his struggle against the Musulmans, could no longer protect him. And so the Church allied itself with the new order of things. In Rome, and in the Empire which it founded, it had no rival. And its power was all the greater inasmuch as the State, being incapable of maintaining its administration, allowed itself to be absorbed by the feudality, the inevitable sequel of the economic regression. All the consequences of this change became glaringly apparent after Charlemagne. Europe, dominated by the Church and the feudality, assumed a new physiognomy, differing slightly in different regions. The Middle Ages—to retain the traditional term—were beginning. The transitional phase was protracted. One may say that it lasted a whole century—from 650 to 750. It was during this period of anarchy that the tradition of antiquity disappeared, while the new elements came to the surface.

This development was completed in 800 by the constitution of the new Empire, which consecrated the break between the West and the East, inasmuch as it gave to the West a new Roman Empire—the manifest proof that it had broken with the old Empire, which continued to exist in Constantinople.

The Carolingian West: The Genesis of Feudal Relationships

David Nicholas

Scholars have long differed over the precise meaning of feudalism. In the following selection David Nicholas surveys this scholarly debate, pointing out some of the problems with the different approaches. He then argues that the term "feudal relations," emphasizing vassalage and the fief as the key components of the feudal bond, is more useful than the term "feudalism."

CONSIDER: *The ways scholars have disagreed over feudalism; why feudal relations might be a better term; the ways this interpretation might be supported by the primary sources in this chapter.*

The Frankish age witnessed the birth of feudal relations, in the stage that the American medievalist Joseph Strayer called the feudalism of the armed retainer, as distinguished from the later feudalism of the counts and other great lords. The term "feudalism" has occasioned considerable dispute among scholars. It is applied by Marxists and some capitalist politicians for any economic or political regime that they consider aristocratic or oppressive. Others have identified it with decentralisation of governmental function, but this ignores the fact that those areas where feudal bonds were most completely developed, France and England, became centralised states, while non-feudal Germany and Italy split into numerous principalities. Forces other than extent of feudalisation were involved in these cases, but lords of feudal vassals had a measure of control over their fiefs that princes did not have over allodial (public, non-feudal) land.

SOURCE: From David Nicholas, *The Evolution of the Medieval World, 312–1500.* Reprinted by permission of Longman Group UK.

Some have defined feudalism very broadly, including the non-honourable bonds of serf to landlord as an economic feudalism. Others prefer to avoid the term entirely, since "feudalism" is a modern word that was not used during the Middle Ages. Much of the confusion comes from the "all or nothing" approach of some historians. Although some lords compiled lists of their fiefholders, there was never a feudal "system." "Feudal relations" seems preferable, for even feudal "ism" suggests more rigidity than was ever present. Feudal relations developed gradually. We learn much about them in the late Merovingian and Carolingian periods, but the sources then say little more until the eleventh century and particularly the twelfth. When the records recommence, they show that feudal bonds had been evolving in many but not all parts of Europe in the intervening period.

For while the word "feudalism" did not exist, Latin and the vernacular languages had words for vassal and fief, the necessary component parts of the feudal bond. Vassalage was a personal tie of man to lord that developed characteristics that set it apart from other such bonds. The vassal, the subordinate party, owed honourable obligations, notably military service, that did not compromise his social rank. In the language of contemporary texts, he was a "free man in a relationship of dependence." Not all vassals held fiefs. Princes throughout the Middle Ages continued to maintain warriors in their households. It is inexact to speak of these people as being in a feudal bond with their lords, for they lived in proximity to their lords and did not hold fiefs. The fief was the proprietary nexus between vassal and lord and was held on conditions of tenure that were sharply different from non-feudal property. Vassals who held fiefs were expected to use the income of those properties to pay the costs of performing their own vassalic obligations. They were not maintained directly in the lords' households. Pope Gregory VII (1073–85), whose vassals included Robert Guiscard, the ruler of much of southern Italy, and who claimed the right to give Hungary and England in fief to their kings, would have been astonished at some scholars' notion that he was fighting for a figment of his imagination. Although there was no feudal system, to deny the existence of vassalage and fiefholding is to deny fact.

An Evaluation of Feudalism

Daniel D. McGarry

Feudalism developed gradually during the Early Middle Ages, becoming a prevailing system in many areas between the ninth and thirteenth centuries. By the Late Middle Ages, the feudal

system was in decline, although elements of it would remain well into the early modern period. Since the Renaissance, scholars have often evaluated medieval feudalism negatively, emphasizing its weakness and localism. In recent decades, scholars have looked at feudalism more positively, emphasizing its adaptiveness to certain historical circumstances. In the following selection Daniel McGarry evaluates the shortcomings and the positive features of feudalism.

CONSIDER: *Whether you agree with McGarry's evaluation of what feudalism's "shortcomings" were and what its "positive" characteristics were; whether the strengths of feudalism outweigh its weaknesses.*

While feudalism had serious shortcomings, it also rendered valuable services. On the negative side, it resulted in numerous small, semi-independent local governments, incapable of providing many needed public services. Usually roads and bridges were inadequately maintained, while excessive tolls and duties were collected, and brigands and pirates flourished. Excessive emphasis was placed upon personal relationships, to the neglect of concepts of the community and public welfare. The components of the body politic were too loosely bound together by oaths and customs, with a minimum of firm enforceable obligations. The central government was too dependent upon voluntary cooperation and moral responsibility. Obligations were often so indeterminate as to admit of easy evasion. Confusion frequently prevailed, private wars were common, and commerce was severely handicapped.

On the positive side, feudalism was a realistic adaptation to existing circumstances: a flexible workable compromise between Germanic and Roman elements. In a time of great insecurity, it provided local defense and government, without entirely sacrificing unity. It was just flexible enough, on the one hand, and just conservative enough on the other, to surmount contemporary challenges yet allow for future reunification. Those states, such as France and England, where feudalism prevailed in the early Middle Ages emerged strong and united at the close of the Middle Ages, whereas those such as Germany and Italy where mixed political patterns were maintained, emerged weak and divided. Feudalism helped to give Western Europe a military proficiency which eventually enabled it to spread its colonies and civilization over the world. It encouraged the contract theory of government, according to which government is the result of a free agreement among the governed; and it contained the principle that all government is limited. Many favorable features of feudalism, first applied only to the upper classes, were progressively extended downward to benefit all the people. Feudal great councils eventually evolved into general representative assemblies, known as Parliaments, Cortes, Estates, Diets, etc. The principle of

"No taxation without representation" or "No new taxes without popular consent" is traceable back to the feudal requirement of the imposition of other than customary aids upon the aristocracy. The modern "code of the gentleman," and many of our ideals of courtesy, good manners, and fair play also derive from feudalism.

Sanctity and Power: The Dual Pursuit of Medieval Women

Jo Ann McNamara and Suzanne F. Wemple

Too often it has been assumed that the position of women changed little throughout the Early Middle Ages. In the following selection two medieval historians, Jo Ann McNamara of Hunter College and Suzanne Wemple of Barnard College, argue that by the ninth century the situation for many women had vastly improved.

CONSIDER: *How marriage customs changed to the benefit of women; the social effects of changes in women's inheritance rights.*

By the ninth century a complex series of social advances had produced a vastly improved situation for the individual woman vis-à-vis the family interest to which she had previously been subordinated. Women were able to ensure their independence within the limits of whatever social sphere they occupied by their control of some property of their own. The Germanic custom of bride purchase practically disappeared. Instead of giving a purchase price to the bride's family, the groom endowed her directly with the bride gift, usually a piece of landed property over which she had full rights. To this, he frequently added the morning gift following the consummation of the marriage. In addition to the economic independence derived through marriage, the women of the ninth century enjoyed an increased capacity to share in the inheritance of property. Women had always been eligible to receive certain movable goods from either their own relatives or from their husbands but now law and practice allowed women to inherit immovables. A reason for this trend

SOURCE: From "Sanctity and Power: The Dual Pursuit of Medieval Women," by Jo Ann McNamara and Suzanne F. Wemple, in *Becoming Visible: Women in European History* (eds. Renate Bridenthal and Claudia Koonz), pp. 103–104. Copyright © 1977 by Houghton Mifflin Company. Reprinted by permission.

may be discerned from a deed from the eighth century in which a doting father left equal shares of his property to his sons and daughters. He justified his act by explaining that discrimination between the sexes was an "impious custom" that ran contrary to God's law and to the love he felt for all of his children.

Women's ability to inherit property had far-reaching social effects, which modern demographers are still investigating. Although a young woman still could not marry a man against her family's will, her independence after marriage was greatly enhanced if she possessed her own property. After their father's death, Charlemagne's daughters were able to withdraw from the court of their brother and lead independent lives because Charlemagne had endowed them with substantial property. As widows, too, women acquired increased status if they were allowed to control their sons' and their deceased husbands' property. The most dramatic example of this permanently affected the political future of England. The daughter of Alfred the Great, Ethelflaeda, widow of the king of Mercia, devoted her long reign to cooperation with her brother in the pursuit of their father's policy of containing the Norse invaders. Together they established a strong, centralized kingdom centered on Wessex. After a life of campaigning against Danish, Irish, and Norwegian enemies, she succeeded in willing the kingdom away from her own daughter, the rightful heiress, and leaving it to her brother. This act destroyed the independence of Mercia with its rival claims to Anglo-Saxon supremacy and assured that the English kingdom would be dominated by Wessex and the line of Alfred. Ironically, Ethelflaeda's indisputable contribution to the future of England deprived another woman of her right to rule.

✴ CHAPTER QUESTIONS

1. In what ways was feudalism an effective answer to problems facing Europeans during the Early Middle Ages? In what ways did feudalism create new problems? Do you think the advantages of feudalism outweighed its disadvantages?

2. How would you justify calling this era a period of decline? What are some of the problems in so interpreting the Early Middle Ages? How might it be described as something other than a decline?

3. In what ways did the West differ politically, militarily, and culturally in the Early Middle Ages from the preceding Roman Empire?

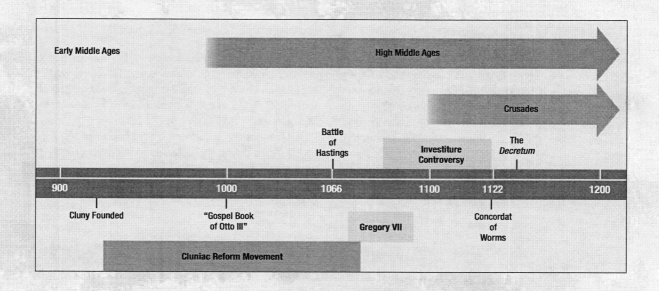

8 The High Middle Ages: The Eleventh and Twelfth Centuries

During the eleventh and twelfth centuries, Western Europe gained new dynamism. The population increased and would continue to do so into the thirteenth century. This was accompanied by an internal expansion, involving increased clearing and farming of land, and an external expansion, with Europeans settling in new lands to the east and venturing on crusades to the Holy Land. Commerce revived, including long-range trade facilitated by newly won control over parts of the Mediterranean formerly dominated by Islam and Byzantium. Towns and cities grew, accompanied by corresponding social and political changes, as urban groups gained power and prestige. Within the Catholic Church, reforms were instituted, such as those initiated by the Cluniac

monasteries. The papacy became more assertive, claiming greater powers and challenging monarchs for authority. In a variety of ways there was a broad cultural revival, perhaps most clearly exemplified by the establishment of new institutions of learning that would develop into universities by the early thirteenth century. Through these and other developments, a more stable civilization was being formed that we can recognize as European.

The sources in this chapter concentrate on three main aspects of the eleventh and twelfth centuries. The first is what many historians feel was the most central issue of the time: What would the relationship between Church and state be? This issue was manifested in the Investiture Controversy, especially in the struggle between Pope

Gregory VII and Emperor Henry IV, but more broadly a controversy that generally marked the High Middle Ages. The second is a broad and deeply significant development, the growth of commerce and industry. The documents show urban revival, growing trade within Europe, and new long-distance commerce. The documents also cast light on the type of individuals most involved—the growing class of merchants. The third is the social and psychological nature of life during this period, a topic that has recently been of particular interest to historians. How was serfdom experienced and viewed? How did people of different classes relate to each other? How were women viewed? In what ways was the psychic life of individuals related to the physical and social environment of the Middle Ages?

A sense of the dynamism characteristic of the High Middle Ages during these two centuries should emerge from these materials. In the next chapter the crusades, which reflect this same expansive dynamism, will be examined.

Primary Sources

Letters: Secular and Ecclesiastical Authority

Pope Gregory VII

Throughout the Middle Ages the line between secular and ecclesiastical authority was often unclear. During the eleventh century, the papacy was growing in stature and power, particularly under Gregory VII's pontificate (1073–1085). Gregory VII, who brought the reforming spirit to his office, soon came into conflict with Emperor Henry IV of the Holy Roman Empire over who had the right to appoint people to high offices in the Church and who had control over properties and revenues connected with ecclesiastical offices. This controversy was not solved until well into the twelfth century, and similar struggles between Church and state continued to arise in succeeding centuries. The following set of papal, propositions, found among the letters of Gregory VII (c. 1075), indicates some of the powers the papacy was claiming for itself during this period.

CONSIDER: *In what matters the papacy asserted its powers and over whom; the ways in which these powers might have threatened the powers of secular rulers.*

The Roman church was founded by God alone.
The Roman bishop alone is properly called universal.
He alone may depose bishops and reinstate them.
His legate, though of inferior grade, takes precedence, in a council, of all bishops and may render a decision of deposition against them.
He alone may use the insignia of empire.

The pope is the only person whose feet are kissed by all princes.
His title is unique in the world.
He may depose emperors.
No council may be regarded as a general one without his consent.
No book or chapter may be regarded as canonical without his authority.
A decree of his may be annulled by no one; he alone may annul the decrees of all.
He may be judged by no one.
No one shall dare to condemn one who appeals to the papal see.
The Roman church has never erred, nor ever, by the witness of Scripture, shall err to all eternity.
He may not be considered Catholic who does not agree with the Roman church.
The pope may absolve the subjects of the unjust from their allegiance.

The Life of Saint Godric: A Merchant Adventurer

Reginald of Durham

Trade and the number of people involved in commerce grew during the eleventh and twelfth centuries, not only in the Mediterranean area but in Northern Europe as well. In some cases individuals were able to start with little and over the years amass considerable wealth. This is illustrated in the following selection from The Life of Saint Godric.

SOURCE: From James Harvey Robinson, ed., *Readings in European History*, vol. I (Boston: Ginn, 1904), p. 274.

SOURCE: G. G. Coulton, *Social Life in Britain from the Conquest to the Reformation* (Cambridge, England: Cambridge University Press, 1918), pp. 415–419.

Godric lived during the twelfth century, closing out his career as a merchant by going on a pilgrimage to Jerusalem and giving his wealth to the Church. His biography was written by a friend and disciple, the monk Reginald of Durham.

CONSIDER: *How this document might be used to show that the main elements of capitalism were present as far back as the twelfth century; what this document shows about the potential for social mobility during the Middle Ages.*

He chose not to follow the life of a husbandman, but rather to study, learn and exercise the rudiments of more subtle conceptions. For this reason, aspiring to the merchant's trade, he began to follow the chapman's way of life, first learning how to gain in small bargains and things of insignificant price; and thence, while yet a youth, his mind advanced little by little to buy and sell and gain from things of greater expense. For, in his beginnings, he was wont to wander with small wares around the villages and farmsteads of his own neighbourhood; but, in process of time, he gradually associated himself by compact with city merchants. Hence, within a brief space of time, the youth who had trudged for many weary hours from village to village, from farm to farm, did so profit by his increase of age and wisdom as to travel with associates of his own age through towns and boroughs, fortresses and cities, to fairs and to all the various booths of the marketplace, in pursuit of his public chaffer. . . . At first, he lived as a chapman for four years in Lincolnshire, going on foot and carrying the smallest wares; then he travelled abroad, first to St. Andrews in Scotland and then for the first time to Rome. On his return, having formed a familiar friendship with certain other young men who were eager for merchandise, he began to launch upon bolder courses, and to coast frequently by sea to the foreign lands that lay around him. Thus, sailing often to and fro between Scotland and Britain, he traded in many divers wares and, amid these occupations, learned much worldly wisdom. . . . For he laboured not only as a merchant but also as a shipman . . . to Denmark and Flanders and Scotland; in all which lands he found certain rare, and therefore more precious, wares, which he carried to other parts wherein he knew them to be least familiar, and coveted by the inhabitants beyond the price of gold itself; wherefore he exchanged these wares for others coveted by men of other lands; and thus he chaffered most freely and assiduously. Hence he made great profit in all his bargains, and gathered much wealth in the sweat of his brow; for he sold dear in one place the wares which he had bought elsewhere at a small price.

Then he purchased the half of a merchant-ship with certain of his partners in the trade; and again by his prudence he bought the fourth part of another ship. At length, by his skill in navigation, wherein he excelled all his fellows, he earned promotion to the post of steersman. . . .

And now he had lived sixteen years as a merchant, and began to think of spending on charity, to God's honour and service, the goods which he had so laboriously acquired. He therefore took the cross as a pilgrim to Jerusalem, and, having visited the Holy Sepulchre, came back to England by way of St. James [of Compostella].

The Art of Courtly Love

Andreas Capellanus

The historian is always faced with a serious problem in writing about social life during the High Middle Ages, for literacy was not widespread and few documents on social life remain. This is the case with sexual practices and the social attitudes of the elite toward the peasants. The historian is forced to rely on documents that deal only indirectly with such topics, such as the following selection from The Art of Courtly Love *(c. 1185), by Andreas Capellanus. It is perhaps a surprise to learn that the author was a chaplain at the court of Marie de France at Troyes. He wrote from and for an aristocratic point of view. Here, Andreas Capellanus comments on the love of peasants.*

CONSIDER: *Evidence in this document for the attitudes of the aristocracy toward peasants; the information provided here about the sexual attitudes and practices of medieval people; what this document indicates about the functions of the medieval clergy.*

CHAPTER XI. THE LOVE OF PEASANTS

But lest you should consider that what we have already said about the love of the middle class applies also to farmers, we will add a little about their love. We say that it rarely happens that we find farmers serving in Love's court, but naturally, like a horse or a mule, they give themselves up to the work of Venus, as nature's urging teaches them to do. For a farmer hard labor and the uninterrupted solaces of plough and mattock are sufficient. And even if it should happen at times, though rarely, that contrary to their nature they are stirred up by Cupid's arrows, it is not expedient that they should be

SOURCE: Andreas Capellanus, *The Art of Courtly Love,* trans. John Jay Parry (New York: Columbia University Press, 1941), pp. 149–150.

instructed in the theory of love, lest while they are devoting themselves to conduct which is not natural to them the kindly farms which are usually made fruitful by their efforts may through lack of cultivation prove useless to us. And if you should, by some chance, fall in love with some of their women, be careful to puff them up with lots of praise and then, when you find a convenient place, do not hesitate to take what you seek and to embrace them by force. For you can hardly soften their outward inflexibility so far that they will grant you their embraces quietly or permit you to have the solaces you desire unless first you use a little compulsion as a convenient cure for their shyness. We do not say these things, however, because we want to persuade you to love such women, but only so that, if through lack of caution you should be driven to love them, you may know, in brief compass, what to do.

The Decretum: Medieval Women— Not in God's Image

Gratian

In the eyes of the medieval Church, the position of women was a problem. On one hand, women were, in theory, spiritual equals to men: their souls were as worthy as men's. On

SOURCE: Excerpts from *Not in God's Image* by Julia O'Faolain and Lauro Martines. Copyright © 1973 by Julia O'Faolain and Lauro Martines. Reprinted by permission of Harper & Row, Publishers, Inc.

the other hand, women were acknowledged as subordinate in various ways to men. In attitudes and in practice, the latter view of women as subject to men predominated. A particularly strong statement of this view can be found in the following selection from the Decretum, a systematization of Church law written around 1140 by Gratian, a jurist from northern Italy.

CONSIDER: *The image of women revealed in this document; how Gratian justifies this view of the position of women; some of the possible consequences of this attitude.*

Women should be subject to their men. The natural order for mankind is that women should serve men and children their parents, for it is just that the lesser serve the greater.

The image of God is in man and it is one. Women were drawn from man, who has God's jurisdiction as if he were God's vicar, because he has the image of the one God. Therefore woman is not made in God's image.

Woman's authority is nil; let her in all things be subject to the rule of man. . . . And neither can she teach, nor be a witness, nor give a guarantee, nor sit in judgment.

Adam was beguiled by Eve, not she by him. It is right that he whom woman led into wrongdoing should have her under his direction, so that he may not fail a second time through female levity. [*Corpus Iuris Canonici*]

Visual Sources

The Gospel Book of Otto III: Church and State

In figure 8.1, this page from an illuminated manuscript, the Gospel Book of Otto III (c. 1000), commemorates Emperor Otto III of the Holy Roman Empire receiving homage from the four parts of the Empire: Sclavinia, Germania, Gallia, and Roma. On Otto's left are two barons, and on his right two members of the clergy. The crowned Otto sits on a throne under a canopy, holding a cross-inscribed orb in his left hand and the scepter in his right, both symbolizing his universal authority. He is clothed in gowns that hark back to Roman imperial costumes. In style and ceremonial arrangement, this picture resembles Byzantine models.

This picture exemplifies the efforts of the Holy Roman emperors to unify the authority of Church and state in their own being and office. Otto is pictured as superior to

separate parts of the empire, feudal lords, and ecclesiastical authorities, himself the legitimate heir to Roman authority and a divinely ordained king. A letter from Berbert of Aurillac supports this: "Ours, ours is the Roman Empire, Italy, fertile in fruits, Lorraine and Germany, fertile in men offer their resources and even the strong kingdoms of the Slavs are not lacking to us. Our august emperor of the Romans art thou, Caesar, who, sprung from the noblest blood of the Greeks [Otto's mother was a Byzantine princess], surpass the Greeks in empire and govern the Romans by hereditary right, but both you surpass in genius and eloquence."

CONSIDER: *Ways suggested by this illuminated manuscript that secular rulers struggled with the Church for authority.*

FIGURE 8.1   (Bayerische Staatsbibliothek, Munich, Germany/Bridgeman Art Library)

The Bayeux Tapestry

This tapestry (figure 8.2), hung in the cathedral at Bayeux in northern France in 1077, was designed to justify the invasion of England by the Norman duke, William the Conqueror, and celebrate his victory over English forces led by King Harold at the Battle of Hastings in 1066.

The top panel presents, from William's point of view, the reason for the invasion. On the left sits William, the sword on his shoulder symbolizing his power as Duke of Normandy. The next figure is Harold, apparently the heir to England's throne, who, after being captured in 1063, swears allegiance to William as part of his ransomed release. To back up that oath, the tapestry shows Harold's hands on religious shrines that contained relics. When Harold broke this oath by ascending to the English throne in 1066, William gained the approval of the pope for his "righteous" invasion of England. On the right, Norman ships embark across the Channel.

In the bottom panel, Harold, third from the left behind his shield, suffers a wound: an arrow to his eye. A mounted Norman cavalryman finishes off the defenseless Harold with his sword. An inscription on the tapestry announces, "King Harold is killed." On the lower border of the tapestry lie some of the many who died in the day-long battle. Two months later, William was crowned the new king.

CONSIDER: *How these images helped justify to viewers how William acquired the English throne.*

Medieval Expansion

The first of these maps (map 8.1) is of a local area in northeastern France. It shows the unplanned growth of settlements during and after the twelfth century. In general, settlements prior to the twelfth century were along old Roman roads or waterways; the newer settlements tended to be in the less desirable areas requiring greater clearing and cultivation. Map 8.2 shows

FIGURE 8.2 (© Erich Lessing/Art Resource, NY)

the growth of settlements in the Black Forest in Germany be-tween the ninth and twelfth centuries; in fact, most of the growth took place during the eleventh and twelfth centuries. In this case, however, much of the settlement was planned and carried out by the dukes of Zähringen and some of the monas-teries under their control, particularly St. Peter and St. George. By the end of the first half of the twelfth century, the Zähringens had founded the strategically located towns of Freiburg, Villin-gen, and Offenburg, which enabled them to gain control over the whole area. The third map (map 8.3) shows a related pat-tern. Here, a series of towns along the road between Paris and Orléans was founded in the twelfth century by French kings anxious to effect their control over the area. Map 8.4 places the information provided by the first three maps in the context of twelfth-century Europe. Together, all four maps reveal the in-ternal expansion of Europe during the eleventh and twelfth cen-turies, how that expansion was connected to geographic and commercial factors, and how political motivations played a role in the pattern of this expansion.

The last map (map 8.5) shows the external expansion of Europe and Christendom during this same period. This was carried out by the newly expanding Byzantine Empire, by the now Christianized Vikings (Normans), by military efforts with directly religious overtones both national (the reconquest in Spain) and international (the crusades to the Holy Land), and by a combination of political and commercial expansion by Italian and north German cities and states.

The external and internal expansions complement each other and provide evidence of the general dynamism of the High Middle Ages and of some of the connections between demographic growth, commercial activity, political consolida-tion, and military assertiveness.

CONSIDER: The ways in which maps can reveal both the expansion of a civilization and how the expansion took place; how differences between the Early and High Middle Ages are revealed when these maps are compared with those in Chapter 6.

MAP 8.1 Unplanned Settlement (France)

MAP 8.2 Planned Settlement (Germany)

MAP 8.3 Strategic Settlement (Paris-Orléans Road)

MAP 8.4 Twelfth-Century Europe

MAP 8.5   External Expansion

Secondary Sources

Medieval Values

Jacques Le Goff

The medieval world was permeated by certain values that colored how people tended to think about the world and to behave in society. Here generalizations are difficult, and in analyzing values scholars often have difficulty leaving their own values aside. In the following selection Jacques Le Goff, a well-known French medievalist, analyzes the fundamental values with which men of the Middle Ages thought, acted, and lived. Here he focuses on their social and political concerns, above all hierarchy, authority, rebellion, and liberty.

SOURCE: From Le Goff & Cochrane, *Medieval Callings*, pp. 33–35, ed. by Jacques Le Goff, trans. by Lydia Cochrane. © 1990 University of Chicago Press. Reprinted by permission of the publisher.

CONSIDER: *What exactly these medieval values were and how they fit together; what "justice" might mean to medieval men; how one's social station might relate to these values.*

. . . [M]en of the Middle Ages thought, acted, and lived with several fundamental values. . . .

Hierarchy: The duty of medieval man was to remain where God had placed him. Rising in society was a sign of pride; demotion was a shameful sin. The organization of society that God had ordained was to be respected, and it was based on the principle of hierarchy. Earthly society, modeled on celestial society, was to reproduce the hierarchy of the angels and the archangels. . . .

Authority and Authorities: On the social and political levels, medieval man had to obey his superiors, who were prelates if he was a cleric, the king, the lord, the city fathers, or community leaders if he was a layman. On the intellectual and mental level he had to show loyalty to the authorities, the first of which was the Bible, followed by authorities imposed by historical Christianity: the Fathers of the church in late antiquity, the university *magistri* in the age of the universities in and after the thirteenth century. The abstract and superior value of *auctoritas*, of authority, inherited from classical antiquity, was imposed upon him, embodied in a great number of different "authorities." The greatest intellectual and social virtue required of medieval man was obedience, justified by religion.

The Rebel: Nevertheless (increasingly after the year 1000, and again after the thirteenth century), a growing number of medieval men refused to accept unchallenged the domination of hierarchical superiors and authorities. For a long time, the principal form of contestation and rebellion was religious: it was heresy. Within the framework of feudalism, it then took the form of the revolt of the vassal against the lord when the latter abused his power or neglected his duties. In the university context contestation was intellectual. Social revolt finally arrived to both city and countryside in the forms of strikes, riots, and workers' and peasants' revolts. The great century for revolt was the fourteenth, from England and Flanders to Tuscany and Rome. When necessary, medieval man had learned how to become a rebel.

Liberty and Liberties: Liberty was one of medieval man's time-honored values. It motivated his principal revolts. The church, paradoxically, gave the signal, as it was under the banner of *Libertas Ecclesiae*—the freedom of the church—that the church, the pope at its head, demanded its independence from a lay world that had subjugated it through feudalization. From the mid-eleventh century, liberty was the password of the great movement for reform begun under Gregory the Great.

Later, aware of their strength and eager to sweep away obstacles to the great surge that had begun with the year 1000, peasants and new city-dwellers demanded and obtained freedom, or, more often, freedoms. The enfranchisement of the serfs corresponded to the concession of charters or liberties to the burghers of the towns and cities. These were above all freedoms (in the plural)—liberties that were actually privileges.

The Mold for Medieval Women: Social Status

Margaret Wade Labarge

Gender alone greatly affected the life of medieval women, but there were several other factors that interacted with gender to influence the sort of life a medieval woman might lead. Perhaps the most important other factor was social status. In the following selection from A Small Sound of the Trumpet: Women in Medieval Life, *Margaret Wade Labarge analyzes the importance of social status for medieval women.*

CONSIDER: *The differences between upper- and lower-class women; how status interacts with gender differences; how the primary sources in this chapter might support Labarge's analysis.*

. . . [S]ocial status was even more important for a medieval woman than her physical inheritance, for it defined how she would be regarded by others, whom she could marry or what form of religious life she might undertake. Status was determined by birth, for medieval thinkers firmly believed that royal and noble blood was indeed different from the substance which pulsed in the veins of the bourgeois and the peasants, and that it should not be intermingled with that of a lower rank. It was this solid conviction which accounted for the fury of widows and wards whose lords sold their marriages and thus their fiefs to men below their own station and explains their willingness to pay large sums to avoid such disparagement. Women shared the status of their family and their husband all the way up and down the social scale, though a married woman was always a step below her husband for he was her lord and master. Nevertheless, such subordination was restricted only to her husband; all other men, if of lower rank, must display respect for her higher status, for actual behaviour was based primarily on the subservience exacted by rank. . . .

The consciousness of their privileged position protected the women of the upper classes, but worked to the disadvantage of those lower down the scale. Courtesy was a noble virtue; it was not considered necessary towards poor townswomen or, even more noticeably, towards peasant women, because their low rank excluded them from consideration. Most men felt that violence, even rape, practised on such base creatures quite literally did not count and should be overlooked. Such an attitude was encouraged by the fact that high tempers and violence were general in the Middle Ages in both sexes. In addition, the law recognized the right of men of all classes to beat their wives, so long as they did not kill them or do excessive

SOURCE: From *A Small Sound of the Trumpet* by Margaret Wade Labarge. Copyright © 1986 by Margaret Wade Labarge. Reprinted by permission of Beacon Press.

damage. It appears to have been a frequently exercised right, for many of the cautionary tales warn women of the wisdom of being humble and not arousing their husband's wrath, lest a beating and permanent disfigurement or worse should follow. The women themselves seem to have been quick with words and occasionally with blows.

The Merchant
Aron Ja. Gurevich

The eleventh and twelfth centuries saw the growth of towns and cities, which marked a new dynamism in Western civilization. One reason for this growth was the revival of commerce. Here the medieval merchant played a central role, but the merchant was important to medieval society in several ways. In the following selection Aron Ja. Gurevich analyzes the roles played by the medieval merchant and the type of person the great merchant was.

CONSIDER: *The ways the merchant supported medieval society; the social and psychological differences between the merchant and others; whether this interpretation is supported by the document on St. Godric.*

The position of men of affairs in medieval society was extremely contradictory. By lending money to the nobles and the monarchs (whose insolvency or refusal to pay often caused the failure of great banks), and by acquiring landed property, concluding marriages with knightly families, and pursuing noble titles and crests, the mercantile patriciate became deeply entrenched in feudal society, to the point of being an inevitable and fundamental element of it. Crafts, commerce, the city, and finance were all organic parts of fully developed feudalism. At the same time, however, money was sapping the traditional bases of aristocratic domination—land and warfare—and pauperizing the artisan class and the peasants, since the great enterprises launched by merchants employed wage-workers. When in the late Middle Ages money became a powerful social force, large-scale international commerce and the spirit of gain that moved the merchants became the heralds of a new economic and social order: capitalism.

In spite of all his efforts to "root himself" in the structure of feudalism and adapt himself to it, the great merchant was a totally different psychological and social type from the feudal lord. He was a knight of profit who risked his life not on the battlefield but in his office or his shop, on board a merchant ship, or in his bank. To the warlike virtues and the impulsive emotivity of the nobles he opposed careful calculation and cause-and-effect thinking;

SOURCE: From Aron Ja. Gurevich, "The Merchant," in *Medieval Callings,* pp. 281–282, ed. by Jacques Le Goff, trans. by Lydia Cochrane. © 1990 University of Chicago Press. Reprinted by permission of the publisher.

to irrationality, he opposed rationality. In the milieu of men of affairs a new type of religious sentiment came to be elaborated in a paradoxical combination of faith in God and fear of castigation in the otherworld, on the one hand, and, on the other, a mercantile approach to "good works" that expected indemnification and compensation, which were to be expressed as material prosperity.

The Making of the Middle Ages: Serfdom
R. W. Southern

For large masses of people serfdom was the overriding condition of life during the Middle Ages. At times observers have tended to romanticize the Middle Ages and the bucolic life of the peasantry. But in the following selection R. W. Southern of Oxford University, author of the highly acclaimed The Making of the Middle Ages, reflects most historians' views in arguing that serfdom was a condition characterized by servitude; the serf's lack of liberty was recognized by contemporaries as harmful and degrading. This selection illustrates the advantages of looking at the Middle Ages from the inside, from the point of view of the people of that time.

CONSIDER: *The evidence Southern provides to support his argument; how this interpretation fits with the selection from The Art of Courtly Love that discusses love and the peasants; conditions that might have mitigated the negative aspects of serfdom.*

To nearly all men serfdom was, without qualification, a degrading thing, and they found trenchant phrases to describe the indignity of the condition. The serf's family was always referred to by lawyers as his brood, his *sequela,* and the poets delighted to exercise their ingenuity in describing the physical deformity of the ideal serf. Hard words break no bones, but they are hard to bear for all that, and they became harder as time went on. Men well knew, however theologians might seem to turn common notions inside out, the difference between the yoke of servitude and the honour of liberty—or, to use the expressive phrase of Giraldus Cambrensis, the *hilaritas libertatis:* "There is nothing," he wrote, "which so stirs the hearts of men and incites them to honourable action like the lightheartedness of liberty; and nothing which so deters and depresses them like the oppression of servitude." If we consider only the practical effects of serfdom and notice how little the lines of economic prosperity follow those of personal status; if we reflect on the many impediments to free action, to which even the mightiest were subjected in such delicate matters as marriage and the bequeathing of property, it may seem surprising that the

SOURCE: R. W. Southern, *The Making of the Middle Ages* (New Haven, CT: Yale University Press, 1953), pp. 106–107.

pride of liberty was so strong, and the contempt for serfdom so general: yet such was the case. However much the hierarchical principle of society forced men into relationships at all levels of society in which rights and restraints were inextricably mixed up, the primitive line which divided liberty from servitude was never forgotten.

Feudal Society: The Psychic World of Medieval People

Marc Bloch

A full picture of the Middle Ages requires a concrete, empathetic sense of how people experienced everyday life at that time. But perhaps the hardest task for the historian is to understand and convey feelings and attitudes of people in the distant past. Few historians have attempted to do this in any "scientific" or rigorous way, although in recent years there has been a growing interest in this kind of scholarship. A pioneering effort in this direction was made by the French medievalist Marc Bloch. In the following selection Bloch relates the physical and social environment of the Middle Ages to the psychic world of the inhabitants of that time.

CONSIDER: *The evidence that supports Bloch's claim that emotional instability was characteristic of the feudal era; how this approach compares with the approaches of Southern and Pirenne.*

The men of the two feudal ages were close to nature—much closer than we are; and nature as they knew it was much less tamed and softened than we see it today. The rural landscape, of which the waste formed so large a part, bore fewer traces of human influence. The wild animals that now only haunt our nursery tales—bears and, above all, wolves—prowled in every wilderness, and even amongst the cultivated fields. So much was this the case that the sport of hunting was indispensable for ordinary security, and almost equally so as a method of supplementing the food supply. People continued to pick wild fruit and to gather honey as in the first ages of mankind. In the construction of implements and tools, wood played a predominant part. The nights, owing to the wretched lighting, were darker; the cold, even in the living quarters of the castles, was more intense. In short, behind all social life there was a background of the primitive, of submission to uncontrollable forces, of unrelieved physical contrasts. There is no means of measuring the influence which such an environment was capable of exerting on the minds of men, but it could hardly have failed to contribute to their uncouthness. . . .

SOURCE: Reprinted from *Feudal Society* by Marc Bloch, trans. L. A. Manyon, University of Chicago Press, 1961, pp. 72–73. Reprinted by permission of The University of Chicago Press. Copyright © 1961.

Infant mortality was undoubtedly very high in feudal Europe and tended to make people somewhat callous toward bereavements that were almost a normal occurrence. As to the life of adults, even apart from the hazards of war it was usually short. . . .

Among so many premature deaths, a large number were due to the great epidemics which descended frequently upon a humanity ill-equipped to combat them; among the poor another cause was famine. Added to the constant acts of violence these disasters gave life a quality of perpetual insecurity. This was probably one of the principal reasons for the emotional instability so characteristic of the feudal era, especially during its first age. A low standard of hygiene doubtless also contributed to this nervous sensibility. . . .

. . . Finally, we must not leave out of account the effects of an astonishing sensibility to what were believed to be supernatural manifestations. It made people's minds constantly and almost morbidly attentive to all manner of signs, dreams, or hallucinations. This characteristic was especially marked in monastic circles where the influence of mortifications of the flesh and the repression of natural instincts were joined to that of a mental attitude vocationally centered on the problems of the unseen. No psychoanalyst has ever examined dreams more earnestly than the monks of the tenth or the eleventh century. Yet the laity also shared the emotionalism of a civilization in which moral or social convention did not yet require well-bred people to repress their tears and their raptures. The despairs, the rages, the impulsive acts, the sudden revulsions of feeling present great difficulties to historians, who are instinctively disposed to reconstruct the past in terms of the rational. But the irrational is an important element in all history and only a sort of false shame could allow its effects on the course of political events in feudal Europe to be passed over in silence.

❧ CHAPTER QUESTIONS

1. For a long time it was believed that the Middle Ages, the years 500 to 1500, constituted an era of little change, offering little in comparison to the Greco-Roman civilization that preceded it and the Renaissance that succeeded it. In what ways do the sources in this chapter *not* support this interpretation?

2. In what ways were developments during the eleventh and twelfth centuries problematic or advantageous to the Church? To the monarchies?

3. What options were available to people in different classes or stations of life—peasants, merchants, Church officials, and kings—to make changes in their lives?

10 The High Middle Ages: The Thirteenth Century

The pinnacle of the High Middle Ages, the thirteenth century was a period in which the dynamic trends already under way during the two preceding centuries came to fruition. Within the Church, new reforming orders such as the Franciscans and Dominicans were founded and the papacy made even more unprecedented claims to power. With these claims the papacy continued to come into conflict with monarchs who had themselves gained in stature and power in certain areas, particularly England and France. Commerce continued to thrive, but by this time merchants, artisans, and even cities were organizing their own institutions, such as guilds and leagues, reflecting their growing power and permanency. The culture of the Middle Ages flourished during this century. Magnificent Gothic cathedrals, some started in the twelfth century, rose throughout Europe. Universities expanded, becoming important centers of learning as well as recruiting grounds for members of the growing state and ecclesiastical bureaucracies. Medieval scholasticism dominated the period intellectually and received its finest statement in the work of St. Thomas Aquinas.

In this chapter some of the connections between religious, political, social, and cultural trends of thirteenth-century Europe are examined. Some documents concentrate primarily on theoretical and practical relations between the Church, the state, and society. How did the papacy justify its claims over secular authority? How did the Church react to the challenges presented by the growing

131

urban centers? How did the Church control its clergy, who had such concrete contact with all classes in traditional society? How was the Church affected by the growing body of and new respect for Classical law and thought?

The documents also shed light on the relations between monarchs, nobles, and towns—the three lay competitors for power. How did the strength of central authority vary in different parts of Europe? How did monarchs, nobles, and towns compete with one another for power and authority? How did the balance between the monarchs, nobles, and towns shift in the Holy Roman Empire under Frederick II? How did the newly assertive cities deal with the development of commerce and urban growth, as seen in the formation of leagues and various urban institutions such as guilds?

Finally, the sources show how some of these relations were reflected in the culture and society of the period. What constituted social injustice? What problems did urban areas have with crime and violence? How was the position of the aristocracy reflected in pictorial art? How was the new respect for Classical law connected to medieval constitutionalism? How did Christian intellectuals relate Classical pagan thought and medieval Christian doctrines in this thirteenth-century environment?

What emerges from these materials is a picture of a flourishing civilization—medieval Europe at its height. During the following century Europe entered a period of disruption and transformation—the Late Middle Ages. This will be examined in the next chapter.

 # Primary Sources

Papal Proclamation of Supremacy

Pope Innocent III

The struggles between Church and state, so apparent during the Investiture Controversy, abated in the twelfth century but did not disappear. Popes continued to claim vast powers for themselves and managed to make some of those claims stick. The pinnacle of papal authority occurred during Innocent III's pontificate (1198–1216). Pope Innocent came into conflict with the rulers of the Empire, England, France, and others over political and religious issues. In the following papal proclamation Innocent III presents a theory for the proper jurisdictions of pontifical authority and royal power.

CONSIDER: *Innocent III's justification for the supremacy of papal authority; how a king might respond to this argument.*

Just as the founder of the universe established two great lights in the firmament of heaven, a greater one to preside over the day and a lesser to preside over the night, so too in the firmament of the universal church, which is signified by the word heaven, He instituted two great dignities, a greater one to preside over souls as if over day and a lesser one to preside over bodies as if over night. These are the pontifical authority and the royal power. Now just as the moon derives its light from the sun and is indeed lower than it in quantity and quality, in position and in power, so too the royal power derives the splendor of its dignity from the pontifical authority.

SOURCE: From Brian Tierney, *The Crisis of Church and State, 1050–1300* (Englewood Cliffs, NA: Prentice-Hall Inc., 1964), p. 132. Copyright © 1964. Reprinted by permission.

A Church Register: Clerical Administration

Archbishop Eudes of Rouen

Much of the administration of the medieval Church was carried out by bishops, the more conscientious of whom made periodic visits to the local clergy and Church establishments in their areas. The following is an excerpt from the register of the Archbishop Eudes of Rouen, who held that office from 1242 to 1267. To judge from his extensive records, he took his responsibilities seriously and rather meticulously attempted to improve the practices of his clergy.

CONSIDER: *The kinds of problems that bothered Eudes; Eudes' view of the proper behavior for the clergy.*

OCTOBER 24. We visited the abbey of St-Etienne-de-Caen, where there are sixty-three monks. All but three are priests. In one of the priories there are rabbit dogs; we forbade the monks who are staying there to become hunters. There are some who do not confess every month; we enjoined them to correct this. It used to be their practice that all those ministering [to the celebrants] at all Masses, save those [Masses] for the dead, received Communion, but this practice, through negligence, has gradually been abandoned; we enjoined the abbot and prior to have this custom more fully observed by all. The cloister is badly kept; we enjoined them to correct this. Traveling

SOURCE: From Jeremiah F. O'Sullivan, ed., *The Register of Eudes of Rouen*, trans. Sydney M. Brown (New York: Columbia University Press, 1964), pp. 43–45, 293.

monks do not observe the fasts of the Rule; we enjoined them to correct this. In the priories they do not observe the fasts of the Rule and they eat meat freely; we enjoined them to correct this. They owe fifteen hundred pounds, but about as much is owed to them; they have an income of four thousand pounds. Total for procuration: seven pounds, ten shillings, ten pence.

JUNE 30. We visited the deanery of Meulan at Chars. We found that the priest at Courdimanche has occasionally celebrated Mass though he is under suspension and that he kept a concubine; he rides horseback dressed in a short mantle, and he runs about too much. Item, the priest at Courcelles does not keep residence well nor is he in the habit of wearing his gown. Item, the priest at Hérouville only rarely wears a gown. Item, the priest at Valmondois sells his services; he is noted for having money, is contentious, and is given to drinking. Item, the priest at Vaux is a trader and had, and still has, a certain vineyard which he holds as security from a certain wastrel to whom he had loaned his too precious coins; he does not say his Hours well and sometimes he comes to Mass straight from his bed. Item, the priest at Chars is ill famed of a certain widow; he runs about too much. . . . Item, the priest at Longuesse is ill famed of Eugénie, his parishioner, and has had children by her; he promised us that if he should be ill famed of these matters again he would regard his church as resigned.

JULY 3. We visited the priory of Notre-Dame-de-Chaumont. Only two monks are there, and there should be three. They do not confess every month as the Statutes of Pope Gregory require. They have no written copy of their Rule, nor a copy of the Statutes. They do not hold chapter, nor do they receive the minor penances. They do not keep the fasts of the Rule; they eat meat when it is not necessary. They use feather beds, though we had warned them about this before. Instead this time, and in the presence of their own abbot of St-Germer, we enjoined them with firmness to correct their deficiencies. They have an income of one hundred pounds; they owe about thirty pounds.

The Rule of St. Francis

St. Francis of Assisi

There were periodic Christian reform movements during the High Middle Ages. The most important movement during the thirteenth century was initiated by the Franciscans, a group of pious laymen who gathered around Francis of Assisi

SOURCE: Oliver J. Thatcher and Edgar H. McNeal, eds. and trans., *A Source Book for Medieval History* (New York: Scribner's, 1905), pp. 499–507.

(c. 1181–1226). Francis, who had been born into a merchant family and was headed for a secular career, had experienced a deeply emotional conversion, given up his worldly goods, and pursued a life of asceticism, preaching, and poverty. He and his followers did not withdraw to a cloistered life, but traveled extensively and were particularly active in urban areas. By 1223, when the following version of St. Francis' rule was adopted, the papacy had officially recognized the Franciscans as an orthodox order.

CONSIDER: *Reasons such an order might be so successful; the functions such an order might perform for society or for the Church; how the record of behavior described in the previous document compares with the standard set up under the Rule of St. Francis.*

This is the rule and life of the Minor Brothers, namely, to observe the holy gospel of our Lord Jesus Christ by living in obedience, in poverty, and in chastity. Brother Francis promises obedience and reverence to Pope Honorius and to his successors who shall be canonically elected, and to the Roman Church. The other brothers are bound to obey brother Francis, and his successors. . . .

I counsel, warn, and exhort my brothers in the Lord Jesus Christ that when they go out into the world they shall not be quarrelsome or contentious, nor judge others. But they shall be gentle, peaceable, and kind, mild and humble, and virtuous in speech, as is becoming to all. They shall not ride on horseback unless compelled by manifest necessity or infirmity to do so. When they enter a house they shall say, "Peace be to this house." According to the holy gospel, they may eat of whatever food is set before them.

I strictly forbid all the brothers to accept money or property either in person or through another. Nevertheless, for the needs of the sick, and for clothing the other brothers, the ministers and guardians may, as they see that necessity requires, provide through spiritual friends, according to the locality, season, and the degree of cold which may be expected in the region where they live. But, as has been said, they shall never receive money or property.

Those brothers to whom the Lord has given the ability to work shall work faithfully and devotedly, so that idleness, which is the enemy of the soul, may be excluded and not extinguish the spirit of prayer and devotion to which all temporal things should be subservient. As the price of their labors they may receive things that are necessary for themselves and the brothers, but not money or property. And they shall humbly receive what is given them, as is becoming to the servants of God and to those who practise the most holy poverty.

The brothers shall have nothing of their own, neither house, nor land, nor anything, but as pilgrims and strangers in this world, serving the Lord in poverty and humility, let them confidently go asking alms. Nor let them be ashamed of this, for the Lord made himself poor for us in this world. This is that highest pitch of poverty which has made you, my dearest brothers, heirs and kings of the kingdom of heaven, which has made you poor in goods, and exalted you in virtues. . . .

I strictly forbid all the brothers to have any association or conversation with women that may cause suspicion. And let them not enter nunneries, except those which the pope has given them special permission to enter. Let them not be intimate friends of men or women, lest on this account scandal arise among the brothers or about brothers.

Summa Theologica

St. Thomas Aquinas

By the thirteenth century much of the intellectual and cultural heritage of Classical times, particularly Aristotelian thought, was being reacquired in Europe. This posed a problem for the Church, for it was not clear whether pagan ideas and the reasoning of Greeks such as Aristotle contradicted the Christian view of the universe as it had developed during the Middle Ages. One of the main tasks of a line of thirteenth-century scholars, among them Albertus Magnus (c. 1193–1280), St. Thomas Aquinas (1225–1274), St. Bonaventure (1221–1274), and Duns Scotus (c. 1265–c. 1308), was to make compatible this pagan thought and Church orthodoxy based on faith. In doing this, these scholastics tended to be encyclopedic, covering almost all the concerns of medieval people. The most encyclopedic and important of these was Aquinas, an Italian Dominican who taught at the University of Paris and elsewhere. In the following selection from his Summa Theologica, *Aquinas addresses the question of whether the existence of God can be proved.*

CONSIDER: *The reasoning used here; the audience being addressed by Aquinas.*

The existence of God can be proved in five ways.

The first and more manifest way is the argument from motion. It is certain, and evidence to our senses, that in the world some things are in motion. Now whatever is in motion is put in motion by another, for nothing can be in motion except it is in potentiality to that towards which it is in motion; whereas a thing moves inasmuch as it is in act. For motion is nothing else than the reduction of something from potentiality to actuality. But nothing can be reduced from potentiality to actuality, except by something in a state of actuality. Thus that which is actually hot, as fire, makes wood, which is potentially hot, to be actually hot, and thereby moves and changes it. Now it is not possible that the same thing should be at once in actuality and potentiality in the same respect, but only in different respects. For what is actually hot cannot simultaneously be potentially hot; but it is simultaneously potentially cold. It is therefore impossible that in the same respect and in the same way a thing should be both mover and moved, *i.e.*, that it should move itself. Therefore, whatever is in motion must be put in motion by another. If that by which it is put in motion be itself put in motion, then this also must needs be put in motion by another, and that by another again. But this cannot go on to infinity, because then there would be no first mover, and, consequently, no other mover; seeing that subsequent movers move only inasmuch as they are put in motion by the first mover; as the staff moves only because it is put in motion by the hand. Therefore it is necessary to arrive at a first mover, put in motion by no other; and this everyone understands to be God.

The second way is from the nature of the efficient cause. In the world of sense we find there is an order of efficient causes. There is no case known (neither is it, indeed, possible) in which a thing is found to be the efficient cause of itself; for so it would be prior to itself, which is impossible. Now in efficient causes it is not possible to go on to infinity, because in all efficient causes following in order, the first is the cause of the intermediate cause, and the intermediate is the cause of the ultimate cause, whether the intermediate cause be several, or one only. Now to take away the cause is to take away the effect. Therefore, if there be no first cause among efficient causes, there will be no ultimate, nor any intermediate cause. But if in efficient causes it is possible to go to infinity, there will be no first efficient cause, neither will there be an ultimate effect, nor any intermediate efficient causes; all of which is plainly false. Therefore it is necessary to admit a first efficient cause, to which everyone gives the name of God.

The third way is taken from possibility and necessity, and runs thus. We find in nature things that are possible to be and not to be, since they are found to be generated, and to corrupt, and consequently, they are possible to be and not to be. But it is impossible for these always to exist, for that which is possible not to be at some time is not. Therefore, if everything is possible not to be, then at one time there could have been nothing in existence. Now if this were true, even now there would be nothing in existence, because that which does not exist only begins to exist by something already existing. Therefore, if at one time nothing was in existence, it would have been

SOURCE: St. Thomas Aquinas, *The Summa Theologica of St. Thomas Aquinas,* Part I, XXI–XXVI, 2nd rev. ed., trans. Fathers of the English Dominican Province (New York: Benziger Brothers, 1920), pp. 24–27.

impossible for anything to have begun to exist; and thus even now nothing would be in existence—which is absurd. Therefore, not all beings are merely possible, but there must exist something the existence of which is necessary. But every necessary thing either has its necessity caused by another, or not. Now it is impossible to go on to infinity in necessary things which have their necessity caused by another, as has been already proved in regard to efficient causes. Therefore we cannot but postulate the existence of some being having of itself its own necessity, and not receiving it from another, but rather causing in others their necessity. This all men speak of as God.

The fourth way is taken from the gradation to be found in things. Among beings there are some more and some less good, true, noble, and the like. But "more" and "less" are predicated of different things, according as they resemble in their different ways something which is the maximum, as a thing is said to be hotter according as it more nearly resembles that which is hottest; so that there is something which is truest, something best, something noblest, and consequently, something which is uttermost being; for those things that are greatest in truth are greatest in being, as it is written in *Metaph*. ii. Now the maximum in any genus is the cause of all in that genus; as fire, which is the maximum of heat, is the cause of all hot things. Therefore there must also be something which is to all beings the cause of their being, goodness, and every other perfection; and this we call God.

The fifth way is taken from the governance of the world. We see that things which lack intelligence, such as natural bodies, act for an end, and this is evident from their acting always, or nearly always, in the same way, so as to obtain the best result. Hence it is plain that not fortuitously, but designedly, do they achieve their end. Now whatever lacks intelligence cannot move towards an end, unless it be directed by some being endowed with knowledge and intelligence; as the arrow is shot to its mark by the archer. Therefore some intelligent being exists by whom all natural things are directed to their end; and this being we call God.

Political Authority: The Emperor, the Princes, and the Towns

Frederick II

The papacy was not the only force competing with royal authority for power during the thirteenth century. Within their realms, kings faced relatively powerful and independent

Source: From Oliver J. Thatcher and Edgar H. McNeal, eds. and trans., *A Source Book for Medieval History* (New York: Scribner's, 1905), pp. 238–240.

princes and cities. This was particularly true in the German lands of the Holy Roman Empire. A development that significantly shifted the balance in favor of independent princes occurred during Frederick II's reign (1212–1250). Frederick was a dynamic emperor who was concerned with acquiring control over his lands in Italy. To enable him to concentrate his efforts there, Frederick made the following grant of privileges to his German princes in 1231.

CONSIDER: *The ways in which this grant strengthened the position of the princes against the emperor; how this grant strengthened the position of the princes against the independent towns; methods that could have been used to strengthen royal authority.*

1. No new castles or cities shall be erected by us or by anyone else to the prejudice of the princes.

2. New markets shall not be allowed to interfere with the interests of former ones.

3. No one shall be compelled to attend any market against his will.

4. Travellers shall not be compelled to leave the old highways, unless they desire to do so.

5. We will not exercise jurisdiction within the banmile of our cities.

6. Each prince shall possess and exercise in peace according to the customs of the land the liberties, jurisdiction, and authority over counties and hundreds which are in his own possession or are held as fiefs from him.

7. Centgrafs shall receive their office from the prince or from the person who holds the land as a fief.

8. The location of the hundred court shall not be changed without the consent of the lord.

9. No nobleman shall be amenable to the hundred court.

10. The citizens who are known as *phalburgii* [*i.e.*, persons or corporations existing outside the city, but possessing political rights within it] shall be expelled from the cities.

11. Payments of wine, money, grain, and other rents, which free peasants have formerly agreed to pay [to the emperor], are hereby remitted, and shall not be collected henceforth.

12. The serfs of princes, nobles, ministerials, and churches shall not be admitted to our cities.

13. Lands and fiefs of princes, nobles, ministerials, and churches, which have been seized by our cities, shall be restored and shall never again be taken.

14. The right of the princes to furnish safe-conduct within the lands which they hold as fiefs from us shall not be infringed by us or by anyone else.

15. Inhabitants of our cities shall not be compelled by our judges to restore any possessions which they may have received from others before they moved there.

16. Notorious, condemned, and proscribed persons shall not be admitted to our cities; if they have been, they shall be driven out.

17. We will never cause any money to be coined in the land of any of the princes which shall be injurious to his coinage.

18. The jurisdiction of our cities shall not extend beyond their boundaries, unless we possess special jurisdiction in the region.

19. In our cities the plaintiff shall bring suit in the court of the accused.

20. Lands or property which are held as fiefs shall not be pawned without the consent of the lord from whom they are held.

21. No one shall be compelled to aid in the fortifying of cities unless he is legally bound to render that service.

22. Inhabitants of our cities who hold lands outside shall pay to their lords or advocates the regular dues and services, and they shall not be burdened with unjust exactions.

23. If serfs, freemen subject to advocates, or vassals of any lord, shall dwell within any of our cities, they shall not be prevented by our officials from going to their lords.

Decrees of the Hanseatic League

Increased trade and the corresponding growth of cities dependent on that trade created common problems and interests, encouraging some cities to make cooperative agreements or form leagues. This cooperation occurred mostly in commercial areas where central royal authority was relatively weak, as in northern Italy, where the Lombard League was formed, and in northern Germany, where the Hanseatic League was established during the thirteenth century. The prominence of the Hanseatic League rose further in the fourteenth and fifteenth centuries. The following are decrees issued by the Hanseatic League between 1260 and 1264.

CONSIDER: *The primary concerns of league members on which they felt they could cooperate; who was perceived as the principal threat to the independence of the towns.*

We wish to inform you of the action taken in support of all merchants who are governed by the law of Lübeck.

(1) Each city shall, to the best of her ability, keep the sea clear of pirates, so that merchants may freely carry on their business by sea. (2) Whoever is expelled from one city because of a crime shall not be received in another. (3) If a citizen is seized [by pirates, robbers, or bandits] he shall not be ransomed, but his sword-belt and knife shall be sent to him [as a threat to his captors]. (4) Any merchant ransoming him shall lose all his possessions in all the cities which have the law of Lübeck. (5) Whoever is proscribed in one city for robbery or theft shall be proscribed in all. (6) If a lord besieges a city, no one shall aid him in any way to the detriment of the besieged city, unless the besieger is his lord. (7) If there is a war in the country, no city shall on that account injure a citizen from the other cities, either in his person or goods, but shall give him protection. (8) If any man marries a woman in one city, and another woman from some other city comes and proves that he is her lawful husband, he shall be beheaded. (9) If a citizen gives his daughter or niece in marriage to a man [from another city], and another man comes and says that she is his lawful wife, but cannot prove it, he shall be beheaded.

This law shall be binding for a year, and after that the cities shall inform each other by letter of what decisions they make.

Ordinances of the Guild Merchants of Southampton

One way medieval merchants responded to the growth of commerce and industry in urban areas was to form guilds. While the specific origin of guilds is unclear—they may at first have been only fraternal-religious groups—by the thirteenth and fourteenth centuries they could be found in most cities. They tended to develop into independent organizations that monopolized commerce and played an important social role in the community. The following selections are taken from ordinances dating back to the thirteenth century of the Guild Merchants of Southampton, England.

CONSIDER: *The ways in which this guild attempted to control commerce and industry; what services the guild performed for its members; how the principles and practices of guilds fit with the argument that capitalism was widespread in medieval times; similarities and differences between the concerns of this guild and those of the Hanseatic League.*

§7. And when a gildsman dies, all those who are of the Gild and are in the city shall attend the service for the dead, and gildsmen shall bear the body and bring it to

SOURCE: From Oliver J. Thatcher and Edgar H. McNeal, eds. and trans., *A Source Book for Medieval History* (New York: Scribner's, 1905), pp. 611–612.

SOURCE: Edward P. Cheyney, ed., "English Towns and Gilds," in *Translations and Reprints from the Original Sources of European History*, vol. II, no. 1, ed. Department of History of the University of Pennsylvania (Philadelphia: University of Pennsylvania Press, 1898), pp. 12–15.

the place of burial. And whoever will not do this shall pay according to his oath, two pence, to be given to the poor. And those of the ward where the dead man shall be ought to find a man to watch over the body the night that the dead shall lie in his house. And so long as the service of the dead shall last, that is to say, the vigil and the mass, there ought to burn four candles of the Gild, each candle of two pounds weight or more, until the body is buried. And these four candles shall remain in the keeping of the steward of the Gild.

§9. And when a gildsman dies, his eldest son or his next heir shall have the seat of his father, or of his uncle, if his father was not a gildsman, and of no other one; and he shall give nothing for his seat. . . .

§11. And if a gildsman shall be imprisoned in England in time of peace, the alderman, with the steward, and with one of the skevins shall go, at the cost of the Gild, to procure the deliverance of the one who is in prison.

§12. And if any gildsman strikes another with his fist; and, is convicted thereof, he shall lose the Gild until he shall have bought it back for ten shillings, and taken the oath of the Gild again like a new member. And if a gildsman strikes another with a stick, or a knife, or any other weapon, whatever it may be, he shall lose the Gild and the franchise, and shall be held as a stranger until he shall have been reconciled to the good men of the Gild and has made recompense to the one whom he has injured; and has paid a fine to the Gild of twenty shillings, and this shall not be remitted.

§15. And if a gildsman reviles or slanders another gildsman, and a complaint of it comes to the alderman, and, if he is reasonably convicted thereof, he shall pay two shillings fine to the Gild, and if he is not able to pay he shall lose the Gild.

§16. And if anyone, who is of the franchise, speaks evil of a gildsman, and is convicted of this before the alderman, he shall pay five shillings for a fine, or lose the franchise.

§19. And no one in the city of Southampton shall buy anything to sell again in the same city, unless he is of the Gild Merchant or of the franchise. . . .

§20. And no one shall buy honey, fat, salt herrings, or any kind of oil, or millstones, or fresh hides, or any kind of fresh skins, unless he is a gildsman; nor keep a tavern for wine, nor sell cloth at retail, except in market or fair days; nor keep grain in his granary beyond five quarters, to sell at retail, if he is not a gildsman; and whoever shall do this and be convicted, shall forfeit all to the king.

§22. If any gildsman falls into poverty and has not the wherewithal to live, and is not able to work or to provide for himself, he shall have one mark from the Gild to relieve his condition when the Gild shall sit. . . .

§23. And no private man or stranger shall bargain for or buy any kind of merchandise coming into the city before a burgess of the Gild Merchant, so long as the gildsman is present and wishes to bargain for and buy this merchandise; and if any one does so and is convicted, that which he buys shall be forfeited to the king.

§24. And anyone who is of the Gild Merchant shall share in all merchandise which another gildsman shall buy or any other person, whoever he is, if he comes and demands part and is there where the merchandise is bought, and also if he gives satisfaction to the seller and gives security for his part. But no one who is not a gildsman is able or ought to share with a gildsman, without the will of the gildsman.

Chambermaids

Bartholomaeus Anglicus

Most women were neither wealthy nor of high position. Few options were available to them. Many had to become servants, serving as chambermaids. The life they faced is described in the following excerpt from a book of writings gathered by a thirteenth-century English Franciscan, Bartholomaeus Anglicus. The book was translated and widely circulated in the fourteenth century.

CONSIDER: *What limitations a chambermaid faced; what penalties could be imposed upon her; ways in which her position might differ from that of a male servant.*

A chambermaid is a servant employed by the master or mistress of the house to do the heaviest and foulest jobs. She is fed coarse food, clad in the meanest cloth, and bears the burden of servitude. If she has children, they are the master's serfs. If she is a serf herself, she may not marry whom she chooses, and anyone who does marry her, falling into servitude, can be sold like an animal by the master. If freed, the serving maid can be recalled to serfdom for ingratitude. Chambermaids are frequently beaten, abused, and tormented, and scarcely given a chance to console themselves by laughter or distractions. . . . Rabanus says that chambermaids have this characteristic: they rebel against their masters and mistresses and get out of hand if they are not kept down. . . . Serfs and that sort are kept in place only through fear.

SOURCE: Excerpts from *Not in God's Image* by Julia O'Faolain and Lauro Martines. Copyright © 1973 by Julia O'Faolain and Lauro Martines. Reprinted by permission of Harper & Row, Publishers, Inc.

Visual Sources

Medieval Life

While there was considerable change throughout the High and Late Middle Ages, many fundamental aspects of life remained much the same. In figure 10.1, a late-medieval illustration by Pol de Limbourg from the Très Riches Heures du Duc de Berry, a book of prayers for each day of the year, shows a typical October day. A peasant sows seeds in a small, recently plowed field. Just behind, a scarecrow in the form of an archer guards another field. In the background flows the Seine with some aristocrats on its bank under the walls of the Louvre, the Gothic castle of the French kings in Paris. The basic reliance on agriculture, the importance of the seasons, the sharp contrast between the social classes, and the increasingly large castles symbolizing military prowess and status remained typical of medieval life.

CONSIDER: *The nature of the peasant's life as portrayed by this artist; how an aristocratic viewer of this illustration might react.*

Secularization and the Medieval Knight

This illustration from a book produced shortly after 1300 (figure 10.2) shows two knights jousting in a tournament. The knights are distinguished by their costumes. The knight on the

FIGURE 10.1 (© Victoria & Albert Museum, London, UK/Bridgeman Art Library)

left falls in defeat with a pierced helmet; the winner suffers only a broken lance. Meanwhile, aristocratic women view the scene in apparent admiration.

This sort of pageantry was growing in a period when the traditional function of knighthood was becoming obsolete. Earlier in the Middle Ages, knights were owners of horses and armor who served in the cavalry and upheld certain chivalric values. According to a twelfth-century source the knight was "to protect the Church, to fight against treachery, to respect the priesthood, to fend off injustice from the poor, to make peace in [his] own province, to shed blood for [his] brethren, and if needs must, to lay down [his] life." By the thirteenth and fourteenth centuries new military tactics diminished the importance of knights, centralizing monarchies weakened their independence, and spreading wealth enabled even the middle class to purchase knighthood. As shown in this picture, however, knighthood still survived and even helped define masculinity and femininity.

The book itself, the Codex Manesse, indicates a growing secularization in society during the thirteenth century. It is a collection of popular poems and songs of chivalry and love written in the vernacular rather than in Latin.

CONSIDER: *The images of masculinity and femininity conveyed by this illustration; any connections between these images and medieval values; the distinctions between the image and reality of medieval knighthood.*

FIGURE 10.2   (Ruprecht-Karls-Universitaat, Heidelberg Universitätsbibliothek)

Secondary Sources

The Outlaws of Medieval Legend: Social Rank and Injustice

Maurice Keen

Today, the social system of the Middle Ages seems unjust, particularly for the poor, who suffered the most. Yet one must be careful in applying modern standards to an earlier era. In the following selection, Maurice Keen of Oxford argues that the poor did not have such a critical view of the social system and the laws that supported such a hierarchical structure. Rather, criticism was directed toward corruption within the system. In his interpretation Keen makes creative use of evidence from medieval ballads and legends.

SOURCE: Maurice Keen, *The Outlaws of Medieval Legend* (London: Routledge and Kegan Paul, 1961), pp. 154–155. Reprinted by permission.

CONSIDER: *The common view or ideal that justified the social system to the medieval mind; what sort of behavior created a sense of injustice in the minds of medieval people.*

The middle ages were profoundly respectful to hereditary rank and they did not question its title to homage. They did on the other hand question the right of those whose actions belied any nobility of mind to the enjoyment of the privileges of noble status. They were not indignant against an unjust social system, but they were indignant against unjust social superiors. The ballad makers accepted this contemporary attitude and echoed it in their poems.

This explains why the ballads have nothing to say of the economic exploitation of the poor, of the tyranny of lords of manors whose bondmen were tied to the soil and bound by immemorial custom to till their land for him. For we might expect, from what we know of the social system of the countryside in the middle ages, to find Robin, as the champion of the poor, freeing serfs from bondage, harbouring runaway villeins in his band, and punishing the stewards of estates whose conduct was every whit as harsh and unjust as that of the offices of the law. But the middle ages did not view social injustice, as we do, in terms of the exploitation of one class by another; they admired the class system as the co-operation for the common well-being of the different estates of men. They recognized three different classes in their society; the knights and lords, whose business it was to protect Christendom in arms, the clerks who had charge of its spiritual well-being and whose duty was prayer, and the common men whose business it was to till the soil. Each rank had its obligation to discharge its proper duties without complaint and, in the case particularly of the first two classes, not to abuse the privileges which its function gave it. That they were made to "swink and toil" gave the peasants no ground for complaint; their occupation, as one preacher quaintly put it, lay in "grobbynge about the erthe, as erynge and dungynge and sowynge and harwying" and "this schuld be do justlie and for a good ende, withoute feyntise or falshede or gruechynge of hire estaat." But those who failed to discharge their duties and abused their position had no right to a place in the system, nor to the profits of association. "They neither labour with the rustics . . . nor fight with the knights, nor pray and chant with the clergy; therefore," says the great Dominican, Bromyard, of such men "they shall go with their own abbot, of whose Order they are, namely the Devil, where no Order exists but horror eternal."

The law's object is ultimately to uphold social justice, and to the middle ages social justice meant a hierarchical social system. The trouble came when those who belonged to a high class used the wealth, which was given them to uphold their proper rank, to corrupt the law and abuse it for their own profit. Their ultimate sin was the use of their originally rightful riches to purchase more than was their due. For this reason, those who were shocked by flagrant injustice into attacking the accepted system criticized not the economic oppression which is almost automatically implied, but the corruption of evil men whose personal greed destroyed the social harmony of what they regarded as the ideal system. The method which these men employed was to buy the law, and to control by their position its application. It is for this reason that the outlaw ballads, whose heroes are the champions of the poor, are silent about the multitudinous economic miseries of the medieval peasant, and are concerned only or at least chiefly with an endless feud against the corrupt representatives of the law. Contemporary opinion diagnosed the disease which was gnawing at society as the personal corruption of those in high rank; that such disease was the inevitable accompaniment of their hierarchic system they simply could not see. This is why the animus in the outlaw ballads is against oppression by those who own the law, not against exploitation by those who own the land.

Life in Cities: Violence and Fear

Jacques Rossiaud

The growth of cities after the eleventh century created what we now recognize as typical urban problems. One such problem was keeping the peace. Cities in Western Europe were often places of violence and fear. As part of a trend toward studying social life, historians have increasingly studied crime and violence in medieval cities. In the following selection Jacques Rossiaud analyzes violent acts in the cities of Western Europe, emphasizing how urban violence fostered anxiety.

CONSIDER: *Who tended to commit most of the violent acts; possible explanations for urban violence; what the effects of this violence might be.*

The history of the cities of Western Europe is shot through with episodes of violence, fear, and revolution, episodes in which family honor, participation in the municipal council, or working conditions were at stake. Such conflicts opposed "magnate" and "popular" factions. In Italy they opposed actual political parties dominated by clans, and in the bigger cities of Flanders they turned into true class wars punctuated by massacres, exilings, and destruction. Such conflicts were frequent between 1250 and 1330, and they resulted everywhere in a defeat of the old rich land and an enlargement of oligarchies. A second wave of unrest of a more clearly social character (the *ciompi* in Florence and Siena, the *maillotins* in Paris, and so forth) battered the urban world in the late fourteenth century. The defeat of the lower orders did not put an end to the tensions, which were transformed into an occasional brief terror, here and there, but were more usually expressed in continual but muted, "atomized" conflicts difficult to distinguish from common delinquency in the documentation. Stones thrown at night through a master's windows, a creditor brutalized, a brawl between two rival groups of workers were easily ascribed to ordinary violence by the judges.

In other words, many city-dwellers, even if they lived through long and difficult periods of tension, escaped the horrors of riots and repression, but they all had to face an atmosphere of violence on an almost daily basis. There is little need to accumulate examples: in Florence, Venice, Paris, Lille, Dijon, Avignon, Tours, or Foix, the judicial archives reveal an impressive series of cold-blooded

SOURCE: From Jacques Rossiaud, "The City-Dweller and Life in Cities and Towns," in *Medieval Callings*, pp. 152–154, ed. by Jacques Le Goff, trans. by Lydia Cochrane. © 1990 University of Chicago Press. Reprinted by permission of the publisher.

vendettas, of *chaudes mêlées* between individuals or groups settled with knives or iron-tipped sticks, and of rapes, often collective, that marked for life poor girls beaten and dragged from their rooms at night.

These violent acts were for the most part committed by youths or adult men, often of modest social condition, but who were indistinguishable from law-abiding citizens. . . .

Wine—drunkenness was often an excuse—does not explain everything, nor do the arms that everyone carried in spite of municipal ordinances. The example came from on high: even in Reims at the beginning of the fourteenth century, the judges were incapable of keeping clans from resolving their quarrels by means of arms. However, civic violence (executions, torture, forcing a criminal to run through the city streets as the crowd jeered and struck him) was offered as a spectacle, and the domestic moral code allowed blows. Justice, what is more, did not inspire belief; it was more dreaded than appreciated, and it was inefficient and costly. When he was scoffed at, the individual turned to immediate vengeance. He did so to safeguard his honor: it was in the name of honor that young men punished girls who, to their minds, transgressed its canons. Like violence, honor was a value widespread in urban societies: prominent citizens were called "honorable." There was no reputation without honor and no honor without authority. The rich man's wealth and friends lent support to his honor; the working man without wealth held his reputation to be an essential capital. . . .

Violence fostered anxiety. On occasion the notables denounced it, but they did not really seek to extirpate it (either in Venice or Dijon). For humble folk this fear added to other obsessions—of being abandoned amid general indifference, as with Dame Poverty, whom Jean de Meun described as covered with an old sack, "a bit apart from the others . . . crouched down and hunched over like a poor dog," sad, shamed, and unloved.

Solitude

Georges Duby

Whether in urban or rural areas, people of the High Middle Ages spent much of their everyday lives in the company of others. What we in our times think of as privacy was not quite the same in medieval society. Not only were living spaces more communal, but people were expected to work, play, and travel in groups. In the following selection from A History of Private Life, *Georges Duby describes this crowded, communal society and the difficulties facing anyone seeking solitude.*

Source: George Duby, "Solitude: Eleventh to Thirteenth Century," in *A History of Private Life,* vol. III, Philippe Aries and Georges Duby, eds. Cambridge, MA: Belknap Press of Harvard University Press, 1987, pp. 509–510.

Consider: *How groups formed in various occupations and activities; how Duby analyzes private space; the problems facing an individual longing for solitude.*

People crowded together cheek by jowl, living in promiscuity, sometimes in the midst of a mob. In feudal residences there was no room for individual solitude, except perhaps in the moment of death. When people ventured outside the domestic enclosure, they did so in groups. No journey could be made by fewer than two people, and if it happened that they were not related, they bound themselves by rites of brotherhood, creating an artificial family that lasted as long as the journey required. By age seven, at which time young aristocratic males were considered persons of sex, they left the woman's world and embarked upon a life of adventure. Yet throughout their lives they remained surrounded, in the strong sense of the word— whether they were dedicated to the service of God and sent to study with a schoolmaster or joined a group of other young men in aping the gestures of a leader, their new father, whom they followed whenever he left his house to defend his rights by force of arms or force of words or to hunt in his forests. Their apprenticeship over, new knights received their arms as a group, a mob organized as a family. (Generally the lord's son was dubbed along with the sons of the vassals.) From that time forth the young knights were always together, linked in glory and in shame, vouching for and standing as hostage for one another. As a group, accompanied by servants and often by priests, they raced from tourney to tourney, court to court, skirmish to skirmish, displaying their loyalties by showing the colors or shouting the same rallying cry. The devotion of these young comrades enveloped their leader in an indispensable mantle of domestic familiarity, an itinerant household.

Thus, in feudal society, private space was divided, composed of two distinct areas: one fixed, enclosed, attached to the hearth; the other mobile, free to move through public space, yet embodying the same hierarchies and held together by the same controls. Within this mobile cell peace and order were maintained by a power whose mission was to organize a defense against the intrusion of the public authorities, for which purpose an invisible wall, as solid as the enclosure that surrounded the house, was erected against the outside world. This power enveloped and restrained the individuals of the household, subjecting them to a common discipline. Power meant constraint. And if private life meant secrecy, it was a secrecy shared by all members of the household, hence fragile and easily violated. If private life meant independence, it was independence of a collective sort. In the eleventh and twelfth centuries collective privacy did exist. But can we detect any signs of personal privacy within the collective privacy?

Feudal society was so granular in structure, composed of such compact curds, that any individual who attempted to remove himself from the close and omnipresent conviviality, to be alone, to construct his own private enclosure, to cultivate his garden, immediately became an object of either suspicion or admiration, regarded as either a rebel or a hero and in either case considered "foreign"—the antithesis of "private." The person who stood apart, even if his intention was not deliberately to commit evil, was inevitably destined to do so, for his very isolation made him more vulnerable to the Enemy's attacks. No one would run such a risk who was not deviant or possessed or mad; it was commonly believed that solitary wandering was a symptom of insanity. Men and women who traveled the roads without escort were believed to offer themselves up as prey, so it was legitimate to take everything they had. In any case, it was a pious work to place them back in some community, regardless of what they might say, to restore them by force to that clearly ordered and well-managed world where God intended them to be, a world composed of private enclosures and of the public spaces between them, through which people moved only in cortege.

Ecological Conditions and Demographic Change

David Herlihy

Most historians feel that the medieval expansion ended between 1300 and 1350 and that changes occurred that marked the following century as one of contraction, disruption, and decline. Traditionally, these changes have been analyzed from political, military, and religious perspectives. In the following selection David Herlihy of Harvard focuses on the economic aspects of this change, particularly the economic limitations that prevented the medieval expansion from continuing much beyond the thirteenth century.

CONSIDER: *Obstacles hindering economic expansion by 1300; the social and political effects that might have stemmed from these economic changes; other factors that might account for the end of the medieval expansion.*

Medieval expansion, however, never achieved a true breakthrough, never reached what some economists today term the stage of "takeoff," in which a built-in capacity for continuing growth is developed. By around 1300, certain obstacles were beginning to hinder economic expansion. One was the relative stagnation of technology. In spite of

SOURCE: David Herlihy, "Ecological Conditions and Demographic Change," in *One Thousand Years: Western Europe in the Middle Ages*, ed. Richard L. DeMolen (Boston: Houghton Mifflin, 1974), p. 32.

important technological discoveries that introduced the Middle Ages, peasants in 1300 were working the land much as their ancestors had several centuries before. However, technological stagnation alone does not seem to have imposed a rigid ceiling on growth. Paradoxically, many peasants in the late thirteenth century were not working the soil according to the best known and available methods. Their chief handicap was not lack of knowledge but lack of capital, for the best methods were based upon the effective use of cattle to supply both labor and manure. Insofar as we can judge, many small cultivators of the thirteenth century could not afford cattle and had to work their plots with their own unaided and inefficient efforts.

A second limitation upon expansion was the failure to develop institutions and values that would maintain appropriate levels of investment, especially in agriculture. In spite of the growth of cities, a large part of Europe's lands was controlled by military and clerical aristocracies, which were not likely to reinvest their profits received in rent. The great landlords were rather prone to spend their rents on conspicuous but economically barren forms of consumption such as manor houses, castles, churches, wars, the maintenance of a lavish style of living. They were also likely to demand from the towns money in loans for such unproductive expenditures.

A third limiting factor seems to have been the growing scarcity of resources, especially good land. As the best soils were taken under cultivation, the still growing population had to rely increasingly upon poorer, marginal lands, which required more effort and capital to assure a good return. The European economy was burdened by a growing saturation in the use of its readily available resources, and it had neither the technology nor the capital to improve its returns from what it possessed. In the opinion of many historians today, this saturation in the use of resources not only ended the economic advance of the central Middle Ages but precipitated a profound demographic and economic crisis in the fourteenth century.

❧ CHAPTER QUESTIONS

1. Some historians have described the thirteenth century as the period in which medieval civilization attained a remarkable balance. In what ways was this period so balanced?

2. In what ways were the main characteristics of the thirteenth century simply a further extension of trends already evident during the eleventh and twelfth centuries? What new developments appeared during the thirteenth century?

3. What evidence does the chapter provide of the struggle for authority that persisted through this period?

11 The Late Middle Ages

The fourteenth century and the first half of the fifteenth saw decline, disruption, and disintegration. This period, usually referred to as the Late Middle Ages, has been described in terms such as "the decline of the Middle Ages" and "the waning of the Middle Ages." Certain developments support these descriptions. Demographically, the population increase of the High Middle Ages was over by the end of the thirteenth century. During the following century population decreased significantly, due in great part to poor harvests, disease, and war. Geographically, European expansion temporarily ended. Religiously, the Church faced a series of problems: The papacy suffered from increasing conflict with powerful European monarchs, heretical movements spread, the Church itself became divided during the Great Schism, and the papacy was threatened by a revolt of its own high clergy in the Conciliar Movement. Economically, wages and prices varied greatly, as did the availability of labor and goods; this disrupted relations among various social groups. Politically, almost unending conflict led to an unusually intense period of wars, the most serious of which was the Hundred Years' War between England and France.

To illustrate the disruptive developments of the Late Middle Ages, the selections in this chapter concentrate on two specific topics: problems facing the Church and the mid-fourteenth-century plague. What was the nature of the Conciliar Movement, which threatened the pope's authority? How was the Church threatened by heresy? How did it deal with heresy? What were the social and psychological consequences of the plague? How was the plague related to religious views of Europeans? How did institutions react to the consequences of the plague?

143

Although this chapter views the Late Middle Ages largely as a period of disruption and decline, it was also a period of continuity. Many aspects of medieval civilization would continue for centuries, evolving only very slowly. To show both the continuity and the decline characteristic of this era, the nature of society in the Late Middle Ages and the psychological characteristics of the period are analyzed. How was this society organized? What were typical members of this society like? What were the attitudes toward women and marriage? How were psychological trends reflected by conceptions of death? What sorts of rebellions occurred?

In sum, the materials paint a picture in marked contrast to our image of the High Middle Ages. But while the decline during the Late Middle Ages was real, the same period witnessed an extraordinary social and cultural revival in Italy, which will be the concern of the next chapter.

Primary Sources

Attack on the Papacy: The Conciliar Movement

From 1378 to 1417 the Catholic Church was divided, with competing popes reigning simultaneously, each claiming authority. In an effort to end this schism, Church councils met at Pisa (1409) and then at Constance (1414–1417). These councils constituted the high point of a developing Conciliar Movement—an effort to place ultimate authority in the hands of a general Church council and diminish the powers of the pope. The council at Pisa worsened the situation by installing a third pope, but at Constance the schism was ended with the election of a single pope, Martin V. He and his successors repudiated the Conciliar Movement over the next few decades. Yet the Conciliar Movement represented a strong current of opinion within the Church and revealed the depth of the problems facing the Church. The following two documents are decrees passed during the Council of Constance at the height of this movement.

CONSIDER: *The intent of the Decree Sacrosancta; why the council felt it necessary also to pass the Decree Frequens; how the council justified its authority.*

DECREE SACROSANCTA

In the name of the Holy and indivisible Trinity; of the Father, Son, and Holy Ghost. Amen.

This holy synod of Constance, forming a general council for the extirpation of the present schism and the union and reformation, in head and members, of the church of God, legitimately assembled in the Holy Ghost, to the praise of Omnipotent God, in order that it may the more easily, safely, effectively and freely bring about the union and reformation of the church of God, hereby determines, decrees, ordains and declares what follows:—

It first declares that this same council, legitimately assembled in the Holy Ghost, forming a general council and representing the Catholic Church militant, has its power immediately from Christ, and everyone, whatever his state or position, even if it be the Papal dignity itself, is bound to obey it in all those things which pertain to the faith and the healing of the said schism, and to the general reformation of the Church of God, in head and members.

It further declares that anyone, whatever his condition, station or rank, even if it be the Papal, who shall contumaciously refuse to obey the mandates, decrees, ordinances or instructions which have been, or shall be issued by this holy council, or by any other general council, legitimately summoned, which concern, or in any way relate to the above mentioned objects, shall, unless he repudiate his conduct, be subjected to condign penance and be suitably punished, having recourse, if necessary, to the other resources of the law.

❧

DECREE FREQUENS

A frequent celebration of general councils is an especial means for cultivating the field of the Lord and effecting the destruction of briars, thorns, and thistles, to-wit, heresies, errors and schism, and of bringing forth a most abundant harvest. The neglect to summon these, fosters and develops all these evils, as may be plainly seen from a recollection of the past and a consideration of existing conditions. Therefore, by a perpetual edict, we sanction, decree, establish and ordain that general councils shall be celebrated in the following manner, so that the next one shall follow the close of this present council at the end of five years. The second shall follow the close of that, at the end of seven years and councils shall thereafter be celebrated every ten years in such places as the Pope shall be required

SOURCE: From James Harvey Robinson, ed., "The Pre-Reformation Period," in *Translations and Reprints from the Original Sources of European History*, vol. III, no. 6, ed. Department of History of the University of Pennsylvania (Philadelphia: University of Pennsylvania Press, 1898), pp. 30–31.

to designate and assign, with the consent and approbation of the council, one month before the close of the council in question, or which, in his absence, the council itself shall designate. Thus, with a certain continuity, a council will always be either in session, or be expected at the expiration of a definite time.

Manual of the Inquisitor
Bernard Gui

Heresy, always a concern for the Church, had by the fourteenth century become such a serious problem that the Church turned to formal institutions such as the Inquisition to deal with it. One of the best-known and longest-lasting heretical movements was that of the Waldensians in southern France and northern Italy. Originally, they were followers of Peter Waldo, who pursued a life of piety and religious belief. The Waldensians were officially condemned in the thirteenth century but survived to be persecuted in the fourteenth century. The following is a selection from the Manual of the Inquisitor, compiled by Bernard Gui, a Dominican monk and bishop who became a zealous inquisitor in southern France from 1307 to 1324.

CONSIDER: *The main crimes of the Waldensians according to Gui; the nature of the threat posed by these crimes; the similarities and differences between the threats posed by this heresy and those of the Conciliar Movement.*

Disdain for ecclesiastical authority was and still is the prime heresy of the Waldenses. Excommunicated for this reason and delivered over to Satan, they have fallen into innumerable errors, and have blended the errors of earlier heretics with their own concoctions.

The misled believers and sacrilegious masters of this sect hold and teach that they are in no way subject to the lord Pope or Roman Pontiff, or to the other prelates of the Roman Church, and that the latter persecute and condemn them unjustly and improperly. Moreover, they declare that they cannot be excommunicated by this Roman Pontiff and these prelates, and that obedience is owed to none of them when they order and summon the followers and masters of the said sect to abandon or abjure this sect, although this sect be condemned as heretical by the Roman Church. . . .

Moreover, the sect does not accept canonical authority, or the decretals or constitutions of the Sovereign Pontiff, any more than the regulations concerning fasts and the observance of the feasts or the decrees of the Fathers. Straying from the straight road, they recognize no authority therein, scorn them, reject and condemn them.

Moreover, the followers of the sect are even more perniciously mistaken concerning the sacrament of penance and the power of the keys. They declare they have received—this is their doctrine and their teaching—from God and none other, like the apostles who held it of Christ, the power of hearing the confessions of men and women who desire to confess to them, of granting them absolution and of prescribing penance. Thus they hear confessions, grant absolution and prescribe penance, although they have not been ordained as priests or clerics by a bishop of the Roman Church and although they are just laymen. They in no way claim to hold this power from the Roman Church, on the contrary, they deny it; and in fact, they hold it neither from God nor from His Church, since they have been cast out from the Church by this very Church, outside which there is neither true penance nor salvation.

Moreover, this same sect hold up to ridicule the indulgences established and granted by the prelates of the Church, saying they are worthless.

Moreover, they are in error with respect to the sacrament of the Eucharist. They claim, not publicly but secretly, that in the sacrament of the altar the bread and wine do not become body and blood of Christ when the priest who celebrates or consecrates is a sinner; and by sinner they mean any man who does not belong to their sect. Moreover, they claim, on the contrary, that any upright man, even a layman, without having received priestly ordination from the hands of a Catholic bishop, may consecrate the body and blood of Christ, provided he be of their sect. They believe that women too can do this, subject to the same condition. Thus they hold that any holy man is a priest.

The Rebellions of 1381
Sir John Froissart

The Late Middle Ages were marked by several rebellions by the lower classes. One of the most important of these was the 1381 rebellion of peasants and artisans in England. Led by John Ball, Wat Tyler, and Jack Straw, the rebellion threatened the upper classes before it was crushed and its leaders were executed. Events of the rebellion are described in the following selection by Sir John Froissart (c. 1333–c. 1400), a French chronicler of the Hundred Years' War between England and France.

SOURCE: Bernard Gui, *Manual of the Inquisitor,* in *Introduction to Contemporary Civilization in the West,* vol. I, 3d ed., ed. Contemporary Civilization Staff of Columbia College, Columbia University (New York: Columbia University Press, 1960), pp. 198–202, 204. Reprinted by permission.

SOURCE: Sir John Froissart, *Chronicles of England, France, Spain,* vol. I, trans. Thomas Johnes (New York: The Colonial Press, 1904), pp. 211–215.

CONSIDER: *Ways John Ball appealed to the poor; how the rebels gained strength; the discontents of the poor; how rebellion might spread throughout England and elsewhere.*

While these conferences were going forward there happened great commotions among the lower orders in England, by which that country was nearly ruined. In order that this disastrous rebellion may serve as an example to mankind, I will speak of all that was done from the information I had at the time. It is customary in England, as well as in several other countries, for the nobility to have great privileges over the commonalty; that is to say, the lower orders are bound by law to plough the lands of the gentry, to harvest their grain, to carry it home to the barn, to thrash and winnow it; they are also bound to harvest and carry home the hay. All these services the prelates and gentlemen exact of their inferiors; and in the counties of Kent, Essex, Sussex, and Bedford, these services are more oppressive than in other parts of the kingdom. In consequence of this the evil disposed in these districts began to murmur, saying, that in the beginning of the world there were no slaves, and that no one ought to be treated as such, unless he had committed treason against his lord, as Lucifer did against God; but they had done no such thing, for they were neither angels nor spirits, but men formed after the same likeness as these lords who treated them as beasts. This they would bear no longer; they were determined to be free, and if they labored or did any work, they would be paid for it. A crazy priest in the country of Kent, called John Ball, who for his absurd preaching had thrice been confined in prison by the Archbishop of Canterbury, was greatly instrumental in exciting these rebellious ideas. Every Sunday after mass, as the people were coming out of church, this John Ball was accustomed to assemble a crowd around him in the marketplace and preach to them. On such occasions he would say, "My good friends, matters cannot go on well in England until all things shall be in common; when there shall be neither vassals nor lords; when the lords shall be no more masters than ourselves. How ill they behave to us! For what reason do they thus hold us in bondage? Are we not all descended from the same parents, Adam and Eve? And what can they show, or what reason can they give, why they should be more masters than ourselves? They are clothed in velvet and rich stuffs, ornamented with ermine and other furs, while we are forced to wear poor clothing. They have wines, spices, and fine bread, while we have only rye and the refuse of the straw; and when we drink it must be water. They have handsome seats and manors, while we must brave the wind and rain in our labors in the field: and it is by our labor they have wherewith to support their pomp. We are called slaves, and if we do not perform our service we are beaten, and

we have no sovereign to whom we can complain or who would be willing to hear us. Let us go to the King and remonstrate with him; he is young, and from him we may obtain a favorable answer, and if not we must ourselves seek to amend our condition."

With such language as this did John Ball harangue the people of his village every Sunday after mass. The archbishop, on being informed of it, had him arrested and imprisoned for two or three months by way of punishment; but the moment he was out of prison, he returned to his former course. Many in the city of London, envious of the rich and noble, having heard of John Ball's preaching, said among themselves that the country was badly governed, and that the nobility had seized upon all the gold and silver. These wicked Londoners, therefore, began to assemble in parties, and to show signs of rebellion; they also invited all those who held like opinions in the adjoining counties to come to London, telling them that they would find the town open to them and the commonalty of the same way of thinking as themselves, and that they would so press the King that there should no longer be a slave in England.

By this means the men of Kent, Essex, Sussex, Bedford, and the adjoining counties, in number about 60,000, were brought to London, under command of Wat Tyler, Jack Straw, and John Ball. . . . At Canterbury the rebels entered the Church of St. Thomas, where they did much damage; they also pillaged the apartments of the archbishop, saying as they were carrying off the different articles, "The Chancellor of England has had this piece of furniture very cheap; he must now give us an account of his revenues, and of the large sums which he has levied since the coronation of the King." After this they plundered the abbey of St. Vincent, and then, leaving Canterbury, took the road toward Rochester. As they passed they collected people from the villages right and left, and on they went like a tempest, destroying all the houses belonging to attorneys, King's proctors, and the archbishop, which came in their way. At Rochester they met with the same welcome as at Canterbury, for all the people were anxious to join them. . . .

In other countries of England the rebels acted in a similar manner, and several great lords and knights, such as the Lord Manley, Sir Stephen Hales, and Sir Thomas Cossington, were compelled to march with them. Now observe how fortunately matters turned out, for had these scoundrels succeeded in their intentions, all the nobility of England would have been destroyed; and after such success as this the people of other nations would have rebelled also, taking example from those of Ghent and Flanders, who at the time were in actual rebellion against their lord; the Parisians, indeed, the same year acted in a somewhat similar manner; upward of 20,000 of them armed themselves with leaden maces and caused a rebellion.

The Decameron: The Plague in Florence

Giovanni Boccaccio

In the middle of the fourteenth century, a devastating plague swept across Europe. In some cities almost half of the population was lost, and for those who were left alive the effects were long-lasting. One survivor was Giovanni Boccaccio (1313–1375), a well-known humanist of the Italian Renaissance. His best-known work is The Decameron, *written between 1348 and 1353 when the plague struck Florence. Boccaccio initiated the work with a description of the plague, an excerpt of which follows.*

CONSIDER: *How people reacted to the plague; the general understanding of the cause of the plague and how it spread.*

In the year then of our Lord 1348, there happened at Florence, the finest city in all Italy, a most terrible plague; which, whether owing to the influence of the planets, or that it was sent from God as a just punishment for our sins, had broken out some years before in the Levant, and after passing from place to place, and making incredible havoc all the way, had now reached the west. There, spite of all the means that art and human foresight could suggest, such as keeping the city clear from filth, the exclusion of all suspected persons, and the publication of copious instructions for the preservation of health; and notwithstanding manifold humble supplications offered to God in processions and otherwise; it began to show itself in the spring of the aforesaid year, in a sad and wonderful manner. Unlike what had been seen in the east, where bleeding from the nose is the fatal prognostic, here there appeared certain tumours in the groin or under the armpits, some as big as a small apple, others as an egg; and afterwards purple spots in most parts of the body; in some cases large and but few in number, in others smaller and more numerous—both sorts the usual messengers of death. To the cure of this malady, neither medical knowledge nor the power of drugs was of any effect; whether because the disease was in its own nature mortal, or that the physicians (the number of whom, taking quacks and women pretenders into the account, was grown very great) could form no just idea of the cause, nor consequently devise a true method of cure; whichever was the reason, few escaped; but nearly all died the third day from the first appearance of the symptoms, some sooner, some later, without any fever or accessory symptoms. What gave the more virulence to this plague, was that, by being communicated from the sick to the hale, it spread daily, like fire when it comes in contact with large masses of combustibles. Nor was it caught only by conversing with, or coming near the sick, but even by touching their clothes, or anything that they had before touched. . . .

These facts, and others of the like sort, occasioned various fears and devices amongst those who survived, all tending to the same uncharitable and cruel end; which was, to avoid the sick, and every thing that had been near them, expecting by that means to save themselves. And some holding it best to live temperately, and to avoid excesses of all kinds, made parties, and shut themselves up from the rest of the world; eating and drinking moderately of the best, and diverting themselves with music, and such other entertainments as they might have within doors; never listening to anything from without, to make them uneasy. Others maintained free living to be a better preservative, and would baulk no passion or appetite they wished to gratify, drinking and revelling incessantly from tavern to tavern, or in private houses (which were frequently found deserted by the owners, and therefore common to every one), yet strenuously avoiding, with all this brutal indulgence, to come near the infected. And such, at that time, was the public distress, that the laws, human and divine, were no more regarded; for the officers, to put them in force, being either dead, sick, or in want of persons to assist them, every one did just as he pleased. A third sort of people chose a method between these two: not confining themselves to rules of diet like the former, and yet avoiding the intemperance of the latter; but eating and drinking what their appetites required, they walked everywhere with odours and nosegays to smell to; as holding it best to corroborate the brain: for the whole atmosphere seemed to them tainted with the stench of dead bodies, arising partly from the distemper itself, and partly from the fermenting of the medicines within them. Others with less humanity, but perchance, as they supposed, with more security from danger, decided that the only remedy for the pestilence was to avoid it: persuaded, therefore, of this, and taking care for themselves only, men and women in great numbers left the city, their houses, relations, and effects, and fled into the country; as if the wrath of God had been restrained to visit those only within the walls of the city; or else concluding, that more ought to stay in a place thus doomed to destruction.

Thus divided as they were in their views, neither did all die, nor all escape; but falling sick indifferently, as well those of one as of another opinion; they who first set the example by forsaking others, now languished themselves without pity. I pass over the little regard that citizens and relations showed to each other; for their terror was such, that a brother even fled from his brother, a wife from her husband, and, what is more uncommon, a parent from his own child. Hence numbers that fell sick could have no help but what the charity of friends, who were very few, or the avarice of servants supplied; and even these were

SOURCE: Giovanni Boccaccio, *The Decameron*, in *Stories of Boccaccio*, trans. John Payne (London: Bibliophilist Library, 1903), pp. 1–6.

scarce and at extravagant wages, and so little used to the business that they were fit only to reach what was called for, and observe when their employer died; and this desire of getting money often cost them their lives. . . .

Not to dwell upon every particular of our misery, I shall observe, that it fared no better with the adjacent country; for, to omit the different boroughs about us, which presented the same view in miniature with the city, you might see the poor distressed labourers, with their families, without either the aid of physicians, or help of servants, languishing on the highways, in the fields, and in their own houses, and dying rather like cattle than human creatures. The consequence was that, growing dissolute in their manners like the citizens, and careless of everything, as supposing every day to be their last, their thoughts were not so much employed how to improve, as how to use their substance for their present support. The oxen, asses, sheep, goats, swine, and the dogs themselves, ever faithful to their masters, being driven from their own homes, were left to roam at will about the fields, and among the standing corn, which no one cared to gather, or even to reap; and many times, after they had filled themselves in the day, the animals would return of their own accord like rational creatures at night.

What can I say more, if I return to the city? unless that such was the cruelty of Heaven, and perhaps of men, that between March and July following, according to authentic reckonings, upwards of a hundred thousand souls perished in the city only; whereas, before that calamity, it was not supposed to have contained so many inhabitants. What magnificent dwellings, what noble palaces were then depopulated to the last inhabitant! what families became extinct! what riches and vast possessions were left, and no known heir to inherit them! what numbers of both sexes, in the prime and vigour of youth, whom in the morning neither Galen, Hippocrates, nor Aesculapius himself, would have denied to be in perfect health, breakfasted in the morning with their living friends, and supped at night with their departed friends in the other world!

Statute of Laborers

King Edward III

The Black Death that struck Florence between 1347 and 1350 came to England, causing a loss of lives so severe that there was an almost immediate shortage of laborers. Under these conditions surviving laborers could demand higher wages and apparently did. This hurt the powerful commercial

SOURCE: Edward P. Cheyney, ed., "England in the Time of Wycliffe," in *Translations and Reprints from the Original Sources of European History*, vol. II, no. 5, ed. Department of History of the University of Pennsylvania (Philadelphia: University of Pennsylvania Press, 1898), pp. 3–4.

and landed classes, who turned for help to government authorities. One response was the Statute of Laborers (1351), issued by King Edward III and directed against changes in prices and wages. An excerpt of this statute follows.

CONSIDER: *The economic and social consequences of the plague in England; the king's response to this economic problem; the standards used to evaluate proper wages.*

The King to the sheriff of Kent, greeting: Because a great part of the people, and especially of workmen and servants, have lately died in the pestilence, many seeing the necessity of masters and great scarcity of servants, will not serve unless they may receive excessive wages, and others preferring to beg in idleness rather than by labor to get their living; we, considering the grievous incommodities which of the lack especially of ploughmen and such laborers may hereafter come, have upon deliberation and treaty with the prelates and the nobles and learned men assisting us, with their unanimous counsel ordained:

That every man and woman of our realm of England, of what condition he be, free or bond, able in body, and within the age of sixty years, not living in merchandize, nor exercising any craft, nor having of his own whereof he may live, nor land of his own about whose tillage he may occupy himself, and not serving any other; if he be required to serve in suitable service, his estate considered, he shall be bound to serve him which shall so require him; and take only the wages, livery, meed, or salary which were accustomed to be given in the places where he oweth to serve, the twentieth year of our reign of England, or five or six other common years next before.

If any reaper, mower, or other workman or servant, of what estate or condition that he be, retained in any man's service, do depart from the said service without reasonable cause or license, before the term agreed, he shall have pain of imprisonment; and no one, under the same penalty, shall presume to receive or retain such a one in his service.

No one, moreover, shall pay or promise to pay to any one more wages, liveries, meed, or salary than was accustomed, as is before said.

The Canterbury Tales

Geoffrey Chaucer

One of the best literary descriptions of representative individuals during the Late Middle Ages comes from Geoffrey Chaucer's Canterbury Tales. Written during the last quarter

SOURCE: Geoffrey Chaucer, *The Canterbury Tales*, trans. David Wright (New York: Random House, 1964), pp. 3–8, 11–12. Copyright © 1964 by David Wright. Reprinted by permission of Literistic, Ltd.

of the fourteenth century by this English poet, soldier, politician, and diplomat, it recounts the tales told by a group of imaginary English pilgrims. In the prologue, excerpted here, Chaucer presents a somewhat stereotypical and subtly sarcastic image of people representative of a medieval world already on the wane.

CONSIDER: *The various roles these people were supposed to play in medieval society according to this document; the extent to which this is both an accurate and a distorted source of medieval history.*

The KNIGHT was a very distinguished man. From the beginning of his career he had loved chivalry, loyalty, honourable dealing, generosity, and good breeding. He had fought bravely in the king's service, beside which he had travelled further than most men in heathen as well as in Christian lands. Wherever he went he was honoured for his valour. . . .

He was always outstandingly successful; yet though distinguished he was prudent, and his bearing as modest as a maid's. In his whole life he never spoke discourteously to any kind of man. He was a true and perfect noble knight. But, speaking of his equipment, his horses were good, yet he was not gaily dressed. He wore a tunic of thick cotton cloth, rust-marked from his coat of mail; for he had just come back from his travels and was making his pilgrimage to render thanks. . . .

There was also a NUN, a Prioress, who smiled in an unaffected and quiet way; . . . At table she showed her good breeding at every point: she never let a crumb fall from her mouth or wetted her fingers by dipping them too deeply into the sauce; and when she lifted the food to her lips she took care not to spill a single drop upon her breast. Etiquette was her passion. So scrupulously did she wipe her upper lip that no spot of grease was to be seen in her cup after she had drunk from it; and when she ate she reached daintily for her food. Indeed she was most gay, pleasant and friendly. She took pains to imitate courtly behaviour and cultivate a dignified bearing so as to be thought a person deserving of respect. Speaking of her sensibility, she was so tender-hearted and compassionate that she would weep whenever she saw a mouse caught in a trap, especially if it were bleeding or dead. . . .

With her she had another NUN, her chaplain and three PRIESTS.

There was a remarkable fine-looking MONK, who acted as estate-steward to his monastery and loved hunting: a manly man, well fitted to be an abbot. He kept plenty of fine horses in his stable, and when he went out riding people could hear the bells on his bridle jingling in the whistling wind as clear and loud as the chapel bell of the small convent of which he was the head. Because the Rule of St Maur or of St Benedict was old-fashioned and somewhat strict, this Monk neglected the old precepts and followed the modern custom. He did not give two pins for the text which says hunters cannot be holy men, or that a monk who is heedless of his Rule—that is to say a monk out of his cloister—is like a fish out of water. In his view this saying was not worth a bean; and I told him his opinion was sound. Why should he study and addle his wits with everlasting poring over a book in cloisters, or work with his hands, or toil as St Augustine commanded? How is the world to be served? Let St Augustine keep his hard labour for himself! Therefore the Monk, whose whole pleasure lay in riding and the hunting of the hare (over which he spared no expense) remained a hard rider and kept greyhounds swift as birds. . . .

Next there was a MERCHANT with a forked beard who rode seated on a high saddle, wearing a many-coloured dress, boots fastened with neat handsome clasps, and upon his head a Flanders beaver hat. He gave out his opinions with great pomposity and never stopped talking about the increase of his profits. In his view the high seas between Harwich and Holland should be cleared of pirates at all costs. He was an expert at the exchange of currency. This worthy citizen used his head to the best advantage, conducting his money-lending and other financial transactions in a dignified manner; none guessed he was in debt. He was really a most estimable man; but to tell the truth his name escapes me. . . .

With us there was a good religious man, a poor PARSON, but rich in holy thoughts and acts. He was also a learned man, a scholar, who truly preached Christ's Gospel and taught his parishioners devoutly. Benign, hardworking, and patient in adversity—as had often been put to the test—he was loath to excommunicate those who failed to pay their tithes. To tell the truth he would rather give to the poor of his parish what had been offered him by the rich, or from his own pocket; for he managed to live on very little. Wide as was his parish, with houses few and far between, neither rain nor thunder nor sickness nor misfortune stopped him from going on foot, staff in hand, to visit his most distant parishioners, high or low. To his flock he set this noble example: first he practised, then he preached. . . . He never looked for ceremony and deference, nor was his conscience of the over-scrupulous and specious sort. He taught the Gospel of Christ and His twelve apostles: but first he followed it himself.

The Goodman of Paris: Instructions on Being a Good Wife

Sources on the history of women during the Late Middle Ages are not abundant, and only recently have historians engaged in a fuller search for them. An exception is the relatively well known Goodman of Paris. Written in the form of a letter by a Parisian merchant to his wife, it was an idealized manual of the duties of a wealthy wife from the point of view of an anonymous merchant. In the following excerpt from this late-fourteenth-century work, the author introduces and outlines what he will be discussing.

CONSIDER: *The position and role of women at this time according to this document; the purposes of marriage according to this author.*

THE FIRST SECTION

The first section of the three is necessary to gain the love of God and the salvation of your soul, and also to win the love of your husband and to give you in this world that peace which should be in marriage. And because these two things, namely the salvation of your soul and the comfort of your husband, be the two things most chiefly necessary, therefore are they here placed first. And this first section contains nine articles.

The first article speaketh of worshipping and thanking our Saviour and his Blessed Mother at your waking and your rising, and of apparelling yourself seemingly.

The second article is of fit companions, and of going to Church, and of choosing your place, of wise behaviour, of hearing mass and of making confession.

The third article is that you should love God and his Blessed Mother and serve them continually and set and keep yourself in their grace.

The fourth article is that you should dwell in continence and chastity, after the ensample of Susanna, of Lucrece, and others.

The fifth article is that you should love your husband (whether myself or another) after the ensample of Sarah, Rebecca and Rachel.

The sixth article is that you should be humble and obedient to him after the ensample of Griselda, of the woman who would not rescue her husband from drowning, and of the Mother of God who answered "fiat" etc., of Lucifer, of the *puys*, of the bailly of Tournay, of the monks and the husbands, of madame d'Andresel, of Chaumont and of the Roman woman.

The seventh that you be careful and heedful of his person.

The eighth that you be silent in hiding his secrets, after the ensample of Papirius, of the woman who laid eight eggs, of the Venetian woman, of the woman who returned from St James (of Compestollo), and of the advocate.

The ninth and last article showeth that if your husband try to act foolishly or so acteth, you must wisely and humbly withdraw him therefrom, like unto Melibeus and dame Jehanne la Quentine.

THE SECOND SECTION

The second section is necessary to increase the profit of the household, gain friends and save one's possessions; to succour and aid oneself against the ill fortunes of age to come, and it contains six [*sic*] articles.

The first article is that you have care of your household, with diligence and perseverence and regard for work; take pains to find pleasure therein and I will do likewise on my part, and so shall we reach the castle whereof it is spoken.

The second article is that at the least you take pleasure and have some little skill in the care and cultivation of a garden, grafting in due season and keeping roses in winter.

The third article is that you know how to choose varlets, doorkeepers, handymen or other strong folk to perform the heavy work that from hour to hour must be done, and likewise labourers etc. And also tailers, shoemakers, bakers, pastry-makers, etc. And in particular how to set the household varlets and chambermaids to work, to sift and winnow grain, clean dresses, air and dry, and how to order your folk to take thought for the sheep and horses and to keep and amend wines.

The fourth article is that you, as sovereign mistress of your house, know how to order dinners, suppers, dishes and courses, and be wise in that which concerns the butcher and the poulterer, and have knowledge of spices.

The fifth article is that you know how to order, ordain, devise and have made all manner of pottages, civeys, sauces and all other meats, and the same for sick folk.

THE THIRD SECTION

The third section tells of games and amusements that be pleasant enough to keep you in countenance and give you something to talk about in company, and contains three articles.

The first article is all concerned with amusing questions, which be shown forth and answered in strange fashion by the hazard of dice and by rooks and kings.

The second article is to know how to feed and fly the falcon.

The third article tells of certain other riddles concerning counting and numbering, which be subtle to find out and guess.

SOURCE: Eileen Power, trans., *The Goodman of Paris* (London: Routledge & Kegan Paul, 1928), pp. 43–46. Reprinted by permission.

The Church Besieged

Some of the problems facing the Church and its sense of being besieged by evil forces are illustrated in this fifteenth-century manuscript illumination (figure 11.1). In the center stands the pope protecting the Church. Above him in the Church, symbolized as a medieval fortress rising up toward the heavens, are Church officials who help defend the Church. The attackers in the foreground are heretics, as indicated by blindness that represents their inability to see the truth. They are flanked by attacking women who represent various cardinal sins.

CONSIDER: *The problems facing the Church and the appropriate cures according to this illumination; any connections between this illumination and the documents on the Conciliar Movement and heresy; how this illumination reveals attitudes toward women.*

The Triumph of Death

With war, famine, and especially plague striking fourteenth- and fifteenth-century Europe, death became a common theme of art. Typically, the plague was viewed as God's punishment

FIGURE 11.1 (© Bibliotheque des Arts Decoratifs, Paris, France/Archives Charmet/The Bridgeman Art Library)

for human sins, and thus only the Church might do something about the plague. Yet religion and everything else seemed impotent against death. This is shown in the numerous illustrations focusing on the theme of death. The engraving shown in figure 11.2 of The Triumph of Death, from Petrarch's Trionfi, was made by a Venetian artist between 1470 and 1480. Here king, clergy, and commoners all fall helplessly under Death's cart. The souls of the dead are taken either by angels, on the upper left, or devils, on the upper right.

CONSIDER: Attitudes toward death reflected by such popular scenes; any ways these scenes reflect attitudes similar to those revealed by Boccaccio.

Food and Crime

Chart 11.1 provides another indication of the disruptions affecting Europe in the fourteenth century. Here the rise and fall in the price of wheat and the number of crimes between 1300 and 1350 in Norfolk, England, are compared. Fluctuations in food supplies are thus revealed, as well as clear connections between the price of wheat and the number of crimes committed.

CONSIDER: How the information in this chart might relate to social, political, or even religious unrest.

Unrest in the Late Middle Ages

This map (map 11.1) gives some idea of the geographic extent of the social and religious unrest in

FIGURE 11.2 (© The British Museum)

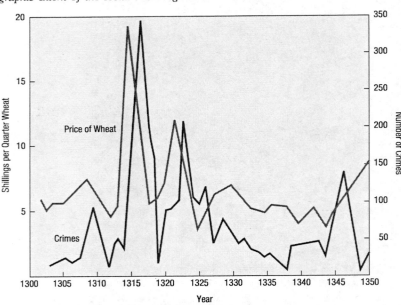

CHART 11.1 Crime and the Price of Wheat in Fourteenth-Century Norfolk, England

fourteenth-century Europe. England was affected by a combination of urban and rural revolts as well as religious heresy. Their geographic locations suggest that the revolts and the heresy may have been connected. What is not shown on this map would also add to the picture of turmoil and unrest: the numerous political and military disturbances, the religious divisions of the Great Schism (1378–1417), the spread of the plague, and the actual disappearance of settlements founded in the three preceding centuries.

CONSIDER: Connections among political disturbances, religious divisions, plagues, and population loss that could be revealed by maps.

MAP 11.1   Social and Religious Unrest in Fourteenth-Century Europe.

Secondary Sources

The Crisis of the Late Middle Ages

Francis Oakley

Most historians agree that during the fourteenth and fifteenth centuries, medieval civilization suffered a crisis. What are less clear are the exact nature of that crisis and its causes. In the following selection Francis Oakley focuses on problems within the Church, wars, and economic difficulties as being the core of the crisis of the Late Middle Ages.

CONSIDER: *Whether the problems within the Church should be considered causes or symptoms of the general crisis; the social consequences of wars and economic depression.*

One of the most persistent features of ecclesiastical life from the early fourteenth century onward had been the extension once more of royal or princely control over the

SOURCE: Reprinted with the permission of Charles Scribner's Sons, an imprint of Macmillan Publishing Company, from *The Medieval Experience* by Francis Oakley. Copyright © 1974 Francis Oakley.

local churches. In ways subtle and not so subtle the work of the Gregorian reformers was being undone, and rulers were moved increasingly to assert their sovereign jurisdiction over all groups and institutions—clergy and churches included—within the territorial boundaries of their states. By the early fifteenth century the kings of France and England, in particular, had become adept at the art of marshaling national antipapal feeling in order to bring pressure on the papacy to concede them a handsome share of the taxes levied on their national churches and of the benefices or ecclesiastical positions belonging thereto. Given the difficulties that the Avignonese popes and the popes of the schism had had to face, they had had little choice but to yield to such diplomatic blackmail, even though by so doing they had committed the church piecemeal to a revolution that would ultimately leave to their successors nothing more than a theoretically supreme authority, the substance of power having passed in fact into the hands of kings, princes, and rulers of city-states like Venice. . . .

Historians have frequently chosen to take this transformation of the church and the accompanying decline of papal fortunes as symptomatic of a more profound crisis in the very soul of medieval civilization itself. It is easy enough to understand why they should have been tempted to do so. The outbreak in 1296 of the war between France and England, which had led so rapidly to the disastrous confrontation with Boniface VIII, had marked the end of a comparatively peaceful era and the beginning of the prolonged struggle between the two major European powers, which, punctuated with intermittent truces and periods of peace, was to drag on well into the fifteenth century. While it lasted it caused a great deal of devastation in France and sponsored in that country a recrudescence of the aristocratic feuds and rival private armies characteristic of the anarchic early phase of feudalism. A similar growth of what has been called "bastard feudalism" occurred in England during the dynastic conflicts between the Yorkist and Lancastrian claimants to the throne which broke out in 1450 after the end of the war with France and which have gone down in history as the "Wars of the Roses." The fourteenth and fifteenth centuries marked, then, at best a pause in the development of the English and French states and at worst a positive setback. Certainly, they witnessed the breakdown of public order and the growth of violence to a degree that would have been unimaginable in the late thirteenth century.

To the social dislocations caused by invasion and civil war must also be added the tribulations consequent to the ending in the early fourteenth century of the great economic boom that had gathered force in the tenth century, accelerated in the eleventh and twelfth centuries, and reached its peak in the thirteenth. Even before the advent of the Black Death (1348–50), population expansion

had ceased, serious and widespread famines had reappeared, and the European economy had begun to slide into a financial crisis and a depression that was to last until the latter part of the fifteenth century and even, in some sectors, into the sixteenth.

The Black Death: A Socioeconomic Perspective

Millard Meiss

Historians have argued that the Black Death, along with other mid-fourteenth-century developments, led to important economic and social changes that characterized the Late Middle Ages. Most concretely, historians point to increasing wages and greater opportunities for social mobility as directly stimulated by the demographic ravages of the plague. In the following selection Millard Meiss makes this interpretation in examining the consequences of the plague in Florence and Siena.

CONSIDER: *The economic and social consequences of the Black Death in northern Italy; the groups that benefited most after the Black Death, and why; the ways in which this interpretation is supported by Boccaccio's account.*

In the immediate wake of the Black Death we hear of an unparalleled abundance of food and goods, and of a wild, irresponsible life of pleasure. Agnolo di Tura writes that in Siena "everyone tended to enjoy eating and drinking, hunting, hawking, and gaming," and Matteo Villani laments similar behavior in Florence. . . .

This extraordinary condition of plenty did not, of course, last very long. For most people the frenzied search for immediate gratification, characteristic of the survivors of calamities, was likewise short-lived. Throughout the subsequent decades, however, we continue to hear of an exceptional difference to accepted patterns of behavior and to institutional regulations, especially among the mendicant friars. It seems, as we shall see, that the plague tended to promote an unconventional, irresponsible, or self-indulgent life, on the one hand, and a more intense piety or religious excitement, on the other. Villani tells us, in his very next sentences, of the more lasting consequences of the epidemic:

"Men thought that, through the death of so many people, there would be abundance of all produce of the land; yet, on the contrary, by reason of men's ingratitude, everything came to unwonted scarcity and remained long thus; . . . most commodities were more costly, by twice or more, than before the plague. And the price of labor, and

SOURCE: From Meiss, Millard, *Painting in Florence and Sienna After the Black Death*, pp. 67–69. Copyright © 1978 by Princeton University Press. Reprinted by permission of Princeton University Press.

the products of every trade and craft, rose in disorderly fashion beyond the double. Lawsuits and disputes and quarrels and riots arose everywhere among citizens in every land, by reason of legacies and successions; . . . Wars and divers scandals arose throughout the world, contrary to men's expectation."

Conditions were similar in Siena. Prices rose to unprecedented levels. The economy of both Florence and Siena was further disrupted during these years by the defection of almost all the dependent towns within the little empire of each city. These towns seized as an opportunity for revolt the fall of the powerful Florentine oligarchy in 1343, and the Sienese in 1355. The two cities, greatly weakened, and governed by groups that pursued a less aggressive foreign policy, made little attempt to win them back.

The small towns and the countryside around the two cities were not decimated so severely by the epidemic, but the people in these regions felt the consequences of it in another way. Several armies of mercenaries of the sort that all the large states had come to employ in the fourteenth century took advantage of the weakness of the cities. . . .

The ravages of the mercenary companies accelerated a great wave of immigration from the smaller towns and farms into the cities that had been initiated by the Black Death. Most of the newcomers were recruits for the woolen industry, who were attracted by relatively high wages. But the mortality offered exceptional opportunities also for notaries, jurists, physicians, and craftsmen. In both Florence and Siena the laws controlling immigration were relaxed, and special privileges, a rapid grant of citizenship, or exemption from taxes were offered to badly needed artisans or professional men, such as physicians. . . .

In addition to bringing into the city great numbers of people from the surrounding towns and country, the Black Death affected the character of Florentine society in still another way. Through irregular inheritance and other exceptional circumstances, a class of *nouveaux riches* arose in the town and also in decimated Siena. Their wealth was accentuated by the impoverishment of many of the older families, such as the Bardi and the Peruzzi, who had lost their fortunes in the financial collapse. In both cities, too, many tradesmen and artisans were enriched to a degree unusual for the *popolo minuto*. Scaramella sees as one of the major conflicts of the time the struggle between the old families and this *gente nuova*. Outcries against both foreigners and the newly rich, never lacking in the two cities, increased in volume and violence. Antagonism to "the aliens and the ignorant" coalesced with antagonism to the new municipal regime; the government, it was said, had been captured by them.

A Psychological Perspective of the Black Death
William L. Langer

Most historians have long been reluctant to view historical developments from a psychological perspective. In recent decades historians have been challenged to apply psychological insights to history. In 1957 William L. Langer, then president of the American Historical Association, issued such a challenge to historians in his presidential address to the annual convention. In the following selection from that address, Langer suggests how modern psychology might be used to interpret the Black Death and related developments.

CONSIDER: *How a psychologist might explain various behaviors related to the Black Death; how* The Triumph of Death *fits with this interpretation.*

The Black Death was worse than anything experienced prior to that time and was, in all probability, the greatest single disaster that has ever befallen European mankind. In most localities a third or even a half of the population was lost within the space of a few months, and it is important to remember that the great visitation of 1348–1349 was only the beginning of a period of pandemic disease with a continuing frightful drain of population. . . .

At news of the approach of the disease a haunting terror seizes the population, in the Middle Ages leading on the one hand to great upsurges of repentance in the form of flagellant processions and on the other to a mad search for scapegoats, eventuating in large-scale pogroms of the Jews. The most striking feature of such visitations has always been the precipitate flight from the cities, in which not only the wealthier classes but also town officials, professors and teachers, clergy, and even physicians took part. The majority of the population, taking the disaster as an expression of God's wrath, devoted itself to penitential exercises, to merciful occupations, and to such good works as the repair of churches and the founding of religious houses. On the other hand, the horror and confusion in many places brought general demoralization and social breakdown. Criminal elements were quick to take over, looting the deserted houses and even murdering the sick in order to rob them of their jewels. Many, despairing of the goodness and mercy of God, gave themselves over to riotous living, resolved, as Thucydides says, "to get out of life the pleasures which could be had speedily and which would satisfy their lusts, regarding their bodies and their wealth alike as transitory." Drunkenness and sexual immorality were the order of the day. "In one

SOURCE: William L. Langer, "The Next Assignment," *The American Historical Review*, vol. LXIII, no. 2 (January 1958), pp. 292–293, 295–298. Reprinted by permission.

house," reported an observer of the London plague of 1665, "you might hear them roaring under the pangs of death, in the next tippling, whoring and belching out blasphemies against God." . . .

The age was marked, as all admit, by a mood of misery, depression, and anxiety, and by a general sense of impending doom. Numerous writers in widely varying fields have commented on the morbid preoccupation with death, the macabre interest in tombs, the gruesome predilection for the human corpse. Among painters the favorite themes were Christ's passion, the terrors of the Last Judgment, and the tortures of Hell, all depicted with ruthless realism and with an almost loving devotion to each repulsive detail. Altogether characteristic was the immense popularity of the Dance of Death woodcuts and murals, with appropriate verses, which appeared soon after the Black Death and which, it is agreed, expressed the sense of the immediacy of death and the dread of dying unshriven. Throughout the fifteenth and sixteenth centuries these pitilessly naturalistic pictures ensured man's constant realization of his imminent fate.

The origins of the Dance of Death theme have been generally traced to the Black Death and subsequent epidemics, culminating in the terror brought on by the outbreak of syphilis at the end of the fifteenth century. Is it unreasonable, then, to suppose that many of the other phenomena I have mentioned might be explained, at least in part, in the same way? We all recognize the late Middle Ages as a period of popular religious excitement or overexcitement, of pilgrimages and penitential processions, of mass preaching, of veneration of relics and adoration of saints, of lay piety and popular mysticism. It was apparently also a period of unusual immorality and

shockingly loose living, which we must take as the continuation of the "devil-may-care" attitude of one part of the population. This the psychologists explain as the repression of unbearable feelings by accentuating the value of a diametrically opposed set of feelings and then behaving as though the latter were the real feelings. But the most striking feature of the age was an exceptionally strong sense of guilt and a truly dreadful fear of retribution, seeking expression in a passionate longing for effective intercession and in a craving for direct, personal experience of the Deity, as well as in a corresponding dissatisfaction with the Church and with the mechanization of the means of salvation as reflected, for example, in the traffic in indulgences.

These attitudes, along with the great interest in astrology, the increased resort to magic, and the startling spread of witchcraft and Satanism in the fifteenth century were, according to the precepts of modern psychology, normal reactions to the sufferings to which mankind in that period was subjected.

⅋ CHAPTER QUESTIONS

1. If you wanted to interpret the Late Middle Ages as a period of decline, what arguments and evidence would you emphasize? If you wanted to interpret this period primarily as one of transition, what arguments and evidence would you emphasize?

2. In what ways was the general character of the Late Middle Ages exemplified by the plague and reactions to it?

Late Middle Ages						
Italian Renaissance						
				Northern Renaissance		
1300	**1350**	**1400**	**1450**	**1500**	**1550**	
		Vergerio		Da Vinci		
	Petrarch	Christine de Pizan			The Prince / The Courtier	
Giotto				"School of Athens"		
		Van Eyck		Raphael		
				Machiavelli		
				Michelangelo		

12 The Renaissance

Although in many ways a period of decline and disintegration, the Late Middle Ages also witnessed an extraordinary outburst of cultural and intellectual creativity known as the Renaissance. The Renaissance started in the fourteenth century in the cities of northern Italy, where scholars and a social elite became more interested in the literature and ideas of ancient Greece and Rome. As interest in Classical civilization grew, so did a tendency to reject many of the ideas and practices of medieval civilization. While remaining deeply religious, people of the Renaissance concerned themselves more with the secular, physical world than medieval people did. The term that best encompasses the meaning of the Renaissance is *humanism:* a new concern with people as powerful, creative individuals in a dynamic secular world. All this was

reflected in the literature, art, and societies of northern Italian cities from the fourteenth century through the beginning of the sixteenth century, when invasions and other problems led to a decline of the Renaissance in Italy.

In Northern Europe the Renaissance started during the fifteenth century and lasted through most of the sixteenth century. This Renaissance was heavily influenced by the earlier Italian Renaissance; indeed, it was common for people to travel south across the Alps and return north with the ideas and styles they were exposed to in northern Italy. Nevertheless, the Northern Renaissance had some roots and characteristics that distinguished it from the Italian Renaissance. Above all, it was more integrated with Christian concerns. For example, more emphasis was placed on learning Classical languages to improve translations of the

Bible, studying Classical literature for its relation to Christian ideals and life, and producing artistic creations with predominantly religious themes.

This chapter concentrates on one broad issue: the Renaissance. Examined here are traits historians define as typical of the Renaissance, such as literary humanism, humanistic education, and humanism in general. What was literary humanism? How was the development of humanism reflected in educational changes such as the new emphasis on the liberal arts? What problems were faced by those involved in humanism? Artistic and political trends that reflect this humanism are also explored. In what ways did Renaissance art differ from medieval art? How are some of the main elements of the Renaissance reflected in the art of the period? How did political theory mirror characteristics of the Renaissance? What was the nature of the

Renaissance in the North? How were some of the connections between medieval concerns and Renaissance style reflected in the art of the Northern Renaissance? Above all, the materials concern efforts by people of that time as well as modern scholars to distinguish the Renaissance as a whole from the preceding Middle Ages. How did important figures of the Italian Renaissance view the Middle Ages? How sharp was the break, if any, with the Middle Ages? How should the Renaissance be interpreted as a whole? Efforts to answer questions such as these have caused considerable scholarly disagreement, most notably over the interpretation by Jacob Burckhardt, which emphasizes the modernity and distinctness of the Italian Renaissance. Secondary sources exemplify this tradition of controversy over the meaning of the Renaissance.

 Primary Sources

A Letter to Boccaccio: Literary Humanism

Francesco Petrarch

Literary humanism, a movement to revive Classical literature and the values expressed in Classical writings, was central to the early Renaissance. This trend, which originated in northern Italy during the fourteenth century, represented a broadening in focus from otherworldly concerns and people as religious beings, which was typical of the Middle Ages, to include the problems of people and nature in this world. The individual most commonly associated with it and perhaps most responsible for its spread was the Florentine Francesco Petrarch (1304–1374). Best known for his love sonnets to Laura, he also collected and translated many Classical works and wrote numerous letters— often extolling the Classical authors and even writing in their style. In the following selection from a 1362 letter to his friend Boccaccio, Petrarch offered reassurance and responded to charges typically made against humanistic learning.

CONSIDER: *The nature of the charges Petrarch is refuting; how Petrarch related humanism to religion; Petrarch's perception of the benefits of literary humanism.*

Neither exhortations to virtue nor the argument of approaching death should divert us from literature; for in a good mind it excites the love of virtue, and dissipates, or

SOURCE: James Harvey Robinson and Henry Winchester Rolfe, *Petrarch: The First Modern Scholar and Man of Letters* (New York: Haskell House, 1898), pp. 391–395.

at least diminishes, the fear of death. To desert our studies shows want of self-confidence rather than wisdom, for letters do not hinder but aid the properly constituted mind which possesses them; they facilitate our life, they do not retard it. Just as many kinds of food which lie heavy on an enfeebled and nauseated stomach furnish excellent nourishment for one who is well but famishing, so in our studies many things which are deadly to the weak mind may prove most salutary to an acute and healthy intellect, especially if in our use of both food and learning we exercise proper discretion. If it were otherwise, surely the zeal of certain persons who persevered to the end could not have roused such admiration. Cato, I never forget, acquainted himself with Latin literature as he was growing old, and Greek when he had really become an old man. Varro, who reached his hundredth year still reading and writing, parted from life sooner than from his love of study. Livius Drusus, although weakened by age and afflicted with blindness, did not give up his interpretation of the civil law, which he carried on to the great advantage of the state. . . .

Besides these and innumerable others like them, have not all those of our own religion whom we should wish most to imitate devoted their whole lives to literature, and grown old and died in the same pursuit? Some, indeed, were overtaken by death while still at work reading or writing. To none of them, so far as I know, did it prove a disadvantage to be noted for secular learning. . . .

While I know that many have become famous for piety without learning, at the same time I know of no one who has been prevented by literature from following the path of holiness. The apostle Paul was, to be sure, accused of having his head turned by study, but the world has long ago passed its verdict upon this accusation. If I may be allowed to speak for myself, it seems to me that, although the path to virtue by the way of ignorance may be plain, it fosters sloth. The goal of all good people is the same, but the ways of reaching it are many and various. Some advance slowly, others with more spirit; some obscurely, others again conspicuously. One takes a lower, another a higher path. Although all alike are on the road to happiness, certainly the more elevated path is the more glorious. Hence ignorance, however devout, is by no means to be put on a plane with the enlightened devoutness of one familiar with literature. Nor can you pick me out from the whole array of unlettered saints, an example so holy that I cannot match it with a still holier one from the other group.

On the Liberal Arts

Peter Paul Vergerio

Closely associated with the rise of literary humanism was a new emphasis on the more broadly defined "liberal arts." This emphasis was manifested in a new concern with education; a change in educational curriculum constituted an institutional development that was enduring and that had wide-ranging effects. The first to express this emphasis systematically in an educational program was Peter Paul Vergerio (1370–1444). He taught in several Italian universities, and in his main treatise, On the Liberal Arts, *he rejected much of the content and methods of medieval education. Vergerio presents his views on the growing importance of the liberal arts in the following selection from a letter written to Ubertinus of Carrara.*

CONSIDER: *What is particularly humanistic rather than scholastic or medieval about this view; how Vergerio justifies his choice of the three subjects in this proposed curriculum; what Petrarch might think of this letter.*

Your grandfather, Francesco I, a man distinguished for his capacity in affairs and for his sound judgment, was in the habit of saying that a parent owes three duties to his children. The first of these is to bestow upon them names of which they need not feel ashamed. For not seldom, out of caprice, or even indifference, or perhaps from a wish to perpetuate a family name, a father in naming his child inflicts upon him a misfortune which clings to him for life. The second obligation is this: to provide that his child be brought up in a city of distinction, for this not only

concerns his future self-respect, but is closely connected with the third and most important care which is due from father to son. This is the duty of seeing that he be trained in sound learning. For no wealth, no possible security against the future, can be compared with the gift of an education in grave and liberal studies. By them a man may win distinction for the most modest name, and bring honour to the city of his birth however obscure it may be. But we must remember that whilst a man may escape from the burden of an unlucky name, or from the contempt attaching to a city of no repute, by changing the one or quitting the other, he can never remedy the neglect of early education. The foundation, therefore, of this last must be laid in the first years of life, the disposition moulded whilst it is susceptible and the mind trained whilst it is retentive.

This duty, common indeed to all parents, is specially incumbent upon such as hold high station. For the lives of men of position are passed, as it were, in public view; and are fairly expected to serve as witness to personal merit and capacity on the part of those who occupy such exceptional place amongst their fellow men. . . .

We come now to the consideration of the various subjects which may rightly be included under the name of "Liberal Studies." Amongst these I accord the first place to History, on grounds both of its attractiveness and of its utility, qualities which appeal equally to the scholar and to the statesman. Next in importance ranks Moral Philosophy, which indeed is, in a peculiar sense, a "Liberal Art," in that its purpose is to teach men the secret of true freedom. History, then, gives us the concrete examples of the precepts inculcated by philosophy. The one shews what men should do, the other what men have said and done in the past, and what practical lessons we may draw therefrom for the present day. I would indicate as the third main branch of study, Eloquence, which indeed holds a place of distinction amongst the refined Arts. By philosophy we learn the essential truth of things, which by eloquence we so exhibit in orderly adornment as to bring conviction to differing minds. And history provides the light of experience— cumulative wisdom fit to supplement the force of reason and the persuasion of eloquence. For we allow that soundness of judgment, wisdom of speech, integrity of conduct are the marks of a truly liberal temper.

The City of Ladies

Christine de Pizan

Most of the great cultural figures of the Renaissance were men. Nevertheless, some women were able to produce works, achieve recognition, and defend women against male

SOURCE: From William Harrison Woodward, *Vittorino da Feltre and Other Humanist Educators* (Cambridge, England: Cambridge University Press; New York: Bureau of Publications, Teachers College, Columbia University, 1963), pp. 96–97, 106–107. Reprinted by permission.

SOURCE: Excerpts from *The Book of the City of Ladies* by Christine de Pizan, translated by Rosalind Brown-Grant (New York: Penguin Putnam, Inc., 1999), pp. 29, 30, 139–141.

detractors. *The most famous of these was Christine de Pizan (c. 1363–c. 1431). Born in Venice, she moved with her family to Paris, where her father became a physician and astrologer at the French royal court. Unusually well educated, she wrote several poems and books, the most widely read of which was* The City of Ladies *(1405). In the following excerpt Christine de Pizan questions an allegorical figure representing Lady Reason about women's political and educational abilities and about men's low opinions of women.*

CONSIDER: *What the common assumptions and arguments about women are; how Christine de Pizan attacks those assumptions and arguments; ways in which her writing embodies traits of the Renaissance.*

35. *AGAINST THOSE WHO CLAIM THAT WOMEN AREN'T INTELLIGENT ENOUGH TO LEARN THE LAW.*

Even though God has often endowed many women with great intelligence, it would not be right for them to abandon their customary modesty and to go about bringing cases before a court, as there are already enough men to do so. Why send three men to carry a burden which two can manage quite comfortably?

"However, if there are those who maintain that women aren't *intelligent* enough to learn the law, I would contradict them by citing numerous examples of women of both the past and the present who were great philosophers and who excelled in many disciplines which are much more difficult than simply learning the laws and the statutes of men. I'll tell you more about these women in a moment. Moreover, in reply to those who think that women are lacking in the ability to govern wisely or to establish good customs, I'll give you examples from history of several worthy ladies who mastered these arts. To give you a better idea of what I'm saying, I'll even cite you a few women from your own time who were widowed and whose competence in organizing and managing their households after their husbands' deaths attests to the fact that an intelligent woman can succeed in any domain."

❧

36. *AGAINST THOSE WHO CLAIM IT IS NOT GOOD FOR WOMEN TO BE EDUCATED.*

After hearing these words I, Christine, said, "My lady, I can clearly see that much good has been brought into the world by women. Even if some wicked women have done evil things, it still seems to me that this is far outweighed by all the good that other women have done and continue to do. This is particularly true of those who are wise and well educated in either the arts or the sciences, whom we mentioned before. That's why I'm all the more amazed at the opinion of some men who state that they are completely opposed to their daughters, wives or other female relatives engaging in study, for fear that their morals will be corrupted."

Rectitude replied, "This should prove to you that not all men's arguments are based on reason, and that these men in particular are wrong. There are absolutely no grounds for assuming that knowledge of moral disciplines, which actually inculcate virtue, would have a morally corrupting effect. Indeed, there's no doubt whatsoever that such forms of knowledge correct one's vices and improve one's morals. How could anyone possibly think that by studying good lessons and advice one will be any the worse for it? This view is completely unthinkable and untenable. I'm not saying that it's a good idea for men or women to study sorcery or any other type of forbidden science, since the Holy Church did not ban people from practising them for nothing. However, it's just that it's not true to say that women will be corrupted by knowing what's right and proper. . . .

Therefore, it is not all men, especially not the most intelligent, who agree with the view that it is a bad idea to educate women. However, it's true that those who are not very clever come out with this opinion because they don't want women to know more than they do. Your own father, who was a great astrologer and philosopher, did not believe that knowledge of the sciences reduced a woman's worth. Indeed, as you know, it gave him great pleasure to see you take so readily to studying the arts. Rather, it was because your mother, as a woman, held the view that you should spend your time spinning like the other girls, that you did not receive a more advanced or detailed initiation into the sciences. But, as that proverb which we've already had occasion to quote says, "What is in our nature cannot be taken away.' Despite your mother's opposition, you did manage to glean some grains of knowledge from your studies, thanks to your own natural inclination for learning. It's obvious to me that you do not esteem yourself any less for having this knowledge: in fact, you seem to treasure it, and quite rightly so."

The Prince

Niccolò Machiavelli

The Italian Renaissance developed in an environment in which politics took on an increasingly competitive, secular tone. Within each Italian state, parties fought for power while at the same time the states fought each other for dominance or advantage. After 1492, Italy was invaded numerous times by Spain,

SOURCE: From *The Prince and the Discourses* by Niccolò Machiavelli, translated by Luigi Ricci and revised by E. R. P. Vincent (1935), pp. 56, 65–66, by permission of Oxford University Press.

France, and the Holy Roman Empire. These developments are reflected in the life and work of the great Renaissance political theorist Niccolò Machiavelli (1469–1527).

Born in Florence when it was under the rule of the Medicis, Machiavelli initiated his career in the Florentine civil service in 1498 during the period when the Medicis were out of power, replaced by a republican government. He rose to important diplomatic posts within the government, but was forced into retirement when the Medici family came back to power in 1512. He never gave up hope of returning to favor, and he wrote his most famous work, The Prince (1513), in part as an application to the Medici rulers for a job in the Florentine government. The book has since become a classic treatise in political theory, above all for the way that it divorces politics from theology and metaphysics. The following selections from The Prince illustrate its style and some of its main themes.

CONSIDER: *The ways in which this work reflects values or practices typical of the Renaissance; how these same principles might be applied to twentieth-century politics.*

It now remains to be seen what are the methods and rules for a prince as regards to his subjects and friends. And as I know that many have written of this, I fear that my writing about it may be deemed presumptuous, differing as I do, especially in this matter, from the opinions of others. But my intention being to write something of use to those who understand, it appears to me more proper to go to the real truth of the matter than to its imagination; and many have imagined republics and principalities which have never been seen or known to exist in reality; for how we live is so far removed from how we ought to live, that he who abandons what is done for what ought to be done, will rather learn to bring about his own ruin than his preservation. A man who wishes to make a profession of goodness in everything must necessarily come to grief among so many who are not good. Therefore it is necessary for a prince, who wishes to maintain himself, to learn how not to be good, and to use this knowledge and not use it, according to the necessity of the case. . . .

It is not, therefore, necessary for a prince to have all the above-named qualities, but it is very necessary to seem to have them. I would even be bold to say that to possess them and always to observe them is dangerous, but to appear to possess them is useful. Thus it is well to seem merciful, faithful, humane, sincere, religious, and also to be so; but you must have the mind so disposed that when it is needful to be otherwise you may be able to change to the opposite qualities. And it must be understood that a prince, and especially a new prince, cannot observe all those things which are considered good in men, being often obliged, in order to maintain the state, to act against faith, against charity, against humanity, and against religion. And, therefore, he must have a mind

disposed to adapt itself according to the wind, and as the variations of fortune dictate, and, as I said before, not deviate from what is good, if possible, but be able to do evil if constrained.

A prince must take great care that nothing goes out of his mouth which is not full of the above-named five qualities, and, to see and hear him, he should seem to be all mercy, faith, integrity, humanity, and religion. And nothing is more necessary than to seem to have this last quality, for men in general judge more by the eyes than by the hands, for every one can see, but very few have to feel. Everybody sees what you appear to be, few feel what you are, and those few will not dare to oppose themselves to the many, who have the majesty of the state to defend them; and in the actions of men, and especially of princes, from which there is no appeal, the end justifies the means. Let a prince therefore aim at conquering and maintaining the state, and the means will always be judged honourable and praised by every one, for the vulgar is always taken by appearances and the issue of the event; and the world consists only of the vulgar, and the few who are not vulgar are isolated when the many have a rallying point in the prince.

The Book of the Courtier
Baldesar Castiglione

In the Italian states, the most prestigious life took place in the courts of rulers. While Machiavelli wrote about methods and rules for the successful prince, others described the qualities necessary for men or women hoping to rise or maintain their position in court life. The most famous of these writers was the Italian diplomat Baldesar Castiglione (1478–1529), who wrote The Book of the Courtier *while a member of the Duke of Urbino's court. In the following excerpt, Castiglione describes first, the best qualities of the courtier—the ideal "Renaissance man"—and second, the virtues and actions best suited to women of the court.*

CONSIDER: *Why Castiglione considers noble birth important; what talents Castiglione thinks are most important for the courtier's success; how a woman's path to success at court differs from a man's.*

"Thus, I would have our Courtier born of a noble and genteel family; because it is far less becoming for one of low birth to fail to do virtuous things than for one of noble birth, who, should he stray from the path of his forebears, stains the family name, and not only fails to achieve anything but loses what has been achieved already. For noble birth is like a bright lamp that makes

SOURCE: Baldesar Castiglione, *The Book of the Courtier,* trans. by Charles S. Singleton (New York: Doubleday, 1959), pp. 28–30, 32–34, 70, 206.

manifest and visible deeds both good and bad, kindling and spurring on to virtue as much for fear of dishonor as for hope of praise. . . .

Besides his noble birth, I would wish the Courtier favored in this other respect, and endowed by nature not only with talent and with beauty of countenance and person, but with that certain grace which we call an 'air,' which shall make him at first sight pleasing and lovable to all who see him; and let this be an adornment informing and attending all his actions, giving the promise outwardly that such a one is worthy of the company and the favor of every great lord." . . .

"But to come to some particulars: I hold that the principal and true profession of the Courtier must be that of arms . . . which I wish him to exercise with vigor; and let him be known among the others as bold, energetic, and faithful to whomever he serves. . . . The more our Courtier excels in this art, the more will he merit praise; although I do not deem it necessary that he have the perfect knowledge of things and other qualities that befit a commander, for since this would launch us on too great a sea, we shall be satisfied, as we have said, if he have complete loyalty and an undaunted spirit, and be always seen to have them. . . .

Therefore, let the man we are seeking be exceedingly fierce, harsh, and always among the first, wherever the enemy is; and in every other place, humane, modest, reserved, avoiding ostentation above all things as well as that impudent praise of himself by which a man always arouses hatred and disgust in all who hear him."

"I would have him more than passably learned in letters, at least in those studies which we call the humanities. Let him be conversant not only with the Latin language, but with Greek as well, because of the abundance and variety of things that are so divinely written therein. Let him be versed in the poets, as well as in the orators and historians, and let him be practiced also in writing verse and prose, especially in our own vernacular; for, besides the personal satisfaction he will take in this, in this way he will never want for pleasant entertainment with the ladies, who are usually fond of such things. . . . These studies, moreover, will make him fluent, and (as Aristippus said to the tyrant) bold and self-confident in speaking with everyone. However, I would have our Courtier keep one precept firmly in mind, namely, in this as in everything else, to be cautious and reserved rather than forward, and take care not to get the mistaken notion that he knows something he does not know."

✄

I think that in her ways, manners, words, gestures, and bearing, a woman ought to be very unlike a man; for just as he must show a certain solid and sturdy manliness, so it is seemly for a woman to have a soft and delicate tenderness, with an air of womanly sweetness in her every movement, which, in her going and staying, and in whatever she says, shall always make her appear the woman without any resemblance to a man.

"Now, if this precept be added to the rules which these gentlemen have taught the Courtier, then I think she ought to be able to follow many such and adorn herself with the best accomplishments, as signor Gasparo says. For I hold that many virtues of the mind are as necessary to a woman as to a man; also, gentle birth; to avoid affectation, to be naturally graceful in all her actions, to be mannerly, clever, prudent, not arrogant, not envious, not slanderous, not vain, not contentious, not inept, to know how to gain and hold the favor of her mistress and of all others, to perform well and gracefully the exercises that are suitable for women. And I do think that beauty is more necessary to her than to the Courtier, for truly that woman lacks much who lacks beauty. Also she must be more circumspect, and more careful not to give occasion for evil being said of her, and conduct herself so that she may not only escape being sullied by guilt but even by the suspicion of it, for a woman has not so many ways of defending herself against false calumnies as a man has."

 Visual Sources

The School of Athens: Art and Classical Culture

Raphael

Raphael's famous fresco in the Vatican, The School of Athens, painted between 1508 and 1511, is one of the most revealing masterpieces of Renaissance art (figure 12.1). It shows the major Greek philosophers arranged in different positions and groups according to their philosophical inclinations. In the center stands Plato, pointing upward to confirm his commitment to his theory of ideas and holding a copy of his Timaeus in his left hand, and Aristotle, pointing downward to indicate his empirical orientation. Correspondingly, the left side of the painting is filled with metaphysical philosophers with a statue of Apollo (patron of poetry) overhead, while the right side shows physical scientists under a statue of Athena (goddess of reason). Socrates is on the left, counting out points on his fingers to a group of younger men. Sprawled on the steps in the center is Diogenes. At the lower left Phythagoras demonstrates his mathematics on a tablet. The figures of Classical authors and gods are actually portraits of Raphael's

FIGURE 12.1 (© Scala/Art Resource, NY)

contemporaries as well. The figure of Plato is probably Leonardo da Vinci. Writing in the center foreground is the brooding, pessimistic philosopher Heraclitus, a portrait of Michelangelo. On the right bending over a geometric diagram is Euclid, a portrait of the architect Bramante. Behind him Ptolemy holds a globe, while on the far right the artist, Raphael, looks out of the picture.

In content, then, this painting is a tribute to Greek philosophy, which played such an important role in the Italian Renaissance. However, it goes further. Raphael belonged to a group of thinkers and artists who met to discuss philosophy, much as in this picture, but as implied in the picture, both the Platonic and Aristotelian points of view were respected in the Renaissance. Moreover, the artists, architects, sculptors, philosophers, and writers who served as models for the figures in this painting knew and communicated with each other; thus this fresco displays the many interconnections of the cultural elite in northern Italy, particularly in Florence. Even this fresco's specific location in the Vatican is revealing. On the opposing wall is another fresco, Raphael's Disputa, which depicts the great Christian theologians of various eras. The placement of these two frescos symbolizes values characteristic of the Renaissance: glorification of pagan culture without

rejecting Christianity. Finally, the use of perspective and the newness of the architectural design exemplify the Renaissance traits of realism and bold innovation.

CONSIDER: The way in which this reflects a society and attitudes different from those of the Middle Ages.

Giovanni Arnolfini and His Bride: Symbolism and the Northern Renaissance

Jan van Eyck

It should not be concluded even in art that the Renaissance constituted a sudden and complete break with the past. Even when in style and subject matter paintings reflect the realism, humanism, and individualism of the Renaissance, they also reflect medieval assumptions and concerns that remained.

This can be seen in a Northern Renaissance masterpiece, Giovanni Arnolfini and His Bride, painted in 1434 by the Flemish artist Jan van Eyck (figure 12.2). The scene appears to be quite secular: Giovanni Arnolfini, an Italian businessman residing in Bruges, is standing with his bride in a private

FIGURE 12.2   (© Erich Lessing/Art Resource, NY)

bridal chamber taking marriage vows (at this time two people could contract a legitimate marriage outside the Church). Around them various objects that might typically be found in such a room are quite realistically depicted. To the medieval eye these objects have well-known symbolic meaning that give this scene considerable religious and cultural significance. The single lighted candle was the traditional nuptial candle, symbolizing Christ and implying divine light. The convex mirror reflected the chamber, testifying to the presence of two witnesses (one of whom was the artist, van Eyck, who tells us just above the mirror that "Jan van Eyck was here"), and represented the all-seeing eye of God. The shoes (to the left), so appropriate for the muddy streets of Bruges, are off, indicating that this couple is standing on holy ground. The dog in the foreground symbolizes fidelity. The ripening peaches to the left on the chest and windowsill represent fertility and perhaps paradise lost. On the post of a chair near the bed is a carved Margaret, patron saint of childbirth. The pose of the couple suggests relationships between husband and wife: He is dominating by his frontal pose; she is deferentially turned toward him.

Thus this painting is both a realistic depiction of two individuals with distinct personalities (as revealed particularly in their faces) in a natural setting and a symbolic representation of the meanings of marriage in the fifteenth century, with all its religious implications. And that this is a portrait of an Italian merchant and his bride in a room furnished with items coming from all areas of Europe, in Bruges, a northern center of banking and commerce, reflects the growing importance and wealth of the middle class and international trade during this period.

CONSIDER: The ways this reflects a society and attitudes similar to those of the Middle Ages.

Wealth, Culture, and Diplomacy
Hans Holbein

Hans Holbein's 1533 painting, The Ambassadors (figure 12.3), reveals the mixture of wealth, culture, and power that were key elements of the Renaissance. It depicts two sumptuously dressed French ambassadors at the Court of King Henry VII of England. Their clothes and stance stress the growing prestige and importance of diplomats in furthering the interests of states. The man on the right is also a French bishop. Part of their mission was to broker an accord between the Catholic church and the Lutheran-sympathizing English monarchy, and the failure of that accord is indicated by the lute (representing the hoped-for harmony) resting on the lower shelf of the table between the two men and its broken string that lies next to the open Lutheran hymn-book. Next to the lute is a terrestrial globe, a surveyor's square, a pair of compasses, and a merchant's arithmetic book, all stressing the themes of intellectual, commercial, and territorial discovery as well as the conflict for lands and wealth among the European powers that were so important during the Renaissance. On the top shelf are instruments and a celestial globe representing the growing interest in understanding the heavens, time, place, and navigation. As a whole, the painting testifies to the cosmopolitan and competitive qualities of Renaissance life and politics among Europe's elites.

CONSIDER: How this painting might fit with the themes of Renaissance humanism and individualism; the significance of Holbein, a German artist, painting this canvas of (and for) French diplomats who were stationed in England.

SOURCE: Hans Holbein, *The Ambassadors*. London, The National Gallery.

Secondary Sources

The Civilization of the Renaissance in Italy
Jacob Burckhardt

Modern interpretations of the Renaissance almost uniformly start with the Swiss historian Jacob Burckhardt's The Civilization of the Renaissance in Italy, first published in 1860. Burckhardt rejected a chronological approach and pictured the Italian Renaissance of the fourteenth and fifteenth centuries as a whole, strikingly distinct from the preceding Middle Ages and clearly a superior civilization. Until the 1920s, historians almost unanimously accepted his interpretation. After that time various aspects of his thesis were attacked, particularly by medievalists. In recent decades, however, Burckhardt's work has gained new respectability, at least as an idealized cultural history of the Italian Renaissance. In any case, all historians who approach this topic must deal with Burckhardt's argument, some of the central points of which appear in the following excerpt.

CONSIDER: What most distinguishes the Italian Renaissance from the preceding Middle Ages according to Burckhardt; any support the primary documents might provide for this argument; how a proud medievalist might respond to this argument.

SOURCE: Jacob Burckhardt, *The Civilization of the Renaissance in Italy*, trans. S. G. C. Middlemore (London: George Allen and Unwin, Ltd.; New York: The Macmillan Co., 1890), p. 129.

FIGURE 12.3 (© Erich Lessing/Art Resource, NY)

In the Middle Ages both sides of human consciousness—that which was turned within as that which was turned without—lay dreaming or half awake beneath a common veil. The veil was woven of faith, illusion, and childish prepossession, through which the world and history were seen clad in strange hues. Man was conscious of himself only as a member of a race, people, party, family, or corporation—only through some general category. In Italy this veil first melted into air; an *objective* treatment and consideration of the state and of all the things of this world became possible. The *subjective* side at the same time asserted itself with corresponding emphasis; man became a spiritual *individual*, and recognised himself as

such. In the same way the Greek had once distinguished himself from the barbarian, and the Arabian had felt himself an individual at a time when other Asiatics knew themselves only as members of a race. . . .

In far earlier times we can here and there detect a development of free personality which in Northern Europe either did not occur at all, or could not display itself in the same manner. . . . But at the close of the thirteenth century Italy began to swarm with individuality; the charm laid upon human personality was dissolved; and a thousand figures meet us each in its own special shape and dress. Dante's great poem would have been impossible in any other country of Europe, if only for the reason that they all still lay under the spell of race. For Italy the august poet, through the wealth of individuality which he set forth, was the most national herald of his time. But this unfolding of the treasures of human nature in literature and art—this many-sided representation and criticism—will be discussed in separate chapters; here we have to deal only with the psychological fact itself. This fact appears in the most decisive and unmistakable form. The Italians of the fourteenth century knew little of false modesty or of hypocrisy in any shape; not one of them was afraid of singularity, of being and seeming unlike his neighbours.

The Myth of the Renaissance
Peter Burke

Many historians attacked Burckhardt's interpretation and the legacy built up around it. These historians argued that Burckhardt overemphasized how modern the Renaissance was. They stressed how much the Renaissance, even in Italy, was still part of the medieval world. Other historians have responded that criticisms of Burckhardt go too far. In the following selection Peter Burke criticizes Burckhardt's idea of the Renaissance as a myth and describes the main objections to it.

CONSIDER: *Why, according to Burke, Burckhardt's idea of the Renaissance is a myth; how a supporter of Burckhardt might respond; whether the sources give greater support to Burckhardt's or Burke's interpretation.*

Jacob Burckhardt defined the period in terms of two concepts, "individualism" and "modernity." "In the Middle Ages," according to Burckhardt, "human consciousness . . . lay dreaming or half awake beneath a common veil. . . . Man was conscious of himself only as a member of a race, people, party, family, or corporation—only through some general category." In Renaissance Italy, however, "this veil first melted into air . . . man became a spiritual *individual,* and recognised himself as such." Renaissance meant modernity. The Italian was, Burckhardt wrote, "the first-born among the sons of modern Europe." The fourteenth-century poet Petrarch was "one of the first truly modern men." The great renewal of art and ideas began in Italy, and at a later stage the new attitudes and the new artistic forms spread to the rest of Europe.

This idea of the Renaissance is a myth. . . .

Burckhardt's mistake was to accept the scholars and artists of the period at their own valuation, to take this story of rebirth at its face value and to elaborate it into a book. To the old formulae of the restoration of the arts and the revival of classical antiquity, he added new ones such as individualism, realism, and modernity. . . .

This nineteenth-century myth of the Renaissance is still taken seriously by many people. Television companies and organisers of package tours still make money out of it. However, professional historians have become dissatisfied with this version of the Renaissance, even if they continue to find the period and the movement attractive. The point is that the grand edifice erected by Burckhardt and his contemporaries has not stood the test of time. More exactly, it has been undermined by the researches of the medievalists in particular. Their arguments depend on innumerable points of detail, but they are of two main kinds.

In the first place, there are arguments to the effect that so-called "Renaissance men" were really rather medieval. They were more traditional in their behaviour, assumptions and ideals than we tend to think—and also more traditional than they saw themselves. Hindsight suggests that even Petrarch, "one of the first truly modern men," according to Burckhardt, had many attitudes in common with the centuries he described as "dark." . . .

In the second place, the medievalists have accumulated arguments to the effect that the Renaissance was not such a singular event as Burckhardt and his contemporaries once thought and that the term should really be used in the plural. There were various "renascences" in the Middle Ages, notably in the twelfth century and in the age of Charlemagne. In both cases there was a combination of literary and artistic achievements with a revival of interest in classical learning, and in both cases contemporaries described their age as one of restoration, rebirth or "renovation."

Machiavelli and the Renaissance
Federico Chabod

Reactions to and appreciations of Machiavelli's thought in The Prince *form an apparently contradictory history in themselves. On the one hand, few thinkers in the history of political theory rank more highly than Machiavelli; he is recognized as being the first modern political theorist. On the other hand, there is a more popular tradition of rejecting his ideas as immoral; the term* Machiavellian *is pejorative, referring to political opportunism and ruthlessness. In the following selection Federico Chabod, an Italian historian who has written extensively on Machiavelli, analyzes Machiavelli and the significance of his ideas.*

SOURCE: From Peter Burke, *The Renaissance,* pp. 1, 3–5. Reprinted with permission by Humanities Press International, Inc., Atlantic Highlands, NJ, 07716; and The Macmillan Press, Ltd.

SOURCE: Federico Chabod, *Machiavelli and the Renaissance,* trans. David Moore (Cambridge, MA: Harvard University Press, 1960), pp. 116–118. Copyright © 1958 by Federico Chabod. Reprinted by permission.

CONSIDER: *Why Machiavelli's ideas are so appropriate to the historical realities of his time; how the selections from* The Prince *support this interpretation of Machiavelli.*

The *leitmotiv* of Machiavelli's posthumous life was his great assertion as a thinker, representing his true and essential contribution to the history of human thought, namely, the clear recognition of the autonomy and the necessity of politics, "which lies outside the realm of what is morally good or evil." Machiavelli thereby rejected the medieval concept of "unity" and became one of the pioneers of modern spirit. . . .

For Machiavelli accepted the political challenge in its entirety; he swept aside every criterion of action not suggested by the concept of *raison d'état*, i.e., by the exact evaluation of the historical moment and the constructive forces which *The Prince* must employ in order to achieve his aim; and he held that the activities of rulers were limited only by their capacity and energy. Hence, he paved the way for absolute governments, which theoretically were completely untrammelled, both in their home and in their foreign policies.

If this was made possible by the Florentine Secretary's recognition of the autonomy of politics, it depended, conversely, on his own peculiar conception of the State, which he identified with the government, or rather with its personal Head. Accordingly, in *The Prince* all his attention was riveted on the human figure of the man who held the reins of government and so epitomized in his person the whole of public life. Such a conception, determined directly by the historical experience which Machiavelli possessed in such outstanding measure and presupposing a sustained effort on the part of the central government, was essential to the success and preeminence of his doctrine.

This was a turning-point in the history of the Christian world. The minds of political theorists were no longer trammelled by Catholic dogma. The structure of the State was not yet threatened in other directions by any revolt of the individual conscience. An entire moral world, if it was not eclipsed, had at any rate receded into the shadows, nor was any other at once forthcoming to take its place and to inspire a new fervour of religious belief; hence, political thought could express itself without being confused by considerations of a different character. It was an era in which unitarian States were being created amid the ruins of the social and political order of the Middle Ages, an era in which it was necessary to place all the weapons of resistance in the hands of those who had still to combat the forces of feudalism and particularism. It was, in short, an era in which it was essential that the freedom and grandeur of political action and the strength and authority of central government should be clearly affirmed. Only thus was it possible to obliterate once and for all the traces of the past and to offer to the society of the future, in the guise of a precept, the weapons which would preserve the life of the united nation in the face of disruptive elements old and new.

This was the great achievement of Niccolò Machiavelli, who accordingly became the legitimate representative of politics and government, the man who was at once admired and hated, followed and opposed, throughout two centuries of European history; and it was on him that the eyes of men were to be fixed, because only he, a poor, weary citizen of a city divided against itself, had proclaimed with an eloquence that was now muted the nature of the arms which the sovereign authority must employ in order to achieve victory.

Northern Sources of the Renaissance
Charles G. Nauert

Most modern scholars argue that there were some differences between the Italian and Northern European Renaissances. Perhaps most obviously, the Northern Renaissance came later. More importantly, while heavily influenced by Italian humanism, humanism in Northern Europe was more tied to Christian culture and concerns. In the following selection Charles Nauert explains differences between the Italian and Northern Renaissance and argues that the North accepted Renaissance culture only when that culture came to suit the particular historical needs of the North.

CONSIDER: *The ways the Northern Renaissance differed from the Italian Renaissance; how Nauert explains these differences.*

The North itself would never have accepted Renaissance culture if that culture had not suited its needs. The reorganized, powerful monarchies of the late fifteenth and early sixteenth centuries needed a new ideal for their servants and courtiers, and the emphasis on public service, on personal merit, and on learning provided an attractive substitute for the traditional manners of the unlettered, unruly, and discredited feudal classes. The new ideal contained enough emphasis on social class and military prowess to make it credible to a society where the hereditary nobility still counted for much. For the kings, it offered the added advantage of servants who were refined and cultivated, and who would wield the pen as well as the sword for their master.

In addition to the monarchs and their courts, other important groups in the North also found humanistic culture attractive. The powerful, self-confident merchant

SOURCE: From Charles G. Nauert, *The Age of Renaissance and Reformation*, pp. 116–117. Reprinted by permission of Charles G. Nauert, Jr. © 1981.

oligarchies that governed the important towns, especially the prospering towns of the Rhine Valley and of south Germany, found in humanism a cultural ideal far more suited to the needs and prejudices of urban magnates than were the chivalric and scholastic traditions of the Middle Ages. The large group of would-be Church reformers found the characteristic Renaissance repudiation of the recent past and the desire to return to the original sources quite attractive, for the Roman past included the apostolic and early patristic age, when the Church was still pure and uncorrupted. . . .

The humanism that grew up in the North was not a mere copy of the Italian culture, but a grafting of Italian elements into a cultural tradition that varied from country to country. Obviously, for example, Germans or even Frenchmen could not revere the ancient Romans as their ancestors in quite the same sense that Italians could.

What did develop everywhere was a revulsion against the heritage of the immediate past (often more open and violent than in Italy because scholastic traditions and a clerical spirit had much greater strength in the North), and the conscious adoption of an idealized Greek and Roman Antiquity as the model for reforming literature, education, and the whole ideal of the educated man. Even more than in Italy, Northern humanists enthusiastically looked to the apostolic and patristic age of the Church as a valuable part of the ancient heritage they sought to restore. This emphasis on ancient Christianity, combined with the widespread movements of lay piety that flourished in the lower Rhine Valley and other parts of Northern Europe, explains why humanism north of the Alps directed much of its reformist activity toward reform of the Church and deepening of personal religious experience.

✎ CHAPTER QUESTIONS

1. In what ways was the Renaissance a new development, strikingly different from the preceding Middle Ages? How might the "newness" of these developments be minimized or reinterpreted as an evolutionary continuation of the Middle Ages?

2. According to the sources in this chapter, what was particularly humanistic about the cultural productions and the attitudes of the Renaissance?

13 The Reformation

The Roman Catholic Church managed to hold together throughout the Middle Ages despite internal discord, heretical movements, and conflicts with secular authorities. In the sixteenth century the Protestant Reformation split it apart. The Reformation was initiated in 1517 by Martin Luther's challenges to official Church doctrine and papal authority. The movement spread in Germany, Northern Europe, and other parts of Europe. By mid-century a related but different form of Protestantism initiated in Geneva by John Calvin had become more dynamic, dominating the struggle against Catholicism in Central Europe and parts of France, Scotland, and England. Meanwhile, Catholic forces fought back politically and militarily under the leadership of the Holy Roman Emperor and Spain, and religiously through the Council of Trent and the Jesuits.

The importance of religious beliefs, the passion involved in the Reformation, and the historical significance of this division in the Western Christian Church have made the Reformation the object of intensive study. Moreover, a relatively large number of Reformation documents have been preserved.

Although representing a broad sampling of Reformation themes, the selections in this chapter center on three related topics. The first involves the much debated question of causes. Clearly, there was a combination of social, religious, political, and economic causes, but which predominated? What were some of the connections among these causes? The second also deals with causes of the Reformation, but from a somewhat different perspective. What moved Luther to reject Catholicism and develop new doctrines? What was the appeal of Lutheranism and Calvinism? In what ways were Catholic organizations such as the Jesuits and Carmelites able to attract members and play such an important role in Catholic reform? The third takes a more comparative perspective, concentrating on the differences and

similarities among the faiths. How closely related were Calvinism and Lutheranism? Why did Lutheranism lose some of its dynamic force while Calvinism spread? How were both Lutheranism and Calvinism related to Catholicism on the one hand and to other Protestant sects on the other? How did the Reformation affect women? What was the nature of Catholic reform during the sixteenth century? Finally, the sources should shed light on the overall significance of the Reformation, one of the most profound revolutions in European history.

 Primary Sources

The Spark for the Reformation: Indulgences

Johann Tetzel

Although there were many causes of the Reformation, the immediate issue that sparked Luther into the position of a reformer was the sale of indulgences. Indulgences were remissions or exemptions for penance in purgatory due to an individual for the sins he had committed in life. They could be granted by the papacy because of the doctrine that it could draw on the treasury of merit or pool of spiritual wealth left by Christ and extraordinarily good Christians over time. As with some other practices of the Church, what was once used primarily for spiritual purposes, such as rewarding acts of penitence, was by the early sixteenth century being "abused" for secular purposes, such as providing money for Church officers. This was apparently the case with the sale of indulgences by Johann Tetzel (c. 1465–1519), a persuasive, popular Dominican friar who was appointed by Archbishop Albert of Mainz in 1517 to sell indulgences in Germany. Proceeds of the sale were to be split between Albert and the papacy. The following is an excerpt from a sermon on indulgences by Tetzel.

CONSIDER: *The most convincing "selling points" made by Tetzel; the requirements for obtaining effective indulgences; how Tetzel might have defended himself against attacks on this sale of indulgences as an abuse.*

SOURCE: From James Harvey Robinson and Merrick Whitcomb, eds., "Period of the Early Reformation in Germany," in *Translations and Reprints from the Original Sources of European History*, vol. II, no. 6, ed. Department of History of the University of Pennsylvania (Philadelphia: University of Pennsylvania Press, 1898), pp. 4–5.

You may obtain letters of safe conduct from the vicar of our Lord Jesus Christ, by means of which you are able to liberate your soul from the hands of the enemy, and convey it by means of contrition and confession, safe and secure from all pains of Purgatory, into the happy kingdom. For know, that in these letters are stamped and engraven all the merits of Christ's passion there laid bare. Consider, that for each and every mortal sin it is necessary to undergo seven years of penitence after confession and contrition, either in this life or in Purgatory.

How many mortal sins are committed in a day, how many in a week, how many in a month, how many in a year, how many in the whole extent of life! They are well-nigh numberless, and those that commit them must needs suffer endless punishment in the burning pains of Purgatory.

But with these confessional letters you will be able at any time in life to obtain full indulgence for all penalties imposed upon you, in all cases except the four reserved to the Apostolic See. Thence throughout your whole life, whenever you wish to make confession, you may receive the same remission, except in cases reserved to the Pope, and afterwards, at the hour of death, a full indulgence as to all penalties and sins, and your share of all spiritual blessings that exist in the church militant and all its members.

Do you not know that when it is necessary for anyone to go to Rome, or undertake any other dangerous journey, he takes his money to a broker and gives a certain per cent—five or six or ten—in order that at Rome or elsewhere he may receive again his funds intact, by means of the letters of this same broker? Are you not willing, then, for the fourth part of a florin, to obtain these letters, by virtue of which you may bring, not your money, but your divine and immortal soul, safe and sound into the land of Paradise?

Justification by Faith

Martin Luther

The early leader of the Reformation was Martin Luther (1483–1546). Born in Germany to a wealthy peasant family, Luther became an Augustinian monk and a professor of theology at the University of Wittenberg. While at this post in 1517, he became involved in the indulgence problem with Tetzel and issued rather academic challenges in his ninety-five theses. News of this act quickly spread, and a major controversy developed. Although originally intending to stimulate only modest reforms within the Catholic Church, Luther soon found himself espousing doctrines markedly differing from those authorized by the Church and taking actions that eventually resulted in his expulsion from the Church.

Luther himself attributed his spiritual evolution to certain crucial experiences. The most important of these was his first formulation of the doctrine of "justification by faith," which constituted the core of his beliefs and much of the basis for Protestantism. In the following excerpts from his autobiographical writings, Luther describes this experience.

CONSIDER: *What Luther meant by "justification by faith"; why this doctrine might have been so appealing to many Catholics; why this doctrine might have been threatening to the Catholic Church.*

I greatly longed to understand Paul's Epistle to the Romans and nothing stood in the way but that one expression, "the justice of God," because I took it to mean that justice whereby God is just and deals justly in punishing the unjust. My situation was that, although an impeccable monk, I stood before God as a sinner troubled in conscience, and I had no confidence that my merit would assuage him. Therefore I did not love a just and angry God, but rather hated and murmured against Him. Yet I clung to the dear Paul and had a great yearning to know what he meant.

Night and day I pondered until I saw the connection between the justice of God and the statement that "the just shall live by his faith." Then I grasped that the justice of God is that righteousness by which through grace and sheer mercy God justifies us through faith. There-upon I felt myself to be reborn and to have gone through open doors into paradise. The whole of Scripture took on a new meaning, and whereas before the "justice of God" had filled me with hate, now it became to be inexpressibly sweet in greater love. This passage of Paul became to me a gate to heaven. . . .

SOURCE: From Roland H. Bainton, *The Age of Reformation* (New York: D. Van Nostrand Co., Inc., 1956), pp. 97–98. Reprinted by permission.

If you have a true faith that Christ is your Saviour, then at once you have a gracious God, for faith leads you in and opens up God's heart and will, that you should see pure grace and overflowing love. This it is to behold God in faith that you should look upon His fatherly, friendly heart, in which there is no anger nor ungraciousness. He who sees God as angry does not see Him rightly but looks only on a curtain, as if a dark cloud had been drawn across his face.

On the Bondage of the Will

Martin Luther

A central distinction between Luther's views and those of Catholicism concerned the power of free will and good works to effect salvation. According to Catholicism, people had the ability to contribute to their own salvation by choosing to engage in good deeds, pious acts, approved behavior, and so forth. Luther rejected this, arguing that people were powerless to effect their own salvation, that salvation was granted only by God out of his mercy. The following is an excerpt from Luther's On the Bondage of the Will, written in 1520 in response to a defense of free will and good works by the famous Christian humanist Erasmus.

CONSIDER: *How Luther's arguments here follow from his ideas about justification by faith; the characteristics of God in Luther's eyes.*

I frankly confess that, for myself, even if it could be, I should not want "free-will" to be given me, nor anything to be left in my own hands to enable me to endeavour after salvation; not merely because in face of so many dangers, and adversities, and assaults of devils, I could not stand my ground and hold fast my "free-will" (for one devil is stronger than all men, and on these terms no man could be saved); but because, even were there no dangers, adversities, or devils, I should still be forced to labour with no guarantee of success, and to beat my fists at the air. If I lived and worked to all eternity, my conscience would never reach comfortable certainty as to how much it must do to satisfy God. Whatever work I had done, there would still be a nagging doubt as to whether it pleased God, or whether He required something more. The experience of all who seek righteousness by works proves that; and I learned it well enough myself over a period of many years, to my own great hurt. But now that God has taken my salvation out of the control of my own will, and put it

Source: Martin Luther, *on the Bondage of the Will,* trans. J. I. Packer and O. R. Jahnston (London: James Clarke & Co., 1957), pp. 313–314. Reprinted by Permission.

under the control of His, and promised to save me, not according to my working or running, but according to His own grace and mercy, I have the comfortable certainty that He is faithful and will not lie to me, and that He is also great and powerful, so that no devils or opposition can break Him or pluck me from Him. "No one," He says, "shall pluck them out of my hand, because my Father which gave them me is greater than all" (John 10.28–29). Thus it is that, if not all, yet some, indeed many, are saved; whereas, by the power of "free-will" none at all could be saved, but every one of us would perish.

Furthermore, I have the comfortable certainty that I please God, not by reason of the merit of my works, but by reason of His merciful favour promised to me; so that, if I work too little, or badly, He does not impute it to me, but with fatherly compassion pardons me and makes me better. This is the glorying of all the saints in their God.

Condemnation of Peasant Revolt

Martin Luther

In 1524 a major peasant revolt broke out in Germany. Longstanding economic and social conflicts came to a head as peasants rose against their lords, the German princes. The peasants expected to be supported by Luther, who had so recently turned on the Church in the name of Christian liberty. Luther's concerns, however, were primarily spiritual; he did not intend his challenge to papal authority to be extended to social and political authority in general. Hesitant at first, Luther clearly sided with the princes as the peasant revolt spread and became more serious. Luther lost much popular support, particularly among peasants, who turned instead to more radical groups like the Anabaptists. But Luther gained important political allies among the princes, who savagely put down the revolt. Lutheranism became cast as a movement that supported strong secular authority. The following is an excerpt from Luther's condemnation of the peasant revolt.

CONSIDER: *Any inconsistency between this document and Luther's previous actions or what Luther says in the other documents; how this helps explain the successes and failures of Lutheranism.*

In my preceding pamphlet [on the "Twelve Articles"] I had no occasion to condemn the peasants, because they promised to yield to law and better instruction, as

SOURCE: From James Harvey Robinson, ed., *Readings in European History*, vol. II (Boston: Ginn, 1904), pp. 106–108.

Christ also demands (Matt. vii. I). But before I can turn around, they go out and appeal to force, in spite of their promises, and rob and pillage and act like mad dogs. From this it is quite apparent what they had in their false minds, and that what they put forth under the name of the gospel in the "Twelve Articles" was all vain pretense. In short, they practice mere devil's work, and it is the arch-devil himself who reigns at Mühlhausen, indulging in nothing but robbery, murder, and bloodshed; as Christ says of the devil in John viii. 44, "he was a murderer from the beginning." Since, therefore, those peasants and miserable wretches allow themselves to be led astray and act differently from what they declared, I likewise must write differently concerning them; and first bring their sins before their eyes, as God commands (Isa. lviii. I; Ezek. ii. 7), whether perchance some of them may come to their senses; and, further, I would instruct those in authority how to conduct themselves in this matter.

With threefold horrible sins against God and men have these peasants loaded themselves, for which they have deserved a manifold death of body and soul.

First, they have sworn to their true and gracious rulers to be submissive and obedient, in accord with God's command (Matt. xxii. 21), "Render therefore unto Caesar the things which are Caesar's," and (Rom. xiii. I), "Let every soul be subject unto the higher powers." But since they have deliberately and sacrilegiously abandoned their obedience, and in addition have dared to oppose their lords, they have thereby forfeited body and soul, as perfidious, perjured, lying, disobedient wretches and scoundrels are wont to do. Wherefore St. Paul judges them, saying (Rom. xiii. 2), "And they that resist shall receive to themselves damnation." The peasants will incur this sentence, sooner or later; for God wills that fidelity and allegiance shall be sacredly kept.

Second, they cause uproar and sacrilegiously rob and pillage monasteries and castles that do not belong to them, for which, like public highwaymen and murderers, they deserve the twofold death of body and soul. It is right and lawful to slay at the first opportunity a rebellious person, who is known as such, for he is already under God's and the emperor's ban. Every man is at once judge and executioner of a public rebel; just as, when a fire starts, he who can extinguish it first is the best fellow. Rebellion is not simply vile murder, but is like a great fire that kindles and devastates a country; it fills the land with murder and bloodshed, makes widows and orphans, and destroys everything, like the greatest calamity. Therefore, whosoever can, should smite, strangle, and stab, secretly or publicly, and should remember that there is nothing more poisonous, pernicious, and devilish than a rebellious man.

Just

Just as one must slay a mad dog, so, if you do not fight the rebels, they will fight you, and the whole country with you.

Third, they cloak their frightful and revolting sins with the gospel, call themselves Christian brethren, swear allegiance, and compel people to join them in such abominations. Thereby they become the greatest blasphemers and violators of God's holy name, and serve and honor the devil under the semblance of the gospel, so that they have ten times deserved death of body and soul, for never have I heard of uglier sins. And I believe also that the devil foresees the judgment day, that he undertakes such an unheard-of measure; as if he said, "It is the last and therefore it shall be the worst; I'll stir up the dregs and knock the very bottom out." May the Lord restrain him! Lo, how mighty a prince is the devil, how he holds the world in his hands and can put it to confusion: who else could so soon capture so many thousands of peasants, lead them astray, blind and deceive them, stir them to revolt, and make them the willing executioners of his malice. . . .

And should the peasants prevail (which God forbid!),—for all things are possible to God, and we know not but that he is preparing for the judgment day, which cannot be far distant, and may purpose to destroy, by means of the devil, all order and authority and throw the world into wild chaos,—yet surely they who are found, sword in hand, shall perish in the wreck with clear consciences, leaving to the devil the kingdom of this world and receiving instead the eternal kingdom. For we are come upon such strange times that a prince may more easily win heaven by the shedding of blood than others by prayers.

Institutes of the Christian Religion: Predestination

John Calvin

Lutheranism was the dominant movement of the first decades of the Reformation. But by mid-century it had lost much of its dynamism and remained confined primarily to major portions of Germany and Scandinavia. Leadership of the expanding Protestant movement in other parts of Europe fell to John Calvin (1509–1564). Born in France and trained as a lawyer and Classical scholar in French universities, Calvin had an important religious experience and adopted many of Luther's doctrines. Because of his views, he fled France for Geneva in the 1530s, eventually establishing a theocratic

Source: John Calvin, *Institutes of the Christian Religion*, vol. II, trans. Henry Beveridge (Edinburgh, Great Britain: Calvin Translation Society, 1845), pp. 529, 534, 540.

government there in the 1540s. While agreeing with most of the doctrines of Lutheranism, Calvin stressed the notion of predestination. This is illustrated in the following excerpt from the Institutes of the Christian Religion *(1536), Calvin's rigorously logical masterpiece, which systematically establishes and explains the Calvinist Christian theology. Here, he stresses the importance of justification by faith and calling—striving to live a good life doing that which one has been called upon by God to do—as evidence that one has already been elected by God for salvation.*

CONSIDER: *How Calvinism avoids the danger of passivity and resignation that might be implied in this conception of predestination; how these views compare with Luther's views on free will and good works; why this doctrine would be threatening to Catholicism.*

The covenant of life is not preached equally to all, and among those to whom it is preached, does not always meet with the same reception. This diversity displays the unsearchable depth of the divine judgment, and is without doubt subordinate to God's purpose of eternal election. But if it is plainly owing to the mere pleasure of God that salvation is spontaneously offered to some, while others have no access to it, great and difficult questions immediately arise, questions which are inexplicable, when just views are not entertained concerning election and predestination. . . .

By predestination we mean the eternal decree of God, by which he determined with himself whatever he wished to happen with regard to every man. All are not created on equal terms, but some are preordained to eternal life, others to eternal damnation; and, accordingly, as each has been created for one or other of these ends, we say that he has been predestinated to life or to death. . . .

We say, then, that Scripture clearly proves this much, that God by his eternal and immutable counsel determined once for all those whom it was his pleasure one day to admit to salvation, and those whom, on the other hand, it was his pleasure to doom to destruction. We maintain that this counsel, as regards the elect, is founded on his free mercy, without any respect to human worth, while those whom he dooms to destruction are excluded from access to life by a just and blameless, but at the same time incomprehensible judgment. In regard to the elect, we regard calling as the evidence of election, and justification as another symbol of its manifestation, until it is fully accomplished by the attainment of glory. But as the Lord seals his elect by calling and justification, so by excluding the reprobate either from the knowledge of his name or the sanctification of his Spirit, he by these marks in a manner discloses the judgment which awaits them. I will here omit many of the fictions which foolish men have devised to overthrow predestination. There is no need of refuting objections which the moment they are produced abundantly betray their hollowness. I will dwell only on those points which either form the subject of dispute among the learned, or may occasion any difficulty to the simple, or may be employed by impiety as specious pretexts for assailing the justice of God.

Constitution of the Society of Jesus

The Catholic Church was not passive in the face of the challenges from Protestant reformers. In a variety of ways the Church reformed itself from within and took the offensive against Protestants in doctrine and deed. Probably the most effective weapon of Catholic reform was the Society of Jesus (the Jesuits) founded by Ignatius Loyola (1491–1556). Loyola, a soldier who had turned to the religious life while recovering from wounds, attracted a group of highly disciplined followers who offered their services to the pope. In 1540, the pope formally accepted their offer. The Jesuits became an arm of the Church in combating Protestantism, spreading Catholicism to foreign lands and gaining influence within Catholic areas of Europe. The following is an excerpt from the Constitution of the Society of Jesus, approved by Pope Paul III in 1540.

CONSIDER: *The characteristics of this organization that help explain its success; how, in tone and content, this document differs from Lutheran and Calvinist documents.*

He who desires to fight for God under the banner of the cross in our society,—which we wish to distinguish by the name of Jesus,—and to serve God alone and the Roman pontiff, his vicar on earth, after a solemn vow of perpetual chastity, shall set this thought before his mind, that he is a part of a society founded for the especial purpose of providing for the advancement of souls in Christian life and doctrine and for the propagation of faith through public preaching and the ministry of the word of God, spiritual exercises and deeds of charity, and in particular through the training of the young and ignorant in Christianity and through the spiritual consolation of the faithful of Christ in hearing confessions; and he shall take care to keep first God and next the purpose of this organization always before his eyes. . . .

All the members shall realize, and shall recall daily, as long as they live, that this society as a whole and in every part is fighting for God under faithful obedience to one most holy lord, the pope, and to the other Roman pontiffs who succeed him. And although we are taught in the gospel and through the orthodox faith to recognize and steadfastly profess that all the faithful of Christ are subject to the Roman pontiff as their head and as the vicar of Jesus Christ, yet we have adjudged that, for the special promotion of greater humility in our society and the perfect mortification of every individual and the sacrifice of our own wills, we should each be bound by a peculiar vow, in addition to the general obligation, that whatever the present Roman pontiff, or any future one, may from time to time decree regarding the welfare of souls and the propagation of the faith, we are pledged to obey without evasion or excuse, instantly, so far as in us lies, whether he send us to the Turks or any other infidels, even to those who inhabit the regions men call the Indies; whether to heretics or schismatics, or, on the other hand, to certain of the faithful.

The Way of Perfection

Teresa of Avila

While the Society of Jesus was the best-known Catholic religious order founded during the Reformation, other orders were founded or reformed and played roles in reasserting the strength of Catholicism. Many of these were women's orders that emphasized meditation, prayer, and mystical religious experiences. The most famous leader of these women's orders was Saint Teresa of Avila (1515–1582), a Spanish saint and founder of the reformed order of Carmelites. The following excerpt is from her book The Way of Perfection.

CONSIDER: *How she reacted to the Lutheran Reformation; ways this religious order and Catholicism might be appealing to women.*

When this convent was originally founded, for the reasons set down in the book which, as I say, I have already written, and also because of certain wonderful revelations by which the Lord showed me how well He would be served in this house, it was not my intention that there should be so much austerity in external matters, nor that it should have no regular income: on the contrary, I should have liked there to be no possibility of want. I acted, in short, like the weak and wretched woman that I am, although I did so with good intentions and not out of consideration for my own comfort.

SOURCE: James Harvey Robinson, ed., *Readings in European History,* vol. II (Boston: Ginn, 1904), pp. 162–163.

SOURCE: E. Allison Peers, ed. and trans., *The Complete Works of Saint Teresa of Jesus,* vol. II (London and New York: Sheed and Ward, 1950), pp. 3, 13.

At about this time there came to my notice the harm and havoc that were being wrought in France by these Lutherans and the way in which their unhappy sect was increasing. This troubled me very much, and, as though I could do anything, or be of any help in the matter, I wept before the Lord and entreated Him to remedy this great evil. I felt that I would have laid down a thousand lives to save a single one of all the souls that were being lost there. And, seeing that I was a woman, and a sinner, and incapable of doing all I should like in the Lord's service, and as my whole yearning was, and still is, that, as He has so many enemies and so few friends, these last should be trusty ones, I determined to do the little that was in me—namely, to follow the evangelical counsels as perfectly as I could, and to see that these few nuns who are here should do the same, confiding in the great goodness of God, Who never fails to help those who resolve to forsake everything for His sake. . . .

It seems over-bold of me to think that I can do anything towards obtaining this. But I have confidence, my Lord, in these servants of Thine who are here, knowing that they neither desire nor strive after anything but to please Thee. For Thy sake they have left the little they possessed, wishing they had more so that they might serve Thee with it. Since Thou, my Creator, art not ungrateful, I do not think Thou wilt fail to do what they beseech of Thee, for when Thou wert in the world, Lord, Thou didst not despise women, but didst always help them and show them great compassion. *Thou didst find more faith and no less love in them than in men, and one of them was Thy most sacred Mother, from whose merits we derive merit, and whose habit we wear, though our sins make us unworthy to do so. We can do nothing in public that is of any use to Thee, nor dare we speak of some of the truths over which we weep in secret, lest Thou shouldst not hear this our just petition. Yet, Lord, I cannot believe this of Thy goodness and righteousness, for Thou art a righteous Judge, not like judges in the world, who, being, after all, men and sons of Adam, refuse to consider any woman's virtue as above suspicion. Yes, my King, but the day will come when all will be known. I am not speaking on my own account, for the whole world is already aware of my wickedness, and I am glad that it should become known; but, when I see what the times are like, I feel it is not right to repel spirits which are virtuous and brave, even though they be the spirits of women.*

Visual Sources

Luther and the New Testament

The frontispiece of Luther's 1546 edition of the New Testament (figure 13.1) reveals much about the Protestant Reformation. First, most words are written in German, not Latin, thus reflecting the Protestant view that the Bible should be read by everyone. The place is Wittenberg, where Luther initiated the Reformation by posting his ninety-five theses in 1517. The year, 1546, was that of Luther's death. In the picture Christ on the cross is flanked by the praying Luther on the right and his patron, the elector of Saxony, on the left. This symbolizes the two unified in the central Protestant belief of justification by faith, the actual political-religious alliance of the two that was so important for the spread of Lutheranism in Germany, and the compatibility of Church and state according to Lutheranism. The general simplicity and lack of ornamentation of this work reflect Lutheranism and part of what it rejected about Catholicism. The book itself, produced mechanically, indicates the importance of the recently invented printing press for the Reformation.

CONSIDER: How this frontispiece might explain or symbolize the causes of the Reformation.

Luther and the Catholic Clergy Debate
Sebald Beham

Both Catholics and Protestants often used art to propagate their views in the Reformation debate. Nuremberg artist Sebald Beham's 1525 woodcut (figure 13.2) appeared in a broadsheet with a text by Hans Sachs entitled Luther and the Artisans. On the left are the "godless"—members of trades, including a painter holding a stick and brush, a bell caster, and a fisherman with his net—all relying on religious commissions from the Catholic church. They complain that Luther has unjustly attacked the clergy for practices such as the sale of indulgences and rental of church lands. They are led by a nun and a priest, who points an accusing finger at Luther. On the right is a group of humble peasants—representing the "common man"—led by Martin Luther, who uses the Bible to answer charges against him and instruct his accusers to seek the kingdom of God. Christ, above in a circle of clouds and holding orb and scepter as Lord of the world, casts his judgment against the clergy by including his scepter to Luther's side.

CONSIDER: What this painting reveals about the Reformation; how this painting compares to the previous illustration.

FIGURE 13.1 (Siftung Luthergedenkstatten in Sachsen-Anhalt)

FIGURE 13.2 (© Bildarchiv Preussischer Kulturbesitz/Art Resource, NY)

Loyola and Catholic Reform

Peter Paul Rubens

In this painting by Peter Paul Rubens (figure 13.3), commissioned by the Jesuits in 1619, Ignatius Loyola is shown preaching and casting out demons from the Church. In the center Loyola, with a halo and backed on his right by the clergy, preaches. He is supported above by angels. To the upper left the demons flee from their victims below, who are both overwhelmed and newly hopeful from the experience.

A comparison with (figure 13.1), the frontispiece of the 1546 edition of Luther's German translation of the New Testament, reveals part of the nature of Catholic reform.

Here, the emphasis is on the Church's intervening between God and man, on the importance of the sacraments, and on the need for an ordained priesthood. The Catholic Church was willing to utilize the wealth and splendor available to it in its cause, as demonstrated not only by Loyola's robes and the grandeur of this Church interior, but in the commissioning of a leading artist like Rubens to paint in the new, elaborate, rich baroque style.

CONSIDER: If you view this picture and the previous two as propaganda pieces, in what ways might they be appealing, and to whom?

FIGURE 13.3 (© Erich Lessing/Art Resource, NY)

Secondary Sources

What Was the Reformation?

Euan Cameron

Historians usually agree that the Reformation comprised the general religious transformations in Europe during the sixteenth century. However, they often disagree on what exactly was at the core of the Reformation. In the following selection Euan Cameron argues that the essence of the Reformation was a combination of religious reformers' protests and laymen's political ambitions.

CONSIDER: *How the protests by churchmen and scholars combined with the ambitions of politically active laymen to become the essence of the Reformation; what this interpretation implies about the causes for the Reformation.*

The Reformation, the movement which divided European Christianity into catholic and protestant traditions, is unique. No other movement of religious protest or reform since antiquity has been so widespread or lasting in its effects, so deep and searching in its criticism of received wisdom, so destructive in what it abolished or so fertile in what it created. . . .

The European Reformation was not a simple revolution, a protest movement with a single leader, a defined set of objectives, or a coherent organization. Yet neither was it a floppy or fragmented mess of anarchic or contradictory ambitions. It was a series of *parallel* movements; within *each* of which various sorts of people with differing perspectives for a crucial period in history combined forces to pursue objectives which they only partly understood.

First of all, the Reformation was a protest by churchmen and scholars, privileged classes in medieval society, against their own superiors. Those superiors, the Roman papacy and its agents, had attacked the teachings of a few sincere, respected academic churchmen which had seemed to threaten the prestige and privilege of clergy and papacy. Martin Luther, the first of those protesting clerics, had attacked "the Pope's crown and the monks' bellies," and they had fought back, to defend their status. The protesting churchmen—the "reformers"—responded to the Roman counter-attack not by silence or furtive opposition, but by publicly denouncing their accusers in print. Not only that: they developed their teachings to make their protest more coherent, and to justify their disobedience.

SOURCE: From Euan Cameron, *The European Reformation*, pp. 1–2, © 1991. Reprinted by permission of Oxford University Press.

Then the most surprising thing of all, in the context of medieval lay people's usual response to religious dissent, took place. Politically active laymen, not (at first) political rulers with axes to grind, but rather ordinary, moderately prosperous householders, took up the reformers' protests, identified them (perhaps mistakenly) as their own, and pressed them upon their governors. This blending and coalition—of reformers' protests and laymen's political ambitions—is the essence of the Reformation. It turned the reformers' movement into a new form of religious dissent: it became not a "schism," in which a section of the catholic Church rose in political revolt against authority, without altering beliefs or practices; nor yet a "heresy," whereby a few people deviated from official belief or worship, but without respect, power, or authority. Rather it promoted a new pattern of worship and belief, publicly preached and acknowledged, which *also* formed the basis of new religious *institutions* for all of society, within the whole community, region, or nation concerned.

A Political Interpretation of the Reformation

G. R. Elton

In more recent times the religious interpretation of the Reformation has been challenged by political historians. This view is illustrated by the following selection from the highly authoritative New Cambridge Modern History. *Here, G. R. Elton of Cambridge argues that while spiritual and other factors are relevant, primary importance for explaining why the Reformation did or did not take hold rests with political history.*

CONSIDER: *How Elton supports his argument; the ways in which Cameron might refute this interpretation.*

The desire for spiritual nourishment was great in many parts of Europe, and movements of thought which gave intellectual content to what in so many ways was an inchoate search for God have their own dignity. Neither of these, however, comes first in explaining why the Reformation took root here and vanished there—why, in fact, this complex of antipapal "heresies" led to a permanent division within the Church that had looked to Rome. This particular place is occupied by politics and

SOURCE: From G. R. Elton, ed., *The New Cambridge Modern History*, vol. II, *The Reformation* (Cambridge, England: Cambridge University Press, 1958), p. 5. Reprinted by permission.

the play of secular ambitions. In short, the Reformation maintained itself wherever the lay power (prince or magistrates) favoured it; it could not survive where the authorities decided to suppress it. Scandinavia, the German principalities, Geneva, in its own peculiar way also England, demonstrate the first; Spain, Italy, the Habsburg lands in the east, and also (though not as yet conclusively) France, the second. The famous phrase behind the settlement of 1555—*cuius regio eius religio*—was a practical commonplace long before anyone put it into words. For this was the age of uniformity, an age which held at all times and everywhere that one political unit could not comprehend within itself two forms of belief or worship.

The tenet rested on simple fact: as long as membership of a secular polity involved membership of an ecclesiastical organisation, religious dissent stood equal to political disaffection and even treason. Hence governments enforced uniformity, and hence the religion of the ruler was that of his country. England provided the extreme example of this doctrine in action, with its rapid official switches from Henrician Catholicism without the pope, through Edwardian Protestantism on the Swiss model and Marian papalism, to Elizabethan Protestantism of a more specifically English brand. But other countries fared similarly. Nor need this cause distress or annoyed disbelief. Princes and governments, no more than the governed, do not act from unmixed motives, and to ignore the spiritual factor in the conversion of at least some princes is as false as to see nothing but purity in the desires of the populace. The Reformation was successful beyond the dreams of earlier, potentially similar, movements not so much because (as the phrase goes) the time was ripe for it, but rather because it found favour with the secular arm. Desire for Church lands, resistance to imperial and papal claims, the ambition to create self-contained and independent states, all played their part in this, but so quite often did a genuine attachment to the teachings of the reformers.

The Catholic Reformation
John C. Olin

The history of the Catholic Church during the sixteenth century is almost as controversial as the history of the Protestant Reformation. Indeed, variations on the terminology used, from "Catholic reform," "Catholic Reformation," and "Catholic revival" to "Counter Reformation" reflect important differences in historians' interpretations of that history. The hub of the controversy is the extent to which reform and revival in the Catholic Church was a reaction to the Protestant Reformation or a product of forces independent of the Protestant Reformation. In the following selection John C. Olin, a historian specializing in Reformation studies, addresses this issue and analyzes the nature of Catholic reform during the sixteenth century.

CONSIDER: *For Olin, the problems in labeling Catholic reform the Counter Reformation; what the inner unity and coherence of the Catholic reform movement was.*

Catholic reform in all its manifestations, potential and actual, was profoundly influenced by the crisis and subsequent schism that developed after 1517. It did not suddenly arise then, but it was given new urgency, as well as a new setting and a new dimension, by the problems that Protestantism posed. What had been, and probably would have remained, a matter of renewal and reform within the confines of religious and ecclesiastical tradition became also a defense of that tradition and a struggle to maintain and restore it. A very complex pattern of Catholic activity unfolded under the shock of religious revolt and disruption. It cannot satisfactorily be labeled the Counter Reformation, for the term is too narrow and misleading. There was indeed a reaction to Protestantism, but this factor, as important as it is, neither subsumes every facet of Catholic life in the sixteenth century nor adequately explains the source and character of the Catholic revival.

Our initial task, then, is to break through the conventional stereotype of Protestant Reformation and Catholic Counter Reformation to view Catholic reform in a more comprehensive and objective way. This will entail consideration of the reaction to schism and the advance of Protestantism, but this subject can neither serve as a point of departure nor be allowed to usurp the stage. The survival of Catholicism and its continued growth suggest another perspective, as do the lives and devotion of so many of the most important Catholic figures of this time. Indeed, if the real significance of the Catholic Reformation must be found in its saints, as has recently been remarked, then emphasis on schism, controversy, and the more secular reflexes of ecclesiastical man may be slightly misplaced.

✂

Certain basic lineaments stand out in the Catholic reform movement, from the days of Savonarola and Ximenes to the close of the Council of Trent. The first and the most obvious was the widespread awareness of the need for reform and the serious efforts made to achieve it. This movement was in the beginning scattered and disparate, a matter of individual initiative and endeavor rather than a coordinated program affecting the church as a whole. Ximenes is the major example of an ecclesiastical or institutional reformer prior to 1517.

SOURCE: John C. Olin, "The Catholic Reformation," in *The Meaning of the Renaissance and Reformation*, ed. Richard L. DeMolen (Boston: Houghton Mifflin Co., 1974), pp. 268, 289–290.

Erasmus and the Christian humanists, however widespread and deep their influence, worked in a private capacity, so to speak, and sought essentially personal reorientation and renewal, though they did envision a broader reform of Christian life and society. With the pontificate of Paul III, Catholic reform became more concerted and official, and reached out to encompass the entire church. The arrival of Contarini in Rome in 1535 ushered in the new era. New blood was infused into the papal administration, the early Jesuits were organized and began their extensive activities, and the General Council was finally convened at Trent. Despite its diversity, the movement had an inner unity and coherence and followed an identifiable and continuous course.

Of what did this inner unity and coherence consist? It was manifested in the first place in the desire for religious reform. . . . [W]hat features distinguish the Catholic reformers and link them in a common endeavor[?] As we see it, two characteristics run like a double rhythm through the Catholic Reformation: the preoccupation of the Catholic reformers with individual or personal reformation, and their concern for the restoration and renewal of the Church's pastoral mission. In short, Catholic reform had a marked personal and pastoral orientation.

The Catholic reformers focused on the individual Christian and his spiritual and moral life. They sought essentially a *reformatio in membris* rather than dogmatic or structural change. The members of Christ's church must lead better Christian lives and be instructed and guided along that path. This is the burden of Savonarola's prophetic preaching, the goal of Erasmus and the Christian humanists, the objective of Ignatius Loyola and his *Spiritual Exercises*. The Theatines, Capuchins, and Jesuits emphasized this in terms of the greater commitment and sanctification of their members. The reforms of Ximenes in Spain, Giberti in Verona, and the Council of Trent for the universal church had this as an underlying purpose in their concern for the instruction and spiritual advancement of the faithful. . . .

Such a focus presupposes concern for the reform of the institutional church as well, for if men are to be changed by religion, then religion itself must be correctly represented and faithfully imparted. Thus the church's pastoral mission—the work of teaching, guiding, and sanctifying its members—must be given primacy and rendered effective. Hence the stress on training priests, selecting good men as bishops and insisting that they reside in their dioceses, instructing the young and preaching the gospel, restoring discipline in the church, and rooting out venality and unworthiness in the service of Christ and the salvation of souls. The Bark of Peter was not to be scuttled or rebuilt, but to be steered back to its original course with its crew at their posts and responsive to their tasks. The state of the clergy loomed large in Catholic reform. If their ignorance, corruption, or neglect had been responsible for the troubles that befell the church, as nearly everyone affirmed, then their reform required urgent attention and was the foundation and root of all renewal. This involved personal reform, that of the priests and bishops who are the instruments of the church's mission, and its purpose and consequence were a matter of the personal reform of the faithful entrusted to their care. The immediate objective, however, was institutional and pastoral. The church itself was to be restored so that its true apostolate might be realized.

The Legacy of the Reformation
Steven E. Ozment

Various historians have identified widespread changes stemming from the Reformation. The most obvious of these were the changes in religious affiliation and the conflicts between Protestants and Catholics that developed. However, there were other cultural and social changes stemming from the Reformation that directly affected daily life. In the following selection Steven Ozment analyzes the legacy of the Reformation, emphasizing how it displaced many of the beliefs, practices, and institutions of daily life.

CONSIDER: *How the changes emphasized by Ozment might have affected daily life; what connections there might be between the Reformation and witchcraft according to Ozment.*

Viewed in these terms, the Reformation was an unprecedented revolution in religion at a time when religion penetrated almost the whole of life. The Reformation constituted for the great majority of people, whose social status and economic condition did not change dramatically over a lifetime, an upheaval in the world as they knew it, regardless of whether they were pious Christians or joined the movement. In the first half of the sixteenth century cities and territories passed laws and ordinances that progressively ended or severely limited a host of traditional beliefs, practices, and institutions that touched directly the daily life of large numbers of people: mandatory fasting; auricular confession; the veneration of saints, relics, and images; the buying and selling of indulgences; pilgrimages and shrines; wakes and processions for the dead and dying; endowed masses in memory of the dead; the doctrine of purgatory; Latin Mass and liturgy; traditional ceremonies, festivals, and holidays; monasteries, nunneries, and mendicant orders; the sacramental status of marriage; extreme unction, confirmation, holy orders, and penance; clerical celibacy; clerical

SOURCE: From Steven E. Ozment, *The Age of Reformation*, pp. 435–436.

immunity from civil taxation and criminal jurisdiction; nonresident benefices; papal excommunication and interdict; canon law; papal and episcopal territorial government; and the traditional scholastic education of clergy. Modern scholars may argue over the degree to which such changes in the official framework of religion connoted actual changes in personal beliefs and habits. Few, however, can doubt that the likelihood of personal change increased with the incorporation of Protestant reforms in the laws and institutions of the sixteenth century. As historians write the social history of the Reformation, I suspect they will discover that such transformations in the religious landscape had a profound, if often indirect, cultural impact.

While the Reformation influenced the balance of political power both locally and internationally, it was not a political revolution in the accepted sense of the term; a major reordering of traditional social and political groups did not result, although traditional enemies often ended up in different religious camps and the higher clergy was displaced as a political elite. The larger social impact of the Reformation lay rather in its effectively displacing so many of the beliefs, practices, and institutions that had organized daily life and given it security and meaning for the greater part of a millennium. Here the reformers continued late medieval efforts to simplify religious, and enhance secular, life. If scholars of popular religion in Reformation England are correct, Protestant success against medieval religion actually brought new and more terrible superstitions to the surface. By destroying the traditional ritual framework for dealing with daily misfortune and worry, the Reformation left those who could not find solace in its message—and there were many—more anxious than before, and especially after its leaders sought by coercion what they discovered could not be gained by persuasion alone. Protestant "disenchantment" of the world in this way encouraged new interest in witchcraft and the occult, as the religious heart and mind, denied an outlet in traditional sacramental magic and pilgrimage piety, compensated for new Protestant sobriety and simplicity by embracing superstitions even more socially disruptive than the religious practices set aside by the Reformation.

Women in the Reformation

Marilyn J. Boxer and Jean H. Quataert

The great figures of the Reformation were men, and traditionally focus has been on their struggles and their doctrines. In recent years scholars have questioned what role women

SOURCE: Excerpted from *Connecting Spheres: Women in the Western World, 1500 to the Present*, edited by Marilyn J. Boxer and Jean H. Quataert. © 1987 by Oxford University Press, Inc.

played in the Reformation and whether the Reformation benefited women socially or in any aspect of public life. These questions are addressed by Marilyn J. Boxer and Jean H. Quataert, both specializing in women's studies, in the following excerpt from their book Connecting Spheres.

CONSIDER: *Ways women helped spread the Reformation; why the Reformation did not greatly change women's place in society.*

Defying stereotypes, women in good measure also were instrumental in spreading the ideas of the religious Reformation to the communities, towns, and provinces of Europe after 1517. In their roles as spouses and mothers they were often the ones to bring the early reform ideas to the families of Europe's aristocracy and to those of the common people in urban centers as well. The British theologian Richard Hooker (c. 1553–1600) typically explained the prominence of women in reform movements by reference to their "nature," to the "eagerness of their affection," not to their intelligence or ability to make conscious choices. Similarly, Catholic polemicists used notions about women's immature and frail "nature" to discredit Protestantism.

The important role played by women in the sixteenth-century Reformation should not surprise us, for they had been equally significant in supporting earlier heresies that challenged the established order and at times the gender hierarchy, too. Many medieval anticlerical movements that extolled the virtues of lay men praised lay women as well. . . .

Since the message of the Reformation, like that of the earlier religious movements, meant a loosening of hierarchies, it had a particular appeal to women. By stressing the individual's personal relationship with God and his or her own responsibility for behavior, it affirmed the ability of each to find truth by reading the original Scriptures. Thus, it offered a greater role for lay participation by women, as well as men, than was possible in Roman Catholicism. . . .

[Nevertheless,] the Reformation did not markedly transform women's place in society, and the reformers had never intended to do so. To be sure, they called on men and women to read the Bible and participate in religious ceremonies together. But Bible-reading reinforced the Pauline view of woman as weak-minded and sinful. When such practice took a more radical turn in the direction of lay prophesy, as occurred in some Reform churches southwest of Paris, or in the coming together of women to discuss "unchristian pieces" as was recorded in Zwickau, reformers—Lutheran and Calvin alike—pulled back in horror. The radical or Anabaptist brand of reform generally offered women a more active role in religious life than did Lutheranism, even allowing them to preach.

"Admonished to Christian righteousness" by more conservative Protestants, Anabaptists were charged with holding that "marriage and whoredom are one and the same thing." The women were even accused of having "dared to deny their husbands' marital rights." During an interrogation one woman explained that "she was wed to Christ and must therefore be chaste, for which she cited the saying, that no one can serve two masters."

The response of the magisterial Reformers was unequivocal. The equality of the Gospel was not to overturn the inequalities of social rank or the hierarchies of the sexual order. As the Frenchman Pierre Viret explained it in 1560, appealing to the old polarities again, the Protestant elect were equal as Christians and believers—as man and woman, master and servant, free and serf. Further, while the Reformation thus failed to elevate women's status, it deprived them of the emotionally sustaining presence of female imagery, of saints and protectors who long had played a significant role at crucial points in their life cycles. The Reformers rejected the special powers of the saints and downplayed, for example, Saints Margaret and Ann, who had been faithful and succoring companions for women in childbirth and in widowhood. With the rejection of Mary as well as the saints, nuns, and abbesses, God the Father was more firmly in place.

→ CHAPTER QUESTIONS

1. What were the most important differences between Catholicism and Protestantism in the sixteenth century? In what ways do these differences explain the appeal of each faith and the causes of the Reformation?

2. Considering the information in the preceding chapter, how might the Reformation be related to some of the intellectual and cultural developments of the Renaissance?

3. In what ways would it be accurate to describe Luther and his doctrines—and indeed the Reformation in general—as more medieval and conservative than humanistic and modern?

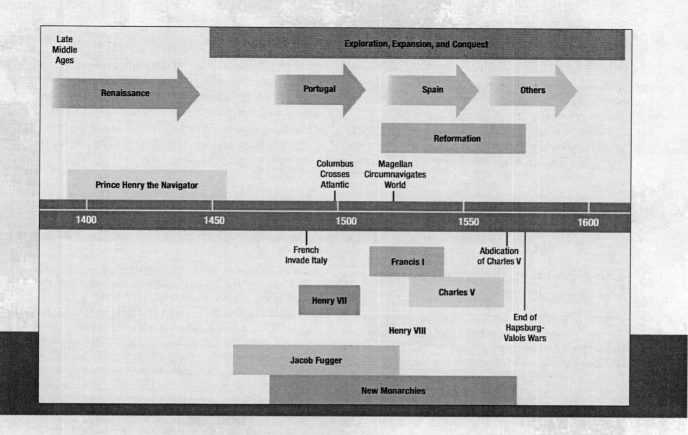

14 Overseas Expansion and New Politics

Between the mid-fifteenth and mid-sixteenth centuries much of Europe gained a new political and economic strength, which had been missing during the Late Middle Ages. This was manifested in a number of ways. First, central governments acquired new authority and power under a series of talented monarchs, often referred to by historians as the "new monarchs." This was particularly so in England, France, and Spain, but even in the Holy Roman Empire, where the emperor was often relatively weak, Emperor Charles V rose in stature and power. Second, European states supported a new wave of expansion into the rest of the world. Led by Portugal and then Spain, these states sent explorers, missionaries, merchants, colonists, and armed forces throughout the world, quickly establishing vast empires. Third, modern diplomacy was developed, enabling states to have recognized representatives with authority and expertise in foreign countries. This reflected and facilitated the new political strength and competitiveness of European states.

Sources in this chapter deal with each of these aspects of the new political and economic strength of fifteenth- and sixteenth-century Europe. In particular, questions related to exploration and expansion are addressed. What were the motives for expansion? Why did the expansion occur at this time? What connections were there between expansion and nationalism? What were the consequences of expansion? Some documents concern political developments of the period, particularly the reign of Charles V, the most renowned ruler of the time. What were his role and position? How were they affected by expansion? What were some of the connections between his position and the new commercial and financial prosperity?

In short, the sources in this chapter reveal a new political and economic strength that relates to the religious, cultural, and intellectual developments covered in the two preceding chapters. While this Renaissance civilization did not represent a complete break with the civilization of the Middle Ages, the selections emphasize what is different and more recognizably "modern" about this period. Historical patterns were being established that would characterize Europe for several succeeding generations, as will be seen in the following chapters.

Primary Sources

The Chronicle of the Discovery and Conquest of Guinea

Gomes Eannes de Azurara

The great geographic expansion and conquests of the fifteenth and sixteenth centuries were initiated by Prince Henry (the Navigator) of Portugal (1394–1460). Although he did not personally participate in the explorations, he established a naval school and base of operations on the southwestern tip of Portugal from which he sent expeditions down the west coast of Africa. One of the clearest explanations of the motives for this effort has been provided by Gomes Eannes de Azurara, a friend of Prince Henry (referred to as "the Lord Infant"), who chronicled the voyages of 1452–1453 at the request of King Alfonso V.

CONSIDER: *The explanations that sound more like rationalizations than reasons for explorations; whether economic, military, and religious motives are complementary or contradictory; ways this document reflects the history of a country engaged with Islam.*

We imagine that we know a matter when we are acquainted with the doer of it and the end for which he did it. And since in former chapters we have set forth the Lord Infant as the chief actor in these things, giving as clear an understanding of him as we could, it is meet that in this present chapter we should know his purpose in doing them. And you should note well that the noble spirit of this Prince, by a sort of natural constraint, was ever urging him both to begin and to carry out very great deeds. For which reason, after the taking of Ceuta he always kept ships well armed against the Infidel, both for war, and because he had also a wish to know the land that lay beyond the isles of Canary and that Cape called

Bojador, for that up to his time, neither by writings, nor by the memory of man, was known with any certainty the nature of the land beyond that Cape. Some said indeed that Saint Brandan had passed that way; and there was another tale of two galleys rounding the Cape, which never returned. But this doth not appear at all likely to be true, for it is not to be presumed that if the said galleys went there, some other ships would not have endeavoured to learn what voyage they had made. And because the said Lord Infant wished to know the truth of this,— since it seemed to him that if he or some other lord did not endeavour to gain that knowledge, no mariners or merchants would ever dare to attempt it—(for it is clear that none of them ever trouble themselves to sail to a place where there is not a sure and certain hope of profit)—and seeing also that no other prince took any pains in this matter, he sent out his own ships against those parts, to have manifest certainty of them all. And to this he was stirred up by his zeal for the service of God and of the King Edward his Lord and brother, who then reigned. And this was the first reason of his action.

The second reason was that if there chanced to be in those lands some population of Christians, or some havens, into which it would be possible to sail without peril, many kinds of merchandise might be brought to this realm, which would find a ready market, and reasonably so, because no other people of these parts traded with them, nor yet people of any other that were known; and also the products of this realm might be taken there, which traffic would bring great profit to our countrymen.

The third reason was that, as it was said that the power of the Moors in that land of Africa was very much greater than was commonly supposed, and that there were no Christians among them, nor any other race of men; and because every wise man is obliged by natural prudence to wish for a knowledge of the power of his enemy; therefore the said Lord Infant exerted himself to cause this to be fully discovered, and to make it known determinately how far the power of those infidels extended.

SOURCE: Gomes Eannes de Azurara, *The Chronicle of the Discovery and Conquest of Guinea*, vol. I, trans. Charles Raymond Beazley and Adgar Prestage (London: The Hakluyt Society, 1896), pp. 27–29.

The fourth reason was because during the one and thirty years that he had warred against the Moors, he had never found a Christian king, nor a lord outside this land, who for the love of our Lord Jesus Christ would aid him in the said war. Therefore he sought to know if there were in those parts any Christian princes, in whom the charity and the love of Christ was so ingrained that they would aid him against those enemies of the faith.

The fifth reason was his great desire to make increase in the faith of our Lord Jesus Christ and to bring to him all the souls that should be saved,—understanding that all the mystery of the Incarnation, Death, and Passion of our Lord Jesus Christ was for this sole end—namely the salvation of lost souls—whom the said Lord Infant by his travail and spending would fain bring into the true path. For he perceived that no better offering could be made unto the Lord than this; for if God promised to return one hundred goods for one, we may justly believe that for such great benefits, that is to say for so many souls as were saved by the efforts of this Lord, he will have so many hundreds of guerdons in the kingdom of God, by which his spirit may be glorified after this life in the celestial realm. For I that wrote this history saw so many men and women of those parts turned to the holy faith, that even if the Infant had been a heathen, their prayers would have been enough to have obtained his salvation. And not only did I see the first captives, but their children and grandchildren as true Christians as if the Divine grace breathed in them and imparted to them a clear knowledge of itself.

Letter to Lord Sanchez, 1493

Christopher Columbus

The voyages of Christopher Columbus (1451–1506) opened the New World to Europe and marked the entry of Spain into the process of exploration, expansion, and conquest initiated by Portugal. Columbus was a Genoese explorer who, after great difficulties, convinced the Spanish monarchs, Queen Isabella and King Ferdinand, to support his voyages across the Atlantic. He expected to discover a western route to Asia and its riches. Instead, he landed on several islands of the Caribbean, which he assumed were part of Asia. The following letter to Lord Raphael Sanchez, treasurer to the Spanish monarchs, was written by Columbus in Lisbon on March 14, 1493, shortly after returning from his first voyage across the Atlantic. In this excerpt, he describes the native people he encountered.

Source: *Select Letters of Christopher Columbus,* trans. and ed. R. H. Hajor (London: The Hakluyt Society, 1847), pp. 6–10.

CONSIDER: *How Columbus viewed the natives; what Columbus was most concerned with; how this letter reflects Columbus' motives.*

The inhabitants of both sexes in this island, and in all the others which I have seen, or of which I have received information, go always naked as they were born, with the exception of some of the women, who use the covering of a leaf, or small bough, or an apron of cotton which they prepare for that purpose. None of them, as I have already said, are possessed of any iron, neither have they weapons, being unacquainted with, and indeed incompetent to use them, not from any deformity of body (for they are well-formed), but because they are timid and full of fear. They carry however in lieu of arms, canes dried in the sun, on the ends of which they fix heads of dried wood sharpened to a point, and even these they dare not use habitually; for it has often occurred when I have sent two or three of my men to any of the villages to speak with the natives, that they have come out in a disorderly troop, and have fled in such haste at the approach of our men, that the fathers forsook their children and the children their fathers. This timidity did not arise from any loss or injury that they had received from us; for, on the contrary, I gave to all I approached whatever articles I had about me, such as cloth and many other things, taking nothing of theirs in return: but they are naturally timid and fearful. As soon however as they see that they are safe, and have laid aside all fear, they are very simple and honest, and exceedingly liberal with all they have; none of them refusing any thing he may possess when he is asked for it, but on the contrary inviting us to ask them. They exhibit great love towards all others in preference to themselves: they also give objects of great value for trifles, and content themselves with very little or nothing in return. I however forbad that these trifles and articles of no value (such as pieces of dishes, plates, and glass, keys, and leather straps) should be given to them, although if they could obtain them, they imagined themselves to be possessed of the most beautiful trinkets in the world. It even happened that a sailor received for a leather strap as much gold as was worth three golden nobles, and for things of more trifling value offered by our men, especially newly coined blancas, or any gold coins, the Indians would give whatever the seller required; as, for instance, an ounce and a half or two ounces of gold, or thirty or forty pounds of cotton, with which commodity they were already acquainted. Thus they bartered, like idiots, cotton and gold for fragments of bows, glasses, bottles, and jars; which I forbad as being unjust, and myself gave them many beautiful and acceptable articles which I had brought with me, taking nothing from them in return; I did this in order that I might the more easily conciliate them, that they might be led to become

Christians, and be inclined to entertain a regard for the King and Queen, our Princes and all Spaniards, and that I might induce them to take an interest in seeking out, and collecting, and delivering to us such things as they possessed in abundance, but which we greatly needed. They practise no kind of idolatry, but have a firm belief that all strength and power, and indeed all good things, are in heaven, and that I had descended from thence with these ships and sailors, and under this impression was I received after they had thrown aside their fears. Nor are they slow or stupid, but of very clear understanding; and those men who have crossed to the neighbouring islands give an admirable description of everything they observed; but they never saw any people clothed, nor any ships like ours. On my arrival at that sea, I had taken some Indians by force from the first island that I came to, in order that they might learn our language, and communicate to us what they knew respecting the country; which plan succeeded excellently, and was a great advantage to us, for in a short time, either by gestures and signs, or by words, we were enabled to understand each other. These men are still travelling with me, and although they have been with us now a long time, they continue to entertain the idea that I have descended from heaven; and on our arrival at any new place they published this, crying out immediately with a loud voice to the other Indians, "Come, come and look upon beings of a celestial race": upon which both women and men, children and adults, young men and old, when they got rid of the fear they at first entertained, would come out in throngs, crowding the roads to see us, some bringing food, others drink, with astonishing affection and kindness. . . . In all these islands there is no difference of physiognomy, of manners, or of language, but they all clearly understand each other, a circumstance very propitious for the realization of what I conceive to be the principal wish of our most serene King, namely, the conversion of these people to the holy faith of Christ, to which indeed, as far as I can judge, they are very favourable and well-disposed.

Memoirs: The Aztecs

Bernal Diaz del Castillo

While many Europeans who first came into contact with non-Western peoples viewed them with arrogance, others were quite impressed with what they saw. This was particularly true of some Spanish observers in Mexico. Before Cortez's conquest of Mexico in 1519, the Aztecs dominated much of the "middle American" world. This selection, written a half-century later by Bernal Diaz (1492–1581), a member of Cortez's conquering army, gives a sense of the Aztec's highly developed civilization and the splendor of their capital.

CONSIDER: *What most impressed Diaz; why Diaz was astonished at the wealth of this civilization; how this account compares with that of Columbus.*

When we gazed upon all this splendour . . . we scarcely knew what to think, and we doubted whether all that we beheld was real. A series of large towns stretched themselves along the banks of the lake, out of which still larger ones rose magnificently above the waters. Innumerable crowds of canoes were plying everywhere around us; at regular distances we continually passed over new bridges, and before us lay the great city of Mexico in all its splendour. . . .

Motecusuma himself, according to his custom, was sumptuously attired, had on a species of half boot, richly set with jewels, and whose soles were made of solid gold. The four grandees who supported him were also richly attired, which they must have put on somewhere on the road, in order to wait upon Motecusuma; they were not so sumptuously dressed when they first came out to meet us. Besides these distinguished caziques, there were many other grandees around the monarch, some of whom held the canopy over his head, while others again occupied the road before him, and spread cotton cloths on the ground that his feet might not touch the bare earth. No one of his suite ever looked at him full in the face; every one in his presence stood with eyes downcast, and it was only his four nephews and cousins who supported him that durst look up. . . .

Our commander, attended by the greater part of our cavalry and foot, all well armed, as, indeed, we were at all times, had proceeded to the Tlatelulco. . . . The moment we arrived in this immense market, we were perfectly astonished at the vast numbers of people, the profusion of merchandise which was there exposed for sale, and at the good police and order that reigned throughout. The grandees who accompanied us drew our attention to the smallest circumstance, and gave us full explanation of all we saw. Every species of merchandise had a separate spot for its sale. We first of all visited those divisions of the market appropriated for the sale of gold and silver wares, of jewels, of cloths interwoven with feathers, and of other manufactured goods; besides slaves of both sexes. . . . Next to these

SOURCE: I. I. Lockhart, trans., *The Memoirs of the Conquistador Bernal de Castillo* (London: J. Hatchard and Son, 1844), pp. 220–221, 235–238.

came the dealers in coarser wares—cotton, twisted thread, and cacao. . . . In one place were sold the stuffs manufactured of nequen; ropes, and sandals; in another place, the sweet maguey root, ready cooked, and various other things made from this plant. In another division of the market were exposed the skins of tigers, lions, jackals, otters, red deer, wild cats, and of other beasts of prey, some of which were tanned. In another place were sold beans and sage, with other herbs and vegetables. A particular market was assigned for the merchants in fowls, turkeys, ducks, rabbits, hares, deer, and dogs; also for fruit-sellers, pastry-cooks, and tripe-sellers. Not far from these were exposed all manner of earthenware, from the large earthen cauldron to the smaller pitchers. Then came the dealers in honey and honey-cakes, and other sweetmeats. Next to these, the timber-merchants, furniture-dealers, with their stores of tables, benches, cradles, and all sorts of wooden implements, all separately arranged. . . .

In this market-place there were also courts of justice, to which three judges and several constables were appointed, who inspected the goods exposed for sale. . . . I wish I had completed the enumeration of all this profusion of merchandise. The variety was so great that it would occupy more space than I can well spare to note them down in; besides which, the market was so crowded with people, and the thronging so excessive in the porticoes, that it was quite impossible to see all in one day. . . .

Indeed, this infernal temple, from its great height, commanded a view of the whole surrounding neighbourhood. From this place we could likewise see the three causeways which led into Mexico. . . . We also observed the aqueduct which ran from Chapultepec, and provided the whole town with sweet water. We could also distinctly see the bridges across the openings, by which these causeways were intersected, and through which the waters of the lake ebbed and flowed. The lake itself was crowded with canoes, which were bringing provisions, manufactures, and other merchandise to the city. From here we also discovered that the only communication of the houses in this city, and of all the other towns built in the lake, was by means of drawbridge or canoes. In all these towns the beautiful white plastered temples rose above the smaller ones, . . . and this, it may be imagined, was a splendid sight.

After we had sufficiently gazed upon this magnificent picture, we again turned our eyes toward the great market, and beheld the vast numbers of buyers and sellers who thronged them. The bustle and noise occasioned by this multitude of human beings was so great that it could be heard at a distance of more than four miles.

Letter to Charles V: Finance and Politics

Jacob Fugger

The explorations and conquests of the fifteenth and sixteenth centuries were connected with the commercial expansion occurring in Europe at the same time. Central to this expansion was the rise of great international financial houses, such as the House of Fugger. The House of Fugger originated in Augsburg, Germany, and the Fuggers established branches throughout Europe and became directly tied not only to the growth of commerce but also to political developments as financiers to royal families. The extent of the Fuggers' political influence is suggested by the tone and content of the following letter, written in 1523, by Jacob Fugger, head of the firm, to Charles V, head of the House of Hapsburg, Holy Roman Emperor, King of Spain, and the most powerful ruler in Europe. The letter refers to the financial support provided by the Fuggers that enabled Charles, rather than his competitor Francis I of France, to be elected Holy Roman Emperor in 1519 by the electoral princes of Germany.

CONSIDER: *The tone of this letter; the interests the Fuggers might have in establishing a relationship with Charles V; Jacob Fugger's options had Charles rejected this request for repayment of the loan.*

Your Imperial Majesty doubtless knows how I and my kinsmen have ever hitherto been disposed to serve the House of Austria in all loyalty to the furtherance of its well-being and prosperity; wherefore, in order to be pleasing to Your Majesty's Grandsire, the late Emperor Maximilian, and to gain for Your Majesty the Roman Crown, we have held ourselves bounden to engage ourselves towards divers princes who placed their Trust and Reliance upon myself and perchance on No Man besides. We have, moreover, advanced to Your Majesty's Agents for the same end a Great Sum of Money, of which we ourselves have had to raise a large part from our Friends. It is well known that Your Imperial Majesty could not have gained the Roman Crown save with mine aid, and I can prove the same by the writings of Your Majesty's Agents given by their own hands. In this matter I have not studied mine own Profit. For had I left the House of Austria and had been minded to further France, I had obtained much money and property, such as was then offered to me. How grave a Disadvantage had in this case accrued to Your Majesty and the House of Austria, Your Majesty's Royal Mind well knoweth.

SOURCE: From Richard Ehrenberg, *Capital and Finance in the Age of the Renaissance: A Study of the Fuggers and Their Connections,* trans. H. M. Lucas (New York: Augustus M. Kelley, 1963), p. 80. Reprinted by permission.

✣ Visual Sources

The Assets and Liabilities of Empire

Frans Fracken II

This painting by Frans Fracken II (figure 14.1) represents the abdication of Emperor Charles V in 1555. In the center sits Charles V with outstretched hands, symbolically giving Spain and the Netherlands to his son Philip on his left and the Empire to his brother Ferdinand on his right. Next to Philip stand various political figures, and below them are banners representing the provinces. In the foreground is an allegorical scene representing Spain's dominance of the sea and the New World. On the left is the bearded Neptune with a globe and his court; on the right is an Indian and other exotic figures and animals offering homage (in the form of gold treasure). The event occurred in Brussels on October 25, 1555, shortly after Charles assented to the Peace of Augsburg, which has been interpreted as a double defeat for him: a recognition of Lutheranism and a political victory for German princes over imperial authority. There Charles made a speech, which included the following statements:

I had no inordinate ambition to rule a multitude of kingdoms, but merely sought to secure the welfare of Germany, to provide for the defense of Flanders, to consecrate my forces to the safety of Christianity against the Turk, and to labor for the extension of the Christian religion. But although such zeal was mine, I was unable to show so much of it as I might have wished, on account of the troubles raised by the heresies of Luther and other innovators of Germany, and on account of serious war into which the hostility and envy of neighboring princes had driven men, and from which I have safely emerged, thanks to the favor of God. . . . I am determined

FIGURE 14.1 (© Rijksmuseum, Amsterdam)

then to retire to Spain, to yield to my son Philip the possession of all my states, and to my brother, the king of the Romans, the Empire. . . . Above all, beware of infection from the sects of neighboring lands. Extirpate at once the germs, if they appear in your midst, for fear lest they may spread abroad and utterly overthrow your state, and lest you may fall into the direst calamities.

CONSIDER: *How this picture and speech reflect the position and predicament of the Hapsburgs during this period.*

The Conquest of Mexico as Seen by the Aztecs

With the exception of a few written documents, most accounts of Aztec culture, like that of Incan and Mayan cultures, come from pictographs, sculptures, and other artifacts. Historical events are often depicted from the point of view of the conqueror rather than the vanquished. Here we see one of the few depictions of the Spanish conquest of the Aztec from the perspective of the conquered people (figure 14.2). In this Aztec manuscript from about 1519 to 1522, shortly after Cortez entered Mexico in 1519, the bloody and brutal suppression of the Aztec is shown in

all its horror. Notice the Aztec offering what appears to be a wreath to Cortez, holding a sword about to be swung.

CONSIDER: *The symbols of conquest and destruction shown in the illustration.*

Exploration, Expansion, and Politics

Aside from the various motivations for the voyages of discovery during the fifteenth and sixteenth centuries, a number of factors combined to make those voyages physically possible when earlier they were not. Technological discoveries significantly improved shipbuilding and navigation. But also important was the understanding and mapping of prevailing ocean currents and winds in relation to land masses. It was much easier to sail with, rather than against, currents and winds, and sailors counted on finding land masses for supplies along the way.

The early voyages tended to take advantage of currents and winds as shown in this map. Thus, for example, early voyages to North America usually took a more southerly route westward across the Atlantic and returned on a more northerly route, while Portuguese ships headed east to the Indian Ocean by following winds and currents to Brazil and then crossed the Atlantic farther south. Prevailing currents

FIGURE 14.2 (Biblioteca Apostolica Vaticana)

MAP 14.1 Overseas Explorations

and winds also explain the difficulty of westward voyages around the tip of South America. These patterns of voyages also shed light on some of the geopolitical results of expansion. For example, even though Portugal's efforts were directed toward an eastern route to the Far East, she acquired Brazil (her only territory in the New World) to the west since it was on a route favored by winds and currents.

CONSIDER: How map 14.1 helps explain the pattern of exploration and colonization by the various European powers.

Map 14.2 shows some of the geopolitical connections of international finance during the sixteenth century. First, it shows the extent of Fugger agencies throughout Europe,

thus indicating how much international finance had grown by this time. Second, it reveals some of the direct connections between industry and finance, for the Fuggers were involved in both and often took mineral concessions or rights in mines as security or repayment for loans. Third, it suggests some of the political connections between the Fuggers and the House of Hapsburg; most of the firm's branches and mines were within Hapsburg lands, and not surprisingly the Fuggers became tied to the Hapsburgs by a series of loans.

CONSIDER: How map 14.2 relates to the letter of Jacob Fugger to Charles V.

 Secondary Sources

The Expansion of Europe
Richard B. Reed

In analyzing the overseas expansion of the fifteenth and sixteenth centuries, historians typically emphasize a combination of economic and religious factors to explain the motivation

behind expansion while focusing on the establishment of adequate knowledge and technology as key conditions for its occurrence. In the following selection Richard B. Reed argues that European expansion was a nationalistic phenomenon, and because of this Portugal was able to become the early leader.

CONSIDER: Why Italy and Germany did not participate in overseas expansion; how one might attack Reed's argument that Portugal was in a better position to initiate expansion than any other country; other factors that might help explain why Portugal led in overseas expansion.

SOURCE: Richard B. Reed, "The Expansion of Europe," in *The Meaning of the Renaissance and Reformation*, ed. Richard L. DeMolen (Boston: Houghton Mifflin, 1974), p. 299. Reprinted by permission.

MAP 14.2   Commercial Expansion and Politics

The expansion of Europe was an intensely nationalistic phenomenon. It was an aspect of the trend, most evident in the late fifteenth and early sixteenth centuries, toward the establishment of strong centralized authority in the "new monarchies," as they have been called, and the emergence of the nation-state. A policy of overseas expansion required a degree of internal stability and national consciousness that only a powerful central government could command. Portugal achieved this position long before her eventual competitors, and under the leadership of the dynamic house of Avis became a consolidated kingdom comparatively free from feudal divisions before the end of the fifteenth century. While Spain was still divided into a number of conflicting political jurisdictions, England and France were preoccupied with their own and each other's affairs, and the Dutch were still an appendage of the Empire, the Portuguese combined the advantages of their natural geographic situation with their political and economic

stability to initiate the age of discovery. Spain in the sixteenth century, and England, France, and the Netherlands in the seventeenth century, became active colonial powers only after each had matured into strong national entities, independent of feudal political and economic restrictions. . . .

The importance of the nation-state in Renaissance expansion is particularly apparent when the Italian city-states are considered. Venice and Genoa, cities that had contributed so many of the medieval travelers and early Renaissance geographers and mapmakers, did not participate directly in Europe's overseas expansion. Yet Italian names dominated the rolls of the early voyagers. Prince Henry employed Venetians and Florentines in his naval establishment, while Columbus, Vespucci, Verrazano, the Cabots, and many others sailed for Spain, France, and England. Italian cartography was the best in Europe until the second half of the sixteenth century, and a high proportion of the books and pamphlets that chronicled new discoveries emanated from the presses of Vicenza, Venice, Rome, and Florence. Italian bankers and merchants were also very active in the commercial life of the principal Iberian cities. A divided Italy was instrumental in making Renaissance expansion possible, but it could not take full advantage of its own endowments. Germans, too, figured prominently in the expansion of the sixteenth century, as the names of Federmann, Staden, Welser, and Fugger attest. But Germany, like Italy, was not united, and the emergence of these two nations as colonial powers had to wait until their respective consolidations in the nineteenth century.

While every nationality in Western Europe was represented in Renaissance expansion, it was by no means an international venture. On the contrary, it was very much an expression of that nationalistic fervor that characterized political developments in the fifteenth and sixteenth centuries. It was primarily a state enterprise, often financed privately but controlled and protected by the governments of the concerned powers. There was no cooperation between nations, and even after the upheaval of the Protestant Reformation, when political loyalties and alignments were conditioned by religious sympathies, there were no colonial alliances that provided for mutual Protestant or Catholic overseas policies.

The Effects of Expansion on the Non-European World

M. L. Bush

While the expansion of Europe was of great significance for European history, it was of even greater consequence for the non-European world touched by the explorers. However, its effects differed greatly in the New World, where the Spanish dominated, and the East, where the Portuguese were the leaders. In the following selection M. L. Bush analyzes these differences.

CONSIDER: *Internal factors in non-Western societies that help explain these differences; contrasts between Portugal and Spain that help explain the different consequences for non-Western societies.*

The Castilian Empire in the West and the Portuguese Empire in the East had very different effects upon the world outside of Europe. In the first place, the Castilian expansion westwards precipitated a series of overseas migrations which were unparalleled in earlier times. For most of the sixteenth century, 1,000 or 2,000 Spaniards settled in the New World each year. Later this was

followed by a large wave of emigrants from northwestern Europe, fleeing from persecution at home to the Atlantic sea-board of North America and the Caribbean, and a final wave of Africans forced into slavery in the West Indies and in Brazil. On the other hand, in the East, there was virtually no settlement in the sixteenth century. Europe impressed itself only by fort, factory and church, by colonial official, trader and missionary.

In the second place, the settlement of the New World had a severe effect upon native peoples, whereas in the East, European influence was very slight until much later times.

In the early 1520s, the conquistadors brought with them smallpox and typhoid. Between them these European diseases soon decimated the Indian population, particularly in the great epidemics of the 1520s, 1540s and 1570s. In central Mexico, for example, an Indian population which numbered 11,000,000 in 1519 numbered no more than 2,500,000 by the end of the century. In addition, the Indian was beset by enormous grazing herds of horned cattle which the white settler introduced. He escaped the herds by working for the white settler, but if this led him to the crowded labour settlements, as it quite often did, he stood less chance of escaping infection. Either through falling hopelessly in debt as a result of desiring the goods of the white man, or through entering the labour settlements on a permanent basis to avoid the herds and also the system of obligatory labour introduced by the Spaniard,[1] there was a strong tendency for the Indian to become europeanised. He became a wage-earner, a debtor and a Christian. The Indian was exploited. But in the law he remained free. Enslavement was practised, but it was not officially tolerated. Moreover, the Franciscan order, a powerful missionary force in the New World, did its best to save the Indian from the evil ways of the white man. In Bartholomew de Las Casas and Francisco de Vitoria, the Indian found influential defenders; and through their schemes for separate Indian Christian communities, he found a partial escape from the white man. But the Indian mission towns, which were permitted by Charles V, were objected to by his successor, Philip II, and they only survived in remote areas.

With few exceptions, the way of life of the surviving Indians was basically changed by the coming of the white man. The outstanding exception was in Portuguese Brazil where the more primitive, nomadic Indians had a greater opportunity to retreat into the bush. There was also less settlement in Brazil, and generally less impression was made because of Portuguese preoccupations elsewhere,

SOURCE: M. L. Bush, *Renaissance, Reformation and the Outer World* (New York: Harper & Row, 1967), pp. 143–145.

---

[1]This system depended upon every Indian village offering a proportion of its menfolk or labour service for a limited amount of time throughout the year.

and also because of their lack of resources for empire-building on the Spanish scale. Furthermore, within the Spanish Empire, the European impressed himself less on the Incas in Peru than upon the Aztecs in Mexico. Because of the slow subjection of Peru, several Inca risings, the nature of the terrain, the smallness of the Spanish community, the process of europeanisation was much slower, and in the long run much less complete. The remnants of the Inca aristocracy became Spanish in their habits and Catholic in their religion, but the peasantry tended to remain pagan. In contrast to these developments, the westernisation of the East was a development of more modern times.

The West impinged upon the East in the sixteenth century mainly through the missionary. With the arrival of St. Francis Xavier in 1542 in India, an impressive process of conversion was begun. Concentrating upon the poor fishermen of the Cape Comorin coast, within ten years he had secured, it was said, 60,000 converts. The Jesuits fixed their attention on the East, choosing Goa as their main headquarters outside of Rome. Little was accomplished in Malaya, Sumatra and China in the sixteenth century, and Christianity soon suffered setbacks in the Moluccas after a promising start; but in Ceylon the conversion of the young king of Kotte in 1557 was a signal triumph, and so were the conversions in Japan. In the 1580s Jesuit missionaries in Japan claimed to have converted 150,000, most of whom, however, were inhabitants of the island of Kyushu.

Christianity was not a new religion in the East. There were extensive communities of Nestorian Christians, but they were regarded as alien as the Muslim by the Europeans. The new Christians by 1583 were supposed to number 600,000. But compared with the expansion of Islam in the East—a process which was taking place at the same time—the expansion of Christianity was a minute achievement.

Finally, the Portuguese sea empire did little to transport Portuguese habits abroad. Their empire was essentially formed in response to local conditions. On the other hand, the Spanish land empire was to a much greater extent reflective of Castilian ways.

In the New World a carefully developed and regulated system of government was established in which it was seen that the care taken to limit the independent power of feudal aristocrats in the Old World should also be applied to the New. There was a firm insistence upon government officials being royal servants. However, the government of the New World became much more regulated from the centre than that of the old. There was less respect for aristocratic privilege. Less power was unreservedly placed in the hands of the nobility. In the New World, in fact, the weaknesses of government, at first, did not lie in the powers and privileges of the nobility but

rather in the cumbersome nature of the government machinery. Nevertheless, in spite of these precautions, the New World, by the early seventeenth century, had become a land of great feudal magnates enjoying, in practice, untrammelled power.

Red, White, and Black: The Peoples of Early America

Gary Nash

Europeans often came into conflict with the peoples they encountered overseas. In the Americas, diverging understanding of the meaning of land ownership and, more broadly, private property, would lead to continual conflict. Europeans took for granted that people had the right to buy and sell land. Yet, this was not the case for Native Americans. In North America, European settlers would fence in land and hunt for private profit. This would undermine the entire livelihood of nomadic tribes that depended on freedom to move, hunt, and establish temporary communities. In the following selection, Gary Nash, a historian of early American history at UCLA, describes the clash of cultures and economic systems between white settlers and the native inhabitants of North America.

CONSIDER: *The differences between the Native American and European world views concerning land and personal identity; in light of what we now know regarding ecological destruction, how you might evaluate the Native American view of the symmetry of nature.*

While Native American and European cultures were not nearly so different as the concepts of "savagery" and "civilization" imply, societies on the eastern and western sides of the Atlantic had developed different systems of values in the centuries that preceded contact. Underlying the physical confrontations that would take place when European and Native American met were incompatible ways of looking at the world. These latent conflicts can be seen in contrasting European and Indian views of man's relationship to his environment, the concept of property, and personal identity.

In the European view the natural world was a resource for man to use. "Subdue the earth," it was said in Genesis, "and have dominion over every living thing that moves on the earth." The cosmos was still ruled by God, of course, and supernatural forces, manifesting themselves in earthquakes, hurricanes, drought, and flood, could not be controlled by man. But a scientific revolution was under way in the early modern period, which

SOURCE: Gary B. Nash, *Red, White and Black: The Peoples of Early America*, 3d ed. (Englewood Cliffs, NJ: Prentice-Hall, 1982), pp. 25–27. Copyright © 1982, 1992. Reprinted by permission of Prentice-Hall.

gave humans more confidence that they could comprehend the natural world—and thus eventually control it. For Europeans the secular and the sacred were distinct, and man's relationship to his natural environment fell into the secular sphere.

In the Indian ethos no such separation of secular and sacred existed. Every part of the natural world was sacred, for Native Americans believed the world was inhabited by a great variety of "beings," each possessing spiritual power and all linked together to form a sacred whole. "Plants, animals, rocks, and stars," explains Murray Wax, "are thus seen not as objects governed by laws of nature but as 'fellows' with whom the individual or band may have a more or less advantageous relationship." Consequently, if one offended the land by stripping it of its cover, the spiritual power in the land—called *manitou* by some woodlands tribes—would strike back. If one overfished or destroyed game beyond one's needs, the spiritual power inhering in fish and animals would take revenge because humans had broken the mutual trust and reciprocity that governed relations between all beings—human and nonhuman. To exploit the land or to treat with disrespect any part of the natural world was to cut oneself off from the spiritual power dwelling in all things and "was thus equivalent to repudiating the vital force in Nature."

Because Europeans regarded the land as a resource to be exploited for man's gain it was easier to regard it as a commodity to be privately held. Private ownership of property became one of the fundamental bases upon which European culture rested. Fences became the symbols of exclusively held property, inheritance became the mechanism for transmitting these "assets" from one generation to another within the same family, and courts provided the institutional apparatus for settling property disputes. In a largely agricultural society property became the basis of political power. In fact, political rights in England derived from the ownership of a specified quantity of land. In addition, the social structure was largely defined by the distribution of property, with those possessing great quantities of it standing at the apex of the social pyramid and the mass of propertyless individuals forming the broad base.

In the Indian world this view of land as a privately held asset was incomprehensible. Tribes recognized territorial boundaries, but within these limits the land was held in common. Land was not a commodity but a part of nature that was entrusted to the living by the Creator. . . . Thus, land was a gift of the Creator, to be used with care, and was not for the exclusive possession of particular human beings.

In the area of personal identity Indian and European values also differed sharply. Europeans were acquisitive, competitive, and over a long period of time had been enhancing the role of the individual. Wider choices and greater opportunities for the individual to improve his status—by industriousness, valor, or even personal sacrifice leading to martyrdom—were regarded as desirable. Personal ambition, in fact, played a large role in the migration of Europeans across the Atlantic in the sixteenth and seventeenth centuries. In contrast, the cultural traditions of Native Americans emphasized the collectivity rather than the individual. Because land and other natural resources were held in common and society was far less hierarchical than in Europe, the accumulative spirit and personal ambition were inappropriate. . . . Hence, individualism was more likely to lead to ostracism than admiration in Indian communities.

✑ CHAPTER QUESTIONS

1. What factors best explain the West's overseas expansion?

2. In what ways was overseas expansion tied to the political and economic developments of the fifteenth and sixteenth centuries?

3. What consequences flowed from this interaction of Western and non-Western civilizations?

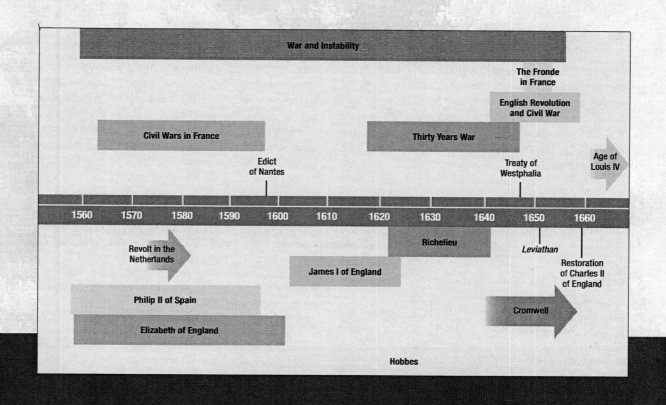

15 War and Revolution: 1560–1660

Between 1560 and 1660 war and revolution broke out throughout Europe. In France different political and religious factions struggled under a weak monarchy in what amounted at times to an extended civil war during the second half of the sixteenth century. Although stronger kings and ministers brought more stability during the seventeenth century, the nobility again rose at mid-century before the final assertion of French absolutism under Louis XIV. In Germany political and religious divisions contributed to the outbreak of a local war in 1618, which quickly turned into a bloody international war lasting thirty years, until it was ended by the Treaty of Westphalia in 1648. Few wars in history have been as devastating to Germany as this; perhaps a third of the people lost their

lives. In England the growing conflict between king and Parliament, further fueled by religious and social divisions, led to a revolution and civil war during the 1640s and the extraordinary rule of Oliver Cromwell during the 1650s. In 1660 relative stability was restored under Charles II. Finally, in the Netherlands extended bloodshed marked the long effort by Spain to retain control over the Dutch, who finally succeeded in gaining complete independence in 1648.

The documents in this chapter deal with three of the upheavals—in France, in Central Europe, and in England—during the period from the mid-sixteenth to mid-seventeenth centuries. What was the nature of the civil wars in sixteenth-century France? In what ways was monarchical absolutism an answer to the political and religious struggles in France? Was the Thirty Years' War in Central Europe primarily a German conflict or a struggle against the predominance of Spain? How important were religious as compared with political causes of this war? Beyond the death and destruction involved, how decisive or significant was this war? What was the nature of the conflict between royal and parliamentary authority in England? How did political theory in England reflect these conflicts? What were some of several consequences of all these struggles?

The materials in this chapter characterize this century as one of extraordinary violence—sometimes directed at women in particular—and struggle for political and religious control. The violence diminishes and a new sense of stability is gained in the second half of the seventeenth century, as will be seen in the next chapter.

Primary Sources

Civil War in France
Ogier Ghiselin de Busbecq

France was one of the first areas in which the turmoil, instability, and war characteristic of the period between 1560 and 1660 occurred. There, political and religious divisions combined to produce a long period of bloodshed and sporadic civil war. The nature and effects of this turmoil are described in the following selection from a letter written in 1575 by Ogier Ghiselin de Busbecq, the Holy Roman Emperor's ambassador to France.

CONSIDER: *Busbecq's perception of the forces and grievances that were threatening to worsen the civil wars that had already broken out; the consequences of the civil wars for various segments of society.*

Ever since the commencement of the civil wars which are distracting the country, there has been a terrible change for the worse. So complete is the alteration, that those who knew France before would not recognise her again. Everywhere are to be seen shattered buildings, fallen churches, and towns in ruins; while the traveller gazes horror-stricken on spots which have but lately been the scenes of murderous deeds and inhuman cruelties. The fields are left untilled: the farmer's stock and tools have been carried off by the soldier as his booty, he is plundered alike by Frenchman and by foreigner. Commerce is crippled; the towns lately thronged with merchants and customers are now mourning their desolation in the midst of closed shops and silent manufactories. Meanwhile, the inhabitants, ground down by ceaseless exactions, are crying out at the immense sums which are being squandered for nought, or applied to purposes for which they were never intended. They demand a reckoning in tones which breathe a spirit of rebellion. Men of experience, members of the oldest families in France, are in many cases regarded with suspicion, and either not allowed to come to Court, or left to vegetate at home. Besides the two parties into which Frenchmen are divided by their religious differences, there are also feuds and quarrels which affect every grade of society.

In the first place, the feeling against the Italians who are in the French service is very strong; the high promotion they have received and the important duties with which they have been intrusted, arouse the jealousy of men who consider them ignorant of French business, and hold that they have neither merit, services, nor birth to justify their appointment. . . .

The feuds which separate the leading families of France are more bitter than those described in ancient tragedy; this is the state of feeling which exists between the Houses of Guise, Vendôme and Bourbon, not to mention that of Montmorency, which, through its alliances and connections, has a considerable party of its own.

Political Will and Testament
Richelieu

The civil wars in France were ended under the rule of Henry IV at the end of the sixteenth century. This strong king prevailed over rival factions and strengthened the French monarchy. But religious conflict and the competition with the nobility for authority were not over in France. Rather, the monarchy was built up toward a position of absolutism under a series of powerful figures, including Cardinal Richelieu (1585–1642), who served as principal adviser to the king between 1624 and 1642 and virtual ruler for most of that period. In the following selection from his Political Will and Testament, *Richelieu presents his view of monarchical power.*

CONSIDER: *How Richelieu justifies monarchical power; how Machiavelli might have responded to this view.*

SOURCE: From Charles Thornton Forster and F. H. Blackburne Daniell, *The Life and Letters of Ogier Ghiselin de Busbecq*, vol. II (London, 1881), pp. 38–40.

SOURCE: Armand Jean du Plessis, Duc de Richelieu, *Political Will and Testament*, vol. II (London, 1695), pp. 45–46.

Power being one of the most necessary ingredients towards the grandeur of kings, and the prosperity of their governments; those who have the chief management of affairs are particularly obliged not to omit anything which may contribute to authorize their master so far as to make all the world reject him.

As goodness is the object of love, power is the cause of dread: and it is most certain, that among all the princes who are capable to stir a state, fear grounded upon esteem and reverence has so much force, that it engages everyone to perform his duty.

If this principle is of great efficacy in respect to the internal part of states, it is to the full as prevailing abroad: subjects and strangers looking with the same eyes upon a formidable power, both the one and the other abstain from offending a prince, whom they are sensible is in a condition to hurt them, if he were so inclined.

I have observed by the by, that the ground of the power I am speaking of must be esteem and respect; . . . that when it is grounded upon any other principle, it is very dangerous; in the case instead of creating a reasonable fear, it inclines men to hate princes, who are never in a worse condition than when it turns to public aversion.

The power which induces men to respect and fear princes with love . . . is a tree which has five divers branches, which all draw their nutriment and substance from one and the same root.

The Prince must be powerful by his reputation.

By a reasonable army always kept on foot.

And by a notable sum of money in his coffers, to supply unexpected exigencies, which often come to pass when they are least expected.

Finally, by the possession of his subjects' hearts. . . .

The Powers of the Monarch in England

James I

In England friction between the monarchy and Parliament increased under the Stuart kings, starting with James I. Already the Scottish monarch, James became King of England on the death of Elizabeth in 1603. James had a scholarly background and a reputation for his strong views about the monarchy. One of his clearest presentations of these views was in a speech to Parliament made in 1610. In it, he comments on the nature of the king's power, not simply in England but everywhere.

Source: From J. R. Tanner, *Constitutional Documents of the Reign of James I, C.E. 1603–1625* (Cambridge, England: Cambridge University Press, 1930), pp. 15–16. Reprinted by permission.

Consider: *How James justifies the high position and vast powers he feels should rightly belong to kings; the limits to monarchical powers.*

The state of Monarchy is the supremest thing upon earth; for kings are not only God's lieutenants upon earth and sit upon God's throne, but even by God himself they are called gods. There be three principal similitudes that illustrate the state of Monarchy: one taken out of the Word of God and the two other out of the grounds of policy and philosophy. In the Scriptures kings are called gods, and so their power after a certain relation compared to the Divine power. Kings are also compared to the fathers of families, for a king is truly *parens patriae*, the politic father of his people. And lastly, kings are compared to the head of his microcosm of the body of man.

Kings are justly called gods for that they exercise a manner or resemblance of Divine power upon earth; for if you will consider the attributes to God you shall see how they agree in the person of a king. God hath power to create or destroy, make or unmake, at his pleasure; to give life or send death; to judge all, and to be judged nor acomptable to none; to raise low things and to make high things low at his pleasure; and to God are both soul and body due. And the like power have kings; they make and unmake their subjects; they have power of raising and casting down; of life and of death; judges over all their subjects and in all causes, and yet acomptable to none but God only. They have power to exalt low things and abase high things, and make of their subjects like men at the chess, a pawn to take a bishop or a knight, and to cry up or down any of their subjects as they do their money. And to the King is due both the affection of the soul and the service of the body of his subjects. . . .

As for the father of a family, they had of old under the Law of Nature *patriam potestatem*, which was *potestatem vitae et necis*, over their children or family, (I mean such fathers of families as were the lineal heirs of those families whereof kings did originally come), for kings had their first original from them who planted and spread themselves in colonies through the world. Now a father may dispose of his inheritance to his children at his pleasure, yea, even disinherit the eldest upon just occasions and prefer the youngest, according to his liking; make them beggars or rich at his pleasure; restrain or banish out of his presence, as he finds them give cause of offence, or restore them in favour again with the penitent sinner. So may the King deal with his subjects.

And lastly, as for the head of the natural body, the head hath the power of directing all the members of the body to that use which the judgment in the head thinks most convenient.

The Powers of Parliament in England

The House of Commons

James' views on monarchical powers were not accepted by members of Parliament. Indeed, from the beginning of his reign through the reign of his son Charles I, king and Parliament struggled over their relative powers. Along with other problems, this struggle culminated in the 1640s with the outbreak of civil war and the eventual beheading of Charles I. The nature of this struggle is partially revealed in the following statements issued by the House of Commons in 1604 to the new king, James I.

CONSIDER: *The powers over which the House of Commons and the king differed; the justifications used by James I and the House of Commons for their claims; any ways in which compromise was possible between these two positions.*

Now concerning the ancient rights of the subjects of this realm, chiefly consisting in the privileges of this House of Parliament, the misinformation openly delivered to your Majesty hath been in three things:

First, That we held not privileges of right, but of grace only, renewed every Parliament by way of donature upon petition, and so to be limited.

Secondly, That we are no Court of Record, nor yet a Court that can command view of records, but that our proceedings here are only to acts and memorials, and that the attendance with the records is courtesy, not duty.

Thirdly and lastly, That the examination of the return of writs for knights and burgesses is without our compass, and due to the Chancery.

Against which assertions, most gracious Sovereign, tending directly and apparently to the utter overthrow of the very fundamental privileges of our House, and therein of the rights and liberties of the whole Commons of your realm of England which they and their ancestors from time immemorable have undoubtedly enjoyed under your Majesty's most noble progenitors, we, the knights, citizens, and burgesses of the House of Commons assembled in Parliament, and in the name of the whole commons of the realm of England, with uniform consent for ourselves and our posterity, do expressly protest, as being derogatory in the highest degree to the true dignity, liberty, and authority of your Majesty's High Court of Parliament, and consequently to the rights of all your Majesty's said subjects and the whole body of this your kingdom: And desire that this our protestation may be recorded to all posterity.

And contrariwise, with all humble and due respect to your Majesty our Sovereign Lord and Head, against those misinformations we most truly avouch,

First, That our privileges and liberties are our right and due inheritance, no less than our very lands and goods.

Secondly, That they cannot be withheld from us, denied, or impaired, but with apparent wrong to the whole state of the realm.

Thirdly, And that our making of request in the entrance of Parliament to enjoy our privilege is an act only of manners, and doth weaken our right no more than our suing to the King for our lands by petition. . . .

Fourthly, We avouch also, That our House is a Court of Record, and so ever esteemed.

Fifthly, That there is not the highest standing Court in this land that ought to enter into competency, either for dignity or authority, with this High Court of Parliament, which with your Majesty's royal assent gives laws to other Courts but from other Courts receives neither laws nor orders.

Sixthly and lastly, We avouch that the House of Commons is the sole proper judge of return of all such writs and of the election of all such members as belong to it, without which the freedom of election were not entire: And that the Chancery, though a standing Court under your Majesty, be to send out those writs and receive the returns and to preserve them, yet the same is done only for the use of the Parliament, over which neither the Chancery nor any other Court ever had or ought to have any manner of jurisdiction.

From these misinformed positions, most gracious Sovereign, the greatest part of our troubles, distrusts, and jealousies have risen.

The Hammer of Witches

Heinrich Krämer and Jacob Sprenger

The upheavals of the period between 1560 and 1660 included growing violence against women in the form of persecuting women as witches. While witch hunting was widespread, it was particularly prevalent in Germany, where both Catholics and Protestants took part in the hunts and prosecutions. Authorities often used witch-hunters' manuals as guides to beliefs about witches. The most influential of these manuals, the Malleus Maleficarum (The Hammer of Witches), was written in 1486 by two Dominican Inquisitors. The following excerpt focuses on why most witches were women.

CONSIDER: *Exactly why, according to these authors, women are more likely than men to be witches; what this reveals about attitudes toward women.*

SOURCE: From J. R. Tanner, *Constitutional Documents of the Reign of James I, C.E. 1603–1625* (Cambridge, England: Cambridge University Press, 1930), pp. 220–222. Reprinted by permission.

SOURCE: Alan C. Kors and Edward Peters, eds. *Witchcraft in Europe, 1100–1700, A Documentary History.* (Philadelphia: University of Pennsylvania Press, 1972), pp. 114, 119, 121, 123.

As for the first question, why a greater number of witches is found in the fragile feminine sex than among men . . . the first reason is, that they are more credulous, and since the chief aim of the devil is to corrupt faith, therefore he rather attacks them . . . the second reason is, that women are naturally more impressionable, and . . . the third reason is that they have slippery tongues, and are unable to conceal from their fellow-women those things which by evil arts they know. . . . But the natural reason is that she is more carnal than a man, as is clear from her many carnal abominations. And it should be noted that there was a defect in the formation of the first woman, since she was formed from a bent rib, that is, a rib of the breast, which is bent as it were in a contrary direction to a man. And since through this defect she is an imperfect animal, she always deceives. . . . And this is indicated by the etymology of the world; for Femina comes from Fe and Minus, since she is ever weaker to hold and preserve the faith. . . . To conclude. All witchcraft comes from carnal lust, which is in women insatiable.

Visual Sources

The Surrender of Breda

Diego Valázquez

The long, draining Thirty Years' War (1618–1648) marked the first half of the seventeenth century. A major component of that complex set of conflicts was the effort of Protestants in Holland to free themselves from their Catholic Spanish overlords.

In this canvass (figure 15.1) commissioned by his monarch, Spanish artist Diego Valázquez celebrates the 1625 victory of Spain's Catholic forces over Protestant

FIGURE 15.1 (© Erich Lessing/Art Resource, NY)

Breda in Holland. The long war between the rebellious Dutch and their Spanish overlords had begun six years earlier. The painting centers on the moment when, after a year-long siege, Breda's commander Justin of Nassau handed over the keys of the city to his graceful counterpart, General Ambrogio Spinola. As indicated by his posture, the Spanish general greets the Dutch commander consolingly and with praise for the brave defense he and his soldiers have mounted. The magnanimity of the victorious Spanish reflects the sense that during the sixteenth and first decades of the seventeenth centuries, Spain's monarchs thought of themselves as the most powerful rulers in Europe, thanks to their glorious history of military conquest. The many long pikes held up vertically symbolize the order and strength of the Spanish forces, although in fact—as was typically the case on all sides of the Thirty Years' War—many of these soldiers were foreign mercenaries. Spinola's grace also suggests the Spanish belief in the ultimate justice of their Catholic cause.

Despite this Spanish victory, General Spinola's overly generous chivalric gesture and terms of surrender allowed the Dutch forces to keep their weapons and remain intact as they exited the town. The Dutch would again turn those forces against the declining armies of Spain and ultimately gain victory in the war.

CONSIDER: *How the vision of "honorable" battle is depicted in this painting; the nature of seventeenth-century warfare suggested by Valázquez's painting.*

War and Violence

Jan Brueghel and Sebastien Vrancx

This painting (figure 15.2), by the Flemish artists Jan Brueghel (1568–1625) and Sebastien Vrancx (1573–1647), is of marauding armies during the Thirty Years' War. This war was a disaster for Germany not only because of its length and viciousness, but because of the common use of mercenary soldiers. In this picture mercenaries, without common uniforms or banners, attack what appears to be a wagon train of civilians probably fleeing on hearing rumors of their approach. Women and children are being attacked by the mercenaries, as are men, whether armed or not. Johann Jakob Christoffel von Grimmelshausen, a contemporary observer of such mercenaries, described them as inflicting "nothing but hurting and harming and being in their turn hurt and harmed, this was their whole purpose and existence. From this nothing could divert them—not winter or summer, snow or ice, heat or cold, wind or rain, mountain or valley, . . . or the very fear of eternal damnation itself. At this task they laboured until at last, in battles,

FIGURE 15.2 (© Erich Lessing/Art Resource, NY)

sieges, assaults, campaigns, or even in their winter quarters, which is the soldiers' paradise, one by one they died, perished and rotted." The picture conveys the sense of almost random, out-of-control violence that was so typical of this period.

CONSIDER: *The ways in which this painting and this observation might be used to describe how the Thirty Years' War was experienced by those involved.*

Leviathan: Political Order and Political Theory

Thomas Hobbes

Although England avoided the Thirty Years' War, it had its own experiences with passionate war and disruption of authority. Between 1640 and 1660 England endured the civil war, the trial and execution of its king, Charles I, the rise to power of Oliver Cromwell, and the return to power of the Stuart king, Charles II. These events stimulated Thomas Hobbes (1588–1679) to formulate one of the most important statements of political theory in history.

Hobbes supported the royalist cause during the civil war and served as tutor to the future Charles II. Applying some of the new philosophical and scientific concepts being developed during the seventeenth century, he presented a theory for the origins and proper functioning of the state and political authority. His main ideas appear in Leviathan (1651), the title page of which appears here (figure 15.3). It shows a giant monarchical figure, with symbols of power and authority, presiding over a well-ordered city and surrounding lands. On close examination one can see that the monarch's body is composed of the citizens of this commonwealth who, according to Hobbes' theory, have mutually agreed to give up their independence to an all-powerful sovereign who will keep order. This is explained in the following selection from Hobbes' book, in which he relates the reasons for the formation of a commonwealth to the nature of authority in that commonwealth.

FIGURE 15.3 (© HIP/Art Resource, NY)

CONSIDER: *Why men form such a commonwealth and why they give such power to the sovereign; how Hobbes' argument compares with that of James I; why both those*

SOURCE: Thomas Hobbes, *Leviathan*, vol. III of *The English Works of Thomas Hobbes*, ed. Sir William Molesworth (London: John Bohn, 1889), pp. 113, 151–153, 157, 159.

favoring more power for the House of Commons and those favoring increased monarchical power might criticize this argument.

Whatsoever therefore is consequent to a time of war, where every man is enemy to every man; the same is consequent to the time, wherein men live without other security, than what their own strength, and their own invention shall furnish them withal. In such condition, there is no place for industry; because the fruit thereof is uncertain: and consequently no culture of the earth; no navigation, nor use of the commodities that may be imported by sea; no commodious building; no instruments of moving, and removing, such things as require much force; no knowledge of the face of the earth; no account of time; no arts; no letters; no society; and which is worst of all, continual fear, and danger of violent death; and the life of man, solitary, poor, nasty, brutish, and short. . . .

The final cause, end, or design of men who naturally love liberty, and dominion over others, in the introduction of that restraint upon themselves, in which we see them live in commonwealths, is the foresight of their own preservation, and of a more contented life thereby; that is to say, of getting themselves out from that miserable condition of war, which is necessarily consequent, as hath been shown in chapter XIII, to the natural passions of men, when there is no visible power to keep them in awe, and tie them by fear of punishment to the performance of their covenants, and observation of those laws of nature set down. . . .

For the laws of nature, as *justice, equity, modesty, mercy,* and, in sum, doing to others, as we would be done to, of themselves, without the terror of some power, to cause them to be observed, are contrary to our natural passions, that carry us to partiality, pride, revenge, and the like. And covenants, without the sword, are but words, and of no strength to secure a man at all. . . .

The only way to erect such a common power, as may be able to defend them from the invasion of foreigners, and the injuries of one another, and thereby to secure them in such sort, as that by their own industry, and by the fruits of the earth, they may nourish themselves and live contentedly; is, to confer all their power and strength upon one man, or upon one assembly of men, that may reduce all their wills, by plurality of voices, unto one will: which is as much as to say, to appoint one man, or assembly of men, to bear their person; and every one to own, and acknowledge himself to be author of whatsoever he that so beareth their person, shall act, or cause to be acted, in those things which concern the common peace and safety; and therein to submit their wills, every one to his will, and their judgments, to his judgment. This is more than consent, or concord; it is a real unity of them all, in one and the same person, made by covenant of every man with every man, in such manner, as if every man should say to every man, *I authorise and give up my right of governing myself, to this man, or to this assembly of men, on this condition, that thou give up thy right to him, and authorise all his actions in like manner.* This done, the multitude so united in one person, is called a COMMONWEALTH, . . . This is the generation of that great LEVIATHAN, or rather, to speak more reverently, of that *mortal god,* to which we owe under the *immortal God,* our peace and defence. For by this authority, given him by every particular man in the

MAP 15.1 Political and Religious Divisions

commonwealth, he hath the use of so much power and strength conferred on him, that by terror thereof, he is enabled to perform the wills of them all, to peace at home, and mutual aid against their enemies abroad. And in him consisteth the essence of the commonwealth; which to define it, is *one person, of whose acts a great multitude, by mutual covenants one with another, have made themselves every one the author, to the end he may use the strength and means of them all, as he shall think expedient, for their peace and common defence.*

And he that carrieth this person, is called SOVEREIGN, and said to have *sovereign power*; and every one besides, his subject.

Germany and the Thirty Years' War

These maps center on circumstances in Germany during the Thirty Years' War. The first (map 15.1) shows the approximate political and religious divisions at the beginning of the war. This map is simplified for clarity in a number of ways. It does not show areas of minority religious allegiance or areas where Protestant sects other than Calvinists or Lutherans made up substantial proportions of the population. It denotes only some of the political divisions, which numbered close to three hundred in this area. The second map (map 15.2) shows the main areas of battle during the Thirty Years' War. Map 15.3 indicates the changes in population, primarily due to war and plague, between 1618 and 1648.

Together, these maps reveal some of the political and religious problems facing Germany. Despite the theoretical existence of the Holy Roman Empire, Germany was in reality the most politically and religiously divided area in seventeenth-century Europe. It is thus not surprising that historians find it difficult to determine the political and religious factors causing this war and the responsibility for its long continuation. Some of the demographic effects are indicated

MAP 15.2   **Main War Zones**

MAP 15.3   **Population Change: 1618–1648**

through a comparison of the main areas of battle and changes in population. Indeed, the continued political and religious division of Germany after this war, along with such massive destruction of the area and the population, helps explain Germany's weakness and inability to unify for the following two centuries.

CONSIDER: *In what ways the geopolitical and religious divisions of Germany explain the duration and extent of damages of the Thirty Years' War; how historians might use these maps to support their interpretations of the causes and significance of the Thirty Years' War.*

Secondary Sources

A Political Interpretation of the Thirty Years' War

Hajo Holborn

Historians have long disagreed about the essential causes of the Thirty Years' War. Some focus on a particular area, such as Germany or Spain; others emphasize a particular set of causes, such as religion or politics; and still others argue that it was only part of a general seventeenth-century crisis affecting all aspects of society. In the following selection Hajo Holborn, a historian known for his work on German history, argues that the war was primarily a political struggle in the German states of the Hapsburgs. He accepts the religious issue as at most a contributing cause.

CONSIDER: *The role religion played in the conflict even though it may not have been primary in causing the war; other factors that might have caused the war.*

It was not a conflict among European powers, not even an acute controversy between the emperor and the princes of the Empire or among these princes themselves that led to the outbreak of the long war that lived on in the memory of the German people as the "Great War" and in the books of the historians as the Thirty Years' War. Rather, it was a struggle between the estates and the monarchy in the territories of the Habsburg dynasty which set fire to all of Germany and to the European continent. Without the grave crisis in the constitutional life of the Empire, the weakness of the German states, and the ambitions of the great powers of Europe, the events that occurred in Bohemia could not have developed into a disaster from which Germany was to emerge crippled and mutilated.

It is difficult to determine to what extent differences in the interpretation of Christian faith were a direct cause of the catastrophe. There is no doubt but that religious motivation was strong in the lives of individuals and societies, and even in the relations among states and nations, in this age. But the confessional war started at a time when enthusiasm for the religious revivals, both Protestant and Catholic, had lost much of its original force and religious ideas had again become conventionalized. Frank skepticism was rare in Germany, but ever larger groups of people had ceased to find in religious ideals the full satisfaction of their human aspirations.

Nevertheless, the reality of heaven and hell was nowhere questioned, nor was the necessity of basing the political and social order on principles that would keep Satan from undoing the work of God. Religious zeal found expression not only in the ghastly fury of witch trials, which reached its climax during these years, but also in the care with which all governments attended to the direction of church life in their dominions. Yet while on the one hand religion deteriorated into superstition, on the other it tended to become formalized and to lose genuineness. Every political action was publicly cloaked in religious terms, but religion seemed to be used more and more to rationalize actions motivated by secular interests.

A Religious Interpretation of the Thirty Years' War

Carl J. Friedrich

An older scholarly tradition attributes primary importance to religion in explaining the causes of the Thirty Years' War. This tradition has been revived by Carl J. Friedrich, a highly respected historian from Harvard. In The Age of the Baroque, 1610–1660, Friedrich places the war in the context of the still strong religious assumptions of the time, arguing that historians who emphasize political causes overlook the importance of this religious context. The following is an excerpt from that work.

CONSIDER: *The evidence Friedrich uses to support his argument; why, according to Friedrich, many historians have rejected the religious interpretation of the war; how Holborn might criticize this argument.*

It has been the fashion to minimize the religious aspect of the great wars which raged in the heart of Europe, over the territory of the Holy Roman Empire of the German Nation. Not only the calculating statecraft of Richelieu and Mazarin, but even Pope Urban VIII's own insistence lent support to such a view in a later age which had come to look upon religion and politics as fairly well separated fields of thought and action. Liberal historians found it difficult to perceive that for baroque man religion and politics were cut from the same cloth, indeed that the most intensely political issues were precisely the religious ones. Gone was the neopaganism of the renaissance, with

SOURCE: Hajo Holborn, *A History of Modern Germany: The Reformation* (New York: Alfred A. Knopf, 1959), pp. 305–306.

SOURCE: Excerpts from *The Age of the Baroque* by Carl J. Friedrich. Copyright 1952 by Harper & Row, Publishers, Inc. Reprinted by permission of HarperCollins Publishers, Inc.

its preoccupation with self-fulfillment here and now. Once again, and for the last time, life was seen as meaningful in religious, even theological, terms, and the greater insight into power which the renaissance had brought served merely to deepen the political passion brought to the struggle over religious faiths.

Without a full appreciation of the close links between secular and religious issues, it becomes impossible to comprehend the Thirty Years' War. Frederick, the unlucky Palatine, as well as Ferdinand, Tilly and Gustavus Adolphus, Maximilian of Bavaria and John George of Saxony, they all must be considered fools unless their religious motivation is understood as the quintessential core of their politics. Time and again, they appear to have done the "wrong thing," if their actions are viewed in a strictly secular perspective. To be sure, men became increasingly sophisticated as the war dragged on; but even after peace was finally concluded in 1648, the religious controversies continued. Ever since the Diet of Augsburg (1555) had adopted the callous position that a man must confess the religion of those who had authority over the territory he lived in—a view which came to be known under the slogan of "*cujus regio, ejus religio*"— the intimate tie of religion and government had been the basis of the Holy Empire's tenuous peace. Born of the spirit of its time—Lutheran otherworldliness combining with Humanistic indifferentism—this doctrine was no more than an unstable compromise between Catholics and Lutherans, the Calvinists being entirely outside its protective sphere. But in the seventeenth century not only the Calvinists, who by 1618 had become the fighting protagonists of Protestantism, but likewise the more ardent Catholics, inspired by the Council of Trent, by the Jesuits and Capuchins, backed by the power of Spain and filled with the ardor of the Counter Reformation, had come to look upon this doctrine as wicked and contrary to their deepest convictions.

When Ferdinand, after claiming the crown of Bohemia by heredity, proceeded to push the work of counter reformation, his strongest motivation was religious; so was the resistance offered by the Bohemian people, as well as Frederick's acceptance of the crown of Bohemia on the basis of an election. Dynastic and national sentiments played their part, surely, but they reinforced the basic religious urge. The same concurrence of religious with dynastic, political, even economic motives persisted throughout the protracted struggle, but the religious did not cease to be the all-pervasive feeling; baroque man, far from being bothered by the contradictions, experienced these polarities as inescapable.

If religion played a vital role in persuading Ferdinand II to dismiss his victorious general, it was even more decisive in inspiring Gustavus Adolphus to enter the war against both the emperor and the League. The

nineteenth century, incapable of feeling the religious passions which stirred baroque humanity and much impressed with the solidified national states which the seventeenth century bequeathed to posterity, was prone to magnify the dynastic and often Machiavellian policies adopted by rulers who professed to be deeply religious, and the twentieth century has largely followed suit in denying the religious character of these wars. But it is precisely this capacity to regard the statesman as the champion of religion, to live and act the drama of man's dual dependence upon faith and power that constituted the quintessence of the baroque.

War and Peace in the Old Regime
M. S. Anderson

Western societies rarely went for long periods of time without becoming involved in wars. However, war was particularly prevalent and destructive in the period between 1618 and 1660. Historians have long debated the causes for these wars. In the following selection, M. S. Anderson, who has written extensively on the Early Modern period, analyzes what war meant to Europeans and the broader significance of war during the seventeenth century.

CONSIDER: *How Europeans perceived the causes, nature, and consequences of war; the distinctions between war and peace; the connections between war and politics.*

In early modern Europe almost everyone regarded war as a normal, perhaps even a necessary, part of human life. Events seemed to bear out this view; in the period 1618–60 every year saw serious armed conflict between states somewhere in Europe, and during a large proportion of it destructive struggles were being waged simultaneously in several parts of the continent. The ubiquity and apparent inevitability of war meant that serious discussion of its causes was rare. As an integral and unavoidable aspect of existence it was received like bad weather or epidemics, as something clearly beyond the power of the ordinary man to avert, something demanding acceptance rather than analysis. Luther's dictum that "war is as necessary as eating, drinking or any other business" reflects in typically blunt terms this matter-of-fact and fatalistic attitude. Nor was there much grasp of the deeper and more lasting effects it might sometimes have. It was only too obvious that in the short term it meant for many death, destruction and loss. But against this was put the venerable and well-established argument that

SOURCE: M. S. Anderson. *War and Society in Europe of the Old Regime, 1618–1789.* (New York: St. Martin's Press, 1988), pp. 13–15.

prolonged peace weakened the moral fibre of a society, making it lax, slothful, even corrupt, whereas war focused and mobilized energies, called forth many of the better qualities of man, and had a generally tonic and purifying effect. It was clear also that a successful war could heighten the personal prestige of a ruler; the vindication of claims put forward by monarchs to disputed territories, to alleged hereditary rights, even merely to precedence over rivals or to specific symbols of such precedence, were by far the most common ostensible causes of conflict. Occasionally it was realized that war might have important long-term economic results, that it might foster the trade of a victorious state against that of its defeated enemies and that economic rivalry might be one of its causes. Struggles inspired simply or even mainly by this kind of material rivalry were not frequent in this period but they did take place. . . . However the idea that war might, through the demands it made on societies and the impetus it gave to the growth of powerful central governments, help fundamentally to change these societies, was still a strange one. . . .

Finally, a clear-cut distinction between war and peace, a dividing line whose crossing was instantly recognizable, was something which was only beginning to emerge. The position of neutrals was still ambiguous, their status poorly guaranteed by embryonic international law and liable to frequent infringements. There was a general belief that a belligerent had some right to march its forces across neutral territory if it made good any damage they caused in the process (the right of *transitus innoxius*). Frontiers were still poorly defined, zones of contact between neighbouring powers rather than lines clearly demarcated. The hold of central governments over officials and commanders in border areas was often still incomplete, so that in these areas locally inspired acts of oppression and outright violence could frequently occur, though usually without involving the states concerned in formal conflict. In this violent age incidents of this kind formed a sort of grumbling undertone to international relations, seldom actively menacing peace between states but always a potential threat. . . .

Armed conflict in early seventeenth-century Europe, therefore, ramified into every aspect of life and was able to do this because it was still in many ways badly defined, because the boundary between peace and war was still fuzzy. But lack of clear definition did nothing to reduce its importance. Most of the governments of Europe were first and foremost, as they had been for generations, machines for waging war. Both the scale on which they fought and the effective control they could exert over their fighting forces were to increase markedly during the seventeenth and early eighteenth centuries.

The Causes of the English Civil War
Conrad Russell

The civil war in England, which broke out in the middle of the seventeenth century, is even more controversial among historians than the Thirty Years' War. At the heart of the controversy are two related issues: first, what the balance of religious, political, economic, and social forces was in causing the civil war; second, what groups or classes can be said to have supported each side. In the following selection Conrad Russell argues that the civil war resulted from a conjunction of three causes of instability: the problem of multiple kingdoms (England and Scotland), the problem of religious division, and the financial pressures on the crown.

CONSIDER: *How Russell's three causes worked together; why Charles' attempt to enforce English religion on Scotland in 1637 was so important.*

[The English Civil War] was the result of three long-term causes of instability, all of them well established before Charles came to the throne, and all of them ones which can be observed to have troubled European, as well as British, monarchies. There is nothing peculiarly British (still less English) about any of them: they were not even exceptionally acute in England. What is peculiar to the two cases of England and the Netherlands is that all of them came to a head at the same time. These three long-term causes were the problem of multiple kingdoms, the problem of religious division, and the breakdown of a financial and political system in the face of inflation and the rising cost of war.

The problem of multiple kingdoms was always a likely cause of instability from 1603 onwards. The temptation to press for greater harmonization was always there, and was always likely to produce serious troubles. In 1603 England encountered . . . the shock of subjection to a supranational authority. . . . [T]he English . . . wished to treat both James and Charles as if they were only kings of a single nation-state called England. Since this was patently not the case, and the kings could not help knowing it, the English were always likely to misread royal actions, and in particular to press their kings to do things which, in British terms, they could not do. When, as in 1637, a British king fell victim to a similar misapprehension, and attempted to govern all Britain as king of England, he found this was something he could not do. . . .

England's basic error in 1603 was the failure to absorb that what had taken place was the union of two sovereign, and therefore legally equal, states. Not even James

---

could really turn Scotland into "North Britain." It was a state with institutions, law, and culture of its own, and one determined to insist that any resulting relationship must be a legally equal partnership. . . .

[T]he problem of religious division . . . derived its explosive force from the belief that religion ought to be enforced. It was a problem of a society which had carried on the assumptions appropriate to a society with a single church into one which had many churches. . . .

But August 1640, when the Scottish army, by entering England, merged the religious problem with the British problem, was too early for it to have cooled enough. One might say of the English Calvinists what Machiavelli said of the Pope in Italy: they were too weak to unite the country, but too strong to allow anyone else to do so. When the Scots entered England, they were able to join forces with a large group of people who preferred Scottish religion to what was coming to be taken for their own.

The strains caused for monarchies by the combination of inflation with the massive increases in the cost of war known collectively as "the military revolution" is also a European theme. The financial difficulties faced, after the conclusion of the long wars of the 1590s, by James VI and I, Philip III of Spain, and Henri IV of France have too much in common to be entirely coincidental. The changes following the regular use of gunpowder, especially the trend to larger-scale fortifications and to larger armies, much increased the economic drain of war. The resulting financial pressures put strain on the principle of consent to taxation everywhere in Europe, and perhaps only the Netherlands, with the advantage of a visible enemy at the gate, were able to combine consent with the levying of taxes on the scale needed. England, because the principle of consent to taxation was so particularly well entrenched, was perhaps put under more constitutional strain by this process than some other powers. . . .

No one, or even two, of these forces was in the event enough: it took the conjunction of all three to drive England into civil war. . . . Both the religious and the financial problem had been plainly visible by the 1550s, and they had not created civil war in ninety years since then. England in 1637 was, no doubt, a country with plenty of discontents, some of them potentially serious, but it was also still a very stable and peaceful one, and one which does not show many visible signs of being on the edge of a major upheaval. . . . The attempt which Charles made in 1637 to enforce English religion on Scotland, was thus by far the likeliest reason for a merging of these three long-term causes of instability. It is difficult to argue that Charles took this risk with his eyes open. It is equally difficult to see what action a king could have taken which would have been better designed to precipitate an English civil war.

The Devil's Handmaid: Women in the Age of Reformations

William Monter

As indicated by the document The Hammer of Witches, *beliefs in witchcraft were widespread during the sixteenth and seventeenth centuries, and authoritative sources supported the belief that most witches were women. Many people were also accused of killing their children (infanticide). For both witchcraft and infanticide, the vast majority of those accused were women. In this selection, William Monter, a historian specializing in the Reformation era, analyzes why witchcraft and infanticide seemed to grow in sixteenth- and seventeenth-century Europe.*

CONSIDER: *Which three developments best explain the growing prosecutions for witchcraft and infanticide during this period; which groups of women were most affected and why.*

Three key developments combined and interacted to shape the male hysteria about witchcraft and infanticide in Reformation Europe. First and foremost, public institutions—state and church alike—were increasingly interfering in daily life. Throughout Protestant and Catholic Europe, the state enforced attendance at church; church officials preached obedience to the state; and both increasingly tried to regulate everyone's behavior. Ecclesiastical courts such as Catholic inquisitions or Calvinist consistories depended heavily on state enforcement of their policies; states like England or France relied on clergymen to provide records of baptisms or to proclaim government edicts from the pulpit.

Secondly, these increasingly active public authorities inhabited a fear-ridden world. Most Protestant and Catholic Europeans still peered at their neighbors from walled towns and fortified castles; Luther's greatest hymn begins, "A Mighty Fortress is our God." We cannot find many material reasons for such pervasive fears at this time; bubonic plague, the great killer of pre-industrial Europe, did most of its damage either before or after the age of reformations. The reformers of Protestant and Catholic Europe, determined to attack all forms of "superstition" (including, of course, witchcraft), reduced the influence of benevolent magic, like exorcisms or special prayers, but provided nothing to replace them. Modern science did not yet exist; official medicine often had no

SOURCE: William Monter, "Protestant Wives, Catholic Saints, and the Devil's Handmaid: Women in the Age of Reformations," in Renate Bridenthal, Claudia Koonz, and Susan Stuard, eds., *Becoming Visible: Women in European History,* First and Second Editions, copyright © 1977 & 1987 by Houghton Mifflin Company. Used with permission.

explanations (and worse, no effective remedies) for many illnesses. Under such conditions, Protestant and Catholic reformers imposed the "Triumph of Lent" on unwed mothers of stillborns, and made old women with deviant dreams into scapegoats for sixteenth-century Christianity's obsession with the Devil.

Finally, the patriarchal theories of late-Renaissance Europe played an important role in determining which groups of women became victims of these obsessions. Accused witches were disproportionately widows, while infanticide defendants were single women; both groups lived outside direct male supervision in this age of reinforced patriarchal nuclear families. Their "unnatural" position aroused suspicion and sometimes fear; neighborhood enmities did the rest.

❧ CHAPTER QUESTIONS

1. Clearly, there were both political and religious aspects to the turmoil between 1560 and 1660. On balance, which do you think were most important? On what evidence have you based your answer? What argument can be formulated that admits the importance of both aspects?

2. How might the themes in this chapter be related to the political and religious developments from the mid-fifteenth to the mid-sixteenth centuries that were the focus of the two preceding chapters?

3. How might the rise of monarchical absolutism be related to the turmoil of this period?

Age of Louis IV

War and Instability

Ancien Regime

Saint-Simon

Frederick William

Death of Louis XIV

1660 1670 1680 1690 1700 1710 1720

Vaux-le-Vicomte

Court Moves to Versailles

Glorious Revolution in England

Two Treatises of Civli Government

Peace of Utrecht

John Locke

16 Aristocracy and Absolutism in the Seventeenth Century

The second half of the seventeenth century was a period of relative political stability in Europe. Although wars still occurred, they lacked the intensity of the preceding period. In the ascendant states, such as France, Prussia, Austria, Russia, and England, central governments were gaining authority. The primary power, and for many states the model of political authority, was France. There, Louis XIV, supported by a strong standing army, a policy of mercantilism, and a growing bureaucracy, wielded absolute power. There were similar situations in Prussia, Austria, and Russia. A different pattern occurred in England, where the central government remained strong while the monarchy itself weakened. There, after the return to power of the Stuart kings between 1660 and 1688, a revolution furthered the authority of Parliament.

During this period, important social, political, and economic changes occurred unevenly and generally benefited those who were already prominent and well to do. Aristocrats lost some of their independence to kings in countries like France and Prussia, but they continued to staff most of the important government offices, to maintain their elevated prestige, and to influence cultural styles and tastes. For most people, the structure of society, the way of life, and the relevant institutions changed little throughout this period.

This chapter concentrates on two broad topics: the growth of central government and Early Modern society. The selections address a number of questions. For the first topic, what was the nature of monarchical absolutism in France? How did it differ from Prussian monarchical absolutism? How did the pattern of monarchical absolutism compare with the growth of parliamentary power in England? What institutions and policies were developed to facilitate the growth of central governments? For the second topic, what was the nature of the family in Early Modern Europe? What were typical attitudes toward childhood? What were the traditional values and patterns of life for commoners during this period?

This dual focus should provide some broad insights into Europe during the seventeenth century and help establish a background for eighteenth-century developments.

 Primary Sources

Austria Over All If She Only Will: Mercantilism

Philipp W. von Hornick

Mercantilism, a loose set of economic ideas and corresponding government policies, was a common component of political absolutism during the seventeenth century. Typical mercantilist goals were the acquisition of bullion, a positive balance of trade, and economic self-sufficiency. An unusually clear and influential statement of mercantilist policies was published in 1684 by Philipp Wilhelm von Hornick. A lawyer and later a government official, Hornick set down what he considered to be the nine principal rules for a proper economic policy. These are excerpted here.

CONSIDER: *The political and military purposes served by encouraging mercantilist policies; the foreign policy decisions such economic policies would support; the political and economic circumstances that would make it easiest for a country to adhere to and benefit from mercantilist policies.*

NINE PRINCIPAL RULES OF NATIONAL ECONOMY

If the might and eminence of a country consist in its surplus of gold, silver, and all other things necessary or convenient for its *subsistence*, derived, so far as possible, from its own resources, without *dependence* upon other countries, and in the proper fostering, use, and application of these, then it follows that a general national *economy* (*Landes-Oeconomie*) should consider how such a surplus, fostering, and enjoyment can be brought about, without *dependence* upon others, or where this is not feasible in every respect, with as little *dependence* as possible upon foreign countries, and sparing use of the country's own cash. For this purpose the following nine rules are especially serviceable.

First, to inspect the country's soil with the greatest care, and not to leave the agricultural possibilities or a single corner or clod of earth unconsidered. Every useful form of *plant* under the sun should be experimented with, to see whether it is adapted to the country, for the distance or nearness of the sun is not all that counts. Above all, no trouble or expense should be spared to discover gold and silver.

Second, all commodities found in a country, which cannot be used in their natural state, should be worked up within the country; since the payment for *manufacturing* generally exceeds the value of the raw material by two, three, ten, twenty, and even a hundred fold, and the neglect of this is an abomination to prudent managers.

Third, for carrying out the above two rules, there will be need of people, both for producing and cultivating the raw materials and for working them up. Therefore, attention should be given to the population, that it may be as large as the country can support, this being a well-ordered state's most important concern, but, unfortunately, one that is often neglected. And the people should be turned by all possible means from idleness to remunerative *professions*; instructed and encouraged in all kinds of *inventions*, arts, and trades; and, if necessary, instructors should be brought in from foreign countries for this.

Fourth, gold and silver once in the country, whether from its own mines or obtained by *industry* from foreign countries, are under no circumstances to be taken out for any purpose, so far as possible, or allowed to be buried in chests or coffers, but must always remain in *circulation*; nor should much be permitted in uses where they are at once *destroyed* and cannot be utilized again. For under these conditions, it will be impossible for a country that has once acquired a considerable supply of cash, especially one that possesses gold and silver mines, ever to sink into poverty; indeed, it is impossible that it should not continually increase in wealth and property. Therefore,

Fifth, the inhabitants of the country should make every effort to get along with their domestic products, to confine their luxury to these alone, and to do without foreign products as far as possible (except where great need leaves no alternative, or if not need, wide-spread, unavoidable abuse, of which Indian spices are an example). And so on.

Sixth, in case the said purchases were indispensable because of necessity or *irremediable* abuse, they should be obtained from these foreigners at first hand, so far as

SOURCE: Philipp W. von Hornick, "Austria Over All If She Only Will," in Arthur Eli Monroe, ed., *Early Economic Thought.* Reprinted by permission of Harvard University Press (Cambridge, MA, 1927), pp. 223–225. Copyright © 1924 by The President and Fellows of Harvard College.

possible, and not for gold or silver, but in exchange for other domestic wares.

Seventh, such foreign commodities should in this case be imported in unfinished form, and worked up within the country, thus earning the wages of *manufacture* there.

Eighth, opportunities should be sought night and day for selling the country's superfluous goods to these foreigners in manufactured form, so far as this is necessary, and for gold and silver; and to this end, *consumption*, so to speak, must be sought in the farthest ends of the earth, and developed in every possible way.

Ninth, except for important considerations, no importation should be allowed under any circumstances of commodities of which there is sufficient supply of suitable quality at home; and in this matter neither sympathy nor compassion should be shown foreigners, be they friends, kinsfolk, *allies*, or enemies. For all friendship ceases, when it involves my own weakness and ruin. And this holds good, even if the domestic commodities are of poorer quality, or even higher priced. For it would be better to pay for an article two dollars which remain in the country than only one which goes out, however strange this may seem to the ill-informed.

A Secret Letter: Monarchical Authority in Prussia

Frederick William, The Great Elector

Seventeenth-century monarchs attained unprecedented authority within their realms, often through the skillful use of policies designed to enhance their power. The most dramatic consolidation of power was made by the head of the Hohenzollerns, Frederick William (1640–1688), known as the "great elector" of Brandenburg-Prussia. He instituted new taxes, developed a trained bureaucracy staffed by members of the nobility, modernized his army, and asserted his own authority over competing claims from the nobility and representative institutions. In 1667 he wrote a secret letter of advice to his son, who was in line to inherit the throne. An excerpt of this letter appears here.

CONSIDER: *The greatest threats to monarchical authority according to Frederick William; the policies Frederick William thought were most important for maintaining power; which of Frederick William's recommendations echo the attitudes expressed in mercantilist doctrines.*

It is necessary that you conduct yourself as a good father to your people, that you love your subjects regardless of their religious convictions, and that you try to promote

their welfare at all times. Work to stimulate trade everywhere, and keep in mind the population increase of the Mark of Brandenburg. Take advantage of the advice of the clergy and nobility as much as you can; listen to them and be gracious to them all, as befits one of your position; recognize ability where you find it, so that you will increase the love and affection of your subjects toward you. But, it is essential that you always be moderate in your attitudes, in order not to endanger your position and lose respect. With those of your own station in life, be careful never to give way in matters of precedence and in all to which you are entitled; on the contrary, hold fast to the eminence of your superior position. Remember that one can lose one's superior position if one allows too great pomposity and too great a show upon the part of members of the court.

Be keenly interested in the administration of justice throughout your land. See to it that justice is maintained for the poor as well as for the rich without discrimination of any kind. See to it that lawsuits are carried out without delay, without procrastination, for in doing this, you will solidify your own position. . . .

Seek to maintain friendly relations with the princes and the nobility of the Empire. Correspond with them frequently and maintain your friendship with them. Be certain not to give them cause for ill-will; try not to arouse emotions of jealousy or enmity, but be sure that you are always in a strong position to maintain your weight in disputes that may arise. . . .

It is wise to have alliances, if necessary, but it is better to rely on your own strength. You are in a weak position if you do not have the means and do not possess the confidence of the people. These are the things, God be praised, which have made me powerful since the time I began to have them. I only regret that, in the beginning of my reign, I forsook these policies and followed the advice of others against my will.

Mémoires: The Aristocracy Undermined in France

Saint-Simon

Louis XIV of France was the most powerful ruler of his time. He had inherited the throne as a child in 1643. He took personal command by 1661, ruling France until his death in 1715. Contemporary rulers viewed him as a model ruler. One of the ways in which he reinforced his position was by conducting a magnificent court life at his palace of Versailles. There, nobles hoping for favors or appointments competed for his attention and increasingly became dependent upon royal whim. One of

SOURCE: From *Documents of German History*, edited by Louis Snyder. Copyright © 1958 by Rutgers, The State University.

SOURCE: Orest Ranum and Patricia Ranum, eds. and trans., *The Century of Louis XIV*. Reprinted by permission of Harper & Row (New York, 1972), pp. 81, 83, 87–88.

those nobles, the Duke of Saint-Simon (1675–1755), felt slighted and grew to resent the king. Saint-Simon chronicled life at Versailles in his Mémoires. In the following excerpt, he shows how Louis XIV used this court life to his own ends.

CONSIDER: *How the king's activities undermined the position of the nobility; the options available to a noble who wanted to maintain or increase his own power; how the king's activities compare with the great elector's recommendations to his son.*

Frequent fetes, private walks at Versailles, and excursions were means which the King seized upon in order to single out or to mortify [individuals] by naming the persons who should be there each time, and in order to keep each person assiduous and attentive to pleasing him. He sensed that he lacked by far enough favors to distribute in order to create a continuous effect. Therefore he substituted imaginary favors for real ones, through jealousy—little preferences which were shown daily, and one might say at each moment—[and] through his artfulness. The hopes to which these little preferences and these honors gave birth, and the deference which resulted from them—no one was more ingenious than he in unceasingly inventing these sorts of things. Marly, eventually, was of great use to him in this respect; and Trianon, where everyone, as a matter of fact, could go pay court to him, but where ladies had the honor of eating with him and where they were chosen at each meal; the candlestick which he had held for him each evening at bedtime by a courtier whom he wished to honor, and always from among the most worthy of those present, whom he named aloud upon coming out from saying his prayers.

Louis XIV carefully trained himself to be well informed about what was happening everywhere, in public places, in private homes, in public encounters, in the secrecy of families or of [amorous] liaisons. Spies and tell tales were countless. They existed in all forms: some who were unaware that their denunciations went as far as [the King], others who knew it; some who wrote him directly by having their letters delivered by routes which he had established for them, and those letters were seen only by him, and always before all other things; and lastly, some others who sometimes spoke to him secretly in his cabinets, by the back passageways. These secret communications broke the necks of an infinity of persons of all social positions, without their ever having been able to discover the cause, often very unjustly, and the King, once warned, never reconsidered, or so rarely that nothing was more [determined]. . . .

In everything he loved splendor, magnificence, profusion. He turned this taste into a maxim for political reasons, and instilled it into his court on all matters. One could please him by throwing oneself into fine food, clothes, retinue, buildings, gambling. These were occasions which enabled him to talk to people. The essence of it

was that by this he attempted and succeeded in exhausting everyone by making luxury a virtue, and for certain persons a necessity, and thus he gradually reduced everyone to depending entirely upon his generosity in order to subsist. In this he also found satisfaction for his pride through a court which was superb in all respects, and through a greater confusion which increasingly destroyed natural distinctions. This is an evil which, once introduced, became the internal cancer which is devouring all individuals—because from the court it promptly spread to Paris and into the provinces and the armies, where persons, whatever their position, are considered important only in proportion to the table they lay and their magnificence ever since this unfortunate innovation—which is devouring all individuals, which forces those who are in a position to steal not to restrain themselves from doing so for the most part, in their need to keep up with their expenditures; [a cancer] which is nourished by the confusion of social positions, pride, and even decency, and which by a mad desire to grow keeps constantly increasing, whose consequences are infinite and lead to nothing less than ruin and general upheaval.

Second Treatise of Civil Government: Legislative Power

John Locke

In England royal absolutism had been under attack throughout the seventeenth century and finally was defeated by the Glorious Revolution of 1688–1689. At that point there was a definitive shift in power to Parliament, which was controlled by the upper classes. John Locke (1632–1704), in his Two Treatises of Civil Government (1690), justified the revolution and the new political constitution of England and expounded political ideas that became influential during the eighteenth and nineteenth centuries. This work and other writings established Locke as a first-rate empirical philosopher and political theorist. In the following selection from his Second Treatise of Civil Government, Locke analyzes legislative power.

CONSIDER: *The purposes for entering into society; the extent of and limitations on legislative power; how Locke justifies his argument; how these ideas are contrary to monarchical absolutism.*

134. The great end of men's entering into society being the enjoyment of their properties in peace and safety, and the great instrument and means of that being the laws established in that society, the first and fundamental positive law of all commonwealths is the establishing of the

SOURCE: John Locke, *Two Treatises of Civil Government* (London: J. M. Dent, Everyman, 1924), pp. 183–184, 189–190.

legislative power, as the first and fundamental natural law which is to govern even the legislative. Itself is the preservation of the society and (as far as will consist with the public good) of every person in it. This legislative is not only the supreme power of the commonwealth, but sacred and unalterable in the hands where the community have once placed it. Nor can any edict of anybody else, in what form soever conceived, or by what power soever backed, have the force and obligation of a law which has not its sanction from that legislative which the public has chosen and appointed; for without this the law could not have that which is absolutely necessary to its being a law, the consent of the society, over whom nobody can have a power to make laws but by their own consent and by authority received from them; and therefore all the obedience, which by the most solemn ties any one can be obliged to pay, ultimately terminates in this supreme power, and is directed by those laws which it enacts. Nor can any oaths to any foreign power whatsoever, or any domestic subordinate power, discharge any member of the society from his obedience to the legislative, acting pursuant to their trust, nor oblige him to any obedience contrary to the laws so enacted or farther than

they do allow, it being ridiculous to imagine one can be tied ultimately to obey any power in the society which is not the supreme.

❧

142. These are the bounds which the trust that is put in them by the society and the law of God and Nature have set to the legislative power of every commonwealth, in all forms of government. First: They are to govern by promulgated established laws, not to be varied in particular cases, but to have one rule for rich and poor, for the favourite at Court, and the countryman at plough. Secondly: These laws also ought to be designed for no other end ultimately but the good of the people. Thirdly: They must not raise taxes on the property of the people without the consent of the people given by themselves or their deputies. And this properly concerns only such governments where the legislative is always in being, or at least where the people have not reserved any part of the legislative to deputies, to be from time to time chosen by themselves. Fourthly: Legislative neither must nor can transfer the power of making laws to anybody else, or place it anywhere but where the people have.

 Visual Sources

The Early Modern Château

The following picture of the château, grounds, and park of Vaux-le-Vicomte in France (figure 16.1) reveals both the wealth of France and certain trends of the seventeenth *century. The château was built between 1657 and 1660 on the orders of France's superintendent of finance, Fouquet, and according to the plans of the architect Le Vau, the painter Lebrun, and the landscape gardener Le Nôtre. With its*

FIGURE 16.1   (© Richard Kalvar/Magnum Photos)

geometric orderliness and balance, it exemplifies the Classical style. In its conquest and manipulation of nature according to the rational plans of humans, it reflects the growing scientific spirit of the age. It also reflects a fundamentally stable society that was still dominated politically, socially, and economically by a small elite. It and buildings like it do not call out for military defense as did medieval castles. It later served as a model for Versailles, which itself became the model of monarchical splendor in seventeenth- and eighteenth-century Europe.

CONSIDER: Why such buildings and parks might have been built and how Saint-Simon might have viewed such projects.

Maternal Care
Pieter de Hooch

This scene of domestic life (figure 16.2) is painted by the seventeenth-century Dutch artist Pieter de Hooch. Entitled Maternal Care, it shows a girl kneeling while her mother examines and delouses her head. The scene takes place in Holland, the most urban and commercial European country. The moderate wealth of the rooms, revealed particularly by the paintings and the quality of the drapes, and the emphasis on cleanliness, privacy, and relative austerity, indicate that this is a middle-class home.

CONSIDER: What the painter intended to communicate to the viewer of this painting.

FIGURE 16.2 (© Rijksmuseum, Amsterdam)

Secondary Sources

Absolutism: Myth and Reality

G. Durand

During the seventeenth century, several monarchs attained such unprecedented power and authority that historians have used the term "absolutism" to describe these political systems. Other historians have argued that the term is misleading, that neither the ambitions of the monarchs nor the results constituted political absolutism. In the following selection G. Durand analyzes the myth and the reality of absolutism.

CONSIDER: *Why Durand prefers to view absolutism as a tendency; how Durand evaluates the goals and attitudes of the monarchs; whether the primary sources by Frederick William and Saint-Simon support Durand's analysis.*

Viewed as a tendency rather than as a political system, absolutism is an undeniable reality. In every state the sovereign sought to free himself from pressure and control. The means were everywhere the same; the monarch tried to rule through councillors whom he chose rather than nobles who claimed such positions as their right. He also tried to recover control of the administration of justice which had been taken over by the feudal nobility and the church. These tendencies produced two institutions common to every state.

First a small, inner or secret council, a cabinet ("Conseil des Affaires"), distinct from the traditional councils which had grown from the division of the functions of the old *Curia Regis*. There is great similarity between, for instance, the *Consejo de Estado* in Castile, the inner circle of the privy council in England, the Austrian Council of State of 1748 and the Imperial council set up by Catherine the Great in 1769.

Second, a system of unifying and centralising judicial institutions. In France the drafting of customary law in the sixteenth century and the publication of the Codes and Great Ordinances in the seventeenth, formed the basis for royal intervention in the judicial process. The procedures of *évocation* to a higher court, or judgement by special commissioners named by the king, were specifically French; but an institution like the *conseil des parties* had its counterpart in the Royal Council of Castile, the English Star Chamber, or the Austrian *Hofrat*.

From this we may infer the existence of a general climate of absolutism, more or less pervasive, which offered the monarch no more than the opportunity to deliberate on matters of state without being affected by intrigue and pressure, and to ensure that the judicial process followed his wishes and directives.

As an actual political system, absolutism is a myth. The monarchs themselves never regarded themselves as absolute, except in the case of the autocrats of Russia, where the lack of fundamental laws, of established customs and corporate orders within the state allowed the growth of a dictatorial form of government. In France, however, even Louis XIV never planned to abolish the Parlement, but merely curbed its pretensions and in December 1655 limited its right of remonstrance; nor did he try to abolish the estates. Monarchs did not try to create a system of institutions which would destroy any possibility of resistance through inertia. They merely sought to restrict the activities of persons who might cause trouble and to set up a new administrative structure parallel to the old; a handful of commissioners directed, urged on and controlled the system inherited from a time when counsel, remonstrance and shared power were the rule. Sovereigns also continued to delegate their administrative powers through the sale of offices, or to farm them out to financial potentates who became virtual states within the state. The kings of Spain suffered the tyranny of their own councils. In practice absolutism seems much more the result of circumstances and personalities than of a deliberate intention to revolutionise the whole structure of the state.

The English Revolution, 1688–1689

George Macaulay Trevelyan

In England two blows to monarchical authority proved to be turning points. The first was the civil war and the execution of Charles I in the 1640s. But although this was a victory for Parliament, the Cromwellian period that followed and the return from exile of Charles II in 1660 cast doubt on the permanence of Parliament's victory. The second was the "Glorious Revolution" of 1688, which removed James II from power without the turmoil of the first revolution. In the following selection Cambridge historian George Macaulay Trevelyan compares the two revolutions and analyzes the significance of the second one. Following the Whig tradition,

SOURCE: From George Durand, "What Is Absolutism?" in *Louis XIV and Absolutism*, pp. 23–24, ed. by Ragnhild Hatton, copyright © 1976 The Macmillan Press, Ltd. Reprinted by permission of the publisher.

SOURCE: George Macaulay Trevelyan, *The English Revolution, 1688–1689*. Reprinted by permission of Oxford University Press (Oxford, England, 1938), pp. 164–166.

Trevelyan views these trends in British history as constructive and progressive. More than most historians, he sees this revolution as an admirable triumph for Parliament.

CONSIDER: *Why the second revolution was a more clear-cut victory for Parliament than the first; factors that contributed to the victory of Parliament.*

The fundamental question at issue in 1688 had been this—Is the law above the King, or is the King above the law? The interest of Parliament was identified with that of the law, because, undoubtedly, Parliament could alter the law. It followed that, if law stood above the King's will, yet remained alterable by Parliament, Parliament would be the supreme power in the State.

James II attempted to make the law alterable wholesale by the King. This, if it had been permitted, must have made the King supreme over Parliament, and, in fact, a despot. The events of the winter of 1688–9 gave the victory to the opposite idea, which Chief Justice Coke and Selden had enunciated early in the century, that the King was the chief servant of the law, but not its master; the executant of the law, not its source; the laws should only be alterable by Parliament—Kings, Lords and Commons together. It is this that makes the Revolution the decisive event in the history of the English Constitution. It was decisive because it was never undone, as most of the work of the Cromwellian Revolution had been undone.

It is true that the first Civil War had been fought partly on this same issue:—the Common Law in league with Parliament had, on the field of Naseby, triumphed over the King in the struggle for the supreme place in the Constitution. But the victory of Law and Parliament had, on that occasion, been won only because Puritanism, the strongest religious passion of the hour, had supplied the fighting force. And religious passion very soon confused the Constitutional issue. Puritanism burst the legal bounds and, coupled with militarism, overthrew law and Parliament as well as the King. Hence the necessity of the restoration in 1660 of the King, law and Parliament together, without any clear definition of their ultimate mutual relations.

Now, in this second crisis of 1688, law and Parliament had on their side not only the Puritan passion, which had greatly declined, but the whole force of Protestant-Anglicanism, which was then at its height, and the rising influence of Latitudinarian scepticism—all arrayed against the weak Roman Catholic interest to which James had attached the political fortunes of the royal cause. The ultimate victor of the seventeenth-century struggle was not Pym or Cromwell, with their Puritan ideals, but Coke and Selden with their secular idea of the supremacy of law. In 1689 the Puritans had to be content with a bare toleration. But law triumphed, and therefore the law-making Parliament triumphed finally over the King.

Centuries of Childhood
Philippe Ariès

Through analysis of paintings such as Maternal Care *by Pieter de Hooch as well as other kinds of evidence, historians have changed our assumptions about attitudes toward childhood in Early Modern times. The most important of these historians is Philippe Ariès. The following is a selection from his* Centuries of Childhood.

CONSIDER: *How this reading relates to Hooch's painting; the differences between the seventeenth-century family, the medieval family, and the modern family according to Ariès.*

Between the end of the Middle Ages and the seventeenth century, the child had won a place beside his parents to which he could not lay claim at a time when it was customary to entrust him to strangers. This return of the children to the home was a great event: it gave the seventeenth-century family its principal characteristic, which distinguished it from the medieval family. The child became an indispensable element of everyday life, and his parents worried about his education, his career, his future. He was not yet the pivot of the whole system, but he had become a much more important character. Yet this seventeenth-century family was not the modern family: it was distinguished from the latter by the enormous mass of sociability which it retained. Where the family existed, that is to say in the big houses, it was a centre of social relations, the capital of a little complex and graduated society under the command of the paterfamilias.

The modern family, on the contrary, cuts itself off from the world and opposes to society the isolated group of parents and children. All the energy of the group is expended on helping the children to rise in the world, individually and without any collective ambition: the children rather than the family.

The World We Have Lost:
The Early Modern Family
Peter Laslett

The family is a tremendously important institution in any society. Changes in its structure and functions occur very slowly and gradually. With the passage of centuries since

SOURCE: Philippe Ariès, *Centuries of Childhood*, trans. Robert Baldick. Reprinted by permission of Alfred A. Knopf, Inc. (New York, 1962), pp. 403–404. Copyright © 1962 by Alfred A. Knopf, Inc.

SOURCE: Excerpt from *The World We Have Lost* by Peter Laslett. Copyright © 1965 by Peter Laslett. Reprinted by permission of Charles Scribner's Sons.

Early Modern times, we can see some sharp differences between the family of that period and the family of today. In the following selection Peter Laslett, a social historian from Cambridge who has written extensively on the Early Modern period, points out these differences.

CONSIDER: *The economic and social functions of the family revealed in this selection; what this document adds to the image of the family provided in the painting by Hooch and the document by Ariès; how the structure of this family differs from that of a typical twentieth-century family.*

In the year 1619 the bakers of London applied to the authorities for an increase in the price of bread. They sent in support of their claim a complete description of a bakery and an account of its weekly costs. There were thirteen or fourteen people in such an establishment: the baker and his wife, four paid employees who were called journeymen, two apprentices, two maidservants and the three or four children of the master baker himself. . . .

The only word used at that time to describe such a group of people was "family." The man at the head of the group, the entrepreneur, the employer, or the manager, was then known as the master or head of the family. He was father to some of its members and in place of father to the rest. There was no sharp distinction between his domestic and his economic functions. His wife was both his partner and his subordinate, a partner because she ran the family, took charge of the food and managed the women-servants, a subordinate because she was woman and wife, mother and in place of mother to the rest.

The paid servants of both sexes had their specified and familiar position in the family, as much part of it as the children but not quite in the same position. At that time the family was not one society only but three societies fused together: the society of man and wife, of parents and children and of master and servant. But when they were young, and servants were, for the most part, young, unmarried people, they were very close to children in their status and their function. . . .

Apprentices, therefore, were workers who were also children, extra sons or extra daughters (for girls could be apprenticed too), clothed and educated as well as fed, obliged to obedience and forbidden to marry, unpaid and absolutely dependent until the age of twenty-one. If apprentices were workers in the position of sons and daughters, the sons and daughters of the house were workers too. John Locke laid it down in 1697 that the children of the poor must work for some part of the day when they reached the age of three. The sons and daughters of a London baker were not free to go to school for many years of their young lives, or even to play as they wished when they came back home. Soon they would find themselves doing what they could in *bolting*, that is sieving flour, or in helping the maidservant with her panniers of loaves on the way to the market stall, or in playing their small parts in preparing the never-ending succession of meals for the whole household.

We may see at once, therefore, that the world we have lost, as I have chosen to call it, was no paradise or golden age of equality, tolerance or loving kindness. It is so important that I should not be misunderstood on this point that I will say at once that the coming of industry cannot be shown to have brought economic oppression and exploitation along with it. It was there already. The patriarchal arrangements which we have begun to explore were not new in the England of Shakespeare and Elizabeth. They were as old as the Greeks, as old as European history, and not confined to Europe. And it may well be that they abused and enslaved people quite as remorselessly as the economic arrangements which had replaced them in the England of Blake and Victoria. When people could expect to live for only thirty years in all, how must a man have felt when he realized that so much of his adult life, perhaps all, must go in working for his keep and very little more in someone else's family?

〜 CHAPTER QUESTIONS

1. What conditions facilitated the development of monarchical absolutism in the seventeenth century? What policies were used by kings to this end?

2. Why might mercantilist doctrines be particularly appealing to seventeenth-century monarchs?

3. How does family life reflect broader social, economic, and political aspects of the seventeenth century?

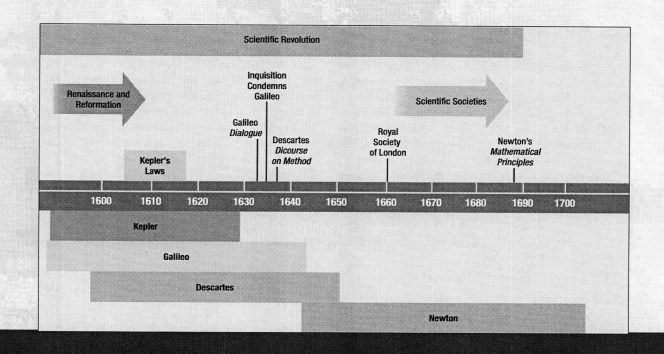

17 The Scientific Revolution

One of the most important intellectual revolutions in Western civilization occurred in the seventeenth century. Building on some sixteenth-century breakthroughs and a more deeply rooted interest in the workings of the natural world, a small elite of thinkers and scientists—Descartes, Galileo, Newton, Kepler, Bacon, and Boyle—established the foundations for the modern sciences of astronomy, mathematics, physics, and chemistry. Although at first their work was known to only a few, their ideas spread widely during the eighteenth century.

In the process of developing the modern sciences, these thinkers challenged the established conception of the universe as well as previous assumptions about knowledge. This ultimately successful challenge, now known as the Scientific Revolution, had a number of key elements. First, the view of the universe as being stable, fixed, and finite, with the earth at its center, gave way to a view of the universe as moving and almost infinite, with the earth merely one of millions of bodies, all subject to the laws of nature. Second, earlier methods for ascertaining the truth, which primarily involved referring to traditional authorities such as Aristotle, Ptolemy, and the Church, were replaced by methods that emphasized scepticism, rationalism, and rigorous reasoning based on observed facts and mathematical laws. Third, although these thinkers remained concerned with their own deeply held religious beliefs, the general scientific orientation shifted from theological questions to secular questions that focused on how things worked.

The primary documents in this chapter emphasize two broad questions that faced these seventeenth-century scientists. First, how can one ascertain the truth? The answers of Descartes, Galileo, and Newton are examined. Second, what is the proper line between science and scriptural authority? Galileo, who came most directly into conflict with Church authorities, provides us with clues.

The secondary documents concentrate on the nature and causes of the Scientific Revolution. In what ways was seventeenth-century science different from the science of earlier centuries? What explains these differences? What were the motives of seventeenth-century scientists?

Most of these intellectual developments were known to only a few throughout Europe. In the eighteenth century these scientific ideas and methods became popularized as part of the intellectual ferment of the Enlightenment.

 Primary Sources

The Discourse on Method

René Descartes

Seventeenth-century science needed new philosophical and methodological standards for truth to replace those traditionally used to support scientific assumptions. These were forcefully provided by René Descartes (1596–1650) in his Discourse on Method (1637). Born and educated in France, but spending his most productive years in Holland, Descartes gained fame as a mathematician, physicist, and metaphysical philosopher. The following excerpt from his Discourse contains the best-known statement of his approach to discovering truth.

CONSIDER: *The ways in which Descartes' approach constitutes a break with traditional ways of ascertaining the truth; the weaknesses of this approach and how a modern scientist might criticize this method; how this approach reflects Descartes' background as a mathematician.*

In place of the multitude of precepts of which logic is composed, I believed I should find the four following rules quite sufficient, provided I should firmly and steadfastly resolve not to fail of observing them in a single instance.

The first rule was never to receive anything as a truth which I did not clearly know to be such; that is, to avoid haste and prejudice, and not to comprehend anything more in my judgments than that which should present itself so clearly and so distinctly to my mind that I should have no occasion to entertain a doubt of it.

The second rule was to divide every difficulty which I should examine into as many parts as possible, or as might be required for resolving it.

The third rule was to conduct my thoughts in an orderly manner, beginning with objects the most simple and the easiest to understand, in order to ascend as it were by steps to the knowledge of the most composite, assuming some order to exist even in things which did not appear to be naturally connected.

The last rule was to make enumerations so complete, and reviews so comprehensive, that I should be certain of omitting nothing.

Those long chains of reasoning, quite simple and easy, which geometers are wont to employ in the accomplishment of their most difficult demonstrations, led me to think that everything which might fall under the cognizance of the human mind might be connected together in a similar manner, and that, provided only one should take care not to receive anything as true which was not so, and if one were always careful to preserve the order necessary for deducing one truth from another, there would be none so remote at which he might not at last arrive, nor so concealed which he might not discover. And I had no great difficulty in finding those with which to make a beginning, for I knew already that these must be the simplest and easiest to apprehend; and considering that, among all those who had up to this time made discoveries in the sciences, it was the mathematicians alone who had been able to arrive at demonstrations—that is to say, at proofs certain and evident—I did not doubt that I should begin with the same truths which they investigated.

Letter to Christina of Tuscany: Science and Scripture

Galileo Galilei

The most renowned scientist at the beginning of the seventeenth century was the Italian astronomer, mathematician, and physicist Galileo Galilei (1564–1642). His discoveries

SOURCE: René Descartes, *The Discourse on Method*, in *The Philosophy of Descartes*, ed. and trans. Henry A. P. Torrey (New York: Henry Holt, 1982), pp. 46–48.

SOURCE: From Galileo Galilei, *Discoveries and Opinions of Galileo*, Stillman Drake, ed. and trans. Reprinted by permission of Doubleday & Company, Inc. (New York, 1957), pp. 182–183. Copyright © 1957 by Stillman Drake.

about gravity, velocity, and the movement of astronomical bodies were grounded in a scientific method that ran contrary to the accepted standards for truth and authority. In the following excerpt from a letter to the Grand Duchess Christina of Tuscany (1615), Galileo defends his ideas and delineates his view of the correct line between science and scriptural authority.

CONSIDER: *According to Galileo's view, the kinds of topics or questions that are appropriately scientific and those that are appropriately theological; how Galileo's views compare with those of Descartes; why Galileo's views are so crucial to the Scientific Revolution.*

I think that in discussions of physical problems we ought to begin not from the authority of scriptural passages, but from sense-experiences and necessary demonstrations; for the holy Bible and the phenomena of nature proceed alike from the divine Word, the former as the dictate of the Holy Ghost and the latter as the observant executrix of God's commands. It is necessary for the Bible, in order to be accommodated to the understanding of every man, to speak many things which appear to differ from the absolute truth so far as the bare meaning of the words is concerned. But Nature, on the other hand, is inexorable and immutable; she never transgresses the laws imposed upon her, or cares a whit whether her abstruse reasons and methods of operation are understandable to men. For that reason it appears that nothing physical which sense-experience sets before our eyes, or which necessary demonstrations prove to us, ought to be called in question (much less condemned) upon the testimony of biblical passages which may have some different meaning beneath their words. For the Bible is not chained in every expression to conditions as strict as those which govern all physical effects; nor is God any less excellently revealed in Nature's actions than in the sacred statements of the Bible. . . .

From this I do not mean to infer that we need not have an extraordinary esteem for the passages of holy Scripture. On the contrary, having arrived at any certainties in physics, we ought to utilize these as the most appropriate aids in the true exposition of the Bible and in the investigation of those meanings which are necessarily contained therein, for these must be concordant with demonstrated truths. I should judge that the authority of the Bible was designed to persuade men of those articles and propositions which, surpassing all human reasoning, could not be made credible by science, or by any other means than through the very mouth of the Holy Spirit.

Yet even in those propositions which are not matters of faith, this authority ought to be preferred over that of all human writings which are supported only by bare assertions or probable arguments, and not set forth in a demonstrative way. This I hold to be necessary and proper to the same extent that divine wisdom surpasses all human judgment and conjecture.

But I do not feel obliged to believe that that same God who has endowed us with senses, reason, and intellect has intended to forgo their use and by some other means to give us knowledge which we can attain by them.

The Papal Inquisition of 1633: Galileo Condemned

Not surprisingly, Galileo found his views under attack from a variety of corners, including important groups within the Church. Ultimately his defense of Copernicanism, which held that the earth was not the center of the universe, was formally condemned by the Church. When he argumentatively summarized these ideas again in his Dialogue Concerning the Two Chief World Systems *(1632), he was brought before the Papal Inquisition, forced to recant his views, and confined to a villa on the outskirts of Florence. The following are some of the main charges against Galileo during his trial for heresy before the Inquisition in 1633.*

CONSIDER: *Why Galileo's views were so threatening to the Church; some of the long-range consequences of such a stance by the Church toward these views.*

We say, pronounce, sentence, and declare that you, the said Galileo, by reason of the matters adduced in trial, and by you confessed as above, have rendered yourself in the judgment of this Holy Office vehemently suspected of heresy, namely, of having believed and held the doctrine—which is false and contrary to the sacred and divine Scriptures—that the Sun is the center of the world and does not move from east to west and that the Earth moves and is not the center of the world; and that an opinion may be held and defended as probable after it has been declared and defined to be contrary to the Holy Scripture; and that consequently you have incurred all the censures and penalties imposed and promulgated in the sacred canons and other constitutions, general and particular, against such delinquents. From which we are content that you be absolved, provided that, first, with a sincere heart and unfeigned faith, you abjure, curse, and detest before us the aforesaid errors and heresies and every other error and heresy contrary to the Catholic and Apostolic Roman Church in the form to be prescribed by us for you.

SOURCE: Excerpt from George Santillana, *The Crime of Galileo*, p. 310. Reprinted by permission of The University of Chicago Press (Chicago, 1955). Copyright © 1955.

Mathematical Principles of Natural Philosophy

Sir Isaac Newton

The greatest scientific synthesis of the seventeenth century was made by Isaac Newton (1642–1727), who was born in England and attained a post as professor of mathematics at Cambridge University. Newton made his most important discoveries early in life. By the beginning of the eighteenth century he was the most admired scientific figure in Europe. He made fundamental discoveries concerning gravity, light, and differential calculus. Most important, he synthesized various scientific findings and methods into a description of the universe as working according to measurable, predictable mechanical laws. Newton's most famous work, Mathematical Principles of Natural Philosophy *(1687), contains his theory of universal gravitation. In the following selection from that work, Newton describes his four rules for arriving at knowledge.*

CONSIDER: *Why Newton's rules might be particularly useful for the experimental sciences; ways these rules differ from those of Descartes.*

RULE I

We are to admit no more causes of natural things than such as are both true and sufficient to explain their appearances.

SOURCE: Sir Isaac Newton, *Mathematical Principles of Natural Philosophy,* trans. Andrew Motte, rev. Florian Cajori (Berkeley, CA: University of California Press, 1947), pp. 398, 400. Reprinted by permission of the University of California Press.

To this purpose the philosophers say that Nature does nothing in vain, and more is in vain when less will serve; for Nature is pleased with simplicity, and affects not the pomp of superfluous causes.

RULE II

Therefore to the same natural effects we must, as far as possible, assign the same causes.

As to respiration in a man and in a beast; the descent of stones in *Europe* and in *America*; the light of our culinary fire and of the sun; the reflection of light in the earth, and in the planets.

RULE III

The qualities of bodies, which admit neither intensification nor remission of degrees, and which are found to belong to all bodies within the reach of our experiments, are to be esteemed the universal qualities of all bodies whatsoever.

For since the qualities of bodies are only known to us by experiments, we are to hold for universal all such as universally agree with experiments; and such as are not liable to diminution can never be quite taken away.

RULE IV

In experimental philosophy we are to look upon propositions inferred by general induction from phenomena as accurately or very nearly true, notwithstanding any contrary hypotheses that may be imagined, till such time as other phenomena occur, by which they may either be made more accurate, or liable to exceptions.

This rule we must follow, that the argument of induction may not be evaded by hypotheses.

 Visual Sources

A Vision of the New Science

One of the most important figures of the Scientific Revolution was the astronomer and mathematician Johannes Kepler (1571–1630). Figure 17.1 shows a page from the front of one of his works, first printed in Nuremberg in 1627, in which the "edifice" of astronomy is presented allegorically. The older but still respectable pillars of astronomy of Hipparchus and Ptolemy give way to the new, sturdy pillars of Kepler's immediate predecessors, Copernicus and Tycho Brahe. In the lower left panel Kepler is pictured in his study; in the center panel is a map of the island where Brahe's observatory was located; in the right-hand panel is a picture of two people working on a printing press. Throughout are various instruments used in astronomy.

The picture reveals much about the Scientific Revolution. The instruments emphasize how important measurement and observation were to the new science. The depiction of the old

and new pillars suggests that the new scientists were replacing if not necessarily challenging the old, accepted scientific authorities by building on the work of their immediate predecessors—here Brahe on Copernicus, and Kepler on Brahe and Copernicus. The importance of communication among scientists is indicated by tribute to the printing press.

CONSIDER: *How this picture illustrates the ways in which seventeenth-century scientists were breaking with earlier scientific assumptions.*

The Anatomy Lesson of Dr. Tulp

Rembrandt van Rijn

This 1632 painting by Dutch artist Rembrandt van Rijn (1606–1669; figure 17.2) shows Dr. Nicholass Tulp using the body of a hanged criminal to give an anatomy lesson.

Public autopsies such as this took place in The Netherlands as well as other areas in seventeenth-century Europe. Typically they were attended by students, colleagues, and ordinary citizens and were held in anatomy theatres such as this one in Amsterdam. The dress of the seven men—all surgeons—observing Dr. Tulp's work suggests that they are taking part in an important official occasion. Their attentive presence—especially of the two surgeons closest to Dr. Tulp—reveals the growing interest in understanding the human body, the effort to associate surgery with science, and the rising prestige of their profession. However, only Dr. Tulp had attended university. In addition to holding a doctorate in medicine and serving here as a teacher, Dr. Tulp was an important public official in Amsterdam: only he wears his hat in the indoor scene.

On the far right stands an open book, suggesting the learning that has gone into this lecture and the growing connections between academic writings about medicine and the facts of the human body. However, during the seventeenth century surgeons did not enjoy high reputations, and confidence in the medical profession in general was, with some good reason, low. Moreover anatomy lessons such as this were held not only for "scientific" purposes. They had to be justified as research to confirm Christian beliefs about God's omnipotence. There were also less solemn aspects to these events: Observers typically paid a fee, and a banquet often followed the autopsy.

CONSIDER: *The changing views toward science and medicine suggested by this painting.*

FIGURE 17.1 (The Burndy Library)

 Secondary Sources

Why Was Science Backward in the Middle Ages?

Michael Postan

The scientific advances of the seventeenth century are commonly considered revolutionary because of their contrast with the previous state of science. One way to gain insight into the origins of the seventeenth-century developments is to look at earlier periods to see whether something was missing then that explains this contrast. In the following selection Michael Postan takes this controversial approach, focusing specifically on the lack of scientific incentives in the Middle Ages.

CONSIDER: *Why scientific incentives were lacking in the Middle Ages; the typically medieval traits that discouraged the men of the Middle Ages from scientific exploration; how the concerns and problems faced by Galileo relate to this argument.*

SOURCE: Michael Postan, "Why Was Science Backward in the Middle Ages?" in *A Short History of Science: Origins and Results of the Scientific Revolution* (London: Routledge and Kegan Paul), pp. 10–17. Reprinted by permission of Routledge and Kegan Paul, Ltd.

FIGURE 17.2   (© Erich Lessing/Art Resource, NY)

It is generally agreed that the Middle Ages preserved for the use of later times the science of the ancients. Therein lies both the scientific achievement and the scientific failure of the medieval civilization. . . . What the Middle Ages took over they did not very much enrich. Indeed so small was their own contribution that historians of science are apt to regard the Middle Ages as something of a pause. . . .

Thus some advance on planes both purely intellectual and technical there was; yet taken together and placed against the vast panorama of medieval life, or indeed against the achievements of Greek and Hellenistic science in the fourth century B.C., or with the scientific activity of the seventeenth century, all these achievements are bound to appear very poor. Why then this poverty?

To this question many answers can be and have been given. But what most of them boil down to is the absence in medieval life of what I should be inclined to call scientific incentives. Students of science sometimes differ about the true inspiration of scientific progress. Some seek and find it in man's intellectual curiosity, in his desire to understand the workings of nature. Others believe that scientific knowledge grew and still grows out of man's attempts to improve his tools and his methods of production; that, in short, scientific truth is a by-product of technical progress. I do not want here to take sides in this particular controversy; what I want to suggest is that the Middle Ages were doubly unfortunate in that both the inspirations, the intellectual as well as the practical, failed more or less.

The easiest to account for is the intellectual. The Middle Ages were the age of faith, and to that extent they were unfavourable to scientific speculation. It is not that scientists as such were proscribed. For on the whole the persecution of men for their scientific ideas was very rare: rare because men with dangerous ideas, or indeed with any scientific ideas at all, were themselves very rare; and it is indeed surprising that there were any at all. This does not mean that there were no intellectual giants. All it means is that in an age which was one of faith, men of intellect and spirit found the calls of faith itself—its elucidation, its controversies, and its conquests—a task sufficient to absorb them. To put it simply, they had no time for occupations like science.

In fact they had neither the time nor the inclination. For even if there had been enough men to engage in activities as mundane as science, there would still be very little reason for them to do so. In times when medieval religious dogma stood whole and unshaken the intellectual objects and the methods of science were, to say the least, superfluous. The purpose of scientific enquiry is to build up piecemeal a unified theory of the universe, of its origin and of its working. But in the Middle Ages was that process really necessary? Did not medieval man already possess in God, in the story of Creation and in the doctrine of Omnipotent Will, a complete explanation of how the world came about and of how, by what means and to what purpose, it was being conducted? Why build up in laborious and painstaking mosaic a design, which was already there from the outset, clear and visible to all?

So much for intellectual incentive. The practical incentive was almost equally feeble. Greater understanding of nature could not come from technical improvements, chiefly because technical improvements were so few. Medieval occupations continued for centuries without appreciable change of method. After the great period of initial development, i.e., after the late eleventh century, the routine of medieval farming in the greater part of Europe became as fixed as the landscape itself. In the history of the smithies, the weaving shops, or the potteries, there were occasional periods of innovation, but taking the Middle Ages as a whole technical improvement was very rare and very slow. For this medieval economic policy was largely to blame. In the course of centuries economic activities got surrounded with a vast structure of bye-laws and regulations. . . . For bye-laws were as a rule based on the technical methods in existence when they were framed; and once framed they were to stand in the way of all subsequent change.

What is more, so deeply ingrained was the spirit of protection that in every local trade the technical methods were treated as a secret. . . . The men of the Middle Ages were unable to do more than they did because they were lacking in scientific incentive. What they achieved in advancing the practical arts of humanity or in preserving and transmitting ancient learning, they did in so far and as long as they were not typically medieval.

Early Modern Europe: Motives for the Scientific Revolution

Sir George Clark

By the seventeenth century, certain broad historical developments had set the stage for individuals to make the discoveries we associate with the Scientific Revolution. In addition,

these individuals were motivated in ways that medieval people were not and used the new and growing body of techniques, materials, and knowledge to make their discoveries. In the following selection, British historian Sir George Clark, a recognized authority on the seventeenth century, examines some of the motives that led people to engage in scientific work.*

CONSIDER: *The distinctions Clark makes among different people engaged in scientific work; why, more than thirteenth- or fourteenth-century people, these seventeenth-century people had a "disinterested desire to know."*

There were an infinite number of motives which led men to engage in scientific work and to clear the scientific point of view from encumbrances; but we may group together some of the most important under general headings, always remembering that in actual life each of them was compounded with the others. There were economic motives. The Portuguese explorers wanted their new instrument for navigation; the German mineowners asked questions about metallurgy and about machines for lifting and carrying heavy loads; Italian engineers improved their canals and locks and harbours by applying the principles of hydrostatics; English trading companies employed experts who used new methods of drawing charts. Not far removed from the economic motives were those of the physicians and surgeons, who revolutionized anatomy and physiology, and did much more good than harm with their new medicines and new operations, though some of them now seem absurd. Like the doctors, the soldiers called science to their aid in designing and aiming artillery or in planning fortifications. But there were other motives far removed from the economic sphere. Jewellers learnt much about precious and semi-precious stones, but so did magicians. Musicians learnt the mathematics of harmony; painters and architects studied light and colour, substances and proportions, not only as craftsmen but as artists. For a number of reasons religion impelled men to scientific study. The most definite and old-established was the desire to reach absolute correctness in calculating the dates for the annual fixed and movable festivals of the Church: it was a pope who presided over the astronomical researchers by which the calendar was reformed in the sixteenth century. Deeper and stronger was the desire to study the wonders of science, and the order which it unravelled in the universe, as manifestations of the Creator's will. This was closer than any of the other motives to the central impulse which actuated them all, the disinterested desire to know.

SOURCE: Sir George Clark, *Early Modern Europe*. Reprinted by permission of The Oxford University Press (Oxford, England, 1957), pp. 164–165.

No Scientific Revolution for Women

Bonnie S. Anderson and Judith P. Zinsser

The Scientific Revolution was generally carried out by men. A few women participated directly in the Scientific Revolution, but they were the exception rather than the rule. The Scientific Revolution was based on principles such as observing, measuring, experimenting, and coming to reasoned conclusions. Were these principles applied by men to change assumptions about women, particularly about female physiology? Bonnie S. Anderson and Judith P. Zinsser address this question in their interpretive survey of women in European history, A History of Their Own.

CONSIDER: *According to Anderson and Zinsser, why there was no Scientific Revolution for women; how perceptions of female physiology relate to broader assumptions about women and men.*

In the sixteenth and seventeenth centuries Europe's learned men questioned, altered, and dismissed some of the most hallowed precepts of Europe's inherited wisdom. The intellectual upheaval of the Scientific Revolution caused them to examine and describe anew the nature of the universe and its forces, the nature of the human body and its functions. Men used telescopes and rejected the traditional insistence on the smooth surface of the moon. Galileo, Leibnitz, and Newton studied and charted the movement of the planets, discovered gravity and the true relationship between the earth and the sun. Fallopio dissected the human body, Harvey discovered the circulation of the blood, and Leeuwenhoek found spermatozoa with his microscope.

For women, however, there was no Scientific Revolution. When men studied female anatomy, when they spoke of female physiology, of women's reproductive organs, of the female role in procreation, they ceased to be scientific. They suspended reason and did not accept the evidence of their senses. Tradition, prejudice, and imagination, not scientific observation, governed their conclusions about women. The writings of the classical authors like Aristotle and Galen continued to carry the same authority as they had when first written, long after they had been discarded in other areas. Men spoke in the name of the new "science" but mouthed words and phrases from the old misogyny. In the name of "science" they gave a supposed physiological basis to the traditional views of women's nature, function, and role. Science affirmed what men had always known, what custom, law, and religion had postulated and justified. With the authority of their "objective," "rational" inquiry they restated ancient premises and arrived at the same traditional conclusions: the innate superiority of the male and the justifiable subordination of the female.

SOURCE: Excerpts from *A History of Their Own,* vol. II, by Bonnie Anderson and Judith Zinsser. Copyright © 1988 by Bonnie Anderson and Judith Zinsser. Reprinted by permission of HarperCollins Publishers, Inc.

❧ CHAPTER QUESTIONS

1. What were the main ways in which the science of the seventeenth century constituted a break from the past? What were some of the main problems facing seventeenth-century scientists in making this break? How did they handle these problems?

2. How would you explain the occurrence of the Scientific Revolution in the seventeenth century rather than in the sixteenth or eighteenth century?

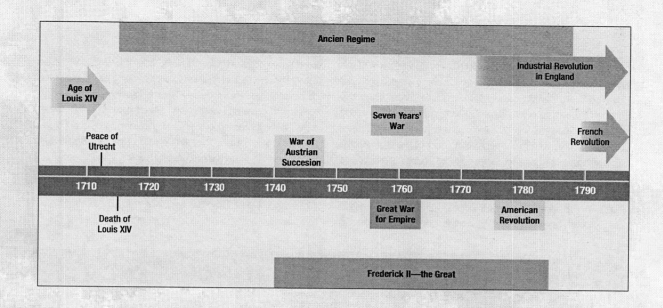

18 Politics and Society in the Ancien Régime

By the time of the death of Louis XIV in 1715, France no longer threatened to overwhelm the rest of Europe. Indeed, during most of the eighteenth century a rough balance of power developed amid the shifting diplomatic alliances and wars. There were two major sets of rivalries among states between 1715 and 1789. In Central Europe, the older Hapsburg Empire was pitted against the newer, assertive Prussia. Although Prussia acquired the status of a major power as a result of this competition, the Hapsburg Empire managed to hold on to most of its lands and to expand at the cost of weaker states like Poland and the Ottoman Empire. Outside of Europe, England and France struggled for supremacy over colonial territories in the Great War for Empire.

During this period preceding the French Revolution, referred to as the "Ancien Régime," most of the same political and social trends that had characterized the second half of the seventeenth century continued, namely, aristocratic dominance, strong monarchies, expanding central governments, and traditional ways of life. Important changes that were initiated—such as agricultural, commercial, and industrial developments that strengthened the middle classes and led to urban growth—were limited in scope and area.

The sources in this chapter center on four aspects of the Ancien Régime between 1715 and 1789. First, the nature and position of the still-dominant aristocracy are examined. What were its responsibilities? What was the position of women within the aristocracy and outside of the aristocracy? Is it true that the aristocracy was frivolous? How did the aristocracy react to pressures from the monarchy on the one side and the middle classes on the other? What were the attitudes of the aristocracy toward the peasantry? Second, the development of the eighteenth-century state is analyzed. What role did Prussia's monarchs play in making her a major power? How did wars contribute to and reflect the growing importance of the state? Third, the importance of commerce and the middle class in England is explored. What were the connections among commerce, the middle classes, and the English aristocracy? What was the relationship between the development of commerce and industry and England's colonial concerns and growing nationalism? What were some of the effects of the commerce in slaves engaged in by the English and others? Fourth, the assumptions most people held during the Ancien Régime are examined.

The sources in this chapter stress the relative political stability that characterized much of the period between 1715 and 1789. Stability was not the rule in intellectual matters, as will be seen in the next chapter.

Primary Sources

Political Testament

Frederick the Great

From a distance it may seem that eighteenth-century monarchs were much like those of the seventeenth century, similar in powers, position, and prestige. On closer examination, however, some differences are evident. Frederick II (the Great) of Prussia (1712–1786) was one of the most admired eighteenth-century monarchs. He ascended the throne in 1740 and ruled actively until his death in 1786. Frederick II continued the Prussian tradition of relying on a strong army to maintain and increase his holdings and prestige. At the same time he reorganized the army and the bureaucracy and introduced new ideas into both the theory and the practice of government. In the following excerpts from his Political Testament *(1752), he sets out his conception of politics and the proper role of the sovereign.*

CONSIDER: *How this conception of the monarch differs from that expressed by seventeenth-century monarchs; why Frederick emphasized the need to protect and support the nobility; who the crown's greatest political rivals for power were; the advantages and disadvantages to the monarch of religious toleration.*

Politics is the science of always using the most convenient means in accord with one's own interests. In order to act in conformity with one's interests one must know what these interests are, and in order to gain this knowledge one must study their history and application. . . . One must attempt, above all, to know the special genius of the people which one wants to govern in order to

SOURCE: Frederick II, *Political Testament,* in *Europe in Review,* eds. George L. Mosse et al. (Chicago: Rand McNally, 1957), pp. 110–112. Reprinted by permission of George L. Mosse.

know if one must treat them leniently or severely, if they are inclined to revolt . . . to intrigue. . . .

[The Prussian nobility] has sacrificed its life and goods for the service of the state, its loyalty and merit have earned it the protection of all its rulers, and it is one of the duties [of the ruler] to aid those [noble] families which have become impoverished in order to keep them in possession of their lands: for they are to be regarded as the pedestals and the pillars of the state. In such a state no factions or rebellions need be feared . . . it is one goal of the policy of this state to preserve the nobility.

A well conducted government must have an underlying concept so well integrated that it could be likened to a system of philosophy. All actions taken must be well reasoned, and all financial, political and military matters must flow towards one goal: which is the strengthening of the state and the furthering of its power. However, such a system can flow but from a single brain, and this must be that of the sovereign. Laziness, hedonism and imbecility, these are the causes which restrain princes in working at the noble task of bringing happiness to their subjects . . . a sovereign is not elevated to his high position, supreme power has not been confined to him in order that he may live in lazy luxury, enriching himself by the labor of the people, being happy while everyone else suffers. The sovereign is the first servant of the state. He is well paid in order that he may sustain the dignity of his office, but one demands that he work efficiently for the good of the state, and that he, at the very least, pay personal attention to the most important problems. . . .

You can see, without doubt, how important it is that the King of Prussia govern personally. Just as it would have been impossible for Newton to arrive at his system of attractions if he had worked in harness with Leibnitz and Descartes, so a system of politics cannot be arrived at and continued if it has not sprung from a single brain. . . . All parts of the government are inexorably linked with each other. Finance, politics and military affairs are inseparable; it does not suffice that one will be well administered; they must all be . . . a Prince who governs personally, who has formed his [own] political system, will not be handicapped when occasions arise where he has to act swiftly: for he can guide all matters towards the end which he has set for himself. . . .

Catholics, Lutherans, Reformed, Jews and other Christian sects live in this state, and live together in peace: if the sovereign, actuated by a mistaken zeal, declares himself for one religion or another, parties will spring up, heated disputes ensue, little by little persecutions will commence and, in the end, the religion persecuted will leave the fatherland and millions of subjects will enrich our neighbors by their skill and industry.

It is of no concern in politics whether the ruler has a religion or whether he has none. All religions, if one examines them, are founded on superstitious systems, more or less absurd. It is impossible for a man of good sense, who dissects their contents, not to see their error; but these prejudices, these errors and mysteries were made for men, and one must know enough to respect the public and not to outrage its faith, whatever religion be involved.

The Complete English Tradesman

Daniel Defoe

During the eighteenth century England was growing in strength and prosperity, particularly in the areas of commerce and manufacturing. A primary beneficiary of these economic developments was the rising commercial middle class. This class was becoming more assertive as the English were becoming more nationalistic. Daniel Defoe (1659c.–1731) speaks about these trends in the following selection from The Complete English Tradesman *(1726). Although best known for* Robinson Crusoe, *Defoe wrote many works and followed a commercial career for some time.*

CONSIDER: *The support Defoe offers for his view that commerce rightly dominates the country economically; how the economic policies that Defoe would recommend compare with policies typical of mercantilism; the connections between commerce and social class in England; the apparent advantages of having colonies and the colonial policies that Defoe's views imply.*

I . . . advance these three points in honour of our country —1. That we are the greatest trading country in the world, because we have the greatest exportation of the

SOURCE: Daniel Defoe, *The Complete English Tradesman*, vols. 17–18 of *The Novels and Miscellaneous Works of Daniel Defoe* (London: Thomas Tegg, 1840–1841), chap. 25.

growth and product of our land, and of the manufacture and labour of our people; and the greatest importation and consumption of the growth, product, and manufactures of other countries from abroad, of any nation in the world.

2. That our climate is the best and most agreeable to live in, because a man can be more out of doors in England than in other countries.

3. That our men are the stoutest and best, because, strip them naked from the waist upwards, and give them no weapons at all but their hands and heels, and turn them into a room or stage, and lock them in with the like number of other men of any nation, man for man, and they shall beat the best men you shall find in the world.

And so many of our noble and wealthy families, as we have shown, are raised by and derived from trade, so it is true, and indeed it cannot well be otherwise, that many of the younger branches of our gentry, and even of the nobility itself, have descended again into the spring from whence they flowed, and have become tradesmen; and thence it is that, as I said above, our tradesmen in England are not, as it generally is in other countries, always of the meanest of our people. Nor is trade itself in England, as it generally is in other countries, the meanest thing that men can turn their hand to; but, on the contrary, trade is the readiest way for men to raise their fortunes and families; and therefore it is a field for men of figure and of good families to enter upon. . . .

As to the wealth of the nation, that undoubtedly lies chiefly among the trading part of the people; and though there are a great many families raised within few years, in the late war, by great employments and by great actions abroad, to the honour of the English gentry, yet how many more families among the tradesmen have been raised to immense estates, even during the same time, by the attending circumstances of the war; such as the clothing, the paying, the victualling and furnishing, &c., both army and navy. And by whom have the prodigious taxes been paid, the loans supplied, and money advanced upon all occasions? By whom are the banks and companies carried on, and on whom are the customs and excises levied? Have not the trade and tradesmen borne the burden of the war? And do they not still pay four million a year interest for the public debts? On whom are the funds levied, and by whom the public credit supported? Is not trade the inexhausted fund of all funds, and upon which all the rest depend?

Again; in how superior a port or figure (as we now call it) do our tradesmen live, to what the middling gentry either do or can support! An ordinary tradesman now, not in the city only, but in the country, shall spend more money by the year, than a gentleman of four or five hundred pounds a year can do, and shall increase and lay up every year too; whereas the gentleman shall at the best stand stock still just where he began, nay, perhaps, decline: and as for the lower gentry, from a hundred pounds a year to three hundred, or thereabouts, though they are often as proud and high in their appearance as the other; as to them, I say, a shoemaker in London shall keep a better house, spend more money, clothe his family better, and yet grow rich too. It is evident where the difference lies; an estate's a pond, but trade's a spring: the first, if it keeps full, and the water wholesome, by the ordinary supplies and drains from the neighbouring grounds, it is well, and it is all that is expected; but the other is an inexhausted current, which not only fills the pond, and keeps it full, but is continually running over, and fills all the lower ponds and places about it.

This being the case in England, and our trade being so vastly great, it is no wonder that the tradesmen in England fill the lists of our nobility and gentry; no wonder that the gentlemen of the best families marry tradesmen's daughters, and put their younger sons apprentices to tradesmen; and how often do these younger sons come to buy the elder sons' estates, and restore the family, when the elder and head of the house, proving rakish and extravagant, has wasted his patrimony, and is obliged to make out the blessing of Israel's family, where the younger son bought the birthright, and the elder was doomed to serve him!

Trade is so far here from being inconsistent with a gentleman, that, in short, trade in England makes gentlemen, and has peopled this nation with gentlemen; for, after a generation or two, the tradesman's children, or at least their grandchildren, come to be as good gentlemen, statesmen, parliamentarian, privy-counsellors, judges, bishops, and noblemen, as those of the highest birth and the most ancient families; as we have shown. . . .

All this confirms what I have said before, viz., that trade in England neither is or ought to be levelled with what it is in other countries; or the tradesmen depreciated as they are abroad, and as some of our gentry would pretend to do in England; but that as many of our best families rose from trade, so many branches of the best families in England, under the nobility, have stooped so low as to be put apprentices to tradesmen in London, and to set up and follow those trades when they have come out of their times, and have thought it no dishonour to their blood. . . .

The greatness of the British nation is not owing to war and conquests, to enlarging its dominions by the sword, or subjecting the people of other countries to our power; but it is all owing to trade, to the increase of our commerce at home, and the extending it abroad.

It is owing to trade, that new discoveries have been made in lands unknown, and new settlements and plantations made, new colonies planted, and new governments formed, in the uninhabited islands, and the uncultivated continent of America; and those plantings and settlements have again enlarged and increased the trade, and thereby the wealth and power of the nation by whom they were discovered and planted; we have not increased our power, or the number of our subjects, by subduing the nations which possess those countries, and incorporating them into our own; but have entirely planted our colonies, and peopled the countries with our own subjects, natives of this island; and, excepting the negroes, which we transport from Africa to America, as slaves to work in the sugar and tobacco plantations, all our colonies, as well in the islands, as on the continent of America, are entirely peopled from Great Britain and Ireland, and chiefly the former; the natives having either removed further up into the country, or, by their own folly and treachery raising war against us, been destroyed and cut off. . . .

The Slave Trade

Anonymous

Part of the commercial prosperity enjoyed by several Western nations was built on the slave trade, which flourished in the seventeenth and eighteenth centuries. Slaves were generally shipped in British vessels, but the French and others engaged in this trade as well. Most slaves were taken across the Atlantic to Europe's colonial holdings, which in turn shipped goods such as sugar, metals, and wood products to the home country. Although there was little widespread opposition to slavery in Europe during the seventeenth and early eighteenth centuries, by the middle of the eighteenth century antislavery sentiments were growing. The following is an account of what was involved in the slave trade, written in 1771 by an anonymous Frenchman who argued for its abolition.

CONSIDER: *The attitudes that permitted and supported the slave trade; the effects of this experience on the blacks; the legacy of this trade for the colonies.*

As soon as the ships have lowered their anchors off the coast of Guinea, the price at which the captains have decided to buy the captives is announced to the Negroes who buy prisoners from various princes and sell them to the Europeans. Presents are sent to the sovereign who rules over that particular part of the coast, and permission to trade is given. Immediately the slaves are brought by inhuman brokers like so many victims dragged to a sacrifice. White men who covet that portion of the human race receive them in a little house they have erected on the shore, where they have entrenched themselves

SOURCE: Leon Apt and Robert E. Herzstein, eds., *The Evolution of Western Society,* vol. II (Hinsdale, IL: The Dryden Press, 1978), pp. 279–280.

with two pieces of cannon and twenty guards. As soon as the bargain is concluded, the Negro is put in chains and led aboard the vessel, where he meets his fellow sufferers. Here sinister reflections come to his mind; everything shocks and frightens him and his uncertain destiny gives rise to the greatest anxiety. At first he is convinced that he is to serve as a repast to the white men, and the wine which the sailors drink confirms him in this cruel thought, for he imagines that this liquid is the blood of his fellows.

The vessel sets sail for the Antilles, and the Negroes are chained in a hold of the ship, a kind of lugubrious prison where the light of day does not penetrate, but into which air is introduced by means of a pump. Twice a day some disgusting food is distributed to them. Their consuming sorrow and the sad state to which they are reduced would make them commit suicide if they were not deprived of all the means for an attempt upon their lives. Without any kind of clothing it would be difficult to conceal from the watchful eyes of the sailors in charge of any instrument apt to alleviate their despair. The fear of a revolt, such as sometimes happens on the voyage from Guinea, is the basis of a common concern and produces as many guards as there are men in the crew. The slightest noise or a secret conversation among two Negroes is punished with utmost severity. All in all, the voyage is made in a continuous state of alarm on the part of the white men, who fear a revolt, and in a cruel state of uncertainty on the part of the Negroes, who do not know the fate awaiting them.

When the vessel arrives at a port in the Antilles, they are taken to a warehouse where they are displayed, like any merchandise, to the eyes of buyers. The plantation owner pays according to the age, strength and health of the Negro he is buying. He has him taken to his plantation, and there he is delivered to an overseer who then and there becomes his tormentor. In order to domesticate him, the Negro is granted a few days of rest in his new place, but soon he is given a hoe and a sickle and made to join a work gang. Then he ceases to wonder about his fate; he understands that only labor is demanded of him. But he does not know yet how excessive this labor will be. As a matter of fact, his work begins at dawn and does not end before nightfall; it is interrupted for only two hours at dinnertime. The food a full-grown Negro is given each week consists of two pounds of salt beef or cod and two pots of tapioca meal, amounting to about two pints of Paris. A Negro of twelve or thirteen years or under is given only one pot of meal and one pound of beef or cod. In place of food some planters give their Negroes the liberty of working for themselves every Saturday; others are even less generous and grant them this liberty only on Sundays and holidays. Therefore, since the nourishment of the Negroes is insufficient, their tendency to cheat

must be attributed to the necessity of finding the food they lack.

Letter to Lady R., 1716: Women and the Aristocracy
Lady Mary Wortley Montagu

During the eighteenth century women continued to remain limited in the economic and political roles they could play, but it was possible for aristocratic women to take up influential social and cultural roles. In particular, many women used letter writing as an art, and from these letters much insight about the position and attitudes of women can be gained. Lady Mary Wortley Montagu (1689–1762) was a well-known British literary figure, writing essays and poetry in addition to her volumes of letters. The following is a selection from a letter written in 1716 to Lady R.

CONSIDER: *The assumptions about marriage among the aristocracy; connections among marriage, love, and economic interests; the position of aristocratic women reflected by this letter.*

No woman dares appear coquette enough to encourage two lovers at a time. And I have not seen any such prudes as to pretend fidelity to their husbands, who are certainly the best natured set of people in the world, and look upon their wives' gallants as favourably as men do upon their deputies, that take the troublesome part of their business off their hands. They have not however the less to do on that account; for they are generally deputies in another place themselves; in one word, 'tis the established custom for every lady to have two husbands, one that bears the name, and another that performs the duties. And these engagements are so well known, that it would be a downright affront, and publicly resented, if you invited a woman of quality to dinner, without, at the same time, inviting her two attendants of lover and husband, between whom she sits in state with great gravity. The submarriages generally last twenty years together, and the lady often commands the poor lover's estate, even to the utter ruin of his family.

These connections, indeed, are as seldom begun by any real passion as other matches; for a man makes but an ill figure that is not in some commerce of this nature; and a woman looks out for a lover as soon as she's married, as part of her equipage, without which she could not be genteel; and the first article of the treaty is establishing the pension, which remains to the lady, in case the gallant should prove inconstant. This chargeable point of honour I look upon as the real foundation of so many

SOURCE: Mary Wortley Montagu, *Works,* vol. II (London: Richard Phillips, 1803), pp. 57–59.

wonderful instances of constancy. I really know some women of the first quality, whose pensions are as well known as their annual rents, and yet nobody esteems them the less; on the contrary, their discretion would be called in question, if they should be suspected to be mistresses for nothing. A great part of their emulation consists in trying who shall get most.

Women of the Third Estate

The vast majority of eighteenth-century Europeans were not members of the aristocracy. More than 90 percent were peasants, artisans, domestics, and laborers—often referred to in France as members of the Third Estate. While both men and women of the Third Estate shared much, women's positions and grievances often differed from those of men. Articulate records of these women's grievances are difficult to find, but the flood of formal petitions preceding the French Revolution of 1789 provides us with some rich sources. The following is a "Petition of the Women of the Third Estate to the King," dated several months prior to the outbreak of the French Revolution.

CONSIDER: *What options seem available to women; the problems identified and solutions proposed; ways in which men's interests and women's interests might clash.*

1 January 1789. Almost all women of the Third Estate are born poor. Their education is either neglected or misconceived, for it consists in sending them to learn from

SOURCE: Excerpts from *Not in God's Image* by Julia O'Faolain and Lauro Martines. Copyright © 1973 by Julia O'Faolain and Lauro Martines. Reprinted by permission of Harper & Row, Publishers, Inc.

teachers who do not themselves know the first word of the language they are supposed to be teaching. . . . At the age of fifteen or sixteen, girls can earn five or six sous a day. If nature has not granted them good looks, they get married, without a dowry, to unfortunate artisans and drag out a grueling existence in the depths of the provinces, producing children whom they are unable to bring up. If, on the other hand, they are born pretty, being without culture, principles, or any notion of morality, they fall prey to the first seducer, make one slip, come to Paris to conceal it, go totally to the bad here, and end up dying as victims of debauchery.

Today, when the difficulty of earning a living forces thousands of women to offer themselves to the highest bidder and men prefer buying them for a spell to winning them for good, any woman drawn to virtue, eager to educate herself, and with natural taste . . . is faced with the choice either of casting herself into a cloister which will accept a modest dowry or of going into domestic service. . . .

If old age overtakes unmarried women, they spend it in tears and as objects of contempt for their nearest relatives.

To counter such misfortunes, Sire, we ask that men be excluded from practicing those crafts that are women's prerogative, such as dressmaking, embroidery, millinery, etc. Let them leave us the needle and the spindle and we pledge our word never to handle the compass or the set-square.

We ask, Sire . . . to be instructed and given jobs, not that we may usurp men's authority but so that we may have a means of livelihood, and so that the weaker among us who are dazzled by luxury and led astray by example should not be forced to join the ranks of the wretched who encumber the streets and whose lewd audacity disgraces both our sex and the men who frequent them.

Visual Sources

Happy Accidents of the Swing

Jean-Honoré Fragonard

The aristocracy remained dominant culturally during the Ancien Régime, commissioning most of the art of the period. It is not surprising, then, that the art reflected aristocratic values and tastes. The Swing by Jean-Honoré Fragonard (figure 18.1) exemplifies a type of painting quite popular among France's eighteenth-century aristocracy.

Fragonard was commissioned by Baron de Saint-Julien in 1767 to paint a picture of his mistress on a swing being pushed by a bishop who did not know that the woman was the baron's mistress, with the baron himself watching from a strategic place of hiding. In the picture the woman on the swing seems well aware of what is happening, flinging off her shoe toward

a statue of the god of discretion in such a way as to cause her gown to billow out revealingly.

This painting reflects a certain religious irreverence on the part of the eighteenth-century aristocracy, for the joke is on the unknowing bishop. The significance of this irreverence is magnified by the fact that Saint-Julien had numerous dealings with the clergy, since he was at this time a government official responsible for overseeing clerical wealth.

The lush setting of the painting and the tenor of the scene suggest the love of romantic luxury and concern for sensual indulgence by this most privileged but soon to be declining part of society.

CONSIDER: *The evidence in this picture of the attitudes of lifestyle of the eighteenth-century French aristocracy.*

FIGURE 18.1　(© Wallace Collection, London, UK, Bridgeman Art Library)

Act of Humanity

Jean Defraine

In Act of Humanity (c. 1783), painter Jean Defraine shows that the old tradition of aristocratic responsibility for social welfare is still upheld in the eighteenth century (figure 18.2). Here, an aristocrat is visiting a family stricken by both illness and poverty. The realistic depiction of poverty is accompanied by the comforting suggestion that its effects can be alleviated through charitable gestures. Such humanitarian acts on the part of the aristocracy were considered one of the few appropriate cures for social problems of the poor.

CONSIDER: How this picture compares with Happy Accidents of the Swing.

The Battle of Fontenoy

C. C. P. Lawson

War, though still common in the eighteenth century, was more controlled and orderly and less vicious than during the first half of the seventeenth century. This is suggested in this painting by C. C. P. Lawson (figure 18.3) of a typical eighteenth-century land battle, The Battle of Fontenoy. Aristocratic traditions are maintained by the commanders, who calmly salute each other before the battle begins. The troops are uniformed and orderly, *apparently under the firm control of officers. The characteristics of eighteenth-century battles depicted here reflect the realities of military tactics and economics. As argued by the modern historian R. J. White in* Europe in the Eighteenth Century *(New York: St. Martin's Press, 1965),*

a supposedly wholesome mixture of aristocrats and scum was the principal substance of the armed forces everywhere in the eighteenth century. Warfare was predominantly defensive, dogged by caution and conducted according to strict rules of procedure. The almost baroque movements of armed forces in the stately game of siege warfare, the rigid adherence to the rules of the game as laid down in *Fighting Instructions* [a standard military manual], which often appear so ludicrous to modern observers, were not invented to charm later generations, but were the offspring of the peculiar necessities of a world of limited material resources and rationally conceived purposes.

CONSIDER: *How the arrangement of the troops in this picture reflects the social structure of the eighteenth century.*

The Atlantic Slave Trade

Many societies were familiar with slavery well before the fifteenth century. Moreover, slave trading from Africa took place to the east and north before it turned west across the Atlantic. However, after the sixteenth century the Atlantic slave trade increased dramatically. Chart 18.1 traces the volume of slave exports from Africa across the Atlantic between the fifteenth and nineteenth centuries.

CONSIDER: *Which periods had the largest volumes of slave exports; how the differences in the slave trade over the centuries might be explained.*

FIGURE 18.2

FIGURE 18.3

Chart 18.1

Period	Volume
1450–1600	367,000
1601–1700	1,868,000
1701–1800	6,133,000
1801–1900	3,330,000
Total	11,698,000

Secondary Sources

Slavery—White, Black, Muslim, Christian

David Brion Davis

From the Western perspective, the focus of African slavery is usually the triangular trade across the Atlantic between Europe, Africa, and the Americas that flourished during the seventeenth and eighteenth centuries. However, the roots of that slave trade go deeper and broader. In the following selection, the American historian David Brion Davis emphasizes the importance of the long history of warfare between Christians and Muslims and the piracy, kidnapping, and enslavement of people from both groups that took place.

CONSIDER: *The significance of the Muslim enslavement of Christians; why the story of the Muslim enslavement of Christians is less well known in the West.*

The origins of African slavery in the New World cannot be understood without some knowledge of the millennium of warfare between Christians and Muslims that took place in the Mediterranean and Atlantic and the piracy and kidnapping that went along with it. In 1627 pirates from the Barbary Coast of North Africa raided distant Iceland and enslaved nearly four hundred astonished residents. In 1617 Muslim pirates, having long enslaved Christians along the coasts of Spain, France, Italy, and even Ireland, captured 1,200 men and women in Portuguese Madeira. Down to the 1640s, there were many more English slaves in Muslim North Africa than African slaves under English control in the Caribbean. Indeed, a 1624 parliamentary proclamation estimated that the Barbary states held at least 1,500 English slaves, mostly sailors captured in the Mediterranean or Atlantic.

The historian Robert C. Davis concludes that between 1580 and 1680 some 850,000 Christian slaves were taken in chains to the Maghreb. The number of enslavements would surely exceed a million if we move down a century to the late eighteenth and early nineteenth centuries, when the question of enslaved white American sailors became a central issue of foreign policy for the administrations of Washington, Adams,

and Jefferson. Only a tiny percentage of Christian slaves were ransomed or converted to Islam; the few who were fortunate enough to get away complained of being fed "nothing but bread and water," of being treated "like dogs," and of being whipped while working as galley slaves or as carriers of heavy rocks in building or repairing public works. Their rate of mortality equaled that of African slaves on the infamous Middle Passage.

This large-scale enslavement of Europeans in the sixteenth and seventeenth centuries did not lead to movements against slavery as an institution. In fact, some of the ransomed European slaves engaged in their own slaving raids against Muslims as a form of revenge. Daniel Defoe's fictional Robinson Crusoe (published in 1719) is on a mid-seventeenth-century slavetrading vessel bound for Guinea when he himself is captured and enslaved by a "Turkish rover of Sallee [Salé]" off the northwest coast of Africa. After two years of enslavement, Crusoe escapes, shoots and kills one naked black "savage," and is then rescued by a humane and charitable Portuguese slave-trading captain, who takes Crusoe to Brazil, where for four years he makes a small fortune as a slaveholding planter.

I do not mean to suggest that the Muslim enslavement of Christians evoked no opposition whatever to slavery. Benjamin Franklin was not the first but simply the most famous man to turn the enslavement of whites by Barbary pirates into a strong and clever antislavery argument; he mocked a proslavery speech in Congress by comparing it to a fictional 1687 speech of the Divan of Algiers defending the "plundering and enslaving" of Christians. But that was in 1790, in the last month of Franklin's life, well after cultural and intellectual changes had already launched antislavery movements in England, America, and France. It is most unlikely that Franklin would have dreamed of writing such a piece in his young manhood, when he in fact owned and sold Negro slaves.

In the preceding centuries, before the rise of humanitarian reform, including the antislavery movement, the continuing enslavement of Christians by Muslims and of Muslims by Christians actually conditioned both groups to accept the institution of slavery on a wider scale and thus prepared the way for the vast Atlantic slave system. In the fifteenth century, for example, Portuguese leaders saw the enslavement and baptism of black Africans as a continuation of the centuries-old reconquest of Iberia and crusade against the Moors.

SOURCE: *The New York Review of Books*, July 5, 2001, p. 51.

The Ancien Régime: Ideals and Realities

John Roberts

It is difficult to look back at past societies with other than our own assumptions. However, people in the Ancien Régime—eighteenth-century Europe—had their own beliefs, values, and perceptions about the world and their place in it. In the following selection John Roberts describes what most eighteenth-century Europeans would take for granted, emphasizing their mental conservatism.

CONSIDER: *The ways in which their assumptions differ from our own; the ways in which they are the same as ours; why their view of innovation and the past is so important.*

What would be taken for granted by most continental Europeans in the eighteenth century and, to some extent, by Englishmen and English settlers abroad, would be assumptions which can be sketched briefly in such propositions as these: God made the world and gave it a moral and social structure; His revelation in Jesus Christ imposes a duty upon society to protect the Church, Christian truth and moral principles in a positive way by promoting sound behaviour and belief and harrying bad; Christianity teaches that the existing structure of society is in principle good and should be upheld; this structure is organized hierarchically and for the most part its hierarchies are hereditary, their apex usually being found in a monarch; privileges and duties are distributed in a manner which can be justified by reference to this hierarchy. It is also true (our list of assumptions could continue) that while the organization of society around hereditary units was a fundamental datum of society under the *ancien régime*, it took for granted respect for other groups in which men came together for religious, professional, economic or social purposes; corporations with these ends were thought the proper regulators of much of daily life—the practice of trade or the enjoyment of legal rights, for example—and the interests of individuals belonging to them came emphatically second to those of these legal persons. . . .

It was also then assumed that much more of personal behaviour should be regulated by law and traditional practice than today. . . .

Social restraint reflected the pervasive anti-individualism of the *ancien régime*. Moreover, moral and ideological truth were thought indivisible and this left little room in theory for the vagaries of the individual. . . .

Across all these assumptions ran an overriding mental conservatism. One of the deepest differences between our own age and the *ancien régime* is the pervading conviction of those times that it was innovation which needed to be justified, not the past. A huge inertia generated by usage, tradition, prescription and the brutal fact of simple ignorance, lay heavily upon the institutions of the eighteenth century. As there had been for centuries, there was a self-evident justification for the ways of our fathers, for the forms and laws they had evolved and set down. One way in which this expressed itself was in an intense legalism, a fascination with old documents, judgments, lineage and inheritance. The higher classes were preoccupied with questions of blood, ancestry and family honour. Yet none of this preoccupation with the past was true historical-mindedness. Men were obsessed with the past as guidance, as precedent, even as spectacle, but not for its own sake. Few men had much sense that they were not looking at the same world as their ancestors.

The Resurgent Aristocracy

Leonard Krieger

Historians have at times exaggerated the importance of the rise of the middle class and the decline of the aristocracy in the eighteenth century. Recently, historians have begun to emphasize the middle of the eighteenth century as a period during which the aristocracy was actually resurgent, making efforts to regain its position and increase its influence—often with considerable success. This view is illustrated in the following selection by Leonard Krieger of the University of Chicago.

CONSIDER: *The evidence Krieger offers for a resurgence of the aristocracy; the ways in which the aristocracy adapted to eighteenth-century political needs.*

In the eighteenth century, surprisingly, aristocracies—or at least important parts of them—were resurgent. Appreciating the principle of what would later become a proverbial prescription for men to join what they could not beat, nobles in the several countries of Europe picked themselves up and began to appropriate commanding positions in the governmental structures of the new states and even in the network of commercial relations. The Whig oligarchy that ruled Britain without serious challenge between the accession of the Hanoverian dynasty in 1714 and George III's assertion of royal influence after 1760 represented a landowning aristocracy that was sponsoring a capitalized and scientific agriculture in response to demands of the market and that had

SOURCE: From John Roberts, *Revolution and Improvement: The Western World, 1775–1847,* pp. 34–35. Copyright © 1976 John Roberts. Reprinted by permission of the Regents of the University of California Press, and the University of California Press.

SOURCE: Reprinted from *Kings and Philosophers, 1689–1789,* by Leonard Krieger, with the permission of W. W. Norton & Company, Inc. Copyright © 1970 by W. W. Norton & Company, Inc.

economic ties with merchants and bankers of the City. The French peers, refueled by Louis XIV's calculated infusion of subsidies, made a serious bid to refashion the monarchy in their own image after the death of the Sun King in 1715, and when this attempt failed, a more economically progressive and modern-minded judicial and administrative aristocracy (*no-blesse de robe* and *noblesse d'office*) rose to continue the counteroffensive on behalf of the privileged. In Russia various sections of the military and landed nobility dictated the succession to the throne—in general they preferred tsarinas in the expectation that they would behave consistently as members of the "weaker sex"—and dominated the social policy of the government from the death of Peter the Great in 1725 through the accession of Catherine the Great in 1762. The long period from 1718 to 1772 that the Swedes euphemistically called their "era of liberty" was actually an age of aristocratic sovereignty, exercised constitutionally in a nominal monarchy through the nobles' oligarchic control over both the *Riksdag*, or parliament, and the bureaucracy. The Dutch gave the same high-flown label to the period from 1702 to 1747, when the small but influential class of Regents, an oligarchy comprised of urban patricians, resumed its sway after the death of William III and kept the office of *stadholder* vacant. The seven provinces that made up the Dutch "Republic" were, in this respect, expanded versions of the independent city-states in Europe. Concentrated mainly in Switzerland and Germany, they too were stabilized during the first half of the eighteenth century under the rule of exclusive patrician oligarchies. . . .

The aristocracies' new lease on life for the eighteenth century was thus predicated upon the modernization of their premises, and they thereby shifted the arena of social conflict from outside to inside the structure of the state. Where they had formerly defended their privileged rights to landownership, manorial lordship, judicial immunities, and tax exemptions by denying the jurisdiction of the central governments, they now defended these privileges by occupying and controlling the governmental agencies which exercised the jurisdiction. This aristocratic penetration of the state ran counter to the standards of general law, equal citizenship, and uniform administration which had served and continued to serve bureaucrats as guides in extending the scope of central government. But the hierarchical tendency was no mere atavism. Despite the obvious and reciprocal hostility between it and the leveling tendency with which it shared the state, the coexistence of the two tendencies, however mismatched in logic, was a faithful response to a fundamental social demand of the age. European society required, for the military security of its inhabitants, for the direction and subsidization of its economy, and for the prevention of religious turbulence and popular disorder, the imposition of unified control over a larger area and more people than the contemporary instruments of government could manage. Hence the employment of the traditional social and corporate hierarchies by the government as extensions of the governing arm into the mass of inhabitants. All people were subject, but some were more subject than others.

Lords and Peasants

Jerome Blum

The aristocracy made up a small percentage of Europe's population. Some 80 to 90 percent of the people were still peasants. While peasants lived in a variety of different circumstances, most lived at not much more than a subsistence level. They were usually thought of as at the bottom of society. In the following selection Jerome Blum analyzes attitudes held toward the peasants by seigniors (lords) and by peasants themselves.

CONSIDER: *How lords viewed peasants in relation to themselves; how the lords' attitudes reflected actual social conditions; possible consequences of the negative attitudes held about peasants.*

With the ownership of land went power and authority over the peasants who lived on the land. There were a multitude of variations in the nature of that authority and in the nature of the peasants' subservience to their seigniors, in the compass of the seigniors' supervision and control, and in the obligations that the peasants had to pay their lords. The peasants themselves were known by many different names, and so, too, were the obligations they owed the seigniors. But, whatever the differences, the status of the peasant everywhere in the servile lands was associated with unfreedom and constraint. In the hierarchical ladder of the traditional order he stood on the bottom rung. He was "the stepchild of the age, the broad, patient back who bore the weight of the entire social pyramid . . . the clumsy lout who was deprived and mocked by court, noble and city." . . .

The subservience of the peasant and his dependence upon his lord were mirrored in the attitudes and opinions of the seigniors of east and west alike. They believed that the natural order of things had divided humankind into masters and servants, those who commanded and those who obeyed. They believed themselves to be naturally superior beings and looked upon those who they believed were destined to serve them as their natural inferiors. At

SOURCE: From Blum, Jerome, *The End of the Old Order in Rural Europe*, pp. 29–31, 44–49. Copyright 1978 by Princeton University Press. Reprinted by permission of Princeton University Press.

best their attitude toward the peasantry was the condescension of paternalism. More often it was disdain and contempt. Contemporary expressions of opinion repeatedly stressed the ignorance, irresponsibility, laziness, and general worthlessness of the peasantry, and in the eastern lands the free use of the whip was recommended as the only way to get things done. The peasant was considered some lesser and sub-human form of life; "a hybrid between animal and human" was the way a Bavarian official put it in 1737. An eyewitness of a rural rising in Provence in 1752 described the peasant as "an evil animal, cunning, a ferocious half-civilized beast; he has neither heart nor honesty. . . ." The Moldavian Basil Balsch reported that the peasants of his land were "strangers to any discipline, order, economy or cleanliness . . . ; a thoroughly lazy, mendacious . . . people who are accustomed to do the little work that they do only under invectives or blows." A counselor of the duke of Mecklenburg in an official statement in 1750 described the peasant there as a "head of cattle" and declared that he must be treated accordingly. . . .

The conviction of their own superiority harbored by the seigniors was often compounded by ethnic and religious differences between lord and peasant. In many parts of central and eastern Europe the masters belonged to a conquering people who had established their domination over the native population. German seigniors ruled over Slavic peasants in Bohemia, Galicia, East Prussia and Silesia, and over Letts and Estonians in the Baltic lands; Polish lords were the masters of Ukrainian, Lithuanian, and White Russian peasants; Great Russians owned manors peopled by Ukrainians and Lithuanians and Poles; Magyars lorded it over Slovaks and Romanians and Slovenes—to list only some of the macroethnic differences. Few peoples of the rest of the world can match Europeans in their awareness of and, generally, contempt for or at least disdain for other ethnic and religious groups. . . . The dominant group, though greatly outnumbered, successfully maintained its cultural identity precisely because it considered the peasants over whom it ruled as lesser breeds of mankind, even pariahs. . . .

Schooling for most peasants was, at best, pitifully inadequate and usually entirely absent, even where laws declared elementary education compulsory. . . . [B]y far the greatest part of Europe's peasantry lived out their lives in darkest ignorance.

The peasants themselves, oppressed, condemned, and kept in ignorance by their social betters, accepted the stamp of inferiority pressed upon them. "I am only a serf" the peasant would reply when asked to identify himself. They seemed without pride or self-respect, dirty, lazy, crafty, and always suspicious of their masters and of the world that lay outside their village. Even friendly observers were put off by the way they looked and by their behavior. One commentator complained in the 1760's that "one would have more pity for them if their wild and brutish appearance did not seem to justify their hard lot."

Women's Work in Preindustrial Europe

Merry E. Wiesner

During the seventeenth and eighteenth centuries, most women worked. However, the types of work available to them and the wages they could earn were more limited than for men. Moreover, women were not perceived as "workers" in the same way that men were. Nevertheless, women's work was essential for Europe's economy and for the growth of capitalism during these centuries. In the following selection, Merry E. Wiesner evaluates the changes in women's work and the meaning of work during the early modern period.

CONSIDER: *The main "generalizations" Wiesner makes about changes in women's work; what Wiesner means by "the meaning of work"; how the gender division between production and reproduction was reinforced.*

Despite wide variety and strong continuities, however, there are a few generalizations we can make about changes in the work of many women in Europe during this period. Occupations that required university education or formal training were closed to women. Women rarely controlled enough financial resources to enter occupations that required large initial capital outlay, and social norms kept them from occupations with political functions. Family responsibilities prevented them from entering occupations that required extensive traveling. These attributes of women's work were true both in 1350 and in 1750, but over these four centuries their meaning changed, for it was exactly those with formal education, political functions, capital investment, or international connections, such as physicians, merchants, bankers, lawyers, government officials, and overseas traders, who were gaining in wealth, power, and prestige.

Indeed, it is in the meaning of work that we can see the most change during this period. Women's productive tasks were increasingly defined as reproductive—as housekeeping—or as assisting—or helping out. Thus a woman who sewed clothes, took in boarders, did laundry, and gathered herbs for pay was increasingly thought of as a housewife, a title that became enshrined in statistical

SOURCE: Merry E. Wiesner, "Spinning Out Capital: Women's Work in Preindustrial Europe, 1350–1750," in Renate Bridenthal et al., eds., *Becoming Visible: Women in European History*, 3rd ed. (New York: Houghton Mifflin Co., 1998), pp. 226–227.

language by the nineteenth century, when her activities were no longer regarded as contributing to the gross national product or relevant to other sorts of economic measurements.

This gender division between production and reproduction was reinforced in the early modern period by parish, city, and state governments, various tasks because these were not really "work," but simply "support." This even included allowing women to sell items that they had produced. Women themselves sometimes adopted the same rhetoric, for they knew that arguing that they had a right to work would be much less effective than describing the children they had to support or how much public money might otherwise be spent if they did not work.

And work women did. A recent study of the London labor market has found that 72 percent of women in 1700 were doing full- or part-time paid work outside the home, most of it low-status work. Historians have posited many reasons for the dramatic development of the European economy and for European expansion around the world. Recently an "Industrious Revolution" has been added to these factors; Europeans are seen as reducing their leisure time and working more in order to have money to purchase consumer goods from around the world. This Industrious Revolution not only involved women; it required their labor. Though it may have been conceptualized as assisting or supporting, women's work provided an enormous pool of labor, in the same way that women and children in developing countries provide the mass of labor for the global market today.

✌ CHAPTER QUESTIONS

1. In what ways did competing groups and historical conditions put pressure on aristocrats who wanted to maintain their position and influence?

2. What were the assets and liabilities of the eighteenth-century aristocracy in the face of pressures to diminish its position and influence?

3. How do eighteenth-century assumptions reflect the nature of politics and society during the Ancien Régime?

4. In what ways was the rise of the Atlantic slave trade related to other developments of the seventeenth and eighteenth centuries?

The Enlightenment

Encyclopedia
The Social Contract

The Social Contract

d'Holbach
Système

Scientific Revolution

French Revolution

| 1710 | 1720 | 1730 | 1740 | 1750 | 1760 | 1770 | 1780 | 1790 |

Voltaire

Rousseau

Diderot

d'Holbach

Joseph II

Kant

Mary Wollstonecraft

19 The Enlightenment

As a period of intellectual history in Western civilization, the eighteenth century is known quite appropriately as the Enlightenment. At that time a group of thinkers, called the *philosophes*, developed and popularized related sets of ideas that formed a basis for modern thought. Their methods emphasized scepticism, empirical reasoning, and satire. They spread their ideas through works ranging from pamphlets to the great *Encyclopedia* and numerous meetings in aristocratic "salons." Although centered in France, this intellectual movement took place throughout Europe.

Most of the *philosophes* believed that Western civilization was on the verge of enlightenment, that reasoning and education could quickly dispel the darkness of the past that had kept people in a state of immaturity. The main objects of their criticism were institutions, such as governments and the Church, and irrational customs that perpetuated old ways of thinking and thus hindered progress. While critical and combative, the *philosophes* were not political or social revolutionaries. Their ideas were revolutionary in many ways, but in practice these thinkers hoped for rather painless change—often through reform from above by enlightened monarchs. Enlightenment thinkers usually admired England, where liberal ideas and practices were most developed.

The sources in this chapter concern three issues. First, what was the nature of Enlightenment thought? What was the professed spirit of the Enlightenment? What patterns of morality were embodied in Enlightenment ideas? In what ways was authority rejected and nature elevated to great importance? Second, how should we characterize the *philosophes?* Who were they? What were their common psychological traits, their religious beliefs, and their interactions? Finally, how did Enlightenment thought affect eighteenth-century politics before the French Revolution? Was there such a phenomenon as "enlightened despotism," and if so, what did it mean?

Together, the sources should reveal an intellectual movement still tied to the traditional society of the Ancien Régime but with strikingly modern characteristics. Toward the end of the eighteenth century, many of the ideas of the Enlightenment played an important role in the French Revolution—the subject of the next chapter.

 Primary Sources

What Is Enlightenment?

Immanuel Kant

One of the most pervasive themes among Enlightenment thinkers was a self-conscious sense of a spirit of enlightenment. This is illustrated in the following excerpt from a short essay by Immanuel Kant (1724–1804) of Köigsberg in East Prussia. Kant, one of the world's most profound philosophers, is particularly known for his analysis of the human mind and how it relates to nature, as set forth in his Critique of Pure Reason *(1781). In the following essay, written in 1784, Kant defines the spirit of the Enlightenment and describes some of its implications.*

CONSIDER: *What Kant means by "freedom" and why he feels freedom is so central to the Enlightenment; how people can become enlightened and the appropriate environment to facilitate this enlightenment; what Kant would consider "mature"; how Kant relates enlightenment and politics.*

Enlightenment is man's leaving his self-caused immaturity. Immaturity is the incapacity to use one's intelligence without the guidance of another. Such immaturity is self-caused if it is not caused by lack of intelligence, but by lack of determination and courage to use one's intelligence without being guided by another. *Sapere Aude!* Have the courage to use your own intelligence! is therefore the motto of the enlightenment.

Through laziness and cowardice a large part of mankind, even after nature has freed them from alien guidance, gladly remain immature. It is because of laziness and cowardice that it is so easy for others to usurp the role of guardians. It is so comfortable to be a minor! If I have a book which provides meaning for me, a pastor who has conscience for me, a doctor who will judge my diet for me and so on, then I do not need to exert myself. I do not have any need to think; if I can pay, others will take over the tedious job for me. The guardians who have kindly undertaken the supervision will see to it that by far the largest part of mankind, including the entire "beautiful sex," should consider the step into maturity, not only as difficult but as very dangerous. . . .

But it is more nearly possible for a public to enlighten itself: this is even inescapable if only the public is given its freedom. . . .

All that is required for this enlightenment is *freedom*; and particularly the least harmful of all that may be called freedom, namely, the freedom for man to make *public use* of his reason in all matters. . . .

The question may now be put: Do we live at present in an enlightened age? The answer is: No, but in an age of enlightenment. Much still prevents men from being placed in a position or even being placed into position to use their own minds securely and well in matters of religion. But we do have very definite indications that this field of endeavor is being opened up for men to work freely and reduce gradually the hindrances preventing a general enlightenment and an escape from self-caused immaturity. In this sense, this age is the age of enlightenment and the age of Frederick (The Great). . . .

I have emphasized the main point of enlightenment, that is of man's release from his self-caused immaturity, primarily *in matters of religion*. I have done this because our rulers have no interest in playing the guardian of their subjects in matters of arts and sciences. Furthermore immaturity in matters of religion is not only most noxious but also most dishonorable. But the point of view of a head of state who favors freedom in the arts and sciences goes even farther; for he understands that there is no danger in legislation permitting his subjects to make *public* use of their own reason and to submit *publicly* their thoughts regarding a better framing of such laws together with a frank criticism of existing *legislation*. We have a shining example of this; no prince excels him whom we admire. Only he who is himself enlightened does not fear spectres when he at the same time has a well-disciplined army at his disposal as a guarantee of public peace. Only he can say what (the ruler of a) free state dare not say: *Argue as much as you want and about whatever you want but obey!*

The System of Nature

Baron d'Holbach

Most Enlightenment thinkers rejected traditional sources of authority such as the Church or custom. Instead, they argued that people should rely on reason, experience, and nature as their guides. Baron d'Holbach (1723–1789) exemplifies this in his varied writings. A German aristocrat and scientist who assumed French citizenship, d'Holbach is best known for his attacks on organized religion and his contributions to Diderot's Encyclopedia. *In the following selection from his* System of Nature *(1770), d'Holbach focuses on the meaning of enlightenment and what should be done to obtain this enlightenment.*

CONSIDER: *Why enlightenment is so important; whether "nature" has a meaning similar to God for d'Holbach; the views about the nature of enlightenment that Kant and d'Holbach share.*

The source of man's unhappiness is his ignorance of Nature. The pertinacity with which he clings to blind opinions imbibed in his infancy, which interweave themselves with his existence, the consequent prejudice that warps his mind, that prevents its expansion, that renders him the slave of fiction, appears to doom him to continual errour. He resembles a child destitute of experience, full of idle notions: a dangerous leaven mixes itself with all his knowledge: it is of necessity obscure, it is vacillating and false:—He takes the tone of his ideas on the authority of others, who are themselves in errour, or else have an interest in deceiving him. To remove this Cimmerian darkness, these barriers to the improvement of his condition; to disentangle him from the clouds of errour that envelop him, that obscure the path he ought to tread; to guide him out of this Cretan labyrinth, requires the clue of Ariadne, with all the love she could bestow on Theseus. It exacts more than common exertion; it needs a most determined, a most undaunted courage—it is never effected but by a persevering resolution to act, to think for himself; to examine with rigour and impartiality the opinions he has adopted. . . .

The most important of our duties, then, is to seek means by which we may destroy delusions that can never do more than mislead us. The remedies for these evils must be sought for in Nature herself; it is only in the abundance of her resources, that we can rationally expect to find antidotes to the mischiefs brought upon us by an ill-directed, by an overpowering enthusiasm. It is time these remedies were sought; it is time to look the evil boldly in the face, to examine its foundations, to scrutinize its super-structure: reason, with its faithful guide experience, must attack in their entrenchments those prejudices to which the human race has but too long been the victim. For this purpose reason must be restored to its proper rank,—it must be rescued from the evil company with which it is associated. . . .

Truth speaks not to these perverse beings:—her voice can only be heard by generous minds accustomed to reflection, whose sensibilities make them lament the numberless calamities showered on the earth by political and religious tyranny—whose enlightened minds contemplate with horrour the immensity, the ponderosity of that series of misfortunes with which errour has in all ages overwhelmed mankind.

The *civilized man*, is he whom experience and social life have enabled to draw from nature the means of his own happiness; because he has learned to oppose resistance to those impulses he receives from exterior beings, when experience has taught him they would be injurious to his welfare.

The *enlightened man*, is man in his maturity, in his perfection; who is capable of pursuing his own happiness; because he has learned to examine, to think for himself, and not to take that for truth upon the authority of others, which experience has taught him examination will frequently prove erroneous. . . .

It necessarily results, that man in his researches ought always to fall back on experience, and natural philosophy: These are what he should consult in his religion—in his morals—in his legislation—in his political government—in the arts—in the sciences—in his pleasures—in his misfortunes. Experience teaches that Nature acts by simple, uniform, and invariable laws. It is by his senses man is bound to this universal Nature; it is by his senses he must penetrate her secrets; it is from his senses he must draw experience of her laws. Whenever, therefore, he either fails to acquire experience or quits its path, he stumbles into an abyss, his imagination leads him astray.

SOURCE: Baron d'Holbach, *The System of Nature*, trans. H. D. Robinson (Boston: J. P. Mendum, 1853), pp. viii–ix, 12–13, 15.

Prospectus for the Encyclopedia of Arts and Sciences

Denis Diderot

More than any other work, the Encyclopedia of Arts and Sciences, *edited by Denis Diderot (1713–1784) and Jean-le-Rond d'Alembert (1717–1783), epitomizes the Enlightenment.*

SOURCE: "The Encyclopedia Announced" from *Major Crises in Western Civilization, Volume II, 1745 to the Nuclear Age* by Richard W. Lyman and Lewis W. Spitz, copyright © 1965 by Harcourt Brace & Company and renewed 1993 by Richard W. Lyman and Lewis W. Spitz, reprinted by permission of the publisher.

Written between 1745 and 1780, it presented to the public the sum of knowledge considered important by Enlightenment thinkers. The critical Enlightenment spirit underlying the Encyclopedia led traditional authorities to condemn it and to suppress it more than once. The following is an excerpt from the Prospectus that appeared in 1750, announcing the forthcoming Encyclopedia. The Prospectus was written by Diderot, a philosopher, novelist, and playwright who had already been in trouble with the authorities for his writings. The Prospectus apparently aroused widespread expectations; even before the first volume of the Encyclopedia appeared, more than a thousand orders for it had been received.

CONSIDER: *What a reader could hope to gain by purchasing the* Encyclopedia *and how these hopes themselves reflect the spirit of the Enlightenment; how this selection from the Prospectus reflects the same ideas expressed by Kant and d'Holbach; how the Enlightenment as described here related to the scientific revolution of the seventeenth century.*

It cannot be denied that, since the revival of letters among us, we owe partly to dictionaries the general enlightenment that has spread in society and the germ of science that is gradually preparing men's minds for more profound knowledge. How valuable would it not be, then, to have a book of this kind that one could consult on all subjects and that would serve as much to guide those who have the courage to work at the instruction of others as to enlighten those who only instruct themselves!

This is one advantage we thought of, but it is not the only one. In condensing to dictionary form all that concerns the arts and sciences, it remained necessary to make people aware of the assistance they lend each other; to make use of this assistance to render principles more certain and their consequences clearer; to indicate the distant and close relationships of the beings that make up nature, which have occupied men; to show, by showing the interlacing both of roots and of branches, the impossibility of understanding thoroughly some parts of the whole without exploring many others; to produce a general picture of the efforts of the human spirit in all areas and in all centuries; to present these matters with clarity; to give to each the proper scope, and to prove, if possible, our epigraph by our success: . . .

The majority of these works appeared during the last century and were not completely scorned. It was found that if they did not show much talent, they at least bore the marks of labor and of knowledge. But what would these encyclopedias mean to us? What progress have we not made since then in the arts and sciences? How many truths discovered today, which were not foreseen then? True philosophy was in its cradle; the geometry of infinity did not yet exist; experimental physics was just appearing; there was no dialectic at all; the laws of sound criticism were entirely unknown. Descartes, Boyle, Huyghens, Newton, Leibnitz, the Bernoullis, Locke, Bayle, Pascal, Corneille, Racine, Bourdaloue, Bossuet, etc., either had not yet been born or had not yet written. The spirit of research and competition did not motivate the scholars: another spirit, less fecund perhaps, but rarer, that of precision and method, had not yet conquered the various divisions of literature; and the academies, whose efforts have advanced the arts and sciences to such an extent, were not yet established. . . . At the end of this project you will find the tree of human knowledge, indicating the connection of ideas, which has directed us in this vast operation.

The Philosophe

Enlightenment thinkers often referred to themselves as "philosophes," which is technically the French word for philosophers. The term had a special meaning bound up with the spirit of the Enlightenment. This is dealt with directly in the following selection, "The Philosopher," from the Encyclopedia. It has traditionally been assumed that Diderot is the author of "The Philosopher," but it may have been written by another person, perhaps Du Marsais. In any case, it is an authoritative treatment of the topic according to Enlightenment precepts.

CONSIDER: *The characteristics of the philosopher; how this compares to Kant's definition of enlightenment and d'Holbach's definition of a civilized or enlightened man; how a twentieth-century philosopher might differ with this definition of a philosopher.*

Other men make up their minds to act without thinking, nor are they conscious of the causes which move them, not even knowing that such exist. The philosopher, on the contrary, distinguishes the causes to what extent he may, often anticipates them, and knowingly surrenders himself to them. In this manner he avoids objects that may cause him sensations that are not conducive to his well being or his rational existence, and seeks those which may excite in him affections agreeable with the state in which he finds himself. Reason is in the estimation of the philosopher what grace is to the Christian. Grace determines the Christian's action; reason the philosopher's.

SOURCE: Merrick Whitcomb, ed., "French Philosophers of the Eighteenth Century," in *Translations and Reprints from the Original Sources of European History,* vol. VI, no. 1, ed. Department of History of the University of Pennsylvania (Philadelphia: University of Pennsylvania Press, 1898), pp. 21–23.

Other men are carried away by their passions, so that the acts which they produce do not proceed from reflection. These are the men who move in darkness; while the philosopher, even in his passions, moves only after reflection. He marches at night, but a torch goes on ahead.

The philosopher forms his principles upon an infinity of individual observations. The people adopt the principle without a thought of the observations which have produced it, believing that the maxim exists, so to speak, of itself; but the philosopher takes the maxim at its source, he examines its origin, he knows its real value, and only makes use of it, if it seems to him satisfactory.

Truth is not for the philosopher a mistress who vitiates his imagination, and whom he believes to find everywhere. He contents himself with being able to discover it wherever he may chance to find it. He does not confound it with its semblance; but takes for true that which is true, for false that which is false, for doubtful that which is doubtful, and for probable that which is only probable. He does more—and this is the great perfection of philosophy; that when he has no real grounds for passing judgment, he knows how to remain undetermined.

The world is full of persons of understanding, even of much understanding, who always pass judgment. They are guessing always, because it is guessing to pass judgment without knowing when one has proper grounds for judgment. They misjudge of the capacity of the human mind; they believe it is possible to know everything, and so they are ashamed not to be prepared to pass judgment, and they imagine that understanding consists in passing judgment. The philosopher believes that it consists in judging well: he is better pleased with himself when he has suspended the faculty of determining, than if he had determined before having acquired proper grounds for his decision.

🙠

The philosophic spirit is then a spirit of observation and of exactness, which refers everything to its true principles; but it is not the understanding alone which the philosopher cultivates; he carries further his attention and his labors.

Man is not a monster, made to live only at the bottom of the sea or in the depths of the forest; the very necessities of his life render intercourse with others necessary; and in whatsoever state we find him, his needs and his well-being lead him to live in society. To that reason demands of him that he should know, that he should study and that he should labor to acquire social qualities.

Our philosopher does not believe himself an exile in the world; he does not believe himself in the enemy's country; he wishes to enjoy, like a wise economist, the goods that nature offers him; he wishes to find his pleasure with others; and in order to find it, it is necessary to assist in producing it; so he seeks to harmonize with those with whom chance or his choice has determined he shall live; and he finds at the same time that which suits him: he is an honest man who wishes to please and render himself useful.

🙠

The philosopher is then an honest man, actuated in everything by reason, one who joins to the spirit of reflection and of accuracy the manners and qualities of society.

Philosophical Dictionary: The English Model

Voltaire

François Marie Arouet, who later adopted the name Voltaire (1694–1778), was certainly the most famous of the philosophes. Writing almost every type of literature, from drama and satire to history and essays, he exhibited most of the main elements of the Enlightenment. One of these was the philosophes' admiration for and idealization of England's political system. Voltaire gained familiarity with England during a three-year visit, from 1726 to 1729, and played an important role in popularizing the ideas of English scientists and the principles of the English political system. The following is an excerpt from his Philosophical Dictionary, *first published in 1764.*

CONSIDER: *What Voltaire admires about the English constitution; the implied criticism of the French political system; whether Voltaire idealizes the English system.*

The English constitution has, in fact, arrived at that point of excellence, in consequence of which all men are restored to those natural rights, which, in nearly all monarchies, they are deprived of. These rights are, entire liberty of person and property; freedom of the press; the right of being tried in all criminal cases by a jury of independent men—the right of being tried only according to the strict letter of the law; and the right of every man to profess, unmolested, what religion he chooses, while he renounces offices, which the members of the Anglican or established church alone can hold. These are denominated privileges. And, in truth, invaluable privileges they are in comparison with the usages of most other nations of the world! To be secure on lying down that you shall rise in possession of the same property with which you retired to rest; that you shall not be torn from the arms of your wife, and from your children, in the dead of night,

SOURCE: Voltaire, *Philosophical Dictionary*, in Voltaire, *Works*, trans. W. F. Fleming (New York: E. R. Dumont, 1901), vol. 5, pp. 293–294.

to be thrown into a dungeon, or buried in exile in a desert; that, when rising from the bed of sleep, you will have the power of publishing all your thoughts; and that, if you are accused of having either acted, spoken, or written wrongly, you can be tried only according to law. These privileges attach to every one who sets his foot on English ground. A foreigner enjoys perfect liberty to dispose of his property and person; and, if accused of any offence, he can demand that half the jury shall be composed of foreigners.

I will venture to assert, that, were the human race solemnly assembled for the purpose of making laws, such are the laws they would make for their security.

A Vindication of the Rights of Woman

Mary Wollstonecraft

While the Enlightenment was dominated by men, there were possibilities for active involvement by women. Several women played particularly important roles as patrons and intellectual contributors to the gatherings of philosophes and members of the upper-middle-class and aristocratic elite held in the salons of Paris and elsewhere. It was, however, far more difficult for a woman to publish serious essays in the Enlightenment tradition. Indeed, Enlightenment thinkers did little to change basic attitudes about the inferiority of women. One person who managed to do both was Mary Wollstonecraft (1759–1797), a British author who in 1792 published A Vindication of the Rights of Woman. *The book was a sharply reasoned attack against the oppression of women and an argument for educational change. In the following excerpt Wollstonecraft addresses the author of a proposed new constitution for France that, in her opinion, does not adequately deal with the rights of women.*

CONSIDER: *Why education is so central to her argument; the ways in which this argument reflects the methods and ideals of the Enlightenment.*

Contending for the rights of woman, my main argument is built on this simple principle, that if she be not prepared by education to become the companion of man, she will stop the progress of knowledge and virtue; for truth must be common to all, or it will be inefficacious with respect to its influence on general practice. And how can woman be expected to co-operate unless she knows why she ought to be virtuous? unless freedom strengthens her reason till she comprehends her duty, and sees in what manner it is connected with her real

SOURCE: Mary Wollstonecraft, *The Rights of Woman* (London: J. M. Dent and Sons, Ltd., 1929), pp. 10–11.

good. If children are to be educated to understand the true principle of patriotism, their mother must be a patriot; and the love of mankind, from which an orderly train of virtues spring, can only be produced by considering the moral and civil interest of mankind; but the education and situation of woman at present shuts her out from such investigations.

In this work I have produced many arguments, which to me were conclusive, to prove that the prevailing notion respecting a sexual character was subversive of morality, and I have contended, that to render the human body and mind more perfect, chastity must more universally prevail, and that chastity will never be respected in the male world till the person of a woman is not, as it were, idolised, when little virtue or sense embellish it with the grand traces of mental beauty, or the interesting simplicity of affection.

Consider, sir, dispassionately these observations, for a glimpse of this truth seemed to open before you when you observed, "that to see one-half of the human race excluded by the other from all participation of government was a political phenomenon, that, according to abstract principles, it was impossible to explain." If so, on what does your constitution rest? If the abstract rights of man will bear discussion and explanation, those of woman, by a parity of reasoning, will not shrink from the same test; though a different opinion prevails in this country, built on the very arguments which you use to justify the oppression of woman—prescription.

Consider—I address you as a legislator—whether, when men contend for their freedom, and to be allowed to judge for themselves respecting their own happiness, it be not inconsistent and unjust to subjugate women, even though you firmly believe that you are acting in the manner best calculated to promote their happiness? Who made man the exclusive judge, if woman partake with him of the gift of reason?

The Age of Reason: Deism

Thomas Paine

Many Enlightenment thinkers were strongly opposed to traditional religious institutions and ideas. Yet only a few went so far as to profess atheism. More typical was some form of deism, a belief in a God who created a rational universe with natural laws but who no longer intervened in the course of events. A good example of this belief is found in the following excerpt from Thomas Paine's Age of Reason *(1794). Paine (1737–1809) was an unusually international person. Born in England, he became an American patriot and later a*

SOURCE: Moncure Daniel Conway, ed., *The Writings of Thomas Paine*, vol. IV (New York: G. P. Putnam's Sons, 1896), pp. 21–23.

member of the French Convention (1792–1793). His most famous works are Common Sense *and* The Rights of Man, *in both of which he justifies revolution. In* The Age of Reason *Paine places himself within the tradition of Enlightenment thought and summarizes his religious views.*

CONSIDER: *Why Paine is so opposed to traditional religious institutions; how this opposition is consistent with other Enlightenment thought; how a sincere, sophisticated member of the Catholic Church might have responded to this.*

As several of my colleagues, and others of my fellow-citizens of France, have given me the example of making their voluntary and individual profession of faith, I also will make mine; and I do this with all that sincerity and frankness with which the mind of man communicates with itself.

I believe in one God, and no more; and I hope for happiness beyond this life.

I believe the equality of man, and I believe that religious duties consist in doing justice, loving mercy, and endeavouring to make our fellow-creatures happy.

But, lest it should be supposed that I believe many other things in addition to these, I shall, in the progress of this work, declare the things I do not believe, and my reasons for not believing them.

I do not believe in the creed professed by the Jewish church, by the Roman church, by the Greek church, by the Turkish church, by the Protestant church, nor by any church that I know of. My own mind is my own church.

All national institutions of churches, whether Jewish, Christian, or Turkish, appear to me no other than human inventions set up to terrify and enslave mankind, and monopolize power and profit.

I do not mean by this declaration to condemn those who believe otherwise; they have the same right to their belief as I have to mine. But it is necessary to the happiness of man, that he be mentally faithful to himself. Infidelity does not consist in believing, or in disbelieving; it consists in professing to believe what he does not believe.

It is impossible to calculate the moral mischief, if I may so express it, that mental lying has produced in society. When a man has so far corrupted and prostituted the chastity of his mind, as to subscribe his professional belief to things he does not believe, he has prepared himself for the commission of every other crime. He takes up the trade of a priest for the sake of gain, and, in order to qualify himself for that trade, he begins with a perjury. Can we conceive anything more destructive to morality than this?

Soon after I had published the pamphlet *Common Sense*, in America, I saw the exceeding probability that a revolution in the system of government would be followed by a revolution in the system of religion. The adulterous connection of church and state, wherever it had taken place, whether Jewish, Christian, or Turkish, had so effectually prohibited, by pains and penalties, every discussion upon established creeds, and upon first principles of religion, that until the system of government should be changed, those subjects could not be brought fairly and openly before the world; but that whenever this should be done, a revolution in the system of religion would follow. Human inventions and priest-craft would be detected; and man would return to the pure, unmixed, and unadulterated belief of one God, and no more.

The Social Contract
Jean Jacques Rousseau

More than anyone else, Jean Jacques Rousseau (1712–1778) tested the outer limits of Enlightenment thought and went on to criticize its very foundations. Born in Geneva, he spent much of his life in France (mainly in Paris), where he became one of the philosophes who contributed to the Encyclopedia. *Yet he also undermined Enlightenment thought by holding that social institutions had corrupted people and that human beings in the state of nature were purer, freer, and happier than they were in modern civilization. This line of thought provided a foundation for the growth of Romanticism in the late eighteenth and early nineteenth centuries. Rousseau's most important political work was* The Social Contract *(1762), in which he argued for popular sovereignty. In the following selection from that work, Rousseau focuses on what he considers the fundamental argument of the book—the passage from the state of nature to the civil state by means of the social contract.*

CONSIDER: *Rousseau's solution to the main problem of* The Social Contract; *the advantages and disadvantages of the social contract; what characteristics of Enlightenment thought are reflected in this selection.*

"The problem is to find a form of association which will defend and protect with the whole common force the person and goods of each associate, and in which each, while uniting himself with all, may still obey himself alone, and remain as free as before." This is the fundamental problem of which *The Social Contract* provides the solution.

The clauses of this contract are so determined by the nature of the act that the slightest modification would make them vain and ineffective; so that, although they have perhaps never been formally set forth, they are everywhere the same and everywhere tacitly admitted

SOURCE: Jean Jacques Rousseau, *The Social Contract and Discourses* (London: J. M. Dent, Everyman Library, 1913), pp. 14–15, 18–19.

and recognised, until, on the violation of the social compact, each regains his original rights and resumes his natural liberty, while losing the conventional liberty in favour of which he renounced it.

These clauses, properly understood, may be reduced to one—the total alienation of each associate, together with all his rights, to the whole community; for, in the first place, as each gives himself absolutely, the conditions are the same for all; and, this being so, no one has any interest in making them burdensome to others.

Moreover, the alienation being without reserve, the union is as perfect as it can be, and no associate has anything more to demand: for, if the individuals retained certain rights, as there would be no common superior to decide between them and the public, each, being on one point his own judge, would ask to be so on all; the state of nature would thus continue, and the association would necessarily become inoperative or tyrannical.

Finally, each man, in giving himself to all, gives himself to nobody; and as there is no associate over whom he does not acquire the same right as he yields others over himself, he gains on equivalent for everything he loses, and an increase of force for the preservation of what he has.

If then we discard from the social compact what is not of its essence, we shall find that it reduces itself to the following terms—

Each of us puts his person and all his power in common under the supreme direction of the general will, and, in our corporate capacity, we receive each member as an indivisible part of the whole.

❧

The passage from the state of nature to the civil state produces a very remarkable change in man, by substituting justice for instinct in his conduct, and giving his actions the morality they had formerly lacked. Then only, when the voice of duty takes the place of physical impulses and right of appetite, does man, who so far had considered only himself, find that he is forced to act on different principles, and to consult his reason before listening to his inclinations. Although, in this state, he deprives himself of some advantages which he got from nature, he gains in return others so great, his faculties are so stimulated and developed, his ideas so extended, his feelings so ennobled, and his whole soul so uplifted, that, did not the abuses of this new condition often degrade him below that which he left, he would be bound to bless continually the happy moment which took him from it for ever, and, instead of a stupid and unimaginative animal, made him an intelligent being and a man.

Let us draw up the whole account in terms easily commensurable. What man loses by the social contract is his natural liberty and an unlimited right to everything he tries to get and succeeds in getting; what he gains is civil liberty and the proprietorship of all he possesses. If we are to avoid mistake in weighing one against the other, we must clearly distinguish natural liberty, which is bounded only by the strength of the individual, from civil liberty, which is limited by the general will; and possession, which is merely the effect of force or the right of the first occupier, from property, which can be founded only on a positive title.

We might, over and above all this, add, to what man acquires in the civil state, moral liberty, which alone makes him truly master of himself; for the mere impulse of appetite is slavery, while obedience to a law which we prescribe to ourselves is liberty. But I have already said too much on this head, and the philosophical meaning of the word liberty does not now concern us.

 # Visual Sources

Frontispiece of the *Encyclopédie*

This illustration (figure 19.1) appeared at the beginning of the 1751 edition to the Encyclopédie. A description guided the reader to its allegorical meanings. In the center and above all other figures stands Truth, "wrapped in a veil, radiant with a light which parts the clouds and disperses them." Close on her left is Reason, who lifts a veil from Truth; below her, Philosophy pulls the veil away. Theology, holding a Bible, kneels at the feet of Truth. On Truth's right is Imagination, "preparing to adorn and crown Truth." Below them are figures representing Geometry, Physics, Astronomy, Optics, Botany, Chemistry, Agriculture, History, and the arts. At the bottom are practitioners who will use the guides above them to make progress. As a whole and in its allegorical detail, this illustration represented the optimistic spirit of the Encyclopédie and the Enlightenment.

CONSIDER: *The meaning of the Enlightenment as represented by this illustration; the connections between first, the ideals of truth, reason, and imagination, second, the sciences and arts, and third, the practitioners depicted in this illustration.*

Experiment with an Air Pump
Joseph Wright

Few paintings provide a better image of the Enlightenment than Experiment with an Air Pump *(1768) by the British artist Joseph Wright (figure 19.2). The experiment takes place in the* center of the picture; its apparent success is evidenced by the dead bird inside a closed glass bowl from which the air has been pumped out. The informally dressed experimenter is carefully observing his work. Around him are members of his family and some well-dressed friends.

The form and content of this picture symbolize the Enlightenment. A small source of light is sufficient to enlighten humanity and reveal the laws of nature. Science is not just for specialists but something amateurs can understand and practice to obtain practical results. That it is a British painting is particularly significant, for the English led in developing useful machines and were identified as having a more pragmatic approach to science and ideas than other peoples. The painting also reveals customary images of the sexes: the experimenter boldly forging on while to his left a friend or associate calmly explains what is happening to a woman and her daughter, whose sensibilities are as appropriately fragile as the dying bird—the main object of their concern.

CONSIDER: Any common themes in this painting and the documents by Kant, d'Holbach, and Diderot.

Propaganda and the Enlightened Monarch

Joseph II of Austria

Emperor Joseph II of Austria (1765–1790) is generally thought to have been one of the most enlightened eighteenth-century kings and indeed considered himself to be an enlightened monarch. Some of what this meant is indicated by this picture Joseph II had painted of himself (figure 19.3). It shows him plowing a field with a farmer and members of his court. To make sure he and his office were recognizable to viewers, Joseph remained appropriately dressed, including

FIGURE 19.1   (© The Granger Collection, New York)

wearing his powdered wig. This scene also affirms the growing interest in agricultural improvements during the eighteenth century, particularly among aristocratic innovators. Joseph II tells of some of his hopes in a number of letters excerpted here.

CONSIDER: What there was about this scene and these letters that could be considered enlightened; any inconsistencies with these statements and the reality of being a monarch; how Kant might have viewed Joseph II.

SOURCE: "Letters of Joseph II," in *The Pamphleteer,* vol. XIX (London, 1882), pp. 282, 288–290.

FIGURE 19.2 (© Art Resource, NY)

FIGURE 19.3 (© Erich Lessing/Art Resource, NY)

Mr. Vice-Chancellor—The present system of taxation in my dominions, and the inequality of the taxes which are imposed on the nation, form a subject too important to escape my attention. I have discovered that the principles on which it is founded are unsound, and have become injurious to the industry of the peasant; that there is neither equality, nor equity, between the hereditary provinces with each other, nor between individual proprietors, and therefore it can no longer continue.

With this view I give you the necessary orders to introduce a new system of taxation, by which the contribution, requisite for the wants of the state, may be effected without augmenting the present taxes, and the industry of the peasant, at the same time, be freed from all impediments.

❧

Since my accession to the throne, I have ever been anxious to conquer the prejudices against my station, and have taken pains to gain the confidence of my people; I have several times since given proof, that the welfare of my subjects is my passion; that to satisfy it, I shun neither labor, nor trouble, nor even vexations, and reflect well on the means which are likely to promote my views; and yet in my reforms, I everywhere find opposition from people, of whom I least expect it.

❧

Sir,—Till now the Protestant religion has been opposed in my states; its adherents have been treated like foreigners; civil rights, possession of estates, titles, and appointments, all were refused them.

I determined from the very commencement of my reign to adorn my diadem with the love of my people, to act in the administration of affairs according to just, impartial, and liberal principles; consequently, I granted toleration, and removed the yoke which had oppressed the protestants for centuries.

Fanaticism shall in future be known in my states only by the contempt I have for it; nobody shall any longer be exposed to hardships on account of his creed; no man shall be compelled in future to profess the religion of the state, if it be contrary to his persuasion, and if he have other ideas of the right way of insuring blessedness.

In future my Empire shall not be the scene of abominable intolerance. Fortunately no sacrifices like those of Calas and Sirven have ever disgraced any reign in this country.

If, in former times, the will of the monarch furnished opportunities for injustice, if the limits of executive power were exceeded, and private hatred acted her part, I can only pity those monarchs who were nothing but kings.

Tolerance is an effect of that beneficent increase of knowledge which now enlightens Europe, and which is owing to philosophy and the efforts of great men; it is a convincing proof of the improvement of the human mind, which has boldly reopened a road through the dominions of superstition, which was trodden centuries ago by Zoroaster and Confucius, and which, fortunately for mankind, has now become the highway of monarchs. Adieu!

 ## Secondary Sources

The Age of Enlightenment
Lester G. Crocker

The Enlightenment owes its substance to the thought of a relatively small group of eighteenth-century philosophes who came from many countries but were centered in France. Although they often argued among themselves, there was a set of approaches and propositions upon which most of them agreed. In the following selection Lester Crocker analyzes what unified the philosophes.

CONSIDER: *How the primary sources support or contradict Crocker's interpretations; why the philosophes were so concerned with Christianity and the Church; the elements of this outlook that make the most sense to you for today's world.*

What we call the Enlightenment gradually took shape in individual minds, over several generations, before it became conscious of itself as a movement during the late 1740's. The principal galvanizing forces were Voltaire's ceaseless efforts in propagandizing and in whipping up "party" spirit, and the prolonged battle over the *Encyclopédie*, which served to unite many of the *philosophes*, as we call the writers who were engaged in furthering the goals of the Enlightenment. The *philosophes* were more often than not at odds among themselves on the answers they proposed to various questions or problems. Their solidarity lay in their awareness of a common foe—the *status quo*, and those who supported it, particularly Christianity and the Church. It lay also in their agreement on what the questions and problems were. The *philosophes* held certain ideas and aims in common. Among these were religious tolerance (belief in toleration of all ideas as well as personal tolerance was not universal among the *philosophes*); the conviction that human life can be improved through the improvement of society, since men are (more or less) shaped by laws and government; the idea that the enlightened group should influence those who govern, both directly and through public opinion. Their stance rested on a base of secularism and

SOURCE: Excerpted from *The Age of Enlightenment*, pp. 2–3, by Lester G. Crocker. Copyright © 1969 by Lester G. Crocker. Reprinted by permission of HarperCollins Publishers, Inc.

humanism. Regardless of their varying religious beliefs, all the *philosophes* held that the proper business (if there was any) of organized churches was the salvation of souls. Science, government, economic policy, even (many thought) moral values and personal morality had to be freed from the dead hand of Christian authority. The Enlightenment was for unfettered critical reason, for social experience to indicate what course men should take in meeting the challenges involved in ameliorating human affairs. God, if he existed, had no influence on these—Bayle had demonstrated that, before the end of the seventeenth century. To the *philosophes*, churches were what we would now call "power groups" and, like all such groups, interested primarily in themselves. Revealed religions were fantasies or downright frauds. Christianity, especially, was hostile to the demands of human nature and pretended (the critics claimed) to direct men away from their self-interest in this life to a mythical paradise in a nonexistent life beyond. Reaction against the Christian world view and religious control of thought had been the very origin of the freethinking (*libertin*) movement in the seventeenth century. The *philosophes* were united by the conviction, above all else, that man must control his own destiny for the sole purpose of a better life on earth and that he must do everything possible to enlarge that control.

The Heavenly City of the Eighteenth-Century Philosophers

Carl L. Becker

Another point of interpretive division among historians of the Enlightenment centers on how modern and secular the philosophes were. Nineteenth- and early-twentieth-century historians argued that the philosophes were more modern than medieval and indeed drew more from the Classical pagan world than from the medieval world. This view still predominates among historians of the period. A famous challenge to this view was made more than sixty years ago by Cornell historian Carl Becker. His book, The Heavenly City of the Eighteenth-Century Philosophers *(1932), became the most influential book on the subject, although today it is no longer as popular as it once was. In the following selection from this work, Becker presents the substance of his thesis.*

CONSIDER: *The ways in which the philosophes were more medieval than modern; the support Becker offers for his argument that there was much Christian philosophy in the*

SOURCE: Carl L. Becker, *The Heavenly City of the Eighteenth-Century Philosophers.* Reprinted by permission of Yale University Press (New Haven, CT, 1932), pp. 29–31, 102–103.

philosophes' writings; how Kant would react to Becker's interpretation.

We are accustomed to think of the eighteenth century as essentially modern in its temper. Certainly, the *Philosophes* themselves made a great point of having renounced the superstition and hocus-pocus of medieval Christian thought, and we have usually been willing to take them at their word. Surely, we say, the eighteenth century was preëminently the age of reason, surely the *Philosophes* were a skeptical lot, atheists in effect if not by profession, addicted to science and the scientific method, always out to crush the infamous, valiant defenders of liberty, equality, fraternity, freedom of speech, and what you will. All very true. And yet I think the *Philosophes* were nearer the Middle Ages, less emancipated from the preconceptions of medieval Christian thought, than they quite realized or we have commonly supposed. . . .

But, if we examine the foundations of their faith, we find that at every turn the *Philosophes* betray their debt to medieval thought without being aware of it. They denounced Christian philosophy, but rather too much, after the manner of those who are but half emancipated from the "superstitions" they scorn. They had put off the fear of God, but maintained a respectful attitude toward the Deity. They ridiculed the idea that the universe had been created in six days, but still believed it to be a beautifully articulated machine designed by the Supreme Being according to a rational plan as an abiding place for mankind. The Garden of Eden was for them a myth, no doubt, but they looked enviously back to the golden age of Roman virtue, or across the waters to the unspoiled innocence of an Arcadian civilization that flourished in Pennsylvania. They renounced the authority of church and Bible, but exhibited a naïve faith in the authority of nature and reason. They scorned metaphysics, but were proud to be called philosophers. They dismantled heaven, somewhat prematurely it seems, since they retained their faith in the immortality of the soul. They courageously discussed atheism, but not before the servants. They defended toleration valiantly, but could with difficulty tolerate priests. They denied that miracles ever happened, but believed in the perfectibility of the human race. We feel that these Philosophers were at once too credulous and too skeptical. They were the victims of common sense. In spite of their rationalism and their humane sympathies, in spite of their aversion to hocus-pocus and enthusiasm and dim perspectives, in spite of their skepticism, their engaging cynicism, their brave youthful blasphemies and talk of hanging the last king in the entrails of the last priest—in spite of all of it, there is more of the Christian philosophy in the writings of the *Philosophes* than has yet been dreamt of in our histories.

Women in the Salons

Bonnie S. Anderson and Judith P. Zinsser

As with the Renaissance and Scientific Revolution, the central figures of the Enlightenment were men. However, some women did directly participate as writers, and perhaps even more importantly, they participated as saloniéres—organizers of gatherings in the salons of homes where Enlightenment figures mingled with women and men of the social and cultural elite. Did the men of the Enlightenment try to change traditional views of women in the same way they tried to change traditional views about men and human nature? In the following selection Bonnie S. Anderson and Judith P. Zinsser address this question.

CONSIDER: *Why, according to Anderson and Zinsser, there was no Enlightenment for women; ways in which the Enlightenment, in the long run, might have benefited women.*

. . . Parisian women established the institution of the salon by the last quarter of the seventeenth century. Aspiring hostesses competed to attract the talented, the witty, and the powerful to their homes. Outside the powerful French court and frequently in opposition to it, these new social circles offered women a new possibility: that of being a salonière, who by her graciousness and skill enabled conversation to flourish, artists to find patrons, and aristocrats to be amused. As a salonière, a woman brought the circles of power into her home. In the environment she created, she could help or hinder not only artistic and literary reputations, but political policies as well. The financial remedies for France's economy were debated in the salons; the king's choices of ministers were strongly influenced by the backing of powerful salonières. Salonières were privy to court secrets; salons were frequented by statesmen and ambassadors as well as intellectuals and artists. Salonières could make or break careers and often provided havens for new political philosophies and the new political opposition to the monarchy. . . .

In the salon, a woman could meet and marry a man of superior social rank or wealth. In the salon, a woman of enterprise could make her way by attracting the famous. The salon became the base of influential women who swayed kings, governments, political opinion, and literary and artistic taste. . . .

Rational conversation, sociability between women and men, delight in the pleasures of this world are the hallmarks of Enlightenment culture. The men who mingled with the Bluestockings and frequented the salons were the men who produced the Enlightenment. It is a tragedy for women that these men, who were aided, sponsored, and lionized by the salonières, produced—with very few exceptions—art and writing which either ignored women completely or upheld the most traditional views of womanhood. Just as there was no Renaissance or Scientific Revolution for women, in the sense that the goals and ideals of those movements were perceived as applicable only to men, so there was no Enlightenment for women. Enlightenment thinkers questioned all the traditional limits on men—and indeed challenged the validity of tradition itself. They championed the rights of commoners, the rights of citizens, the rights of slaves, Jews, Indians, and children, but not those of women. Instead, often at great cost to their own logic and rationality, they continued to reaffirm the most ancient inherited traditions about women: that they were inferior to men in the crucial faculties of reason and ethics and so should be subordinated to men. In philosophy and in art, men of the Enlightenment upheld the traditional ideal of woman: silent, obedient, subservient, modest, and chaste. The salonière—witty, independent, powerful, well-read, and sometimes libertine—was condemned and mocked. A few Enlightenment thinkers did question and even reject subordinating traditions about women. But those who argued for a larger role for women—like the English-woman Mary Wollstonecraft in her *Vindication of the Rights of Woman* (1792), the French Marquis de Condorcet in his *Admission of Women to Civic Rights* (1790), the German Theodor von Hippel in his *On the Civic Improvement of Women* (1792), the Spaniard Josefa Amar y Borbón in her *Discourse in Defense of Women's Talent and Their Capacity for Government and Other Positions Held by Men* (1786)—prompted outrage and then were forgotten. Instead, most philosophers and writers reiterated the most limiting traditions of European culture regarding women, often in works which condemned traditional behavior for men.

The Problem of Enlightened Absolutism

H. M. Scott

Historians have long debated exactly how much the Enlightenment influenced monarchs of the time. Traditionally, there has been considerable acceptance of the view that monarchs such as Joseph II of Austria and Frederick II of Prussia were enlightened. In recent decades this view was seriously narrowed and questioned to the point where many historians felt that enlightened despotism and enlightened absolutism were no longer terms that could usefully be applied to these eighteenth-century monarchs. More recently, other historians have come to the conclusion that the term is useful. In the following selection H. M. Scott surveys this controversy and concludes that enlightened absolutism was real.

CONSIDER: *The characteristics of enlightened absolutism; why Joseph II (see the visual sources in this chapter) and Frederick II (see the primary sources in the preceding chapter) might be considered enlightened monarchs; how enlightened absolutism differs from seventeenth-century absolutism (see sources in Chapter 16).*

Few historical concepts have had their obituaries written more frequently than enlightened absolutism, yet so obstinately refuse to die. In its classical form, the theory of enlightened absolutism asserted that during the second half of the eighteenth century the domestic policies of most European states were influenced and even dictated by the ideas of the Enlightenment and were therefore sharply distinguished from what had gone before. Government became a systematic and rational attempt to apply the best recent knowledge to the task of ruling, while the main aim of internal policy came to be the improvement of educational opportunities, social conditions and economic life. . . .

Together, rulers and their influential advisers carried through a wide-ranging series of reforms, the principal inspiration for which was the political philosophy of the Enlightenment. Administrations and legal and fiscal systems were modernised; commercial and economic development was encouraged; efforts were made to improve agriculture and even to abolish the institution of serfdom; state control over the Catholic Church was extended and a determined attempt was made to channel some of its wealth into increased and improved pastoral activity; teaching in universities was brought up to date; and the provision of secondary and primary education was vastly increased. These reforms, and the amount of success achieved, were remarkable in the context of the later eighteenth century, and the sense of social responsibility which lay behind many of these measures was also novel and striking. Though the precise policies adopted varied from country to country, a common explanation was found in the movement of ideas known as the European Enlightenment, which was at its peak exactly when the policies of enlightened absolutism were being pursued: the middle decades of the eighteenth century until the outbreak of the French Revolution in 1789.

During the past two generations, the historical reputation of enlightened absolutism has undergone remarkable vicissitudes, above all in Anglo-American historical writing about later eighteenth-century Europe. It first rose to prominence during the 1930s, and for a generation thereafter was widely accepted among historians. By the 1960s, however, the tide was beginning to turn and the sceptics, who saw only the conventional aims of state-building in these policies and regarded the enlightened professions which accompanied them as mere window-dressing, were gaining the ascendant. The critics of enlightened absolutism argued that few monarchs, and certainly none of the major rulers, could afford to adhere blindly to an enlightened blueprint and ignore, or even neglect, the demands of self-defence. The competitive states-system within which the great powers operated required large and powerful armies and administrative and fiscal systems to support them. These priorities preempted much of the scope for enlightened reform. Above all, critics of the notion of enlightened absolutism argued that the success of these initiatives was often incomplete and could, at times, be very limited indeed. . . .

During the 1970s, the widespread assumption that enlightened absolutism was a fiction came to be challenged by a growing number of monographic studies of particular countries which make clear that the reforms of this period were influenced by ideas and were not simply another stage in the growth of the absolutist state. This trend has increased during the 1980s. . . .

[I]t has become clear that enlightened absolutism is not an idea in the mind of historians. The remarkable extent and the considerable success of the reforming initiatives is now established beyond question.

❧ CHAPTER QUESTIONS

1. What core of ideas and attitudes most clearly connects Enlightenment thinkers as revealed in these sources? How do these ideas relate to eighteenth-century society and institutions?

2. What policies would an eighteenth-century ruler have to pursue to fit to the greatest degree the ideas and assumptions of Enlightenment thinkers? What hindrances were faced by monarchs who wanted to be more enlightened?

3. What ideas and attitudes of Enlightenment thinkers do you think remain valid for the problems facing today's world? What Enlightenment ideas and attitudes no longer seem valid or appropriate?

4. In what ways do the sources support the argument that together, the Scientific Revolution and the Enlightenment constitute a single intellectual revolution of great long-term significance?

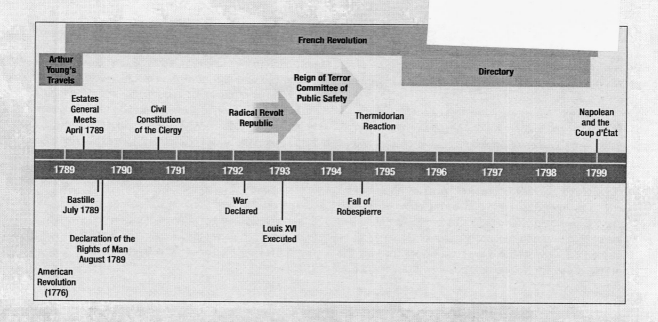

20 The French Revolution

In 1789 the French Revolution ended the relative political and social stability of the Ancien Régime. This, and the earlier American Revolution, led to political and social changes that swept through Western civilization in the nineteenth and twentieth centuries.

Although the causes of the French Revolution are deep and controversial, most agree it was precipitated by financial problems that led Louis XVI to call a meeting of an old representative institution, the Estates General, in 1789. A struggle for power soon developed between a resurgent aristocracy and a rising middle class, both demanding support from the king. In an environment where peasants were turning against the aristocracy in the countryside and crowds were resorting to violence in Paris, the king managed to alienate both sides. Revolutionary legislation soon followed. By 1792 France was a constitutional monarchy,

feudalism was abolished, liberal principles echoing Enlightenment thought were formally recognized, Church lands were confiscated, and government administration was reorganized. The country was at war internally with counterrevolutionary forces and externally with much of the rest of Europe.

A second revolution in 1792 set France on a more radical course. Louis XVI was executed, and the government was declared a republic. Real power rested in the hands of the small Committee of Public Safety, which attacked internal dissent through the Reign of Terror and external wars through national mobilization. The period ended with a return to a more moderate course in 1794 and 1795, known as the Thermidorian Reaction. With power in the hands of the well-to-do middle class, an uneasy balance was maintained between forces clamoring for more radical policies and those wishing to return the monarchy until 1799, when Napoleon Bonaparte rose to power by means of a *coup d'état*.

Historians are fascinated by revolutions, for change is unusually rapid and dramatic. They are particularly interested in the causes of revolutions. In this chapter several primary documents address questions related to the causes of the French Revolution. What were some early signs of revolutionary discontent? What complaints were voiced by the middle class and by the commoners—the Third Estate? How did leaders of this Third Estate see themselves? Related secondary documents explore some of the interpretive debates over the revolution: Was this mainly a social revolution? What was the influence of politics on the French Revolution? Other sources examine the course and effects of the French Revolution. What happened is of particular importance, since the French Revolution was seen as a model for other revolutions and hoped-for revolutions. What were the main changes enacted during the revolution? How can we explain the most radical phase—the Reign of Terror? What role did women play in revolutionary events? What part did nationalism play in revolutionary developments?

In short, the selections should provide broad insights into the nature and significance of the French Revolution, which more than any other event marks a dividing line between the Early Modern and the Modern eras of Western civilization.

 # Primary Sources

Travels in France: Signs of Revolution

Arthur Young

In one sense, the French Revolution came as a great surprise. One of the last places people might have expected a revolution to occur was in a country so advanced and with such a stable monarchy as France. Yet to some sensitive observers of the time, the signs of revolution were at hand during the late 1780s. One of these observers was Arthur Young (1741–1820), a British farmer and diarist, best known for his writings on agricultural subjects. Between 1787 and 1789 he traveled extensively throughout France, keeping a diary of his experiences. In the following selection from that diary, Young notes deep dissatisfactions among the French.

CONSIDER: *The problems and dissatisfactions that gave the French a sense of impending revolution; the specific problems that seemed most likely to lead to a revolutionary crisis and the steps that might have been taken to avoid such a crisis; how Young felt about these problems and dissatisfactions.*

PARIS, OCTOBER 17, 1787

One opinion pervaded the whole company, that they are on the eve of some great revolution in the government: that every thing points to it: the confusion in the finances great; with a *deficit* impossible to provide for without the states-general of the kingdom, yet no ideas formed of what would be the consequence of their meeting: no minister existing, or to be looked to in or out of power, with such decisive talents as to promise any other remedy than palliative ones: a prince on the throne, with excellent dispositions, but without the resources of a mind that could govern in such a moment without ministers: a court buried in pleasure and dissipation; and adding to the distress, instead of endeavouring to be placed in a more independent situation: a great ferment amongst all ranks of men, who are eager for some change, without knowing what to look to, or to hope for: and a strong leaven of liberty, increasing every hour since the American revolution; altogether form a combination of circumstances that promise e'er long to ferment into motion, if some master hand, of very superior talents, and inflexible courage, is not found at the helm to guide events, instead of being driven by them. It is very remarkable, that such conversation never occurs, but a bankruptcy is a topic: the curious question on which is, *would a bankruptcy occasion a civil war, and a total overthrow of the government?* These answers that I have received to this question, appear to be just: such a measure, conducted by a man of abilities, vigour, and firmness, would certainly not occasion either one or the other. But the same measure, attempted by a man of a different character, might possibly do both. All agree, that the states of the kingdom cannot assemble without more liberty being the consequence; but I meet with so few men that have any just ideas of freedom, that I question much the species of this new liberty that is to arise. They know not how to value the privileges of THE PEOPLE: as to the nobility and the clergy, if a revolution added any thing to their scale, I think it would do more mischief than good. . . .

SOURCE: Arthur Young, *Arthur Young's Travels in France During the Years 1787, 1788, 1789*, 4th ed., ed. Miss Betham-Edwards (London: Bell, 1892), pp. 97–98, 124, 134.

RENNES, SEPTEMBER 2, 1788

The discontents of the people have been double, first on account of the high price of bread, and secondly for the banishment of the parliament. The former cause is natural enough, but why the people should love their parliament was what I could not understand, since the members, as well as of the states, are all noble, and the distinction between the *noblesse* and *roturiers* no where stronger, more offensive, or more abominable than in Bretagne. They assured me, however, that the populace have been blown up to violence by every art of deception, and even by money distributed for that purpose. The commotions rose to such a height before the camp was established, that the troops here were utterly unable to keep the peace. . . .

NANTES, SEPTEMBER 22, 1788

Nantes is as *enflammé* in the cause of liberty, as any town in France can be; the conversations I witnessed here, prove how great a change is effected in the minds of the French, nor do I believe it will be possible for the present government to last half a century longer, unless the clearest and most decided talents are at the helm. The American revolution has laid the foundation of another in France, if government does not take care of itself.

The Cahiers: Discontents of the Third Estate

Pressured by discontent and financial problems, Louis XVI called for a meeting of the Estates General in 1789. This representative institution, which had not met for 175 years, reflected the traditional formal divisions in French society: the First Estate, the clergy; the Second Estate, the nobility; and the Third Estate, all the rest from banker and lawyer to peasant. In anticipation of the meeting of the Estates General, the king requested and received cahiers, lists of grievances drawn up by local groups of each of the three Estates. These cahiers have provided historians with an unusually rich source of materials revealing what was bothering people just before the outbreak of the revolution in 1789. The following is an excerpt from a cahier from the Third Estate in Carcassonne.

CONSIDER: *How these grievances of the Third Estate compare to the grievances noted by Young; why these grievances might be revolutionary; the ways in which these grievances are peculiar to the Third Estate and not shared by the First and Second Estates.*

SOURCE: "Cahier of the Grievances, Complaints, and Protests of the Electoral District of Carcassonne . . ." From James Harvey Robinson, ed., *Readings in European History,* vol. II (Boston: Ginn, 1904), pp. 399–400.

8. Among these rights the following should be especially noted: the nation should hereafter be subject only to such laws and taxes as it shall itself freely ratify.

9. The meetings of the Estates General of the kingdom should be fixed for definite periods, and the subsidies judged necessary for the support of the state and the public service should be noted for no longer a period than to the close of the year in which the next meeting of the Estates General is to occur.

10. In order to assure to the third estate the influence to which it is entitled in view of the number of its members, the amount of its contributions to the public treasury, and the manifold interests which it has to defend or promote in the national assemblies, its votes in the assembly should be taken and counted by head.

11. No order, corporation, or individual citizen may lay claim to any pecuniary exemptions. . . . All taxes should be assessed on the same system throughout the nation.

12. The due exacted from commoners holding fiefs should be abolished, and also the general or particular regulations which exclude members of the third estate from certain positions, offices, and ranks which have hitherto been bestowed on nobles either for life or hereditarily. A law should be passed declaring members of the third estate qualified to fill all such offices for which they are judged to be personally fitted.

13. Since individual liberty is intimately associated with national liberty, his Majesty is hereby petitioned not to permit that it be hereafter interfered with by arbitrary orders for imprisonment. . . .

14. Freedom should be granted also to the press, which should however be subjected, by means of strict regulations, to the principles of religion, morality, and public decency.

What Is the Third Estate?

Emmanuel Joseph Sieyès

Before the Estates General met, issues arose among the Estates, particularly over whether the combined First and Second Estates should be able to hold the preponderance of power when the Estates General met. One of the most wide-ranging attacks on the privileged orders and assertion of

SOURCE: From Merrick Whitcomb, ed., "French Philosophers of the Eighteenth Century," in *Translations and Reprints from the Original Sources of European History,* vol. VI, no. 1, ed. Department of History of the University of Pennsylvania (Philadelphia: University of Pennsylvania Press, 1898), pp. 34–35.

Third Estate rights came from Emmanuel Joseph Sieyès (1748–1836). A clergyman strongly influenced by Enlightenment ideas, Sieyès was eventually elected as a representative of the Third Estate and played an active role in events throughout the revolutionary and Napoleonic periods. The following is a selection from his pamphlet, What Is the Third Estate?, *which was published in January 1789 and gained quick popularity.*

CONSIDER: *The basis for the attack by Sieyès on the nobility; why members of the bourgeoisie might find this pamphlet very appealing; how the tone and content of this pamphlet compare with the cahier.*

It suffices here to have made it clear that the pretended utility of a privileged order for the public service is nothing more than a chimera; that with it all that which is burdensome in this service is performed by the Third Estate; that without it the superior places would be infinitely better filled; that they naturally ought to be the lot and the recompense of ability and recognized services, and that if privileged persons have come to usurp all the lucrative and honorable posts, it is a hateful injustice to the rank and file of citizens and at the same time a treason to the public weal.

Who then shall dare to say that the Third Estate has not within itself all that is necessary for the formation of a complete nation? It is the strong and robust man who has one arm still shackled. If the privileged order should be abolished, the nation would be nothing less, but something more. Therefore, what is the Third Estate? Everything; but an everything shackled and oppressed. What would it be without the privileged order? Everything, but an everything free and flourishing. Nothing can succeed without it, everything would be infinitely better without the others. . . .

What is a nation? A body of associates, living under a common law, and represented by the same legislature, etc.

Is it not evident that the noble order has privileges and expenditures which it dares to call its rights, but which are apart from the rights of the great body of citizens? It departs there from the common order, from the common law. So its civil rights make of it an isolated people in the midst of the great nation. This is truly *imperium in imperio.*

In regard to its political rights, these also it exercises apart. It has its special representatives, which are not charged with securing the interests of the people. The body of its deputies sit apart; and when it is assembled in the same hall with the deputies of simple citizens, it is none the less true that its representation is essentially distinct and separate; it is a stranger to the nation, in the first place, by its origin, since its commission is not derived from the people; then by its object, which consists of defending not the general, but the particular interest.

The Third Estate embraces then all that which belongs to the nation; and all that which is not the Third Estate, cannot be regarded as being of the nation. What is the Third Estate? It is the whole.

Revolutionary Legislation: Abolition of the Feudal System

During the summer of 1789, France was swept with a variety of revolutionary activities. The Third Estate had successfully formed the National Assembly. On July 14 a mob had stormed the Bastille, an act that symbolized a violent tearing down of the Ancien Régime and the beginning of the popular revolution. In the countryside the peasantry rose against the nobility. Faced with these pressures, elements of the nobility in the National Assembly moved on August 4 and 5 to abolish their own feudal rights and privileges. In sum, these laws constituted a formal repudiation of the feudal system and many of the institutions of the Ancien Régime. The following selection comes from that legislation.

CONSIDER: *The extent to which these measures satisfied the grievances of the Third Estate as expressed in the* cahier *and the pamphlet by Sieyès; why members of the nobility proposed and supported these measures themselves; whether these measures should be interpreted as a repudiation of the monarchy as an institution or specifically of Louis XVI as the king.*

ARTICLE I. The National Assembly hereby completely abolishes the feudal system. It decrees that, among the existing rights and dues, . . . all those originating in or representing real or personal serfdom or personal servitude, shall be abolished without indemnification.

❧

IV. All manorial courts are hereby suppressed without indemnification. . . .

V. Tithes of every description, as well as the dues which have been substituted for them . . . are abolished, on condition, however, that some other method be devised to provide for the expenses of divine worship, the support of the officiating clergy, for the assistance of the poor, for repairs and rebuilding of churches and parsonages, and for the maintenance of all institutions, seminaries, schools, academies, asylums, and organizations to which the present funds are devoted.

❧

SOURCE: From James Harvey Robinson, ed., "The French Revolution, 1789–1791," in *Translations and Reprints from the Original Sources of European History*, vol. I, no. 5, ed. Department of History of the University of Pennsylvania (Philadelphia: University of Pennsylvania Press, 1898), pp. 2–5.

VII. The sale of judicial and municipal offices shall be suppressed forthwith. Justice shall be dispensed *gratis.*

IX. Pecuniary privileges, personal or real, in the payment of taxes are abolished forever. Taxes shall be collected from all the citizens, and from all property, in the same manner and in the same form. . . .

X. . . . All the peculiar privileges, pecuniary or otherwise, of the provinces, principalities, districts, cantons, cities and communes, are once for all abolished and are absorbed into the law common to all Frenchmen.

XI. All citizens, without distinction of birth, are eligible to any office or dignity, whether ecclesiastical, civil or military; and no profession shall imply any derogation.

XVII. The National Assembly solemnly proclaims the King, Louis XVI, the *Restorer of French Liberty.*

XVIII. The National Assembly shall present itself in a body before the King, in order to submit to him the decrees which have just been passed, to tender to him the tokens of its most respectful gratitude. . . .

XIX. The National Assembly shall consider, immediately after the constitution, the drawing up of the laws necessary for the development of the principles which it has laid down in the present decree.

The Declaration of the Rights of Man and Citizen

No document better summarizes the ideals underlying the French Revolution than The Declaration of the Rights of Man and Citizen. *After an extended discussion, this document was passed by the National Assembly on August 27, 1789; later a revised version of it was incorporated into the Constitution of 1791. Its provisions are a combination of general statements about human rights and specific statements about what the government should and should not do. This document corresponds to the American Declaration of Independence. It is also viewed more broadly as containing the general principles for democratic revolutions in the eighteenth and nineteenth centuries.*

CONSIDER: *How this document reflects ideals of the Enlightenment; at which social groups this document was aimed; who would suffer most from or be most infuriated by its pro-*

SOURCE: James Harvey Robinson, ed., "The French Revolution, 1789–1791," in *Translations and Reprints from the Original Sources of European History,* vol. I, no. 5, ed. Department of History of the University of Pennsylvania (Philadelphia: University of Pennsylvania Press, 1898), pp. 6–8.

visions; the ways in which this document is inconsistent with monarchical government; how a monarch might retain meaningful powers while still conforming to this document.

The representatives of the French people, organized as a National Assembly, believing that the ignorance, neglect or contempt of the rights of man are the sole cause of public calamities and of the corruption of governments, have determined to set forth in a solemn declaration the natural, inalienable and sacred rights of man, in order that this declaration, being constantly before all the members of the social body, shall remind them continually of their rights and duties; in order that the acts of the legislative power, as well as those of the executive power, may be compared at any moment with the ends of all political institutions and may thus be more respected; and, lastly, in order that the grievances of the citizens, based hereafter upon simple and incontestable principles, shall tend to the maintenance of the constitution and redound to the happiness of all. Therefore the National Assembly recognizes and proclaims, in the presence and under the auspices of the Supreme Being, the following rights of man and of the citizen:—

ARTICLE 1. Men are born and remain free and equal in rights. Social distinctions may only be founded upon the general good.

2. The aim of all political association is the preservation of the natural and imprescriptible rights of man. These rights are liberty, property, security and resistance to oppression.

3. The principle of all sovereignty resides essentially in the nation. No body nor individual may exercise any authority which does not proceed directly from the nation.

4. Liberty consists in the freedom to do everything which injures no one else; hence the exercise of the natural rights of each man has no limits except those which assure to the other members of the society the enjoyment of the same rights. These limits can only be determined by law.

5. Law can only prohibit such actions as are hurtful to society. Nothing may be prevented which is not forbidden by law, and no one may be forced to do anything not provided for by law.

6. Law is the expression of the general will. Every citizen has a right to participate personally or through his representative in its formation. It must be the same for all, whether it protects or punishes. All citizens, being equal in the eyes of the law, are equally eligible to all dignities and to all public positions and occupations, according to their abilities, and without distinction except that of their virtues and talents.

7. No person shall be accused, arrested or imprisoned except in the cases and according to the forms prescribed by law. Any one soliciting, transmitting, executing or causing to be executed any arbitrary order shall be punished. But any citizen summoned or arrested in virtue of the law shall submit without delay, as resistance constitutes an offence.

8. The law shall provide for such punishments only as are strictly and obviously necessary, and no one shall suffer punishment except it be legally inflicted in virtue of a law passed and promulgated before the commission of the offence.

9. As all persons are held innocent until they shall have been declared guilty, if arrest shall be deemed indispensable, all harshness not essential to the securing of the prisoner's person shall be severely repressed by law.

10. No one shall be disquieted on account of his opinions, including his religious views, provided their manifestation does not disturb the public order established by law.

11. The free communication of ideas and opinions is one of the most precious of the rights of man. Every citizen may, accordingly, speak, write and print with freedom, but shall be responsible for such abuses of this freedom as shall be defined by law.

12. The security of the rights of man and of the citizen requires public military force. These forces are, therefore, established for the good of all and not for the personal advantage of those to whom they shall be entrusted.

13. A common contribution is essential for the maintenance of the public forces and for the cost of administration. This should be equitably distributed among all the citizens in proportion to their means.

14. All the citizens have a right to decide, either personally or by their representatives, as to the necessity of the public contribution; to grant this freely; to know to what uses it is put; and to fix the proportion, the mode of assessment, and of collection, and the duration of the taxes.

15. Society has the right to require of every public agent an account of his administration.

16. A society in which the observance of the law is not assured, nor the separation of powers defined, has no constitution at all.

17. Since property is an inviolable and sacred right, no one shall be deprived thereof except where public necessity, legally determined, shall clearly demand it, and then only on condition that the owner shall have been previously and equitably indemnified.

Declaration of the Rights of Woman and the Female Citizen

Olympe de Gouges

While men of the French Revolution stood for principles of natural rights, equality before the law, and universal liberties, few favored applying those principles to women. However, several women and women's organizations struggled to win rights for women that corresponded to those gained by men. Olympe de Gouges (1743–1793), a self-educated daughter of a butcher and an author of several pamphlets and plays, was one of the most famous of these women. The following excerpts are from her September 1791 pamphlet, which she modeled on the National Assembly's Declaration of the Rights of Man and Citizen. Her critical writings would eventually bring her into conflict with Robespierre and the Jacobins. Charged for counterrevolutionary activities, she was arrested and executed in 1793.

CONSIDER: *What Gouges demands; the arguments and language she uses to support her demands.*

Mothers, daughters, sisters [and] representatives of the nation demand to be constituted into a national assembly. Believing that ignorance, omission, or scorn for the rights of woman are the only causes of public misfortunes and of the corruption of governments, [the women] have resolved to set forth in a solemn declaration the natural, inalienable, and sacred rights of woman. . . .

ARTICLE 1

Woman is born free and lives equal to man in her rights. Social distinctions can be based only on the common utility.

ARTICLE 4

Liberty and justice consist of restoring all that belongs to others; thus, the only limits on the exercise of the natural rights of woman are perpetual male tyranny; these limits are to be reformed by the laws of nature and reason.

ARTICLE 6

The laws must be the expression of the general will; all female and male citizens must contribute either personally or through their representatives to its formation; it must be the same for all: male and female citizens, being equal in the eyes of the law, must be equally admitted to all honors, positions, and public employment according to their capacity and without other distinctions besides those of their virtues and talents.

SOURCE: Olympe de Gouges, "The Declaration of the Rights of Women," in *Women in Revolutionary Paris, 1789–1795*, Darline Gay Levy, et al., eds. (Urbana, IL: University of Illinois Press, 1980), pp. 89–93.

ARTICLE 11

The free communication of thoughts and opinions is one of the most precious rights of woman, since the liberty assures the recognition of children by their fathers. Any female citizen thus may say freely, I am the mother of a child which belongs to you, without being forced by a barbarous prejudice to hide the truth; [an exception may be made] to respond to the abuse of this liberty in cases determined by the law.

ARTICLE 17

Property belongs to both sexes whether united or separate; for each it is an inviolable and sacred right; no one can be deprived of it, since it is the true patrimony of nature, unless the legally determined public need obviously dictates it, and then only with a just and prior indemnity.

POSTSCRIPT

Woman, wake up; the tocsin of reason is being heard throughout the whole universe; discover your rights. The powerful empire of nature is no longer surrounded by prejudice, fanaticism, superstition, and lies. The flame of truth has dispersed all the clouds of folly and usurpation. Enslaved man has multiplied his strength and needs recourse to yours to break his chains. Having become free, he has become unjust to his companion. Oh, women, women! When will you cease to be blind? What advantage have you received from the Revolution? A more pronounced scorn, a more marked disdain. In the centuries of corruption you ruled only over the weakness of men. The reclamation of your patrimony, based on the wise decrees of nature—what have you to dread from such a fine undertaking? The bon mot of the legislator of the marriage of Cana? Do you fear that our French legislators, correctors of that morality, long ensnared by political practices now out of date, will only say again to you: women, what is there in common between you and us? Everything, you will have to answer. If they persist in their weakness in putting this non sequitur in contradiction to their principles, courageously oppose the force of reason to the empty pretensions of superiority; unite yourselves beneath the standards of philosophy; deploy all the energy of your character, and you will soon see these haughty men, not groveling at your feet as servile adorers, but proud to share with you the treasures of the Supreme Being. Regardless of what barriers confront you, it is in your power to free yourselves; you have only to want to. Let us pass not to the shocking tableau of what you have been in society; and since national education is in question at this moment, let us see whether our wise legislators will think judiciously about the education of women.

The Declaration of Independence

The American Revolution preceded the French Revolution by a few years. Yet its priority in time does not give it priority in historical importance. At that time America was at the fringes of Western civilization while France was at its heart. Nevertheless, the American Revolution influenced the French Revolution in a variety of ways. One similarity between the two is their two great declarations: the American Declaration of Independence (1776) and the French Declaration of the Rights of Man and Citizen (1789). Although it is uncertain whether the French were directly influenced by the American document, both are products of common ideas of the late eighteenth century and show evidence of a strong relationship between these ideas and revolutionary activities in Western civilization. The Declaration of Independence was written primarily by Thomas Jefferson. The following selection comes from the beginning of this document.

CONSIDER: *The usefulness of this standard for evaluating the legitimacy of a revolution; similarities between the French and American declarations; how these two documents differ in purpose and substance.*

When in the Course of human events, it becomes necessary for one people to dissolve the political bonds which have connected them with another, and to assume among the powers of the earth, the separate and equal station to which the Laws of Nature and of Nature's God entitle them, a decent respect to the opinions of mankind requires that they should declare the causes which impel them to the separation.—We hold these truths to be self-evident, that all men are created equal, that they are endowed by their Creator with certain unalienable Rights, that among these are Life, Liberty and the pursuit of Happiness.—That to secure these rights, Governments are instituted among Men, deriving their just powers from the consent of the governed,—That whenever any Form of Government becomes destructive of these ends, it is the Right of the People to alter or to abolish it, and to institute new Government, laying its foundation on such principles and organizing its powers in such form, as to them shall seem most likely to effect their Safety and Happiness. Prudence, indeed, will dictate that Governments long established should not be changed for light and transient causes; and accordingly all experience hath shewn, that mankind are more disposed to suffer, while evils are sufferable, than to right themselves by abolishing the forms to which they are accustomed. But when a long train of abuses and usurpations, pursuing invariably the same Object evinces a design to reduce them under

SOURCE: *The Declaration of Independence, 1776* (Washington, D.C.: U.S. Department of State, 1911), pp. 3–8.

absolute Despotism, it is their right, it is their duty, to throw off such Government, and to provide new Guards for their future security.—Such has been the patient sufferance of these Colonies; and such is now the necessity which constrains them to alter their former Systems of Government.

Speech to the National Convention—February 5, 1794: The Terror Justified

Maximilien Robespierre

Between 1793 and 1794, France experienced the most radical phase of the revolution, known as the Reign of Terror. During this period France was essentially ruled by the twelve-member Committee of Public Safety elected by the National Convention every month. The outstanding member of this committee was Maximilien Robespierre (1758–1794), a provincial lawyer who rose within the Jacobin Club and gained a reputation for incorruptibility and superb oratory. Historians have argued over Robespierre, some singling him out as a bloodthirsty individual with the major responsibility for the executions during the Reign of Terror, others seeing him as a sincere, idealistic, effective revolutionary leader called to the fore by events of the time. In the following speech to the National Convention on February 5, 1794, Robespierre defines the revolution and justifies extreme actions, including terror, in its defense.

CONSIDER: *What Robespierre means when he argues that terror flows from virtue; how the use of terror relates to the essence of the revolution; how this speech might be interpreted as an Enlightenment attack on the Ancien Régime carried to its logical conclusion.*

It is time to mark clearly the aim of the Revolution and the end toward which we wish to move; it is time to take stock of ourselves, of the obstacles which we still face, and of the means which we ought to adopt to attain our objectives. . . .

What is the goal for which we strive? A peaceful enjoyment of liberty and equality, the rule of that eternal justice whose laws are engraved, not upon marble or stone, but in the hearts of all men.

We wish an order of things where all low and cruel passions are enchained by the laws, all beneficent and generous feelings aroused; where ambition is the desire to merit glory and to serve one's fatherland; where distinctions are born only of equality itself; where the citizen is subject to the magistrate, the magistrate to the people,

SOURCE: Raymond P. Stearns, ed., *Pageant of Europe*. Reprinted by permission of Harcourt Brace Jovanovich, Inc. (New York, 1947), pp. 404–405.

the people to justice; where the nation safeguards the welfare of each individual, and each individual proudly enjoys the prosperity and glory of his fatherland; where all spirits are enlarged by the constant exchange of republican sentiments and by the need of earning the respect of a great people; where the arts are the adornment of liberty, which ennobles them; and where commerce is the source of public wealth, not simply of monstrous opulence for a few families.

In our country we wish to substitute morality for egotism, probity for honor, principles for conventions, duties for etiquette, the empire of reason for the tyranny of customs, contempt for vice for contempt for misfortune, pride for insolence, the love of honor for the love of money . . . that is to say, all the virtues and miracles of the Republic for all the vices and snobbishness of the monarchy.

We wish in a word to fulfill the requirements of nature, to accomplish the destiny of mankind, to make good the promises of philosophy . . . that France, hitherto illustrious among slave states, may eclipse the glory of all free peoples that have existed, become the model of all nations. . . . That is our ambition; that is our aim.

What kind of government can realize these marvels? Only a democratic government. . . . But to found and to consolidate among us this democracy, to realize the peaceable rule of constitutional laws, it is necessary to conclude the war of liberty against tyranny and to pass successfully through the storms of revolution. Such is the aim of the revolutionary system which you have setup. . . .

Now what is the fundamental principle of democratic, or popular government—that is to say, the essential mainspring upon which it depends and which makes it function? It is virtue: I mean public virtue . . . that virtue which is nothing else but love of fatherland and its laws. . . .

The splendor of the goal of the French Revolution is simultaneously the source of our strength and of our weakness: our strength, because it gives us an ascendancy of truth over falsehood, and of public rights over private interests; our weakness, because it rallies against us all vicious men, all those who in their hearts seek to despoil the people. . . . It is necessary to stifle the domestic and foreign enemies of the Republic or perish with them. Now in these circumstances, the first maxim of our politics ought to be to lead the people by means of reason and the enemies of the people by terror.

If the basis of popular government in time of peace is virtue, the basis of popular government in time of revolution is both virtue and terror: virtue without which terror is murderous, terror without which virtue is powerless. Terror is nothing else than swift, severe, indomitable justice; it flows, then, from virtue.

A Soldier's Letters to His Mother: Revolutionary Nationalism

François-Xavier Joliclerc

Despite tremendous internal difficulties, including counter-revolutionary movements in a number of provinces, French armies held back foreign forces after war broke out in 1792, but by 1794 the French forces had made gains even beyond the 1789 borders. Part of the reason for this success was the nationalistic enthusiasm that developed along with the revolution. This nationalism is demonstrated by the following letters from François-Xavier Joliclerc, a conscript in the French army, to his mother.

CONSIDER: *The divisions within French society revealed in these letters; why such sentiments among soldiers are so important and how political leaders or military strategists might capitalize on them; whether the nationalism revealed in these letters is inherent in the nature of the French Revolution or in any particular phase of that revolution.*

13 December, 1793

My dear mother,

You continue to point out to me, in all your letters, that we must get out of the army, cost what it may. Here are the difficulties and the obstacles that I can see.

First of all, it is difficult to find replacements despite the enormous sums that are expended for this purpose. Secondly, we have just had a call-up of men eighteen to twenty-five; and the call-up of those from twenty-five to thirty-five is being prepared. As soon as we got home, we would have to get ready to go back, regretting the money we had spent. Thirdly, when *la patrie* calls us to her defense, we ought to fly there as if running to a good meal. Our life, our wealth, and our talents do not belong to us. It is to the nation, *la patrie*, that all that belongs.

I know well that you and all the others in our village do not share these sentiments. They are not aroused by the cries of an outraged fatherland, and all that they do results from being compelled to. But I have been brought up in conscience and thought, and have always been republican in spirit, although obliged to live in a monarchy. These principles of love for *la patrie, la liberté, la république,* are not only engraved in my heart, but are deeply etched and will remain there as long as it will please the Supreme Being to sustain in me the breath of life.

Even if it cost me three quarters of my possessions to have you share these sentiments with me, I would gladly part with them and consider it a very small sacrifice. Oh, if only one day you could know the price of liberty and lose your senseless attachment to material things.

30 May, 1794

What about my lot? I am at my post, where I ought to be, and every good man who knows what's what ought to fly to the aid of his country in danger. If I should perish there, you ought to rejoice. Can one make a finer sacrifice than to die for one's country? Can one die for a more just, glorious, and fairer cause? No! Would you rather see me die on a mattress of straw in my bed at Froidefontaine [his home village] working with wood or stone?

No, dear mother. Think that I am at my post and you will be consoled. If your conscience reproaches you in some way, sell even the last of your petticoats for *la patrie*. She is our only rudder, and it is she who guides us and gives us happiness. . . .

Your son, Joliclerc

SOURCE: From Ludwig F. Schaefer, Daniel P. Resnick, and George F. Netterville, eds., *The Shaping of Western Civilization*, vol. II, trans. Daniel P. Resnick (New York: Holt, Rinehart and Winston, Inc., 1970), p. 216. Reprinted by permission of the editors.

 # Visual Sources

Allegory of the Revolution

Jeaurat de Bertray

Jeaurat de Bertray's Allegory of the Revolution (figure 20.1) is literally a jumble of historical and revolutionary symbols. At the top is a portrait of Jean Jacques Rousseau, at the time considered by many the spiritual and intellectual father of the French Revolution, even though he never advocated revolution and died eleven years before it began. Below him are the new flags of the French Republic, the one on the left with the nationalistic words "love of country." Further to the left is a triangular monument to Equality, below it two maidens representing Goodness and Good Faith, and in the center a bundle of rods and arms topped by a red liberty cap, all symbolizing a fair, forceful republican government. Just below is paper money, the assignats, that helped finance the revolution and pay off debts, and in the center right grows a liberty tree. To the right are two unfinished pillars, the first dedicated to the

FIGURE 20.1   An Allegory of the Revolution in Honor of Rousseau. (© Snark/Art Resource, NY)

regeneration of morals and The Declaration of the Rights of Man and Citizen, *the second to the French Revolution. Just below them and in the background are symbols of forceful determination to uphold and defend the revolution: a guillotine, a cannon, and a soldier. In the right foreground is a peasant wearing a liberty cap and sowing a field. This painting pulls together many symbols and elements of the revolutionary ideology. It was painted in 1794, the time of the most radical phase of the revolution.*

CONSIDER: *Connections between this picture,* The Declaration of the Rights of Man and Citizen, *and the Enlightenment; the ways in which the Ancien Régime is rejected symbolically in this picture.*

Henri de la Rochjacquelein
Pierre-Narcisse Guérin

As events developed during France's revolutionary years, the new republican government had to battle not only foreign troops, but also uprisings within France. The most serious of these erupted in the Vendée region of western France. Years later, Pierre-Narcisse Guérin (1774–1833) would celebrate the cause of the Vendée rebels.

As suggested by Guérin's painting of Henri Duverger (figure 20.2), comte de la Rochejacquelein (1772–1794), the Vendée peasants, led by local nobles and clergy, rebelled in the name of "our king, our priests, and the Old Regime." Guérin depicts the young aristocratic general Rochejacquelein amid

FIGURE 20.2   (© Réunion des Musées Nationaux/Art Resource, NY)

one of the close-quarter battles that defined the Vendée revolt. Standing firm in tall boots and yellow pants, a white sash around his waist and his wounded right arm in a sling, Rochejacquelein fires a gun point-blank at the enemy, whose bayonets we see just inches away. Behind Rochejacquelein stand his equally determined but more modestly dressed peasant guerrilla followers, one with a rifle, another with only a pitchfork to stress the popularity of this rebellion. Above flies the white flag of the rebel Royalist cause, echoed by the sacred heart pinned to the general's chest.

Rochejacquelein would survive this battle only to be killed in 1794. However, the uprising he helped lead spread until revolts broke out in some sixty of France's eighty-three depart-

ments. These all-too-real enemies outside and within France's borders threatened the fledgling Republic.

CONSIDER: How this painting portrays the rebel Royalist cause; how supporters of the French Revolution might have viewed this painting.

Internal Disturbances and the Reign of Terror

Understanding of the Reign of Terror has often been distorted by an image of random and purposeless brutality. One way to gain clearer insights into the Terror is through the use of

MAP 20.1   Internal Disturbances

Legend:
- No Major Disturbances
- Numerous Riots, Royalist Guerrilla Activity, and Threats of Civil War or Foreign Invasion
- Major Insurrections and Invasions
- Areas of Significant Civil War Activity

FRANCE

MAP 20.2   The Incidence of the Terror

Legend:
- Fewer Than 10 Executions
- 10 to 50 Executions
- 50 to 100 Executions
- More Than 100 Executions

FRANCE

maps and statistics, which reveal where the Terror occurred, how intensive it was, and who its victims were. Maps 20.1 and 20.2 compare the amount of civil disturbance facing government officials and the number of executions occurring in the various departments of France during the period of the Terror. The two pie charts (charts 20.1 and 20.2) compare the estimated percentages of France's population belonging to

the various classes in 1789 and during the Terror from March 1793 to August 1794.

CONSIDER: How these maps and charts support an argument that the Reign of Terror was not random or purposeless; the hypotheses that might be drawn from these maps and charts about the causes or effects of the Terror.

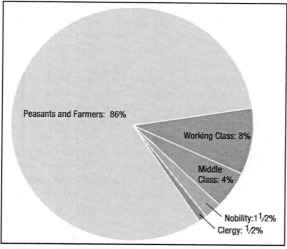

CHART 20.1   Classes in France

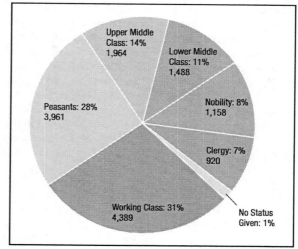

CHART 20.2   Executions During the Reign of Terror

Secondary Sources

The Coming of the French Revolution

Georges Lefebvre

Probably no event in modern history has been interpreted at greater length and with greater passion than the French Revolution. The historiographic tradition related to this event is so extensive that numerous books and articles have been written on this historiography itself. A central controversy involves the cause or causes of the revolution and is dealt with in the following selection from The Coming of the French Revolution *by Georges Lefebvre. Lefebvre held the prestigious chair of French revolutionary history at the Sorbonne until his death in 1959. His work on the French Revolution continues to be highly respected.*

CONSIDER: *The most important cause of the French Revolution, according to Lefebvre; how this interpretation relates the revolution in France to areas outside of France; how social, economic, and political factors are linked in this interpretation of the French Revolution; how this view is supported by the primary documents.*

The ultimate cause of the French Revolution of 1789 goes deep into the history of France and of the western world. At the end of the eighteenth century the social

SOURCE: From Georges Lefebvre, *The Coming of the French Revolution,* pp. 1–3. Copyright 1947 by Princeton University Press. Reprinted by permission of Princeton University Press.

structure of France was aristocratic. It showed the traces of having originated at a time when land was almost the only form of wealth, and when the possessors of land were the masters of those who needed it to work and to live. It is true that in the course of age-old struggles (of which the Fronde, the last revolt of the aristocracy, was as recent as the seventeenth century) the king had been able gradually to deprive the lords of their political power and subject nobles and clergy to his authority. But he had left them the first place in the social hierarchy. Still restless at being merely his "subjects," they remained privileged persons.

Meanwhile the growth of commerce and industry had created, step by step, a new form of wealth, mobile or commercial wealth, and a new class, called in France the bourgeoisie, which since the fourteenth century had taken its place as the Third Estate in the General Estates of the kingdom. This class had grown much stronger with the maritime discoveries of the fifteenth and sixteenth centuries and the ensuing exploitation of new worlds, and also because it proved highly useful to the monarchical state in supplying it with money and competent officials. In the eighteenth century commerce, industry and finance occupied an increasingly important place in the national economy. It was the bourgeoisie that rescued the royal treasury in moments of crisis. From its ranks were recruited most members of the liberal professions and most public employees. It had developed a new ideology which the "philosophers" and "economists" of the time had simply put into definite form. The role of the nobility had correspondingly declined; and the clergy, as the ideal which it proclaimed lost prestige, found its authority growing weaker. These groups preserved the highest rank in the legal structure of the country, but in reality economic power, personal abilities and confidence in the future had passed largely to the bourgeoisie. Such a discrepancy never lasts forever. The Revolution of 1789 restored the harmony between fact and law. This transformation spread in the nineteenth century throughout the west and then to the whole globe, and in this sense the ideas of 1789 toured the world.

The Revolution of the Notables

Donald M. G. Sutherland

Georges Lefebvre's interpretation for the causes of the French Revolution became part of what has been called the "classical view" of the origins of the revolution. In recent years this view has been strongly criticized by increasing numbers of historians, most of whom reject Lefebvre's social-economic view in favor of a more political analysis. In the following selection Donald M. G. Sutherland reviews this controversy.

CONSIDER: *The basis for the attack on the classical view; why "exclusivism" is so important for these interpretations; how a representative of the classical view might respond.*

There was a time when historians could be fairly confident in describing the origins of the French Revolution. The operative concept was "aristocratic reaction." It meant several things at once. Politically, it referred to the undermining of the absolutism of Louis XIV which was thought to have subverted the independence and privileges of the aristocracy. The parlements, the regional sovereign and appeal courts of which that of Paris was by far the most important, were the driving forces behind the noble offensive. They were able to transform their right of registering laws and edicts into a veto on progressive royal legislation. The Crown was consequently much weaker. This had implications in the social sphere as well. In the course of the eighteenth century, the aristocracy ended up monopolizing the highest offices in government, the military, the Church and judiciary. This in turn had its effects on the bourgeoisie. No longer able to advance to the top of the major social and political institutions of the day, the bourgeoisie became increasingly alienated from the state and from respectable society. Frustrated from achieving its highest ambitions, its loyalties

SOURCE: From Donald Sutherland, *France, 1789–1815,* pp. 15–18, © 1986 Oxford University Press. Reprinted by permission of HarperCollins Publishers, Ltd., and Oxford University Press.

strained, ever open to suggestive criticisms of the system, it was well placed to take advantage of the political crisis of 1788–9 to overthrow the old order altogether. One of the many crises of the Old Regime was a crisis of social mobility.

The argument was irresistibly attractive, partly because of its internal elegance and partly because it explained so much. It made sense of the reign of Louis XIV, the eighteenth century and the Revolution too. The struggle between revolution and counterrevolution could be reduced to two actors, the bourgeoisie and the aristocracy, who had first come to blows in the closing years of the reign of Louis XIV. The aristocracy lost, of course, and specialists of the nineteenth century could move on to the next round, the struggle between the bourgeoisie and the working class.

Unfortunately, research and reflective criticism over the past twenty years have rendered the classical view of the origins of the Revolution utterly untenable. In the first place, it assumes rather than demonstrates the aristocracy's progressive monopoly of high posts. It assumes, too, that the society of the seventeenth century was more open than its successor but relies on incomplete evidence and a limited range of contemporary complaints. The Duc de Saint-Simon's famous observation that Louis XIV raised up the "vile bourgeoisie" turns out to be untrue in the case of the episcopate, partially true but grossly misleading of the ministry and unknown in the case of the officer corps of the army. . . .

Closer examination of some of the major signs of noble exclusivism shows that restrictions were often aimed at excluding the rich parvenu nobles, not a rising bourgeoisie. . . . The Old Regime aristocracy was thus comparatively young and was in a constant process of renewal.

The doors of the Second Estate were well oiled to men of talent but above all to those with money. Society was therefore capable of absorbing the most thrusting, entrepreneurial and ambitious men of the plutocracy. . . .

The effect of the revisionist critique of the classical interpretation has been to reassert the importance of the political origins of the Revolution. If the nobility had always been a dominant class, if whatever trends there were towards exclusivism are problematic to interpret, if opportunities for advancement were far greater than was ever suspected, and if nobles and bourgeois shared similar economic functions and interests, the notion that the Revolution originated in a struggle between two distinct classes has to be abandoned. Politics remains. Both groups could agree to unite to overthrow absolutism in favour of a liberal constitution but, according to which revisionist historian one follows, they fell out either over means or because of a failure of political leadership or the form the political crisis took, or even over something as amorphous as "style."

Loaves and Liberty: Women in the French Revolution

Ruth Graham

Historians have long recognized that women played an important role in certain aspects of the French Revolution. But only in the last twenty years have extensive examinations been made of the significance of the French Revolution for women's history. The following selection by Ruth Graham is a good example of this work.

CONSIDER: *Any connections between sex and class lines in the French Revolution; the ways in which women became a "revolutionary force unprecedented in history" during the revolution; what Graham means by women's victories and defeats.*

It would be wrong to assume that because women had come into the Revolution in 1789 asking for bread and liberty and had come out in 1795 with starvation and restriction of their movements, they had gained nothing. They won laws protecting their rights in marriage, property, and education. True, women were denied political rights in the French Revolution (as were the majority of men when the Convention scrapped the democratic constitution of 1793) but nowhere else at the time did women share political rights with men.

Although women were a cohesive group during the Revolution, they responded mainly to the needs of their class and were never an autonomous force. The ideology of the revolutionary authorities who distrusted women's political movements derived seemingly from Rousseau, but actually from the facts of their lives: France's small-scale, home-based economy needed middle- and working-class women to contribute their special skills and labor to their families. Women were not yet a large, independent group in the working class.

In the early days of the French Revolution, women from the middle classes (as can be seen from cahiers written by them) welcomed the restoration of their natural rights as wives and mothers to participate in society as men's "natural companions." Women of the urban poor—wage earners, artisans of women's crafts, owners of small enterprises, such as the market women—agitated for bread rather than for women's rights. There is, however, evidence that "respectable" middle-class women joined them. Although these movements crossed class lines, which were perhaps not rigidly fixed, they did not cross sex lines. When men participated, as they did in the October Days of 1789, they came as armed escorts or separate detachments.

As the Revolution entered its more radical phase, as economic crisis followed war and civil strife, the polarization between the rich and the poor sharpened the older stuggle between aristocrat and patriot. During the last days of the National Convention, the women who surged into the hall crying "Bread and the Constitution of 1793!" truly represented the poor, whom the upper classes and their women now feared. The bread riots belonged to the women of the poor, who incited their men to insurrection, but the insurrection belonged to both of them, the sans-culottes and their women.

Yet, the Revolution had called upon women to make great sacrifices and they did; in consequence, women became a revolutionary force unprecedented in history. The men in power feared women who challenged the Revolution's failure to guarantee bread for the poor. So feared were the women of the French Revolution that they became legendary—they became Mme. Defarge later to those who feared revolution itself.

A new elite of the upper middle class, men of wealth and talent, rose to power in the four years of the Directory following the dissolution in 1795 of the National Convention. Their women had no political rights but emerged as influential ladies of the salon, such as the brilliant writer Mme. de Staë, and Mme. Tallien, former wife of an aristocrat and now derisively called "Our Lady of Thermidor," as a symbol of the reaction. One of these ladies, Josephine de Beauharnais, the widow of a general, became the mistress of one of the Directors before she married the young Napoleon Bonaparte, who soon afterward became general of the armies in Italy.

Outside of Paris, away from the glamour of these women, middle-class morality prevailed. Napoleon subscribed to this morality. When he became emperor in 1804, he wrote laws into his code to strengthen the authority of the husband and father of the family as a safeguard for private property. Women lost whatever rights they had gained in the Revolution, for now they had to obey their husbands unconditionally. Napoleon left women the right to divorce (for Napoleon to use against Josephine when she failed to provide him an heir), but this right was taken from them after 1815 by the restoration of the Bourbon monarchy.

What could not be taken from women was their memory of victories during the French Revolution: their march to Versailles in the October Days, their petitions to the legislature, their club meetings, their processions, their insurrections. Their defeats served as lessons for next time. "We are simple women," a woman was reported to have said at a club meeting in the days of the

SOURCE: Ruth Graham, "Loaves and Liberty: Women in the French Revolution," in *Becoming Visible: Women in European History,* ed. Renate Bridenthal and Claudia Koonz (Boston: Houghton Mifflin, 1977), pp. 251–253.

uprising of the Paris Commune in May 1871, nearly a century later, "but not made of weaker stuff than our grandmothers of '93. Let us not cause their shades to blush for us, but be up and doing, as they would be were they living now."

An Evaluation of the French Revolution

William Doyle

Although most would say that rapid and vast changes occurred during the French Revolution, it is difficult to evaluate the extent to which these changes were more apparent than real. Many historians have concluded that while the revolution stood for much, most of the promises made by the revolution were not carried out. Others argue that much that has been attributed to the revolution would probably have come about anyway. In the following selection William Doyle attempts to strike a balance between what was and was not accomplished by the revolution.

CONSIDER: *How Doyle determines what changes would in all probability have come about in any case; what Doyle attributes directly to the revolution; how Doyle's argument might be used by those opposing revolutions in general.*

The shadow of the Revolution, therefore, fell across the whole of the nineteenth century and beyond. Until 1917 few would have disputed that it was the greatest revolution in the history of the world; and even after that its claims to primacy remain strong. It was the first modern revolution, the archetypal one. After it, nothing in the European world remained the same, and we are all heirs to its influence. And yet, it can be argued, much that was attributed to it would in all probability have come about in any case. Before 1789 there were plenty of signs that the structure of French society was evolving towards domination by a single élite in which property counted for more than birth. The century-long expansion of the bourgeoisie which underlay this trend already looked irreversible; and greater participation by men of property in government, as constant experiments with provincial assemblies showed, seemed bound to come. Meanwhile many of the reforms the Revolution brought in were already being tried or thought about by the absolute monarchy—law codification, fiscal rationalization, diminution of venality, free trade, religious toleration. With all these changes under way or in contemplation,

SOURCE: From William Doyle, *The Oxford History of the French Revolution*, pp. 423–425. Copyright 1989. Reprinted by permission of Oxford University Press.

the power of government looked set for steady growth, too—which ironically was one of the complaints of the despotism-obsessed men of 1789. In the Church, the monastic ideal was already shrivelling and the status of parish priests commanding more and more public sympathy. Economically, the colonial trade had already peaked, and failure to compete industrially with Great Britain was increasingly manifest. In other structural areas, meanwhile, the great upheaval appears to have made no difference at all. Conservative investment habits still characterized the early nineteenth century, agricultural inertia and unentrepreneurial business likewise. And in international affairs, it is hard to believe that Great Britain would not have dominated the world's seas and trade throughout the nineteenth century, that Austro-Prussian rivalry would not have run much the course it did, or that Latin America would not have asserted its independence in some form or other, if the French Revolution had never happened. In all these fields, the effect was to accelerate or retard certain trends, but not to change their general drift.

Against all this, it is equally hard to believe that the specifically anti-aristocratic, anti-feudal revolutionary ideology of the Rights of Man would have emerged as it did without the jumble of accident, miscalculation, and misunderstanding which coalesced into a revolution in specifically French circumstances. It is equally hard to believe that anything as extraordinary as dechristianization would have occurred without the monumental misjudgement which produced the Revolution's quarrel with the Catholic Church. Without that quarrel, the dramatic revival in the authority of the papacy also seems inconceivable. Representative government may well have been on the horizon, but how long would the ideal of popular democracy have taken to establish itself without the example of the sansculotte movement? It certainly transformed and widened out of all recognition the cause of parliamentary reform in England—although the blood-stained figure of the sansculotte probably galvanized conservative resistance on the other side. Above all, the revolutionaries' decision to go to war, which all historians agree revolutionized the Revolution, destroyed an established pattern of warfare in a way no old regime government would otherwise have promoted. Arming the people was the last thing they would have dreamed of. The emergencies of that war in turn produced the scenes which have indelibly marked our memory of the Revolution: the Terror. Massacres were nothing new, and the worst ones of the 1790s occurred outside France. But there was something horribly new and unimaginable in the prospect of a government systematically executing its opponents by the cartload for months on end, and by a device which, however humane in concept, made the streets run with blood. And this occurred in what had passed for the most civilized country in Europe, whose writers had taught the eighteenth century to pride itself on its increasing mildness, good sense, and humanity. This great drama transformed the whole meaning of political change, and the contemporary world would be inconceivable if it had not happened.

In other words it transformed men's outlook.

🙠 CHAPTER QUESTIONS

1. What seems to have motivated many of the revolutionaries, as revealed by the demands made prior to the French Revolution and the actions taken during the revolution?

2. What factors help explain why this revolution occurred in France, one of the most prosperous and powerful nations of Europe? What does this explanation add to the significance of the revolution?

3. With the advantage of hindsight, what might the monarchy have done to retain control and minimize revolutionary changes?

4. In what ways should the French Revolution be considered a middle-class revolution or a revolution of the notables?

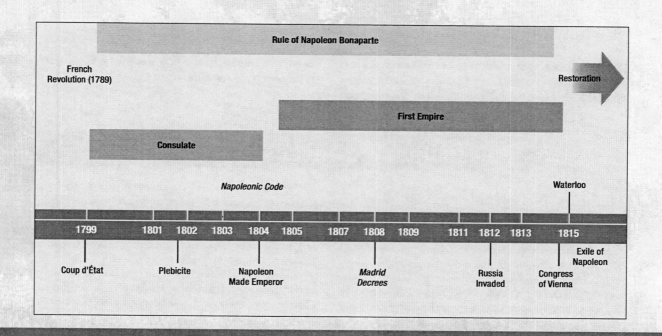

21 The Age of Napoleon

In 1799 members of the ruling Directory conspired with the well-known military leader Napoleon Bonaparte (1769–1821) to take over the French government by means of a *coup d'état*. It was successful, and Napoleon quickly asserted his own dominance over others. By 1802 he had full power, and by 1804 he was the self-proclaimed Emperor Napoleon I.

The period from 1799 to 1815 is generally known as the Age of Napoleon. Rising with opportunities presented by the French Revolution, Napoleon gained power not only in France, but directly and indirectly throughout much of continental Europe. Within France he crushed threats from both radicals and royalists who wanted to extend or reverse the French Revolution. Through administrative reforms,

codification of laws, and settlement with the Church, he institutionalized some of the changes brought about by the revolution and took the heart out of others. Backed by the ideological force of the revolution and strong nationalism, his armies extended French rule, institutions, and influence throughout Europe. In 1814 Napoleon's forces, weakened by overextension and a disastrous Russian campaign, were defeated by a coalition of European powers. After Napoleon's defeat, the major powers, meeting at Vienna, attempted to establish a new stability that would minimize the revolutionary and Napoleonic experiences.

The sources in this chapter focus on the principal interpretive debate connected with Napoleon: How should Napoleon and his policies be understood? Is Napoleon best viewed as a moderate defender of the French Revolution or as an enlightened despot in the eighteenth-century tradition? To provide insight into these issues, the selections will examine Napoleon's rise to power and his ideas, external policies, and internal institutions.

 Primary Sources

Memoirs: Napoleon's Appeal
Madame de Remusat

Napoleon was neither the candidate of those longing to turn France to a more revolutionary course nor the favorite of those who wanted to return France to the legitimacy of the Ancien Régime. He came to power promising to uphold both revolutionary principles and order. Scholars have analyzed the question of why he was able to rise to power. Some see him as a military and political genius; others argue that he was an opportunist who took advantage of circumstances as they arose. One of the earliest analyses of Napoleon's rise to power was written by Madame de Remusat (1780–1821). As a lady in waiting to Empress Josephine and wife of a Napoleonic official, she observed Napoleon firsthand and described him in her Memoirs.

CONSIDER: *Why, according to Remusat, Napoleon was so appealing to the French; the means Napoleon used to secure his power.*

I can understand how it was that men worn out by the turmoil of the Revolution, and afraid of that liberty which had long been associated with death, looked for repose under the dominion of an able ruler on whom fortune was seemingly revolved to smile. I can conceive that they regarded his elevation as a degree of destiny and fondly believed that in the irrevocable they should find peace. I may confidently assert that those persons believed quite sincerely that Bonaparte, whether as consul or emperor, would exert his authority to oppose the intrigue of faction and would save us from the perils of anarchy.

None dared to utter the word "republic," so deeply had the Terror stained that name; and the government of the Directory had perished in the contempt with which its chiefs were regarded. The return of the Bourbons could only be brought about by the aid of a revolution; and the slightest disturbance terrified the French people, in whom enthusiasm of every kind seemed dead. Besides, the men in whom they had trusted had one after the other deceived them; and as, this time, they were yielding to force, they were at least certain that they were not deceiving themselves.

SOURCE: From James Harvey Robinson, ed., *Readings in European History*, vol. II (Boston: Ginn, 1904), pp. 491–492.

The belief, or rather the error, that only despotism could at that epoch maintain order in France was very widespread. It became the mainstay of Bonaparte; and it is due to him to say that he also believed it. The factions played into his hands by imprudent attempts which he turned to his own advantage. He had some grounds for his belief that he was necessary; France believed it, too; and he even succeeded in persuading foreign sovereigns that he constituted a barrier against republican influences, which, but for him, might spread widely. At the moment when Bonaparte placed the imperial crown upon his head there was not a king in Europe who did not believe that he wore his own crown more securely because of that event. Had the new emperor granted a liberal constitution, the peace of nations and of kings might really have been forever secured.

Memoirs: Napoleon's Secret Police
Joseph Fouché

Although historians have found various aspects of Napoleonic rule admirable, most condemn Napoleon's use of the secret police. Joseph Fouché, Duke of Otranto (1763–1820), headed this institution for most of the period between 1802 and 1810. Fouché combined the attributes of a powerful politician, a police officer, and an opportunist. In the following selection from his Memoirs, Fouché boasts of his accomplishments.

CONSIDER: *The credibility of this document; whether it was reasonable of Napoleon to have Fouché carry out these activities.*

With regard to the interior, an important spring was wanted, that of the general police, which might have rallied the past round the present, and guaranteed the security of the empire. Napoleon himself perceived the void, and, by an imperial decree of the 10th July, reestablished me at the head of the police; at the same time investing me with stronger functions than those which I had possessed, before the absurd fusion of the police with the department of justice. . . .

It will not be doubted that I had salaried spies in all ranks and orders; I had some of both sexes, hired at the rate of a thousand or two thousand francs per

SOURCE: Joseph Fouché, *Memoirs* (London: Gibbings and Co., 1894), pp. 188–191.

month, according to their importance and their services. I received their reports directly in writing, having a conventional mark. Every three months, I communicated my list to the emperor, in order that there might be no double employment; and also in order that the nature of the service, occasionally permanent, often temporary, might be rewarded either by places or remunerations.

As to the government's police abroad, it had two essential objects, namely, to watch friendly powers, and counteract hostile governments. In both cases, it was composed of individuals purchased or pensioned, and commissioned to reside near each government, or in each principal town, independent of numerous secret agents sent into all countries, either by the minister of foreign affairs, or by the emperor himself.

I also had my foreign spies. It was in my cabinet, also, that the foreign gazettes, prohibited to the perusal of the French people, were collected, abstracts of which were made for my own use. By that means, I held in my hands the most important strings of foreign politics; and I discharged, in conjunction with the chief of the government, a task capable of controlling or balancing that of the minister charged with foreign relations.

I was thus far from limiting my duties to *espionnage*. All the state prisons were under my control, as well as the *gendarmerie*. The delivery of the *visa* of passports belonged to me. To me was assigned the duty of watching amnestied individuals and foreigners. I established general commissariats in the principal towns of the kingdom, which extended the net-work of the police over the whole of France, and especially our frontiers.

My police acquired so high a renown, that the world went so far as to pretend that I had, among my secret agents, three nobles of the *ancien régime*, distinguished by princely titles, and who daily communicated to me the result of their observations.

I confess that such an establishment was expensive; it swallowed up several millions, the funds of which were secretly provided from taxes laid upon gambling and prostitution, and from the granting of passports. Notwithstanding all that has been said against gambling, reflecting and firm minds must allow, that in the actual state of society, the legal converting of vice into profit is a necessary evil. . . .

It became necessary to organize the gambling-houses upon a much larger scale, for the produce of them was not solely destined to reward my moving phalanxes of spies. I nominated as superintendent-general of the gambling-houses in France, Perrein the elder, who already farmed them, and who, after the coronation, extended his privilege over all of the chief towns of the empire, upon condition of paying fourteen million yearly, independent of three thousand francs daily to the minister of the police, which, however, did not remain entirely in his hands.

Napoleon's Diary

Napoleon's accomplishments and place in history are explained in part by the type of individual he was. The principal sources of information on his personality are his diaries, memoirs, and letters, particularly the portions in which he reflects on himself. The following selection comes from diary entries made between 1798 and 1817.

CONSIDER: *Napoleon's opinions about what made him successful; Napoleon's analysis of his power and his personality; how Napoleon wants to be remembered.*

Paris, January 1, 1798

Paris has a short memory. If I remain longer doing nothing, I am lost. In this great Babylon one reputation quickly succeeds another. After I have been seen three times at the theatre, I shall not be looked at again; I shall therefore not go very frequently.

Paris, January 29, 1798

I will not remain here; there is nothing to be done. They will listen to nothing. I realize that if I stay my reputation will soon be gone. All things fade here, and my reputation is almost forgotten; this little Europe affords too slight a scope; I must go to the Orient; all great reputations have been won there. If the success of an expedition to England should prove doubtful, as I fear, the army of England will become the army of the East, and I shall go to Egypt.

The Orient awaits a man!

Milan, June 17, 1800

I have just reached Milan, somewhat fatigued.

Some Hungarian grenadiers and German prisoners passing by, who had already been prisoners in the campaigns of 1796 and 1797, recognized the First Consul. Many began to shout, with apparent enthusiasm: "Vive Bonaparte!"

What a thing is imagination! Here are men who don't know me, who have never seen me, but who only knew of me, and they are moved by my presence, they would do anything for me! And this same incident arises in all centuries and in all countries! Such is fanaticism! Yes, imagination rules the world. The defect of our modern institutions is that they do not speak to the imagination. By that alone can man be governed; without it he is but a brute.

December 30, 1802

My power proceeds from my reputation, and my reputation from the victories I have won. My power would fall

SOURCE: R. M. Johnston, ed., *The Corsican: A Diary of Napoleon's Life in His Own Words* (Boston: Houghton Mifflin Co., 1910), pp. 74, 140, 166, 492, 496.

if I were not to support it with more glory and more victories. Conquest has made me what I am; only conquest can maintain me.

Friendship is only a word; I love nobody; no, not even my brothers. Perhaps Joseph a little; even then it's a matter of habit, it's because he is my elder.—Duroc? Ah, yes, I love him; but why? His character attracts me: he is cool, dry, severe; and Duroc never sheds tears. As for me, you don't suppose I care; I know perfectly well I have no real friends. As long as I remain what I am, I shall have as many as I need so far as the appearance goes. Let the women whimper, that's their business, but for me, give me no sentiment. A man must be firm, have a stout heart, or else leave on one side war and government.

Saint Helena, March 3, 1817

In spite of all the libels, I have no fear whatever about my fame. Posterity will do me justice. The truth will be known; and the good I have done will be compared with the faults I have committed. I am not uneasy as to the result. Had I succeeded, I would have died with the reputation of the greatest man that ever existed. As it is, although I have failed, I shall be considered as an extraor-

dinary man: my elevation was unparalleled, because unaccompanied by crime. I have fought fifty pitched battles, almost all of which I have won. I have framed and carried into effect a code of laws that will bear my name to the most distant posterity. I raised myself from nothing to be the most powerful monarch in the world. Europe was at my feet. I have always been of opinion that the sovereignty lay in the people. In fact, the imperial government was a kind of republic. Called to the head of it by the voice of the nation, my maxim was, *la carriére est ouverte aux talent* without distinction of birth or fortune, and this system of equality is the reason that your oligarchy hates me so much.

Saint Helena, August 28, 1817

Jesus was hanged, like so many fanatics who posed as a prophet, a messiah; there were several every year. What is certain is that at that epoch opinion was setting towards a single God, and those who first preached the doctrine were well received: circumstances made for it. It is just like in my case, sprung from the lower ranks of society I became an emperor, because circumstances, opinion, were with me.

Visual Sources

Napoleon Crossing the Alps
Jacques Louis David

Jacques Louis David was a leading painter of the late eighteenth and early nineteenth centuries and one of the first great painters to consciously devote his talents to the art of propaganda. A republican during the French Revolution, he painted a number of pictures supportive of the revolution and what it stood for. David argued that "the arts should . . . contribute forcefully to the education of the public" and that art "should have grandeur and a moral"; if a painting is properly presented, the "marks of heroism and civic virtue offered the eyes of the people will electrify its soul, and plant the seeds of glory and devotion to the fatherland."

When Napoleon rose to power, David became a Bonapartist. In 1800 he was asked by Napoleon to paint a picture of him leading his army across the Alps. The result, Napoleon Crossing the Alps (figure 21.1), shows Napoleon in a heroic pose on a white charger following the glorious footsteps of Hannibal and Charlemagne (whose names are carved in the rocks below) across the Alps. Napoleon is pointing upward, probably both to heaven and to the top of the mountains, while a wind blows at his back—a traditional symbol of victory. Under the horse's belly are troops and cannon moving up the trail. In reality, Napoleon wisely rode a sure-footed mule.

He also posed only briefly for David, informing him that "it is the character and what animates the physiognomy that needs to be painted. No one inquires if the portraits of great men are likenesses. It is enough that their genius lives in them."

CONSIDER: *The way this painting and the circumstances surrounding its execution by David illustrate connections between politics and art of the period.*

Bonaparte Visiting the Plague Victims at Jaffa
Antoine-Jean Gros

Despite the British victory at Aboukir Bay in Egypt, which annihilated French sea power, Napoleon retained hopes of conquering the Near East by land. In February 1799, French forces moved northeast from Cairo to Gaza and Nazareth. Despite some victories, the campaign failed to establish French control over the area. Nevertheless, Napoleon tried to transform these disappointments by promoting paintings that created images of success in this campaign.

In 1804 Antoine-Jean Gros (1771–1835) presented a scene from the Near Eastern campaigns of 1799 that showed the heroic Napoleon displaying humanism, charity, and nobility. The painting (figure 21.2) records Napoleon, after the battle of

Jaffa, entering the mosque courtyard (with its horseshoe arches and pointed arcades) of a pest house (plague hospital) at the Palestinian city of Jaffa in the Holy Land on March 11, 1799. Within lay victims of the bubonic plague, which had recently broken out among Arab defenders of the city and spread to the French. When the plague struck, Napoleon at first had his chief medical officer Desgenettes (just behind and to the right of Napoleon, who stands at the center of the painting) deny the presence of the sickness. Here Napoleon tries to stop the panic and inspire his troops by showing that he is not afraid of contamination and that the victims will be well cared for. At this moment the apparently immune and clearly fearless Napoleon reaches out and even touches the dreaded buboes (an inflamed swelling of the lymphatic glands that usually preceded death) of a French victim, perhaps conveying a sense that his touch might miraculously heal the stricken man. Just behind Napoleon, to the left, a more cautious officer holds a handkerchief to his face to ward off the stench of disease and death. In the foreground lay the dead and the agonized dying. At the left, an Arab physician in white robes attends the sick and an assistant carries bread for distribution to the needy. To the right, a blind man, leaning against a column, tries to approach Napoleon, and on the extreme bottom right a doctor, while caring for a soldier, succumbs himself. In the background are the white cubic houses and rising minarets of Jaffa. High in the center from the top of a Franciscan monastery flies triumphantly the French tricolor.

The surrounding facts differ from the historical image presented by this painting. During the battle of Jaffa, Napoleon had agreed to protect the lives of enemy soldiers if they capitulated. But upon laying down their arms, Napoleon ordered the 3,000 prisoners massacred and plundered the town. By May 1799, French forces had retreated back to Egypt.

FIGURE 21.1   (© Réunion des Musées Nationaux/Art Resource, NY)

CONSIDER: The message the artist intended to convey to viewers; how high quality art might be used for propaganda purposes.

 Secondary Sources

France Under Napoleon: Napoleon as Enlightened Despot

Louis Bergeron

As with most charismatic figures, it has been difficult to evaluate Napoleon objectively from a historical perspective. Even before his death, a number of myths were developing about

SOURCE: From Bergeron, Louis, *France Under Napoleon*. Copyright 1981 by the Princeton University Press.

him. Since then much of the debate among scholars has dealt with whether Napoleon should be considered a defender or a destroyer of the revolution, whether his rise to power reversed the revolutionary tide or consolidated it. In the following selection the French historian Louis Bergeron focuses on the consequences for France of Napoleon's rule and argues that he should be viewed more as an eighteenth-century enlightened despot than as anything else.

CONSIDER: Why Bergeron calls Napoleon the last of the enlightened despots and a prophet of the modern state; what, according to Bergeron, was beyond Napoleon's control;

FIGURE 21.2 (© Réunion des Musées Nationaux/Art Resource, NY)

whether the primary and visual sources support Bergeron's interpretation.

There is thus no doubt about the interpretation to be given to the historic role of Napoleon Bonaparte. For the rest of the world, indeed, he remained the fearsome prop-agator of the Revolution, or the admirable instrument of reason governing the world, of progress of the spirit in its long "discourse with time" (Hegel). But for France? . . . Bonaparte belongs to the Revolution, surely, in matters that seemed irreversible at the time—civil equality, the destruction of feudalism, the ruin of the privileged position of the Catholic Church. As for the rest, the enjoyment of liberties, the form of political institutions, there had been since 1789 so much instability, so many contradictions between grand principles and the practice of governments, so much persistent uncertainty on the outcome of the war and the unity of the nation, that the field lay open for a strong man who, on condition of preserving the essential conquests of the Revolution, would do something new in the matter of government and refuse to be embarrassed by scruples. By anchoring France securely to the shores that the Constituent Assembly had been unwilling to leave,

Bonaparte accomplished somewhat late in the day that "revolution from above" of which the old monarchy had been incapable. The political trade-off was a certain number of amputations of the immediate Revolutionary inheritance, a few backward movements, and disconcerting borrowings from the Old Régime. In a sense, the dynamism of Bonaparte and his rigorous administration revived the experiment of enlightened despotism, somewhat belatedly, since in the setting of Western Europe it was already a bit out of date. . . .

It was his political genius, as it is generally agreed to call it, to combine his own clear and strongly held per-sonal ideas and convictions, reinforced by his great indi-vidual prestige, with a sure sense of the necessary and the possible in revolutionary France—after ten years of revolution. "My policy is to govern men as the great number wish to be governed. That, I think, is the way to recognize the sovereignty of the people." While implacably suppressing the most actively opposed minorities, he overcame the apathy and the wait-and-see attitude of the majority of the French. In matters of social hierarchy and the administrative system he forced upon the French, who from citizens were soon to become subjects again, a coherent construction which he intended to be permanent, and which reflected his taste for uniformity, symmetry and efficiency, the signs of a rational organization in which a single mind transmitted impulses to the most distant members. What we see as rigid or even oppressive in the survivals of the Napoleonic system were at the time the source of its strength, making of it a model to be envied, and one of unequaled modernity.

Napoleon Bonaparte and the Legacy of the French Revolution

Martyn Lyons

In recent years, some historians have taken a fresh look at Napoleon and the significance of his régime. In addition to examining his words and deeds, they stress the historical context of his rise to power and the break from the Old Régime of the Bourbon monarchy. In the following selection, Martyn Lyons argues that Napoleon was not an enlightened despot but rather the founder of the modern state, and that his régime was the fulfillment of the "bourgeois" Revolution of 1789–1799.

CONSIDER: *What Lyons means by founder of the modern state; how he disagrees with Bergeron and others who argue that Napoleon was an enlightened despot; in what ways Napoleon's régime was a fulfilment of the "bourgeois" Revolution of 1789–1799.*

Throughout this evolution, two main themes stand out. Napoleon was, as he is often described, the founder of the modern state. His régime was also the fulfilment of the bourgeois Revolution of 1789–99.

The new state, which emerged from the Revolution and was shaped by Napoleon, was a secular state, without a trace of the divine sanction which had been one of the ideological props of the old régime monarchy. It was a state based on a conscripted army and staffed by a professional bureaucracy. Administration was "rationalised," in the sense that corruption and favouritism were officially outlawed. The affairs of all citizens were dealt with in principle on a basis of equality and according to fixed regulations, instead of being at the mercy of a monarch's whim. Above all, the modern state was a well-informed state, which used its own machinery to collect data on the lives and activities of its subjects. As it knew them better, it policed them more closely and it taxed them more efficiently. . . .

In Napoleon's hands, however, the state had become the instrument of dictatorship. Although lip service was still paid to the princple of popular sovereignty, Napoleon

SOURCE: Martyn Lyons, *Napoleon Bonaparte and the Legacy of the French Revolution* (New York: St. Martin's Press, 1994), pp. 295–298.

negated its democratic essence by claiming that he alone embodied the indivisible rights of the people. He manipulated a series of plebiscites to consolidate his personal authority. Bonapartism was not, then, a military dictatorship, for its power was characteristically derived from repeated consultations with the popular will, in 1800, 1802, 1804 and 1815. It was, however, a régime which brought parliamentary life to an end and expressed utter contempt for the liberal intellectuals who defended the representative style of democracy. The imperial years of Bonapartism were anti-parliamentary and anti-liberal. In addition, the information media were strictly controlled by Napoleon's popular dictatorship. . . .

To compare Napoleon with the Bourbons is to sin by anachronism. Turning Napoleon into the last of the Enlightened Absolutists of the late eighteenth century means ignoring the momentous events that separate them. The French Revolution was a decisive historical rupture which places Louis XVI and Napoleon Bonaparte in totally different spheres. The historical role of the Enlightened Absolutists had been to rationalise the confused and creaking old régime state structure. Their aim was to squeeze more resources from it, without disturbing its fundamental framework which was based on inequality and privilege. They had no intention of undermining the society of orders itself. On the contrary, they stood at its pinnacle, and its existence justified their authority.

When Bonaparte came to power, the society of orders had been completely transformed by the French Revolution. Legal privilege and tax exemptions had been destroyed—a fact which Napoleon emphatically confirmed. Bonaparte's task was not to extract more resources from a traditional social structure; that traditional social structure, along with noble privilege, the guilds, the Parlements and provincial autonomies, had been swept away by the Revolution. The role of the Enlightened Absolutists was to rationalise the Old Régime, but Napoleon's was to rationalise the new one. His task was not to safeguard the social prestige of the aristocracy (to which the monarchies were dedicated, and to whom in 1789 Louis XVI had linked his own fate). Napoleon's role was rather to build the institutions which would realise new forms of equality of opportunity. . . .

Its social basis is what distinguishes the Napoleonic régime from the Bourbon monarchy, and makes it the heir of the Revolution. The social foundations of the Napoleonic régime, as this book has argued, lay in the bourgeois and peasant revolution of 1789.

The Consulate and Empire rested on the support of the *notables*, whom the régime itself helped to define and cultivate. The *notables* were gathered from the successful revolutionary bourgeoisie of landowners, professional men and administrators, together with elements of the commercial and manufacturing élites. They supported Napoleon because he preserved the social gains of the Revolution. He himself was an enduring symbol of careers open to talent. He perpetuated the abolition of seigneurialism and of aristocratic privilege. He confirmed the material gains of the bourgeoisie, especially the sale of the *biens nationaux*. He established a legal code which embodied equality before the law, and he introduced a system of secondary education which served the interests of the professional and administrative élite. The creation of the new imperial nobility seemed to many to be a retrograde step, but it could also be interpreted as an assertion of new social priorities. The new imperial nobility was intended to bury the old. The society of orders was obsolete and archaic. Instead of birth and connections, society now declared its new criteria for distinguished status: propertied wealth, personal talent and service to the state. . . . Napoleon was the consolidator of the bourgeois Revolution, but he was not the passive instrument of any class or social group.

Women and the Napoleonic Code

Bonnie G. Smith

However they evaluate Napoleon and his rule, most historians point to the set of rationally organized laws—the Napoleonic Code—as one of Napoleon's most important and lasting legacies. The Code embodied many principles of the Enlightenment and the French Revolution, and the Code was modified and adopted outside of France in Europe and the Western Hemisphere. While it has been generally considered a progressive legal system, historians now point out that it may have represented a step back for women. In the following selection from her comprehensive survey, Changing Lives: Women in European History Since 1700, *Bonnie G. Smith analyzes the significance of the Napoleonic Code for women.*

CONSIDER: *Ways the Code made women legally and economically dependent on men; what concept of woman's proper role the Code supported; what concept of man's proper role the Code supported.*

First, women acquired the nationality of their husbands upon marriage. This made a woman's relationship to the state an indirect one because it was dependent on her husband's. Second, a woman had to reside where her husband desired. Women could not participate in lawsuits

SOURCE: From Bonnie G. Smith, *Changing Lives: Women in European History Since 1700*, pp. 120–122. Copyright 1989 by D. C. Heath and Co. Reprinted by permission of the publisher.

or serve as witnesses in court or as witnesses to civil acts such as births, deaths, and marriages. Such a reduction in woman's civil status enhanced that of the individual male. Moreover, the Code reduced, if not eliminated, male accountability for sexual acts and thrust it squarely on women. For example, men were no longer susceptible to paternity suits or legally responsible for the support of illegitimate children. Women were weakened economically if they bore illegitimate children, whereas men were not so affected if they fathered them. Finally, female adultery was punished by imprisonment and fines unless the husband relented and took his wife back. Men, however, suffered no such sanctions unless they brought their sexual partner into the home. The sexual behavior of women was open to scrutiny and prescribed by law, whereas that of men, almost without exception, had no criminal aspect attached to it. Thus male sexuality was accepted with few limitations, but women's was only acceptable if it remained within strict domestic boundaries. The Napoleonic Code institutionalized the republican responsibility of women to generate virtue—a term that began to acquire sexual overtones to its civic definition.

The Napoleonic Code also defined the space women would occupy in the new regime as marital, maternal, and domestic—all public matters would be determined by men. This circumscription was made more effective by the way the property law undercut the possibilities for women's economic independence and existence in a world beyond the home. In general, a woman had no control over property. Even if she was married under a contract that ensured a separate accounting of her dowry, her husband still had administrative control of funds. This administrative power of the husband and father replaced arbitrary patriarchal rule and was more in tune with modern ideas of government. Instead of serving the king's whim, governmental officials served the best interests of the nation just as the father increased the well-being of the family. This kind of economic control of women held in all classes. Women's wages went to their husbands, and market women and others engaged in business could not do so without permission from their husbands. Once a woman gained permission she did acquire some kind of legal status, in that a business woman could be sued. On the other hand, she had no control of her profits—these always passed to her husband, and court records demonstrate the continuing enforcement of this kind of control. Moreover, the husband's right to a business woman's property meant that the property passed to his descendants rather than hers. All of these provisions meant that, in the strictest sense, women could not act freely or independently.

The Napoleonic Code influenced many legal systems in Europe and the New World and set the terms for the treatment of women on a widespread basis. Establishing male power by transferring autonomy and economic goods from women to men, the Code organized gender roles for more than a century. "From the way the Code treats women, you can tell it was written by men," so older women reacted to the new decree. Women's publications protested the sudden repression after a decade of more equitable laws. Even in the 1820s, books explaining the Code to women always recognized their anger. The justification for the Code's provisions involved reminders about men's chivalrous character and women's weakness. Arguments were based on nature both to invoke the equality of all men and to reinforce the consequences of women's supposed physical inferiority. Looking at nature, one writer saw in terms of gender man's "greater strength, his propensity to be active and assertive in comparison to woman's weakness, lack of vigor and natural modesty." At the time the Code was written, the codifiers were looking at nature in two ways. In theorizing about men alone, nature was redolent of abstract rights. As far as women were concerned, however, nature became empirical in that women had less physical stature than men. Although short men were equal to tall men, women were simply smaller than men and thus were unequal.

According to jurists, therefore, women needed protection, and this protection was to be found within the domicile. The law, they maintained, still offered women protection from individual male brutality, in the rare cases when that might occur. Legislators thus used the law officially to carve out a private space for women in which they had no rights. At the same time, law codes were supposed to protect women from the abuses allowed in the first place. The small number of abuses that might result were not seen as significant drawbacks by the jurists. They saw the Code as "insuring the safety of patrimonies and restoring order in families." It mattered little to them that the old regime carried over for women in the form of an "estate"—a term that indicated an unchangeable lifetime situation into which people were born and would always remain. Estates had been abolished for men in favor of mobility, but it continued for women.

By the time the Napoleonic Code went into effect, little remained of liberal revolutionary programs for women except the provisions for equal inheritance by sisters and brothers. The Code cleared the way for the rule of property and for individual triumph. It ushered in an age of mobility, marked by the rise of the energetic and heroic. The Code gave women little room for that kind of acquisitiveness or for heroism. Instead, women's realm was to encompass virtue, reproduction, and family.

❧ CHAPTER QUESTIONS

1. Considering the materials in this chapter, how would you explain Napoleon's rise to power and his effective exercise of it?

2. In what ways did Napoleon preserve and support the principles of the French Revolution? In what ways did he undermine these principles?

22 Industrialization and Social Change

The Industrial Revolution, which transformed economic life in the West, began in England in the eighteenth century. After the Napoleonic period it spread to Western Europe, and by the end of the nineteenth century it had touched most of Western civilization. The Industrial Revolution was characterized by unprecedented economic growth, the factory system of production, and the use of new, artificially powered machines for transportation and mechanical operations. The potential was tremendous; for the first time, human beings had the ability to produce far more than was needed to sustain a large percentage of the population. Whether that potential would be realized, and at what cost, remained to be seen.

In the wake of industrialization came great social changes. The middle and working classes were most affected by industrialization, and both grew in number and social influence as did the urban areas in which they worked and lived. But it was the middle class that benefited most, enjoying a rising standard of living, increased prestige, and growing political influence. Whether the working class benefited from industrialization during the early decades is a matter for debate among historians. Clearly it was this class that bore the burdens of urban social problems: overcrowded slums, poor sanitation, insufficient social services, and a host of related problems. The aristocracy, the peasantry, and the artisans—classes tied to the traditional agricultural economy and older means of production—slowly diminished in numbers and social importance as industrialization spread.

The selections in this chapter deal with the economic and social aspects of industrialization. Much-debated questions of economic history are addressed. Why did industrialization occur first in England? How did England differ from other areas that were relatively advanced economically? Most of the documents concern the human consequences of industrialization, questions of social history. The most popular area of interest, the effect of industrialization on the workers directly involved, is explored. What were the working conditions in the factories? How did industrialization affect the overall lifestyle of these people? Did their standard of living improve or diminish as a result of industrialization? The middle class is also examined, especially middle-class attitudes and values. How did the middle class view industrialization? What were its attitudes toward money? How did the attitudes of and toward women change?

This chapter centers on industrialization in the first half of the nineteenth century. It should be recognized that industrialization spread unevenly, and it was not until the second half of the nineteenth century and even the beginning of the twentieth century that industrialization spread to many areas in Southern and Eastern Europe.

 Primary Sources

Testimony for the Factory Act of 1833: Working Conditions in England

Industrialization carried with it broad social and economic changes that were quickly felt by those involved. The most striking changes were in the working conditions in the new factories and mines. During the first decades of industrialization, there was little government control over working conditions and few effective labor organizations; laborers were thus at the mercy of factory owners who were pursuing profit in a competitive world. Investigations into conditions in factories and mines conducted by the British Parliament in the 1830s and 1840s led eventually to the enactment of legislation, such as the Factory Act of 1833. These parliamentary investigations provide us with extensive information about working conditions and attitudes toward them. The following selection contains three excerpts from a parliamentary commission's investigations into child labor in factories. The first is a summary by the commission of medical examiners from northeastern England. The second is the testimony of John Wright, a steward in a silk factory. The third is the testimony of William Harter, a silk manufacturer.

CONSIDER: *What these people perceived as the worst abuses of factory labor; the causes of the poor working conditions; how Harter might defend himself against the charges that he was abusing the working class; what biases the witnesses might hold.*

SOURCE: Commission for Inquiry into the Employment of Children in Factories, *Second Report, with Minutes of Evidence and Reports by the Medical Commissioners*, vol. V, Session 29 January–20 August, 1833 (London: His Majesty's Printing Office, 1833), pp. 5, 26–28.

TESTIMONY OF THE COMMISSION OF MEDICAL EXAMINERS

The account of the physical condition of the manufacturing population in the large towns in the North-eastern District of England is less favourable. It is of this district that the Commissioners state, "We have found undoubted instances of children five years old sent to work thirteen hours a day; and frequently of children nine, ten, and eleven consigned to labour for fourteen and fifteen hours." The effects ascertained by the Commissioners in many cases are, "deformity," and in still more "stunted growth, relaxed muscles, and slender conformation:" "twisting of the ends of the long bones, relaxation of the ligaments of the knees, ankles, and the like." "The representation that these effects are so common and universal as to enable some persons invariably to distinguish factory children from other children is, I have no hesitation in saying, an exaggerated and unfaithful picture of their general condition; at the same time it must be said, that the individual instances in which some one or other of those effects of severe labour are discernible are rather frequent than rare. . . .

"Upon the whole, there remains no doubt upon my mind, that under the system pursued in many of the factories, the children of the labouring classes stand in need of, and ought to have, legislative protection against the conspiracy insensibly formed between their masters and parents, to tax them to a degree of toil beyond their strength.

"In conclusion, I think it has been clearly proved that children have been worked a most unreasonable and cruel length of time daily, and that even adults have been expected to do a certain quantity of labour which scarcely any human being is able to endure. I am of opinion no child under fourteen years of age should work in a factory of any description for more than eight hours a day.

From fourteen upwards I would recommend that no individual should, under any circumstances, work more than twelve hours a day; although if practicable, as a physician, I would prefer the limitation of ten hours, for all persons who earn their bread by their industry."

TESTIMONY OF JOHN WRIGHT

How long have you been employed in a silk-mill?—More than thirty years.

Did you enter it as a child?—Yes, betwixt five and six.

How many hours a day did you work then?—The same thirty years ago as now.

What are those hours?—Eleven hours per day and two over-hours: over-hours are working after six in the evening till eight. The regular hours are from six in the morning to six in the evening, and two others are two over-hours: about fifty years ago they began working over-hours. . . .

Why, then, are those employed in them said to be in such a wretched condition?—In the first place, the great number of hands congregated together, in some rooms forty, in some fifty, in some sixty, and I have known some as many as 100, which must be injurious to both health and growing. In the second place, the privy is in the factory, which frequently emits an unwholesome smell; and it would be worth while to notice in the future erection of mills, that there be betwixt the privy door and the factory wall a kind of a lobby of cage-work. 3rdly, The tediousness and the everlasting sameness in the first process preys much on the spirits, and makes the hands spiritless. 4thly, The extravagant number of hours a child is compelled to labour and confinement, which for one week is seventy-six hours. . . . 5thly, About six months in the year we are obliged to use either gas, candles, or lamps, for the longest portion of that time, nearly six hours a day, being obliged to work amid the smoke and soot of the same; and also a large portion of oil and grease is used in the mills.

What are the effects of the present system of labour?—From my earliest recollections, I have found the effects to be awfully detrimental to the well-being of the operative; I have observed frequently children carried to factories, unable to walk, and that entirely owing to excessive labour and confinement. The degradation of the workpeople baffles all description: frequently have two of my sisters been obliged to be assisted to the factory and home again, until by-and-by they could go no longer, being totally crippled in their legs. And in the next place, I remember some ten or twelve years ago working in one of the largest firms in Macclesfield, (Messrs. Baker and Pearson,) with about twenty-five men, where they were scarce one half fit for His Majesty's service. Those that are straight in their limbs are stunted in their growth; much inferior to their fathers in point of strength. 3dly, Through excessive labour and confinement there is often a total loss of appetite; a kind of

langour steals over the whole frame—enters to the very core—saps the foundation of the best constitution—and lays our strength prostrate in the dust. In the 4th place, by protracted labour there is an alarming increase of cripples in various parts of this town, which has come under my own observation and knowledge. . . .

Are all these cripples made in the silk factories?—Yes, they are, I believe. . . .

TESTIMONY OF WILLIAM HARTER

What effect would it have on your manufacture to reduce the hours of labour to ten?—It would instantly much reduce the value of my mill and machinery, and consequently of far prejudice my manufacture.

How so?—They are calculated to produce a certain quantity of work in a given time. Every machine is valuable in proportion to the quantity of work which it will turn off in a given time. It is impossible that the machinery could produce as much work in ten hours as in twelve. If the tending of the machines were a laborious occupation, the difference in the quantity of work might not always be in exact proportion to the difference of working time; but in my mill, and silk-mills in general, the work requires the least imaginable labour; therefore it is perfectly impossible that the machines could produce as much work in ten hours as in twelve. The produce would vary in about the same ratio as the working time.

Sybil, or the Two Nations: Mining Towns

Benjamin Disraeli

Nineteenth-century novels contain some of the most effective descriptions of industrial life. In addition to providing such description, Sybil, or the Two Nations *(1845), written by Benjamin Disraeli (1804–1881), a novelist and politician who also served as prime minister of England (1867–1868, 1874–1880), illustrates the thinking of a group of reforming Tory aristocrats, sometimes referred to as Young England. They hoped to gain working-class support against their political competitors, the liberal Whigs. In the following selection from this novel, Disraeli describes Marney, a rural mining town.*

CONSIDER: *The physical consequences of industrialization for the land and the town; the worst aspects of industrial labor, according to Disraeli; how this description compares with Engels' views in the following excerpt; who, if anyone, Disraeli would blame for all this.*

SOURCE: Benjamin Disraeli, *Sybil, or the Two Nations* (New York: M. Walter Dunne, 1904), pp. 198–200.

The last rays of the sun contending with clouds of smoke that drifted across the country, partially illumined a peculiar landscape. Far as the eye could reach, and the region was level, except where a range of limestone hills formed its distant limit, a wilderness of cottages, or tenements that were hardly entitled to a higher name, were scattered for many miles over the land; some detached, some connected in little rows, some clustering in groups, yet rarely forming continuous streets, but interspersed with blazing furnaces, heaps of burning coal, and piles of smouldering ironstone; while forges and engine chimneys roared and puffed in all directions, and indicated the frequent presence of the mouth of the mine, and the bank of the coal-pit. Notwithstanding the whole country might be compared to a vast rabbit warren, it was nevertheless intersected with canals, crossing each other at various levels; and though the subterranean operations were prosecuted with so much avidity that it was not uncommon to observe whole rows of houses awry, from the shifting and hollow nature of the land, still, intermingled with heaps of mineral refuse, or of metallic dross, patches of the surface might here and there be recognised, covered, as if in mockery, with grass and corn, looking very much like those gentlemen's sons that we used to read of in our youth, stolen by the chimneysweeps, and giving some intimations of their breeding beneath their grimy livery. But a tree or a shrub, such an existence was unknown in this dingy rather than dreary region.

It was the twilight hour; the hour at which in southern climes the peasant kneels before the sunset image of the blessed Hebrew maiden; when caravans halt in their long course over vast deserts, and the turbaned traveller, bending in the sand, pays his homage to the sacred stone and the sacred city; the hour, not less holy, that announces the cessation of English toil, and sends forth the miner and the collier to breathe the air of earth, and gaze on the light of heaven.

They come forth: the mine delivers its gang and the pit its bondsmen; the forge is silent and the engine is still. The plain is covered with the swarming multitude: bands of stalwart men, broad-chested and muscular, wet with toil, and black as the children of the tropics; troops of youth, alas! of both sexes, though neither their raiment nor their language indicates the difference; all are clad in male attire; and oaths that men might shudder at issue from lips born to breathe words of sweetness. Yet these are to be, some are, the mothers of England! But can we wonder at the hideous coarseness of their language, when we remember the savage rudeness of their lives? Naked to the waist, an iron chain fastened to a belt of leather runs between their legs clad in canvas trousers, while on hands and feet an English girl, for twelve, sometimes for sixteen hours a day, hauls and hurries tubs of coals up subterranean roads, dark, precipitous, and plashy; circumstances that seem to have escaped the notice of the Society for the Abolition of Negro Slavery. Those worthy gentlemen, too, appear to have been singularly unconscious of the sufferings of the little trappers, which was remarkable, as many of them were in their own employ.

See, too, these emerge from the bowels of the earth! Infants of four and five years of age, many of them girls, pretty and still soft and timid; entrusted with the fulfilment of responsible duties, the very nature of which entails on them the necessity of being the earliest to enter the mine and the latest to leave it. Their labour indeed is not severe, for that would be impossible, but it is passed in darkness and in solitude. They endure that punishment which philosophical philanthropy has invented for the direst criminals, and which those criminals deem more terrible than the death for which it is substituted. Hour after hour elapses, and all that reminds the infant trappers of the world they have quitted, and that which they have joined, is the passage of the coal-waggons for which they open the air-doors of the galleries, and on keeping which doors constantly closed, except at this moment of passage, the safety of the mine and the lives of the persons employed in it entirely depend.

The Condition of the Working Class in England

Friedrich Engels

To many contemporaries, child labor in factories and mines under harsh conditions was the most shocking change in working conditions brought on by industrialization. However, several investigators documented a whole range of problems facing England's industrial working class. One of the most famous of these investigators was Friedrich Engels (1820–1895), the son of a German textile manufacturer. Engels moved to England in the 1840s, where in addition to learning about business he traveled through cities visiting working-class areas and interviewing people. He would soon become a collaborator with his friend, Karl Marx, and one of the founders of modern socialism. The following excerpt is from the book that arose from his studies, The Condition of the Working Class in England, first published in 1845. Here Engels focuses on worker's living environment in England's industrial cities.

CONSIDER: *What Engels considers the worst health conditions facing the poor; Engels' analysis of how the environment affects the poor mentally as well as physically; how this description adds to the testimony before the commission on child labor (in a previous excerpt).*

SOURCE: Friedrich Engels, *The Condition of the Working Class in England,* trans. and ed. by W. O. Henderson and W. H. Chaloner. (Stanford, CA: Stanford University Press, 1968), pp. 110–111.

The way in which the vast mass of the poor are treated by modern society is truly scandalous. They are herded into great cities where they breathe a fouler air than in the countryside which they have left. They are housed in the worst ventilated districts of the towns; they are deprived of all means of keeping clean. They are deprived of water because this is only brought to their houses if someone is prepared to defray the cost of laying the pipes. River water is so dirty as to be useless for cleansing purposes. The poor are forced to throw into the streets all their sweepings, garbage, dirty water, and frequently even disgusting filth and excrement. The poor are deprived of all proper means of refuse disposal and so they are forced to pollute the very districts they inhabit. And this is by no means all. There is no end to the sufferings which are heaped on the heads of the poor. It is notorious that general overcrowding is a characteristic feature of the great towns, but in the working-class quarters people are packed together in an exceptionally small area. Not satisfied with permitting the pollution of the air in the streets, society crams as many as a dozen workers into a single room, so that at night the air becomes so foul that they are nearly suffocated. The workers have to live in damp dwellings. When they live in cellars the water seeps through the floor and when they live in attics the rain comes through the roof. The workers' houses are so badly built that the foul air cannot escape from them. The workers have to wear poor and ragged garments and they have to eat food which is bad, indigestible and adulterated. Their mental state is threatened by being subjected alternately to extremes of hope and fear. They are goaded like wild beasts and never have a chance of enjoying a quiet life. They are deprived of all pleasures except sexual indulgence and intoxicating liquors. Every day they have to work until they are physically and mentally exhausted. This forces them to excessive indulgence in the only two pleasures remaining to them. If the workers manage to survive this sort of treatment it is only to fall victims to starvation when a slump occurs and they are deprived of the little that they once had.

How is it possible that the poorer classes can remain healthy and have a reasonable expectation of life under such conditions? What can one expect but that they should suffer from continual outbreaks of epidemics and an excessively low expectation of life? The physical condition of the workers shows a progressive deterioration.

Self-Help: Middle-Class Attitudes

Samuel Smiles

Middle-class liberals were not totally unaware of the consequences of industrialization for society. Doctrines were developed that reflected and appealed to their attitudes. Such

SOURCE: Samuel Smiles, *Self-Help* (Chicago: Belford, Clarke, 1881), pp. 21–23, 48–49.

doctrines served to justify the position of the middle class, to support policies it usually favored, and to rationalize the poor state of the working class. Many of these doctrines appeared in Self-Help, the popular book by Samuel Smiles, a physician, editor, secretary of two railroads, and author. First published in 1859, Self-Help became a best-seller in England and was translated into many languages. The following excerpt is a good example of the individualism and moral tone that appear throughout the book.

CONSIDER: *How Smiles justifies his assertion that self-help is the only answer to problems; how Smiles would analyze the situation of the working class and how he would react to the testimony presented to the parliamentary commission on child labor.*

"Heaven helps those who help themselves" is a well tried maxim, embodying in a small compass the results of vast human experience. The spirit of self-help is the root of all genuine growth in the individual; and, exhibited in the lives of many, it constitutes the true source of national vigor and strength. Help from without is often enfeebling in its effects, but help from within invariably invigorates. Whatever is done *for* men or classes, to a certain extent takes away the stimulus and necessity of doing for themselves; and where men are subjected to over-guidance and over-government, the inevitable tendency is to render them comparatively helpless.

Even the best institutions can give a man no active help. Perhaps the most they can do is, to leave him free to develop himself and improve his individual condition. But in all times men have been prone to believe that their happiness and well-being were to be secured by means of institutions rather than by their own conduct. Hence the value of legislation as an agent in human advancement has usually been much overestimated. To constitute the millionth part of a Legislature, by voting for one or two men once in three or five years, however conscientiously this duty may be performed, can exercise but little active influence upon any man's life and character. Moreover, it is every day becoming more clearly understood, that the function of Government is negative and restrictive, rather than positive and active; being resolvable principally into protection—protection of life, liberty, and property. Laws, wisely administered, will secure men in the enjoyment of the fruits of their labor, whether of mind or body, at a comparatively small personal sacrifice; but no laws, however stringent, can make the idle industrious, the shiftless provident, or the drunken sober. Such reforms can only be effected by means of individual action, economy, and self-denial; by better habits, rather than by greater rights. . . .

Indeed, all experience serves to prove that the worth and strength of a State depend far less upon the form of its institutions than upon the character of its men. For the nation is only an aggregate of individual conditions, and civilization itself is but a question of the personal improvement of the men, women, and children of whom society is composed.

National progress is the sum of individual industry, energy, and uprightness, as national decay is of individual idleness, selfishness, and vice. What we are accustomed to decry as great social evils, will for the most part be found to be but the outgrowth of man's own perverted life; and though we may endeavor to cut them down and extirpate them by means of Law, they will only spring up again with fresh luxuriance in some other form, unless the conditions of personal life and character are radically improved. If this view be correct, then it follows that the highest patriotism and philanthropy consist, not so much in altering laws and modifying institutions, as in helping and stimulating men to elevate and improve themselves by their own free and independent individual action.

One of the most strongly marked features of the English people is their spirit of industry, standing out prominent and distinct in their past history, and as strikingly characteristic of them now as at any former period. It is this spirit, displayed by the commons of England, which has laid the foundations and built up the industrial greatness of the empire. This vigorous growth of the nation has been mainly the result of the free energy of individuals, and it has been contingent upon the number of hands and minds from time to time actively employed within it, whether as cultivators of the soil, producers of articles of utility, contrivers of tools and machines, writers of books, or creators of works of art. And while this spirit of active industry has been the vital principle of the nation, it has also been its saving and remedial one, counteracting from time to time the effects of errors in our laws and imperfections in our constitution.

The career of industry which the nation has pursued, has also proved its best education. As steady application to work is the healthiest training for every individual, so is it the best discipline of a state. Honorable industry travels the same road with duty; and Providence has closely linked both with happiness. The gods, says the poet, have placed labor and toil on the way leading to the Elysian fields. Certain it is that no bread eaten by man is so sweet as that earned by his own labor, whether bodily or mental. By labor the earth has been subdued, and man redeemed from barbarism; nor has a single step in civilization been made without it. Labor is not only a necessity and a duty, but a blessing: only the idler feels it to be a curse. The duty of work is written on the thews and muscles of the limbs, the mechanism of the hand, the nerves and lobes of the brain—the sum of whose healthy action is satisfaction and enjoyment. In the school of labor is taught the best practical wisdom; nor is a life of manual employment, as we shall hereafter find, incompatible with high mental culture.

Father Goriot: Money and the Middle Class
Honoré de Balzac

With industrialization the middle class rose in status and wealth. Increasingly, money became a common denominator in society, and the middle class was in a position to benefit from this. But the emphasis on money had its painful side even for the relatively wealthy. Few have focused on this more profoundly and broadly than the French novelist Honoré de Balzac, who himself struggled with financial problems for much of his life. The following is an excerpt from his Father Goriot (1834), in which Goriot, an old bourgeois, bemoans the way his daughters are treating him now that he is no longer so rich.

CONSIDER: *How Goriot sees money as both the cause for and the solution to his problems; the connections Balzac makes between money, social structure, and family life; how a worker might react to Goriot's problems.*

"Ah! if I were rich still, if I had kept my money, if I had not given all to them, they would be with me now; they would fawn on me and cover my cheeks with their kisses! I should be living in a great mansion; I should have grand apartments and servants and a fire in my room; and *they* would be about me all in tears, and their husbands and their children. I should have had all that; now—I have nothing. Money brings everything to you; even your daughters. My money. Oh! where is my money? If I had plenty of money to leave behind me, they would nurse me and tend me; I should hear their voices; I should see their faces. Ah, God! who knows? They both of them have hearts of stone. I love them too much; it was not likely that they should love me. A father ought always to be rich; he ought to keep his children well in hand, like unruly horses. I have gone down on my knees to them. Wretches! this is the crowning act that brings the last ten years to a proper close. If you but knew how much they made of me just after they were married. (Oh! this is cruel torture!) I had just given them each eight hundred thousand francs; they were bound to be civil to me after that, and their husbands too were civil. I used to go to their houses: it was, 'My kind father' here, 'My dear father' there. There was always a place for me at their tables. I used to dine with their husbands now and then, and they were very respectful to me. I was still worth something, they thought. How should they know? I had not said anything about my affairs. It is worth while to be civil to a man who has given his daughters eight hundred thousand francs apiece; and they showed me every attention then—but it was all for my money.

SOURCE: Honoré de Balzac, *Father Goriot* (New York: Century Co., 1904), pp. 264–265.

Grand people are not great. I found that out by experience! I went to the theatre with them in their carriage; I might stay as long as I cared to stay at their evening parties. In fact, they acknowledged me their father; publicly they owned that they were my daughters. But I always was a shrewd one, you see, and nothing was lost upon me. Everything went straight to the mark and pierced my heart. I saw quite well that it was all sham and pretence, but there is no help for such things as these. I felt less at my ease at their dinner-table than I did downstairs here. I had nothing to say for myself. So these grand folks would ask in my son-in-law's ear, 'Who may that gentleman be?'—'The father-in-law with the dollars; he is very rich.'—'The devil, he is!' they would say, and look again at me with the respect due to my money."

Woman in Her Social and Domestic Character

Elizabeth Poole Sandford

Industrialization also had its effects on middle-class women. As the wealth and position of these women rose in a changing economic environment, previous models of behavior no longer applied. A variety of books and manuals appeared to counsel middle-class women on their proper role and behavior. The following is an excerpt from one of these, Woman in Her Social and Domestic Character *(1842), written by Mrs. John Sandford.*

CONSIDER: *Woman's ideal function in relation to her husband, according to this document; by implication, the role of the middle-class man in relation to his wife; possible explanations for this view of women.*

The changes wrought by Time are many. It influences the opinions of men as familiarity does their feelings; it has a tendency to do away with superstition, and to reduce every thing to its real worth.

It is thus that the sentiment for woman has undergone a change. The romantic passion which once almost deified her is on the decline; and it is by intrinsic qualities that she must now inspire respect. She is no longer the queen of song and the star of chivalry. But if there is less of enthusiasm entertained for her, the sentiment is more rational, and, perhaps, equally sincere; for it is in relation to happiness that she is chiefly appreciated.

And in this respect it is, we must confess, that she is most useful and most important. Domestic life is the chief source of her influence; and the greatest debt society

SOURCE: Mrs. John Sandford (Elizabeth Poole Sandford), *Woman in Her Social and Domestic Character* (Boston: Otis, Broaders and Co., 1842), pp. 5–7, 15–16.

can owe to her is domestic comfort: for happiness is almost an element of virtue; and nothing conduces more to improve the character of men than domestic peace. A woman may make a man's home delightful, and may thus increase his motives for virtuous exertion. She may refine and tranquillize his mind,—may turn away his anger or allay his grief. Her smile may be the happy influence to gladden his heart, and to disperse the cloud that gathers on his brow. And in proportion to her endeavors to make those around her happy, she will be esteemed and loved. She will secure by her excellence that interest and regard which she might formerly claim as the privilege of her sex, and will really merit the deference which was then conceded to her as a matter of course. . . .

Perhaps one of the first secrets of her influence is adaptation to the tastes, and sympathy in the feelings, of those around her. This holds true in lesser as well as in graver points. It is in the former, indeed, that the absence of interest in a companion is frequently most disappointing. Where want of congeniality impairs domestic comfort, the fault is generally chargeable on the female side. It is for woman, not for man, to make the sacrifice, especially in indifferent matters. She must, in a certain degree, be plastic herself if she would mould others. . . .

To be useful, a woman must have feeling. It is this which suggests the thousand nameless amenities which fix her empire in the heart, and render her so agreeable, and almost so necessary, that she imperceptibly rises in the domestic circle, and becomes at once its cement and its charm.

❧

Nothing is so likely to conciliate the affections of the other sex as a feeling that woman looks to them for support and guidance. In proportion as men are themselves superior, they are accessible to this appeal. On the contrary, they never feel interested in one who seems disposed rather to offer than to ask assistance. There is, indeed, something unfeminine in independence. It is contrary to nature, and therefore it offends. We do not like to see a woman affecting tremors, but still less do we like to see her acting the amazon. A really sensible woman feels her dependence. She does what she can; but she is conscious of inferiority, and therefore grateful for support. She knows that she is the weaker vessel, and that as such she should receive honor. In this view, her weakness is an attraction, not a blemish.

In every thing, therefore, that women attempt, they should show their consciousness of dependence. If they are learners, let them evince a teachable spirit; if they give an opinion, let them do it in an unassuming manner. There is something so unpleasant in female self-sufficiency that it not unfrequently deters instead of persuading, and prevents the adoption of advice which the judgment even approves.

Women and the Working Class

Flora Tristan

As industrialization spread, working-class organizations developed. Opposed by governments and by the middle classes, these organizations faced great difficulties in creating a following and maintaining their existence. For the most part the new labor unions paid little attention to women and were dominated by men. However, there were women like Flora Tristan (1803–1844) who recognized the connections between the emancipation of women and forming working-class unions. In The Workers' Union (1844), Tristan made the following appeal to French workers.

CONSIDER: *The ways this might appeal to workers and particularly to working-class women; how this differs from the attitude of Elizabeth Poole Sandford or Samuel Smiles.*

(1) To constitute the working class by setting up a compact, solid, and indissoluble union.

(2) The workers' union to choose and pay a defender who shall represent the working class before the nation [workers were without the voting franchise because of the 200-franc tax requirement], so as to establish universal acceptance of this class' right to exist [as an organization].

(3) To proclaim the legitimacy of hands (*bras*) as property, 25 million French workers having no property other than their hands.

(4) To secure the recognition of every man and woman's right to work.

(5) To secure the recognition of every man and woman's right to moral, intellectual, and vocational training.

(6) To examine the possibilities of organizing the labor force in present social conditions.

(7) To construct workers' union buildings in every department of France which shall provide intellectual and vocational training for working-class children and admit working men and women who have been disabled on the job or are sick or old.

(8) To proclaim the urgent necessity of giving working-class women moral, intellectual, and vocational training so that they may improve the morals of the men.

(9) To proclaim the fact that juridical equality between men and women is the only means of achieving the unity of humanity.

SOURCE: Flora Tristan, *L'Union Ouvriére*, 2nd ed. (Paris, 1844), p. 108, in Julia O'Faolain and Lauro Martines, eds., *Not in God's Image.* Copyright © 1973 by Julia O'Faolain and Lauro Martines. Reprinted by permission of Harper & Row, Publishers, Inc.

 ## Visual Sources

Gare Saint Lazare

Claude Monet

From a visual standpoint, industrial civilization was strikingly different from its predecessor. The 1877 painting (figure 22.1) of a railroad station in the heart of nineteenth-century Paris by the French Impressionist Claude Monet epitomizes the new industrial civilization. Steam, powerful engines, rapid transportation, and structures of iron and glass, all in an expanding urban environment, contrast sharply with the typical rural or urban images of previous eras.

CONSIDER: *The associations that a nineteenth-century viewer might have upon viewing this painting.*

FIGURE 22.1 (© Fogg Art Museum, Harvard University Art Museums, USA, Bequest from the Collection of Maurice Wertheim, Class of 1906/Bridgeman Art Library)

FIGURE 22.2 (© National Trust/Art Resource, NY)

Iron and Coal

William Bell Scott

In the caption to his 1860 painting of industrial activity in Tyneside, England (figure 22.2), British artist William Bell Scott (1811–1891) proudly proclaims: "In the Nineteenth Century the Northumbrians show the World what can be done with Iron and Coal." He may have painted the picture in response to a plea in a publication complaining that in most paintings "we miss . . . the poetry of the things about us; our railways, factories, mines, roaring cities, steam vessels, and the endless novelties and wonders produced everyday." Certainly this mid-nineteenth century painting celebrates these industrial "things." The foreground setting is an engineering workshop. In the center, three muscular workers hammer out molten iron. On the right is a drawing of a steam engine built by Robert Stephenson and Co., and indeed an example of that steam engine is crossing Stephenson's High Level Bridge in the background to the right. In the left foreground, a girl sits on an Armstrong gun with her father's lunch and an arithmetic book in her lap. In the shop are other industrial objects made of iron: an anchor, a marine air pump, and a heavy chain with a pulley. In back of the three workers a boy who works in the mines stands with a Davy safety lamp and looks down on the docks below. On the river a coal barge passes.

CONSIDER: *What image of industrial activity this painting presents to the viewer; what other images of industrial activity might an artist present.*

Illustration from *Life and Adventures of Michael Armstrong*

The following illustration (figure 22.3) is from a novel, Life and Adventures of Michael Armstrong (1840), by the well-known British author, Mrs. Frances Trollope. The illustration depicts several of the main elements of the Industrial Revolution in England. It shows the inside of a textile factory—a factory in the most advanced of the new industries. Thanks to mechanization and artificial power, a few workers can now do the work of many. The workers—men, women, and children—are obviously poor. In the background stands the stern middle-class owner talking with others of his class while in the foreground a child worker embraces his middle-class counterpart for some kindness he has displayed. The scene is reflective of the typical middle-class view of the poor and poverty—as problems of morals, to be treated with pity and philanthropic concern but not yet requiring substantial social or economic change.

CONSIDER: *The ways in which this illustration reflects aspects of industrialization touched on by other documents in this chapter; the similarities and differences between this illustration and Figure 18.2 in Chapter 18.*

Industrialization and Demographic Change

A comparison of maps 22.1 and 22.2, which show the population density of England in 1801 and 1851, respectively, reveals the relatively rapid increase in population and urbanization in certain areas of England during this period. The third map (map 22.3) shows where industry (mainly textiles, metallurgy, and mining) was concentrated in 1851. A comparison of all three maps reveals the connections among shifting population density, urbanization, and industrialization during this period of early, rapid modernization of England's economy.

CONSIDER: *What some of the geopolitical consequences of these connections between demographic and economic changes might be; what some of the social consequences of these same connections might be.*

FIGURE 22.3   (© Bettmann/Corbis)

MAP 22.1   Population Density: England, 1801

MAP 22.2   Population Density: England, 1851

MAP 22.3   Concentration of Industry in England, 1851

Secondary Sources

The Making of Economic Society: England, the First to Industrialize

Robert L. Heilbroner

Although it is clear that industrialization occurred first in England, it is not apparent why this should be so. During the eighteenth century France was prosperous and economically advanced. Other countries such as Belgium and the Netherlands possessed certain economic advantages over England and might have industrialized earlier but did not. In the following selection Robert Heilbroner, an economist and economic

historian, addresses the question of why England was first and points out the differences between England and most other European nations in the eighteenth century.

CONSIDER: *Why Heilbroner stresses the role of the "New Men" over the other factors he lists; any disadvantages England had to overcome; whether it was simply the circumstances that gave rise to the "New Men" or whether it was the "New Men" who took advantage of the circumstances when most men in most other nations would not have.*

Why did the Industrial Revolution originally take place in England and not on the continent? To answer the question we must look at the background factors which distinguished England from most other European nations in the eighteenth century.

SOURCE: Robert L. Heilbroner, *The Making of Economic Society.* Reprinted by permission of Prentice-Hall, Inc. (Englewood Cliffs, NJ, 1980), pp. 76–77, 80–81.

The first of these factors was simply that England was relatively wealthy. In fact, a century of successful exploration, slave-trading, piracy, war, and commerce had made her the richest nation in the world. Even more important, her riches had accrued not merely to a few nobles, but to a large upper-middle stratum of commercial bourgeoisie. England was thus one of the first nations to develop, albeit on a small scale, a prime requisite of an industrial economy: a "mass" consumer market. As a result, a rising pressure of demand inspired a search for new techniques.

Second, England was the scene of the most successful and thoroughgoing transformation of feudal society into commercial society. A succession of strong kings had effectively broken the power of the local nobility and had made England into a single unified state. As part of this process, we also find in England the strongest encouragement to the rising mercantile classes. Then too, as we have seen, the enclosure movement, which gained in tempo in the seventeenth and eighteenth centuries, expelled an army of laborers to man her new industrial establishments.

Third, England was the locus of a unique enthusiasm for science and engineering. The famous Royal Academy, of which Newton was an early president, was founded in 1660 and was the immediate source of much intellectual excitement. Indeed, a popular interest in gadgets, machines, and devices of all sorts soon became a mild national obsession: *Gentlemen's Magazine*, a kind of *New Yorker* of the period, announced in 1729 that it would henceforth keep its readers "abreast of every invention"— a task which the mounting flow of inventions soon rendered quite impossible. No less important was an enthusiasm of the British landed aristocracy for scientific farming: English landlords displayed an interest in matters of crop rotation and fertilizer which their French counterparts would have found quite beneath their dignity.

Then there were a host of other background causes, some as fortuitous as the immense resources of coal and iron ore on which the British sat; others as purposeful as the development of a national patent system which deliberately sought to stimulate and protect the act of invention itself. In many ways, England was "ready" for an Industrial Revolution. But perhaps what finally translated the potentiality into an actuality was the emergence of a group of new men who seized upon the latent opportunities of history as a vehicle for their own rise to fame and fortune. . . .

Pleasant or unpleasant, the personal characteristics fade beside one overriding quality. These were all men interested in expansion, in growth, in investment for investment's sake. All of them were identified with technological progress, and none of them disdained the productive process. An employee of Maudslay's once remarked, "It was a pleasure to see him handle a tool of any kind, but he was *quite splendid* with an 18-inch file." Watt was tireless in experimenting with his machines; Wedgwood stomped about his factory on his wooden leg scawling, "This won't do for Jos. Wedgwood," wherever he saw evidence of careless work. Richard Arkwright was a bundle of ceaseless energy in promoting his interests, jouncing about England over execrable roads in a post chaise driven by four horses, pursuing his correspondence as he traveled.

"With us," wrote a French visitor to a calico works in 1788, "a man rich enough to set up and run a factory like this would not care to remain in a position which he would deem unworthy of his wealth." This was an attitude entirely foreign to the rising English industrial capitalist. His work was its own dignity and reward; the wealth it brought was quite aside. Boswell, on being shown Watt and Boulton's great engine works at Soho, declared that he never forgot Boulton's expression as the latter declared, "I sell here, sir, what all the world desires to have—Power."

The new men were first and last *entrepreneurs*— enterprisers. They brought with them a new energy, as restless as it proved to be inexhaustible. In an economic, if not a political, sense, they deserve the epithet "revolutionaries," for the change they ushered in was nothing short of total, sweeping, and irreversible.

The Industrial Revolution in Russia

Peter N. Stearns

Before 1850 the industrial revolution was confined to Britain and a few limited areas in the West. Between 1850 and 1870, the coal mines, iron foundries, textile factories, steam engines, and railroads that had made Britain an industrial giant spread broadly into Western and Central Europe and North America. However, outside of these areas, no industrial revolution occurred until after the 1870s. Many historians have suggested reasons for this disparity between these areas of the West and elsewhere. In the following selection, Peter Stearns suggests reasons Russia was slow to industrialize.

CONSIDER: *What opportunities were available for industrial development in Russia; why, nevertheless, Russia did not industrialize sooner.*

Russia began to receive an industrial outreach from the West within a few decades of the advent of the industrial revolution. British textile machinery was imported beginning in 1843. Ernst Knoop, a German immigrant to Britain who had clerked in a Manchester cotton factory, set himself up as export agent to the Russians. He also

---

SOURCE: Peter N. Stearns, *The Industrial Revolution in World History* (Boulder, CO: Westview Press, 1993), pp. 72–73.

sponsored British workers who installed the machinery in Russia and told any Russian entrepreneur brash enough to ask not simply for British models but for alterations or adaptations: "That is not your affair; in England they know better than you." Despite the snobbism, a number of Russian entrepreneurs set up small factories to produce cotton, aware that even in Russia's small urban market they could make a substantial profit by underselling traditional manufactured cloth. Other factories were established directly by Britons.

Europeans and Americans were particularly active in responding to calls by the tsar's government for assistance in establishing railway and steamship lines. The first steamship appeared in Russia in 1815, and by 1820 a regular service ran on the Volga River. The first public railroad, joining St. Petersburg to the imperial residence in the suburbs, opened in 1837. In 1851 the first major line connected St. Petersburg and Moscow, along a remarkably straight route desired by Tsar Nicholas I himself. American engineers were brought in, again by the government, to set up a railroad industry so that Russians could build their own locomotives and cars. . . .

But Russia did not then industrialize. Modern industrial operations did not sufficiently dent established economic practices. The nation remained overwhelmingly agricultural. High percentage increases in manufacturing proceeded from such a low base that they had little general impact. Several structural barriers impeded a genuine industrial revolution. Russia's cities had never boasted a manufacturing tradition; there were few artisans skilled even in preindustrial methods. Only by the 1860s and 1870s had cities grown enough for an artisan core to take shape—in printing, for example—and even then large numbers of foreigners (particularly Germans) had to be imported. Even more serious was the system of serfdom that kept most Russians bound to agricultural estates. While some free laborers could be found, most rural Russians could not legally leave their land, and their obligation to devote extensive work service to their lords' estates reduced their incentive even for agricultural production. Peter the Great had managed to adapt serfdom to a preindustrial metallurgical industry by allowing landlords to sell villages and the labor therein for expansion of ironworks. But this mongrel system was not suitable for change on a grander scale, which is precisely what the industrial revolution entailed.

Furthermore, the West's industrial revolution, while it provided tangible examples for Russia to imitate, also produced pressures to develop more traditional sectors in lieu of structural change. The West's growing cities and rising prosperity claimed rising levels of Russian timber, hemp, tallow, and, increasingly, grain. These were export goods that could be produced without new technology and without altering the existing labor system. Indeed, many landlords boosted the work-service obligations of the serfs in order to generate more grain production for sale to the West. The obvious temptation was to lock in an older economy—to respond to new opportunity by incremental changes within the traditional system and to maintain serfdom and the rural preponderance rather than to risk fundamental internal transformation.

Early Industrial Society: Progress or Decline?

Peter Stearns and Herrick Chapman

One of the most persistent debates over the early stages of the Industrial Revolution is whether a higher standard of living resulted for factory workers. A number of "optimistic" historians, relying primarily on statistical evidence such as wage rates, prices, and mortality rates, have argued that even during the early period factory workers experienced a rising standard of living. A group of more "pessimistic" historians, emphasizing qualitative data such as descriptions of the psychological, social, and cultural impact of the factory on workers' lives, argues that the standard of living declined for these workers during the first half of the nineteenth century. In the following selection Peter Stearns and Herrick Chapman focus on this debate, concluding that, at least for many workers, material conditions were modestly better.

CONSIDER: *The aspects of this selection that optimistic historians would emphasize and how pessimistic historians might respond; whether increased wage rates are a meaningful measure without a consideration of the psychological and social costs of that extra money.*

The question of whether conditions deteriorated or were improved by early factory employment has been hotly debated, particularly in the case of the British industrial revolution. There is evidence on both sides. Many have tried to prove that early industry was evil; others have asserted its beneficence. Even during the Industrial Revolution itself the question was argued with much partisan feeling. The issue is not merely an academic one. In order to understand the workers themselves, it is vital to know whether they experienced a deterioration in conditions as they entered industry. That the workers were in misery from a modern point of view cannot be denied; that they were severely limited in their conditions is obvious; but whether they felt themselves to be miserable, judging by the standards they knew, is far from clear. . . .

Furthermore, in England and elsewhere, rural conditions had usually been declining before the Industrial Revolution began. This was, after all, the main impulse for peasants to accept factory jobs. Peasant standards of living were low anyway; preindustrial society was simply poor. And the people entering industry were often drawn from the lowest categories of the peasantry. These were the people who suffered most from expanding population and declining domestic industry. There was deterioration of material conditions in the early industrial period, but it occurred primarily in the countryside among the landless and the domestic producers and among the unskilled in the slums of cities like London. When they found factory employment, workers seldom could note a significant worsening of their situation: many factory workers actually gained some ground in standard of living.

The worst problem for factory workers, as for the poorer classes even in premodern times, was the instability of conditions. Sick workers were rarely paid and sometimes lost their jobs. With age workers' skill and strength declined, and so did their earnings. Old workers, lacking property to fall back on, suffered from falling wages and frequent unemployment. Machine break-downs caused days and even weeks of unemployment. Most important, recurrent industrial slumps plunged many workers into profound misery. Wages fell, sometimes by as much as 50 percent; up to a quarter of the labor force lost their jobs. Some returned to the countryside to seek work or to roam in bands to find food. Some survived on charity; the charity rolls of manufacturing cities often embraced over half the working class, though only meager support was offered. Some sold or pawned their possessions. All reduced expenses by eating potatoes instead of bread and ignoring rent payments. Old age, finally, could bring disaster. Working-class life was thus punctuated by a number of personal and general crises, creating a sense of insecurity that haunted workers even in better times.

In prosperous years the worst feature of the average worker's material standard of living was housing. Rural cottages had often been flimsy and small, befouled by animals, but city housing was sometimes worse. . . .

With poor housing and urban crowding, along with the pressures of factory work itself, many workers were in poor health. Rates of infant mortality were high, and many workers had a life expectancy at birth only half as high as that of their employers. . . .

Unquestionably factory wages were better than those of the countryside. Highly skilled male workers, many of them former artisans, were paid three to six times as much as ordinary laborers. For early mechanization did not eliminate the need for skill, though it reduced the percentage of skilled workers and changed the skills required. Hence the men who built and installed machines or puddled iron or ran the more complex spinning machines required years to learn their trade fully. But even lesser-skilled workers could command a money wage that was higher than what was available in the countryside or to the transient workers of the cities. There was little left over for purchases beyond food, housing, and clothing. A bit of tobacco or a small contribution to a mutual aid group were all that the ordinary worker could afford. However, wages tended to go up with time. They definitely rose in England after 1840. The main factory centers in France saw an increase in real wages in the 1830s and 1840s, and there was improvement in Germany in the 1840s and 1850s, in Russia in the 1890s.

So it is safe to conclude that material conditions, though bad, provided modest gains and some solace for many workers during the early industrial period as a whole. On the average, conditions were better than the new workers' traditions had led them to expect.

The Family and Industrialization in Western Europe

Michael Anderson

The tremendous growth of interest in social history over the past twenty years has stimulated scholars from other disciplines to address historical questions. A number of sociologists have applied methods from their own discipline to social aspects of nineteenth-century industrialization. In the following selection Michael Anderson, a sociologist from the University of Edinburgh, discusses the effects of industrialization on the working-class family.

CONSIDER: *The specific ways in which the process of industrialization affected working-class families; how Anderson's interpretation might support the "optimists" or the "pessimists" in their debate over the effects of the Industrial Revolution on the working class; how the effects on middle-class families might differ.*

In industrial areas, then, the close interdependence of parents and children which was so important in peasant societies gave way, and this was reflected in changes in family relationships. The early stages of industrialization, however, probably changed relationships between husbands and wives much less, though freedom from such close supervision and a more private domestic situation may have allowed rather more affection to develop between them than had been the case in preindustrial peasant families. Husband and wife were no

SOURCE: Michael Anderson, "The Family and Industrialization in Western Europe," *The Forum Series.* Reprinted by permission of Forum Press (St. Louis, MO, 1978), p. 14. Copyright © 1978 by Forum Press.

longer cooperating in the same productive task, but this had never been universal anyway. There was, however, a continued need and possibility for both husbands and wives to work as producers to keep the family above the subsistence line. In a few areas wives actually left the house to work in the factories. More usually, as women had always done, the wives of factory workers worked at home producing small items of clothing, processing some kind of food or drink, taking in the middle class's washing, or running a small shop or lodging house. The manifold needs of an industrial community were thus met in a way which contributed to working class family solidarity while allowing mothers to supervise and care (perhaps rather better than before) for small children during the lengthening period before they were able to enter the labor force themselves.

Initially, then, it was only in a few areas, especially those specializing in mining, machine-making, metal manufacturing, shipbuilding and sawmilling, that a change occurred in the economic status of women and with it in their family situation. In these areas there were not enough openings for female wage employment and, in consequence, many women were forced into the almost totally new situation of full-time housewife. However, as more and more traditional tasks were taken over by the application of factory production methods to clothing and food preparation, the home increasingly became confined to consumption. Only then did the distinction between male productive work outside the home and female consumption-oriented work inside the home become common among the working class.

Though the evidence is patchy, it seems that, at least in some areas, this had an effect on relationships between husbands and wives. Since the husband became the only income producer, the rest of the family became more dependent on him than he was on them. Whatever the husband did, the wife had little power to resist. While the family as a whole relied materially on the father, he needed them only to the extent that he could obtain from them emotional or other rewards which he could not obtain elsewhere or to the extent to which public opinion in the neighborhood was effective in controlling his behavior (And with the weakened community control of large industrial cities, neighborhood control was often weak.). Thus, in the working class, the idea that a woman's place was in the home and that her role was essentially an inferior domestic one is not of great antiquity. Rather it seems only to have developed as a response to a major shift in the power balance between husbands and wives which reflected the new employment situation of late-nineteenth- and early-twentieth-century industrial society.

✋ CHAPTER QUESTIONS

1. Do you feel that industrialization should be considered a great boon, a mixed blessing, or a disaster for nineteenth-century Europeans? Why?

2. In retrospect, what policies might governments have adopted to minimize the pains of industrialization? What factors acted against the adoption of such policies?

3. In a debate over how industrialization should be evaluated, what would the arguments of middle-class liberals be? Of industrial workers? Of women?

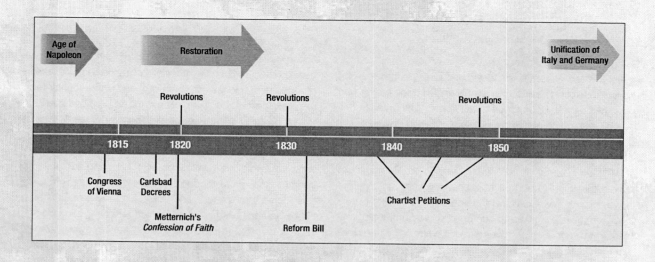

23 Reaction, Reform, Revolution, and Romanticism: 1815–1848

The European powers met at the Congress of Vienna (1814–1815) to decide how to proceed now that Napoleon had been defeated. Conservative sentiments, exemplified by the views of Prince Metternich of Austria, predominated at this congress. Although the final settlement was not punitive or humiliating to France, it did represent an effort by conservative leaders to reject changes instituted during the revolutionary and Napoleonic periods, to restore traditional groups and governments to power, and to resist liberalism and nationalism. As a result of this and other developments, the aristocracy regained some of its prominence, monarchs such as Louis XVIII (brother of Louis XVI) returned to power, and armies intervened (as in Spain and Italy) to crush threats to the status quo.

Nevertheless, movements for national liberation and liberal reform surfaced during the 1820s, 1830s, and 1840s. In the 1820s and 1830s, Greece and Belgium gained independence and less successful nationalistic movements arose in Italy and Poland. Liberalism, encompassing demands for greater freedom, constitutional government, and political rights, was particularly strong in Western Europe. In England a series of legislative acts in the 1830s and 1840s clearly recognized liberal demands. In France a revolution in 1830 brought to power groups more open to liberal ideas.

A climax came in 1848, when revolutions erupted across Europe. Although each revolution was different, in general the middle and working classes demanded changes in the name of nationalism or liberalism. At first, established governments weakened or fell, but the revolutionaries found it difficult to remain unified once power was in their hands. Soon groups standing for authoritarian rule took advantage of this disunity and regained power.

The conservatism and liberalism that characterized so many of the political developments of this period were reflected in certain artistic and literary styles. Romanticism was the most important of these, reflecting, in different ways, both conservatism and liberalism. From its beginning in the late eighteenth century, it spread until it became the dominant cultural movement of the first half of the nineteenth century. Romanticism rejected the formalism of the previously dominant Classical style, refused to be limited by Enlightenment rationalism or the stark realism of everyday life, and emphasized emotion and freedom.

The sources in this chapter focus first on conservatism: What were some of the main characteristics of conservatism? What did it stand against? What policies fit with conservative attitudes? In what ways did the Congress of Vienna reflect the conservatism of the period? The next set of documents looks at liberalism and movements for reform: What did liberalism mean in the first half of the nineteenth century? What reforms did liberals demand? What was the nature of reform movements, as exemplified by Chartism in England? Third are the revolutions of 1848: In what ways did the revolutions of 1848 bring to a head some of the main trends of the period? Who might be considered the "winners" and "losers" in these revolutions? Finally sources on the nature of Romanticism, particularly as it is revealed in literature and art are reviewed: What were some of the ties between Romanticism and conservatism? How was Romanticism related to liberal and even revolutionary ideals? What emerges from these selections is a picture of Europeans trying to deal politically and culturally with the legacy of the French Revolution and the Enlightenment.

 Primary Sources

Secret Memorandum to Tsar Alexander I, 1820: Conservative Principles

Prince Klemens von Metternich

The outstanding leader of the conservative tide that rose with the fall of Napoleon was Prince Klemens von Metternich (1773–1859). From his post as Austrian Minister of Foreign Affairs, Metternich hosted the Congress of Vienna and played a dominating role within Austria and among the conservative states of Europe between 1815 and 1848. Both in principle and in practice, he represented a conservatism that rejected the changes wrought by the French Revolution and stood against liberalism and nationalism. The following is an excerpt from a secret memorandum that Metternich sent to Tsar Alexander I of Russia in 1820, explaining his political principles. While not a sophisticated statement of political theory, it does reflect key elements of conservative attitudes and ideas.

CONSIDER: *What threats Metternich perceives; how Metternich connects "presumption" with the middle class; how this document reflects the experience of the revolutionary and Napoleonic periods; the kinds of policies that would logically flow from these attitudes.*

SOURCE: Prince Richard Metternich, ed., *Memoirs of Prince Metternich, 1815–1829*, vol. III, trans. Mrs. Alexander Napier (New York: Charles Scribner's Sons, 1881), pp. 454–455, 458–460, 468–469.

"L'Europe," *a celebrated writer has recently said,* "fait aujourd'hui pitié à l'homme d'esprit et horreur à l'homme vertueux."[1]

It would be difficult to comprise in a few words a more exact picture of the situation at the time we are writing these lines!

Kings have to calculate the chances of their very existence in the immediate future; passions are let loose, and league together to overthrow everything which society respects as the basis of its existence; religion, public morality, laws, customs, rights, and duties, all are attacked, confounded, overthrown, or called in question. The great mass of the people are tranquil spectators of these attacks and revolutions, and of the absolute want of all means of defense. A few are carried off by the torrent, but the wishes of the immense majority are to maintain a repose which exists no longer, and of which even the first elements seem to be lost. . . .

Having now thrown a rapid glance over the first causes of the present state of society, it is necessary to point out in a more particular manner the evil which threatens to deprive it, at one blow, of the real blessings, the fruits of genuine civilisation, and to disturb it in the midst of its enjoyments. This evil may be described in one word—presumption; the natural effect of the rapid

---

[1] Europe . . . is pitied by men of spirit and abhorred by men of virtue.

progression of the human mind towards the perfecting of so many things. This it is which at the present day leads so many individuals astray, for it has become an almost universal sentiment.

Religion, morality, legislation, economy, politics, administration, all have become common and accessible to everyone. Knowledge seems to come by inspiration; experience has no value for the presumptuous man; faith is nothing to him; he substitutes for it a pretended individual conviction, and to arrive at this conviction dispenses with all inquiry and with all study; for these means appear too trivial to a mind which believes itself strong enough to embrace at one glance all questions and all facts. Laws have no value for him, because he has not contributed to make them, and it would be beneath a man of his parts to recognise the limits traced by rude and ignorant generations. Power resides in himself; why should he submit himself to that which was only useful for the man deprived of light and knowledge? That which, according to him, was required in an age of weakness cannot be suitable in an age of reason and vigour amounting to universal perfection, which the German innovators designate by the idea, absurd in itself, of the Emancipation of the People! Morality itself he does not attack openly, for without it he could not be sure for a single instant of his own existence; but he interprets its essence after his own fashion, and allows every other person to do so likewise, provided that other person neither kills nor robs him.

In thus tracing the character of the presumptuous man, we believe we have traced that of the society of the day, composed of like elements, if the denomination of society is applicable to an order of things which only tends in principle towards individualising all the elements of which society is composed. Presumption makes every man the guide of his own belief, the arbiter of laws according to which he is pleased to govern himself, or to allow some one else to govern him and his neighbours; it makes him, in short, the sole judge of his own faith, his own actions, and the principles according to which he guides them. . . .

The Governments, having lost their balance, are frightened, intimidated, and thrown into confusion by the cries of the intermediary class of society, which, placed between the Kings and their subjects, breaks the sceptre of the monarch, and usurps the cry of the people—the class so often disowned by the people, and nevertheless too much listened to, caressed and feared by those who could with one word reduce it again to nothingness.

We see this intermediary class abandon itself with a blind fury and animosity which proves much more its own fears than any confidence in the success of its enterprises, to all the means which seem proper to assuage its thirst for power, applying itself to the task of persuading Kings that their rights are confined to sitting upon a throne, while those of the people are to govern, and to attack all that centuries have bequeathed as holy and worthy of man's respect—denying, in fact, the value of the past, and declaring themselves the masters of the future. We see this class take all sorts of disguises, uniting and subdividing as occasion offers, helping each other in the hour of danger, and the next day depriving each other of all their conquests. It takes possession of the press, and employs it to promote impiety, disobedience to the laws of religion and the State, and goes so far as to preach murder as a duty for those who desire what is good.

The Carlsbad Decrees, 1819: Conservative Repression

One way political leaders tried to assert conservatism against any perceived threats such as liberalism or nationalism was through international cooperation and action, a policy known as the Concert of Europe. Another way was through taking internal measures against the same threats, such as occurred in Germany in 1819 with the issuance of the Carlsbad Decrees. These decrees were pushed through the Diet of the German Confederation by Austria and Prussia, but particularly by Prince Metternich, in reaction to nationalist student movements against the principles of the Congress of Vienna. The following excerpts from those decrees concern the universities, the press, and all "revolutionary plots."

CONSIDER: *The purposes of these decrees and the means used to effect these purposes; whether these decrees are consistent with attitudes expressed by Metternich in the "confession of faith" he makes in his secret memorandum to Tsar Alexander I; the consequences of the effective enforcement of these decrees.*

PROVISIONAL DECREE RELATING TO THE UNIVERSITIES, UNANIMOUSLY ADOPTED SEPTEMBER 20, 1819

§2. The confederated governments mutually pledge themselves to remove from the universities or other public educational institutions all teachers who, by obvious deviation from their duty or by exceeding the limits of their functions, or by the abuse of their legitimate influence over the youthful minds, or by propagating harmful doctrines hostile to public order or subversive of existing

SOURCE: From James Harvey Robinson, ed., "The Reaction after 1815 and European Policy of Metternich," in *Translations and Reprints from the Original Sources of European History*, vol. I, no. 3, ed. Department of History of the University of Pennsylvania (Philadelphia: University of Pennsylvania Press, 1898), pp. 16–20.

governmental institutions, shall have unmistakably proved their unfitness for the important office intrusted to them. . . .

§3. Those laws which have for a long period been directed against secret and unauthorized societies in the universities, shall be strictly enforced. These laws apply especially to that association established some years since under the name Universal Students' Union (*Allgemeine Burschenschaft*), since the very conception of the society implies the utterly unallowable plan of permanent fellowship and constant communication between the various universities. The duty of especial watchfulness in this matter should be impressed upon the special agents of the government.

✍

PRESS LAWS FOR FIVE YEARS

§1. So long as this decree shall remain in force no publication which appears in the form of daily issues or as a serial not exceeding twenty sheets of printed matter shall go to press in any state of the Union without the previous knowledge and approval of the state officials.

✍

§6. . . . The Diet shall have the right, moreover, to suppress on its own authority, without being petitioned, such writings included in Section 1, in whatever German state they may appear, as in the opinion of a commission appointed by it, are inimical to the honor of the Union, the safety of individual states or the maintenance of peace and quiet in Germany. There shall be no appeal from such decisions and the governments involved are bound to see that they are put into execution.

✍

ESTABLISHMENT OF AN INVESTIGATING COMMITTEE AT MAINZ

ARTICLE I. Within a fortnight, reckoned from the passage of this decree, there shall convene, under the auspices of the Confederation, in the city and federal fortress of Mainz, an Extraordinary Commission of Investigation to consist of seven members including the chairman.

ARTICLE II. The object of the Commission shall be a joint investigation, as thorough and extensive as possible, of the facts relating to the origin and manifold ramifications of the revolutionary plots and demagogical associations directed against the existing Constitutional and internal peace both of the Union and of the individual states: of the existence of which plots more or less clear evidence is to be had already, or may be produced in the course of the investigation.

English Liberalism

Jeremy Bentham

The roots of liberalism are deep and varied, stretching back to the writings of John Locke in the seventeenth century and further. By the time liberalism started to flourish during the nineteenth century, it had a particularly strong English tradition. Perhaps the most influential of the early-nineteenth-century English liberals was Jeremy Bentham (1748–1832). He is best known as the author of the theory of utilitarianism and for advocating reform of many English institutions. The ideas and efforts of Bentham and his followers, who include James Mill and John Stuart Mill, formed one of the mainstreams of English liberalism and liberal reform in the nineteenth century. The first of the following two selections comes from Bentham's An Introduction to the Principles of Morals and Legislation *(1789) and focuses on the principle of utility. The second is from his* Manual of Political Economy *(1798) and indicates his views toward governmental economic policy.*

CONSIDER: *What exactly Bentham means by the principle of utility; what, according to the principle of utility, the proper role of government in general is; his explanation for the proper role of the government in economic affairs.*

I. Nature has placed mankind under the governance of two sovereign masters, *pain* and *pleasure*. It is for them alone to point out what we ought to do, as well as to determine what we shall do. On the one hand the standard of right and wrong, on the other chains of causes and effects, are fastened to their throne. They govern us in all we do, in all we say, in all we think: every effort we can make to throw off our subjection, will serve to demonstrate and confirm it. In words a man may pretend to abjure their empire: but in reality he will remain subject to it all the while. The *principle of utility* recognizes this subjection, and assumes it for the foundation of that system, the object of which is to rear the fabric of felicity by the hands of reason and of law. Systems which attempt to question it, deal in sounds instead of sense, in caprice instead of reason, in darkness instead of light.

But enough of metaphor and declamation: it is not by such means that moral science is to be improved.

II. The principle of utility is the foundation of the present work: it will be proper therefore at the outset to give an explicit and determinate account of what is meant by it. By the principle of utility is meant that principle which approves or disapproves of every action whatsoever, according to the tendency which it appears

SOURCES: Jeremy Bentham, *An Introduction to the Principles of Morals and Legislation* (Oxford: Clarendon Press, 1876), pp. 1–3; John Bowring, ed., *Bentham's Works,* vol. III (Edinburgh: William Tait, 1843), pp. 33–35.

to have to augment or diminish the happiness of the party whose interest is in question: or, what is the same thing in other words, to promote or to oppose that happiness. I say of every action whatsoever; and therefore not only of every action of a private individual, but of every measure of government.

III. By utility is meant that property in any object, whereby it tends to produce benefit, advantage, pleasure, good, or happiness (all this in the present case comes to the same thing) or (what comes again to the same thing) to prevent the happening of mischief, pain, evil, or unhappiness to the party whose interest is considered: if that party be the community in general, then the happiness of the community: if a particular individual, then the happiness of that individual.

IV. The interest of the community is one of the most general expressions that can occur in the phraseology of morals: no wonder that the meaning of it is often lost. When it has a meaning, it is this. The community is a fictitious *body,* composed of the individual persons who are considered as constituting as it were its *members.* The interest of the community then is, what?—the sum of the interests of the several members who compose it.

V. It is in vain to talk of the interest of the community, without understanding what is the interest of the individual. A thing is said to promote the interest, or to be *for* the interest, of an individual, when it tends to add to the sum total of his pleasures: or, what comes to the same thing, to diminish the sum total of his pains.

VI. An action then may be said to be conformable to the principle of utility, or, for shortness sake, to utility (meaning with respect to the community at large) when the tendency it has to augment the happiness of the community is greater than any it has to diminish it.

VII. A measure of government (which is but a particular kind of action, performed by a particular person or persons) may be said to be conformable to or dictated by the principle of utility, when in like manner the tendency which it has to augment the happiness of the community is greater than any which it has to diminish it. . . .

❧

The practical questions, therefore, are how far the end in view is best promoted by individuals acting for themselves? and in what cases these ends may be promoted by the hands of government?

With the view of causing an increase to take place in the mass of national wealth, or with a view to increase of the means either of subsistence or enjoyment, without some special reason, the general rule is, that nothing ought to be done or attempted by government. The motto, or watchword of government, on these occasions, ought to be—*Be quiet.*

For this quietism there are two main reasons:

1. Generally speaking, any interference for this purpose on the part of government is needless. The wealth of the whole community is composed of the wealth of the several individuals belonging to it taken together. But to increase his particular portion is, generally speaking, among the constant objects of each individual's exertions and care. Generally speaking, there is no one who knows what is for your interest so well as yourself—no one who is disposed with so much ardour and constancy to pursue it.

2. Generally speaking, it is moreover likely to be pernicious, viz. by being unconducive, or even obstructive, with reference to the attainment of the end in view. Each individual bestowing more time and attention upon the means of preserving and increasing his portion of wealth, than is or can be bestowed by government, is likely to take a more effectual course than what, in his instance and on his behalf, would be taken by government.

It is, moreover, universally and constantly pernicious in another way, by the restraint or constraint imposed on the free agency of the individual. . . .

. . . With few exceptions, and those not very considerable ones, the attainment of the maximum of enjoyment will be most effectually secured by leaving each individual to pursue his own maximum of enjoyment, in proportion as he is in possession of the means. Inclination in this respect will not be wanting on the part of any one. Power, the species of power applicable to this case—viz. wealth, pecuniary power—could not be given by the hand of government to one, without being taken from another; so that by such interference there would not be any gain of power upon the whole.

The gain to be produced in this article by the interposition of government, respects principally the head of knowledge. There are cases in which, for the benefit of the public at large, it may be in the power of government to cause this or that portion of knowledge to be produced and diffused, which, without the demand for it produced by government, would either not have been produced, or would not have been diffused.

We have seen above the grounds on which the general rule in this behalf—*Be quiet*—rests. Whatever measures, therefore, cannot be justified as exceptions to that rule, may be considered as *non agenda* on the part of government. The art, therefore, is reduced within a small compass: *security* and *freedom* are all that industry requires. The request which agriculture, manufactures and commerce present to governments, is modest and reasonable as that which Diogenes made to Alexander: *"Stand out of my sunshine."* We have no need of favour—we require only a secure and open path.

Liberalism: Progress and Optimism

The Economist, 1851

Liberals usually believed in progress and were optimistic about their own times and the future. By mid-century, liberalism was most widespread in England, Europe's dominant economic power. English liberals living in the mid-nineteenth century were therefore particularly confident and proud, as indicated by the following excerpts from two 1851 articles published in The Economist. This journal appealed to England's prosperous middle class.

CONSIDER: *What liberals considered the great improvements of the first half of the nineteenth century; who benefited most from these changes; how conservatives or socialists might respond.*

Economists are supposed to be, by nature and occupation, cold, arithmetical, and unenthusiastic. We shall not, we hope, do discredit to this chapter when we say that we consider it a happiness and a privilege to have had our lot cast in the first fifty years of this century. . . .

It has witnessed a leap forward in all the elements of material well-being such as neither scientific vision nor poetic fancy ever pictured. It is not too much to say that, in wealth, in the arts of life, in the discoveries of science and their application to the comfort, the health, the safety, and the capabilities of man, in public and private morality, in the diffusion if not in the advancement of knowledge, in the sense of social charity and justice, in religious freedom, and in political wisdom,—the period of the last fifty years has carried us forward faster and further than any other half-century in modern times . . . in many of the particulars we have enumerated, it has witnessed a more rapid and astonishing progress than *all* the centuries which have preceded it. In several vital points the difference between the 18th and the 19th century, is greater than between the first and the 18th, as far as civilised Europe is concerned.

❧

When we refer to a few only of the extraordinary improvements of the half century just elapsed—such as the 35 years' peace, so far as morals are concerned; such as the philanthropic and just conviction that the welfare of the multitude, not of one or two classes, is the proper object of social solicitude; the humane direction which the mind has received towards the abolition of slavery; the amelioration of all penal systems, and the doubts that have been generated of their utility; the advances in religious toleration, and in forbearing one with another: and such as the application of steam to locomotives on water and land, and the consequent vast extension of communication all over the world, so far as physics are concerned;—such as the invention and general introduction of gas; the use of railroads and electric telegraphs; the extended application of machinery to all the arts of life, almost putting an end to very severe injurious bodily toil, except in agriculture, in which, though the labourers are speedily doubled up with rheumatism, and become, from poverty and excessive labour in all kinds of weather, prematurely old, great improvements have nevertheless been made:—when we refer to a few events of this kind, we become convinced that the half century just elapsed is more full of wonders than any other on record.

SOURCE: *The Economist* (London), vol. IX, January 4, 1851, p. 5; January 18, 1851, p. 57.

The First Chartist Petition: Demands for Change in England

Movements for reform occurred throughout Europe between 1815 and 1848 despite the efforts of conservatives to quash them. Eventually almost all countries in Europe experienced the revolutions conservatives feared so much. One exception was England, but even there political movements threatened to turn into violent revolts against the failure of the government to change. The most important of these was the Chartist movement, made up primarily of members of the working class who wanted reforms for themselves. The following is an excerpt from the first charter presented to the House of Commons in 1838. Subsequent charters were presented in 1842 and 1848. In each case the potential existed for a mass movement to turn into a violent revolt, and in each case Parliament rejected the Chartist demands. Only later in the century were most of these demands met.

CONSIDER: *The nature of the Chartists' demands; by what means the Chartists hoped to achieve their ends; how Metternich might analyze these demands.*

Required, as we are universally, to support and obey the laws, nature and reason entitle us to demand that in the making of the laws the universal voice shall be implicitly listened to. We perform the duties of freemen; we must have the privileges of freemen. Therefore, we demand universal suffrage. The suffrage, to be exempt from the corruption of the wealthy and the violence of the powerful, must be secret. The assertion of our right necessarily involves the power of our uncontrolled exercise. We ask for the reality of a good, not for its

SOURCE: From R. G. Gammage, *History of the Chartist Movement,* 2nd ed. (Newcastle-on-Tyne, England: Browne and Browne, 1894), pp. 88–90.

semblance, therefore we demand the ballot. The connection between the representatives and the people, to be beneficial, must be intimate. The legislative and constituent powers, for correction and for instruction, ought to be brought into frequent contact. Errors which are comparatively light, when susceptible of a speedy popular remedy, may produce the most disastrous effects when permitted to grow inveterate through years of compulsory endurance. To public safety, as well as public confidence, frequent elections are essential. Therefore, we demand annual parliaments. With power to choose, and freedom in choosing, the range of our choice must be unrestricted. We are compelled, by the existing laws, to take for our representatives men who are incapable of appreciating our difficulties, or have little sympathy with them; merchants who have retired from trade and no longer feel its harrassings; proprietors of land who are alike ignorant of its evils and its cure; lawyers by whom the notoriety of the senate is courted only as a means of obtaining notice in the courts. The labours of a representative who is sedulous in the discharge of his duty are numerous and burdensome. It is neither just, nor reasonable, nor safe, that they should continue to be gratuitously rendered. We demand that in the future election of members of your honourable house, the approbation of the constituency shall be the sole qualification, and that to every representative so chosen, shall be assigned out of the public taxes, a fair and adequate remunerative for the time which he is called upon to devote to the public service. The management of his mighty kingdom has hitherto been a subject for contending factions to try their selfish experiments upon. We have felt the consequences in our sorrowful experience. Short glimmerings of uncertain enjoyment, swallowed up by long and dark seasons of suffering. If the self-government of the people should not remove their distresses, it will, at least, remove their repinings. Universal suffrage will, and it alone can, bring true and lasting peace to the nation; we firmly believe that it will also bring prosperity. May it therefore please your honourable house, to take this our petition into your most serious consideration, and to use your utmost endeavours, by all constitutional means, to have a law passed, granting to every male of lawful age, sane mind, and unconvicted of crime, the right of voting for members of parliament, and directing all future elections of members of parliament to be in the way of secret ballot, and ordaining that the duration of parliament, so chosen, shall in no case exceed one year, and abolishing all property qualifications in the members, and providing for their due remuneration while in attendance on their parliamentary duties.

"And your petitioners shall ever pray."

An Eyewitness Account of the Revolutions of 1848 in Germany
Annual Register, 1848

In 1848 revolutions broke out throughout Europe. The February Revolution in France seemed to act as a spark for revolutions elsewhere, particularly in the German states. Indeed, within a few days of the outbreak in France, the established governments of the German states were faced with demands for change, demonstrations, and revolutions. The following is an account by an eyewitness of some of the events in Germany during March 1848, as reported in the London Annual Register.

CONSIDER: *Whether this indicates any pattern to the revolutionary activities; the nature of the demands for change; how the established governments reacted.*

In order to give a clear and distinct narrative of the complicated events which have taken place during the present year in Germany, we have had to consider carefully the question of arrangement; for, independently of the revolutionary movements in the separate kingdoms, there has been a long-sustained attempt to construct a new German nationality on the basis of a Confederation of all the states, with one great Parliament or Diet, and a Central Executive at Frankfort. . . .

It was in the southwestern states of Germany that the effects of the French Revolution began first to manifest themselves. On the 29th of February the Grand Duke of Baden received a deputation from his subjects who demanded liberty of the press, the establishment of a national guard, and trial by jury. They succeeded in their object, and M. Welcker, who had distinguished himself as a Liberal leader, was appointed one of the ministers.

On the 3d of March, the Rhenish provinces, headed by Cologne, followed the same example. On the 4th similar demonstrations took place at Wiesbaden and Frankfort, and on the 5th at Düsseldorf. At Cologne, on the 3d of March, the populace asembled in crowds before the Stadthaus, or town hall, where the town council were sitting, and demanded the concession of certain rights, which were inscribed on slips of paper and handed about amongst the mob. They were as follows: (1) Universal suffrage; all legislation and government to proceed from the people. (2) Liberty of the press and freedom of speech. (3) Abolition of the standing army and the armament of the people, who are to elect their own officers. (4) Full rights of public

SOURCE: Louis L. Snyder, ed., *Documents of German History* (New Brunswick, NJ: Rutgers University Press, 1958), pp. 174–175.

meeting. (5) Protection to labor, and a guarantee for the supply of all necessaries. (6) State education for all children.

The military were, however, called out, and the streets were cleared without much difficulty.

At Wiesbaden, in Nassau, a large concourse of people met opposite the palace on the 4th, and demanded a general arming of the people under their own elective leaders; entire liberty of the press; a German Parliament; right of public meeting; public and oral trial by jury; the control of the duchy domain; convocation of the second chamber to frame a new electoral law on the basis of population, and to remove all restrictions on religious liberty. The Duke was absent at Berlin, but the Duchess, from the balcony of the palace, assured the people that their demands would be fully conceded by the Duke, her stepson. Subsequently appeared a proclamation in which the Duchess *guaranteed* the concession of these demands; and on the same day, in the afternoon, the Duke returned, and, immediately addressing the people, he ratified all the concessions made by the Duchess and his ministers.

The Tables Turned: The Glories of Nature

William Wordsworth

Romantic themes were reflected in poetry as much as in other cultural forms. The British poet William Wordsworth (1770–1850) focused early on romantic themes in his work. He emphasized the connection between the individual and the glories of nature. Wordsworth gained much recognition in his own lifetime and was eventually appointed Poet Laureate of England. The following poem, "The Tables Turned," was first published in 1798.

SOURCE: Edward Dowden, ed., *The Poetical Works of William Wordsworth*, vol. IV (London: George Bell and Sons, 1893), pp. 198–199.

CONSIDER: *How this poem might be viewed as a rejection of the Enlightenment; the ways in which this poem relates to themes stressed by Châteaubriand in an excerpt later in this chapter.*

Up! up! my Friend, and quit your books;
Or surely you'll grow double:

Up! up! my Friend, and clear your looks;
Why all this toil and trouble?

The sun, above the mountain's head,
A freshening lustre mellow
Through all the long green fields has spread,
His first sweet evening yellow.

Books! 'tis a dull and endless strife:
Come, hear the woodland linnet,
How sweet his music! on my life,
There's more of wisdom in it.

And hark! how blithe the throstle sings!
He, too, is no mean preacher:
Come forth into the light of things,
Let Nature be your Teacher.

She has a world of ready wealth,
Our minds and hearts to bless—
Spontaneous wisdom breathed by health,
Truth breathed by cheerfulness.

One impulse from a vernal wood
May teach you more of man,
Of moral evil and of good,
Than all the sages can.

Sweet is the lore which Nature brings;
Our meddling intellect
Mis-shapes the beauteous forms of things:—
We murder to dissect.

Enough of Science and of Art;
Close up those barren leaves;
Come forth, and bring with you a heart
That watches and receives.

Visual Sources

Abbey Graveyard in the Snow

Caspar David Friedrich

Abbey Graveyard in the Snow (*figure 23.1*) *was painted by the well-known North German artist Caspar David Friedrich in 1819. In the center are the ruins of a Gothic choir of a monastic church surrounded by a snow-covered graveyard*

and leafless winter forest. To the left a procession of monks follows a coffin into the ruins.

This painting exemplifies many elements typical of Romanticism, particularly German Romanticism. The scene, while visually accurate, goes beyond realism: The light is too perfectly placed, the church remains are too majestic, the surrounding forest is too symmetrical a frame, and the funeral procession is out of place (funerals did not take place in ruins). By implication, this painting rejects the limits of Enlightenment rationalism and the reality of nineteenth-century urban life. Instead, a Romantic version of the Middle Ages, the spirituality of nature, and the glories of Christianity are evoked. The Romantic longing to be overwhelmed by eternal nature is suggested, particularly by the rendering of small human figures in a large landscape. Romanticism typically exalted the emotional over the rational, even if it was a melancholy sensitivity that was being displayed.

CONSIDER: *The ways in which the Romanticism of this painting is consistent with that of Wordsworth's poetry, and with Châteaubriand's description of a Gothic cathedral, which follows.*

FIGURE 23.1 (Bildarchiv Preussischer Kulturbesitz /Art Resource, NY)

The Genius of Christianity

René de Châteaubriand

The Romantic movement of the late eighteenth century and first half of the nineteenth century was in part a rebellion against new trends such as rationalism, urbanization, and secularism. Many historians have noted specific connections between Romanticism and conservatism, particularly in the longing for a less complex life, the respect for traditional religion, and the sense of unity between rural life and human institutions. This is illustrated in the following selection from The Genius of Christianity *by René de Châteaubriand (1768–1848), a conservative French politician and writer. Published in 1802, it gained considerable popularity and helped Châteaubriand achieve a leading position among French conservatives. Here Châteaubriand describes the Gothic churches of the Middle Ages.*

CONSIDER: *Why this description might appeal to members of the aristocracy and the Catholic Church; by implication, the aspects of Châteaubriand's own times that he was attacking; how this complements Friedrich's painting.*

You could not enter a Gothic church without feeling a kind of awe and a vague sentiment of the Divinity. You were all at once carried back to those times when a

SOURCE: Viscount de Châteaubriand, *The Genius of Christianity,* trans. Charles I. White (Baltimore, MD: John Murphy, 1856), pp. 385–387.

fraternity of cenobites, after having meditated in the woods of their monasteries, met to prostrate themselves before the altar and to chant the praises of the Lord, amid the tranquillity and the silence of night. Ancient France seemed to revive altogether; you beheld all those singular costumes, all that nation so different from what it is at present; you were reminded of its revolutions, its productions, and its arts. The more remote were these times the more magical they appeared, the more they inspired ideas which always end with a reflection on the nothingness of man and the rapidity of life. . . .

The forests of Gaul were, in their turn, introduced into the temples of our ancestors, and those celebrated woods of oaks thus maintained their sacred character. Those ceilings sculptured into foliage of different kinds, those buttresses which prop the walls and terminate abruptly like the broken trunks of trees, the coolness of the vaults, the darkness of the sanctuary, the dim twilight of the aisles, the secret passages, the low doorways,—in a word, every thing in a Gothic church reminds you of the labyrinths of a wood; every thing excites a feeling of religious awe, of mystery, and of the Divinity.

The two lofty towers erected at the entrance of the edifice overtop the elms and yew-trees of the church-yard, and produce the most picturesque effect on the azure of heaven. Sometimes their twin heads are illumined by the first rays of dawn; at others they appear crowned with a capital of clouds or magnified in a foggy atmosphere. The birds themselves seem to make a mistake in regard to them, and to take them for the trees of the forest; they hover over their summits, and perch upon their pinnacles. But, lo! confused noises suddenly issue from the top of these towers and scare away the affrighted birds. The Christian architect, not content with building forests, has been desirous to retain their murmurs; and, by means of the organ and of bells, he has attached to the Gothic temple the very winds and thunders that roar in the recesses of the woods. Past ages, conjured up by these religious sounds, raise their venerable voices from the bosom of the stones, and are heard in every corner of the ancient Sibyl; loud-tongued bells swing over your head, while the vaults of death under your feet are profoundly silent.

Liberty Leading the People: Romanticism and Liberalism

Eugène Delacroix

A number of historical themes of the first half of the nineteenth century are combined in Liberty Leading the People *(1830) by the French painter Eugène Delacroix (figure 23.2).*

The painting shows an important event of the revolution of 1830 in Paris—revolutionaries fighting off government troops at a bridge in the center of the city. The revolutionaries are led by a feminine figure symbolizing liberty and carrying a Republican flag in one hand, a gun in the other. She is followed by people of all classes and ages.

In both style and content this painting reveals some of the connections between liberalism and Romanticism. The scene represents the high moral purposes of the revolution: the people struggling for the ideals of liberalism and nationalism. Despite the turmoil of the event, the people's faces convey a calm, firm assurance of the rightness and the outcome of their liberal cause. At the same time, the style of the painting is in the Romantic tradition, above all in its emphasis on heroism and the attainment of ideal goals—here liberal goals—beyond the normal expectations of life.

CONSIDER: *The ways in which this painting represents what Metternich and the Congress of Vienna struggled against.*

FIGURE 23.2 (© Erich Lessing/Art Resource, NY)

Working Class Disappointments: Rue Transnonain, April 15, 1834

Honoré Daumier

The 1830 revolutions may have brought victories to the middle class in some countries, but the working class was soon disappointed. In the years after 1830, the new regime in France not only did little to ease conditions for workers but actually passed legislation restricting their rights to organize. In 1834, outraged by the institution of the repressive Law on Associations (which would ban all unauthorized associations with more than 20 members in the name of order) and suffering from brutal labor conditions (silk weavers usually worked 16 to 20 hours a day), a workers' insurrection erupted in Lyon. After four days of bloodshed that left hundreds dead, government troops put down the uprising. A smaller insurrection also broke out in Paris, where armed insurgents began building barricades on the streets. This too was put down by government troops.

In this 1834 lithograph (figure 23.3), Honoré Daumier (1808–1879), a republican critic of the government and illustrator for two political periodicals, depicted the aftermath of this action, focusing on an event at 12 rue Transnonain in a working-class neighborhood of Paris. There, government troops believed they were being fired upon from an apartment house window. On the night of April 14–15, they stormed up the stairs to the apartment complex and shot, stabbed, and clubbed to death eight innocent men, a woman, and a child. Daumier shows the dead victims strewn in a bedroom. In the center, next to an overturned chair and propped up on the bed, lies a father whose body is riddled with wounds. Beneath him is his infant, his bashed-in bleeding skull showing from under the nightshirt. On the right is the dead grandfather and in the darkened left is the body of the mother. On the floor are the bloody footprints of the murderers. French officials quickly confiscated all the copies of this print they could find.

CONSIDER: What this reveals about the policies of even the more "liberal" governments that came to power during the 1830 revolutions; why governmental officials tried to confiscate all copies of this print.

FIGURE 23.3 (Rue Transnonian, *15 avril 1834*, Rosenwald Collection, Image © 2006 Board of Trustees, National Gallery of Art, Washington, DC)

Secondary Sources

The Congress of Vienna

Hajo Holborn

Hindsight allows historians to evaluate diplomatic events with a sharply critical eye. Often great settlements between nations have been criticized for not taking into account the historical forces that would soon undo the stability that the peace treaties were supposed to establish. Although this critical view applies to the Congress of Vienna, there are historians who see it as relatively successful, particularly in comparison with the settlement after World War I. One of these historians is Hajo Holborn of Yale University. In the following selection Holborn evaluates the Congress of Vienna from the point of view of what was realistic for the parties at that time.

CONSIDER: *Why Holborn feels that the Congress of Vienna produced a constructive peace treaty; how other historians might criticize this view.*

The Vienna settlement created a European political system whose foundations lasted for a full century. For a hundred years there occurred no wars of world-wide scope like those of the twenty-odd years after 1792. Europe experienced frightful wars, particularly between 1854 and 1878, but none of them was a war in which all the European states or even all the great European powers participated. The European wars of the nineteenth century produced shifts of power, but they were shifts within the European political system and did not upset that system as such.

The peace settlement of Vienna has more often been condemned than praised. The accusation most frequently levelled against the Congress of Vienna has been that it lacked foresight in appraising the forces of modern nationalism and liberalism. Foresight is, indeed, one of the main qualities that distinguishes the statesman from the mere political professional. But even a statesman can only build with the bricks at hand and cannot hope to construct the second floor before he has modelled the first by which to shelter his own generation. His foresight of future developments can often express itself only by cautious attempts at keeping the way open for an evolution of the new forces.

It is questionable how successful the Congress of Vienna was in this respect. None of the Congress representatives was a statesman or political thinker of the first historic rank. All of them were strong partisans of conservatism or

outright reaction, and they found the rectitude of their convictions confirmed by the victory of the old powers over the revolutionary usurper. Still, they did not make a reactionary peace. They recognized that France could not live without a constitutional charter, and they knew, too, that the Holy Roman Empire was beyond resurrection. The new German Confederation represented a great improvement of the political conditions of Germany if one remembers that in Germany as well as in Italy the national movements were not strong enough to serve as pillars of a new order. In eastern Europe, furthermore, the modern ideas of nationality had hardly found more than a small academic and literary audience. A peace treaty cannot create new historical forces; it can only place the existing ones in a relationship most conducive to the maintenance of mutual confidence and least likely to lead to future conflict. The rest must be left to the ever continuing and never finished daily work of the statesmen.

In this light the Vienna settlement was a constructive peace treaty.

Western Liberalism

E. K. Bramsted and K. J. Melhuish

Although liberalism varied throughout Europe in accordance with the circumstances facing each country, there were broad similarities among the various liberal ideas and demands during the first half of the nineteenth century. In the following selection E. K. Bramsted and K. J. Melhuish summarize the common elements of liberal doctrine and attitudes in Europe.

CONSIDER: *How these doctrines and attitudes differ from conservatism; why liberalism would be more appealing to the middle class than to the aristocracy or the working class.*

In spite of the variations in the three main strands of liberalism, the features which classic liberals from Locke to John Stuart Mill had in common should not be overlooked. Rooted largely in the outlook of Enlightenment there was a constant emphasis on man's fundamental rationality and reasonableness. Privileges of the ruling strata based on mere tradition and custom were questioned and often rejected. Everywhere we encounter a strong urge to expand the rights of the individual and to reduce the powers of the State and of the government. However widely their arguments differed, liberal thinkers of the period . . . argued mainly in favour of the rights and the social usefulness of the individual citizen and stressed the need for parliamentary control of the powers of the government and of the accountability of its civil servants. Throughout, liberalism presumed a pluralism of existing political and religious opinions; everywhere it tended to make a plea for the rights of minorities, rights which should be protected. Civil disabilities on account of religious or political dissent were to be abolished, provided the dissenters kept their activities within the rule of the law. The right to own property and the obligation of the government to safeguard it were essential features of the liberal ideology. It was not accidental that most liberals insisted on property qualifications to be attached to the right to vote. . . .

While by no means all liberals shared Guizot's famous slogan *"Enrichissez vous!,"*[2] people without property were not much respected by most of them, but were regarded as the concern of charity, if not of socialists and anarchists. Instead liberals busied themselves with the belief in a rational political order, based on a constitution and promoted by a government with limited powers. Ministers were to be responsible to Parliament.

The belief in progress, in an advancing civilization, was another characteristic of most liberal thought. . . . The continuous improvement of mankind, helped by the advance of science and the new self-confidence of the diligent middle classes, was never seriously doubted.

The European Revolutions, 1848–1851

Jonathan Sperber

The revolutions of 1848 have been at the center of historical debate for a long time. To some, 1848 represents the end of the system set up by the Congress of Vienna; to others, it represents the great battle between the forces of liberalism and conservatism; and to still others, it represents the point at which liberalism, nationalism, socialism, and Romanticism met. Perhaps the most persistent historiographical tradition views 1848 as a point at which history made a "wrong" turn. Aspects of this historical debate are summarized in the following selection by Jonathan Sperber.

CONSIDER: *The differences between the three major interpretative traditions concerning the revolutions of 1848; which of these interpretations makes the most sense to you.*

---

[2]Make yourself wealthy.

SOURCE: Jonathan Sperber, *The European Revolutions, 1848–1851.* Cambridge: Cambridge University Press, 1994, pp. 1–2.

The European revolutions of 1848 have not always received the kindest of treatment at the hands of historians. Gentle mockery, open sarcasm and hostile contempt have frequently set the tone for narrative and evaluation. More favorable treatments of the period have not been much of an improvement, since their poetic interpretations have subtly downgraded the revolutions as serious political movements, not to be compared to the real business of 1789 and 1917. We might point to three major interpretative traditions.

One is characterized by its description of 1848 as the "romantic revolution." Historians writing along these lines apostrophize the barricade fighting born from a combination of youthful enthusiasm and romantic poetry; they evoke a revolution reaching its climax in the brief euphoria of liberation in March 1848, the "springtime of the peoples" as the contemporary German phrase described it. In this version, attention is often focused on the romantically heroic deeds of individual great figures: Lajos Kossuth travelling from village to village in the Hungarian plain, to rally the peasants against the invading Habsburg armies; Giuseppe Garibaldi leading the improvised armies of the Roman Republic against the French expeditionary force; Daniele Manin single handedly rallying the Venetians to fight the Austrians against terrible odds. It was all great and glorious, but primarily in gesture and pathos—whether it really accomplished anything is quite another matter.

Rather darker is another version of the 1848 revolutions, that views them primarily as farce, a revolution made by revolutionaries who were at best incompetent dilettantes, at worst cowards and blowhards who stole away from the scene when the going got rough. This version features the story of the Parisian revolutionary observing from his window a demonstrating crowd go by, springing up from his chair, and rushing out, proclaiming, "I am their leader; I must follow them." Another typical victim of retrospective contempt is the Frankfurt National Assembly, the all-German parliament. Historians have had their fun with the "professors' parliament," mocking its lengthy debates about whether Germany should be a *Bundesstaat* or a *Staatenbund,* noting how, after a year of deliberation, the deputies voted to name the King of Prussia emperor, only to discover that he had no interest in the post.

The third and probably most substantial of the historians' versions of 1848 directs attention to the failure of the revolutions of that year to establish new regimes, pointing out that after a shorter or longer—and usually shorter—interval, the authorities overthrown at the onset of the revolution returned to power. Historians working in this tradition contrast the failed revolutions of the mid-nineteenth century with the more successful ones in 1789 and 1917, and offer a variety of explanations for the differences.

The Revolutions of 1848

John Weiss

The scholarly debate over the revolutions of 1848 continues, but in recent years several historians have suggested a new interpretation. The following selection by John Weiss is an example of this new trend. Here he deemphasizes the role of liberalism, stressing instead the role played by artisans and peasants in the revolutions.

CONSIDER: *According to Weiss, the social and economic causes of the revolutions; how Weiss supports his conclusion that it is misleading to label these revolutions liberal.*

The revolutions of 1848 were the last in Europe, excluding those caused by defeat in war. Their suppression also marked the last triumph of the semi-feudal varieties of conservatism discussed previously. It is misleading to label these revolutions liberal, as is usually done. The revolutions were started and maintained by artisans and peasants who were either fighting to maintain some elements of the traditional order, or whose status had been dislocated by the intrusion of liberal commercial capitalism. It is true that liberals assumed leadership once the outbreaks had started, but they wanted reform, not revolution. Moreover, the liberals did not represent the middle class as a whole, but only the politically aware professional groups—lawyers, civil servants, educators and students. There was no mass following for liberal reforms in Europe, and the middle classes in general had no clearly perceived class enemy blocking their social mobility as in 1789. Consequently they were much more wary of the potential for social upheaval from below.

SOURCE: From John Weiss, *Conservatism in Europe*, p. 56. Reprinted by permission of Thames & Hudson, Ltd.

The liberal leaders of the revolutions were isolated from their own class and, as it turned out, had little to offer the artisans and peasants in revolt that could not as easily have been granted by conservatives. Only in Hungary and Italy, where nationalism incited mass risings against the Austrians, were the revolutions truly violent and sweeping. Elsewhere, we find only urban revolts accompanied by sporadic peasant uprisings. Excluding France, frightened conservative élites were never overthrown; they merely made paper concessions and withdrew temporarily until the weakness of the revolutionaries was evident, whereupon they returned in force. East of France traditionalists could still dominate the forms of social upheaval characteristic of pre-industrial society. In 1848 the industrial proletariat played almost no role whatsoever, and the outbreaks had familiar traditional causes: 1846 and 1847 were the years of the most terrible crop failures of nineteenth-century Europe, from which stemmed famine, inflation, shrinking markets and unemployment.

❧ CHAPTER QUESTIONS

1. In a debate between liberals and conservatives of the early nineteenth century over how the French Revolution should be evaluated, what points would each side make?

2. In what ways might conservatives find Romanticism to their liking? What aspects of Romanticism might appeal to liberals?

3. Analyze nineteenth-century conservatism, liberalism, and Romanticism as alternative ways in which Europeans attempted to deal with the changes in Western civilization that had been occurring since the second half of the eighteenth century.

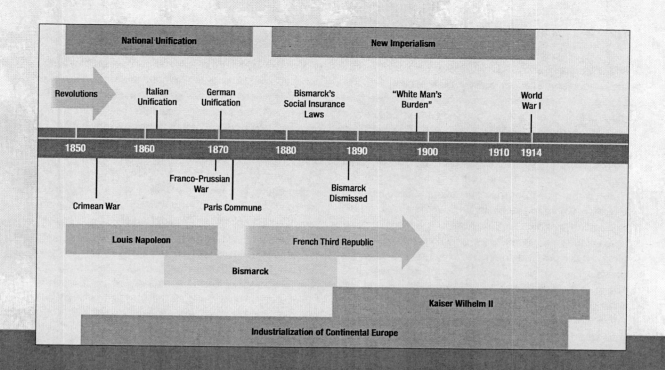

24 The National State, Nationalism, and Imperialism: 1850–1914

Between 1850 and 1914 Europe was characterized politically by the development of the national state, the spread of nationalism, and the rise of the "new imperialism." The development of the national state took place after 1848. Governments, responding to economic and social pressures, increased their involvement in the economic and social life of their countries. This was apparent both in liberal England and in more conservative France under Louis Napoleon. There were similar trends during the national unification movements in Italy and particularly in Germany, where the state took on a wide range of new functions.

Nationalism had deep roots, notably in the experience of and reactions to the French Revolution and the Napoleonic invasions. Nationalism also played a central role in the revolutions of 1848. During the second half of the nineteenth century, nationalism continued to grow and to be capitalized upon by national governments. The most striking manifestations of nationalism came in the successful unification movements in Italy and Germany.

The rise of the new imperialism occurred in the latter decades of the nineteenth century. The European powers engaged in a sudden quest for control over new territories in Asia and Africa. Explorers, missionaries, traders, troops, and government officials quickly followed one another into these lands and established direct political control. In this process the West greatly increased its dominance over much of the rest of the world, bringing Western culture and institutions to the indigenous societies whether they wanted it or not.

The sources in this chapter explore each of these three developments. Some of the documents concentrate on the growth of the national state, particularly in Germany, where the authoritarian government expanded in an effort to adapt to the social and economic pressures of the times. Some of the questions addressed are: How did the government in Germany react to demands for social legislation? What was the role of conservative forces in the German unification process, and how did other powers deal with Prussia's drive to unify Germany? Other documents concern nationalism, particularly its meaning, its appeal, and its connections to liberalism and conservatism. What role did nationalism play in the unification movements in Germany and Italy? How was nationalism tied to the new imperialism of the period? Finally, most of the selections deal with imperialism, for not only was imperialism of far-reaching significance for much of the world, it has been a topic of considerable debate among historians. What were the nationalistic and economic motives for imperialism? What were some of the attitudes toward imperialism, particularly as reflected in materials glorifying it as a Christian and humanitarian movement? What roles did women play in colonial societies?

Throughout these selections there is evidence for an increasing competitiveness among European states and political strains within those states. As will be seen in Chapter 26, these contributed to the outbreak of World War I and the revolutions that accompanied it.

Primary Sources

Speeches on Pragmatism and State Socialism

Otto von Bismarck

The revolutions of 1848 were ultimately a blow to idealistic reform. Thereafter, governments pursued more limited goals. They tended to resort to more authoritarian measures, to avoid doctrinaire policies, and even to adopt certain programs of opposing groups in the hopes of weakening determined opposition to the government. Otto von Bismarck (1815–1898) did this in Germany. Born into a noble Prussian family, Bismarck rose to the position of chief minister under the king in 1862. The first selection below is from an 1862 speech to the Reichstag, in which he argues that the idealism of 1848 must be replaced by a conservative realism.

Bismarck remained in power until 1890. During this time he and his conservative supporters faced opposition from some liberals and from a growing number of socialists representing the working class. In the 1880s Bismarck supported some of the workers' demands for social insurance

SOURCE: Louis L. Snyder, ed., *Documents of German History* (New Brunswick, NJ: Rutgers University Press, 1958), p. 202; William H. Dawson, *Bismarck and State Socialism* (London: Swan Sonnenschein and Co., 1890), pp. 29, 34–35, 63–64, 118–119.

and pushed through such legislation as the German Workers' Insurance Laws. The remaining excerpts below Bismarck's speeches indicate the rationale behind these policies.

CONSIDER: *What Bismarck means when he says the great questions of the day will be decided by iron and blood; how Bismarck justifies his support of "socialist" policies; why Bismarck would support such policies; what conservatives have to gain and who stands to lose by enactment of these policies.*

IRON AND BLOOD

. . . It is true that we can hardly escape complications in Germany, although we do not seek them. Germany does not look to Prussia's liberalism, but to her power. The south German States—Bavaria, Württemberg, and Baden—would like to indulge in liberalism, and because of that no one will assign Prussia's role to them! Prussia must collect her forces and hold them in reserve for an opportune moment, which has already come and gone several times. Since the Treaty of Vienna, our frontiers have not been favorably designed for a healthy body politic. Not by speeches and majorities will the great questions of the day be decided—that was the mistake of 1848 and 1849—but by iron and blood.

STATE SOCIALISM

Herr Richter has called attention to the responsibility of the State for what it does. But it is my opinion that the State can also be responsible for what it does not do. I do not think that doctrines like those of *"Laissez-faire, laissez-aller,"* "Pure Manchesterdom in politics," "He who is not strong enough to stand must be knocked down and trodden to the ground," "To him that hath shall be given, and from him that hath not shall be taken away even that which he hath,"—that doctrines like these should be applied in the State, and especially in a monarchically, paternally governed State. On the other hand, I believe that those who profess horror at the intervention of the State for the protection of the weak lay themselves open to the suspicion that they are desirous of using their strength—be it that of capital, that of rhetoric, or whatever it be—for the benefit of a section, for the oppression of the rest, for the introduction of party domination, and that they will be chagrined as soon as this design is disturbed by any action of the Government.

✌

Give the working-man the right to work as long as he is healthy; assure him care when he is sick; assure him maintenance when he is old. If you do that, and do not fear the sacrifice, or cry out at State Socialism directly the words "provision for old age" are uttered,—if the State will show a little more Christian solicitude for the working-man, then I believe that the gentlemen of the Wyden (Social-Democratic) programme will sound their bird-call in vain, and that the thronging to them will cease as soon as working-men see that the Government and legislative bodies are earnestly concerned for their welfare.

Yes, I acknowledge unconditionally a right to work, and I will stand up for it as long as I am in this place. But here I do not stand upon the ground of Socialism, which is said to have only begun with the Bismarck Ministry, but on that of the Prussian common law.

✌

Many measures which we have adopted to the great blessing of the country are Socialistic, and the State will have to accustom itself to a little more Socialism yet. We must meet our needs in the domain of Socialism by reformatory measures if we would display the wisdom shown in Prussia by the Stein-Hardenberg legislation respecting the emancipation of the peasantry. That was Socialism, to take land from one person and give it to another—a much stronger form of Socialism than a monopoly. But I am glad that this Socialism was adopted, for we have as a consequence secured a free and very well-to-do peasantry, and I hope that we shall in time do something of the sort for the labouring classes. Whether I, however, shall live to see it—with the general opposition which is, as a matter of principle, offered to me on all sides, and which is wearying me—I cannot say. But you will be compelled to put a few drops of social oil into the recipe which you give to the State—how much I do not know. . . . The establishment of the freedom of the peasantry was Socialistic; Socialistic, too, is every expropriation in favour of railways; Socialistic to the utmost extent is the aggregation of estates—the law exists in many provinces—taking from one and giving to another, simply because this other can cultivate the land more conveniently; Socialistic is expropriation under the Water Legislation, on account of irrigation, etc., where a man's land is taken away from him because another can farm it better; Socialistic is our entire poor relief, compulsory school attendance, compulsory construction of roads, so that I am bound to maintain a road upon my lands for travellers. That is all Socialistic, and I could extend the register further; but if you believe that you can frighten any one or call up specters with the word "Socialism," you take a standpoint which I abandoned long ago, and the abandonment of which is absolutely necessary for our entire imperial legislation.

✌

The whole matter centres in the question, Is it the duty of the State, or is it not, to provide for its helpless citizens? I maintain that it is its duty, that it is the duty not only of the *"Christian* State," as I ventured once to call it when speaking of "practical Christianity," but of every State. It would be foolish for a corporation to undertake matters which the individual can attend to alone; and similarly the purposes which the parish can fulfill with justice and with advantage are left to the parish. But there are purposes which only the State as a whole can fulfill. To these belong national defence, the general system of communications, and, indeed, everything spoken of in article 4 of the constitution. To these, too, belong the help of the necessitous and the removal of those just complaints which provide Social Democracy with really effective material for agitation. This is a duty of the State, a duty which the State cannot permanently disregard. . . . As soon as the State takes this matter [of insurance] in hand—and I believe it is its duty to take it in hand—it must seek the cheapest form of insurance, and, not aiming at profit for itself, must keep primarily in view the benefit of the poor and needy. Otherwise we might leave the fulfillment of certain State duties—such as poor relief, in the widest sense of the words, is amongst others—like education and national defence with more right to share companies, only asking ourselves, Who will do it most cheaply? who will do it most effectively? If provision for the necessitous in a greater degree than is possible with the present poor relief legislation is a State duty, the State must take the matter in hand; it cannot rest content with the thought that a share company will undertake it.

If an establishment employing twenty thousand or more workpeople were to be ruined . . . we could not allow these men to hunger. We should have to resort to real State Socialism and find work for them, and this is what we do in every case of distress. If the objection were right that we should shun State Socialism as we would an infectious disease, how do we come to organise works in one province and another in case of distress—works which we should not undertake if the labourers had employment and wages? In such cases we build railways whose profitableness is questionable; we carry out improvements which otherwise would be left to private initiative. If that is Communism, I have no objection at all to it; though with such catchwords we really get no further.

The Duties of Man

Giuseppe Mazzini

Nationalism, a growing force since the French Revolution, tended to be associated with liberal and humanitarian ideals during the first half of the nineteenth century. After 1848 it became more pragmatic and conservative, as illustrated by the unification of Germany and Italy. Yet it was still based on some of the earlier ideals. These ideals are illustrated in both the life and writings of the Italian patriot Giuseppe Mazzini (1805–1872). Mazzini was a revolutionary for most of his life and strove continuously for an independent and united Italian Republic. His revolutionary efforts in the 1830s and 1840s failed; unification was ultimately accomplished under the more pragmatic leadership of Cavour in the 1860s. But his ideas represented a strong strain of mid-nineteenth-century nationalism both in Italy and in other countries. The following is an excerpt from Mazzini's most famous essay, The Duties of Man, *addressed to Italian workingmen.*

CONSIDER: *The bases for Mazzini's nationalism; why these ideas might be appealing to the Italian working class; why Bismarck might approve of these ideas and whether there is anything he might reject.*

SOURCE: Emilie Ashurst Venturi, *Joseph Mazzini: A Memoir* (London: Alexander & Shepheard, 1875), pp. 312–315.

Your first duties—first as regards importance—are, as I have already told you, towards Humanity. You are *men* before you are either citizens or fathers. If you do not embrace the whole human family in your affection, if you do not bear witness to your belief in the Unity of that family, consequent upon the Unity of God, and in that fraternity among the peoples which is destined to reduce that unity to action; if, wheresoever a fellow-creature suffers, or the dignity of human nature is violated by falsehood or tyranny—you are not ready, if able, to aid the unhappy, and do not feel called upon to combat, if able, for the redemption of the betrayed or oppressed—you violate your law of life, you comprehend not that Religion which will be the guide and blessing of the future.

But what can each of you, singly, *do* for the moral improvement and progress of Humanity? You can from time to time give sterile utterance to your belief; you may, on some rare occasions, perform some act of *charity* towards a brother man not belonging to your own land;—no more. But charity is not the watchword of the Faith of the Future. The watchword of the faith of the future is *Association*, and fraternal co-operation of all towards a common aim; and this is as far superior to all charity, as the edifice which all of you should unite to raise would be superior to the humble hut each one of you might build alone, or with the mere assistance of lending and borrowing stone, mortar, and tools.

But, you tell me, you cannot attempt united action, distinct and divided as you are in language, customs, tendencies, and capacity. The individual is too insignificant, and Humanity too vast. The mariner of Brittany prays to God as he puts to sea: *Help me, my God! my boat is so small and thy ocean so wide!* And this prayer is the true expression of the condition of each one of you, until you find the means of infinitely multiplying your forces and powers of action.

This means was provided for you by God when he gave you a country; when, even as a wise overseer of labour distributes the various branches of employment according to the different capacities of the workmen, he divided Humanity into distinct groups or nuclei upon the face of the earth, thus creating the germ of Nationalities. Evil governments have disfigured the divine design. Nevertheless you may still trace it, distinctly marked out—at least as far as Europe is concerned—by the course of the great rivers, the direction of the higher mountains, and other geographical conditions. They have disfigured it by their conquests, their greed, and their jealousy even of the righteous power of others; disfigured it so far that if we except England and France—there is not perhaps a single country whose present boundaries correspond to that design.

These governments did not, and do not, recognise any country save their own families or dynasty, the egotism of caste. But the Divine design will infallibly be realized. Natural divisions, and the spontaneous, innate tendencies of the peoples, will take the place of the arbitrary divisions sanctioned by evil governments. The map of Europe will be redrawn. The countries of the Peoples, defined by the vote of free men, will arise upon the ruins of the countries of kings and privileged castes, and between these countries harmony and fraternity will exist. And the common work of Humanity, of general amelioration and the gradual discovery and application of its Law of life, being distributed according to local and general capacities, will be wrought out in peaceful and progressive development and advance. Then may each one of you, fortified by the power and the affection of many millions, all speaking the same language, gifted with the same tendencies, and educated by the same historical tradition, hope, even by your own single effort, to be able to benefit all Humanity.

O my brothers, love your Country! Our country is our Home, the house that God has given us, placing therein a numerous family that loves us, and whom we love; a family with whom we sympathise more readily, and whom we understand more quickly than we do others; and which, from its being centred round a given spot, and from the homogeneous nature of its elements, is adapted to a special branch of activity. Our country is our common workshop, whence the products of our activity are sent forth for the benefit of the whole world; wherein the tools and implements of labour we can most usefully employ are gathered together: nor may we reject them without disobeying the plan of the Almighty, and diminishing our own strength.

Militant Nationalism

Heinrich von Treitschke

The idea of nationalism and nationalistic movements gained great power throughout the nineteenth century. While favored by a variety of liberal and conservative thinkers and groups during the first half of the century, nationalism became more militant, extreme, and racist in the second half of the century, particularly in central Europe. One of the most influential proponents of this militant nationalism in Germany was Heinrich von Treitschke (1834–1896), a historian at the University of Berlin. In the following selections from his works, Treitschke puts forth his views on national character, the state, war, and Jews.

CONSIDER: *What might be appealing about these views; possible reasons for Treitschke's views of the English and Jews; what policies might logically flow from these ideas.*

ON THE GERMAN CHARACTER

Depth of thought, idealism, cosmopolitan views; a transcendent philosophy which boldly oversteps (or freely looks over) the separating barriers of finite existence; familiarity with every human thought and feeling, the desire to traverse the worldwide realm of ideas in common with the foremost intellects of all nations and all times. All that has at all times been held to be characteristic of the Germans and has always been praised as the essence of German character and breeding. . . .

ON THE STATE

The state is a moral community, which is called upon to educate the human race by positive achievement. Its ultimate object is that a nation should develop in it, a nation distinguished by a real national character. To achieve this state is the highest moral duty for nation and individual alike. All private quarrels must be forgotten when the state is in danger.

At the moment when the state cries out that its very life is at stake, social selfishness must cease and party hatred be hushed. The individual must forget his egoism, and feel that he is a member of the whole body.

The most important possession of a state, its be-all and end-all, is power. He who is not man enough to look this truth in the face should not meddle in politics. The state is not physical power as an end in itself, it is power to protect and promote the higher interests. Power must justify itself by being applied for the greatest good of mankind. It is the highest moral duty of the state to increase its power.

The true greatness of the state is that it links the past with the present and future; consequently, the individual has no right to regard the state as a means for attaining his own ambitions in life. Every extension of the activities of the state is beneficial and wise if it arouses, promotes, and purifies the independence of free and reasoning men; it is evil when it kills and stunts the independence of free men. It is men who make history. . . .

Only the truly great and powerful states ought to exist. Small states are unable to protect their subjects against external enemies; moreover, they are incapable

SOURCE: Louis L. Snyder, ed., *Documents of German History* (New Brunswick, NJ: Rutgers University Press, 1958), pp. 259–62.

of *Kultur* in great dimensions. Weimar produced a Goethe and a Schiller; still these poets would have been greater had they been citizens of a German national state. . . .

ON WAR

The idea of perpetual peace is an illusion supported only by those of weak character. It has always been the weary, spiritless, and exhausted ages which have played with the dream of perpetual peace. A thousand touching portraits testify to the sacred power of the love which a righteous war awakes in noble nations. It is altogether impossible that peace be maintained in a world bristling with arms, and even God will see to it that war always recurs as a drastic medicine for the human race. Among great states the greatest political sin and the most contemptible is feebleness. It is the political sin against the Holy Ghost.

War is elevating because the individual disappears before the great conception of the state. The devotion of the members of a community to each other is nowhere so splendidly conspicuous as in war.

Modern wars are not waged for the sake of goods and chattels. What is at stake is the sublime moral good of national honor, which has something in the nature of unconditional sanctity, and compels the individual to sacrifice himself for it.

ON THE ENGLISH

The hypocritical Englishman, with the Bible in one hand and a pipe of opium in the other, possesses no redeeming qualities. The nation was an ancient robber-knight, in full armor, lance in hand, on every one of the world's trade routes.

The English possess a commercial spirit, a love of money which has killed every sentiment of honor and every distinction of right and wrong. English cowardice and sensuality are hidden behind unctuous, theological fine talk which is to us free-thinking German heretics among all the sins of English nature the most repugnant. In England all notions of honor and class prejudices vanish before the power of money, whereas the German nobility has remained poor but chivalrous. That last indispensable bulwark against the brutalization of society—the duel—has gone out of fashion in England and soon disappeared, to be supplanted by the riding whip. This was a triumph of vulgarity. The newspapers, in their accounts of aristocratic weddings, record in exact detail how much each wedding guest has contributed in the form of presents or in cash; even the youth of the nation have turned their sports into a business, and contend for valuable prizes, whereas the German students wrought havoc on

their countenances for the sake of a real or imaginary honor.

ON JEWS

The Jews at one time played a necessary role in German history, because of their ability in the management of money. But now that the Aryans have become accustomed to the idiosyncrasies of finance, the Jews are no longer necessary. The international Jew, hidden in the mask of different nationalities, is a disintegrating influence; he can be of no further use to the world. It is necessary to speak openly about the Jews, undisturbed by the fact that the Jewish press befouls what is purely historical truth.

Does Germany Need Colonies?
Friedrich Fabri

Imperialism swept through Europe with extraordinary force in the late nineteenth century. Probably the most apparent motive for the new imperialism was economic. With each conquest, people expected to develop new commerce and particularly new markets for manufactured goods. But there was another, perhaps even more important motive: nationalism. The step between the increasingly assertive nationalism of the time and the new imperialism was a short one. Both of these views are reflected by Friedrich Fabri in his 1879 pamphlet, "Does Germany Need Colonies?" A former inspector of a German missionary association in South West Africa, Fabri emphasizes Germany's "cultural mission" in becoming an imperial power.

CONSIDER: *What arguments Fabri mounts to justify Germany's acquisition of colonies; what Fabri means by Germany's "cultural mission" and how that relates to imperialism.*

Should not the German nation, so seaworthy, so industrially and commercially minded, more than other peoples geared to agricultural colonization, and possessing a rich and available supply of labor, all these to a greater extent than other modern culture-peoples, should not this nation successfully hew a new path on the road of imperialism? We are convinced beyond doubt that the colonial question has become a matter of life-or-death for the development of Germany. Colonies will have a salutary effect on our economic situation as well as on our entire national progress.

SOURCE: Louis L. Snyder, *The Imperialism Reader* (New York: D. Van Nostrand, 1962), pp. 18–20 as excerpted.

Here is a solution for many of the problems that face us. In this new Reich of ours there is so much bitterness, so much unfruitful, sour, and poisoned political wrangling, that the opening of a new, promising road of national effort will act as a kind of liberating influence. Our national spirit will be renewed, a gratifying thing, a great asset. A people that has been led to a high level of power can maintain its historical position only as long as it understands and proves itself to be *the bearer of a culture-mission*. At the same time, this is the only way to stability and to the growth of national welfare, the necessary foundation for a lasting expansion of power.

At one time Germany contributed only intellectual and literary activity to the tasks of our century. That era is now over. As a people we have become politically minded and powerful. But if political power becomes the primal goal of a nation, it will lead to harshness, even to barbarism. We must be ready to serve for the ideal, moral, and economic culture-tasks of our time. The French national-economist, Leroy Beaulieu, closed his work on colonization with these words: "That nation is the greatest in the world which colonizes most; if she does not achieve that rank today, she will make it tomorrow."

No one can deny that in this direction England has by far surpassed all other countries. Much has been said, even in Germany, during the last few decades about the "disintegrating power of England." Indeed, there seems to be something to it when we consider the Palmerston era and Gladstonian politics. It has been customary in our age of military power to evaluate the strength of a state in terms of its combat-ready troops. But anyone who looks at the globe and notes the steadily increasing colonial possessions of Great Britain, how she extracts strength from them, the skill with which she governs them, how the Anglo-Saxon strain occupies a dominant position in the overseas territories, he will begin to see the military argument as the reasoning of a philistine.

The fact is that England tenaciously holds on to its world-wide possessions with scarcely one-fourth the manpower of our continental military state. That is not only a great economic advantage but also a striking proof of the solid power and cultural fiber of England. . . .

It would be wise for us Germans to learn about colonial skills from our Anglo-Saxon cousins and to begin a friendly competition with them. When the German Reich centuries ago stood at the pinnacle of the states of Europe, it was the Number One trade and sea power. If the New Germany wants to protect its newly won position of power for a long time, it must heed its *Kultur*-mission and, above all, delay no longer in the task of renewing the call for colonies.

The White Man's Burden
Rudyard Kipling

Imperialism was often glorified both by those actively involved in it and by the public at home. Part of this glorification involved perceiving imperialism as a Christian and nationalistic venture. More broadly it involved portraying imperialism as a heroic deed carried out by idealistic leaders of Western civilization in an effort to spread the "benefits" of "true civilization" to "less advanced" peoples of the world. One of the most popular expressions of this is found in the writings of Rudyard Kipling (1865–1936), particularly in his poem "The White Man's Burden," written in 1899 to celebrate the American annexation of the Philippines.

CONSIDER: *What Kipling means by "the White Man's burden"; how Kipling justifies imperialism; why such a justification might be so appealing.*

Take up the White Man's burden—
　　Send forth the best ye breed—
Go, bind your sons to exile
　　To serve your captives' need;
To wait, in heavy harness,
　　On fluttered folk and wild—
Your new-caught sullen peoples,
　　Half devil and half child.

Take up the White Man's burden—
　　In patience to abide,
To veil the threat of terror
　　And check the show of pride;
By open speech and simple,
　　An hundred times made plain,
To seek another's profit
　　And work another's gain.

Take up the White Man's burden—
　　The savage wars of peace—
Fill full the mouth of Famine,
　　And bid the sickness cease;
And when your goal is nearest
　　(The end for others sought)
Watch sloth and heathen folly
　　Bring all your hope to nought.

Take up the White Man's burden—
　　No iron rule of kings,

SOURCE: Rudyard Kipling, "The White Man's Burden," *McClure's Magazine*, vol. XII, no. 4 (February 1899), pp. 290–291.

But toil of serf and sweeper—
    The tale of common things.
The ports ye shall not enter,
    The roads ye shall not tread,
Go, make them with your living
    And mark them with your dead.

Take up the White Man's burden,
    And reap his old reward—
The blame of those ye better
    The hate of those ye guard—
The cry of hosts ye humour
    (Ah, slowly!) toward the light:—
"Why brought ye us from bondage,
    Our loved Egyptian night?"

Take up the White Man's burden—
    Ye dare not stoop to less—
Nor call too loud on Freedom
    To cloke your weariness.
By all ye will or whisper,
    By all ye leave or do,
The silent sullen peoples
    Shall weigh your God and you.

Take up the White Man's burden!
    Have done with childish days—
The lightly-proffered laurel,
    The easy ungrudged praise:
Comes now, to search your manhood
    Through all the thankless years,
Cold, edged with dear-bought wisdom,
    The judgment of your peers.

Controlling Africa: The Standard Treaty

Royal Niger Company

Europeans used many means to gain control over African lands, the most obvious being force. However, more subtle means included "treaties," or what the Europeans could consider "legal contracts." During the scramble for Africa, African chieftains signed hundreds of these documents. The following document is an example of one of these "standard treaties" issued in the 1880s by the British firm, the Royal Niger Company. The company had already been granted a trade monopoly over the area around the Niger River in

SOURCE: Edwart Hertslet, ed., *The Map of Africa by Treaty*, 2nd ed. (London: Her Majesty's Stationary Office, 1896), vol. I, pp. 467–468.

West Africa by the British government and was competing with the French for control over that area. The treaties would eventually form the basis for creating the British colony of Nigeria.

CONSIDER: *What the treaties offered to each side; what the Africans were giving up; why the British found this way of gaining control so appealing.*

We, the undersigned Chiefs of _____, with the view to the bettering of the condition of our country and people, do this day cede to the Royal Niger Company, for ever, the whole of our territory extending from _____.

We also give to the said Royal Niger Company full power to settle all native disputes arising from any cause whatever, and we pledge ourselves not to enter into any war with other tribes without the sanction of the said Royal Niger Company.

We understand that the said Royal Niger Company have full power to mine, farm, and build in any portion of our country.

We bind ourselves not to have any intercourse with any strangers or foreigners except through the said Royal Niger Company.

In consideration of the foregoing, the said Royal Niger Company (Chartered and Limited) bind themselves not to interfere with any of the native laws or customs of the country, consistently with the maintenance of order and good government.

The said Royal Niger Company agree to pay native owners of land a reasonable amount for any portion they may require.

The said Royal Niger Company bind themselves to protect the said Chiefs from the attacks of any neighboring aggressive tribes.

The said Royal Niger Company also agree to pay the said Chiefs _____ measures native value.

We, the undersigned witnesses, do hereby solemnly declare that the _____ Chiefs whose names are placed opposite their respective crosses have in our presence affixed their crosses of their own free will and consent, and that the said _____ has in our presence affixed his signature.

Done in triplicate at _____, this _____ day of _____, 188 _____.

Declaration by interpreter I, _____, of _____, do hereby solemnly declare that I am well acquainted with the language of the country, and that on the _____ day of _____, 188 _____, I truly and faithfully explained the above Agreement to all the Chiefs present, and that they understood its meaning.

Visual Sources

Imperialism Glorified

George Harcourt

The following 1900 painting by George Harcourt (figure 24.1) conveys some of the meaning of imperialism to Europeans. First displayed at the Royal Academy in 1900, it shows British soldiers leaving by train for the Boer War in South Africa. The soldiers are clearly cast in the role of masculine heroes, both in their own eyes and in the eyes of civilians, young and old. This is further evidenced by the couple in the center, representing the epitome of sentimentalized British masculinity and femininity. For many, imperialism enabled Europeans to have a sense of adventure and to prove their superiority to themselves and the rest of the world. Avoided in this picture is the reality of the bloodshed and exploitation to be experienced by these same soldiers and the populations of the colonized lands.

CONSIDER: *How this painting fits with Kipling's description of "the White Man's burden."*

FIGURE 24.1 (© Bettmann/Corbis)

FIGURE 24.2 (© New York Public Library/Art Resource, NY)

American Imperialism in Asia: Independence Day 1899

The Spanish-American War of 1898 led to the Spanish defeat and withdrawal from Cuba, Puerto Rico, and the Philippines. It also occasioned an impassioned debate in the United States about whether America should follow in Europe's footsteps and acquire colonies. The "liberation" of the Philippines led to a ten-year war against Philippine insurgents who fought for independence from both Spain and the United States. American imperialists were interested in the Philippines in large part because it gave them access to trade and investments in other Asian countries, especially the fabled China market that would be able to buy untold quantities of American goods. In this cartoon (figure 24.2) we see Uncle Sam about to bayonet a Filipino youth who is trying to defend himself with a sword, suggesting the massive difference in power between the U.S. Army and the Philippine insurgents. In back of Uncle Sam, then President McKinley waves the flag, suggesting the patriotism and jingoism that was seen to be behind American imperialism.

CONSIDER: *How Americans were able to rationalize their support for colonialism with their long opposition to European imperialism.*

Imperialism in Africa

Map 24.1 shows the approximate divisions among indigenous peoples in the centuries prior to European colonization. Map 24.2 (on p. 122) highlights political and cultural divisions in nineteenth-century Africa prior to 1880. Map 24.3 (on p. 123) shows the colonial partition of Africa between 1880 and 1914.

Together these maps indicate a number of things about imperialism in Africa. First, the manner and speed with which Africa was divided demonstrate the intense competition involved in this late-nineteenth-century imperial expansion. Second, the European partition of Africa did not take account of the already established social, political, cultural, and ethnic divisions among Africans. From this geopolitical perspective alone, one can imagine some of the disruption to native societies and cultures caused by imperialism. Third, these maps help explain problems experienced by Africans after decolonization occurred. The new African nations were generally formed on the basis of the arbitrary political lines established by European colonizers. Thus many African countries had to deal with persisting divisions and rivalries among their populations, stemming from the nineteenth-century partition of Africa.

CONSIDER: *How these maps help explain the effects of imperialism on Africans.*

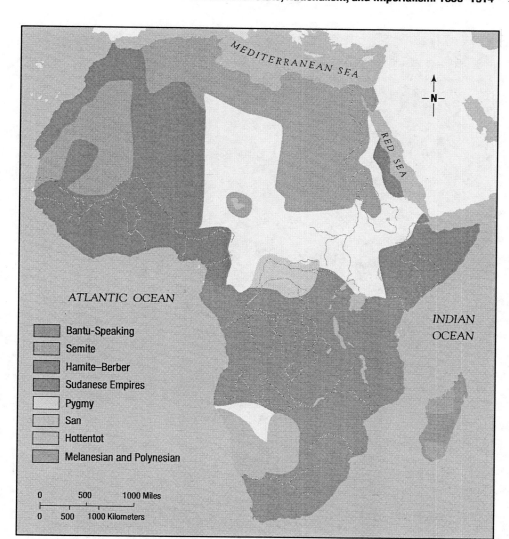

MAP 24.1   Divisions Among Indigenous Peoples

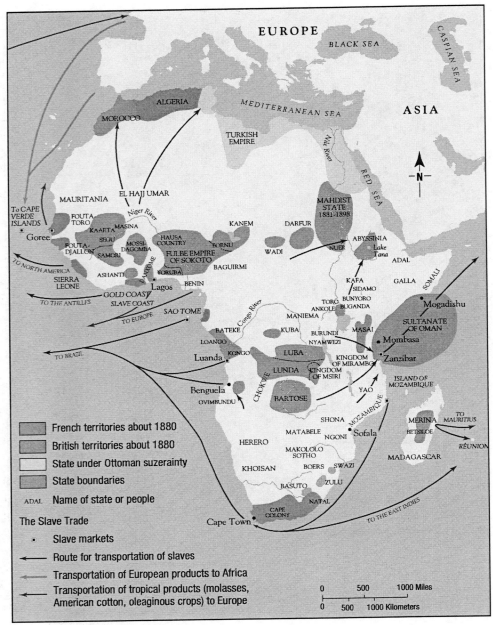

MAP 24.2 Political and Cultural Divisions

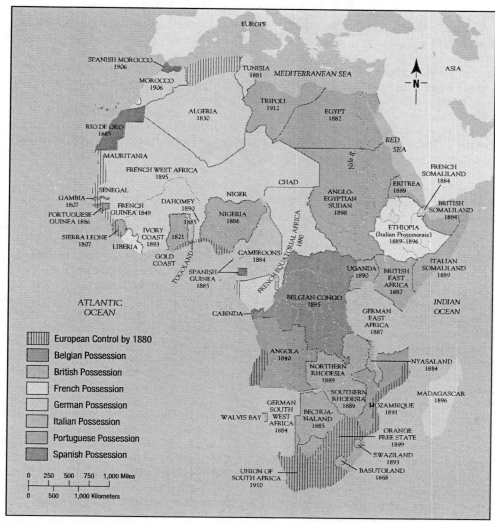

MAP 24.3   European Control of Africa

Secondary Sources

A Sterner Plan for Italian Unity: Nationalism, Liberalism, and Conservatism

Raymond Grew

During the first half of the nineteenth century, nationalism was most often connected to liberalism. After the revolu-

SOURCE: Raymond Grew, *A Sterner Plan for Italian Unity*. Reprinted by permission of Princeton University Press (Princeton, NJ, 1963), pp. 465–466. Copyright © 1963 by Princeton University Press.

tions of 1848 there were increasing ties between nationalism and conservatism, particularly in the movements for national unification. In the following selection Raymond Grew, an advocate of comparative history from the University of Michigan, analyzes the relationships among nationalism, liberalism, and conservatism in a comparative context.

CONSIDER: *How nationalism could appeal to both liberals and conservatives; why, during the second half of the nineteenth century, liberal ideals were often sacrificed in the name of nationalism.*

Insofar as politics was the public battle of ideas and interests, then nationalism was a denial of politics. For in stressing the values of unity, loyalty, and duty, nationalism saw political dispute as a source of weakness. It denied that there was conflict in the true interests of classes, groups or regions. The effect of nationalism was therefore inherently conservative in that it provided reason for supporting anyone thought to wield the power of the state effectively in behalf of national unity and strength, Disraeli or Gladstone, Napoleon III or Bismarck. Since order and unity, the cry of the political conservative, are essential to a strong state, and since, to the nationalist, most worthy ends required that strength, the nationalist was always tempted under pressure to move toward the political right, to sacrifice liberty to unity, discussion to authority, ends to means.

Yet the origins of nationalism were usually liberal and reformist; for everywhere it was a demand for change, the doctrine of the modernizers who, while they had too much to lose to want a social revolution, were self-consciously aware that theirs was an "underdeveloped" country. Nationalism could make its denial of politics effective because its ends were so clear, so easily defined in the model of the modern state. For the French that model had been England; for the Italians it was England and France. Italian nationalists were usually liberals, but their liberalism was primarily an admiration for the achievements of the liberal state. Because their model already existed, they looked directly to it, anxious to achieve an efficient bureaucracy, a responsible government, a progressive economic structure, all based on accepted and universally applied laws. Nationalism was a program to obtain these things quickly, not to evolve toward them but, if necessary, to superimpose them. The hurry to achieve these goals where nationalism itself was seriously opposed made a doctrinaire concern for means appear pedantic and unrealistic. Italian nationalists needed nothing so brutal as cynicism to justify "postponement" of controversy or the choice of practical means, though often this meant whittling away at the practices necessary to viable liberalism.

German Unification

David Blackbourn

As in the case of Italy, nationalism in Germany during the first half of the nineteenth century was closely connected to liberalism. This was particularly so in the early stages of the revolutions of 1848. But with the failure of liberal

SOURCE: David Blackbourn, *The Long Nineteenth Century: A History of Germany, 1780–1918* (New York: Oxford University Press, 1998), pp. 247–248.

nationalists to gain the concrete changes they strove for, steps toward unification over the next two decades followed a path blazed by Bismarck and the conservatives, who used three wars to help achieve unity in 1871. In the following selection, David Blackbourne analyzes the international environment that allowed the drive for German unification to succeed.

CONSIDER: *Why the great powers allowed Prussia to unify Germany without intervening; why Russia and Great Britain were "distracted"; what the other powers might have done to counter Prussia.*

Germany was unified as a result of three wars that created a new power in the centre of Europe. Why did the other great powers allow this to come about? An important part of the answer is obviously the success of Prussian arms when put to the test. It cannot be emphasized too much that unification was, in the last resort, achieved on the battlefield. But other elements smoothed the Prussian path to success. Russia had suffered military humiliation in the Crimean war, and was absorbed during the 1860s in a bout of internal reforms. Early Russian industrialization also depended on Russo-German trade, and placed a premium on good relations with the emerging German power. . . . Britain had pressing colonial problems; it was primarily suspicious of French ambitions on the Continent, and viewed the emerging Germany as a power that neither threatened fundamental British interests nor possessed a significant navy. Add to this the general British approval of national self-determination (as in Italy), the high regard for German culture, and Gladstone's concern with domestic issues, and it is clear why British sympathizers comfortably outnumbered those suspicious of Prussian "militarism." If we turn to the two powers directly defeated by Prussia on the road to unification, it is their weakness rather than their benevolent neutrality that requires emphasis. Austria was desperately isolated in this period. Vienna had failed to repair the alliance with Russia, broken by the Crimean war; and the great irony of the Austrian position, as well as the central weakness, was the fact that its principal ally, Prussia, was also its archrival in German affairs. Compounding these problems were the perpetual difficulties created by the subject nation-alities of the far-flung Habsburg monarchy, Hungarians, Italians and Slavs. This was an important part of the background to 1866; then, during the Franco-Prussian war, the restlessness of the Czechs and Poles pushed Vienna into a more pro-"German" stance. Last, but not least, France under Napoleon III was the loose cannon in European affairs, an adventurist power that excited universal suspicion and found none to mourn its fate in 1870.

The Age of Empire

Eric J.Hobsbawn

Imperialism has been interpreted from a number of perspectives since the early twentieth century. The way that scholars view imperialism often reveals much about their own political and ideological views. Some of the earliest interpretations, such as those by J. H. Hobson and V. I. Lenin, were economic. They criticized imperialism as an outgrowth of capitalism, Hobson from the perspective of a liberal socialist, Lenin as a Marxist theorist and political leader. Economic interpretations of imperialism, often in newer versions, remain popular. This is illustrated in the following selection by the British historian E. J. Hobsbawn, who has written extensively on nineteenth-century Western civilization.

CONSIDER: *Why Hobsbawn considers economic results irrelevant to economic motives for imperialism; why Hobsbawn calls imperialism a natural by-product of the international economy; why political actions are secondary to the economic motives for imperialism.*

A more convincing general motive for colonial expansion was the search for markets. The fact that this was often disappointed is irrelevant. The belief that the "overproduction" of the Great Depression could be solved by a vast export drive was widespread. Businessmen, always inclined to fill the blank spaces on the map of world trade with vast numbers of potential customers, would naturally look for such unexploited areas: China was one which haunted the imagination of salesmen—what if every one of those 300 millions bought only one box of tin-tacks?—and Africa, the unknown continent, was another. The Chambers of Commerce of British cities in the depressed early 1880s were outraged by the thought that diplomatic negotiations might exclude their traders from access to the Congo basin, which was believed to offer untold sales prospects, all the more so as it was being developed as a paying proposition by that crowned businessman, King Leopold II of the Belgians. . . .

But the crux of the global economic situation was that a number of developed economies simultaneously felt the same need for new markets. If they were sufficiently strong their ideal was "the open door" on the markets of the underdeveloped world; but if not strong enough, they hoped to carve out for themselves territories which, by virtue of ownership, would give national business a monopoly position or at least a substantial advantage. Partition of the unoccupied parts of the

Third World was the logical consequence. In a sense, this was an extension of the protectionism which gained ground almost everywhere after 1879. . . . To this extent the "new imperialism" was the natural by-product of an international economy based on the rivalry of several competing industrial economies, intensified by the economic pressures of the 1880s. It does not follow that any particular colony was expected to turn into Eldorado by itself, though this is what actually happened in South Africa, which became the world's greatest gold-producer. Colonies might simply provide suitable bases or jumping-off points for regional business penetration. . . .

At this point the economic motive for acquiring some colonial territory becomes difficult to disentangle from the political action required for the purpose, for protectionism of whatever kind is economy operating with the aid of politics. . . . Once rival powers began to carve up the map of Africa or Oceania, each naturally tried to safeguard against an excessive portion (or a particularly attractive morsel) going to the others. Once the status of a great power thus became associated with raising its flag over some palm-fringed beach (or, more likely, over stretches of dry scrub), the acquisition of colonies itself became a status symbol, irrespective of their value.

Imperialism as a Nationalistic Phenomenon

Carlton J. H. Hayes

Although the economic interpretation of imperialism has not lost its strength, other views have been offered recently as supplements and sometimes as direct alternatives to an economic interpretation. A direct alternative appears in the following selection by Carlton J. H. Hayes. One of the earliest historians to develop a sophisticated understanding of nationalism, Hayes argues that economic motives were at best secondary; on the whole, imperialism was a nationalistic phenomenon.

CONSIDER: *The evidence Hayes uses to reject economic interpretations of nationalism; how Hobsbawn might reply to this interpretation; the ways in which this view fits with the documents on nationalism in this chapter.*

The founding of new colonial empires and the fortifying of old ones antedated the establishment of neomercantilism, and that the economic arguments adduced

SOURCE: From *The Age of Empire* by Eric Hobsbawn. Copyright © 1987 by E. J. Hobsbawn. Reprinted by permission of Pantheon Books, a division of Random House, Inc.

SOURCE: Excerpted from *A Generation of Materialism, 1871–1900,* pp. 223–224, by Carlton J. H. Hayes. Copyright 1941 by Harper & Row Publishers, Inc. Copyright renewed 1969 by Mary Evelyn Hayes. Reprinted by permission of HarperCollins Publishers, Inc.

in support of imperialism seem to have been a rationalization *ex post facto*. In the main, it was not Liberal parties, with their super abundance of industrials and bankers, who sponsored the outward imperialistic thrusts of the '70's and early '80's. Instead, it was Conservative parties, with a preponderantly agricultural clientele notoriously suspicious of moneylenders and big business, and, above all, it was patriotic professors and publicists regardless of political affiliation and unmindful of personal economic interest. These put forth the economic arguments which eventually drew bankers and traders and industrialists into the imperialist camp.

Basically the new imperialism was a nationalistic phenomenon. It followed hard upon the national wars which created an all-powerful Germany and a united Italy, which carried Russia within sight of Constantinople, and which left England fearful and France eclipsed. It expressed a resulting psychological reaction, an ardent desire to maintain or recover national prestige. France sought compensation for European loss in oversea gain. England would offset her European isolation by enlarging and glorifying the British Empire. Russia, halted in the Balkans, would turn anew to Asia, and before long Germany and Italy would show the world that the prestige they had won by might inside Europe they were entitled to enhance by imperial exploits outside. The lesser powers, with no great prestige at stake, managed to get on without any new imperialism, though Portugal and Holland displayed a revived pride in the empires they already possessed and the latter's was administered with renewed vigor. . . .

Most simply, the sequence of imperialism after 1870 appears to have been, first, pleas for colonies on the ground of national prestige; second, getting them; third, disarming critics by economic argument; and fourth, carrying this into effect and relating the results to the neomercantilism of tariff protection and social legislation at home.

The Tools of Empire

Daniel R. Headrick

Recently some historians have focused on exactly how the spread of imperial rule took place during the second half of the 19th century. They argue that the tools of colonial conquest constituted an important explanation for that burst of colonial expansion occurring when it did. In the following selection from his influential book, The Tools of Empire: Technology

SOURCE: Daniel R. Headrick, *The Tools of Empire: Technology and European Imperialism in the Nineteenth Century* (New York: Oxford University Press, 1981), pp. 205–206.

and European Imperialism in the Nineteenth Century, Daniel R. Headrick focuses on the ways key inventions and innovations enabled Europeans to conquer new lands with such relative ease.

CONSIDER: *How, according to Headrick, technology helps explain the events of imperial expansion; whether Headrick's argument undermines an economic or nationalistic interpretation of imperialism or adds to those interpretations.*

Imperialism in the mid-century was predominantly a matter of British tentacles reaching out from India toward Burma, China, Malaya, Afghanistan, Mesopotamia, and the Red Sea. Territorially, at least, a much more impressive demonstration of the new imperialism was the scramble for Africa in the last decades of the century. Historians generally agree that from a profit-making point of view, the scramble was a dubious undertaking. Here also, technology helps explain events.

Inventions are most easily described one by one, each in its own technological and socioeconomic setting. Yet the inner logic of innovations must not blind us to the patterns of chronological coincidence. Though advances occurred in every period, many of the innovations that proved useful to the imperialists of the scramble first had an impact in the two decades from 1860 to 1880. These were the years in which quinine prophylaxis made Africa safer for Europeans; quick-firing breechloaders replaced muzzleloaders among the forces stationed on the imperial frontiers; and the compound engine, the Suez Canal, and the submarine cable made steamships competitive with sailing ships, not only on government-subsidized mail routes, but for ordinary freight on distant seas as well. Europeans who set out to conquer new lands in 1880 had far more power over nature and over the people they encountered than their predecessors twenty years earlier had; they could accomplish their tasks with far greater safety and comfort. . . .

What the breechloader, the machine gun, the steamboat and steamship, and quinine and other innovations did was to lower the cost, in both financial and human terms, of penetrating, conquering, and exploiting new territories. So cost-effective did they make imperialism that not only national governments but lesser groups as well could now play a part in it. The Bombay Presidency opened the Red Sea Route; the Royal Niger Company conquered the Caliphate of Sokoto; even individuals like Macgregor Laird, William Mackinnon, Henry Stanley, and Cecil Rhodes could precipitate events and stake out claims to vast territories which later became parts of empires. It is because the flow of new technologies in the nineteenth century made imperialism so cheap that it reached the threshold of acceptance among the peoples and governments of Europe, and led nations to become empires. Is this not as important a factor in the scramble for Africa as the political, diplomatic, and business motives that historians have stressed?

Gender and Empire

Margaret Strobel

While most of the Europeans who served as soldiers, officials, and administrators in overseas colonies were men, women also traveled to the colonies, lived there, and participated in these overseas societies. Their position as unequals to men in their own societies but superior to colonized men and women added complexity to their roles and to controversies over imperial practices. In the following selection, Margaret Strobel analyzes the situation facing these women and how they related to colonized peoples in Africa and Asia.

CONSIDER: *The ways European women benefited from imperialism; how these women may have viewed imperialism differently than men.*

European women had a complex, varied, and often contradictory relationship to the African and Asian territories controlled by the European powers in the nineteenth and twentieth centuries. As members of the "inferior sex" within the "superior race" (to use contemporary formulations), women were afforded options by imperialism that male dominance in the colonies then limited. By the twentieth century, some European women were attacking aspects of the racial, political, and economic inequalities of the colonial relationship. But the vast majority of them supported and contributed to the imperial venture. These women benefited from the economic and political subjugation of indigenous peoples and shared many of the accompanying attitudes of racism, paternalism, ethnocentrism, and national chauvinism. For most of them,

life in the colonies provided opportunities not found in Europe, where their options were limited by their social class, a "shortage" of marriageable men, difficulty in finding adequate employment, or the lack of "heathen souls" to be converted. At the same time, women continuously experienced, sometimes challenged, and sometimes reproduced the economic, political, and ideological subordination of women. As wives of colonial officials, they subordinated their lives to a male-centered administrative environment. As educators of indigenous women, they reproduced the European notions of bourgeois or Victorian domesticity and female dependence. Even missionary women, whose commitment to career and calling was in some ways a challenge to those very notions, accepted the patriarchal ideology and bureaucracy of the Church and promoted conventional European gender roles to African and Asian women. . . .

In one sense, European women's marginal status within a male-dominated colonial society and structure provided an opportunity. People outside the dominant culture have a different perspective that derives from their different experience and position within the social structure. Perhaps European women's marginal position within the dominant colonial society enabled them to see aspects of imperialism differently. European women frequently saw the needs of indigenous women where male administrators were blind to them. Some chose to use their skills, enhanced power, and status as members of the colonizing society on behalf of indigenous people. In so doing, they contributed, if not always intentionally, to the dismantling of the empire.

✺ CHAPTER QUESTIONS

1. What historical links are there between nationalism, the national state, and imperialism during the nineteenth century? How might all three be connected to industrialization?

2. How would you explain the rise of imperialism in the late nineteenth century?

3. In what ways have some of our perceptions of imperialism changed since the late nineteenth century?

SOURCE: Margaret Strobel, "Gender, Race, and Empire in Nineteenth- and Twentieth-Century Africa and Asia," in Renate Bridenthal et al., eds., *Becoming Visible: Women in European History,* 3rd ed. (New York: Houghton Mifflin Co., 1998), pp. 390, 410.

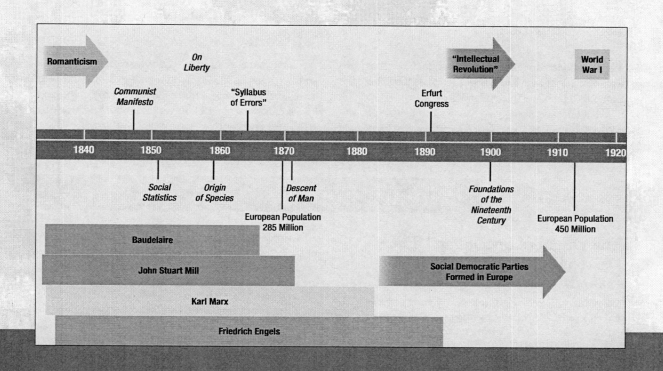

25 Culture, Thought, and Society: 1850–1914

From the mid–nineteenth century to 1914 the urban middle class dominated Europe socially and culturally. It was this class that was benefiting most from the continuing industrialization of the period. As the urban middle class grew in numbers and wealth, it asserted its own values and assumptions. Increasingly this class set the standards of lifestyle, thought, and culture. At the same time, these standards were attacked from all sides, particularly by those sensitive to the problems of the working class. The contrast between the standards being established by the middle class and the challenges to those standards marks this period as one of great social, cultural, and intellectual ferment.

The selections in this chapter exemplify some of the main social, cultural, and intellectual developments of this period. Three broad questions are addressed. First, what were some of the main elements of the middle-class style of life? Some of the materials show how this lifestyle was reflected in the physical setting of the middle class; others concentrate on the role women and the family played in this style of life. Second, what were some of the dominant intellectual currents favored by the middle class? Here liberalism as it was evolving toward the end of the century and ideas generally referred to as Social Darwinism are examined. Third, what were some of the main challenges to middle-class ideas and institutions? The most pervasive of these were Marxism and related social doctrines, but there were also conservative challenges, such as those from the Catholic Church and the challenges of racism.

What emerges from these sources is a picture of a dynamic society with a vast array of cultural and intellectual developments. In the decades following the outbreak of World War I, many would look back to this period as one of unusual progress. Some of the twentieth-century developments that in retrospect make the second half of the nineteenth century seem such a positive time will be examined in the next chapter.

 Primary Sources

The Origin of Species and The Descent of Man

Charles Darwin

The nineteenth century was a period of great scientific ideas and discoveries. Perhaps the most important and certainly the most controversial was Darwin's theory of evolution. Charles Darwin (1809–1882), a British naturalist, gathered data while on voyages in the southern Pacific. He used those data to develop his theory of evolution by natural selection. This theory of evolution, particularly as applied to human beings, challenged Biblical accounts of creation. He argued that all life, including human life, evolved from lower forms. Evolution was slow and extended over a much longer period than had been assumed. Natural selection, or survival of the fittest, determined how species evolved. Darwin first formulated his findings and theory in an 1844 essay. However, it was only after 1859, when he published The Origin of Species by Means of Natural Selection, *that his ideas became well known and widely controversial. The first of two selections below is from that book. The second is from* The Descent of Man, *which he published in 1871.*

CONSIDER: *Why his ideas might be so welcome by some, so disturbing to others; the possible psychological impact of his ideas; how those favoring Biblical accounts might respond.*

. . . [C]an we doubt (remembering that many more individuals are born than can possibly survive) that individuals having any advantage, however slight, over others, would have the best chance of surviving and of procreating their kind? On the other hand, we may feel sure that any variation in the least degree injurious would be rigidly destroyed. This preservation of favourable individual differences and variations, and the destruction of those which are injurious, I have called Natural Selection, or the Survival of the Fittest. . . .

SOURCES: Charles Darwin, *The Origin of Species by Means of Natural Selection,* 6th ed. (London: John Murray, 1872), pp. 63, 85; Charles Darwin, *The Descent of Man* (New York: D. Appleton and Co., 1883), pp. 606–607, 619.

Natural selection acts solely through the preservation of variations in some way advantageous, which consequently endure. Owing to the high geometrical rate of increase of all organic beings, each area is already fully stocked with inhabitants; and it follows from this, that as the favoured forms increase in number, so, generally, will the less favoured decrease and become rare. Rarity, as geology tells us, is the precursor to extinction.

❧

The main conclusion here arrived at, and now held by many naturalists who are well competent to form a sound judgment, is that man is descended from some less highly organized form. The grounds upon which this conclusion rests will never be shaken, for the close similarity between man and the lower animals in embryonic development, as well as in innumerable points of structure and constitution, both of high and of the most trifling importance,—the rudiments which he retains, and the abnormal reversions to which he is occasionally liable,—are facts which cannot be disputed. They have long been known, but until recently they told us nothing with respect to the origin of man. Now when viewed by the light of our knowledge of the whole organic world, their meaning is unmistakable. The great principle of evolution stands up clear and firm, when these groups of facts are considered in connection with others, such as the mutual affinities of the members of the same group, their geographical distribution in past and present times, and their geological succession. It is incredible that all these facts should speak falsely. He who is not content to look, like a savage, at the phenomena of nature as disconnected, cannot any longer believe that man is the work of a separate act of creation. . . .

We have seen that man incessantly presents individual differences in all parts of his body and in his mental faculties. These differences or variations seem to be induced by the same general causes, and to obey the same laws as with the lower animals. In both cases similar laws of inheritance prevail. Man tends to increase at a greater rate than his means of subsistence; consequently he is occasionally subjected to a severe struggle for existence, and natural selection will have effected whatever lies within its scope. A succession of strongly-marked variations of a similar nature is by no means requisite; slight fluctuating differences in the individual suffice for the work of natural selection. . . .

[M]an with all his noble qualities, with sympathy which feels for the most debased, with benevolence which extends not only to other men but to the humblest living creature, with his god-like intellect which has penetrated into the movements and constitution of the solar system—with all these exalted powers—Man still bears in his bodily frame the indelible stamp of his lowly origin.

Social Statics: Liberalism and Social Darwinism

Herbert Spencer

The works of Herbert Spencer (1820–1903) epitomize the assertive liberal philosophy favored by successful mid-nineteenth-century industrialists. This was a period in which capitalism was relatively unrestrained and social legislation was only in its infancy. It was also the beginning of thinking from a biological and evolutionary perspective, as best evidenced by the publication of Charles Darwin's Origin of Species *in 1859. Spencer reflected all this in his massive writings. He rose from being a railroad engineer to become editor of the London* Economist—*which espoused the views of industrial capitalism—and an independent author. Always a supporter of laissez-faire, he was best known for his advocacy of social evolution and acceptance of Darwinian ideas applied to society (Social Darwinism). Modern scholars consider him a founder of sociology. The following is an excerpt from* Social Statics *first published in 1851.*

CONSIDER: *Why Spencer's views would be so appealing to the industrial middle class; on what grounds certain groups might oppose these views; the social policies that would flow from these ideas; ways these views reflect Darwin's ideas.*

Pervading all Nature we may see at work a stern discipline which is a little cruel that it may be very kind. . . . It seems hard that an unskillfulness which with all his efforts he cannot overcome, should entail hunger upon the artizan. It seems hard that a labourer incapacitated by sickness from competing with his stronger fellows, should have to bear the resulting privations. It seems hard that widows and orphans should be left to struggle for life or death. Nevertheless, when regarded not separately but in connexion with the interests of universal humanity, these harsh fatalities are seen to be full of beneficence—the same beneficence which brings to early graves the children of diseased parents, and singles out the intemperate and the debilitated as the victims of an epidemic.

There are many very amiable people who have not the nerve to look this matter fairly in the face. Disabled as they are by their sympathies with present suffering, from duly regarding ultimate consequences, they pursue a course which is injudicious, and in the end even cruel. We do not consider it true kindness in a mother to gratify her child with sweetmeats that are likely to make it ill. We should think it a very foolish sort of benevolence which led a surgeon to let his patient's disease progress to a fatal issue, rather than inflict pain by an operation. Similarly, we must call those spurious philanthropists who, to prevent present misery, would entail greater misery on future generations. That rigorous necessity which, when allowed to operate, becomes so sharp a spur to the lazy and so strong a bridle to the random, these paupers' friends would repeal, because of the wailings it here and there produces. Blind to the fact that under the natural order of things society is constantly excreting its unhealthy, imbecile, slow, vacillating, faithless members, these unthinking, though well-meaning, men advocate an interference which not only stops the purifying process, but even increases the vitiation—absolutely encourages the multiplication of the reckless and incompetent by offering them an unfailing provision, and *discourages* the multiplication of the competent and provident by heightening the difficulty of maintaining a family. And thus, in their eagerness to prevent the salutary sufferings that surround us, these sigh-wise and groan-foolish people bequeath to posterity a continually increasing curse.

On Liberty

John Stuart Mill

During the second half of the nineteenth century, liberalism in theory and practice started to change. In general, it became less wedded to laissez-faire policies and less optimistic than it was during the first half of the nineteenth century. This change is reflected in the thought of John Stuart Mill (1806–1873). He was the most influential British thinker of the mid-nineteenth century and probably the leading liberal theorist of the period. When he was young he favored the early liberalism of his father, James Mill, a well-known philosopher, and Jeremy Bentham, the author of utilitarianism. Over time he perceived difficulties with this early liberalism and new dangers. He modified his liberal ideas, a change that would later be reflected in liberal political policies of the late

SOURCE: Herbert Spencer, *Social Statics* (New York: D. Appleton and Co., 1896), pp. 149–151.

SOURCE: John Stuart Mill, *Utilitarianism, Liberty, and Representative Government* (London: J. M. Dent and Sons Ltd., Everyman Library, 1910), pp. 66–68.

nineteenth and early twentieth centuries. In the following selection from On Liberty *(1859), his most famous work, Mill analyzes this evolution of liberalism starting with the aims of liberals during the first half of the nineteenth century.*

CONSIDER: *What Mill feels was the essence of early liberalism; what crucial changes occurred to transform liberalism; what Mill means by tyranny of the majority.*

The aim, therefore, of patriots was to set limits to the power which the ruler should be suffered to exercise over the community; and this limitation was what they meant by liberty. It was attempted in two ways. First, by obtaining a recognition of certain immunities, called political liberties or rights, which it was to be regarded as a breach of duty in the ruler to infringe, and which if he did infringe, specific resistance, or general rebellion, was held to be justifiable. A second, and generally a later expedient, was the establishment of constitutional checks, by which the consent of the community, or of a body of some sort, supposed to represent its interests, was made a necessary condition to some of the more important acts of the governing power. To the first of these modes of limitation, the ruling power, in most European countries, was compelled, more or less, to submit. It was not so with the second; and, to attain this, or when already in some degree possessed, to attain it more completely, became everywhere the principal object of the lovers of liberty. And so long as mankind were content to combat one enemy by another, and to be ruled by a master, on condition of being guaranteed more or less efficaciously against his tyranny, they did not carry their aspirations beyond this point.

A time, however, came, in the progress of human affairs, when men ceased to think it a necessity of nature that their governors should be an independent power, opposed in interest to themselves. It appeared to them much better that the various magistrates of the State should be their tenants or delegates, revocable at their pleasure. In that way alone, it seemed, could they have complete security that the powers of government would never be abused to their disadvantage. By degrees this new demand for elective and temporary rulers became the prominent object of the exertions of the popular party, wherever any such party existed; and superseded, to a considerable extent, the previous efforts to limit the power of rulers. As the struggle proceeded for making the ruling power emanate from the periodical choice of the ruled, some persons began to think that too much importance had been attached to the limitation of the power itself, *That* (it might seem) was a resource against rulers whose interests were habitually opposed to those of the people. What was now wanted was, that the rulers should be identified with the people; that their interest and will should be the interest and will of the nation. The

nation did not need to be protected against its own will. There was no fear of its tyrannising over itself. Let the rulers be effectually responsible to it, promptly removable by it, and it could afford to trust them with power of which it could itself dictate the use to be made. Their power was but the nation's own power, concentrated, and in a form convenient for exercise. This mode of thought, or rather perhaps of feeling, was common among the last generation of European liberalism, in the Continental section of which it still apparently predominates. . . .

In time, however, a democratic republic came to occupy a large portion of the earth's surface, and made itself felt as one of the most powerful members of the community of nations; and elective and responsible government became subject to the observations and criticisms which wait upon a great existing fact. It was now perceived that such phrases as "self-government," and "the power of the people over themselves," do not express the true state of the case. The "people" who exercise the power are not always the same people with those over whom it is exercised; and the "self-government" spoken of is not the government of each by himself, but of each by all the rest. The will of the people, moreover, practically means the will of the most numerous or the most active *part* of the people; the majority, or those who succeed in making themselves accepted as the majority; the people, consequently, *may* desire to oppress a part of their number; and precautions are as much needed against this as against any other abuse of power. The limitation, therefore, of the power of government over individuals loses none of its importance when the holders of power are regularly accountable to the community, that is, to the strongest party therein. This view of things, recommending itself equally to the intelligence of thinkers and to the inclination of those important classes in European society to whose real or supposed interests democracy is adverse, has had no difficulty in establishing itself; and in political speculations "the tyranny of the majority" is now generally included among the evils against which society requires to be on its guard.

Like other tyrannies, the tyranny of the majority was at first, and is still vulgarly, held in dread, chiefly as operating through the acts of the public authorities. But reflecting persons perceived that when society is itself the tyrant—society collectively over the separate individuals who compose it—its means of tyrannising are not restricted to the acts which it may do by the hands of its political functionaries. Society can and does execute its own mandates: and if it issues wrong mandates instead of right, or any mandates at all in things with which it ought not to meddle, it practises a social tyranny more formidable than many kinds of political oppression, since, though not usually upheld by such extreme penalties, it leaves fewer means of escape, penetrating much more deeply into the details of life, and enslaving the soul itself. Protection, therefore, against the tyranny of the magistrate is not enough: there needs protection also against the tyranny of the prevailing opinion and feeling; against the tendency of society to impose, by other means than civil penalties, its own ideas and practices as rules of conduct on those who dissent from them; to fetter the development, and, if possible, prevent the formation, of any individuality not in harmony with its ways, and compel all characters to fashion themselves upon the model of its own. There is a limit to the legitimate interference of collective opinion with individual independence: and to find that limit, and maintain it against encroachment, is as indispensable to a good condition of human affairs, as protection against political despotism.

Women as Chemists [Pharmacists]

Our Sisters

Most occupations were defined as inappropriate for middle-class women. What few occupations were appropriate were often explained to middle-class women in "how to" guides that appeared in books and women's magazines, often written by women. The following is an excerpt from "What to Do with Our Daughters, or Remunerative Employment of Women— Women as Chemists [Pharmacists]," an 1897 article published in Our Sisters, *a popular magazine addressed to middle-class women.*

CONSIDER: *What makes pharmacy appropriate for women; what kinds of activities are inappropriate for women as pharmacists and women in general.*

The Pharmaceutical Society, in opening up its ranks to women, has provided them with an eminently suitable calling. There is no lack of persons of both sexes who still loudly proclaim that a woman doctor is a thing unsexed. These persons could scarcely bring their arguments to bear against Pharmacy, and maintain that there is anything essentially unfeminine in the making up of drugs and pills. The calling of a chemist does not necessitate the possession on the part of a woman of all those faculties and qualities generally summed up as "strong-mindedness." In the peaceful seclusion of a drug shop, a woman chemist, unlike a doctor or a nurse, is not brought face to face with those stern realities: disease, pain, deformity, death. True, she works in with the doctor and the nurse, and her share in the healing of the sick is

SOURCE: "What to Do with Our Daughters, or Remunerative Employment of Women—Women as Chemists," *Our Sisters*, February 1897, pp. 85–86, in Eleanor S. Riemer and John C. Fout, eds., *European Women: A Documentary History, 1789–1945* (New York: Schocken Books, 1980), p. 45.

responsible enough; but for all that, her life work involves no such wear and tear, no such physical and mental strain, no such constant demands upon her endurance, patience, and staying power. Should her services be required for an operation to which some chemists devote attention, namely, tooth drawing, and should she not feel equal to the occasion, she need only refer the sufferer from toothache either to a dentist or a male colleague around the corner!

The Communist Manifesto

Karl Marx and Friedrich Engels

Although initially only one of many radical doctrines, Marxism proved to be the most dynamic and influential challenge to industrial capitalism and middle-class civilization in general. Its most succinct and popular statement is contained in the Communist Manifesto, written by Karl Marx (1818–1883) and Friedrich Engels (1820–1895) and first published in 1848. Karl Marx was born in Germany, studied history and philosophy, and entered a career as a journalist, writer, and revolutionary. For most of his life he lived in exile in London. His collaborator, Friedrich Engels, was also born in Germany and lived in England, but there he helped manage his family's cotton business in Manchester. Their doctrines directly attacked the middle class and industrial capitalism, presenting communism as a philosophically, historically, and scientifically justified alternative that would inevitably replace capitalism. They saw themselves as revolutionary leaders of the growing proletariat (the working class). The following is a selection from the Communist Manifesto.

CONSIDER: *The appeal of the ideas presented here; the concrete policies advocated by Marx and Engels; the historical and intellectual trends reflected in the Manifesto.*

A specter is haunting Europe—the specter of Communism. All the powers of old Europe have entered into a holy alliance to exorcise this specter; Pope and Czar, Metternich and Guizot, French radicals and German police spies.

Where is the party in opposition that has not been decried as Communistic by its opponents in power? Where the opposition that has not hurled back the branding reproach of Communism, against the more advanced opposition parties, as well as against its reactionary adversaries?

Two things result from this fact.

I. Communism is already acknowledged by all European powers to be in itself a power.

SOURCE: Karl Marx and Friedrich Engels, *Manifesto of the Communist Party*, 2nd ed. (New York: National Executive Committee of the Socialist Labor Party, 1898), pp. 30–32, 41–43, 60.

II. It is high time that Communists should openly, in the face of the whole world, publish their views, their aims, their tendencies, and meet this nursery tale of the Specter of Communism with a Manifesto of the party itself.

To this end the Communists of various nationalities have assembled in London, and sketched the following manifesto to be published in the English, French, German, Italian, Flemish and Danish languages.

❧

In what relation do the Communists stand to the proletarians as a whole?

The Communists do not form a separate party opposed to other working class parties.

They have no interests separate and apart from those of the proletariat as a whole.

They do not set up any sectarian principles of their own by which to shape and mould the proletarian movement.

The Communists are distinguished from the other working class parties by this only: 1. In the national struggles of the proletarians of the different countries, they point out and bring to the front the common interests of the entire proletariat, independently of all nationality. 2. In the various stages of development which the struggle of the working class against the bourgeoisie has to pass through, they always and everywhere represent the interests of the movement as a whole.

The Communists, therefore, are on the one hand, practically, the most advanced and resolute section of the working class parties of every country, that section which pushes forward all others; on the other hand, theoretically, they have over the great mass of the proletariat the advantage of clearly understanding the line of march, the conditions, and the ultimate general results of the proletarian movement.

The immediate aim of the Communists is the same as that of all the other proletarian parties: formation of the proletariat into a class, overthrow of the bourgeois supremacy, conquest of political power by the proletariat.

The theoretical conclusions of the Communists are in no way based on ideas or principles that have been invented, or discovered, by this or that would-be universal reformer.

They merely express, in general terms, actual relations springing from an existing class struggle, from a historical movement going on under our very eyes. The abolition of existing property relations is not at all a distinctive feature of Communism.

All property relations in the past have continually been subject to historical change, consequent upon the change in historical conditions.

The French revolution, for example, abolished feudal property in favor of bourgeois property.

The distinguishing feature of Communism is not the abolition of property generally, but the abolition of bourgeois property. But modern bourgeois private property is the final and most complete expression of the system of producing and appropriating products, that is based on class antagonisms, on the exploitation of the many by the few.

In this sense the theory of the Communists may be summed up in the single sentence: Abolition of private property.

We have seen above that the first step in the revolution by the working class is to raise the proletariat to the position of the ruling class; to win the battle of democracy.

The proletariat will use its political supremacy to wrest, by degrees, all capital from the bourgeoisie; to centralize all instruments of production in the hands of the State, *i.e.*, of the proletariat organized as the ruling class; and to increase the total of productive forces as rapidly as possible.

Of course, in the beginning this cannot be effected except by means of despotic inroads on the rights of property and on the conditions of bourgeois production; by means of measures, therefore, which appear economically insufficient and untenable, but which, in the course of the movement, outstrip themselves, necessitate further inroads upon the old social order and are unavoidable as a means of entirely revolutionizing the mode of production.

These measures will, of course, be different in different countries.

Nevertheless in the most advanced countries the following will be pretty generally applicable:

1. Abolition of property in land and application of all rents of land to public purposes.

2. A heavy progressive or graduated income tax.

3. Abolition of all right of inheritance.

4. Confiscation of the property of all emigrants and rebels.

5. Centralization of credit in the hands of the State, by means of a national bank with State capital and an exclusive monopoly.

6. Centralization of the means of communication and transport in the hands of the State.

7. Extension of factories and instruments of production owned by the State; the bringing into cultivation of waste lands, and the improvement of the soil generally in accordance with a common plan.

8. Equal liability of all to labor. Establishment of industrial armies, especially for agriculture.

9. Combination of agriculture with manufacturing industries: gradual abolition of the distinction between town and country, by a more equable distribution of the population over the country.

10. Free education for all children in public schools. Abolition of children's factory labor in its present form. Combination of education with industrial production, etc., etc.

When, in the course of development, class distinctions have disappeared and all production has been concentrated in the hands of a vast association of the whole nation, the public power will lose its political character. Political power, properly so called, is merely the organized power of one class for oppressing another. If the proletariat during its contest with the bourgeoisie is compelled, by the force of circumstances, to organize itself as a class, if, by means of a revolution, it makes itself the ruling class, and, as such, sweeps away by force the old conditions of production, then it will, along with these conditions, have swept away the conditions for the existence of class antagonisms, and of classes generally, and will thereby have abolished its own supremacy as a class.

In place of the old bourgeois society with its classes and class antagonisms we shall have an association in which the free development of each is the condition for the free development of all.

Socialist Women: Becoming a Socialist

Anna Maier

Between 1850 and 1914 numerous working-class women joined unions and various working-class political organizations. As socialism became more popular in the last decades of the nineteenth century, more and more working-class women were attracted to socialist organizations. At first, most socialist leaders took little account of the specific needs of women workers, but over time more attention was paid to women's issues and women gained leadership roles within socialist organizations. In the following selection Anna Maier describes how she became a socialist by joining the Social Democrats in Austria during the 1890s.

CONSIDER: *What experiences led Anna Maier to become a socialist; the consequences of her becoming a socialist.*

SOURCE: Adelheid Popp, ed., *A Commemorative Book: Twenty Years of the Austrian Women Workers' Movement* (Vienna, 1912), pp. 107–109, in Eleanor S. Riemer and John C. Fout, eds., *European Women: A Documentary History, 1789–1945* (New York: Schocken Books, 1980), pp. 94–95.

When I turned thirteen my mother took me by the hand and we went to see the manager of a tobacco factory to get me a job. The manager refused to hire me but my mother begged him to change his mind, since she explained, my father had died. I was hired. When I was getting ready to go to work the next day, my mother told me that I was to keep quiet and do what I was told. That was easier said than done. The treatment you received in this factory was really brutal. Young girls were often abused or even beaten by the older women. I rebelled strongly against that. I tried anything that might help improve things for me. As a child I was very pious and used to listen enthusiastically to the priests telling stories from the Bible. So, when things were going badly for me [at work], I would go to church on Sundays where I prayed so intently that I saw or heard nothing going on around me. When I went back to work on Monday, things were not any better and sometimes they were worse. I asked myself: Can there be a higher power that rewards good and punishes evil? I said to myself, no, that cannot be.

Several years went by. The *Women Workers' Newspaper* [*Arbeiterinnen-Zeitung*] began to appear and a few issues were smuggled into the factory by one of the older women. The more I was warned to stay away from this woman, the more I went to her to ask her if she would lend me a copy of the newspaper since I didn't have enough money to buy my own. At that time work hours were very long and the pay was very low. When my friend lent me a copy of the newspaper, I had to keep it hidden and I couldn't even let my mother see it if I took it home. I came to understand many things, my circle of acquaintances grew and when a political organization was founded in Sternberg, the workers were urged to join—only the men, the women were left out. A party representative came to us since I was already married by then. When he came by for the third time I asked him if I wasn't mature enough to become a member of the organization. He was embarrassed but replied: "When do you want to?" So I joined and I am a member of the party to this day.

I attended all the meetings, took part in all the demonstrations and it was not long before I was punished by the manager of the factory. I was taken off a good job and put in a poorer one just because I had become a Social Democrat. Nothing stopped me though; I said to myself, if this official is against it, out of fear to be sure, then it can't be all bad. When the tobacco workers' union was founded in November 1899, I joined and we had some big battles before we were able to make progress. Through these two organizations I have matured into a class-conscious fighter and I am now trying to win over mothers to the cause so that future children of the proletariat will have a happier youth than I had.

Why We Are Militant

Emmeline Pankhurst

The movement for female suffrage had deep roots in the nineteenth century, but gained force toward the end of the century. Various women's organizations in the West circulated petitions, led marches, and held demonstrations to support their demands for the right to vote. In the years before World War I, women's groups became more militant in the face of refusals by governmental officials to act. In Britain, Emmeline Pankhurst (1858–1928) helped organize the Women's Social and Political Union, which conducted assaults on private property and hunger strikes to promote the cause of women's suffrage. In the following excerpt from a 1913 speech, Pankhurst explains why her group is so militant.

CONSIDER: *The problems facing women who wanted to gain the right to vote; how Pankhurst explains why it became necessary for women to revolt; what arguments government officials might use to oppose Pankhurst.*

I know that in your minds there are questions like these; you are saying, "Woman Suffrage is sure to come; the emancipation of humanity is an evolutionary process, and how is it that some women, instead of trusting to that evolution, instead of educating the masses of people of their country, instead of educating their own sex to prepare them for citizenship, how is it that these militant women are using violence and upsetting the business arrangements of the country in their undue impatience to attain their end?" . . .

Meanwhile, during the '80's, women, like men, were asking for the franchise. Appeals, larger and more numerous than for any other reform, were presented in support of Woman's Suffrage. Meetings of the great corporations, great town councils, and city councils, passed resolutions asking that women should have the vote. More meetings were held, and larger, for Woman Suffrage than were held for votes for men, and yet the women did not get it. Men got the vote because they were and would be violent. The women did not get it because they were constitutional and law-abiding. Why, is it not evident to everyone that people who are patient where mis-government is concerned may go on being patient! Why should anyone trouble to help them? I take to myself some shame that through all those years, at any rate from the early '80's, when I first came into the Suffrage movement, I did not learn my political lessons.

I believed, as many women still in England believe, that women could get their way in some mysterious manner, by purely peaceful methods. We have been so accustomed, we women, to accept one standard for men and another standard for women, that we have even applied that variation of standard to the injury of our political welfare.

Having had better opportunities of education, and having had some training in politics, having in political life come so near to the "superior" being as to see that he was not altogether such a fount of wisdom as they had supposed, that he had his human weaknesses as we had, the twentieth century women began to say to themselves. "Is it not time, since our methods have failed and the men's have succeeded, that we should take a leaf out of their political book?" . . .

Well, I say the time is long past when it became necessary for women to revolt in order to maintain their self respect in Great Britain. The women who are waging this war are women who would fight, if it were only for the idea of liberty—if it were only that they might be free citizens of a free country—I myself would fight for that idea alone. But we have, in addition to this love of freedom, intolerable grievances to redress. . . .

Well, in Great Britain, we have tried persuasion, we have tried the plan of showing (by going upon public bodies, where they allowed us to do work they hadn't much time to do themselves) that we are capable people. We did it in the hope that we should convince them and persuade them to do the right and proper thing. But we had all our labour for our pains, and now we are fighting for our rights, and we are growing stronger and better women in the process. We are getting more fit to use our rights because we have such difficulty in getting them.

Syllabus of Errors

Pope Pius IX

Critics of middle-class liberalism were not limited to those demanding more rapid, radical changes such as the Marxists. From the time of the French Revolution, the conservative Catholic Church was usually hostile to most of the changes favored by the middle class and by doctrines of liberalism. Indeed, in the decades just after mid-century, when it had become apparent that traditional society was on the wane, the Church became more intransigent than ever. In 1864 Pius IX, who served as pope from 1846 to 1878, issued the famous "Syllabus of Errors," in which most of the major forces of the

SOURCE: Jane Marcus, ed., *Suffrage and the Pankhursts* (New York: Routledge and Kegan Paul, 1987), pp. 153–156.

SOURCE: From William E. Gladstone, *The Vatican Decrees in Their Bearing on Civil Allegiance: A Political Expostulation* (New York: Harper and Brothers, 1875), pp. 109–129.

nineteenth century were formally rejected. The following excerpts from that document should be read with care; they present views the Church specifically rejected as errors, not views accepted by the Church.

CONSIDER: *Why Pius IX took this stand; the dilemma faced by Catholics who were also middle class and liberal; the groups that might favor the Church's view as expressed here.*

15. Every man is free to embrace and profess the religion he shall believe true, guided by the light of reason.

16. Men may in any religion find the way of eternal salvation, and obtain eternal salvation.

❧

39. The commonwealth is the origin and source of all rights, and possesses rights which are not circumscribed by any limits.

❧

45. The entire direction of public schools, in which the youth of Christian states are educated, except (to a certain extent) in the case of episcopal seminaries, may and must appertain to the civil power, and belong to it so far that no other authority whatsoever shall be recognized as having any right to interfere in the discipline of the schools, the arrangement of the studies, the taking of degrees, or the choice and approval of the teachers.

❧

47. The best theory of civil society requires that popular schools open to the children of all classes, and, generally, all public institutes intended for instruction in letters and philosophy, and for conducting the education of the young, should be freed from all ecclesiastical authority, government, and interference, and should be fully subject to the civil and political power, in conformity with the will of rulers and the prevalent opinions of the age.

❧

56. Moral laws do not stand in need of the divine sanction, and there is no necessity that human laws should be conformable to the laws of nature, and receive their sanction from God.

57. Knowledge of philosophical things and morals, and also civil laws, may and must depart from divine and ecclesiastical authority.

❧

78. In the present day, it is no longer expedient that the Catholic religion shall be held as the only religion of the State, to the exclusion of all other modes of worship.

❧

80. The Roman Pontiff can and ought to reconcile himself to, and agree with, progress, liberalism, and civilization as lately introduced.

Foundations of the Nineteenth Century: Racism

Houston Stewart Chamberlain

During the second half of the nineteenth century, elements of nationalism, Darwinism, and Romanticism were combined by various writers to produce racist theories and provide justification for the growth of racist views. One of the most famous of these writers was Houston Stewart Chamberlain (1855–1927), an Englishman who moved to Germany and became a naturalized German. There he wrote Foundations of the Nineteenth Century *(1900), which soon became a popular success. In it he stressed the importance of racism for the development of civilization. The following selection from that book deals with the "German race."*

CONSIDER: *The characteristics of the "German race"; the ways in which this selection reflects racist thought; how this might relate to German nationalism.*

Let us attempt a glance into the depths of the soul. What are the specific intellectual and moral characteristics of this Germanic race? Certain anthropologists would fain teach us that all races are equally gifted; we point to history and answer: that is a lie! The races of mankind are markedly different in the nature and also in the extent of their gift, and the Germanic races belong to the most highly gifted group, the group usually termed Aryan. Is this human family united and uniform by bonds of blood? Do these stems really all spring from the same root? I do not know and I do not much care; no affinity binds more closely than elective affinity, and in this sense the Indo-European Aryans certainly form a family. . . .

Physically and mentally the Aryans are pre-eminent among all peoples; for that reason they are by right, as the Stagirite expresses it, the lords of the world. Aristotle puts the matter still more concisely when he says, "Some men are by nature free, others slaves"; this perfectly expresses the moral aspect. For freedom is by no means an

SOURCE: Houston Stewart Chamberlain, *Foundations of the Nineteenth Century,* vol. I (New York: Howard Fertig, 1968), pp. 542–543.

abstract thing, to which every human being has fundamentally a claim; a right to freedom must evidently depend upon capacity for it, and this again presupposes physical and intellectual power. One may make the assertion, that even the mere conception of freedom is quite unknown to most men. Do we not see the *homo syriacus* develop just as well and as happily in the position of slave as of master? Do the Chinese not show us another example of the same nature? Do not all historians tell us that the Semites and half-Semites, in spite of their great intelligence, never succeeded in founding a State that lasted, and that because every one always endeavoured to grasp all power for himself, thus showing that their capabilities were limited to despotism and anarchy, the two opposites of freedom?

Judaism in Music: Anti-Semitism

Richard Wagner

One of the darkest aspects of racist thought during the second half of the nineteenth century was its growing stress on anti-Semitism. Anti-Semitism has a long history, but it welled up with new strength after mid-century, particularly in Germany, where it became an important social and political force. An example of this bitter anti-Semitism comes from the pen of the great German composer, Richard Wagner (1813–1883). The following is an excerpt from "Judaism in Music," an article he published in a German journal in 1850.

CONSIDER: *The elements of Wagner's anti-Semitism; the support he uses for his arguments against the Jew; how this relates to the ideas of Houston Stewart Chamberlain.*

SOURCE: Louis L. Snyder, ed., *Documents of German History* (New Brunswick, NJ: Rutgers University Press, 1958), pp. 192–193.

It is necessary for us to explain the *involuntary repugnance* we possess for the nature and personality of the Jews. . . . According to the present constitution of the world, the Jew in truth is already more than emancipate: He rules, and will rule, as long as Money remains the power before which all our doings and our dealings lose their force. . . . The public art taste has been brought between the busy fingers of the Jews, who reside over an art bazaar. . . . The Jew's outward appearance always has something disagreeably foreign about it. . . .

The Jew speaks the language of the nation in whose midst he dwells from generation to generation, but he always speaks it as an alien. Our whole European art and civilization have remained to the Jew a foreign tongue. In this speech, this art, the Jew can only after-speak and after-patch—cannot truly make a poem of his words, an artwork of his doings. In the peculiarities of Semitic pronunciation the first thing that strikes our ear as quite outlandish and unpleasant, in the Jew's production of the voice sounds, is a creaking, squeaking, buzzing snuffle. . . . The Jew who is innately incapable of enouncing himself to us artistically through either his outward appearance or his speech, and least of all through his singing, has, nevertheless, been able in the widest-spread of modern art varieties, to wit, in Music, to reach the rulership of public taste. . . . Control of money through usury has led the Jews to power, for modern culture is accessible to none but the well-to-do. . . .

The Jews have never produced a true poet. [Heinrich Heine] reached the point where he duped himself into a poet, and was rewarded by his versified lies being set to music by our own composers. He was the conscience of Judaism, just as Judaism is the evil conscience of our modern civilization.

Visual Sources

The Hatch Family: The Upper Middle Class

Eastman Johnson

The following 1871 portrait of the Hatch family by the American artist Eastman Johnson (figure 25.1) shows a number of elements of the condition, style of life, and values of the upper middle class. Both the quality and quantity of the furnishings and the clothes indicate how materially well to do this family is. The clothes and demeanor convey the strong sense of propriety; yet the activities of the children

and the position of their toys denote how child-centered this family is. The appropriate gender roles are suggested: the father at center right in an authoritative pose, with pen in hand sitting at his desk, the grandfather on the left, keeping up on the news by reading a paper, the mother on the right, generally surveying her children, and the grandmother on the left, knitting. The large painting on the left as well as the sculptures on the right show this family to be properly supportive and appreciative of the arts. The large bookcase on the right indicates a respect for literature and learning. Heavy curtains largely block out the outside world; values

FIGURE 25.1   (The Metropolitan Museum of Art, Gift of Frederick H. Hatch, 1926)

of domesticity and privacy are evident.

CONSIDER: *What lessons the nineteenth-century viewer might learn from this portrait.*

The Ages of Woman

This mid-nineteenth-century French engraving (figure 25.2) shows an idealized image of the ages of woman. In the center, three religious scenes represent the purity of woman's origins, place on earth, and final destination. Around this foundation is the woman at nine ages, from the happy playful child of ten years old to the solitary honorable grandmother of ninety years old. In between she is shown in her role as a middle-class wife, mother, and grandmother.

CONSIDER: *What image of women's proper nature and role this conveys to nineteenth-century viewers; how this fits with the Eastman Johnson portrait and the analysis of European women by Riemer and Fout that follows; how an image of the ages of man might differ.*

FIGURE 25.2   (© Musee Nat. des Arts et Traditions Populaires, Paris, France, Lauros/Giraudon/Bridgeman Art Library)

Lunch Hour: The Working Class
Käthe Kollwitz

Accompanying the rise to prominence of the upper middle class was the growth of the urban working class, the two economically dependent on each other but in strikingly different conditions. This 1909 drawing by the German artist Käthe Kollwitz (figure 25.3), entitled Lunch Hour, *gives an impression of the condition and spirit of the German working class. The workers seem to be part of an almost undifferentiated mass, dully and similarly clothed, eating low-quality meals in uncomfortable circumstances, and above all displaying a physical and psychological fatigue and a pervasive sense of discouragement.*

CONSIDER: *How this drawing relates to the views of Marx and Engels.*

The Stages of a Worker's Life

Léon Frédéric

Léon Frédéric (1856–1940), for a time Belgium's most famous painter, tried to encompass all stages of a worker's life in this large 1895 triptych (figure 25.4). In the foreground of the central panel, children on the right play cards while on the left they carry and nibble bread. Their parents and young couples stand just behind them; in the background are the aged members of the working class whose ultimate fate is marked by the distant but approaching funeral coach. The left side panel depicts the man's work world, where men of all ages, from adolescence to old age, engage in manual labor or observe it. In the foreground they are

FIGURE 25.3 (Käthe Kollwitz: *Lunch Hour*. Black charcoal and ink on paper. Nagel/Timm 469. Private Collection. Photo courtesy Galerie St. Etienne, New York)

digging while in the middle ground they struggle with heavy beams. Behind them are the factories where they work. The right side panel shows women's world, all mothering and

FIGURE 25.4 (Réunion des Musées Nationaux/Art Resource, NY)

nurturing with babies in their arms and at their breasts. Behind them are market stalls where they shop. Here is a vision of workers' lives in a nutshell: hard manual labor for men, childrearing and food preparation for women, and at the end old age and death for all.

CONSIDER: Whether this seems like a realistic depiction of workers' lives; how, in content and tone, a corresponding depiction of middle-class lives might look.

The City

Jacob Steinhardt

During the decades surrounding the turn of the century, great cities like Brussels, Paris, Milan, London, and Berlin became thriving embodiments of modern life. But many artists revealed disturbing undersides to these modern urban centers.

The 1913 canvas, The City (figure 25.5), by German expressionist artist Jacob Steinhardt (1887–1968) is one apt example. In this painting, throngs of people and modern streetcars push through the city boulevards at night. Electric lights from street lamps and store windows blaze; around corners, people half-disappear into shadows. In the left foreground, a man sleeps, perhaps dreaming. Above him a distracted nude woman (probably a prostitute) sits framed at a window, while above her haunting figures revel and lean out to ogle the action. Buildings loom over the people below. The scene evokes the frenzy, decadence, and danger of the modern city—the dark side of the years leading up to the "Great War."

CONSIDER: How this painting suggests the stresses of city life during the years before World War I.

FIGURE 25.5 (© Bildarchiv Preussischer Kulturbesitz/Art Resource, NY)

 ## Secondary Sources

The Decline of Political Liberalism

F. H. Hinsley

Despite the apparent failures of 1848, political liberalism was at its zenith during the middle of the nineteenth century. By the last two decades of the century it was clearly on the decline or was at least evolving in striking new ways. This

SOURCE: F. H. Hinsley, "Introduction," in *The New Cambridge Modern History*, vol. XI, F. H. Hinsley, ed. (Cambridge, England: Cambridge University Press, 1962), pp. 32–34. Reprinted by permission of the publisher.

evolution is analyzed in the following selection from The New Cambridge Modern History by F. H. Hinsley of Cambridge.

CONSIDER: The causes of the decline of political liberalism; the intellectual or ideological developments that occurred in the second half of the nineteenth century, as reflected by the decline of political liberalism.

The politics of the age was distinguished, even in the least authoritarian of states, as much by the growth of authority as by the extension of democracy; and less by the extension of democracy and the democratisation of government than by an advance towards the democratisation of government policies and of the political context in which governments operated. It is these facts which account for the collapse of liberalism—for its exhaustion in more democratic countries as well as for its frustration in less democratic circumstances and its distortion in situations that were in between.

In the advanced countries of western Europe during the 1870's, when liberalism was at its zenith in its European home, liberal governments, abandoning the liberal opposition to the power of the state and seeing the state as the most effective means of securing the liberal conception of freedom in changed circumstances, accepted the early steps towards the inevitable extension of the functions of government and the use of unprecedented state compulsion on individuals for social ends—embracing the notion of state education, legalising trade unions, justifying public health measures, adopting even insurance and factory legislation. No governments in such countries, whatever their political complexion, could, indeed, have opposed such developments. From the end of the 1870's, however, they were overrun and overturned in those countries by the further progress of those twin forces, the masses and the modern state. Every advance in the role of the state, every new aspect of the social problem, every recognition of the emergence of the masses, every new turn of policy—whether towards protectionism and imperialism or towards social regulation and the extension of the franchise—conflicted with the liberal belief in freedom of contract and of enterprise, in free trade, in individual liberty, in public economy, in the minimum of government interference. Liberalism's great contribution, the constitutional state, and its guiding principles, the freedom of the individual, legal equality and conflict with the Church, were—to the varying extents that they had been already established in these states—taken over by more empirical and conservative politicians. Liberalism became more doctrinaire and more narrowly associated with urban and big business interests—even while industrial organisation itself, with the movement from personal to corporate control, was deserting it. The liberal parties split into moderate (national, social or imperialist) and radical wings on these current issues and lost office. Liberal rule or its equivalent ended in Great Britain in 1885, in Germany in 1878, in Austria and the Netherlands in 1879, in Sweden in 1880, in Belgium in 1884, in France in 1885. In Italy under Depretis and Crispi and in some states beyond western Europe liberal parties remained in power. But, liberal only in name, they embraced protectionism and imperialism, undertook social regulation and retained of the old liberal creed only opposition to the extension of the franchise and to the pretensions of the Church. In these states, as in even more authoritarian countries, authentic liberalism remained a relevant if a weakened basis for opposition to established authority. But even in that role, and even when it was not proscribed by the increased possibilities of repression, it was doomed to frustration by the growth of the need for social regulation and strong government and by the demand for those things by the mass of the population.

The Unfinished Revolution: Marxism Interpreted

Adam B. Ulam

Critical analyses of Marx and Marxism abound and from almost all points of view. From the historian's perspective, one of the most useful ways to approach Marx and Marxism is to place both in their historical context. This is done in the following excerpt from The Unfinished Revolution *by Adam Ulam, a professor of government at Harvard who has written extensively on the history of Marxism and the Soviet Union. Here he attempts to explain aspects of both the content and the appeal of Marxism by pointing to intellectual traditions affecting Marx and social realities conditioning those who accepted it.*

CONSIDER: *Why Marxism is most appealing during the early period of industrialization; how Ulam would explain the apparent failure of Marxism to take hold in twentieth-century nations such as the United States; what Ulam means when he calls Marx a child of rationalistic optimism; how a more pro-Marxist scholar might respond to this interpretation.*

Here, then, is a theory attuned even more closely than other parts of Marxism to the facts and feelings of an early period of industrialization. The class struggle is the salt of Marxism, its most operative revolutionary part. As a historical and psychological concept, it expresses a gross oversimplification, but it is the oversimplification of a genius. The formula of the class struggle seizes the essence of the mood of a great historical moment—a revolution in basic economy—and generalizes it into a historical law. It extracts the grievances of groups of politically conscious workers in Western Europe, then a very small part of the whole proletariat, and sees in it the portent and meaning of the awakening of the whole working class everywhere. The *first* reaction of the worker to industrialization, his feelings of

SOURCE: Adam B. Ulam, *The Unfinished Revolution* (New York: Random House, Inc., 1960), pp. 42–44. Reprinted by permission of the author.

grievance and impotence before the machine, his employer, and the state which stands behind the employer, are assumed by Marx to be typical of the general reactions of the worker to industrialization. What does change in the process of the development of industry is that the worker's feeling of impotence gives way to class consciousness, which in turn leads him to class struggle and socialism. Marx's worker is the historical worker, but he is the historical worker of a specific period of industrial and political development.

Even in interpreting the psychology of the worker of the transitional period, Marx exhibited a rationalistic bias. The worker's opposition to the capitalist order is a total opposition to its laws, its factories, and its government. But this revolutionary consciousness of the worker is to take him next to Marxist socialism, where he will accept the factory system and the state, the *only* difference being the abolition of capitalism. Why shouldn't the revolutionary protest of the worker flow into other channels: into rejection of industrialism as well as capitalism, into rejection of the socialist as well as the capitalist state? It is here that Marx is most definitely the child of his age, the child of rationalistic optimism: the workers will undoubtedly translate their anarchistic protests and grievances into a sophisticated philosophy of history. They will undoubtedly realize that the forces of industrialism and modern life, which strip them of property, status, and economic security, are in themselves benevolent in their ultimate effects and that it is only capitalism and the capitalists which make them into instruments of oppression. The chains felt by the proletariat are the chains of the industrial system. The chains Marx urges them to throw off are those of capitalism. Will the workers understand the difference? And if they do, will they still feel that in destroying capitalism they have a "world to win"?

European Women

Eleanor S. Riemer and John C. Fout

In recent years many historians have pointed out the limitations facing middle-class women between 1850 and 1914. As investigations into women's history have multiplied and deepened, new interpretations have been made. In the following selection the historians Eleanor S. Riemer and John C. Fout argue that middle-class women during this period increasingly questioned their roles and often expanded their activities into new, important areas.

Source: From *European Women: A Documentary History, 1789–1945,* edited by Eleanor S. Riemer and John C. Fout. Copyright © 1980 by Schocken Books, Inc. Reprinted by permission of Schocken Books, published by Pantheon Books, a division of Random House, Inc.

CONSIDER: *How middle-class women's maternal and housewifely roles were justified; ways in which middle-class women expanded their roles; how middle-class women's new roles affected their attitudes.*

Middle-class women, too, faced new situations and challenges in the nineteenth and twentieth centuries. Although some lower-middle-class women continued to work alongside their shopkeeper husbands as they had in the past, most married middle-class women did not, and never expected to have to work for wages. Their lives were centered on caring for their children and homes. But most middle-class women did not lead leisured existences. Indeed, they found that the demands on their time and energy increased as modernization progressed, and middle-class families' standards for cleanliness, food preparation, and physical comfort were upgraded.

Middle-class women's maternal and housewifely roles were justified in the nineteenth century by a twofold conception of women's nature and capabilities. On the one hand, women were considered passive creatures who were physically and intellectually inferior to men. Thus, women needed protection and direction from their fathers and husbands. On the other hand, women, because they were nonaggressive and sexually passive and were removed from the contamination of the competitive workaday world, were deemed morally superior to men and were to be respected for that. A woman's unique capability and greatest responsibility in life was caring for the moral and spiritual needs of her family.

The contradictions within this ideal and women's attempts to reconcile or dispel them are recurring and major themes in the documents. From the middle of the nineteenth century large numbers of middle-class women consciously and methodically expanded their maternal and moral roles—and thus their sphere of competence—outside their homes to society at large. One way they accomplished this was by transforming middle-and upper-class women's traditional, and often haphazard, charitable work into organized movements for social reform. These women became increasingly interested in the problems of poor women and children. They believed they understood and shared many of the concerns of working-class mothers and considered these women and their children the primary victims of the economic and social dislocations caused by urbanization and the new industrial order.

Through their social welfare and reform work, middle-class women gained a sense of both their own competence and their limitations in a world controlled by men. Many also realized that although women of their class expected to be dependent wives, economic and social realities were such that there was no guarantee women would be supported by men throughout their lives. Many came to believe that their own limited educations and the restrictions placed on them by the law and the ideals of ladylike conduct left women ill-equipped for the roles they might have to—or want to—play in life. Thus, the reform of society and reforms for women became closely identified and often were confronted simultaneously by organized women all over Europe.

✑ CHAPTER QUESTIONS

1. Give support for the argument that the nineteenth century was above all a middle-class century.

2. What common elements are there among the various criticisms of the middle class, its ideas, and its lifestyle?

3. How would you explain the rise of Marxist and socialist ideas and movements during the second half of the nineteenth century?

4. Contrast the ways in which the social, cultural, and economic changes of the period affected men and women.

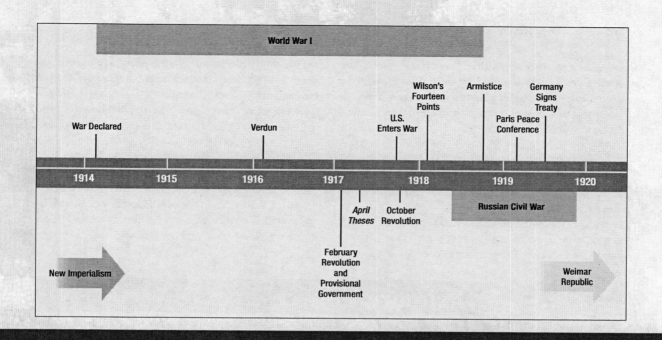

26 War and Revolution: 1914–1920

Historians usually mark the end of the nineteenth century not at the turn of the century but with the outbreak of World War I in 1914. Although a number of wars took place after 1815, none covered all of Europe, none was long, and none was very costly. Indeed, many Europeans optimistically believed that the Western nations had become too economically interdependent and culturally mature to become involved in massive wars ever again. At the outbreak of World War I no one expected it to be so widespread or long-lasting. In fact, the fighting continued for four years before the war was finally concluded. The destruction was so unprecedented and the fighting so brutal that many people questioned whether Western civilization had progressed at all. The war was such a strain that the most modernized nations, England, France, and

Germany, for example, mobilized the total resources of their societies, while less modernized nations like Russia were unable to support the effort.

Revolutions occurred in a number of areas, most notably in Germany, the Austro-Hungarian Empire, and Russia. The revolutions in Russia were the most significant. In March 1917 the tsarist government was swept from power by relatively moderate, liberal groups. In November of that year the new Provisional Government was toppled by the Bolsheviks, who initiated a Communist regime that proved surprisingly resilient. Under this government, the Soviet Union was to become a significant force in world politics.

In some ways the Paris Peace Conference in 1919 brought the period to a close, but the problems facing diplomats and heads of state meeting in Versailles were

147

overwhelming. The Soviet Union was not invited to the conference, and the Germans were virtually ignored. Few left the conference satisfied, and many harbored resentments that would color domestic and international politics during the 1920s and 1930s.

This chapter focuses on World War I and the Russian Revolution. With World War I, the two major issues for historians are the cause and the settlement. What caused this apparently unwanted war to break out and who, if anyone, was most to blame? Was the Peace of Paris a success or a failure? Some of the selections also explore tactics used to fight the war, people's experiences during the war, and the results of the war. Other documents deal with the ways the war affected women. With the Russian Revolution, the question is not only why it occurred but also how and why the Bolsheviks—through most of 1917 only a small party— were ultimately able to gain and maintain power against extremely long odds. A number of documents illustrate Lenin's strategy and Bolshevik policy as well as the variety of scholarly efforts to answer these questions.

Many feel that the events during this period of war constituted a fundamental break with the past. The significance of World War I and the Russian Revolution are shown in the developments in the two decades that followed. These will be covered in Chapters 27 and 28.

 # Primary Sources

Reports from the Front: The Battle for Verdun, 1916

The widely anticipated short war typified by heroic offensive thrusts failed to materialize. Instead, it turned into a long, extraordinarily brutal struggle. On the Western front, opposing armies slaughtered each other from their trenches. There are numerous reports of life at the front, such as the following account by a French Army officer of the battle for Verdun in 1916.

CONSIDER: *Why the defense was at such an advantage; why there was a willingness to sacrifice so much for such small advances.*

The Germans attacked in massed formation, by big columns of five or six hundred men, preceded by two waves of sharpshooters. We had only our rifles and our machine guns, because the 75's could not get to work.

Fortunately the flank batteries succeeded in catching the Boches on the right. It is absolutely impossible to convey what losses the Germans must suffer in these attacks. Nothing can give the idea of it. Whole ranks are mowed down, and those that follow them suffered the same fate. Under the storm of machine gun, rifle and 75 fire, the German columns were plowed into furrows of death. Imagine if you can what it would be like to rake water. Those gaps filled up again at once. That is enough to show with what disdain of human life the German attacks are planned and carried out.

In these circumstances German advances are sure. They startle the public, but at the front nobody attaches any importance to them. As a matter of fact, our trenches are so near those of the Germans that once the barbed wire is destroyed the distance between them can be covered in a few minutes. Thus, if one is willing to suffer a loss of life corresponding to the number of men necessary to cover the space between the lines, the other trench can always be reached. By sacrificing thousands of men, after a formidable bombardment, an enemy trench can always be taken.

There are slopes on Hill 304 where the level of the ground is raised several meters by mounds of German corpses. Sometimes it happens that the third German wave uses the dead of the second wave as ramparts and shelters. It was behind ramparts of the dead left by the first five attacks, on May 24th, that we saw the Boches take shelter while they organized their next rush.

We make prisoners among these dead during our counterattacks. They are men who have received no hurt, but have been knocked down by the falling of the human wall of their killed and wounded neighbors. They say very little. They are for the most part dazed with fear and alcohol, and it is several days before they recover.

Dulce et Decorum Est: Disillusionment

Wilfred Owen

The experience of World War I was profoundly disillusioning to those who believed in nineteenth-century ideals. After World War I, Europe was no longer characterized by the sense of optimism, progress, and glory that had typified Europe for most of the period between the eighteenth century and 1914. This is

SOURCE: From *Source Records of the Great War*, vol. IV, ed. Charles F. Horne (New York: National Alumni, 1923), pp. 222–223.

SOURCE: C. Day Lewis, *Collected Poems of Wilfred Owen*. Reprinted by permission of New Directions and Chatto & Windus, p. 55. Copyright © Chatto & Windus, Ltd., 1946, 1963, and The Owen Estate.

evidenced in war poems that no longer glorified the struggle but instead conveyed a sense of the horror and futility about it. One of the best of these antiwar poets was Wilfred Owen, born in England in 1893 and killed in action in 1918, one week before the armistice. The following poem has the ironic ending, "It is sweet and proper to die for one's country."

CONSIDER: The psychological consequences of war for the soldiers; other ways this same disillusionment might be shown in novels, plays, paintings, or even historical analyses of the time.

DULCE ET DECORUM EST

Bent double, like old beggars under sacks,
Knock-kneed, coughing like hags, we cursed through sludge,
Till on the haunting flares we turned our backs
And towards our distant rest began to trudge.
Men marched asleep. Many had lost their boots
But limped on, blood-shod. All went lame; all blind;
Drunk with fatigue; deaf even to the hoots
Of tired, outstripped Five-Nines that dropped behind.

Gas! Gas! Quick, boys!—An Ecstasy of fumbling,
Fitting the clumsy helmets just in time;
But someone still was yelling out and stumbling
And flound'ring like a man in fire or lime . . .
Dim, through the misty panes and thick green light,
As under a green sea, I saw him drowning.
In all my dreams, before my helpless sight,
He plunges at me, guttering, choking, drowning.

If in some smothering dreams you too could pace
Behind the wagon that we flung him in,
And watch the white eyes writhing in his face,
His hanging face, like a devil's sick of sin;
If you could hear, at every jolt, the blood
Come gargling from the froth-corrupted lungs,
Obscene as cancer, bitter as the cud
Of vile, incurable sores on innocent tongues,—
My friend, you would not tell with such high zest
To children ardent for some desperate glory,
The old Lie: Dulce et decorum est
Pro patria mori.

The Home Front

Evelyn Blücher

As each year of the war dragged on, support from the home front became more crucial. For most people living away from the battle lines, conditions usually grew worse as the military drew resources and supplies for the armed forces. In the

following selection, Evelyn Blücher, an English wife of a German officer, describes the difficulties of life in Berlin during the winter of 1917.

CONSIDER: What seemed to bother people on the home front most; differences in the hardships faced by people in the countryside; what powers governments needed to manage the home fronts.

In a small town near here, a sad little ceremony took place the other day. The ancient church bell, which had rung the people from the cradle to the grave for 300 years and more, was requisitioned by the military authorities. The grief felt by the inhabitants was so great that they determined to do their ancient friend all the honor that they could; and after having performed the regular funeral service for the dead over it, a procession was formed, headed by the priest in his vestments, with his acolytes swinging their incense, and the inhabitants following the bell, which was covered with wreaths and flowers and handed over to the military authorities under tears and protestations.

As coffee and tea have entirely run out, all sorts of berries and leaves are being used as a surrogate. Chestnuts are used for feeding the deer, and it is interesting to see the children, who are not old enough to work otherwise, busy plucking and collecting the different things.

Nothing seems to be left unused—salad-oil being extracted from every kind of fruit-stone, and an excellent oil for greasing machinery is being pressed from the seeds of sunflowers. It is marvelous how much has been produced in this way, and it is only a pity we cannot use the latter for cooking and eating purposes too.

The difficulty of getting butter is increasing daily, and one has to use all one's power of persuasion to be able to entice a miserable quarter of a pound of it, after having begged in vain at quite a number of small peasants' houses. . . .

Lighting will prove a great problem this winter, as there is almost no petroleum or methylated spirits to be had; gas-light is next to impossible, on account of the small quantity allowed, and electric-light is also limited. . . .

This darkness is especially unpleasant for the people in the town who have to wait for the vegetables and fruit coming in from the country. Our gardener, who goes in daily, tells me that they stand for hours and hours patiently waiting to get but a pound of cabbage, onions, etc., which are all very scarce indeed. Luckily for the purchasers, maximum prices have been settled on all eatables, or it would be impossible for the poorer classes to get anything at all. . . .

The food question is always the most important topic of the day. The less there is of it, the more do we talk of it. The Austrians have already eaten up their stores, and are grumbling and turning to Germany for fresh supplies.

SOURCE: Evelyn Blücher, *An English Wife in Berlin* (New York: E. P. Dutton, 1920), pp. 183–184, 231.

It is rather like turning from a sandy desert to a rocky mountain for nourishment. . . .

We ourselves have little to eat but smoked meat and dried peas and beans, but in the towns they are considerably worse off. The potatoes have come to a premature end, and in Berlin the population have now a portion of 1 lb. per head a week, and these even are bad. The cold winds of this wintry June have retarded the growth of vegetables, and there is almost nothing to be had. We are all waiting hungrily for the harvest and the prospect of at least more bread and flour.

Program of the Provisional Government in Russia

In the spring of 1917 a revolution finally toppled the disintegrating tsarist government in Russia. A relatively moderate, liberal Provisional Government was formed under the leadership of men like Prince Lvov and Paul Miliukov. While the Provisional Government had to share and even compete for power with the more radical workers' political organizations—the soviets—it initially acted with speed to make important changes. The following is the early program of the Provisional Government, issued on March 16, 1917.

CONSIDER: *The attitudes revealed by this document; the nature of the reforms initiated; what this implies about the problems under the tsarist government and the discontents that supported the revolution.*

Citizens, the Provisional Executive Committee of the members of the Duma, with the aid and support of the garrison of the capital and its inhabitants, has triumphed over the dark forces of the Old Régime to such an extent as to enable it to organize a more stable executive power. . . .

The Cabinet will be guided in its actions by the following principles:

1. An immediate general amnesty for all political and religious offenses, including terrorist acts, military revolts, agrarian offenses, etc.

2. Freedom of speech and press; freedom to form labor unions and to strike. These political liberties should be extended to the army in so far as war conditions permit.

3. The abolition of all social, religious and national restrictions.

4. Immediate preparation for the calling of a Constituent Assembly, elected by universal and secret vote, which shall determine the form of government and draw up the Constitution for the country.

SOURCE: Frank A. Golder, ed., *Documents of Russian History, 1914–1917,* trans. Emanuel Aronsberg (New York: Prentice-Hall, Inc., 1927).

5. In place of the police, to organize a national militia with elective officers, and subject to the local self-government body.

6. Elections to be carried out on the basis of universal, direct, equal, and secret suffrage.

7. The troops that have taken part in the revolutionary movement shall not be disarmed or removed from Petrograd.

8. On duty and in war service, strict military discipline should be maintained, but when off duty, soldiers should have the same public rights as are enjoyed by other citizens.

The Provisional Government wishes to add that it has no intention of taking advantage of the existence of war conditions to delay the realization of the above-mentioned measures of reform.

April Theses: The Bolshevik Opposition

V. I. Lenin

Faced with a continuing war and deep discontent, the Provisional Government soon came under attack by people like Vladimir Ilyich Lenin (1870–1924), who called for more radical changes. Lenin, who spent much of his life as a revolutionary—often in exile—had risen to the leadership of the Bolshevik faction of the Russian Marxists. He combined the skills of a superb Marxist theoretician and a revolutionary organizer. In April 1917 the Germans aided his return to Russia in an effort to weaken the new government there. On his arrival, Lenin presented his April Theses, at first criticized by Russian Marxists but eventually accepted by the Bolshevik Central Committee.

CONSIDER: *Why Lenin rejects support for the Provisional Government; to whom this program might be appealing and why; the ways in which this program is particularly Marxist.*

1. In our attitude towards the war, which under the new government of Lvov and Co. unquestionably remains on Russia's part a predatory imperialist war owing to the capitalist nature of that government, not the slightest concession to a "revolutionary defencism" is permissible. . . .

2. The specific feature of the present situation in Russia is that the country is *passing* from the first stage of the revolution—which, owing to the insufficient class-consciousness and organisation of the proletariat,

SOURCE: From V. I. Lenin, *Collected Works,* vol. XXIV (Moscow: Progress Publishers, 1964), pp. 21–24. Reprinted by permission of the Copyright Agency of the U.S.S.R placed power in the hands of the bourgeoisie—to its *second* stage, which must place power in the hands of the proletariat and the poorest sections of the peasants. . . .

3. No support for the Provisional Government; . . .

5. Not a parliamentary republic—to return to a parliamentary republic from the Soviets of Workers' Deputies would be a retrograde step—but a republic of Soviets of Workers', Agricultural Labourers' and Peasants' Deputies throughout the country, from top to bottom. Abolition of the police, the army and the bureaucracy.

   The salaries of all officials, all of whom are elective and displaceable at any time, not to exceed the average wage of a competent worker.

6. The weight of emphasis in the agrarian programme to be shifted to the Soviets of Agricultural Labourers' Deputies.

   Confiscation of all landed estates.

   Nationalisation of *all* lands in the country, the land to be disposed of by the local Soviets of Agricultural Labourers' and Peasants' Deputies. The organisation of separate Soviets of Deputies of Poor Peasants.

   The setting up of a model farm on each of the large estates (ranging in size from 100 to 300 dessiatines, according to local and other conditions, and to the decisions of the local bodies) under the control of the Soviets of Agricultural Labourers' Deputies and for the public account.

7. The immediate amalgamation of all banks in the country into a single national bank, and the institution of control over it by the Soviet of Workers' Deputies.

8. It is not our *immediate* task to "introduce" socialism, but only to bring social production and the distribution of products at once under the *control* of the Soviets of Workers' Deputies.

Speech to the Petrograd Soviet— November 8, 1917: The Bolsheviks in Power

V. I. Lenin

The Provisional Government fell in a revolution in November 1917. Under the leadership of Lenin and Leon Trotsky (1877–1940), the tightly organized Bolsheviks quickly took control. On November 8, 1917, Lenin made the following speech to a meeting of the Petrograd Soviet.

Source: Frank A. Golder, ed., *Documents of Russian History, 1914–1917,* Emanuel Aronsberg, trans. Reprinted by permission of Prentice-Hall, Inc., pp. 618–619. Copyright © 1927 by Prentice-Hall, Inc.

CONSIDER: *The policies Lenin supported and how they compare with the program in his April Theses; the ways in which Lenin was relying on forces outside of Russia to sustain the initial success of this revolution.*

Comrades, the workmen's and peasants' revolution, the need of which the Bolsheviks have emphasized many times, has come to pass.

What is the significance of this revolution? Its significance is, in the first place, that we shall have a soviet government, without the participation of bourgeoisie of any kind. The oppressed masses will of themselves form a government. The old state machinery will be smashed into bits and in its place will be created a new machinery of government by the soviet organizations. From now on there is a new page in the history of Russia, and the present, third Russian revolution shall in its final result lead to the victory of Socialism.

One of our immediate tasks is to put an end to the war at once. But in order to end the war, which is closely bound up with the present capitalistic system, it is necessary to overthrow capitalism itself. In this work we shall have the aid of the world labor movement, which has already begun to develop in Italy, England, and Germany.

A just and immediate offer of peace by us to the international democracy will find everywhere a warm response among the international proletariat masses. In order to secure the confidence of the proletariat, it is necessary to publish at once all secret treaties.

In the interior of Russia a very large part of the peasantry has said: Enough playing with the capitalists; we will go with the workers. We shall secure the confidence of the peasants by one decree, which will wipe out the private property of the landowners. The peasants will understand that their only salvation is in union with the workers.

We will establish a real labor control on production.

We have now learned to work together in a friendly manner, as is evident from this revolution. We have the force of mass organization which has conquered all and which will lead the proletariat to world revolution.

We should now occupy ourselves in Russia in building up a proletarian socialist state.

Long live the world-wide socialistic revolution.

The Fourteen Points

Woodrow Wilson

Each nation entered World War I for its own mixture of pragmatic and idealistic reasons. In considering their war aims and a possible peace settlement, governments did not

Source: Woodrow Wilson, "Fourteen Points," *Congressional Record,* vol. LVI, part I (1918), Washington, D.C.: U.S. Government Printing Office, pp. 680–681.

anticipate the changes that would occur in this unexpectedly long and costly war. By 1918 various governments had fallen and the United States had entered the conflict. On January 8, 1918, in an address to a joint session of the U.S. Congress, President Woodrow Wilson (1856–1924) presented his Fourteen Points, a delineation of American war aims and proposals for a peace settlement. The Fourteen Points served as a basis for debate at the Paris Peace Conference in 1919 and represented the most idealistic statement of what might be gained in a final peace settlement.

CONSIDER: *The ideals that hold these points together; the grievances recognized and unrecognized in these points; the assumptions about what measures would preserve peace in the postwar world.*

We entered this war because violations of right had occurred which touched us to the quick and made the life of our own people impossible unless they were corrected and the world secured once for all against their recurrence. What we demand in this war, therefore, is nothing peculiar to ourselves. It is that the world be made fit and safe to live in; and particularly that it be made safe for every peace-loving nation which, like our own, wishes to live its own life, determine its own institutions, be assured of justice and fair dealing by the other peoples of the world as against force and selfish aggression. All the peoples of the world are in effect partners in this interest, and for our own part we see very clearly that unless justice be done to others it will not be done to us. The program of the world's peace, therefore, is our program; and that program, the only possible program, as we see it, is this:

  I. Open covenants of peace, openly arrived at, after which there shall be no private international understandings of any kind but diplomacy shall proceed always frankly and in the public view.

  II. Absolute freedom of navigation upon the seas, outside territorial waters, alike in peace and in war, except as the seas may be closed in whole or in part by international action. . . .

  III. The removal, so far as possible, of all economic barriers and the establishment of an equality of trade conditions among all the nations consenting to the peace and associating themselves for its maintenance.

  IV. Adequate guarantees given and taken that national armaments will be reduced to the lowest point consistent with domestic safety.

  V. A free, open-minded, and absolutely impartial adjustment of all colonial claims, based upon a strict observance of the principle that in determining all such questions of sovereignty the interests of the populations concerned must have equal weight with the equitable claims of the government whose title is to be determined.

  VI. The evacuation of all Russian territory and such a settlement of all questions affecting Russia as will secure the best and freest cooperation of the other nations of the world in obtaining for her an unhampered and unembarrassed opportunity for the independent determination of her own political development and national policy and assure her of a sincere welcome into the society of free nations under institutions of her own choosing; and, more than a welcome, assistance also of every kind that she may need and may herself desire. . . .

  VII. Belgium, the whole world will agree, must be evacuated and restored, without any attempt to limit the sovereignty which she enjoys in common with all other free nations. . . .

  VIII. All French territory should be freed and the invaded portions restored, and the wrong done to France by Prussia in 1871 in the matter of Alsace-Lorraine, which has unsettled the peace of the world for nearly fifty years, should be righted, in order that peace may once more be made secure in the interest of all.

  IX. A readjustment of the frontiers of Italy should be effected along clearly recognizable lines of nationality.

  X. The peoples of Austria-Hungary, whose place among the nations we wish to see safeguarded and assured, should be accorded the freest opportunity of autonomous development.

  XI. Rumania, Serbia, and Montenegro should be evacuated; occupied territories restored; Serbia accorded free and secure access to the sea; and the relations of the several Balkan states to one another determined by friendly counsel along historically established lines of allegiance and nationality; and international guarantees of the political and economic independence and territorial integrity of the several Balkan states should be entered into.

  XII. The Turkish portions of the present Ottoman Empire should be assured a secure sovereignty, but the other nationalities which are now under Turkish rule should be assured an undoubted security of life and an absolutely unmolested opportunity of autonomous development. . . .

  XIII. An independent Polish state should be erected which should include the territories inhabited by indisputably Polish populations. . . .

XIV. A general association of nations must be formed under specific covenants for the purpose of affording mutual guarantees of political independence and territorial integrity to great and small states alike.

In regard to these essential rectifications of wrong and assertions of right we feel ourselves to be intimate partners of all the governments and peoples associated together against the Imperialists. We cannot be separated in interest or divided in purpose. We stand together until the end. . . .

We have no jealousy of German greatness, and there is nothing in this program that impairs it. We grudge her no achievement or distinction of learning or of pacific enterprise such as have made her record very bright and very enviable. We do not wish to injure her or to block in any way her legitimate influence or power. . . .

Neither do we presume to suggest to her any alteration or modification of her institutions. But it is necessary. . . . that we should know whom her spokesmen speak for when they speak to us, whether for the Reichstag majority or for the military party and the men whose creed is imperial domination. . . .

An evident principle runs through the whole program I have outlined. It is the principle of justice to all peoples and nationalities, and their right to live on equal terms of liberty and safety with one another, whether they be strong or weak. . . . The people of the United States could act upon no other principle; and to the vindication of this principle they are ready to devote their lives, their honor, and everything that they possess. The moral climax of this the culminating and final war for human liberty has come, and they are ready to put their own strength, their own highest purpose, their own integrity and devotion to the test.

Visual Sources

World War I: The Front Lines

The following figure (figure 26.1) displays the physical and psychological realities of life on the Western front during World War I. The war is being fought from trenches with soldiers at machine guns guarding land made barren by artillery barrages, throwing hand grenades at the often unseen enemy, and using poison gas (note the gas mask). It is difficult to find in such a scene a sense of a progressive civilization, of the dignity of the individual, or of reasoned interaction among nations— the ideals held by nineteenth-century Western civilization. Considering the use of such weapons, we can easily imagine the carnage and the sense of futility that resulted from the "heroic" offensive charges of the foot soldiers that were so common for most of the war.

CONSIDER: *How this supports the description of life on the front lines during the Verdun battle.*

The Paths of Glory
C. R. W. Nevinson

The brutality of World War I ended dreams of heroic battles and courageous military deeds. The 1917

painting (figure 26.2) by English artist C. R. W. Nevinson (1889–1946), with its ironic title, The Paths of Glory, spoke eloquently to this disturbing reality.

In this image, the bodies of two British soldiers—easily identified by their brown uniforms and flat helmets—lie in a desolate battlefield in northern France. This battle has ended, and it is unclear how their anonymous deaths contributed to the war or to any supposed glory. The only

FIGURE 26.1

FIGURE 26.2   (© Snark/Art Resource, NY)

objects left standing are the wooden stakes holding up the rows of barbed wire that have entangled these two individuals. Already the bodies are dissolving into earth. "Words such as glory, honor, courage, or hallow [became] obscene" in the face of the carnage that resulted, wrote the American author and veteran Ernest Hemingway. Nevinson's painting, echoing these sentiments, was hung in a British gallery in March 1918. Military authorities immediately condemned it.

CONSIDER: *Why British military authorities condemned this painting; how this image might represent the realities of battle during World War I.*

World War I: The Home Front and Women

The following picture of a British war plant (figure 26.3) gives an idea of how industrialization and technology have helped turn any extended war into a massive strain. Large factories had to be built or converted to the production of war munitions, here heavy artillery shells. A new labor force had to be trained, often involving a change of values: Here women and older men

predominate to make up for the drain on manpower caused by the armed services. Finally, this picture suggests the enormous logistical organization and government cooperation with capitalist enterprises necessary to keep a modern war effort going.

The need for labor on the home front resulted in large numbers of women entering the labor force or changing jobs. The following two charts indicate the changing employment of women in Great Britain between 1914 and 1918: chart 26.1 for all employment, chart 26.2 for industrial employment.

FIGURE 26.3   (© The Imperial War Museum)

Chart 26.1 Women in the Labor Force, Great Britain, 1914–1918

Numbers of women working	In July 1914	In July 1918	In July 1918, over (+) or under (−) numbers in July 1914
On their own account or as employers	430,000	470,000	+40,000
In industry	2,178,600	2,970,000	+792,000
In domestic service	1,658,000	1,258,000	−400,000
In commerce, etc.	505,500	934,500	+429,000
In national and local government, including education	262,200	460,200	+198,000
In agriculture	190,000	228,000	+38,000
In employment of hotels, public houses, theatres, etc.	181,000	220,000	+39,000
In transport	18,200	117,200	+99,000
In other, including professional employment and as home workers	542,500	652,500	+110,000
Altogether in occupations	5,966,000	7,311,000	+1,345,000
Not in occupations but over 10	12,946,000	12,496,000	−450,000
Under 10	4,809,000	4,731,000	−78,000
Total females	23,721,000	24,538,000	+817,000

Chart 26.2 Women in Industry, Great Britain, 1914–1918

Trades	Estimated number of females employed in July 1914	Estimated number of females employed in July 1918	Difference between numbers of females employed in July 1914, and July 1918	Percentage of females to total number of workpeople employed — July 1914	Percentage of females to total number of workpeople employed — July 1918	Estimated number of females directly replacing males in Jan. 1918
Metal	170,000	594,000	+424,000	9	25	195,000
Chemical	40,000	104,000	+64,000	20	39	35,000
Textile	863,000	827,000	−36,000	58	67	64,000
Clothing	612,000	568,000	−44,000	68	76	43,000
Food, drink, and tobacco	196,000	235,000	+39,000	35	49	60,000
Paper and printing	147,500	141,500	−6,000	36	48	21,000
Wood	44,000	79,000	+35,000	15	32	23,000
China and earthenware	32,000					
Leather	23,100	197,100	+93,000	4	10	62,000
Other	49,000					
Government establishments	2,000	225,000	+223,000	3	47	197,000
Total	2,178,600	2,970,600	+792,000	26	37	704,000

SOURCE: *Women in Industry: Report of the War Cabinet Committee on Women in Industry* (London: His Majesty's Stationery Office, 1919).

CONSIDER: *The ways in which a modern war effort affects a nation's people and economy, even though the war is being fought on foreign soil; the potential significance for women of these changes in employment.*

Revolutionary Propaganda

This 1922 poster (figure 26.4) celebrating the fifth anniversary of the Russian revolution reflects some of the message and appeal of the Communists during the revolution of 1917 and the years that followed. Here Lenin, in a worker's suit, tie, and cap, stands on a globe as if leading a worldwide Communist revolution. He proclaims, "Let the ruling class tremble before the Communist revolution." Behind him the rising sun marks the glorious dawn of the communist era. To his left and right, together in alliance, are agricultural and industrial workers—the revolutionary mainstays and beneficiaries of the new order—carrying a banner proclaiming, "Proletariat of All Countries, Unite." Below are the tools of their trades and symbols of Russia's Communist revolution— the hammer and sickle.

CONSIDER: *What might be particularly appealing about this poster; what image of the Russian revolution it incorporates.*

FIGURE 26.4 (© Sovfoto/Eastfoto)

 Secondary Sources

The Origins of World War I: Militant Patriotism

Roland N. Stromberg

Almost before World War I was over, scholars were debating its causes. With the depth of emotional involvement characterizing this war, objective evaluation was difficult. Scholars often had difficulty distinguishing analysis of causes from placement of blame. In recent years many scholars have been struck by the almost universal enthusiasm with which people greeted the news that war had been declared in August 1914. This has led some scholars to reevaluate traditional interpretations of the causes for World War I and emphasize the underlying social forces that led people to welcome its outbreak. In the following selection Roland

SOURCE: Roland N. Stromberg, *Europe in the Twentieth Century* (Englewood Cliffs, NJ: Prentice-Hall, Inc., 1980), pp. 43–44, 74.

Stromberg, a historian of modern Europe at the University of Wisconsin, examines various attempts to explain the outbreak of war and suggests that the willingness of European peoples to go to war may have been more important than "the system of sovereign states" or any other cause for World War I.

CONSIDER: *The explanations that Stromberg rejects and why he rejects them; how militant patriotism played a role in the outbreak of the war.*

No wonder the sudden outbreak of a major international war at the beginning of August caught everyone by surprise. The sobering lesson was that war could happen without anybody seeming to want it or to will it. All kinds of myths grew up later, as bewildered people attempted to explain the outbreak of war. As usual, conspiracy theories flourished. In particular it was alleged that the Germans plotted war; Wilhelm II, the unhappy German monarch, was depicted in the Allied countries as a monster with tentacles reaching out to ensnare small countries. That "Prussian militarism" was the canker in the olive branch became an article of faith in France and England and later, after she had joined the war, in the United States. For their part, the Germans believed that jealous neighbors plotted to encircle and destroy a country whose only crime was her economic success.

Then, too, the theory arose that the capitalistic economic system, far from being a force for peace, had engineered the war because war was profitable or because there was competition for markets and raw materials. Although they may contain germs of truth, all such simple-minded "devil theories" must be dismissed as inadequate to the serious study of events, more interesting as folklore than as history.

Though it is tempting to look for it, no single all-embracing cause can successfully explain the war or any other major historical event. . . .

The states of Europe were like individuals living in a primeval state of nature marked by incessant strife between one and another. They acknowledged no higher authority that might have forced them to keep the peace. What was called "international law" was not in fact binding on them, being backed by no more than a moral or customary sanction. . . .

More and more people had acquired a larger stake in defending the state. This was the natural result of democratization and increase in wealth. However imperfectly or inequitably these had come about, the large majority of citizens had some interest in defending the political community of which they were a part. All over Europe, 1914 was to prove that the masses as well as the classes were militantly patriotic when they thought their country was being attacked. . . .

Virtually no one had expected war; it came with dramatic suddenness. When it did come, . . . a sense of joy rather than of gloom prevailed. Huge cheering crowds surrounded the kaiser, stood outside Buckingham Palace, saluted departing French troops at the railroad stations, made love publicly in St. Petersburg. A Parisian observer on August 2 described a "human torrent, swelling at every corner" screaming, shouting, singing the "Marseillaise." In Berlin, crowds passed through the streets incessantly for two days singing "Deutschland über alles" and "Wacht am Rhein." A mob attacked the German embassy in St. Petersburg. An "indescribable crowd" blocked the streets around government offices in London a few minutes after midnight August 4–5, and continued to fill the streets for days. It was with exultation, not sorrow, that the peoples of Europe greeted the war, a fact that in the last analysis may go farther to explain its coming than all the details of diplomacy. . . .

Germany and the Coming of War
Hartmut Pogge von Strandmann

In an attempt to understand the origins of World War I and why it lasted so long, many scholars focus on the role of Germany, but differ greatly on what the underpinnings of German involvement were. In the following selection Hartmut Pogge von Strandmann analyzes what made war acceptable to the German population and what sustained the war efforts for four years.

CONSIDER: *Ways in which forces for war within Germany were part of Europeanwide developments; why, according to the author, there was support for the war effort in Germany; how this analysis of Germany compares to Stromberg's analysis for the origins of the war.*

However strongly the political and military leadership was influenced by the public and its political debates, the war was not started for domestic reasons nor to defend a social status quo. The concept of expansion based on a military victory found enough support to command a consensus among the military, political, and business leaders of Wilhelmine Germany. The drive to the east and to the west was underpinned by an imperialist culture which spread the virtues of Social Darwinism, the conquest of markets, the penetration of spheres of influence, competition between capitalist partners, the winning of living-space, and the rising power of the state. Buoyed up by an assumed military superiority, general economic strength and particular industrial vigour, widespread optimism and a mood of belligerence, the military and political leaders found, when they made the decision to push for war, that this was an acceptable option to many Germans, possibly even to the majority. The notion of "cultural despair" is of limited value. There were no signs of panic and no indications that Wilhelmine Germany could not continue to muddle through politically for years to come. Confidence, determination, and the belief in victory were the ingredients of a willingness to fight an expansionist war, disguised as a defensive or preventive action, which was widely shared by political and military leaders, political groupings, as well as large sectors of the population. This consensus enabled Germany to sustain the war effort until the military defeats of August and September 1918.

SOURCE: From Hartmut Pogge von Strandmann, "Germany and the Coming of War," in *The Coming of the First World War*, p. 123, eds. R. J. W. Evans and Hartmut Pogge von Strandmann. © 1988 Oxford University Press. Reprinted by permission of Oxford University Press.

The Revolution in War and Diplomacy

Gordon A. Craig

The technology and tactics used in World War I were strikingly different from those used in previous wars. This, combined with the war's length and the waning distinction between civilian and military targets, made it difficult for people to perceive the enemy in terms other than extreme hatred. This was reflected in the demands for retribution made both during and at the end of the war, inevitably affecting the peace settlements that followed. In the following selection Gordon Craig of Princeton and Stanford, a noted military and diplomatic historian who has done extensive work on German history, analyzes these attitudes and their causes while comparing World War I with previous wars.

CONSIDER: *How the primary documents on the experience of World War I relate to this interpretation; why it was difficult for governments of belligerent nations to compromise; whether this description of what happened in World War I is likely to be true for almost any extended twentieth-century war.*

The war of 1914 was the first total war in history, in the sense that very few people living in the belligerent countries were permitted to remain unaffected by it during its course. This had not been true in the past. Even during the great wars against Napoleon many people could go on living as if the world were at peace. . . .

This kind of detachment, which was true also of the wars in Central Europe in the 1860s, was wholly impossible during World War I. This was, for one thing, the first war in which the distinction between soldier and civilian broke down, a development that was partly due to the expansion of warfare made possible by . . . technological innovations. . . . When dirigibles began to drop bombs over London and submarines began to sink merchant ships, war had invaded the civilian sphere and the battle line was everywhere. . . .

Moreover . . . precisely because war became so total and was so prolonged, it also became ideological, taking on a religious cast that had not characterized warfare in the West since the Thirty Years' War. . . .

The civilian . . . could not look the enemy in the face and recognize him as another man; he knew only that it was "the enemy," an impersonal, generalized concept, that was depriving him of the pleasures of peace. As his

own discomfort grew, his irritation hardened into a hatred that was often encouraged by government propagandists who believed that this was the best way of maintaining civilian morale. Before long, therefore, the enemy was considered to be capable of any enormity and, since this was true, any idea of compromise with him became intolerable. The foe must be beaten to his knees, no matter what this might cost in effort and blood; he must be made to surrender unconditionally; he must be punished with peace terms that would keep him in permanent subjection.

The result of this was . . . that rational calculation of risk versus gain, of compromise through negotiation . . . became virtually impossible for the belligerent governments.

Women, Work, and World War I

Bonnie S. Anderson and Judith P. Zinsser

As men were drawn into the armed forces during World War I and there were new demands for arms and other goods to support the war effort, the demand for women workers grew. Women entered the work force in great numbers, often taking jobs previously offered only to men. Historians have pointed to this as a crucial change for women, but recently other historians question how much women, in the long run, benefited from their experiences as workers during World War I. In the following excerpt from A History of Their Own, Bonnie S. Anderson and Judith P. Zinsser argue that the changes for women were fewer and less long-lasting than generally assumed.

CONSIDER: *Why, according to Anderson and Zinsser, changes for women were more apparent than real, more short-term than long-lasting; how employers, governments, and the mass media undermined changes for women; how this document relates to the visual sources on the home front and women.*

The improved standard of living, smaller family size, maternity benefits, protective legislation, unions, and new jobs comprised the most important changes in the lives of urban working-class women between the 1870s and the 1920s. Compared to these changes, the impact of World War I (1914–1918) on these women's lives was relatively minor. While middle- and upper-class women often reported that the war freed them from nineteenth-century attitudes limiting both work and personal life, working-class

SOURCE: Gordon A. Craig, "The Revolution in War and Diplomacy," Jack J. Roth, ed., *World War I: A Turning Point in Modern History.* Reprinted by permission of Alfred A. Knopf, Inc., pp. 12–14. Copyright © 1967 by Alfred A. Knopf, Inc.

SOURCE: Excerpts from *A History of Their Own*, vol. II, by Bonnie Anderson and Judith Zinsser. Copyright © 1988 by Harper & Row, Publishers, Inc., pp. 112–114. Reprinted by permission of Harper & Row, Publishers, Inc.

women's lives changed relatively little. Unlike more privileged women, working-class women were used to earning income outside the home, and their entry into war
work was more likely to be exploitative than liberating.
Unlike more privileged women, working-class women
and girls had rarely been shielded by a "double standard"
of sexual behavior for women and men; rather, working-
class women made the maintenance of the double standard possible for men of property. For working-class
women in the cities, the growth of the new white-collar
job was the one new trend fostered by the war which was
not reversed afterward. Otherwise, World War I brought
only a temporary suspension of the normal conditions of
work outside the home, and traditional patterns returned
in the postwar era.

As soon as the war broke out, European governments
moved to suspend protective legislation for women for
the duration. Just as nations expected working-class men
to serve in the military, so they exhorted working-class
women to serve in the factories, taking the places of the
men who had joined the armed forces. Drawn by high
wages as well as patriotism, women thronged into these
new, previously male jobs. . . .

Governments initially insisted that women receive
equal pay for doing a job formerly done by a man, but this
policy was largely ineffective: factories tended to divide
up jobs into smaller operations and pay women at a lesser
rate. Women's industrial wages rose during the war, both
relative to men's and absolutely, but they still remained
measurable as a percentage of male earnings. In Paris,
women in metallurgy earned only 45 percent of what
men earned before the war; by 1918, the women earned
84 percent of what men earned. In Germany, women's
industrial earnings relative to men's rose by about 5 percent. Both women and men seemed to view the changes
brought by the war as temporary. After the war, the men
would return to their jobs, the women would leave men's
work, and all would return to normal. . . .

As soon as the war was over, all belligerent governments acted quickly to remove women from "men's" jobs.
In England, these women were made "redundant" and let
go; in France, they were offered a bonus payment if they
left factory work; and in Germany, the government issued
regulations calling for women to be dismissed before men
if necessary. These policies were effective: by 1921, fewer
French and English women worked in industry than had
before the war. Women's earnings decreased to return to
lower percentages of men's, and the promise of "equal
remunerations for work of equal value" made in the
Versailles Treaty of 1919 remained a dead letter. Mass
media concentrated on the relatively superficial changes
in women's clothing, hair styles, and use of cosmetics and
ignored the deeper continuities which structured most
women's lives.

Peace and Diplomacy
Arthur Walworth

*Historians have traditionally condemned the settlement of
World War I worked out at Versailles. They usually argue that
it compared poorly with the previous Vienna settlement ending
the Napoleonic Wars. Yet some historians have challenged this
view, arguing that the circumstances of peacemaking were extraordinarily difficult at the end of World War I. In the following selection Arthur Walworth analyzes the pressures and
obstacles facing the peacemakers.*

CONSIDER: *The choices and compromises the diplomats
would have to make; in these circumstances, what the diplomats might have done; how Walworth's interpretation compares to that of Craig.*

A belligerent spirit of nationalism, fortified by the patriotic
sacrifices that war had called forth, ran strong and limited
the freedom of the peacemakers to pursue the distant goals
of idealists. The prevailing hatred toward the defeated enemy made it difficult for diplomats to make a rational
peace without being denounced as "pro-German." The
wisest of the statesmen realized, after the cessation of the
fighting, that unless they were able to reverse the baneful
psychology of wartime quickly, no enduring peace could
be signed, much less dictated.

Furthermore, the European democracies during the
war had set up obstacles that would embarrass the diplomats in the making of peace. Under the necessity of
survival the governments of the Allied powers had made
secret commitments to the satisfaction of national aspirations. The 1915 Treaty of London, concluded in order to
bring Italy into the conflict on the side of the Allies, had
promised that nation a frontier that would place hundreds of thousands of Austrians and Slavs under Italian
rule. To persuade the Japanese to step up their naval
activity, Japan had been offered concessions in China and
a share of Germany's islands in the Pacific. Although
agreements to which Russia was a party became invalid
when the Soviet government made peace with Germany,
nevertheless the interests of France, Great Britain, and
Italy in the lands of the Ottoman Empire remained as
they had been defined in understandings reached in 1916
and 1917. These secret understandings gained force from
popular indignation against the violations of treaty obligations at the time of the outbreak of war in 1914.

The settlement at the war's end could not disregard
the commitments and the national aspirations that existed in 1919 and that no one could expect to alter

SOURCE: From Arthur Walworth, *Wilson and His Peacemakers*,
pp. xii–xiii. Copyright 1986 W. W. Norton. Reprinted by permission of
W. W. Norton & Company, Inc.

quickly. Compromises were inevitable. For one thing, there had to be an accommodation among various prescriptions for dealing with the German enemy. At the end of the war the European diplomats were of two minds about a policy to preserve the peace. One, the more appealing to the English-speaking authorities, would avoid peace terms that might incite violent reactions among the vanquished and also would provide for a continuing process of adjustment. The other, advocated by the French, would create alliances with a preponderance of military power that could put down any opposition. During the long war of attrition France's deficiency in manpower had worsened; it was clear that the French nation, fighting alone, could not hope to withstand another onset of German might.

The Russian Revolution
Robert Service

Historians often respond to the challenge of explaining the occurrence of a major revolution by constructing a complex set or theory of causes. For Marxist historians, the Russian Revolution was of extraordinary importance. These historians and others point to long-term economic and social factors as crucial in causing this revolution. Many historians, however, argue that the causes were more immediate and less complex. Robert Service, a respected author of several works on Russian history, takes a middle ground, focusing on a few circumstances as the key causes for the revolution. In the following selection, Service analyzes the revolution that toppled the tsar's government in February 1917, as well as the rise to power of Lenin and the Bolsheviks in October 1917.

CONSIDER: *The problems facing the Russian Empire; how Tsar Nicholas II placed himself in "double jeopardy"; why the Bolsheviks resorted to terror.*

Under the tsars, the Russian Empire faced many problems and approval of the state's demands and purposes was largely absent from society. The technological gap was widening between Russia and the other capitalist powers. Military security posed acute problems; administrative and educational co-ordination remained frail. Political parties had little impact on popular opinion, and the State Duma was to a large extent ignored. Furthermore, the traditional propertied classes made little effort to engender a sense of civic community among the poorer members of society. While most Russians lacked a strong sense of nationhood, several non-Russian nations had a sharp sense of national resentment. The Russian Empire was a restless, unintegrated society.

SOURCE: Robert Service, *A History of Twentieth-Century Russia* (Cambridge, MA: Harvard University Press, 1998), pp. 545–547.

Nicholas II, the last tsar, had put himself in double jeopardy. He had seriously obstructed and annoyed the emergent elements of a civil society: the political parties, professional associations and trade unions. But he also stopped trying to suppress them entirely. The result was a constant challenge to the tsarist regime. The social and economic transformation before the First World War merely added to the problems. Those groups in society which had undergone impoverishment were understandably hostile to the authorities. Other groups had enjoyed improvement in their material conditions; but several of these, too, posed a danger since they felt frustrated by the nature of the political order. It was in this situation that the Great War broke out and pulled down the remaining stays of the regime. The result was the February Revolution of 1917 in circumstances of economic collapse, administrative dislocation and military defeat. Vent was given to a surge of local efforts at popular self-rule; and workers, peasants and military conscripts across the empire asserted their demands without impediment.

These same circumstances made liberalism, conservatism and fascism impractical for a number of years ahead: some kind of socialist government was by far the likeliest outcome in those years. Yet it was not inevitable that the most extreme variant of socialism—Bolshevism—should take power. What was scarcely avoidable was that once the Bolsheviks made their revolution, they would not be able to survive without making their policies even more violent and regimentative than they already were. Lenin's party had much too little durable support to remain in government without resort to terror. This in turn placed limits on their ability to solve those many problems identified by nearly all the tsarist regime's enemies as needing to be solved. The Bolsheviks aspired to economic competitiveness, political integration, inter-ethnic co-operation, social tranquillity, administrative efficiency, cultural dynamism and universal education. But the means they employed inevitably vitiated their declared ends.

❧ CHAPTER QUESTIONS

1. In what ways was World War I an outgrowth of the major trends of the late nineteenth century? Why is World War I nevertheless often considered a dividing line between the nineteenth and twentieth centuries?

2. What role did World War I play in explaining the Russian Revolution and the Bolsheviks' rise to power?

3. What was there about the causes and process of World War I that made the peace settlement at the end of the war so difficult?

27 Democracy, Depression, and Instability: The 1920s and 1930s

The two decades following World War I were marked by instability and uncertainty. Except in Russia, where the Bolsheviks had taken power, it appeared that liberal democracy had been established throughout Europe as a result of World War I. But soon a trend toward authoritarianism appeared, with many nations suffering from political fluctuations. The economic problems left from World War I and the immediate postwar period did not disappear despite a brief period of fragile prosperity in the mid-1920s. In 1929 the stock market crash in New York initiated the Great Depression in the United States, which quickly spread to Europe. Huge numbers of people suffered economically, and governments were pressured to effect radical solutions to the problems.

Not surprisingly, there were great social strains through all of this. The difficulty of recovering from World War I was exacerbated by this political and economic instability. Swept by uncertainty about the present and the future, society seemed to polarize into opposing classes and around competing ideologies.

A similar uncertainty characterized intellectual trends. The optimism and faith in rationality typical of the eighteenth and nineteenth centuries gave way to movements such as relativism in the physical and social sciences, Freudianism in psychology, and seeming anarchy in the arts. The West was no longer so confident, and events of the 1920s and 1930s added to that lack of confidence.

161

The selections in this chapter exemplify these trends. Historians usually focus on Germany during the 1920s in describing the general unrest and the efforts made to respond to it. What was the nature of the political and economic disorder in Germany during the 1920s? In what ways was there a sense that things were out of hand and that the population was composed of many opposing factions? The Great Depression dealt the worst blow to the industrial economy. How did the Depression make the future of capitalism uncertain? What policies were pursued by governments to deal with the Depression? How was the Depression related to political disorder during the 1930s? What was the long-term significance of the Depression? Finally, a general sense of disillusionment and uncertainty characterized intellectual life. In what ways was disillusionment particularly strong for the generation that came of age in 1914? In what ways was there a feeling that nineteenth-century ideals were gone and that twentieth-century people might be worse off than their predecessors?

A gloomy picture of life during the 1920s and 1930s emerges from these materials. The growth of totalitarianism during this period, to be examined in the next chapter, will add to this negative image.

 # Primary Sources

The Road Back
Erich Maria Remarque
and
Restless Days
Lilo Linke

With the establishment of the Weimar Republic at the end of World War I, Germany had a government system much like those of the other Western democracies. But the German government was burdened with tremendous economic problems, continued social turmoil, and inexperienced politicians laboring with the legacy of World War I. This society and its mood are particularly well reflected in the cultural productions of the period, for example, in the following selections from Erich Maria Remarque and Lilo Linke. Remarque, whose All Quiet on the Western Front *(1929) and* The Road Back *(1931) were two of the most popular books of the period, was a German soldier during World War I. The first selection is from* The Road Back, *which focuses on the life in Germany faced by the returning soldier. The second selection is from Linke's autobiography,* Restless Days.

CONSIDER: *Any connections between World War I and subsequent economic problems; the political problems facing the Weimar Republic; how such an environment might prove fertile for the rise of a political figure like Hitler.*

Demonstrations in the streets have been called for this afternoon. Prices have been soaring everywhere for months past, and the poverty is greater even than it was during the war. Wages are insufficient to buy the bare necessities of life, and even though one may have the money it is often impossible to buy anything with it. But ever more and more gin palaces and dance halls go up, and ever more and more blatant is the profiteering and swindling.

Scattered groups of workers on strike march through the streets. Now and again there is a disturbance. A rumour is going about that troops have been concentrated at the barracks. But there is no sign of it as yet.

Here and there one hears cries and counter-cries. Somebody is haranguing at a street corner. Then suddenly everywhere is silence.

A procession of men in the faded uniforms of the front-line trenches is moving slowly toward us.

It is formed up by sections, marching in fours. Big white placards are carried before: *Where is the Fatherland's gratitude?—The War Cripples are starving.*

The men with one arm are carrying the placards, and they look around continually to see if the procession is still coming along properly behind them, for they are the fastest.

These are followed by men with sheep dogs on short, leather leads. The animals have the red cross of the blind at their collars. . . .

Behind the blind come the men with one eye, the tattered faces of men with head wounds: wry, bulbous mouths, faces without noses and without lower jaws, entire faces one great red scar with a couple of holes where formerly were a mouth and a nose. But above this desolation, quiet, questioning, sad human eyes.

On these follow the long lines of men with legs amputated. Some already have artificial limbs that spring forward obliquely as they walk and strike clanking on the pavement, as if the whole man were artificial, made up of iron and hinges. Others have their trouser legs looped up and made fast with safety pins. These go on crutches or sticks with black rubber pads.

Then come the shakers, the shell-shocked. Their hands, their heads, their clothes, their bodies quake as though they still shudder with horror. They no longer have control of themselves; the will has been extinguished, the muscles and nerves have revolted against the brain, the eyes become void and impotent.

❦

It was no good to go on assuming that a common basis for all the different groups and classes in Germany could be found. The break between them became daily wider and more irreparable. The plebiscite of the Right "against the Young Plan and the war-guilt lie" proved just as unsuccessful as those arranged in former years by the Left, but the poison of the defamatory agitation remained in the body of the community, and we watched its effects with anxiety.

In my own family the political antagonism was growing past endurance. In October Fritz had finished his apprenticeship in an old-established export house, at the precise moment when the firm went bankrupt—a minor incident compared with such events as the breakdown of the Frankfurt General Insurance Company and the Civil Servants' Bank or the enforced reorganization and amalgamation of the Deutsche Bank and the DiscontoGesellschaft, which all happened in the course of the year and dangerously damaged the whole economic life of Germany. Yet for my brother the bankruptcy of his firm overshadowed all other happenings, since it meant that he lost his job. His three years' training was in vain—there was not a single export firm which was not forced to dismiss as many of its employees as possible. . . .

"Yes, that's just it—millions! If it isn't my fault, whose fault is it? I tell you—your friends, the French, the English, the Americans, all those damnable nations who inflict on us one dishonorable penalty after the other— they are to blame for all this. Before the war the whole world bought German goods. My firm exported to Africa, to the German colonies. Hundreds of thousands we turned over every year. But they have robbed us of our colonies, of all our foreign markets. They have stolen the coal-mines in the Saar and in Upper Silesia, they squeeze millions of marks out of our bleeding country. We'll never rise again unless we free ourselves by another war."

"Don't be foolish, Fritz. Things are bad in the whole world."

"I don't care about the world, I care only about Germany, which you and your pacifists have delivered into the hands of our enemies. I despise you, you are not worthy to call yourself a German."

With Germany's Unemployed
Heinrich Hauser

No nation was hit harder by the Great Depression than Germany. By 1932 it had more than six million unemployed workers and countless people wandering homeless along its streets and roads. Many sought help in city shelters. The plight of these people—like that of millions in other nations—is reflected in the following account by Heinrich Hauser.

CONSIDER: *Who Hauser observed along Germany's highways; the psychological effects of the hardships on these people; how such conditions might lead many to turn to Adolf Hitler and the Nazis.*

An almost unbroken chain of homeless men extends the whole length of the great Hamburg-Berlin highway.

There are so many of them moving in both directions, impelled by the wind or making their way against it, that they could shout a message from Hamburg to Berlin by word of mouth. . . . All the highways in Germany over which I traveled this year presented the same aspect. . . .

But most of the hikers paid no attention to me. They walked separately or in small groups, with their eyes on the ground. And they had the queer, stumbling gait of barefooted people, for their shoes were slung over their shoulders. Some of them were guild members,— carpenters with embroidered wallets, knee breeches, and broad felt hats; milkmen with striped red shirts, and bricklayers with tall black hats,—but they were in a minority. Far more numerous were those whom one could assign to no special profession or craft—unskilled young people, for the most part, who had been unable to find a place for themselves in any city or town in Germany, and who had never had a job and never expected to have one. There was something else that had never been seen before—whole families that had piled all their goods into baby carriages and wheelbarrows that they were pushing along as they plodded forward in dumb despair. It was a whole nation on the march.

I saw them—and this was the strongest impression that the year 1932 left with me—I saw them, gathered into groups of fifty or a hundred men, attacking fields of potatoes. I saw them digging up the potatoes and throwing them into sacks while the farmer who owned the field watched them in despair and the local policeman looked on gloomily from the distance. I saw them staggering toward the lights of the city as night fell, with their sacks on their backs. What did it remind me of? Of the War, of

SOURCE: Heinrich Hauser, "With Germany's Unemployed," *Living Age*, vol. 344, no. 4398 (March 1933), pp. 27–29, 37–38.

the worst periods of starvation in 1917 and 1918, but even then people paid for the potatoes. . . .

I entered the huge Berlin municipal lodging house in a northern quarter of the city. . . .

My next recollection is sitting at table in another room on a crowded bench that is like a seat in a fourth-class railway carriage. Hundreds of hungry mouths make an enormous noise eating their food. The men sit bent over their food like animals who feel that someone is going to take it away from them. They hold their bowl with their left arm part way around it, so that nobody can take it away, and they also protect it with their other elbow and with their head and mouth, while they move the spoon as fast as they can between their mouth and the bowl. The portions, for men on a normal diet, would be extraordinarily large. There must be about a quart of stew in each bowl, and it's not bad, either. There is fat and strength in it. But I am only halfway through mine when all my neighbors have finished and are looking at me enviously. I give the rest to the Saxon, who looks at me in amazement. "Stomach ache," I say. In the twinkling of an eye the rest has disappeared.

Wash basins are brought in on the other side of the room. Everyone washes his own bowl here, for he will need it again for his morning meal.

Program of the Popular Front— January 11, 1936

The Great Depression of the 1930s was a major blow to Western stability. In many areas it led to the fall of established governments and the rise of right-wing groups. In France in 1934, Socialists and Communists, in part fearing the rise of fascism, drew together into the Popular Front. In 1936, under the leadership of Léon Blum (1872–1950), the Popular Front came to power, but only for about two years. The following is an excerpt from the program of the Popular Front, January 11, 1936.

CONSIDER: *The ways in which this document reflects the turmoil of public life during the 1930s; how the Popular Front proposes to deal with the Depression; to what groups such a program would most appeal and why.*

I. *Defence of Freedom.*
  1. A general amnesty.
  2. Measures against the Fascist Leagues:
     (*a*) The effective disarmament and dissolution of all semi-military formations, in accordance with the law.

SOURCE: From David Thomson, *Democracy in France.* Reprinted by permission of Oxford University Press (Oxford, England, 5th ed., 1969), pp. 310–314.

(*b*) The enforcement of legal measures in cases of incitement to murder or any attempt against the safety of the State. . . .
  4. The Press:
     (*a*) The repeal of the laws and decrees restricting freedom of opinion. . . .
        (iii) Measures ending the private monopoly of commercial advertising and the scandals of financial advertising, and preventing the formation of newspaper trusts.
     (*c*) Organization by the State of wireless broadcasts with a view to assuring the accuracy of wireless news and the equality of political and social organizations in relation to radio.
  5. Trade Union Liberties:
     (*a*) Application and observance of trade union freedom for all.
     (*b*) Recognition of women's labour rights. . . .
II. *Defence of Peace.*
  1. Appeal to the people, and especially the working classes, for collaboration in the maintenance and organization of peace.
  2. International collaboration within the framework of the League of Nations for collective security, by defining the aggressor and by joint application of sanctions in cases of aggression.
  3. Ceaseless endeavour to pass from armed peace to disarmed peace, first by a convention of limitation, and then by the general, simultaneous and effectively controlled reduction of armaments.
  4. Nationalization of war industries and suppression of private trade in armaments.
  5. Repudiation of secret diplomacy; international action and public negotiation to bring back to Geneva the states which have left it, without weakening the essential principles of the League of Nations, which are the principles of collective security and indivisible peace. . . .
III. *Economic Demands.*
  1. Restoration of purchasing power destroyed or reduced by the crisis.
     (*a*) Against unemployment and the crisis in industry.
        (i) Establishment of a national unemployment fund.
        (ii) Reduction of the working week without reduction of the weekly wage.
        (iii) Bringing your workers into employment by establishing a system of adequate pensions for aged workers.

(iv) Rapid execution of a public works programme, both urban and rural, linking local investments with schemes financed by the State and local authorities. . . .

2. Against the robbery of investors and for the better organization of credit:

(a) Regulation of banking business. . . .

(c) In order to remove credit and investment from the control of the economic oligarchy, the Bank of France must cease to be a private concern, and "The Bank of France" must become "France's Bank.". . .

IV. *Financial Purification.* . . .

3. Democratic reform of the system of taxation as to relax the fiscal burden blocking economic recovery, and raising revenue by measures against large fortunes. Rapid steepening of income tax on incomes above 75,000 francs a year; reorganization of death duties; special taxes on monopoly profits, but in such a way as to have no effects on retail prices. Measures against tax evasions, in connexion with transferable ("bearer") securities.

The Revolt of the Masses

José Ortega y Gasset

The disillusionment of the 1920s and 1930s, often associated with the effects of World War I, is reflected in many of the more profound attempts to understand Western civilization and the human condition. But this intellectual trend should not be seen only as a reaction to World War I. In The Revolt of the Masses (1930), one of the most influential works of the period, José Ortega y Gasset (1883–1955) laments the population increase, the rise of the "masses," and the decline of the elite, cultured, liberal civilization of the nineteenth century. Ortega, a strong liberal and antimonarchist, became professor of metaphysics at the University of Madrid in 1910 and Spain's leading intellectual. Anticipating the defeat of the Republicans, he fled Spain in 1936. In the following excerpt from The Revolt of the Masses, he introduces the themes he will deal with in the rest of the book.

CONSIDER: *Why the rise to power of the masses is so serious; how Ortega distinguishes the "masses" from the "qualified minorities"; whether he presents a valid criticism of modern democracy.*

SOURCE: Fosé Ortega y Gasset, *The Revolt of the Masses.* Reprinted by permission of W. W. Norton & Co., Inc. (New York, 1932), pp. 11, 16, 18.

There is one fact which, whether for good or ill, is of utmost importance in the public life of Europe at the present moment. This fact is the accession of the masses to complete social power. As the masses, by definition, neither should nor can direct their own personal existence, and still less rule society in general, this fact means that actually Europe is suffering from the greatest crisis that can afflict peoples, nations, and civilisation. Such a crisis has occurred more than once in history. Its characteristics and its consequences are well known. So also is its name. It is called the rebellion of the masses. . . .

There exist, then, in society, operations, activities, and functions of the most diverse order, which are of their very nature special, and which consequently cannot be properly carried out without special gifts. For example: certain pleasures of an artistic and refined character, or again the functions of government and of political judgment in public affairs. Previously these special activities were exercised by qualified minorities, or at least by those who claimed such qualification. The mass asserted no right to intervene in them; they realised that if they wished to intervene they would necessarily have to acquire those special qualities and cease being mere mass. They recognised their place in a healthy dynamic social system. . . .

The characteristic of the hour is that the commonplace mind, knowing itself to be commonplace, has the assurance to proclaim the rights of the commonplace and to impose them wherever it will. As they say in the United States: "to be different is to be indecent." The mass crushes beneath it everything that is different, everything that is excellent, individual, qualified and select. Anybody who is not like everybody, who does not think like everybody, runs the risk of being eliminated. And it is clear, of course, that this "everybody" is not "everybody." "Everybody" was normally the complex unity of the mass and the divergent, specialised minorities. Nowadays, "everybody" is the mass alone. Here we have the formidable fact of our times, described without any concealment of the brutality of its features.

Civilization and Its Discontents

Sigmund Freud

Psychoanalysis became one of the most powerful intellectual influences in the twentieth century. In part, it was based on the older eighteenth- and nineteenth-century optimism about

SOURCE: Sigmund Freud, *Civilization and its Discontents,* in *The Standard Edition of the Complete Psychological Works of Sigmund Freud,* James Strachey, trans. and ed. Reprinted by permission of W. W. Norton & Co., Inc. (New York, 1961), pp. 58–59, 92, The Hogarth Press, Ltd., Sigmund Freud Copyrights Ltd., and The Institute of Psycho-Analysis.

the power of human rationality and scientific investigation: It assumed that human behavior could be even more deeply understood than before through scientific observation and that rational understanding could alleviate pain and problems. In other ways, however, it reflected the late-nineteenth- and early-twentieth-century attack on rationality: It argued that much of human behavior is irrational, unconscious, and instinctual. Finally, it echoed some of the pessimism fostered by the experience of World War I: Civilization was increasingly threatened by deep, antisocial drives such as those for sex or aggression. Sigmund Freud (1856–1939), the person most responsible for developing psychoanalysis, was a Viennese neurologist who became increasingly interested in psychoanalysis as a theory of human behavior, as a method of investigation, and as a treatment for certain illnesses. The following is a selection from Civilization and Its Discontents *(1929), written in the aftermath of World War I and toward the end of Freud's life. In it Freud speaks of the fragility of civilization.*

CONSIDER: *How this selection reflects the experience of World War I; the ways in which this document reflects and contributes to the sense of uncertainty common in this period; similarities between Ortega and Freud.*

The element of truth behind all this, which people are so ready to disavow, is that men are not gentle creatures who want to be loved, and who at the most can defend themselves if they are attacked; they are, on the contrary, creatures among whose instinctual endowments is to be reckoned a powerful share of aggressiveness. As a result, their neighbour is for them not only a potential helper or sexual object, but also someone who tempts them to satisfy their aggressiveness on him, to exploit his capacity for work without compensation, to use him sexually without his consent, to seize his possessions, to humiliate him, to cause him pain, to torture and to kill him. *Homo homini lupus.*[1] Who, in the face of all his experience of life and of history, will have the courage to dispute this assertion? As a rule this cruel aggressiveness waits for some provocation or puts itself at the service of some other purpose, whose goal might also have been reached by milder measures. In circumstances that are favourable to it, when the mental counter-forces which ordinarily inhibit it are out of action, it also manifests itself spontaneously and reveals man as a savage beast to whom consideration towards his own kind is something alien. Anyone who calls to mind the atrocities committed during racial migrations or the invasions of the Huns, or by the people known as

Mongols under Jenghiz Khan and Tamerlane, or at the capture of Jerusalem by the pious Crusaders, or even, indeed, the horrors of the recent World War—anyone who calls these things to mind will have to bow humbly before the truth of this view.

The existence of this inclination to aggression, which we can detect in ourselves and justly assume to be present in others, is the factor which disturbs our relations with our neighbour and which forces civilization into such a high expenditure [of energy]. In consequence of this primary mutual hostility of human beings, civilized society is perpetually threatened with disintegration. The interest of work in common would not hold it together; instinctual passions are stronger than reasonable interests. Civilization has to use its utmost efforts in order to set limits to man's aggressive instincts and to hold the manifestations of them in check by psychical reaction-formations. Hence, therefore, the use of methods intended to incite people into identifications, and aim-inhibited relationships of love, hence the restriction upon sexual life, and hence too the ideal's commandment to love one's neighbour as oneself—a commandment which is really justified by the fact that nothing else runs so strongly counter to the original nature of man. In spite of every effort, these endeavours of civilization have not so far achieved very much. It hopes to prevent the crudest excesses of brutal violence by itself assuming the right to use violence against criminals, but the law is not able to lay hold of the more cautious and refined manifestations of human aggressiveness.

❧

The fateful question for the human species seems to me to be whether and to what extent their cultural development will succeed in mastering the disturbance of their communal life by the human instinct of aggression and self-destruction. It may be that in this respect precisely the present time deserves a special interest. Men have gained control over the forces of nature to such an extent that with their help they would have no difficulty in exterminating one another to the last man. They know this, and hence comes a large part of their current unrest, their unhappiness and their mood of anxiety. And now it is to be expected that the other of the two "Heavenly Powers," eternal Eros, will make an effort to assert himself in the struggle with his equally immortal adversary. But who can foresee with what success and with what result?[2]

---

[1] "Man is a wolf to man." Derived from Plautus, *Asinaria* II, iv, 88.

[2] The final sentence was added in 1931—when the menace of Hitler was already becoming apparent.

Visual Sources

Decadence in the Weimar Republic

George Grosz

The following 1921 drawing by the German artist George Grosz (figure 27.1) shows some of the problems facing Western societies, particularly Germany, shortly after World War I. The wealthy few indulge in leisure activities while guards protect their factories. The rest of the people are crippled veterans, bankrupt businessmen, old women, young children, and the poor. They appear to feel isolated, distrustful, and out of place. The subject matter of this drawing is typical of art and literature that attacked capitalism and militarism between the wars.

CONSIDER: *How this drawing relates to the selection by Linke or the one by Remarque.*

Unemployment and Politics in the Weimar Republic

Economic and political developments often go hand in hand. Many historians argue that this was particularly the case in Germany during the 1920s and

FIGURE 27.1   (© The Granger Collection, New York)

Chart 27.1 Elections to the German Reichstag, 1924–1932						
	May 4, 1924	*December 7, 1924*	*May 20, 1928*	*September 14, 1930*	*July 31, 1932*	*November 6, 1932*
Number of Eligible Voters (in millions)	38.4	39.0	41.2	43.0	44.2	44.2
Votes Cast (in millions)	29.7	30.7	31.2	35.2	37.2	35.7
National Socialist German Workers Party	1,918,000 6.6%	908,000 3%	810,000 2.6%	6,407,000 18.3%	13,779,000 37.3%	11,737,000 33.1%
German Nationalist People's Party (Conservative)	5,696,000 19.5%	6,209,000 20.5%	4,382,000 14.2%	2,458,000 7%	2,187,000 5.9%	3,131,000 8.8%
Center Party (Catholic)	3,914,000 13.4%	4,121,000 13.6%	3,712,000 12.1%	4,127,000 11.8%	4,589,000 12.4%	4,230,000 11.9%
Democratic Party (The German State Party)	1,655,000 5.7%	1,921,000 6.3%	1,506,000 4.9%	1,322,000 3.8%	373,000 1%	339,000 1%
Social Democratic Party	6,009,000 20.5%	7,886,000 26%	9,153,000 29.8%	8,576,000 24.5%	7,960,000 21.6%	7,251,000 20.4%
Communist Party	3,693,000 12.6%	2,712,000 9%	3,265,000 10.6%	4,590,000 13.1%	5,370,000 14.3%	5,980,000 16.9%

early 1930s. Chart 27.1 and Chart 27.2 deal with the
Weimar Republic in Germany between 1924 and 1932. The
first shows election results by political parties to the Reichstag;
the second shows unemployment figures.

CONSIDER: The relationship between unemployment and
voting patterns.

Unemployment During the Great Depression, 1930–1938

While the Great Depression of the 1930s had worldwide consequences, it didn't affect all countries equally. One way of
comparing the course of the Depression in different countries
is to examine national unemployment, perhaps the most telling

Chart 27.2 Unemployment in Germany, 1924–1932

1924	1928	1930	July 31, 1932	October 31, 1932
978,000	1,368,000	3,076,000	5,392,000	5,109,000

SOURCE: Joachim Remak, ed., *The Nazi Years: A Documentary History* (Englewood Cliffs, NJ: Simon & Schuster, Inc., 1969), p. 44.

Chart 27.3 National Unemployment, 1930–1938

Year	Germany		Japan	
	Number	Percentage	Number	Percentage
1930	3,075,580	—	369,408	5.3%
1931	4,519,704	23.7%	422,755	6.1
1932	5,575,492	30.1	485,681	6.8
1933	4,804,428	25.8	408,710	5.6
1934	2,718,309	14.5	372,941	5.0
1935	2,151,039	11.6	356,044	4.6
1936	1,592,655	8.1	338,365	4.3
1937	912,312	4.5	295,443	3.7
1938 (June)	429,475	2.0	230,262	2.9

Year	Great Britain		United States	
	Number	Percentage	Number	Percentage
1930	1,464,347	11.8%	4,340,000	8.7%
1931	2,129,359	16.7	8,020,000	15.9
1932	2,254,857	17.6	12,060,000	23.6
1933	2,110,090	16.4	12,830,000	24.9
1934	1,801,913	13.91	1,340,000	21.7
1935	1,714,844	13.1	10,610,000	20.1
1936	1,497,587	11.2	9,030,000	16.9
1937	1,277,928	9.4	7,700,000	14.3
1938 (Nov.)	1,529,133	10.8	10,390,000	19.0

Frauen!

Adolf Hitler!

FIGURE 27.2 (Library of Congress [LC-US ZC4-3236])

index of the depth of the Great Depression and its social consequences. Chart 27.3 traces unemployment numbers and unemployment as a percentage of the civilian labor force in four countries between 1930 and 1938.

CONSIDER: *Which countries suffered more than others; where unemployment persisted the longest; possible reasons why Japan was not hit so hard as other countries.*

Unemployment and the Appeal to Women

The Nazi party used unemployment as part of its political appeal to women, as revealed in the following 1931 poster (figure 27.2). It states: "Women! Millions of Men Are Without Work. Millions of Children Are Without a Future. Save the German Family! Vote for Adolf Hitler!"

CONSIDER: *Why certain political parties gained and others lost as unemployment grew during the Depression years; how these charts relate to the drawing by Grosz, the selections by Linke and Remarque, and the Nazi poster; ways this poster was designed to appeal, in particular to German women.*

❧ Secondary Sources

The Generation of 1914: Disillusionment

Robert Wohl

The end of World War I raised hopes and expectations among large numbers of people. In a few years those hopes and expectations turned into disappointment and disillusionment, coloring the two decades between World Wars I and II. In the following selection Robert Wohl analyzes the origins and meaning of this disillusionment, focusing on the shared experiences of the generation of Europeans who were born during the 1890s and who had to shoulder much of the burden of the war.

SOURCE: Reprinted by permission of the publishers from *The Generation of 1914* by Robert Wohl. Cambridge, MA: Harvard University Press. Copyright © 1979 by the President and Fellows of Harvard College.

CONSIDER: *Why the first few years of peace were so crucial for the creation of cynicism and disillusionment among survivors of the war; the forms disillusionment took; possible consequences of the developments of 1917–1920 according to Wohl.*

When we think of the army of returning veterans during the 1920s, we see them through the eyes of Remarque and Hemingway as a generation of men crippled, both physically and morally, by their service in the war. Many no doubt were. Yet it is a fact that the famed cynicism and disillusionment of the survivors were, to a great extent, a product of the first few years of peace. To understand this mood of disillusionment we must recall the attitudes and expectations that soldiers brought home with them, attitudes and expectations that were also widespread among the younger population as a whole.

Many soldiers had, like Omodeo, come to think that the war must have a secret meaning that only the future would reveal; they found it necessary to believe that their sacrifice and suffering would not be in vain; and they clung to the hope that the war would turn out to have been a rite of purification with positive results. Sensing this feeling and realizing its importance, political leaders in all countries encouraged the fighting and civilian sectors of the population to expect from peace not merely an end to bloodshed but a real alteration and improvement in the tenor and quality of life. It was said, and widely believed, that class barriers would fall; that selfishness would give way to cooperation; that harmony would reign; that conflict among nations would cease; and that everyone's sacrifice and suffering would somehow be compensated.

These expectations were often encapsulated in the word "revolution," but people of different social backgrounds assigned very different meanings to the term. Governments encouraged these hopes with their propaganda, and in 1918 Wilson came to incarnate the dream of renovation. The Wilsonian vision of a world safe for democracy merged with the equally vague idea of a revolution carried out by returning soldiers in the name of the values of manhood and self-sacrifice they had discovered on the battlefield. . . .

Disillusionment comes in many forms. The special form it took in Europe in the 1920s had to do with the development of the political situation and the frustration of apocalyptic hopes. Between 1917 and 1920 a revolutionary wave broke over every European country. Armies grew restive and mutinied; urban populations staged riots and insurrections over dwindling food supplies and rising prices; unions swelled in membership far beyond their prewar size; and workers began to challenge factory owners for the control of production. . . .

This disillusionment was felt by men and women of all age-groups in all parts of Europe; but the feeling of betrayal and defeat was especially strong among returning veterans born in the 1890s. They suffered from a tremendous sense of anticlimax, and the younger they were the more disoriented they felt. . . .

The developments of 1917–1920 engendered disappointment and frustration; they gave rise to bitterness and cynicism; but among young war veterans, the dream of cultural and political renewal did not die. Brought up in a crepuscular atmosphere of cultural crisis, subjected while still young to the ordeal of the war, witnesses during the immediate postwar years to a wave of revolution that swept away century-old empires and shook to its foundations every European institution, intellectuals born in the last two decades of the nineteenth century could not divest themselves of the feeling that the apocalypse had only been postponed and that any restoration

of the postwar era would be temporary. The survival of the revolutionary regime in Russia, the creation of Communist parties throughout Europe, the victory of the Fascist movement in Italy, the collapse of parliamentary government in Spain, the difficulties that Great Britain and France experienced in regaining their prewar dynamism, and the onset of the worldwide economic crisis in 1929 confirmed these intellectuals in their belief that the world of their childhood was dead and that a new postwar world was being born.

Government and the Governed: The Interwar Years
R. H. S. Crossman

Many scholars saw the 1920s as a period of failure and missed opportunities. This was particularly true of liberal or left-wing scholars from Western democracies, for they looked for the origins of the disastrous rise of dictatorships and the Great Depression in those years. The following selection by R. H. S. Crossman exemplifies this perspective. Educated at Oxford, Crossman became a leading figure in the Labour Party's left wing and wrote numerous works on philosophy and politics. Here, in a work published in 1940, Crossman analyzes the period between 1918 and 1933.

CONSIDER: *Opportunities that were missed in 1918 and 1919; policies that the Western democracies might have initiated during this period that could have changed the course of events.*

Seen in retrospect, the period from 1918–1933 is marked by a growing lethargy in the victor nations. Neither at home nor abroad did democracy undertake a single great constructive enterprise. Victory seemed to have deprived France and Britain of their dynamic: their Conservatives ceased to be ardent imperialists, and their Socialists lost their revolutionary fervour. A spirit of collective pacifism possessed them, and made the people content with the lazy approval of high ideals, the verbal condemnation of injustice, chicanery and oppression. Holding all the power, the Western democracies disdained to use it, so long as the status quo was in any way tolerable. The attitude of America was not dissimilar, except that here the League idea was rejected and the Monroe doctrine was still regarded as America's contribution to world peace.

A myth is only justifiable if it stimulates to action. But "Collective Pacifism" was a sedative, not a stimulant. It intoxicated the democracies with a feeling of moral

SOURCE: R. H. S. Crossman, *Government and the Governed.* Reprinted by permission of G. P. Putnam's Sons (New York, 1940), pp. 255–257. Copyright © 1940 by G. P. Putnam's Sons.

superiority and well-being, while it sapped their sense of responsibility. Gradually statesmen and peoples alike began to believe that the League of Nations was a force able to do the work which previously fell to the various nations. Instead of relying on themselves and on cooperation with their allies, they began to rely on the League to preserve peace. Since the League had no coercive power at its disposal, this trust was wholly unjustified.

No one Party or section of the population can be blamed for this collapse of democratic morale. The great opportunity had been missed in 1918–19: and it was difficult for the Western democracies to recover from that failure. They had encouraged nationalism as the basis of government; they had retained economic imperialism and permitted international finance to function independently of government policy. In brief, they had as far as possible returned to pre-war conditions. Having done so, they sought to humanize them. That they failed is an indication that good intentions and kindness, unbacked by resolution and knowledge, may disguise injustices but never eradicate them. Kindness and good-will no doubt console the patient suffering from cancer, but they will not cure the cancer; and the patient whose practitioner only displays these qualities, may, in his intolerable agonies, turn to a quack and curse the Christian humanity which his practitioner displays.

The Great Depression in Europe

James M. Laux

Most scholars agree that the Great Depression was very important, but they disagree over its precise significance. For Marxists, it was the greatest in a series of periodic economic crises inevitably flowing from the capitalist system and an indication that this system would soon collapse. For liberal economic historians, it was an indictment of conservative, nationalistic economic policies that would be forced to give way to modern Keynesian policies characterized by greater government activity and planning. For others, it was a crucial cause of the rise of Nazism and World War II itself. In the following selection James Laux analyzes the impact of the Great Depression, emphasizing various changes in attitude that stemmed from it.

CONSIDER: *Whether, as some scholars argue, the Great Depression forced governments to modify laissez-faire just enough to save capitalism as a whole; why economic planning appeared more attractive after the experience of the Depression.*

SOURCE: James M. Laux, from "The Great Depression in Europe" (*The Forum Series*). Reprinted by permission of Forum Press (St. Louis, MO, 1974), pp. 13–14. Copyright © 1974 by Forum Press.

The Depression, perhaps, had the most serious impact in Europe on people's thinking about economic matters. Looking back on the experience, most Europeans agreed that the orthodoxy of laissez-faire no longer held. They would not again accept the view that a government must interfere as little as possible in the operation of the economic system. Governments must accept wider responsibilities than balancing their own budgets. The value of the currency in terms of gold must give way to economic expansion if the two appear to conflict. Laissez-faire already was wheezing and laboring in the 1920s; after the decade of the 1930s it was nearly prostrate. As so often happens, a philosophy came along to justify this changed attitude, a new approach to theoretical economics worked out by the Englishman John Maynard Keynes. The most influential economist of the twentieth century, Keynes published his classic work in 1936, *The General Theory of Employment, Interest and Money*. He argued that governments can and should manipulate capitalist economies, by running surpluses or deficits, by investing heavily in public works, by changing the size of the money and credit supply, and by altering rates of interest. In his analysis he emphasized the total economy, the relations among savings, investment, production, and consumption, what is called macroeconomics, rather than an investigation of a single firm or sector. A critic of socialism, Keynes scorned the significance of government ownership of production facilities, but promoted government intervention in an economy to make capitalism work better.

Bolstering this view were the remarkable production achievements of many European industrial states during the two world wars. In these crises national economies expanded military production enormously under government direction. Many asked why such techniques could not be applied in peacetime also, but to make consumer products rather than tools of destruction.

The upshot was that by 1945 if not 1939 most Europeans abandoned the idea that they lived at the mercy of an impersonal economic system whose rules could not be changed and accepted the proposition that the economy could operate the way people wanted it to. From this it was a short step to the concept of planning the future development of the economy—both the whole and particular segments of it. Economic planning became an acceptable posture for capitalist societies and enjoyed a considerable reputation. Some of those who supported it perhaps underestimated the possible merits of free markets as guiding production decisions and did seem to assume that planners somehow possess more wisdom than ordinary human beings.

Economic nationalism was a more immediate result of the Depression—the policy that short-run national economic interests have highest priority and that international economic cooperation and trade must give way before narrowly conceived national interests. Economic nationalism showed its sharpest teeth in those European states where political nationalism reached a peak—Germany, Italy, and the Soviet Union. Its strength declined in western Europe after the Second World War as people saw once again that economic prosperity among one's neighbors could bring great benefits to oneself. In an expanding continental or world economy everyone can get richer. But one wonders if economic nationalism may not revive in western Europe, especially if it seems a popular policy in a crisis.

The Great Depression had important political repercussions too. In Germany, the Depression's tragic gloom made the dynamism of the Nazi movement seem more attractive. It is difficult to imagine the Nazis achieving power without the Depression and its pervasive unemployment in the background. In France, the Depression convinced many that the regime of the Third Republic had lost its élan and relevance to twentieth-century problems, but the lack of a widely popular alternative meant that the Republic could limp along until a disastrous military defeat brought it down. In Britain, the Depression was less serious and no fundamental challenge to the political regime developed. The Conservatives held power for most of the interwar period and their failure to work actively to absorb the large unemployment that continued there until late in the 1930s brought widespread rancor and bitterness against them. Doubts as to the Conservatives' ability to manage a peacetime economy led to the first majority Labour government in the 1945 election. More profoundly, the years of heavy unemployment bred a very strong anticapitalist sentiment in much of British labor, a sentiment that led them after the war to demand moves toward socialism, such as nationalization of major industries.

The Depression helped convince Europeans that their governments must try to manage their economies. Most agreed that full employment and expanding output should be the goals. They did not agree on the means to achieve these ends.

❧ CHAPTER QUESTIONS

1. Which developments focused on in this chapter are most closely related to the experience and results of World War I?

2. In what ways do the trends of the 1920s and 1930s support the argument that Western civilization reached its apogee between 1789 and 1914 and that starting with World War I it was clearly on the decline? What factors might be pointed out to mitigate or counter this interpretation?

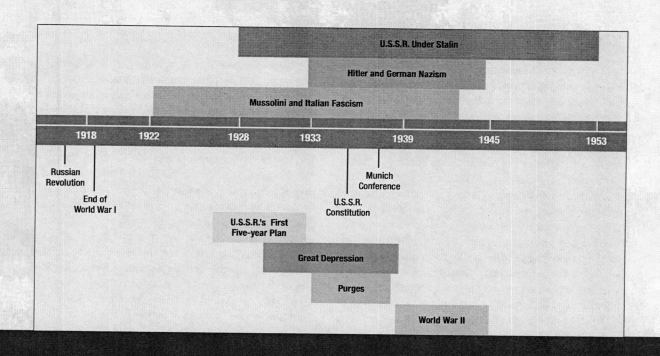

28 Communism, Fascism, and Authoritarianism

The end of World War I and the arrangements made at the Paris Peace Conference in 1919 seemed to represent success for parliamentary democracy. But during the 1920s and 1930s, that success proved to be more apparent than real. The 1917 revolution had already brought a Communist regime to power in Russia. During the following two decades, Communist parties spread throughout Europe and were perceived as a great threat, but they did not come to power outside of the Soviet Union. Authoritarian movements of the right became the most immediate danger to parliamentary democracy. The first of these movements was Mussolini's fascism, which became dominant in Italy in 1922. By the end of the decade regimes in Eastern and Southern Europe were becoming more authoritarian. This trend

became stronger during the Depression of the 1930s. There was a retreat toward nationalistic economic policies and greater central control by governments attempting to deal with the despair, destruction, and dislocation accompanying the Depression. In Central, Eastern, and Southern Europe, the Depression fueled already strong tendencies toward dictatorships and fascism. The most extreme of rightist ideology was Hitler's Nazism, which became dominant in Germany in 1933. By the end of that decade, Europe was embroiled in a new World War even greater than World War I.

Historians and social scientists looking at this period sometimes focus on the rise of "totalitarianism." This is a controversial term that is hard to evaluate objectively. Generally, it refers to a form of government that shares certain traits. It rejects individualism, a single party is in power, and the state controls almost all aspects of life (economic activities, social organizations, cultural institutions, the military, and politics). It has one official, revolutionary ideology, and terror, propaganda, and mass communications are used as tools of power. Yet there have been important differences among states that have been called totalitarian. Communism in Russia under Stalin and its professed opposite, Nazism in Germany, sprang from different sources and ideologies. Even though German Nazism and Italian fascism resembled each other, some scholars question whether Italian fascism was thorough and effective enough to be considered totalitarian. Other nationalistic authoritarian regimes of the right, from Eastern Europe to Spain and Portugal, shared only certain elements of fascism. Nevertheless, many scholars still argue that the concept of totalitarianism does provide us with a tool to use in interpreting important developments between the two world wars.

This chapter addresses a number of broad questions. What were the main features of these regimes? How were they similar to and different from one another? How can their appeal and the power they commanded over people be explained? In what ways were they related to nineteenth- and early-twentieth-century trends?

The selections in this chapter survey Communism, fascism, and authoritarianism from a variety of perspectives. What characteristics do these regimes share and how do these regimes differ from parliamentary systems? The selections on Mussolini and Italian fascism focus on the ideology of fascism and its historical place. An effort is made to distinguish German Nazism from Italian fascism, to analyze Nazism's appeal, to understand the extremes—including the policy of genocide—possible under such a system, and to evaluate the role of Hitler in shaping Nazism. Three of the most controversial aspects of Stalin and Russian communism are examined: Stalin's justification for the policy against the *kulaks* in 1929, his analysis of democracy as part of his defense of the 1936 Soviet Constitution, and his massive purges of the 1930s.

In addition to offering broad insights into Communism, fascism, and authoritarianism during the 1920s and 1930s, the selections in this chapter provide some of the background of World War II, which will be covered in the next chapter.

Primary Sources

The Doctrine of Fascism

Benito Mussolini

Italy was the first European power to turn to fascism. The country was one of the victors in World War I, but the war was costly and Italy did not gain much. After the war the country was marked by instability, weak governments, and an apparent threat from the left. Benito Mussolini (1883–1945), a former leader of the Socialist party and a veteran of the war, organized the Italian Fascist party in 1919. Strongly nationalistic, the party stood against the Versailles Treaty, left-wing radicalism, and the established government. After leading his Blackshirts in a march on Rome in 1922, Mussolini was invited by King Victor Emmanuel III to form a government. Over the next few years Mussolini effectively eliminated any opposition and installed his fascist state system, which would last some twenty years. The following document contains excerpts from "The Political and Social Doctrine of Fascism," an article signed by Mussolini and written with the philosopher Giovanni Gentile that originally appeared in the Enciclopedia Italiana *in 1932. It describes the ideological foundations of Italian fascism. These excerpts emphasize the rejection of traditional democracy, liberalism, and socialism as well as faith in the authoritarian, fascist state.*

CONSIDER: *The greatest sources of appeal in the doctrine according to Mussolini; the ways in which this doctrine can be considered a rejection of major historical trends that had been developing over the previous century; the government policies that would logically flow from such a doctrine.*

Fascism, the more it considers and observes the future and the development of humanity quite apart from political considerations of the moment, believes neither in the possibility nor the utility of perpetual peace. It thus repudiates the doctrine of Pacifism—born of a renunciation of the struggle and an act of cowardice in the face of sacrifice. War alone brings up to its highest tension all human energy and puts the stamp of nobility upon the peoples who have the courage to meet it. . . .

The Fascist accepts life and loves it, knowing nothing of and despising suicide; he rather conceives of life as duty and struggle and conquest, life which should be high and full, lived for oneself, but above all for others—those who are at hand and those who are far distant, contemporaries, and those who will come after. . . .

SOURCE: Benito Mussolini, "The Political and Social Doctrine of Fascism," *International Conciliation*, No. 306 (January 1935), pp. 7–17. Originally published by the Carnegie Endowment for International Peace, as part of the *International Conciliation Series*.

Such a conception of life makes Fascism the complete opposite of that doctrine, the base of so-called scientific and Marxian Socialism, the materialist conception of history. . . . Fascism, now and always, believes in holiness and in heroism; that is to say, in actions influenced by no economic motive, direct or indirect. . . .

Fascism repudiates the conception of "economic" happiness, to be realized by Socialism and, as it were, at a given moment in economic evolution to assure to everyone the maximum of well-being. Fascism denies the materialist conception of happiness as a possibility, and abandons it to its inventors, the economists of the first half of the nineteenth century. . . .

After Socialism, Fascism combats the whole complex system of democratic ideology, and repudiates it, whether in its theoretical premises or in its practical application. Fascism denies that the majority, by the simple fact that it is a majority, can direct human society; it denies that numbers alone can govern by means of a periodical consultation, and it affirms the immutable, beneficial, and fruitful inequality of mankind, which can never be permanently leveled through the mere operation of a mechanical process such as universal suffrage. . . .

Fascism denies, in democracy, the absurd conventional untruth of political equality dressed out in the garb of collective irresponsibility, and the myth of "happiness" and indefinite progress. But if democracy may be conceived in diverse forms—that is to say, taking democracy to mean a state of society in which the populace are not reduced to impotence in the State—Fascism may write itself down as "an organized, centralized, and authoritative democracy."

Fascism has taken up an attitude of complete opposition to the doctrines of Liberalism, both in the political field and the field of economics. . . . Fascism uses in its construction whatever elements in the Liberal, Social, or Democratic doctrines still have a living value; it maintains what may be called the certainties which we owe to history, but it rejects all the rest—that is to say, the conception that there can be any doctrine of unquestioned efficacy for all times and all peoples. Given that the nineteenth century was the century of Socialism, of Liberalism, and of Democracy, it does not necessarily follow that the twentieth century must also be a century of Socialism, Liberalism, and Democracy: political doctrines pass, but humanity remains; and it may rather be expected that this will be a century of authority, a century of the Left, a century of Fascism. For if the nineteenth century was a century of individualism (Liberalism always signifying individualism) it may be expected that this will be the century of collectivism, and hence the century of the State. It is a perfectly logical deduction that a new doctrine can utilize all the still vital elements of previous doctrines. . . .

The foundation of Fascism is the conception of the State, its character, its duty, and its aim. Fascism conceives of the State as an absolute, in comparison with which all individuals or groups are relative, only to be conceived of in their relation to the State. The conception of the Liberal State is not that of a directing force, guiding the play and development, both material and spiritual, of a collective body, but merely a force limited to the function of recording results: on the other hand, the Fascist State is itself conscious, and has itself a will and a personality—thus it may be called the "ethic" State. . . .

If every age has its own characteristic doctrine, there are a thousand signs which point to Fascism as the characteristic doctrine of our time. For if a doctrine must be a living thing, this is proved by the fact that Fascism has created a living faith; and that this faith is very powerful in the minds of men, is demonstrated by those who have suffered and died for it.

Fascism has henceforth in the world the universality of all those doctrines which, in realizing themselves, have represented a stage in the history of the human spirit.

Mein Kampf
Adolf Hitler

The most extreme and racist form of fascism arose in Germany under the Nazis, led by Adolf Hitler (1889–1945). After serving in World War I, Hitler joined and soon took control of the small National Socialist German Workers party. In the early 1930s, after years of relative obscurity, the Nazi party gained popularity with a nationalistic program attacking the Versailles Treaty, the Weimar Republic, the Communists, and above all the Jews. In 1933 Hitler was appointed chancellor and Germany was soon transformed into a Nazi state. Hitler's ideology, his mental processes, and some of the ideas behind Nazism are illustrated in his rather formless book Mein Kampf ("My Struggle"). It was written in 1924 while he was in jail for his efforts to overthrow the government of Bavaria in southern Germany. With the growing popularity of the Nazi party in the early 1930s, the book became a best-seller. In these selections from Mein Kampf, Hitler displays his anti-Semitism, argues that a racial analysis is central to an understanding of history, and indicates his vision of German expansion eastward at the expense of Russia.

SOURCE: Adolf Hitler, *Mein Kampf,* R. Manheim, trans. Reprinted by permission of Houghton Mifflin Company (New York, 1943), pp. 290–296, 300–302, 305–308, 312–320, 323–327, 580–583, 649–655, and the Hutchinson Publishing Group Ltd. (London, 1943). Copyright © 1943 and © renewed 1971 by Houghton Mifflin Co. (U.S. Rights), and by the Hutchinson Publishing Group Ltd. (Canadian Rights).

CONSIDER: *How Hitler connects the Jews, the Marxists, and German expansion eastward; on what points Mussolini might agree with Hitler here; the ways in which these ideas might be appealing, popular, or acceptable in the historical circumstances of Germany in the early 1930s.*

If we were to divide mankind into three groups, the founders of culture, the bearers of culture, the destroyers of culture, only the Aryan could be considered as the representative of the first group. From him originate the foundations and walls of all human creation, and only the outward form and color are determined by the changing traits of character of the various peoples. He provides the mightiest building stones and plans for all human progress and only the execution corresponds to the nature of the varying men and races. . . .

Blood mixture and the resultant drop in the racial level is the sole cause of the dying out of old cultures; for men do not perish as a result of lost wars, but by the loss of that force of resistance which is contained only in pure blood.

All who are not of good race in this world are chaff. . . .

With satanic joy in his face, the black-haired Jewish youth lurks in wait for the unsuspecting girl whom he defiles with his blood, thus stealing her from her people. With every means he tries to destroy the racial foundations of the people he has set out to subjugate. Just as he himself systematically ruins women and girls, he does not shrink back from pulling down the blood barriers for others, even on a large scale. It was and it is Jews who bring the Negroes into the Rhineland, always with the same secret thought and clear aim of ruining the hated white race by the necessarily resulting bastardization, throwing it down from its cultural and political height, and himself rising to be its master.

For a racially pure people which is conscious of its blood can never be enslaved by the Jew. In this world he will forever be master over bastards and bastards alone.

And so he tries systematically to lower the racial level by a continuous poisoning of individuals.

And in politics he begins to replace the idea of democracy by the dictatorship of the proletariat.

In the organized mass of Marxism he has found the weapon which lets him dispense with democracy and in its stead allows him to subjugate and govern the peoples with a dictatorial and brutal fist.

He works systematically for revolutionization in a twofold sense: economic and political.

Around peoples who offer too violent a resistance to attack from within he weaves a net of enemies, thanks to his international influence, incites them to war, and finally, if necessary, plants the flag of revolution on the very battlefields.

In economics he undermines the states until the social enterprises which have become unprofitable are taken from the state and subjected to his financial control.

In the political field he refuses the state the means for its self-preservation, destroys the foundations of all national self-maintenance and defense, destroys faith in the leadership, scoffs at its history and past, and drags everything that is truly great into the gutter.

Culturally he contaminates art, literature, the theater, makes a mockery of natural feeling, overthrows all concepts of beauty and sublimity, of the noble and the good, and instead drags men down into the sphere of his own base nature.

Religion is ridiculed, ethics and morality represented as outmoded, until the last props of a nation in its struggle for existence in this world have fallen.

Now begins the great last revolution. In gaining political power the Jew casts off the few cloaks that he still wears. The democratic people's Jew becomes the blood-Jew and tyrant over peoples. In a few years he tries to exterminate the national intelligentsia and by robbing the peoples of their natural intellectual leadership makes them ripe for the slave's lot of permanent subjugation.

The most frightful example of this kind is offered by Russia, where he killed or starved about thirty million people with positively fanatical savagery, in part amid inhuman tortures, in order to give a gang of Jewish journalists and stock exchange bandits domination over a great people.

The end is not only the end of the freedom of the peoples oppressed by the Jew, but also the end of this parasite upon the nations. After the death of his victim, the vampire sooner or later dies too. . . .

⊱

And so we National Socialists consciously draw a line beneath the foreign policy tendency of our pre-War period. We take up where we broke off six hundred years ago. We stop the endless German movement to the south and west, and turn our gaze toward the land in the east. At long last we break off the colonial and commercial policy of the pre-War period and shift to the soil policy of the future.

If we speak of soil in Europe today, we can primarily have in mind only *Russia* and her vassal border states.

Here Fate itself seems desirous of giving us a sign. By handing Russia to Bolshevism, it robbed the Russian nation of that intelligentsia which previously brought about and guaranteed its existence as a state. For the organization of a Russian state formation was not the result of the political abilities of the Slavs in Russia, but only a wonderful example of the state-forming efficacy of the German element in an inferior race. Numerous mighty empires on earth have been created in this way. Lower nations led by Germanic organizers and overlords have more than once grown to be mighty state formations and have endured as long as the racial nucleus of the creative state race maintained itself. For centuries Russia drew nourishment from this Germanic nucleus of its upper leading strata. Today it can be regarded as almost totally exterminated and extinguished. It has been replaced by the Jew. Impossible as it is for the Russian by himself to shake off the yoke of the Jew by his own resources, it is equally impossible for the Jew to maintain the mighty empire forever. He himself is no element of organization, but a ferment of decomposition. The Persian empire in the east is ripe for collapse. And the end of Jewish rule in Russia will also be the end of Russia as a state. We have been chosen by Fate as witnesses of a catastrophe which will be the mightiest confirmation of the soundness of the folkish theory.

Nazi Propaganda Pamphlet

Joseph Goebbels

Propaganda was strongly emphasized by the Nazis as a method of acquiring and maintaining power. Joseph Goebbels (1897–1945), an early leader in the Nazi party, was made chief of propaganda in 1929, minister for propaganda and national enlightenment in 1933, and a member of Hitler's cabinet council in 1938. The following is an excerpt from a 1930 pamphlet, written by Goebbels, describing why the Nazis are nationalists, "socialists," and against Jews and Marxists.

CONSIDER: *How this document reflects the character of life in Germany during the 1920s; to whom this document was designed to appeal and in what ways it might be a convincing piece of propaganda; in tone, quality, and ideas, how this compares with Mussolini's "Doctrine of Fascism"; how Nazi "socialism" differs from more traditional or Marxist conceptions of socialism.*

WHY ARE WE NATIONALISTS?

We are NATIONALISTS because we see in the NATION the only possibility for the protection and the furtherance of our existence.

The NATION is the organic bond of a people for the protection and defense of their lives. He is nationally minded who understands this IN WORD AND IN DEED.

Today, in GERMANY, NATIONALISM has degenerated into BOURGEOIS PATRIOTISM, and its power exhausts itself in tilting at windmills. It says GERMANY and means MONARCHY. It proclaims FREEDOM and means BLACK-WHITE-RED.

WE ARE NATIONALISTS BECAUSE WE, AS GERMANS, LOVE GERMANY. And because we love Germany, we demand the protection of its national spirit and we battle against its destroyers.

SOURCE: From Louis L. Snyder, *The Weimar Republic.* Reprinted by permission of D. Van Nostrand Co. (New York, 1966), pp. 201–203. Copyright © 1966 by Litton Educational Publishing, Inc.

WHY ARE WE SOCIALISTS?

We are SOCIALISTS because we see in SOCIALISM the only possibility for maintaining our racial existence and through it the reconquest of our political freedom and the rebirth of the German state. SOCIALISM has its peculiar form first of all through its comradeship in arms with the forward-driving energy of a newly awakened nationalism. Without nationalism it is nothing, a phantom, a theory, a vision of air, a book. With it, it is everything, THE FUTURE, FREEDOM, FATHERLAND!

It was a sin of the liberal bourgeoisie to overlook THE STATE-BUILDING POWER OF SOCIALISM. It was the sin of MARXISM to degrade SOCIALISM to a system of MONEY AND STOMACH.

SOCIALISM IS POSSIBLE ONLY IN A STATE WHICH IS FREE INSIDE AND OUTSIDE.

DOWN WITH POLITICAL BOURGEOIS SENTIMENT: FOR REAL NATIONALISM!

DOWN WITH MARXISM: FOR TRUE SOCIALISM!

UP WITH THE STAMP OF THE FIRST GERMAN NATIONAL SOCIALIST STATE!

AT THE FRONT THE NATIONAL SOCIALIST GERMAN WORKERS PARTY!

WHY DO WE OPPOSE THE JEWS?

We are ENEMIES OF THE JEWS, because we are fighters for the freedom of the German people. THE JEW IS THE CAUSE AND THE BENEFICIARY OF OUR MISERY. He has used the social difficulties of the broad masses of our people to deepen the unholy split between Right and Left among our people. He has made two halves of Germany. He is the real cause for our loss of the Great War.

The Jew has no interest in the solution of Germany's fateful problems. He CANNOT have any. FOR HE LIVES ON THE FACT THAT THERE HAS BEEN NO SOLUTION. If we would make the German people a unified community and give them freedom before the world, then the Jew can have no place among us. He has the best trumps in his hands when a people lives in inner and outer slavery. THE JEW IS RESPONSIBLE FOR OUR MISERY AND HE LIVES ON IT.

That is the reason why we, AS NATIONALISTS and AS SOCIALISTS, oppose the Jew. HE HAS CORRUPTED OUR RACE, FOULED OUR MORALS, UNDERMINED OUR CUSTOMS, AND BROKEN OUR POWER.

THE JEW IS THE PLASTIC DEMON OF THE DECLINE OF MANKIND.

WE ARE ENEMIES OF THE JEWS BECAUSE WE BELONG TO THE GERMAN PEOPLE. THE JEW IS OUR GREATEST MISFORTUNE.

It is not true that we eat a Jew every morning at breakfast.

It is true, however, that he SLOWLY BUT SURELY ROBS US OF EVERYTHING WE OWN.

THAT WILL STOP, AS SURELY AS WE ARE GERMANS.

The German Woman and National Socialism [Nazism]

Guida Diehl

From the beginning, the Nazi party stood against any expansion of women's political or economic roles. Indeed, the Nazi policy was to keep women in their own separate sphere as mothers and wives and remove them from jobs and politics—the man's sphere. Nevertheless, many women supported the Nazi party and joined Nazi women's organizations. The following selection is from a book published in 1933 by Guida Diehl, a leader of pro-Nazi women's organizations.

CONSIDER: *The ways this might appeal to German women; how this fits with other ideals of Nazism.*

This tumultuous age with all its difficulties and challenges must create a new type of woman capable of partaking in the achievements of the Third Reich and of fulfilling the womanly task that awaits her.

Let us not forget that this new woman holds her honor high above all else. A man's honor rests on fulfilling the tasks of public life entrusted to him. He safeguards his honor by doing his work honorably and with firmness of character and pride. A woman's honor rests on the province specifically entrusted to her, for which she is responsible, the province where new life is to grow: love, marriage, family, motherhood. A woman who does not accept this responsibility, who misuses this province for mere enjoyment, who will not let herself be proudly wooed before she surrenders—which is nature's way—who does not in marriage provide a new generation with the basis of a family—such a woman desecrates her honor. For we live in a time when womanly worth and dignity, womanly honor and pride, are of the utmost importance for the future of the nation, for the next generation. Therefore, the proud safeguarding of her honor must be an essential characteristic of this new type of woman. The German man wants to look up again to the German maid, the German woman. He wants to admire in her this dignity, this pride, this safeguarding of her honor and her heroic fighting spirit along with her native, cheerful simplicity. He wants to know again that German women and German fidelity go hand in hand, and that it is worthwhile to live and die for such German womanhood.

The Theory and Practice of Hell: The Nazi Elite

Eugene Kogon

The SS was Hitler's special corps, serving as his bodyguard and elite police force. Members of the SS usually became extremely dedicated to the ideas and practices of Nazism and carried out its precepts with extraordinary ruthlessness. The following is a statement from an SS officer recorded in a 1937 interview conducted by Eugene Kogon, less than one year before Kogon was arrested and taken to the concentration camp at Buchenwald. The officer was being trained as one of the elite of the Nazi state. Here he reveals his assumptions as a committed follower of Hitler and Nazism.

CONSIDER: *The role this officer assumes the SS will play in the Nazi state and the ways this role was particularly appropriate to a fascist system; how this document helps account for the appeal of the SS to those deciding to join it; how the ideas revealed here might serve as psychological justification for some of the atrocities committed by the SS.*

"What we trainers of the younger generation of Führers aspire to is a modern governmental structure on the model of the ancient Greek city states. It is to these aristocratically run democracies with their broad economic basis of serfdom that we owe the great cultural achievements of antiquity. From five to ten percent of the people, their finest flower, shall rule; the rest must work and obey. In this way alone can we attain that peak performance we must demand of ourselves and of the German people.

"The new Führer class is selected by the SS—in a positive sense by means of the National Political Education Institutes (*Napola*) as a preparatory stage, of the *Ordensburgen* as the academies proper of the coming Nazi aristocracy, and of a subsequent active internship in public affairs; in a negative sense by the extermination of all racially and biologically inferior elements and by the radical removal of all incorrigible political opposition that refuses on principle to acknowledge the philosophical basis of the Nazi State and its essential institutions.

"Within ten years at the latest it will be possible for us in this way to dictate the law of Adolf Hitler to Europe, put a halt to the otherwise inevitable decay of the continent, and build up a true community of nations, with Germany as the leading power keeping order."

SOURCE: Guida Diehl, *The German Woman and National Socialism* (Eisenach, 1933), pp. 111–113, in Eleanor S. Riemer and John C. Fout, eds., *European Women: A Documentary History, 1789–1945* (New York: Schocken Books, 1980), pp. 108–109.

SOURCE: Excerpt from *The Theory and Practice of Hell* by Eugene Kogon. Copyright © 1950 by Farrar, Straus & Giroux, Inc. Reprinted by permission of Farrar, Straus & Giroux, Inc.

The Informed Heart: Nazi Concentration Camps

Bruno Bettelheim

Organized, official racial persecution, particularly of the Jews, was a direct consequence of Nazi theories, attitudes, and practices. During the 1920s and early 1930s, however, the extent of the persecution was unanticipated. The most extreme form of this occurred in the late 1930s, with the introduction of forced labor and concentration camps, later to be followed by camps in which a policy of literal extermination was pursued resulting in the killing of millions of Jews and others. In the following selection Bruno Bettelheim, a psychoanalyst in Austria at the time and later a leading psychoanalyst in the United States, describes his experiences in the concentration camps at Dachau and Buchenwald. He focuses on the dehumanizing processes involved and some of the ways prisoners adapted in an effort to survive.

CONSIDER: *The methods used to gain control over the prisoners; the psychological means developed by Bettelheim and other prisoners to cope with and survive this experience; how the existence, nature, and functioning of these camps reflect the theory and practice of Nazi totalitarianism.*

Usually the standard initiation of prisoners took place during transit from the local prison to the camp. If the distance was short, the transport was often slowed down to allow enough time to break the prisoners. During their initial transport to the camp, prisoners were exposed to nearly constant torture. The nature of the abuse depended on the fantasy of the particular SS man in charge of a group of prisoners. Still, they all had a definite pattern. Physical punishment consisted of whipping, frequent kicking (abdomen or groin), slaps in the face, shooting, or wounding with the bayonet. These alternated with attempts to produce extreme exhaustion. For instance, prisoners were forced to stare for hours into glaring lights, to kneel for hours, and so on.

From time to time a prisoner got killed, but no prisoner was allowed to care for his or another's wounds. The guards also forced prisoners to hit one another and to defile what the SS considered the prisoners' most cherished values. They were forced to curse their God, to accuse themselves and one another of vile actions, and their wives of adultery and prostitution. . . .

The purpose of this massive initial abuse was to traumatize the prisoners and break their resistance; to change at least their behavior if not yet their personalities. This could be seen from the fact that tortures became less and less violent to the degree that prisoners stopped resisting and complied immediately with any SS order, even the most outrageous. . . .

It is hard to say just how much the process of personality change was speeded up by what prisoners experienced during the initiation. Most of them were soon totally exhausted; physically from abuse, loss of blood, thirst, etc.; psychologically from the need to control their anger and desperation before it could lead to a suicidal resistance. . . .

If I should try to sum up in one sentence what my main problem was during the whole time I spent in the camps, it would be: to protect my inner self in such a way that if, by any good fortune, I should regain liberty, I would be approximately the same person I was when deprived of liberty. So it seems that a split was soon forced upon me, the split between the inner self that might be able to retain its integrity, and the rest of the personality that would have to submit and adjust for survival. . . .

I have no doubt that I was able to endure the horrors of the transport and all that followed, because right from the beginning I became convinced that these dreadful and degrading experiences were somehow not happening to "me" as a subject, but only "me" as an object. . . .

All thoughts and feelings I had during the transport were extremely detached. It was as if I watched things happening in which I took part only vaguely. . . .

This was taught me by a German political prisoner, a communist worker who by then had been at Dachau for four years. I arrived there in a sorry condition because of experiences on the transport. I think that this man, by then an "old" prisoner, decided that, given my condition, the chances of my surviving without help were slim. So when he noticed that I could not swallow food because of physical pain and psychological revulsion, he spoke to me out of his rich experience: "Listen you, make up your mind: do you want to live or do you want to die? If you don't care, don't eat the stuff. But if you want to live, there's only one way: make up your mind to eat whenever and whatever you can, never mind how disgusting. Whenever you have a chance, defecate, so you'll be sure your body works. And whenever you have a minute, don't blabber, read by yourself, or flop down and sleep."

Witness to the Holocaust

Fred Baron

In the 1940s, the Nazis instituted the "final solution" to exterminate Jews and others that Hitler considered enemies of the state. The Nazis built several huge death camps, employing terror and factory-like methods to kill their victims. Only a few survived, but some who did managed to tell the story. One of these was Fred Baron, an Austrian Jew who was sent to the death camp at Auschwitz in occupied Poland. Here he tells of his deportation and experiences at the camp.

CONSIDER: *The methods used by Nazis to gain obedience and effect extermination; the nature of life for those in the camps.*

Deportation: I was marched with the local Jewish population—men, women, and children—eight or ten hours, to a small railroad station. Nobody told us where we were going. We were forced into railroad cars, 100 to 120 in one car, like sardines, without food, without water, without any sanitary facility. The cars were sealed and we stood there for maybe half a day before even moving. Finally, began the slow trip to nowhere.

There were children in our car, and old people. People got sick, died, and some went insane. It was an absolute, indescribable hell. I really don't know how many days and nights we were in that living hell on wheels.

When we finally stopped, they tore open the railroad cars and we were blinded by light, because our eyes were just not used to light any more. We saw funny-looking characters wearing striped pajama-like uniforms with matching caps, with great big sticks in their hands. They were screaming and yelling in all languages to jump out of the cars.

I didn't know where I was. All around us were barracks and barbed wire and machine gun towers, and in the distance I saw what looked like a huge factory with black smoke coming out of chimneys. I noticed a peculiar smell in the air and also a fine dust, subduing the light. The sunshine was not bright but there were birds singing. It was a beautiful day.

We were marched through a meadow filled with yellow flowers and one of the fellows next to me just turned and walked straight into the meadow. The guards cried out to him to stop, but he didn't hear or he didn't want to. He just kept slowly marching into the meadow, and then they opened up with machine guns and the man fell down dead. And that was my reception to Auschwitz.

Auschwitz: We were separated, men and women, and formed rows of fives. I found myself in front of a very elegantly dressed German officer. He was wearing boots and white gloves and he carried a riding whip, and with the whip he was pointing left or right, left or right. Whichever direction he pointed, guards pushed the person in front of him either left or right. I was twenty-one years old and in pretty good shape, but older people were sent to the other side and marched away.

We had to undress and throw away all belongings except our shoes. We were chased through a cold shower, and we stood shivering in the night air until we were told to march to a barracks. We were handed prisoner uniforms—a jacket, pants, and a sort of beanie—and a

metal dish. We didn't really know what happened yet. We were absolutely numb.

A non-Jewish kapo, an Austrian with a hard, weather-beaten face, told us, "You have arrived at hell on earth." He had been in prison since 1938, and he gave us basic concepts on how to stay alive.

"Don't trust anybody," he said, "don't trust your best friend. Look out for yourself. Be selfish to the point of obscenity. Try and stay alive from one minute to the other one. Don't let down for one second. Always try and find out where the nearest guards are and what they are doing. Don't volunteer for anything. And don't get sick, or you will be a goner in no time."

Auschwitz was gigantic—row and rows of barracks as far as the eye could see, subdivided by double strings of electric barbed wire. There were Hungarians and Polish Jews and a great number of Greeks, many Dutch Jews, some French, Germans.

Food was our main interest in life. In the morning we received what they called coffee—black water. We worked until noon, then we got a bowl of soup. In the evening we received another bowl of either vegetable or soup, a little piece of bread, and sometimes a tiny little piece of margarine or sugar or some kind of sausage. And that was the food for the day.

Suicides happened all the time, usually by hanging, at night. One fellow threw himself in front of a truck. It just broke his arm, but the S.S. guards beat him to a pulp, and in the morning he was dead.

A tremendous number of transports were coming in. The gas chambers could not keep up, so they were burning people in huge pits. Some of the smaller children were thrown in alive. We could hear the screams day and night, but sometimes the human mind can take just so much and then it just closes up and refuses to accept what is happening just 100, 200 feet away.

Problems of Agrarian Policy in the U.S.S.R.: Soviet Collectivization

Joseph Stalin

Joseph Stalin (1879–1953) rose from his working-class origins to become a leading member of the Bolsheviks before the 1917 revolution, the general secretary of the Russian Communist party in 1922, and the unchallenged dictator of the U.S.S.R. by 1929. In 1927 Stalin and the leadership of the Russian Communist party decided on a policy for the planned industrialization of the U.S.S.R.—the First Five-Year Plan. At the same time they decided on a policy favoring the collectivization

SOURCE: J. V. Stalin, "Problems of Agrarian Policy in the U.S.S.R.," in *Problems of Leninism*, ed. J. V. Stalin (Moscow: Foreign Languages, 1940), pp. 303–305, 318–321. Reprinted by permission of the Copyright Agency of the U.S.S.R.

of agriculture. By 1929 Stalin made that policy more drastic, using massive coercion against the kulaks (relatively rich independent peasants). Kulaks resisted this enforced collectivization and widespread death and destruction resulted. Nevertheless, by 1932 much of Russian agriculture was collectivized. The following is an excerpt from a 1929 speech delivered by Stalin at the Conference of Marxist Students of the Agrarian Question. In it he explains and justifies the policy of collectivization and the need to eliminate the kulaks as a class.

CONSIDER: The relations of this policy toward the kulaks to the policy for the planned industrialization of the U.S.S.R.; how Stalin justifies this policy as "socialist" as opposed to "capitalist"; the differences between Stalin's attitudes and ideas toward the kulaks and Hitler's toward the Jews.

Can we advance our socialized industry at an accelerated rate while having to rely on an agricultural base, such as is provided by small peasant farming, which is incapable of expanded reproduction, and which, in addition, is the predominant force in our national economy? No, we cannot. Can the Soviet government and the work of Socialist construction be, for any length of time, based on two *different* foundations; on the foundation of the most large-scale and concentrated Socialist industry and on the foundation of the most scattered and backward, small-commodity peasant farming? No, they cannot. Sooner or later this would be bound to end in the complete collapse of the whole national economy. What, then, is the solution? The solution lies in enlarging the agricultural units, in making agriculture capable of accumulation, of expanded reproduction, and in thus changing the agricultural base of our national economy. But how are the agricultural units to be enlarged? There are two ways of doing this. There is the *capitalist* way, which is to enlarge the agricultural units by introducing capitalism in agriculture—a way which leads to the impoverishment of the peasantry and to the development of capitalist enterprises in agriculture. We reject this way as incompatible with the Soviet economic system. There is a second way: the *Socialist* way, which is to set up collective farms and state farms, the way which leads to the amalgamation of the small peasant farms into large collective farms, technically and scientifically equipped, and to the squeezing out of the capitalist elements from agriculture. We are in favour of this second way.

And so, the question stands as follows: either one way or the other, either *back*—to capitalism or *forward*—to Socialism. There is no third way, nor can there be. The "equilibrium" theory makes an attempt to indicate a third way. And precisely because it is based on a third (non-existent) way, it is Utopian and anti-Marxian. . . .

Now, as you see, we have the material base which enables us to *substitute* for kulak output the output of the collective farms and state farms. That is why our offensive against the kulaks is now meeting with undeniable

success. That is how the offensive against the kulaks must be carried on, if we mean a real offensive and not futile declamations against the kulaks.

That is why we have recently passed from the policy of *restricting* the exploiting proclivities of the kulaks to the policy of *eliminating the kulaks as a class.*

Well, what about the policy of expropriating the kulaks? Can we permit the expropriation of kulaks in the regions of solid collectivization? This question is asked in various quarters. A ridiculous question! We could not permit the expropriation of the kulaks as long as we were pursuing the policy of restricting the exploiting proclivities of the kulaks, as long as we were unable to launch a determined offensive against the kulaks, as long as we were unable to substitute for kulak output the output of the collective farms and state farms. At that time the policy of not permitting the expropriation of the kulaks was necessary and correct. But now? Now the situation is different. Now we are able to carry on a determined offensive against the kulaks, to break their resistance, to eliminate them as a class and substitute for their output the output of the collective farms and state farms. Now, the kulaks are being expropriated by the masses of poor and middle peasants themselves, by the masses who are putting solid collectivization into practice. Now, the expropriation of the kulaks in the regions of solid collectivization is no longer just an administrative measure. Now, the expropriation of the kulaks is an integral part of the formation and development of the collective farms. That is why it is ridiculous and fatuous to expatiate today on the expropriation of the kulaks. You do not lament the loss of the hair of one who has been beheaded.

There is another question which seems no less ridiculous: whether the kulak should be permitted to join the collective farms. Of course not, for he is a sworn enemy of the collective-farm movement. Clear, one would think.

Report to the Congress of Soviets, 1936: Soviet Democracy

Joseph Stalin

In 1936 a new constitution for the U.S.S.R. was established. Although in form it was democratic and apparently rather liberal, in fact it did nothing to challenge Stalin's power or the Communist party as the only legitimate political organization. Part of the problem has to do with differing conceptions of the word "democracy." In the following selection from his report to the Extraordinary Eighth Congress of Soviets of the U.S.S.R. in 1936, Stalin defends the constitution, comparing the meanings of "democracy" and "political freedom" in the U.S.S.R. with their significance in other societies.

SOURCE: James H. Meisel and Edward S. Kozera, eds., *Materials for the Study of the Soviet System* (Ann Arbor, MI: The George Wahr Publishing Co., 1950), pp. 236–237. Reprinted by permission of the publisher.

CONSIDER: *The concerns revealed by this document; why Stalin goes to such pains to justify the new constitution; the legitimacy of the distinction made between democracy in capitalist countries and democracy in the U.S.S.R.*

I must admit that the draft of the new Constitution does preserve the regime of the dictatorship of the working class, just as it also preserves unchanged the present leading position of the Communist Party of the U.S.S.R. [Loud applause.] If the esteemed critics regard this as a flaw in the Draft Constitution, that is only to be regretted. We Bolsheviks regard it as a merit of the Draft Constitution. [Loud applause.]

As to freedom for various political parties, we adhere to somewhat different views. A party is a part of a class, its most advanced part. Several parties, and, consequently, freedom for parties, can exist only in a society in which there are antagonistic classes whose interests are mutually hostile and irreconcilable—in which there are, say, capitalists and workers, landlords and peasants, kulaks and poor peasants, etc. But in the U.S.S.R. there are no longer such classes as the capitalists, the landlords, the kulaks, etc. In the U.S.S.R. there are only two classes, workers and peasants, whose interests—far from being mutually hostile—are, on the contrary, friendly. Hence there is no ground in the U.S.S.R. for the existence of several parties, and, consequently, for freedom for these parties. In the U.S.S.R. there is ground only for one party, the Communist Party. In the U.S.S.R. only one party can exist, the Communist Party, which courageously defends the interests of the workers and peasants to the very end. . . .

They talk of democracy. But what is democracy? Democracy in capitalist countries, where there are antagonistic classes, is, in the last analysis, democracy for the strong, democracy for the propertied minority. In the U.S.S.R., on the contrary, democracy is democracy for the working people, i.e., democracy for all. But from this it follows that the principles of democratism are violated, not by the draft of the new Constitution of the U.S.S.R., but by the bourgeois constitutions. That is why I think that the Constitution of the U.S.S.R. is the only thoroughly democratic Constitution in the world.

Visual Sources

Nazi Mythology

Richard Spitz

The following (figure 28.1) is an example of Nazi propaganda art, with its characteristic blend of realistic style and romantic vision. It shows Nazi soldiers and civilian folk marching in brotherly comradeship toward Valhalla, the final resting place of Aryan heroes. Above them, Nazi flags and wounded soldiers are being lifted together toward the same heavens. Stereotypes, rather than distinct individuals, are shown: The soldiers all look almost the same, and on the right there are representatives of civilian youth, middle-aged and elderly people, farmers, and workers. Those being glorified are all males and almost all soldiers. Viewers of this picture are supposed to feel proud, to feel that sacrifices for the state will be rewarded and that the greatest glory comes from military service. In subject and style, this picture represents a rejection of the major twentieth-century artistic trends.

CONSIDER: *How this picture fits the image and ideals of Nazism as reflected in the documents by Hitler and Goebbels and the statements of the SS officer.*

Socialist Realism

K. I. Finogenov

The following example of socialist realism (figure 28.2) has great similarities to Nazi art: its realistic style, its romantic vision, its propagandistic purpose. In this case, however, the emphasis on economic themes is greater than that on military themes. Painted in 1935 by K. I. Finogenov, it shows Communist party and government leaders, led by Stalin, on a modern Soviet farm. On the right an expert checks the soil. In the background a new tractor is displayed. All the figures are relatively well dressed; no one looks like a peasant farmer.

CONSIDER: *How this picture relates to the role of the government in the Soviet Union and to Stalin's place in it; what insight into the agricultural policy during the 1930s the picture is supposed to convey; how the image presented here fits with Stalin's explanation of collectivization; how this picture compares with that of Joseph II in Chapter 19 (figure 19.3).*

Authoritarianism and Totalitarianism, 1919–1937

The following map (map 28.1) shows the spread of authoritarian and totalitarian governments in Europe between 1919 and 1937. Although no firm rules apply here, those countries retaining parliamentary democratic forms of government generally had a longer tradition of democratic institutions, were more satisfied winners in World War I,

FIGURE 28.1   (Photograph by Garner. Courtesy of Army Art Collection, U.S. Army Center of Military History)

FIGURE 28.2   (© Tass/Sovfoto/Eastfoto)

MAP 28.1   The Spread of Authoritarian Governments

and were located in more advanced industrialized areas in northwestern Europe.

CONSIDER: Taking account of the relevant geography, historical background, and experience of World War I, the commonalities of two or more countries that became dictatorships or changed to right-wing authoritarian regimes.

Secondary Sources

Fascism in Western Europe

H. R. Kedward

Both fascism and communism, as they were practiced during the first half of the twentieth century, are traditionally categorized as totalitarian systems. Yet fascism is typically placed on the extreme right of the political spectrum, communism on the extreme left. Indeed, the two usually consider each other archenemies. In the following selection H. R. Kedward, a British historian at the University of Sussex, takes account of these facts in developing and diagraming a working political definition of fascism.

CONSIDER: *Why the extreme left should be placed next to the extreme right on the political spectrum, even though they consider each other enemies; the historical developments that justify using the second diagram for the twentieth century and*

SOURCE: H. R. Kedward, *Fascism in Western Europe: 1900–1945.* Reproduced by kind permission of Blackie and Son Ltd. (Bishopbriggs, Glasgow, 1971), pp. 240–241.

the first for the nineteenth century; the characteristics of fascism according to Kedward.

It could be argued that the best way to define fascism is not in a positive but in a negative way, by references to its opposites, but this too presents difficulties. At one time its opposite was naturally assumed to be communism, since fascism was said to be on the extreme Right of politics and communism on the extreme Left. This appeared self-evident when the traditional semicircle of political parties was drawn, i.e.:

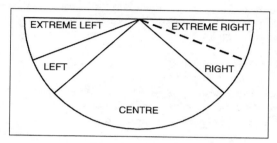

Such a diagram served the political scene of the 19th century when socialism was on the extreme Left and autocratic conservatism on the extreme Right, but in the 20th century a new diagram is needed in the form of a circle, i.e.:

This circular image does greater justice to the realities of 20th-century politics by recognizing that extreme Left and extreme Right, communism and fascism, converge at many points and are in some cases indistinguishable. Doriot, for example, moved with ease from French communism to his Fascist P.P.F. without changing his attitudes or methods, and most of the conclusions on Nazi culture . . . could be applied to Stalinism. The circle, however, does not minimize the differences which kept the two systems apart. Travelling the longest route round the circle, it is a very long way indeed from extreme Left to extreme Right. Thus communism and fascism are as distinct in some respects as they are similar in others.

This was most clearly apparent in the Spanish Civil War. If one looked at methods, the Communists were as violent, as authoritarian and as tightly organized as the Fascists; they were both supported by dictators, Stalin on the one hand and Hitler and Mussolini on the other, and they were both as intolerant of any deviation from the party line. They were next to each other on the circle. But if one looked at this history and their ideology the two had little in common: the Communists stood in the Marxist tradition and aimed at proletarian revolution, while the Fascists had their national values and a vision of an organic society. They were quite distinct.

Fascism therefore will only be partly defined by its opposition to communism. It is perhaps more profitable to look for its political opposites across the circle in the centre, where one finds progressive conservatism, liberalism and radical individualism. It is at least historically true that in the countries where these political attitudes were most entrenched—Britain, France and Belgium—neither fascism nor communism came to power.

The Rise of Fascism
F. L. Carsten

Historians have employed a variety of perspectives in an effort to understand the rise of fascism during the two decades following World War I. Focusing on the appeal of fascism, several historians have analyzed what social classes and groups of people supported fascist movements. In the following selection F. L. Carsten argues that while fascism appealed to all social groups, certain groups responded more strongly to it than others.

CONSIDER: *Why fascism might have been particularly appealing to the lower middle classes; what other groups it appealed to and why.*

Unlike many middle-class or working-class parties, the Fascists appealed to all social groups, from the top to the bottom of the social scale. Excluded were only those who were their favourite objects of attack: the profiteers, the parasites, the financial gangsters, the ruling cliques, the rapacious capitalists, the reactionary landowners. But even there exceptions were made if it suited the Leader's book. There is no doubt, however, that certain social groups responded much more strongly to the Fascist appeal than others. This is particularly true of those who were uprooted and threatened by social and economic change, whose position in society was being undermined, who had lost their traditional place, and were frightened of the future. These were, above all, the lower middle classes—or rather certain groups within them: the artisans and independent tradesmen, the small farmers, the lower grade government employees and white-collar workers. Perhaps even more important in the early stages were the former officers and non-commissioned officers of the first world war for whom no jobs were waiting, who had got accustomed to the use of violence, and felt themselves deprived of their "legitimate" rewards. In Italy, in Germany, and elsewhere the "front" generation played a leading part in the rise of Fascism. For its members fighting was a way of life which they transferred to the domestic scene. They loved battles for their own sake. It is no accident that the most important Fascist movements had their origin in the year 1919, the year of the Hungarian and Munich Soviet republics, of civil war which aroused fear and hatred in many hearts. Those who had been badly frightened did not easily forget. The occupation of the factories in northern Italy in the following year had the same effect. . . .

Apart from the groups already mentioned, there were the youngsters at school and university who became ardent believers in Fascism at an early stage. They were fed up with the existing society, bored with their daily duties, and strongly attracted by a movement which promised a radical change, which they could invest with a romantic halo. These youths came from middle-class or lower middle-class families. They could not easily find the way into the Communist camp. But they found the weak and changing governments of the post-war period utterly unattractive. In the Weimar Republic, in the post-war Italian kingdom, in the corrupt governments of Rumania, in the powerless governments of Spain, there was nothing to fire the enthusiasm of youth: they were dreary and pedestrian, the offices filled with mediocrities and time-servers. It was this, rather than any economic threat, that led so many idealist students into the Fascist camp. Similarly, many young officers and soldiers of the post-war generation were attracted by visions of national greatness and the promise of a revision of the peace treaties. A perusal of the autobiographical notes compiled by men who joined the National Socialist Party in its early years shows that pride of place belongs to a strong nationalism, the desire to see Germany strong and united again, freed from the "chains of Versailles", and also from the faction fights and the 'horse-trading' of the political parties. This often went together with hatred of the Communists and Socialists, and with anti-Semitism. Those who joined the Party were usually very young; they loved the frequent fights and battles in which they got involved together with their comrades, as well as the uniforms and the propaganda marches.

Hitler and Nazism
Klaus P. Fischer

It is difficult to analyze Nazism without focusing on its leader, Adolf Hitler. The close connection between Nazism and Hitler raises two questions of particular importance for historians. First, what was the role of the individual in shaping history—here, of Hitler in shaping German Nazism? Second, to what extent were Hitler and Nazism uniquely German developments related to particular characteristics of Germany's past? Klaus Fischer, a German historian and author of the widely respected Nazi Germany: A New History, addresses these issues. In this excerpt, he focuses in particular on who supported Hitler.

CONSIDER: *Whether Hitler and Nazism should be considered as uniquely German or as an extreme of a broader historical trend affecting the West as a whole during the 1920s and 1930s; who made up the "hard core" of his followers; the role played by Hitler in creating the appeal of Nazism.*

With the appointment of Adolf Hitler as chancellor, Germany would be plunged into an abyss, a dark age of unprecedented evil. Although Hitler's much-heralded Thousand-Year Reich would last for only twelve years, the world has never witnessed the perpetration of so much evil in such a short period. The historiographic effect has been to produce a series of optical illusions in the eyes of many historians who have described the rise and fall of the Third Reich. The evil that Hitler unleashed had the effect of magnifying the Twelve-Year Reich within the stream of history, prompting many historians to postulate fallacious or misleading theories of political causation and psychological motivation. Since the amount of destruction the Nazis unleashed on the world was so great, historians have assumed that such evil must be rooted deeply in German history and in the German character, an assumption that, ironically, inspired some slanderous explanations of the sort that Nazi racialists had developed as their own stock-in-trade during the Third Reich. For some Germanophobic historians the Nazi experience still serves as *the* pivot around which explanations about German history as a whole are formulated. At its most extreme, this has resulted in the practice of twisting many personalities or events in German history into a prefiguration of Adolf Hitler and Auschwitz. And what has been perpetrated on the past has also been extended into the future, for Hitler's shadow is still stretching beyond the present into the future.

SOURCE: Klaus P. Fischer, *Nazi Germany: A New History* (New York: The Continuum Publishing Co., 1995), pp. 259–262.

The opposite of the Germanophobic approach is the exculpatory, which holds that the Nazi experience was an aberration unrelated to previous events or institutions in German history. Some even claim that it was a unique event, an eruption of evil whose roots reside outside historical time and place. These arguments are as inauthentic as their opposite, though they may satisfy some Germans who would like to believe that they were unwitting and innocent victims of Hitler's lust for aggression. Dodging behind various covers—ignorance (we knew nothing), obeying orders, comparative trivialization (you were as bad as we were), or simple denial—some revisionist historians have tried to whitewash the record by claiming that the Nazis, though perhaps misguided, wanted the best for Germany and did not commit most of the heinous crimes attributed to them by their opponents. . . .

It is important to remind ourselves that Hitler was not Germany and Germany was not Hitler, as one ridiculous Nazi slogan insisted. If this is the case, who supported Hitler and what was the nature of the movement he inspired? . . . The followers by conviction represented the hard core of the Nazi movement. They were overwhelmingly male, and there is some justification to the famous Nazi boast that National Socialism was "a male event." The hard core consisted largely of recalcitrant and demobilized soldiers who could not reconcile their inherited militarism with the democratic beliefs of the Weimar Republic. . . .

If economic stability had been restored and maintained during the Weimar Republic, the Nazi movement would have never amounted to anything more than a small, xenophobic group of unregenerate misfits, but with the economic collapse, first of 1923 and then of 1929, it began to amalgamate misguided sympathizers who joined out of economic self-interest because they had been frightened into believing that the only alternative was the destruction of the middle class and the triumph of Communism. In order of precedent, the following groups were amalgamated step-by-step into the Nazi movement—the lower middle classes, who were afraid of being deprived of their social status; substantial elements of the more prosperous *Mittlestand* who fell victim to scare tactics that their businesses or possessions were subject to immanent expropriation by Communism; and disenchanted workers whose loyalty to nation exceeded their loyalty to class.

In the end, however, it was Hitler's organizational and charismatic genius that made it possible for the Nazi Party to attract a broad segment of the German population. Party membership lists and electoral data reveal that the Nazi Party was able to appeal beyond its hardcore followers and attract apparently incompatible social groups. Hitler seems to have known intuitively that voting patterns are shaped not only by class affiliation but by group prejudices. Hitler reasoned that if he could successfully nationalize the masses, indoctrinating them with ethnic prejudices, he could effectively diffuse economic divisions and reintegrate heterogeneous elements into one national community. . . .

The Weimar Republic failed because there were not enough strongly committed republicans to save it. In normal times, the republic might have been able to muddle through, as illustrated by its modest resurgence in the middle years (1924–29); but in times of turbulent and chaotic changes, its weaknesses became fatal liabilities. Amid a climate of mutual fear and paranoia, many Germans regressed to a "quick-fix," authoritarian solution; and given the predominance of right-wing, nationalistic attitudes, such a solution was bound to originate from the political right.

Hitler's Willing Executioners
Daniel J. Goldhagen

One of the most emotionally charged debates has long been over responsibility for the Holocaust, which cost so many lives. The question involves not only who made the key decisions instituting the policy of extermination, but who carried out that policy, who supported it, who knew, and who should have known. One of the most controversial and wide-read books addressing these issues is the recently published Hitler's Willing Executioners: Ordinary Germans and the Holocaust, *by Harvard scholar Daniel J. Goldhagen. Here he points to the role of antisemitic beliefs held by "ordinary" Germans in ultimately causing the slaughter of the Jews.*

CONSIDER: *How Goldhagen's views differ from those of Fischer (in the previous selection) and other historians; how Goldhagen's argument might be supported or attacked; why these views might be so controversial.*

This revision calls for us to acknowledge what has for so long been generally denied or obscured by academic and non-academic interpreters alike: Germans' antisemitic beliefs about Jews were the central causal agent of the Holocaust. They were the central causal agent not only of Hitler's decision to annihilate European Jewry (which is accepted by many) but also of the perpetrators' willingness to kill and to brutalize Jews. The conclusion of this book is that antisemitism moved many thousands of "ordinary" Germans—and would have moved millions more, had they been appropriately positioned—to slaughter Jews.

SOURCE: Daniel Johah Goldhagen, *Hitler's Willing Executioners: Ordinary Germans and the Holocaust* (New York: Alfred A. Knopf, Inc., 1996), pp. 9–10, 416–417.

Not economic hardship, not the coercive means of a totalitarian state, not social psychological pressure, not invariable psychological propensities, but ideas about Jews that were pervasive in Germany, and had been for decades, induced ordinary Germans to kill unarmed, defenseless Jewish men, women, and children by the thousands, systematically and without pity. . . . [T]he perpetrators, "ordinary Germans," were animated by antisemitism, by a particular *type* of antisemitism that led them to conclude that the Jews *ought to die*. The perpetrators' beliefs, their particular brand of antisemitism, though obviously not the sole source, was, I maintain, a most significant and indispensable source of the perpetrators' actions and must be at the center of any explanation of them. Simply put, the perpetrators, having consulted their own convictions and morality and having judged the mass annihilation of Jews to be right, did not *want* to say "no.". . .

This, it must be emphasized, is not a monocausal account of the perpetration of the Holocaust. Many factors were necessary for Hitler and others to have conceived the genocidal program, for them to have risen to the position from which they could implement it, for its undertaking to have become a realistic possibility, and for it then to have been carried out. Most of these elements are well understood. This book has focused on one of a number of the causes of the Holocaust, the least well-understood one, namely the crucial motivational element which moved the German men and women, without whom it would and could not have occurred, to devote their bodies, souls, and ingenuity to the enterprise. With regard to the *motivational* cause of the Holocaust, for the vast majority of perpetrators, a monocausal explanation does suffice.

When focusing on only the motivational cause of the Holocaust, the following can be said. The claim here is that this virulent brand of German racial antisemitism was in *this historical instance* causally sufficient to provide not only the Nazi leadership in its decision making but also the perpetrators with the requisite motivation to participate willingly in the extermination of the Jews.

Dictatorship in Russia: Stalin's Purges

Stephen J. Lee

In 1934 a colleague of Stalin was assassinated by a member of the Communist party. Shortly afterward, Stalin initiated mass purges of the Communist party. By 1939, when the purges had ended, vast numbers of people had been executed

Source: From Stephen J. Lee, *The European Dictatorships, 1918–1945*, pp. 53–55. Copyright 1987. Reprinted by permission of the authors and Methuen & Co. as publishers.

or imprisoned. Analysts have tried to explain these purges in a variety of ways. In the following selection Stephen Lee describes this historical controversy.

Consider: *How the interpretations differ; which interpretation makes the most sense to you; whether purges, or their like, are an inherent or predictable characteristic of any totalitarian regime.*

The most spectacular and notorious of all Stalin's policies was his deliberate creation of a state of total terror. His direct responsibility for this has never been questioned and plenty of evidence was provided by Khrushchev in 1956. . . .

Although the enormity of Stalin's purges defy a completely logical explanation, a number of motives have been suggested. One is that Stalin had a disastrously flawed personality. Khrushchev, for example, later emphasized his brutality, vindictiveness, pathological distrust and "sickly" suspicion. More recently, Tucker has maintained that, in addition to serving a political function, the trials also rationalized "Stalin's own paranoid tendency." A second reason for the purges is that Stalin was never one to resort to half measures. He aimed to wipe out the entire generation of Bolsheviks who had assisted Lenin between 1917 and 1924. This alone would guarantee Stalin as the sole heir to Lenin and would secure his position for a lifetime. Most of the threats to his power were latent and would possibly not reveal themselves for several years. They should, nevertheless, be dealt with as soon as possible. Since these latent threats were impossible to identify, a large number of people who would ultimately prove innocent of any form of opposition to Stalin, would also have to go. It was only by having such a clean sweep that Stalin could make sure of eradicating those who would be a threat. . . .

A third explanation of the purges is that they were ideologically necessary. Stalin argued that he was merely continuing the tactics of Lenin in 1918 and that he was accelerating the move towards a "classless society." If this desirable aim of Communism were to be achieved, class conflict would have to be intensified so that it could be ended the more quickly. The state would achieve its objectives "not through the weakening of its power but through it becoming as strong as possible so as to defeat the remnants of the dying classes and to defend itself against capitalist encirclement."

This brings us to the most frequently discussed aspect of Stalin's purges: how were they affected by the external situation? Two very different answers have been provided.

The first is that Stalin was obsessed with the fear that the west would smash the Soviet regime before his industrialization programme was complete. It therefore made sense to adopt a pragmatic approach to foreign policy; Germany, the main threat, could be won over by a temporary policy of cooperation. Stalin found it no more difficult to collaborate with Fascism than with any other European system, for he regarded it merely as a variant of western capitalism. The old-style Bolsheviks, by contrast, were profoundly anti-Fascist and saw Hitler as a far more deadly enemy than either France or Britain. According to R. Tucker and R. Conquest, Stalin therefore considered it essential to remove the anti-Hitler element to make possible the accommodation with Germany which eventually materialized in August 1939, in the Nazi-Soviet Non-Aggression Pact.

I. Deutscher puts a different cast. Stalin's main worry was that his regime would be destroyed from *within*—by internal revolt. There seemed little chance of this happening in 1936. Unless, of course, some major external catastrophe occurred, which could lead to a revival of the scenario of the First World War; military crisis could well bring about a revolution. Stalin's solution was therefore to destroy any elements within Russia which could possibly take advantage of such a situation. The show trials dealt with these potential threats by magnifying the charge against them.

❧ CHAPTER QUESTIONS

1. In light of the evidence and interpretations presented in this chapter about these authoritarian regimes, how would you explain their appeal or relative success in the twentieth century? In what ways should Italian fascism, German Nazism, and Russian communism be distinguished here?

2. Considering some of the theories and practices of these governments during the 1920s, 1930s, and 1940s, would you conclude that "totalitarianism" almost inevitably leads to violence and war, or rather that it happens to involve violence and war because of particular historical circumstances of the times? In this respect, should fascism be distinguished from communism? Why or why not?

3. In what ways do Italian fascism and German Nazism differ in theory and practice from liberal democracy? In what ways does Russian communism differ from both?

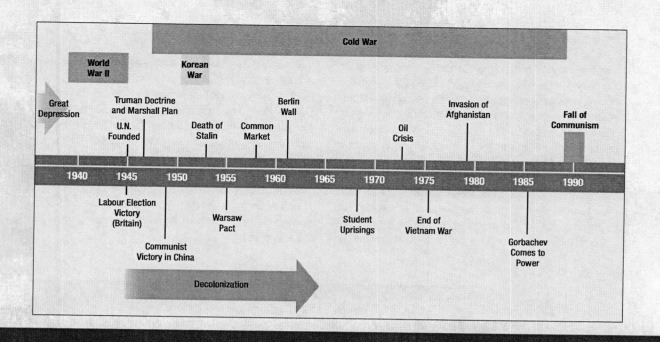

29 World War II and the Postwar World

World War II broke out in 1939 and was even more destructive than World War I. In 1945 Europe emerged from the war facing an overwhelming task of recovery. It had lost her position of dominance in the world, reflected in the successful independence movement among its colonies and the rise of the two new superpowers: the United States and the Soviet Union. Nevertheless, by the early 1960s, Europe had greatly recovered from the war and was enjoying considerable prosperity.

This chapter deals with five developments between 1939 and the early 1960s. First, almost all of Western civilization became embroiled in the war that broke out in 1939 and that did not end until two atomic bombs were dropped on Japan in 1945. What were the origins of World War II?

What connections between Hitler, Nazism, and appeasement might have led to the outbreak of the war in 1939? How did people experience the war?

Second, by 1947 the growing hostility between the United States and the Soviet Union became formalized in speeches, policies, and alliances, resulting in a division between Eastern and Western Europe and more broadly between Communist and non-Communist countries throughout the world: The Cold War had broken out. The Cold War remains a controversial issue among American historians as well as between Western and Soviet scholars. Why did it occur? What policies characterized the Cold War?

Third, Europe recovered from World War II more rapidly than expected. By the 1950s most countries were back on their feet, thanks in part to aid from the superpowers. By the early 1960s Western Europe was enjoying unprecedented prosperity and relative political and social stability. What were some of the political and social changes that occurred in this process of recovery? How are they exemplified by the establishment of a Labour government in Britain in 1945?

Fourth, European powers were unable to hold on to all their colonies in the two decades following the war. What were some of the arguments made and the strategies used in the struggle over decolonization? What role did the United Nations play in this struggle? How were problems in the Middle East related to the struggle over decolonization and the actions of the United Nations?

Fifth, several social and cultural developments marked this era. One of the most important of these was feminism. Art and the media took new turns during this period, challenging viewers' expectations. What was the nature of these developments? How did they reflect the rapid pace of historical change during this period?

While these developments have undergone some modification in the last thirty years, they remain part of the present along with other trends that will be examined in the final chapter.

Primary Sources

The Battle of Britain

Mrs. Robert Henrey

In July 1940 the Germans unleashed massive air attacks against Britain in preparation for an invasion of the island nation. For almost two months, the Germans bombed London every night. In cellars and subway stations, the British people holed up while their planes and antiaircraft guns fought off the Germans. By November, the British had won the Battle of Britain. The following excerpt is from account by Mrs. Robert Henrey, who lived in London's West End and survived the attacks.

CONSIDER: *The effects of the bombings on the morale of the British people; the symbolic importance of St. Paul's Cathedral.*

Bombs fell by day as well as by night. We became accustomed to the sudden drone of an airplane in the middle of the morning, the screech of a bomb, the dull crash of its explosion and the smell of cordite that filled the air a moment later. The sight of a burned-out bus unexpectedly in Berkeley Square, the ruins of a shop still half-hidden in a cloud of dust, streets that were impassable because of time bombs, enemy planes that burst in mid air sending down large chunks of fuselage, the pilots gliding down with their parachutes, became the normal things of life. . . . Almost every night some landmark near us would go up in dust. . . .

From the very first night of the battle for London [1940], because of the fires in the east which lit up the dome, St. Paul's Cathedral had become a symbol of London's defiance. As long ago as the night of the 12th September a large delayed-action bomb hurtled down south of the granite posts and buried itself twenty-seven feet deep. Everybody knew that if it exploded there would be nothing left of St. Paul's. For three days men worked to dig it out. Then it was driven in state to Hackney Marches on a lorry under the command of Lt. Davies, a Canadian who became a national hero.

Even for a very ordinary housewife living with her baby in the West End, St. Paul's could never for long be out of her mind. Almost every evening from the flat roof of Carrington House we peered east and prayed that it might stand.

A German Soldier at Stalingrad

William Hoffman

In June 1941 German forces turned eastward and invaded the Soviet Union. The German war machine advanced quickly until the Russian winter and Soviet resistance slowed them down. In June 1942 the Germans went on the offensive again. In August they reached the outskirts of Stalingrad, a crucial industrial city on the Volga River. The battle raged for six months and was so fierce that the city was virtually destroyed. More than a million Soviet soldiers and civilians lost their lives. In the end Russian forces managed to trap what remained of Germany's exhausted Six Army, win the battle of Stalingrad, and turn the tide on the eastern front.

The following are excerpts from the diary of a German soldier, William Hoffman, who lost his life in the fighting.

SOURCE: Mrs. Robert Henrey, *London Under Fire, 1940–1945* (London: J. M. Dent, The Orion Publishing Group, 1969), pp. 43–44.

SOURCE: Vasili Chuikov, *The Battle for Stalingrad* (Chelmsford, U.K.: Grafton Books, HarperCollins Publishers Ltd., 1964), pp. 248–254.

CONSIDER: *Hoffman's attitudes about the war in Russia, German prospects, and Hitler during July and August 1942; Hoffman's view of the Russians; the causes for Hoffman's discouragement and despair during September, October, and November 1942.*

July 3, 1942. . . . Today, after we'd had a bath, the company commander told us that if our future operations are as successful, we'll soon reach the Volga, take Stalingrad and then the war will inevitably soon be over. Perhaps we'll be home by Christmas.

July 29 1942. . . . The company commander says the Russian troops are completely broken, and cannot hold out any longer. To reach the Volga and take Stalingrad is not so difficult for us. The Führer knows where the Russians' weak point is. Victory is not far away. . . .

August 2. . . . What great spaces the Soviets occupy, what rich fields there are to be had here after the war's over! Only let's get it over with quickly. I believe that the Führer will carry the thing through to a successful end.

September 4. We are being sent northward along the front towards Stalingrad. We marched all night and by dawn had reached Voroponovo Station. We can already see the smoking town. It's a happy thought that the end of the war is getting nearer. That's what everyone is saying. If only the days and nights would pass more quickly . . .

September 5. Our regiment has been ordered to attack Sadovaya station—that's nearly in Stalingrad. Are the Russians really thinking of holding out in the city itself? We had no peace all night from the Russian artillery and aeroplanes. Lots of wounded are being brought by. God protect me . . .

September 8. Two days of non-stop fighting. The Russians are defending themselves with insane stubbornness. Our regiment has lost many men. . . .

September 13. . . . The Russians are fighting desperately like wild beasts, don't give themselves up, but come up close and then throw grenades. Lieutenant Kraus was killed yesterday, and there is no company commander.

September 16. Our battalion, plus tanks, is attacking. . . . Barbarism. The battalion is suffering heavy losses. . . .

September 18. . . . The Russians inside are condemned men; the battalion commander says: "The commissars have ordered those men to die in the elevator."

If all the buildings of Stalingrad are defended like this then none of our soldiers will get back to Germany. I had a letter from Elsa today. She's expecting me home when victory's won.

October 10. The Russians are so close to us that our planes cannot bomb them. We are preparing for a decisive attack. The Führer has ordered the whole of Stalingrad to be taken as rapidly as possible.

October 22. We have lost many men; every time you move you have to jump over bodies. You can scarcely breathe in the daytime: there is nowhere and no one to remove the bodies, so they are left there to rot. Who would have thought three months ago that instead of the joy of victory we would have to endure such sacrifice and torture, the end of which is nowhere in sight? . . .

The soldiers are calling Stalingrad the mass grave of the Wehrmacht [German army]. There are very few men left in the companies.

October 28. Every soldier sees himself as a condemned man. The only hope is to be wounded and taken back to the rear. . . .

November 10. A letter from Elsa today. Everyone expects us home for Christmas. In Germany everyone believes we already hold Stalingrad. How wrong they are. If they could only see what Stalingrad has done to our army.

November 18. Our attack with tanks yesterday had no success. After our attack the field was littered with dead.

November 21. The Russians have gone over to the offensive along the whole front. Fierce fighting is going on. So, there it is—the Volga, victory and soon home to our families! We shall obviously be seeing them next in the other world.

The Truman Doctrine and the Marshall Plan

During World War II the Soviet Union and the United States were allied against their common enemies, the Axis powers. Shortly after the end of the war, animosity began to reappear between the former allies. By 1947 that animosity had risen to

SOURCE: U.S. Congress, *Congressional Record*, 80th Congress, 1st Session (Washington, D.C.: U.S. Government Printing Office, 1947), vol. 93, p. 1981.

SOURCE: U.S. Congress, Senate Committee on Foreign Relations, *A Decade of American Foreign Policy: Basic Documents, 1941–1949* (Washington, D.C.: U.S. Government Printing Office, 1950), pp. 1270–1271.

the point where it was formalized in government programs and international policies; the Cold War had broken out. In the United States this was most clearly announced in two policy decisions excerpted here. The first is a speech delivered by President Truman on March 12, 1947, to Congress, concerning proposed aid to Greece and Turkey, which appeared in danger of falling under the influence of the Soviet Union. The principles contained in this speech became known as the Truman Doctrine. The second is a statement made by Secretary of State George C. Marshall on November 10, 1947, to Senate and House Committees on Foreign Relations, proposing massive aid to Europe. This proposal became known as the Marshall Plan.

CONSIDER: *The American perception of the Soviet Union and its allies; the purposes of this foreign policy; how the Soviet Union would probably perceive and react to this foreign policy.*

The peoples of a number of countries of the world have recently had totalitarian regimes forced upon them against their will. The Government of the United States had made frequent protests against coercion and intimidation, in violation of the Yalta agreement, in Poland, Rumania, and Bulgaria. I must also state that in a number of other countries there have been similar developments.

At the present moment in world history nearly every nation must choose between alternative ways of life. The choice is too often not a free one.

One way of life is based upon the will of the majority, and is distinguished by free institutions, representative government, free elections, guaranties of individual liberty, freedom of speech and religion, and freedom from political oppression.

The second way of life is based upon the will of a minority forcibly imposed upon the majority. It relies upon terror and oppression, a controlled press and radio, fixed elections, and the suppression of personal freedoms.

I believe that it must be the policy of the United States to support free peoples who are resisting attempted subjugation by armed minorities or by outside pressures.

I believe that we must assist free peoples to work out their own destinies in their own way.

I believe that our help should be primarily through economic and financial aid, which is essential to economic stability and orderly political processes.

☙

As a result of the war, the European community which for centuries had been one of the most productive and indeed creative portions of the inhabited world was left prostrate. This area, despite its diversity of national cultures and its series of internecine conflicts and wars, nonetheless enjoys a common heritage and a common civilization.

The war ended with the armies of the major Allies meeting in the heart of this community. The policies of three of them have been directed to the restoration of that European community. It is now clear that only one power, the Soviet Union, does not for its own reasons share this aim.

We have become involved in two wars which have had their origins in the European continent. The free peoples of Europe have fought two wars to prevent the forcible domination of their community by a single great power. Such domination would have inevitably menaced the stability and security of the world. To deny today our interest in their ability to defend their own heritage would be to disclaim the efforts and sacrifices of two generations of Americans. We wish to see this community restored as one of the pillars of world security; in a position to renew its contribution to the advancement of mankind and to the development of a world order based on law and respect for the individual.

The record of the endeavors of the United States Government to bring about a restoration of the whole of that European community is clear for all who wish to see. We must face the fact, however, that despite our efforts, not all of the European nations have been left free to take their place in the community of which they form a natural part.

Thus the geographic scope of our recovery program is limited to those nations which are free to act in accordance with their national traditions and their own estimates of their national interests. If there is any doubt as to this situation, a glance at the present map of the European continent will provide the answer.

The present line of division in Europe is roughly the line upon which the Anglo-American armies coming from the west met those of the Soviet Union coming from the east. To the west of that line the nations of the continental European community have been grappling with the vast and difficult problems resulting from the war in conformity with their own national traditions without pressure or menace from the United States or Great Britain. Developments in the European countries to the east of that line bear the unmistakable imprint of an alien hand.

The Cold War: A Soviet Perspective

B. N. Ponomaryov

The Cold War and indeed modern history were seen differently in the Soviet Union than in the West. The following excerpt is from History of the Communist Party of the

SOURCE: B. N. Ponomaryov et al., *History of the Communist Party of the Soviet Union*, Andrew Rothstein, trans. (Moscow: Foreign Languages Publishing House, 1960), pp. 599, 606–12.

Soviet Union (1960), *an official publication of the Soviet government. Here the focus is on the end of World War II and the early Cold War period.*

CONSIDER: *The elements of this interpretation most likely to be accepted by Western non-Marxist historians; how this interpretation differs from Truman's and Marshall's perceptions; how these differences help explain the existence of the Cold War.*

As a result of the war the capitalist system sustained enormous losses and became weaker. *The second stage of the general crisis of capitalism set in,* manifesting itself chiefly in a new wave of revolutions. Albania, Bulgaria, Eastern Germany, Hungary, Czechoslovakia, Poland, Rumania and Yugoslavia broke away from the system of capitalism. . . .

In their relations with the People's Democracies the Communist Party and the Soviet Government strictly adhered to the principle of non-interference in their internal affairs. The U.S.S.R. recognised the people's governments in these States and supported them politically. True to its internationalist duty, the U.S.S.R. came to the aid of the People's Democracies with grain, seed and raw materials, although its own stocks had been badly depleted during the war. This helped to provide the population with foodstuffs and also to speed up the recommissioning of many industrial enterprises. The presence of the Soviet armed forces in the People's Democracies prevented domestic counter-revolution from unleashing a civil war and averted intervention. The Soviet Union paralysed the attempts of the foreign imperialists to interfere in the internal affairs of the democratic States. . . .

The U.S.A. decided to take advantage of the economic and political difficulties in the other leading capitalist countries and bring them under its sway. Under the pretext of economic aid the U.S.A. began to infiltrate into their economy and interfere in their internal affairs. Such big capitalist countries as Japan, West Germany, Italy, France and Britain all became dependent on the U.S.A. to a greater or lesser degree. The people of Western Europe were confronted with the task of defending their national sovereignty against the encroachments of American imperialism. . . .

The radical changes that took place after the second world war substantially altered the political map of the world. There emerged *two* main *world* social and political camps: the *Socialist* and democratic camp, and the *imperialist* and anti-democratic camp. . . .

The ruling circles of the U.S.A., striving for world supremacy, openly declared that they could achieve their aims only from "positions of strength." The American imperialists unleashed the so-called cold war, and sought to kindle the flames of a third world war. In 1949, the U.S.A. set up an aggressive military bloc known as the North Atlantic Treaty Organisation (NATO). As early as 1946, the Western States began to pursue a policy of splitting Germany, which was essentially completed in 1949 with the creation of a West German State. Subsequently they set out to militarise West Germany. This further deepened the division of Germany and made her reunification exceptionally difficult. A dangerous hotbed of war began to form in Europe. In the Far East the United States strove to create a hotbed of war in Japan, stationing its armed forces and building military bases on her territory.

In 1950, the United States resorted to open aggression in the Far East. It occupied the Chinese island of Taiwan, provoked an armed clash between the Korean People's Democratic Republic and South Korea and began an aggressive war against the Korean people. The war in Korea was a threat to the People's Republic of China, and Chinese people's volunteers came to the assistance of the Korean people.

The military adventure of the U.S.A. in Korea sharply aggravated international tension. The U.S.A. started a frantic arms drive and stepped up the production of atomic, thermonuclear, bacteriological and other types of weapons of mass annihilation. American military bases, spearheaded primarily against the U.S.S.R., China and the other Socialist countries, were hastily built at various points of the capitalist world. Military blocs were rapidly knocked together. The threat of a third world war with the use of mass destruction weapons increased considerably.

The Berlin Wall

Jens Reich

Perhaps the most striking symbol of the Cold War that divided Europe was the Berlin Wall. In 1961, the East German government, under orders from Moscow, erected a 100-mile heavily armed wall in Berlin to keep its citizens from fleeing to the West. Berlin had served as an escape route for 2.6 million people, especially professionals and the well educated who sought a higher standard of living and broader cultural options in West Berlin and Western Europe. In the following selection, Jens Reich, a 22-year-old student in East Berlin in 1961, describes his reactions when the wall went up.

CONSIDER: *What Reich means by "Wall-Sickness"; the significance of the Berlin Wall to people such as Reich.*

SOURCE: Jens Reich, "Reflections on Becoming an East German Dissident, on Loosing the Wall and a Country," in *Spring in Winter, The 1989 Revolutions,* ed. by Gwyn Prins (Manchester, U.K.: Manchester University Press, 1990) (Dist. by St. Martin's Press), pp. 75–77.

I was a student in East Berlin before 13th August, 1961, before the day of "The Wall." I came to Berlin in 1956, as a boy of 17. I had lived in a rather dull provincial town and after Halberstadt, Berlin was like a revelation for me. . . . And then we had West Berlin. What a thrill! Cinemas, theatres, the Philharmonie. . . . I took everybody who came to visit me in Berlin. And I remember the coming of The Wall.

I mention all these details, which I remember so clearly, in order give a sense of the shock that we suffered when The Wall came upon us one night. There we were in Berlin, at the crossroads between East and West, at the juncture of two fundamentally different cultures, and suddenly we were locked up like canaries in a cage. Literally from one day to the next, from being a vibrant and cultured city, Berlin subsided into the drowsy torpor of a midsummer afternoon in the provinces. We were imprisoned in a dull, flat country.

In the first years no foreign earth was available to us at all. Czechoslovakia, Poland and the Soviet Union could only be visited by professional people. Bulgaria and Romania opened for tourists in the mid-sixties; but prices were steep and they were holiday resorts rather than centres of European culture. To reach West Germany was a venture that most probably ended in prison for *Republik-flucht*, or worse, for the Border Guards shot mercilessly at people trying to climb over "The Wall."

To call it a wall doesn't really do it justice. It was an entire system of watch towers, barbed wire, searchlights, pierced steel plate (to call it "wire mesh" gives the wrong impression of what was called "The Wire" within "The Wall"), strips sown with land-mines, free-fire zones covered by automatic guns, dog runs with ferocious, hungry dogs, armed Border Guard launches on the river to stop swimmers—all this apparatus of containment as well as concrete walls and passages. . . .

"Wall-sickness" was the eternal, lamenting analysis of our life blighted and circumscribed by *Die Mauer*. It came from being in a cage in the centre of Europe. Wall-sickness was boredom. We felt condemned to utter, excruciating dullness, sealed off from everything that happened in the world around us. Wall-sickness was loneliness, the feeling that you were condemned to die without having ever seen Naples, or Venice, or Paris, or London.

Some people could not stand the prospect of a life of such tedium and literally went mad. People would sometimes do crazy irrational things. You might go to the border, for example, draw your identity card and announce that you wanted "to be rid of this shitty country," a gesture with the guaranteed outcome of years in prison, but done in the hope that West Germany would buy you out sooner or later (often later!). Wall-sickness was the anguish of deprivation of a whole generation born between 1930 and 1950. We knew what we had lost.

British Labor's Rise to Power

Harry W. Laidler

During World War II governments became involved in social and economic activities to an unprecedented degree. Although with the end of the war this changed to some degree, there was still significant acceptance of government involvement in society. In Great Britain this was combined with an increasing acceptance of the Labor party, whose strength had been growing since the end of World War I. In the elections of 1945, this party, made up of a combination of Socialist and trade-union groups, gained a majority and took office, replacing the Conservatives led by Winston Churchill. The new government initiated policies that substantially changed the relationship between the government and the people during the period following World War II. Excerpts from the Labor party platform set forth shortly before the 1945 elections are presented here.

CONSIDER: *The ways in which this platform constituted a major assault on capitalism and laissez-faire; how this platform might reflect the experience of the Great Depression and the world wars; how a Conservative might argue against this platform.*

The Labor party is a socialist party, and proud of it. Its ultimate purpose at home is the establishment of the socialist commonwealth of Great Britain—free, democratic, efficient, progressive, public-spirited, its material resources organized in the service of the British people.

But socialism cannot come overnight, as the product of a week-end revolution. The members of the Labor party, like the British people, are practical-minded men and women.

There are basic industries ripe and over-ripe for public ownership and management in the direct service of the nation. There are many smaller businesses rendering good service which can be left to go on with their useful work.

There are big industries not yet ripe for public ownership which must nevertheless be required by constructive supervision to further the nation's needs and not to prejudice national interests by restrictive antisocial monopoly or cartel agreements—caring for their own capital structures and profits at the cost of a lower standard of living for all.

In the light of these considerations, the Labor party submits to the nation the following industrial program:

1. *Public Ownership of the Fuel and Power Industries.* For a quarter of a century the coal industry, producing Britain's most precious national raw material, has

SOURCE: Harry W. Laidler, "British Labor's Rise to Power," in *League for Industrial Democracy Pamphlet Series* (New York: League for Industrial Democracy, 1945), pp. 24–25. Reprinted by permission of the publisher.

been floundering chaotically under the ownership of many hundreds of independent companies. Amalgamation under public ownership will bring great economies in operation and make it possible to modernize production methods and to raise safety standards in every colliery in the country. Public ownership of gas and electricity undertakings will lower charges, prevent competitive waste, open the way for co-ordinated research and development, and lead to the reforming of uneconomic areas of distribution. Other industries will benefit.

2. *Public Ownership of Inland Transport.* Co-ordination of transport services by rail, road, air and canal cannot be achieved without unification. And unification without public ownership means a steady struggle with sectional interests or the entrenchment of a private monopoly, which would be a menace to the rest of industry.

3. *Public Ownership of Iron and Steel.* Private monopoly has maintained high prices and kept inefficient high-cost plants in existence. Only if public ownership replaced private monopoly can the industry become efficient.

These socialized industries, taken over on a basis of fair compensation, to be conducted efficiently in the interests of consumers, coupled with proper status and conditions for the workers employed in them.

4. *Public Supervision of Monopolies and Cartels* with the aim of advancing industrial efficiency in the service of the nation. Anti-social restrictive practices will be prohibited.

5. *A First and Clear-cut Program for the Export Trade.* We would give State help in any necessary form to get our export trade on its feet and enable it to pay for the food and raw materials without which Britain must decay and die. But State help on conditions—conditions that industry is efficient and go-ahead. Laggards and obstructionists must be led or directed into a better way. Here we dare not fail.

6. *The Shaping of Suitable Economic and Price Controls* to secure that first things shall come first in the transition from war to peace and that every citizen (including the demobilized Service men and women) shall get fair play. There must be priorities in the use of raw materials, food prices must be held, homes for the people must come before mansions, necessities for all before luxuries for the few. We do not want a short boom followed by collapse as after the last war; we do not want a wild rise in prices and inflation, followed by a smash and widespread unemployment. It is either sound economic controls—or smash.

Declaration Against Colonialism
The General Assembly of the United Nations

Most colonized peoples gained their independence from Western powers during the twenty years that followed World War II. This reflected both the weakness of Europe after the war and the strength of anti-imperialist sentiments around the world. Yet the process of decolonization was difficult in itself and was complicated by the ideological differences that divided nations. In 1960, after a bitter debate, the United Nations adopted the following "Declaration Against Colonialism." Although no nation voted against the resolution, Australia, Belgium, the Dominican Republic, France, Great Britain, Portugal, South Africa, Spain, and the United States abstained.

CONSIDER: *Possible reasons these nations abstained; justifications used by nations for not giving up their colonial possessions; what this declaration reveals about the strengths and weaknesses of the United Nations.*

The General Assembly.

Mindful of the determination proclaimed by the peoples of the world in the Charter of the United Nations to reaffirm faith in fundamental human rights, in the dignity and worth of the human person, in the equal rights of men and women and of nations large and small and to promote social progress and better standards of life in larger freedom,

Conscious of the need for the creation of conditions of stability and well-being and peaceful and friendly relations based on respect for the principles of equal rights and self-determination of all peoples, and of universal respect for, and observance of, human rights and fundamental freedoms for all without distinction as to race, sex, language or religion,

Recognizing the passionate yearning for freedom in all dependent peoples and the decisive role of such peoples in the attainment of their independence,

Aware of the increasing conflicts resulting from the denial of or impediments in the way of the freedom of such peoples, which constitute a serious threat to world peace,

Considering the important role of the United Nations in assisting the movement for independence in Trust and Non-Self-Governing Territories,

Recognizing that the people of the world ardently desire the end of colonialism in all its manifestations,

Convinced that the continued existence of colonialism prevents the development of international economic cooperation, impedes the social, cultural and economic

SOURCE: General Assembly of the United Nations, "Declaration Against Colonialism," *Official Records of the General Assembly,* Fifteenth Session, Resolution 1514, December 14, 1960.

development of dependent peoples and militates against the United Nations ideal of universal peace,

Affirming that peoples may, for their own ends, freely dispose of their natural wealth and resources without prejudice to any obligations arising out of international economic co-operation, based upon the principle of mutual benefit, and the international law,

Believing that the process of liberation is irresistible and irreversible and that, in order to avoid serious crises, an end must be put to colonialism and all practices of segregation and discrimination associated therewith,

Welcoming the emergence in recent years of a large number of dependent territories into freedom and independence, and recognizing the increasingly powerful trends towards freedom in such territories which have not yet attained independence,

Convinced that all peoples have an inalienable right to complete freedom, the exercise of their sovereignty and the integrity of their national territory,

Solemnly proclaims the necessity of bringing to a speedy and unconditional end colonialism in all its forms and manifestations;

And to this end

Declares that:

1. The subjection of peoples to alien subjugation, domination and exploitation constitutes a denial of fundamental human rights, is contrary to the Charter of the United Nations and is an impediment to the promotion of world peace and co-operation.

2. All peoples have the right to self-determination; by virtue of that right they freely determine their political status and freely pursue their economic, social and cultural development.

3. Inadequacy of political, economic, social or educational preparedness should never serve as a pretext for delaying independence.

4. All armed action or repressive measures of all kinds directed against dependent peoples shall cease in order to enable them to exercise peacefully and freely their right to complete independence, and the integrity of their national territory shall be respected.

5. Immediate steps shall be taken, in Trust and Non-Self-Governing Territories or all other territories which have not yet attained independence, to transfer all powers to the peoples of those territories, without any conditions or reservations, in accordance with their freely expressed will and desire, without any distinction as to race, creed or color, in order to enable them to enjoy complete independence and freedom.

6. Any attempt aimed at the partial or total disruption of the national unity and the territorial integrity of a country is incompatible with the purposes and principles of the Charter of the United Nations.

7. All States shall observe faithfully and strictly the provisions of the Charter of the United Nations, the Universal Declaration of Human Rights and the present Declaration on the basis of equality, noninterference in the internal affairs of all States, and respect for the sovereign rights of all peoples and their territorial integrity.

The Balfour Declaration, U.N. Resolution 242, and A Palestinian Memoir: Israel, Palestine, and the Middle East

Since World War II, the Middle East has been a center of violent conflict as well as a source of great concern for the world. One of the main sources of conflict has been the struggle over the creation of Israel and the Palestinian problem that resulted. The roots of this Israeli–Palestinian struggle stretch back at least as far as the late nineteenth century when the Zionist movement—a movement to make Palestine the national home of the Jews—began. The struggle over the creation of Israel came to a head in 1948 when the British, who controlled Palestine, left it in the hands of the United Nations. A United Nations resolution and the first Arab–Israeli war resulted in the creation of Israel, a massive number of Palestinian refugees, and decades of conflict between Arabs and Israelis.

The first of the following three documents on this topic is the Balfour Declaration, a 1917 letter from British Foreign Secretary Balfour to Walter Rothschild, the representative of British Jewry. The letter was used by Zionists to support immigration to Palestine and to obligate the British to create a Jewish homeland there. The second document is Resolution 242 (passed by the United Nations in 1967), which recognized Israel's existence and its need for security but at the same time called on Israel to withdraw from the territories captured in the 1967 Arab–Israeli War. The third document contains excerpts from a memoir of a Palestinian exile, Fawaz Turki. He describes the flight from Palestine in 1948, the years of exile that followed, and his continuing sense of Palestinian consciousness.

CONSIDER: *Why the Balfour Declaration was so important and why the Palestinians rejected it; why Israel has been reluctant to accept U.N. Resolution 242; the source and importance of Turki's sense of Palestinian consciousness.*

SOURCES: *International Documents on Palestine*, 1968, Zuhair Diab, ed. (New York, 1971); Fawaz Turki, *The Disinherited: Journal of a Palestinian Exile* (New York: Monthly Review Press, 1972), pp. 43–45, 54, as excerpted.

THE BALFOUR DECLARATION

Dear Lord Rothschild,

I have much pleasure in conveying to you, on behalf of His Majesty's Government, the following declaration of sympathy with Jewish Zionist aspirations which has been submitted to, and approved by, the Cabinet.

"His Majesty's Government view with favour the establishment in Palestine of a national home for the Jewish people, and will use their best endeavours to facilitate the achievement of this object, it being clearly understood that nothing shall be done which may prejudice the civil and religious rights of existing non-Jewish communities in Palestine, or the rights and political status enjoyed by Jews in any other country,"

I should be grateful if you would bring this declaration to the knowledge of the Zionist Federation.

Yours sincerely,
Arthur James Balfour

U.N. RESOLUTION 242

The Security Council . . .

1. *Affirms* that that the fulfilment of Charter principles requires the establishment of a just and lasting peace in the Middle East which should include the application of both the following principles:
   (i) Withdrawal of Israel armed forces from territories occupied in the recent conflict;
   (ii) Termination of all claims or states of belligerency and respect for and acknowledgement of the sovereignty, territorial integrity and political independence of every State in the area and their right to live in peace within secure and recognized boundaries free from threats or acts of force;
2. *Affirms further* the necessity
   (a) For guaranteeing freedom of navigation through international waterways in the area;
   (b) For achieving a just settlement of the refugee problem;
   (c) For guaranteeing the territorial inviolability and political independence of every State in the area, through measures including the establishment of demilitarized zones.

A PALESTINIAN MEMOIR

A breeze began to blow as we moved slowly along the coast road, heading to the Lebanese border—my mother and father, my two sisters, my brother and I. Behind us lay the city of Haifa, long the scene of bombing, sniper fire, ambushes, raids, and bitter fighting between Palestinians and Zionists. Before us lay the city of Sidon and indefinite exile. Around us the waters of the Mediterranean sparkled in the sun. Above us eternity moved on unconcerned, as if God in his heavens watched the agonies of men, as they walked on crutches, and smiled. And our world had burst, like a bubble, a bubble that had engulfed us within its warmth. From then on I would know only crazy sorrow and watch the glazed eyes of my fellow Palestinians burdened by loss and devastated by pain.

April 1948. And so it was the cruelest month of the year, but there were crueler months, then years. . . .

After a few months in Sidon, we moved again, a Palestinian family of six heading to a refugee camp in Beirut, impotent with hunger, frustration, and incomprehension. But there we encountered other families equally helpless, equally baffled, who like us never had enough to eat, never enough to offer books and education to their children, never enough to face an imminent winter. In later years, when we left the camp and found better housing and a better life outside and grew up into our early teens, we would complain about not having this or that and would be told by our mothers: "You are well off, boy! Think of those still living there in the camps. Just think of them and stop making demands." We would look out the window and see the rain falling and hear the thunder. And we would remember. We would understand. We would relent as we thought "of those still living there."

Man adapts. We adapted, the first few months, to life in a refugee camp. In the adaptation we were also reduced as men, as women, as children, as human beings. At times we dreamed. Reduced dreams. Distorted ambitions. One day, we hoped, our parents would succeed in buying two beds for me and my sister to save us the agonies of asthma, intensified from sleeping on blankets on the cold floor. One day, we hoped, there would be enough to buy a few pounds of pears or apples as we had done on those special occasions when we fought and sulked and complained because one of us was given a smaller piece of fruit than the others. One day soon, we hoped, it would be the end of the month when the UNRWA rations arrived and there was enough to eat for a week. One day soon, we argued, we would be back in our homeland.

The days stretched into months and those into a year and yet another. Kids would play in the mud of the winters and the dust of the summers, while "our problem" was debated at the UN and moths died around the kerosene lamps. . . .

Our Palestinian consciousness, instead of dissipating, was enhanced and acquired a subtle nuance and a new dimension. It was buoyed by two concepts: the preservation of our memory of Palestine and our acquisition of education. We persisted in refusing the houses and monetary compensation offered by the UN to settle us in our host countries. We wanted nothing short of returning to our homeland. And from Syria, Lebanon, and Jordan, we would see, a few miles, a few yards, across the border, a land where we had been born, where we had lived, and where we felt the earth. "This is my land," we would shout, or cry, or sing, or plead, or reason. And to that land a people had come, a foreign community of colonizers, aided by a Western world in a hurry to rid itself of guilt and shame, demanding independence from history, from heaven, and from us.

The Second Sex
Simone de Beauvoir
and
A Feminist Manifesto
Redstockings

It is increasingly recognized that women, both individually and in organizations, have been struggling for changes for a long time. The effort to gain consciousness and understanding of what it means to be a woman—politically, socially, economically, and sexually—has become central to women's struggles for change in the mid-twentieth century. The most important book in Europe and probably all of the West to explore this effort is The Second Sex, *by Simone de Beauvoir, first published in France in 1949. In this book de Beauvoir, a well-known French novelist, social critic, and existential philosopher, argues that women have been forced into a position subordinate to men in numerous obvious and subtle ways. During the 1960s and 1970s women's struggle for change spread and took on a new militancy. Throughout the West, women were arguing for change in what came to be known, especially in the United States, as the women's liberation movement. Numerous women's organizations formed, and many issued publications stating their views.*

The first of the following two selections on the liberation of women is from The Second Sex. *De Beauvoir stresses the status and role of woman as the "Other" in comparison to man. The second selection is an example of one of the more radical statements of feminism. It was issued in July 1969 by* Redstockings, *an organization of New York feminists.*

CONSIDER: *How de Beauvoir relates women to "Negroes" and proletarians; the handicaps facing women according to de Beauvoir; the primary demands of the Redstockings; how this group justifies its demands; how men might react to this selection.*

The parallel drawn . . . between women and the proletariat is valid in that neither ever formed a minority or a separate collective unit of mankind. And instead of a single historical event it is in both cases a historical

SOURCES: Simone de Beauvoir, *The Second Sex,* H. M. Parshley, trans. Reprinted by permission of Alfred A. Knopf, Inc., pp. xvii–xxii, xxvii. Copyright © 1952 by Alfred A. Knopf, Inc.; Redstockings, July 7, 1969, mimeograph.

development that explains their status as a class and accounts for the membership of *particular individuals* in that class. But proletarians have not always existed, whereas there have always been women. They are women in virtue of their anatomy and physiology. Throughout history they have always been subordinated to men, and hence their dependency is not the result of a historical event or a social change—it was not something that *occurred.* The reason why otherness in this case seems to be an absolute is in part that it lacks the contingent or incidental nature of historical facts. A condition brought about at a certain time can be abolished at some other time, as the Negroes of Haiti and others have proved; but it might seem that a natural condition is beyond the possibility of change. In truth, however, the nature of things is no more immutably given, once for all, than is historical reality. If woman seems to be the inessential which never becomes the essential, it is because she herself fails to bring about this change. Proletarians say "We"; Negroes also. Regarding themselves as subjects, they transform the bourgeois, the whites, into "others." But women do not say "We," except at some congress of feminists or similar formal demonstration; men say "women," and women use the same word in referring to themselves. They do not authentically assume a subjective attitude. The proletarians have accomplished the revolution in Russia, the Negroes in Haiti, the Indo-Chinese are battling for it in Indo-China; but the women's effort has never been anything more than a symbolic agitation. They have gained only what men have been willing to grant; they have taken nothing, they have only received.

The reason for this is that women lack concrete means for organizing themselves into a unit which can stand face to face with the correlative unit. They have no past, no history, no religion of their own; and they have no such solidarity of work and interest as that of the proletariat. They are not even promiscuously herded together in the way that creates community feeling among the American Negroes, the ghetto Jews, the workers of Saint-Denis, or the factory hands of Renault. They live dispersed among the males, attached through residence, housework, economic condition, and social standing to certain men—fathers or husbands—more firmly than they are to other women. If they belong to the bourgeoisie, they feel solidarity with men of that class, not with proletarian women; if they are white, their allegiance is to white men, not to Negro women. The proletariat can propose to massacre the ruling class, and a sufficiently fanatical Jew or Negro might dream of getting sole possession of the atomic bomb and making humanity wholly Jewish or black; but women cannot even dream of exterminating the males. The bond that unites her to her oppressors is not comparable to any other. The division of the sexes is a biological fact, not an event in human history. Male and female stand opposed within a primordial *Mitsein,* and woman has not broken it. The couple is a fundamental unity with its two halves riveted together, and the cleavage of society along the line of sex is impossible. Here is to be found the basic trait of woman: she is the Other in a totality of which the two components are necessary to one another. . . .

Now, woman has always been man's dependent, if not his slave; the two sexes have never shared the world in equality. And even today woman is heavily handicapped, though her situation is beginning to change. Almost nowhere is her legal status the same as man's, and frequently it is much to her disadvantage. Even when her rights are legally recognized in the abstract, long-standing custom prevents their full expression in the mores. In the economic sphere men and women can almost be said to make up two castes; other things being equal, the former hold the better jobs, get higher wages, and have more opportunity for success than their new competitors. In industry and politics men have a great many more positions and they monopolize the most important posts. In addition to all this, they enjoy a traditional prestige that the education of children tends in every way to support, for the present enshrines the past—and in the past all history has been made by men. At the present time, when women are beginning to take part in the affairs of the world, it is still a world that belongs to men—they have no doubt of it at all and women have scarcely any. To decline to be the Other, to refuse to be a party to a deal—this would be for women to renounce all the advantages conferred upon them by their alliance with the superior caste. Man-the-sovereign will provide woman-the-liege with material protection and will undertake the moral justification of her existence; thus she can evade at once both economic risk and the metaphysical risk of a liberty in which ends and aims must be contrived without assistance. Indeed, along with the ethical urge of each individual to affirm his subjective existence, there is also the temptation to forgo liberty and become a thing. This is an inauspicious road, for he who takes it—passive, lost, ruined—becomes henceforth the creature of another's will, frustrated in his transcendence and deprived of every value. But it is an easy road; on it one avoids the strain involved in undertaking an authentic existence. When man makes of woman the *Other,* he may, then, expect her to manifest deep-seated tendencies toward complicity. Thus, woman may fail to lay claim to the status of subject because she lacks definite resources, because she feels the necessary bond that ties her to man regardless of reciprocity, and because she is often very well pleased with her role as the *Other.*

Now, what peculiarly signalizes the situation of woman is that she—a free and autonomous being like all human creatures—nevertheless finds herself living in a world where men compel her to assume the status of the Other. They propose to stabilize her as object and to doom her to immanence since her transcendence is to be overshadowed and forever transcended by another ego (*conscience*) which is essential and sovereign. The drama of woman lies in this conflict between the fundamental aspirations of every subject (ego)—who always regards the self as the essential—and the compulsions of a situation in which she is the inessential.

〜

I. After centuries of individual and preliminary political struggle, women are uniting to achieve their final liberation from male supremacy. Redstockings is dedicated to building their unity and winning our freedom.

II. Women are an oppressed class. Our oppression is total, affecting every facet of our lives. We are exploited as sex objects, breeders, domestic servants, and cheap labor. We are considered inferior beings, whose only purpose is to enhance men's lives. Our humanity is denied. Our prescribed behavior is enforced by the threat of physical violence.

Because we have lived so intimately with our oppressors, in isolation from each other, we have been kept from seeing our personal suffering as a political condition. This creates the illusion that a woman's relationship with her man is a matter of interplay between two unique personalities, and can be worked out individually. In reality, every such relationship is a *class* relationship, and the conflicts between individual men and women are *political* conflicts that can only be solved collectively.

III. We identify the agents of our oppression as men. Male supremacy is the oldest, most basic form of domination. All other forms of exploitation and oppression (racism, capitalism, imperialism, and the like) are extensions of male supremacy: men dominate women, a few men dominate the rest. All power structures throughout history have been male-dominated and male-oriented. Men have controlled all political, economic, and cultural institutions and backed up this control with physical force. They have used their power to keep women in an inferior position. *All men* receive economic, sexual, and psychological benefits from male supremacy. *All men* have oppressed women.

IV. Attempts have been made to shift the burden of responsibility from men to institutions or to women themselves. We condemn these arguments as evasions. Institutions alone do not oppress; they are merely tools of the oppressor. To blame institutions implies that men and women are equally victimized, obscures the fact that men benefit from the subordination of women, and gives men the excuse that they are forced to be oppressors. On the contrary, any man is free to renounce his superior position provided that he is willing to be treated like a woman by other men.

We also reject the idea that women consent to or are to blame for their own oppression. Women's submission is not the result of brainwashing, stupidity, or mental illness but of continual, daily pressure from men. We do not need to change ourselves, but to change men.

The most slanderous evasion of all is that women can oppress men. The basis for this illusion is the isolation of individual relationships from their political context and the tendency of men to see any legitimate challenge to their privileges as persecution.

V. We regard our personal experience, and our feelings about that experience, as the basis for an analysis of our common situation. We cannot rely on existing ideologies as they are all products of male supremacist culture. We question every generalization and accept none that are not confirmed by our experience.

Our chief task at present is to develop female class consciousness through sharing experience and publicly exposing the sexist foundation of all our institutions. Consciousness-raising is not "therapy," which implies the existence of individual solutions and falsely assumes that the male-female relationship is purely personal, but the only method by which we can ensure that our program for liberation is based on the concrete realities of our lives. The first requirement for raising class consciousness is honesty, in private and in public, with ourselves and other women.

VI. We identify with all women. We define our best interest as that of the poorest, most brutally exploited woman.

We repudiate all economic, racial, educational, or status privileges that divide us from other women. We are determined to recognize and eliminate any prejudices we may hold against other women.

We are committed to achieving internal democracy. We will do whatever is necessary to ensure that every woman in our movement has an equal chance to participate, assume responsibility, and develop her political potential.

VII. We call on all our sisters to unite with us in struggle.

We call on all men to give up their male privileges and support women's liberation in the interests of our humanity and their own.

In fighting for our liberation we will always take the side of women against their oppressors. We will not ask what is "revolutionary" or "reformist," only what is good for women.

The time for individual skirmishes has passed. This time we are going all the way.

Visual Sources

The Destruction of Europe

The following map (map 29.1) shows the destruction inflicted on Dresden in the Anglo-American bombing raid of February 13–14, 1945, during the last stages of World War II. As in other "area bombings" made by Allied forces during the war, thousands of civilians were killed in this raid. This shows the blurring of civilian and military targets and the growing use of terror in modern warfare. Military targets such as factories, railway bridges, railway marshaling yards, main railway lines, troop bunkers and barracks, arsenals, and command headquarters were

MAP 29.1   Dresden, 1945

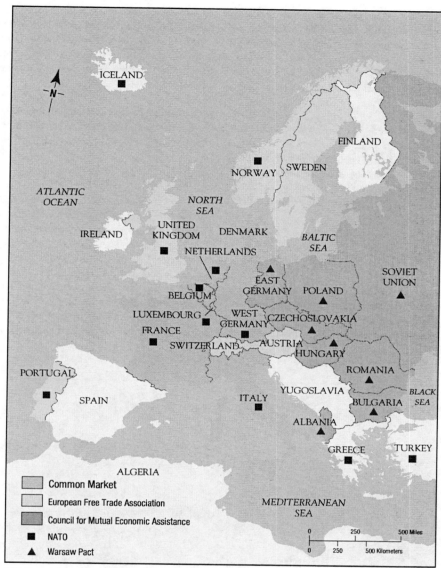

MAP 29.2   The Economic and Military Division of Europe

for the most part not significantly damaged. Instead, the destruction was concentrated on the heavily populated inner city, which was almost completely leveled by fires from incendiary bombing.

CONSIDER: The possible explanations for this raid and its effects; how warfare conducted in this manner seems to contradict the classic ideals of Western civilization concerning the value of the individual and individual rights.

The Cold War and European Integration

Map 29.2 gives some idea of the movements toward the Cold War and toward European integration in the two decades following World War II. Militarily, West and East divided into NATO, led by the United States, and the Warsaw Pact Organization, led by the U.S.S.R. Economically, Western European nations became increasingly tied together through organizations such as the Benelux Customs Union, the European Coal and Steel Community, the European Economic Community (Common Market), and the European Free Trade Association; the East joined in the Council for Mutual Economic Assistance (Comecon). Although military cooperation and economic cooperation were not always linked together, such linkage often did take place.

CONSIDER: *The geographic logic, if any, of the political and economic decisions that were made by the various countries; how maps of the world indicating regional economic cooperation, military alliances, political upheavals, and international "hotspots" might show the extent and intensity of the Cold War and regional cooperation even more fully than this map of Europe.*

Decolonization in Asia and Africa

Weakened by World War II and faced with growing movements for national liberation, Western imperial powers were forced to start giving up their colonial holdings in the late 1940s. As indicated by map 29.3, the process of decolonization was in some ways rapid—witness the large areas that gained independence in the few years around 1960—and in some ways delayed—it took some three decades for the process to be almost complete with some areas (e.g., Namibia, Hong Kong) still under external control into the 1990s.

CONSIDER: *Possible explanations for some areas gaining independence sooner, others later; possible problems new countries faced following independence.*

Televised Violence

Most observers agree that television has had a great impact on the lives of people within Western civilization and throughout the world, but exactly what that impact has been is open to debate. The following picture (figure 29.1) illustrates one of the most controversial issues that have been raised. It shows a television camera crew filming the live action in Vietnam. Here the crew and troops surround a nine-year-old girl burned by an aerial napalm attack in 1972. The images filmed by such crews were displayed on daily newscasts in America and elsewhere, giving civilians a

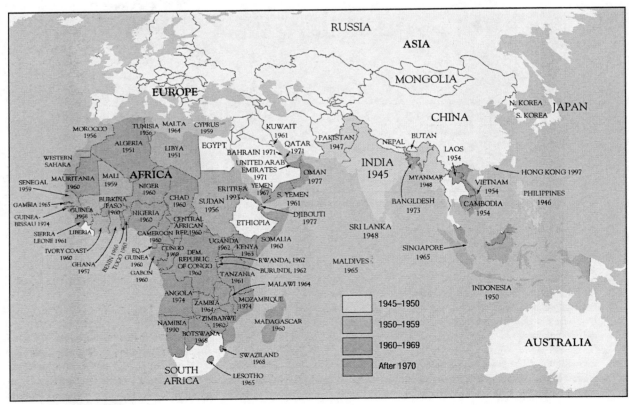

MAP 29.3 Decolonization in Asia and Africa

FIGURE 29.1   (© AP Wide World Photos)

virtual firsthand, up-to-the-minute, perhaps overly realistic impression of what the war was like. However, critics argue that because such images became so common, because they were displayed just before and just after the most mundane of other television shows (typically, situation comedies), and because they were viewed so often from the comfort of a living room, the image of a very real war may have come to seem unreal. Indeed, one must wonder whether this picture itself is not part of a staged scene for a movie (as was the case with a scene the audience sees being filmed in *Apocalypse Now,* a major movie of 1979–1980).

CONSIDER: *Other ways in which the media in the twentieth century have affected people's perception and understanding of war.*

Number 1

Jackson Pollock

Twentieth-century artistic styles have tended to become increasingly removed from popular tastes and from what the general public has been used to expecting from art. This was particularly the case

with the style of action painting or abstract expressionism, which came to the fore shortly after World War II. The leading painter in this school of art was Jackson Pollock (1912–1956), who executed this work (figure 29.2), entitled *Number 1, in 1948. In 1950 Pollock was interviewed by Francis V. O'Connor, a well-known art critic; a selection from that interview follows.*

CONSIDER: *How Pollock's statements and this painting reflect some of the trends of twentieth-century history.*

Mr. Pollock, in your opinion, what is the meaning of modern art?

Modern art to me is nothing more than the expression of contemporary aims of the age that we're living in.

Did the classical artists have any means of expressing their age?

Yes, they did it very well. All cultures have had means and techniques of expressing their immediate aims—the Chinese, the Renaissance, all cultures. The thing that interests me is that today painters do not have to go to a subject matter outside of themselves. Most modern painters work from a different source. They work from within.

Would you say that the modern artist has more or less isolated the quality which made the classical works of art valuable, that he's isolated it and uses it in a purer form?

Ah—the good ones have, yes.

Mr. Pollock, there's been a good deal of controversy and a great many comments have been made regarding your method of painting. Is there something you'd like to tell us about that?

My opinion is that new needs need new techniques. And the modern artists have found new ways and new means of making their statements. It seems to me that

FIGURE 29.2   (Digital Image © The Museum of Modern Art/Licensed by Scala/Art Resource, NY. © 2006 The Pollock-Krasner Foundation/Artists Rights Society (ARS), New York)

the modern painter cannot express this age, the airplane, the atom bomb, the radio, in the old forms of the Renaissance or of any other past culture. Each age finds its own technique.

Which would also mean that the layman and the critic would have to develop their ability to interpret the new techniques.

Yes—that always somehow follows. I mean, the strangeness will wear off and I think we will discover the deeper meanings in modern art.

I suppose every time you are approached by a layman they ask you how they should look at a Pollock painting, or any other modern painting—what they look for—how do they learn to appreciate modern art?

I think they should not look for, but look passively—and try to receive what the painting has to offer and not bring a subject matter or preconceived idea of what they are to be looking for.

Would it be true to say that the artist is painting from the unconscious, and the—canvas must act as the unconscious of the person who views it?

The unconscious is a very important side of modern art and I think the unconscious drives do mean a lot in looking at paintings.

Then deliberately looking for any known meaning or object in an abstract painting would distract you immediately from ever appreciating it as you should?

I think it should be enjoyed just as music is enjoyed—after a while you may like it or you may not. But—it doesn't seem to be too serious. I like some flowers and others, other flowers I don't like. I think at least it gives—I think at least give it a chance.

Well, I think you have to give anything that sort of chance. A person isn't born to like good music, they have to listen to it and gradually develop an understanding of it or liking for it. If modern painting works the same way—a person would have to subject himself to it over a period of time in order to be able to appreciate it.

I think that might help, certainly.

Mr. Pollock, the classical artists had a world to express and they did so by representing the objects in that world. Why doesn't the modern artist do the same thing?

H'm—the modern artist is living in a mechanical age and we have a mechanical means of representing objects in nature such as the camera and photograph. The modern artist, it seems to me, is working and expressing an inner world—in other words—expressing the energy, the motion, and other inner forces.

Would it be possible to say that the classical artist expressed his world by representing the objects, whereas the modern artist expresses his world by representing the effects the objects have upon him?

Yes, the modern artist is working with space and time, and expressing his feelings rather than illustrating.

 # Secondary Sources

Appeasement at Munich Attacked

George F. Kennan

The traditional view in the debate over who was responsible for the outbreak of World War II is that Hitler was emboldened by the unnecessarily weak policy of appeasement pursued by the Western democracies during the 1930s. One element of this appeasement was the Munich Conference of 1938 at which England and France agreed to the dismemberment of Czechoslovakia in return for Hitler's promise to demand no further territories. In the following selection George F. Kennan, former U.S. ambassador to the Soviet Union and Pulitzer Prize winner for a two-volume work on Soviet-American relations, presents the traditional view of appeasement.

CONSIDER: *From the point of view of the French and British statesmen actually participating in the Munich*

SOURCE: George F. Kennan, *Russia and the West Under Lenin and Stalin* (Boston: Atlantic–Little, Brown, 1961), p. 322. Reprinted by permission of Little, Brown and Company.

Conference of 1938 whether Kennan's criticism is justified; the implications of the argument about the causes of or blame for World War II.

The Munich agreement was a tragically misconceived and desperate act of appeasement at the cost of the Czechoslovak state, performed by Chamberlain and the French premier, Daladier, in the vain hope that it would satisfy Hitler's stormy ambition, and thus secure for Europe a peaceful future. We know today that it was unnecessary—unnecessary because the Czech defenses were very strong, and had the Czechs decided to fight they could have put up considerable resistance; even more unnecessary because the German generals, conscious of Germany's relative weakness at that moment, were actually prepared to attempt the removal of Hitler then and there, had he persisted in driving things to the point of war. It was the fact that the Western powers and the Czechoslovak government did yield at the last moment, and that Hitler once again achieved a bloodless triumph, which deprived the generals of any excuse for such a move. One sees again, as so often in the record of history, that it sometimes pays to stand up manfully to one's problems, even when no certain victory is in sight.

The Origins of the Second World War: Appeasement Defended
A. J. P. Taylor

The traditional view attacking appeasement as unjustified and a major cause of World War II has been questioned from different perspectives. Perhaps the most controversial perspective comes from A. J. P. Taylor, a popular, outspoken British historian who has written extensively on modern European history. In the following selection from The Origins of the Second World War, *Taylor argues that the appeasers have been unfairly faulted for their policies.*

CONSIDER: *The ways that Taylor and Kennan would disagree about the legitimacy of appeasement rather than the facts of appeasement; the implications of Taylor's argument about the causes of or blame for World War II; the advantages and dangers of looking at appeasement in the 1930s as a historical lesson to be learned for dealing with more recent circumstances.*

He got as far as he did because others did not know what to do with him. Here again I want to understand the "appeasers," not to vindicate or to condemn them. Historians do a bad day's work when they write the appeasers off as stupid or as cowards. They were men confronted with real problems, doing their best in the circumstances of their time. They recognised that an independent and powerful Germany had somehow to be fitted into Europe. Later experience suggests that they were right. At any rate, we are still going round and round the German problem. Can any sane man suppose, for instance, that other countries could have intervened by armed force in 1933 to overthrow Hitler when he had come to power by constitutional means and was apparently supported by a large majority of the German people? Could anything have been designed to make him more popular in Germany, unless perhaps it was intervening to turn him out of the Rhineland in 1936? The Germans put Hitler into power; they were the only ones who could turn him out. Again the "appeasers" feared that the defeat of Germany would be followed by a Russian domination over much of

Europe. Later experience suggests that they were right here also. Only those who wanted Soviet Russia to take the place of Germany are entitled to condemn the "appeasers"; and I cannot understand how most of those who condemn them are now equally indignant at the inevitable result of their failure.

Nor is it true that the "appeasers" were a narrow circle, widely opposed at the time. To judge by what is said now, one would suppose that practically all Conservatives were for strenuous resistance to Germany in alliance with Soviet Russia and that all the Labour party were clamouring for great armaments. On the contrary, few causes have been more popular. Every newspaper in the country applauded the Munich settlement with the exception of *Reynolds' News.* Yet so powerful are the legends that even when I write this sentence down I can hardly believe it. Of course the "appeasers" thought firstly of their own countries as most statesmen do and are usually praised for doing. But they thought of others also. They doubted whether the peoples of eastern Europe would be best served by war. The British stand in September 1939 was no doubt heroic; but it was heroism mainly at the expense of others. The British people suffered comparatively little during six years of war. The Poles suffered catastrophe during the war, and did not regain their independence after it. In 1938 Czechoslovakia was betrayed. In 1939 Poland was saved. Less than one hundred thousand Czechs died during the war. Six and a half million Poles were killed. Which was better—to be a betrayed Czech or a saved Pole? I am glad Germany was defeated and Hitler destroyed. I also appreciate that others paid the price for this, and I recognise the honesty of those who thought the price too high.

A World at Arms
Gerhard L. Weinberg

The issues involved with appeasement, which have so often been a focus for analysis, lead to the broader questions of why war broke out in 1939 and whether it could have been prevented. To answer these questions, historians often look back to the whole era that began with the outbreak of World War I in 1914. In the following selection, Gerhard Weinberg of the University of Michigan compares the two wars and emphasizes the differences that separate them. He also leaves no doubt whom he holds responsible for World War II.

SOURCES: A. J. P. Taylor, *The Origins of the Second World War,* 2nd ed. (New York: Atheneum Publishers, 1965), pp. 291–292. Reprinted by permission of the publisher.

SOURCES: Gerhard L. Weinberg, *A World At Arms: A Global History of World War II.* Cambridge, U.K.: Cambridge University Press, 1994, pp. 1–2, 43–44.

CONSIDER: *In what ways the causes and nature of the two wars differed; how Weinberg's interpretation compares to those of Kennan and Taylor.*

Although this book contains a chapter on the background of World War II, it defines that war as beginning in 1939 in Europe. While some have argued that the war was merely a continuation of World War I after a temporary interruption created by the armistice of 1918, and that the whole period from 1914 to 1945 should be seen as the age of a new European civil war, a Thirty-one Years War if you will, such a perspective ignores not only the very different origins and nature of the prior conflict but obscures instead of illuminating the special character of the second one. If an important by-product of both wars was the weakening of Europe and its hold on the world, the *intentions* of the belligerents were fundamentally different. It is true that these changed somewhat in the course of each of these lengthy struggles, but a basic differentiation remains.

In World War I, the two sides were fighting over their relative roles in the world, roles defined by possible shifts in boundaries, colonial possessions, and military and naval power. It is true that the Austro-Hungarian empire anticipated the elimination of Serbia's independent status, and Germany very quickly came to the conclusion that Belgium would never regain its independence, but beyond this expected disappearance of two of the smaller states which had emerged from larger constructions during the nineteenth century, the other powers—and most especially the major ones—were all expected to survive, even if trimmed by the winners. In this sense, the war, however costly and destructive in its *methods*, was still quite traditional in its aims.

It is also true that the fighting itself, with its unprecedented casualties, its incredible costs, the appearance of such new weapons as poison gas, airplanes, tanks, and submarines, as well as vast shifts in world economic patterns, ended up completely transforming the pre-war world and doing so in ways that none of the belligerents had anticipated. The effects on winners and losers alike were colossal, and the pre-war world could not be revived even if some made valiant and sometimes counterproductive efforts to do so. But neither side had either intended or preferred the massive changes which resulted from the ability of the modern state to utilize the social and mechanical technologies developed in the preceding two centuries to draw vast human and material resources out of their respective societies and employ them—and thereby use them up—in the cauldron of battle.

In World War II, all this was very different indeed. The *intent* was different from the start. A total reordering of the globe was at stake from the very beginning, and the leadership on both sides recognized this. The German dictator Adolf Hitler had himself explicitly asserted on May 23, 1939, that the war he intended would be not for the Free City of Danzig but for living space in the East; his Foreign Minister similarly assured Italy's Foreign Minister that it was war, not Danzig, that Germany wanted. When Germany had conquered Poland and offered a temporary peace to Britain and France, those countries responded by making it clear, as British Prime Minister Neville Chamberlain explained, that there could be no agreement with a German government led by Hitler, a man who had regularly broken his promises. If Chamberlain, who has often been derided for allegedly not grasping the true nature of the National Socialist challenge, saw the issues so clearly, the historian decades later ought not to close his or her eyes to the reality of a very different war. This was, in fact, a struggle not only for control of territory and resources but about who would live and control the resources of the globe and which peoples would vanish entirely because they were believed inferior or undesirable by the victors.

It was in this way that the two wars which originated in Europe differed greatly from each other even if separated by only two decades. . . .

No appeals from prospective neutrals could move Hitler. He not only would not put off war for one day, he was in such a hurry that he gave the orders to begin hostilities hours earlier than the German military timetable required. To justify war in the eyes of the German public, he shared in the preparation of demands on Poland that might sound reasonable to his people—and that he ordered withheld until after they were no longer valid. He would not again run the "danger" of having his ostensible demands agreed to, or made the basis for real negotiations, or be met with counter-offers. Now that there was no longer any chance of splitting the Western Powers from Poland, his focus of attention was on the German home front in the coming war, a reflection of his belief that it had been the collapse there which had produced defeat in the preceding great conflict. . . .

On the morning of September 1 the German offensive into Poland began. . . . To the thunderous applause of the representatives of the German people, he announced that Germany was once more at war.

Almost every nation eventually participated in the new war, some as victims of attack, some as eager attackers themselves, some at the last moment in order to participate in the post-war world organization. A flood of blood and disaster of unprecedented magnitude had been let loose on the world. If the details of military operations and the localities of combat were often vastly different from those of World War I, the fearful anticipation that a new war would be as horrendous or quite likely even worse than the last proved all too accurate. There would be, however, no agitated discussion this time, as there had been after the crisis of 1914, of the question of who was responsible for the outbreak of war. It was all too clear that Germany had taken the initiative and that others had tried, perhaps too much, but certainly very hard, to avert another great conflict. There would be no second "war guilt" debate.

Origins of the Cold War

James L. Gormly

The period between the end of World War II and the mid-1960s was marked by the Cold War between the two superpowers emerging from World War II, the United States and the U.S.S.R. Initially American historians analyzed the Cold War with assumptions not too different from policymakers': The United States was only responding defensively to an aggressive Soviet Union intent on spreading its control and Communist ideology over the world. But by the 1960s other interpretations were being offered, most notably a revisionist position holding the Cold War to be at least in part a result of an aggressive, provocative American foreign policy. In the following selection James Gormly describes the competing interpretations and suggests how the controversy might be analyzed.

CONSIDER: *Whether the Cold War was inevitable or could have been avoided; how the speeches by Truman and Marshall support one side or the other; which view makes the most sense to you.*

Those who place the major responsibility for the Cold War on the Soviet Union argue that Stalin, as dictator and leader of a totalitarian system, easily could have moderated the nation's interests to meet U.S. objections and ensure peace. According to this view, if the generalissimo was not an expansionist wanting to overrun central and Western Europe, he should have articulated the defensive and limited nature of his goals to the Truman administration and the American public. Instead, the Russians would not accept the U.S. vision for a stable and prosperous world or trust that Washington accepted the legitimacy of the Soviet Union and recognized its need for some degree of influence over regions along its borders. Moscow needed "a hostile international environment" to maintain control and the integrity of the Soviet state. Thus, Stalin was either an expansionist or unwilling to communicate his aims, and the United States, supported by Britain, had no other option than to react aggressively. . . .

Other analysts place a large amount of the blame on the United States and its unwillingness to accept expressed Soviet needs and to articulate to the Russians and Stalin that Washington trusted them and recognized the legitimacy of their system and state. Some explain U.S. behavior as an outgrowth of the American Open Door ideology, which sought to ensure for the nation's businesses access to world markets. Still others credit U.S. actions to a general arrogance of power that translated the country's tremendous economic and military strength and accomplishments into a moral, ideological superiority. According to this theory, many Soviets feared that the West still hoped to destroy their state. To convince them that America intended to be a friend and thereby avoid the Cold War, the United States should have shelved its presumptuousness and global goals and demonstrated an affirmation of the Soviet Union's right to rule and enjoy the fruits of its victory. To ease fears and mistrust, Washington needed to recognize Russia's new borders, its diplomatic equality, and its spheres of influence in Eastern Europe. Instead, the U.S. government continued to follow the path suggested by Ambassador Harriman, who stated that the administration should supply assistance to the Soviets only if they "played the international game with us in accordance with our standards." . . .

Given the situation, the belief that U.S. actions divided the world into two camps and necessitated a rapid Sovietization of Eastern Europe seems as logical as the view that Russian expansionism forced the United States to institute its containment policy. To evaluate and assess either theory fully and to determine if the Cold War international system could have been avoided requires an examination of Soviet records, but, even without such information, and using existing American and British documents, one can conclude that U.S. policymakers made few efforts after the Potsdam Conference to reassure Moscow that mutual cooperation was possible and that Washington had no intention of seeking the destruction of the Soviet state.

The Positive Role of the United Nations in a Split World

Dag Hammarskjöld

One of the most idealistic institutions stemming from World War II was the United Nations, formed by agreement of the major powers in 1945 and eventually including most nations of the world. Its primary purpose is to preserve peace, which

SOURCES: From James L. Gormly, *From Potsdam to the Cold War*, pp. 220–223. Copyright 1990 by Scholarly Resources, Inc. Reprinted by permission of Scholarly Resources, Inc.

SOURCES: Dag Hammarskjöld, "The Positive Role of the United Nations in a Split World," *United Nations Review*, vol. VII, no. 4 (October 1960), pp. 24–25. Reprinted by permission of the *UN Chronicle*.

has become even more pressing with the proliferation of nuclear weapons. But despite some successes, the United Nations has come under attack for favoring policies in opposition to a perceived national interest and for being unable to take effective action when armed conflicts broke out. In the following selection Dag Hammarskjöld, secretary-general of the United Nations from 1953 to 1961, analyzes and defends the position and actions of the UN.

CONSIDER: *Why, according to Hammarskjöld, the UN has been unable to resolve many major international problems; how one might respond to this argument; whether policies such as those enunciated by Truman and Marshall support or conflict with the goals and efforts of the UN.*

With its constitution and structure, it is extremely difficult for the United Nations to exercise an influence on problems which are clearly and definitely within the orbit of present-day conflicts between power blocs. If a specific conflict is within that orbit, it can be assumed that the Security Council is rendered inactive, and it may be feared that even positions taken by the General Assembly would follow lines strongly influenced by considerations only indirectly related to the concrete difficulty under consideration. Whatever the attitude of the General Assembly and the Security Council, it is in such cases also practically impossible for the Secretary-General to operate effectively with the means put at his disposal, short of risking seriously to impair the usefulness of his office for the Organization in all the other cases for which the services of the United Nations Secretariat are needed.

This clearly defines the main field of useful activity of the United Nations in its efforts to prevent conflicts or to solve conflicts. Those efforts must aim at keeping newly arising conflicts outside the sphere of bloc differences. Further, in the case of conflicts on the margin of, or inside, the sphere of bloc differences, the United Nations should seek to bring such conflicts out of this sphere through solutions aiming, in the first instance, at their strict localization. In doing so, the Organization and its agents have to lay down a policy line, but this will then not be for one party against another, but for the general purpose of avoiding an extension or achieving a reduction of the area into which the bloc conflicts penetrate. . . .

Those who look with impatience at present-day efforts by the United Nations to resolve major international problems are inclined to neglect, or to misread, the significance of the efforts which can be made by the United Nations in the field of practical politics in order to guide the international community in a direction of growing stability. They see the incapacity of the United Nations to resolve the major bloc conflicts as an argument against the very form of international cooperation which the

Organization represents. In doing so, they forget what the Organization has achieved and can achieve, through its activities regarding conflicts which are initially only on the margin of, or outside, the bloc conflicts, but which, unless solved or localized, might widen the bloc conflicts and seriously aggravate them. Thus the Organization in fact also exercises a most important, though indirect, influence on the conflicts between the power blocs by preventing the widening of the geographical and political area covered by these conflicts and by providing for solutions whenever the interests of all parties in a localization of conflict can be mobilized in favor of its efforts.

The Wretched of the Earth
Frantz Fanon

When discussing colonialism in the decades following World War II, most historians focus on its political and economic consequences. Some observers, however, point to the deeper psychological consequences of colonialism. The best known of these observers was Frantz Fanon (1925–1961), a French psychiatrist from the French West Indies whose writings supported the Algerian rebels in their struggle for independence from France after World War II. In his book The Wretched of the Earth *(1961), Fanon argues that colonialism had its greatest impact on the people physically involved in it: the foreign occupiers (settlers) and the colonized (natives). In the following excerpt from that book, Fanon emphasizes the great physical and psychological gap between these two groups.*

CONSIDER: *What connections there are between the physical and the psychological gaps separating settlers and natives; the attitudes of the settlers toward the natives; the attitudes of the natives toward the settlers and their institutions.*

The colonial world is a world cut in two. The dividing line, the frontiers are shown by barracks and police stations. In the colonies it is the policemen and the soldier who are the official, instituted go-betweens, the spokesmen of the settler and his rule of oppression. . . .

It is obvious here that the agents of government speak the language of pure force. The intermediary does not lighten the oppression, nor seek to hide the domination; he shows them up and puts them into practice with the clear conscience of an upholder of the peace; yet he is the bringer of violence into the home and into the mind of the native. . . .

The settler's town is a strongly-built town, all made of stone and steel. It is a brightly-lit town; the streets are covered with asphalt, and the garbage-cans swallow all

SOURCES: Frantz Fanon, *The Wretched of the Earth,* trans. Constance Farrington. Copyright © 1963 by Presence Africaine. Used by permission of Grove Weidenfeld.

the leavings, unseen, unknown and hardly thought about. The settler's feet are never visible, except perhaps in the sea; but there you're never close enough to see them. His feet are protected by strong shoes although the streets of his town are clean and even, with no holes or stones. The settler's town is a well-fed town, an easy-going town; its belly is always full of good things. The settler's town is a town of white people, of foreigners.

The town belonging to the colonised people, or at least the native town, the negro village, the medina, the reservation, is a place of ill fame, peopled by men of evil repute. They are born there, it matters little where or how; they die there, it matters not where, nor how. It is a world without spaciousness; men live there on top of each other, and their huts are built one on top of the other. The native town is a hungry town, starved of bread, of meat, of shoes, of coal, of light. The native town is a crouching village, a town on its knees, a town wallowing in the mire. It is a town of niggers and dirty arabs. The look that the native turns on the settler's town is a look of lust, a look of envy; it expresses his dreams of possession—all manner of possession: to sit at the settler's table, to sleep in the settler's bed, with his wife if possible. The colonised man is an envious man. And this the settler knows very well; when their glances meet he ascertains bitterly, always on the defensive "They want to take our place." It is true, for there is no native who does not dream at least once a day of setting himself up in the settler's place.

This world divided into compartments, this world cut in two is inhabited by two different species. The originality of the colonial context is that economic reality, inequality and the immense difference of ways of life never come to mask the human realities. When you examine at close quarters the colonial context, it is evident that what parcels out the world is to begin with the fact of belonging to or not belonging to a given race, a given species. . . .

It is not enough for the settler to delimit physically, that is to say with the help of the army and the police force, the place of the native. As if to show the totalitarian character of colonial exploitation the settler paints the native as a sort of quintessence of evil. Native society is not simply described as a society lacking in values. It is not enough for the colonist to affirm that those values have disappeared from, or still better never existed in, the colonial world. The native is declared insensible to ethics; he represents not only the absence of values, but also the negation of values. . . .

The Church in the colonies is the white people's Church, the foreigner's Church. She does not call the native to God's ways but to the ways of the white man, of the master, of the oppressor. And as we know, in this matter many are called but few chosen.

✠ CHAPTER QUESTIONS

1. To what extent do the trends described in this chapter give further support to the argument that Western civilization has been on the decline since World War I in comparison to the heights it reached in the nineteenth century? What developments might be cited to refute this argument?

2. How might one make an argument that the fundamental historical shift in the last two hundred years did not come with World War I but rather with World War II, as indicated by the consequences of that war and the developments of the postwar period?

3. Do you think the Cold War was caused primarily by developments related to World War II or by the ideological differences between Communist and non-Communist countries? Were there any ways in which the Cold War might have been averted?